ESCAPE FROM VIOLENCE

ESCAPE FROM VIOLENCE
Conflict and the Refugee Crisis in the Developing World

Aristide R. Zolberg
Astri Suhrke
Sergio Aguayo

New York   Oxford
OXFORD UNIVERSITY PRESS
1989

Oxford University Press

Oxford   New York   Toronto
Delhi   Bombay   Calcutta   Madras   Karachi
Kuala Lumpur   Singapore   Hong Kong   Tokyo
Nairobi   Dar es Salaam   Cape Town
Melbourne   Auckland
and associated companies in
Berlin   Ibadan

Copyright © 1989 by Oxford University Press, Inc.

First issued as an Oxford University Press paperback, 1992

Published by Oxford University Press, Inc.,
200 Madison Avenue, New York, New York 10016

Library of Congress Cataloging-in-Publication Data
Zolberg, Aristide R.
Escape from violence: conflict and the refugee crisis
in the developing world /
Aristide R. Zolberg, Astri Suhrke, Sergio Aguayo.
p.   cm.
Includes bibliographies and index.
ISBN 0-19-505592-6
ISBN 0-19-507916-7 (PBK)
1. Refugees—Developing countries.
2. International relief—Developing countries.
I. Suhrke, Astri.
II. Aguayo, Sergio.
III. Title.
HV640.4.D44Z65 1989
362.8'7'091724—dc19   88-25156

9 8 7 6 5 4 3 2 1

Printed in the United States of America
on acid-free paper

PREFACE

Widely perceived as an unprecedented crisis, the number of refugees originating in the developing world since the 1970s has generated urgent concern throughout the West. Such concern is an ambiguous mixture of compassion for the plight of the unfortunates who have been cast adrift and of fear that they will come pouring in. But not only does that fear constantly threaten to undermine the exercise of compassion, it also shows that the affluent countries of the West will neither admit all who seek entry nor give sufficient relief to those who find havens in the developing world itself. This is equally true of neighboring countries in Asia, Africa, and Latin America, which in fact bear the brunt of the crisis.

This book seeks to foster a more critical and realistic understanding of the refugee phenomenon, so as to clarify the obligations of the more fortunate of the world toward others in great need, and the ways in which these are best implemented. We shall attempt to explain why the developing world today is producing so many refugees; why they sometimes come in a flood and sometimes in a trickle; where they go; and why they sometimes return and sometimes do not.

This is the first attempt to provide a comprehensive, theoretically grounded explanation of refugee flows. Social scientists who analyze the causes and consequences of international migrations generally exclude refugee movements, because they believe that the two types of population movement are fundamentally different.

It has long been recognized that migration is governed by social and economic forces that themselves are somewhat regular and thus are amenable to theoretical analysis. By contrast, however, refugee flows are unruly in that they result from events such as civil strife, abrupt changes of regime, arbitrary governmental decisions, or international war, all of which are generally considered singular and unpredictable occurrences. This is reflected, for example, in the differing articles, "Migrations" and "Refugees," in the *International Encyclopedia of the Social Sciences* (1968). The first consists of sections by a sociologist and an economist, who review theories seeking to explain population movements generally; the second consists of two sections: one, on "World Problems," was written by a political scientist specializing in international law and organization, and was focused on the development of the Office of the United Nations High Commissioner for Refugees; another was on "Adjustment and Assimilation" of refugees.[1]

When concern over refugees began to mount in the late 1970s, the only analytic framework dealing with such movements was Egon F. Kunz's "Kinetic models," which are, however, formalistic and very abstract.[2] Several publications followed, but it is noteworthy that in the two special issues of journals devoted to the subject, one ignores the question of causation altogether, and the other devotes only one article to it—incidentally, a preliminary formulation by A. R. Zolberg of the approach used in this book.[3]

Indeed, the assumption in this book is that refugee flows, like other international population movements, are patterned by identifiable social forces and hence can be viewed as structured events that result from broad historical processes. Although the flows are irregular, the events that trigger them are themselves manifestations of persistent trends in the developing world. A further step toward their analysis is to map both the different situations that produce refugees and the characteristics of the flows and to organize them into typologies. We have done this here by surveying the major refugee-producing regions and discussing in more detail a variety of case studies. On the basis of our findings, we demonstrate that different types of social conflict give rise to different types of refugee flows and that the patterns of conflict are themselves intimately related to more general economic and political conditions, not only in the countries from which the refugees originate, but also in the world at large.

This emphasis on conflict patterns differs from that on typologies in political science, which generally focus on types of political regime. Our approach is more suitable in this case, however, because in the developing world, regimes come and go (e.g., civilian or military, democratic or authoritarian), whereas the conflicts that produce this instability are themselves enduring. The use of conflict patterns also makes it possible to analyze a given country as a field of social activity within which a number of distinct conflicts are taking place at the same time, possibly generating diverse types of refugee flows concurrently.

We attribute considerable weight to factors external to the country in which the refugees originate, thereby challenging the prevailing "internalist" view of the root causes of such flows—that the crucial factors are internal to the state of origin. In contrast with this, our regional studies indicate that usually the causes are more complex and include numerous instances of egregious external intervention. Beyond this, the internal factors themselves often are part of patterns of social change determined by a combination of closely intertwined external and internal processes. In addition, as we shall show, the refugee and immigration policies of outside countries and organizations play a poorly understood but significant role in triggering the flows and shaping their course.

Why then has the internalist conceptualization dominated both scholarly and public discourse about refugees? Because international law is founded on the notion that the world is divided into a finite set of states with mutually exclusive jurisdiction over segments of territory and clusters of population, there is a tendency to assume that social causation can also be located precisely within or among particular states. For reasons that will be elucidated in Chapter 1, this has generally suited the purposes of the receiving countries of the West, which collectively also shaped the international institutions that deal with refugees and that in turn operate under political constraints that foreclose attribution of responsibility for causing the flows. The research literature also reflects these conventional legal assumptions and diplomatic obfuscations, a neglect that has contributed to the inadequacy of proposals to deal with the "refugee crisis."

We therefore hope that the reconceptualization proposed here, simultaneously structural and transnational, will not only stimulate further discussion among academic specialists but will also spill over into the policy arena so as to broaden the terms of reference of the current debates. To some extent, this began to happen even before the publication of this book. Initial efforts were summarized by Charles B. Keely, who as far back as 1981 commented that "the structural analyses of Zolberg and Suhrke reduce the feeling of helplessness and support an approach to refugee policy and programs that departs from recent practices."[4] We hope to have lived up to his generous characterization. Another encouraging sign is Leon Gordenker's *Refugees in International Politics* (1987), which is concerned primarily with the scope and limits of the international "refugee system" but which devotes some attention to "the novel nature of recent refugee incidents" as well as their "causal elements" and, in so doing, takes into account some of our earlier formulations.[5]

The term *refugee* is ambiguous and has given rise to protracted controversies, and thus, before analyzing refugee flows, we must identify as precisely as possible the category of persons with whom we are concerned. Although few question that "refugees" deserve special care, even a perfunctory survey of the contemporary scene will reveal widespread disagreement within and among countries on the criteria for determining refugee status. And even when the criteria are agreed on, the very nature of social reality renders it difficult to objectify them so as to provide unambiguous guidance for officials. Our first chapter is therefore entitled "Who Is a Refugee?" We answer the question by retracing the European historical origins of contemporary legal definitions and practices and then assessing them in the light of current realities. We then provide a definition that is both realistic and theoretically valid, as well as firmly grounded in humanitarian concern.

This is followed by a number of detailed regional studies, covering most of sub-Saharan Africa, Asia, and Latin America, from approximately 1960 to the present (Part Two, Chapters 2 to 8). The only major region not covered is the Middle East, which lies outside our collective competence. We do, however, refer at various points to the Palestinians, because their case is historically important to the development of international institutions and because, at a more analytic level, it is relevant as a distinctive pattern of response by the refugees to their predicament. Each of the chapters is constructed around case studies selected either because of their intrinsic importance to the region in question or because they provide special insights into the relationships with which we are concerned.

From a social science perspective, these regional studies are designed to validate our hypotheses, but they also are meant to serve a practical purpose. The public's fear of refugees is closely related to the notion that flows have rapidly increased in recent years and will probably continue to do so in the future. Although nobody can comfortably predict future numbers, a more precise identification of those patterns of social conflict that are characteristic of different regions of the developing world, together with an assessment of their incidence and bearing on the generation of refugee flows, can yield sober projections more useful for decision makers and the concerned public.

These studies provide the foundation for the more general analyses presented in Part Three. Our examination of the relationships between social conflict and the formation of refugee flows is elaborated in Chapter 9, in which we also assess the likely incidence of various patterns. Finally, in Chapter 10, we discuss the policy implications of our findings for individual states and international organizations.

Keely's comments, published in 1981, reveal the long period of gestation required to complete this study. In fact, he identified theoretical affinities in the work of Suhrke and

Zolberg even before they decided to collaborate. They became acquainted in 1981 while preparing papers for a "state of the art" conference organized by Mary M. Kritz of the Rockefeller Foundation.[6]

Suhrke came to the subject by way of research on ethnic conflict in Southeast Asia and takes this opportunity to thank Charles Morrison, at the East–West Center in Honolulu, who in 1979 as a staff member in the U.S. Senate, was instrumental in commissioning research on the impact of the Indochinese refugees on the ASEAN countries. As one of the few academic experts on Southeast Asia on the U.S. East Coast, Suhrke was asked to conduct the study.

Zolberg, a former Africanist, came to refugees by way of research on the role of states in determining and controlling international population movements and takes this opportunity also to thank Gerhard Casper of the University of Chicago Law School, who involved him in that subject (with the promised book still to be completed).

In 1982, Zolberg and Suhrke drew up a formal research proposal, focusing on Asia and Africa, which obtained generous funding from the Ford and Rockefeller foundations. Special thanks are due also to Paul Balaran (Ford) and again Mary M. Kritz, who not only recommended approval of the project but also urged that it be broadened to cover Latin America. On the advice of Patricia Weiss Fagen, the original duo enlisted Sergio Aguayo, who was writing a book on Central American refugees.[7] As is evident from any "before" and "after" comparison, inclusion of the Latin American refugee experience led to a revision of the theoretical arguments previously developed on the basis of Asia and Africa alone. The resulting work is therefore genuinely the output of a trio.

Our research began in late 1983. Over the next two years, we proceeded along two tracks, carrying on research on our respective case studies while simultaneously elaborating the common framework, which at times took on the air of a flying circus (with a bow to Monty Python). Although our grant did not allow us to do extensive field work, Suhrke and Aguayo were able to take advantage of various opportunities to make firsthand observations.

In March 1984, Suhrke and Zolberg presented a preliminary version of the framework of this book, based on case studies of Ethiopia and Afghanistan, at the Center for Migration and Population Studies, Harvard University (Oded Stark, director).[8] Following especially constructive comments from Myron Weiner, they prepared a revised version for delivery at the American Political Science Association meetings the following fall, where they benefited further from the insights of Crawford Young and Art Hansen. In the summer of 1984 the trio embarked on a combined research and lecture tour in Western Europe. Particularly stimulating were the seminar discussions organized by Barbara Harrell-Bond, director of the Refugee Research Center at Oxford University, and the late Hedley Bull; Göran Melander at the University of Lund; and Catherine de Wenden at the Centre d'Etude des Relations Internationales in Paris. Other helpful visits included the British Refugee Group (London), the Refugee Documentation Center (Bonn), the Peace Research Institute (Frankfurt), the Office of the UNHCR (Geneva), and the Independent Commission on International Humanitarian Issues (Geneva), whose report parallels the theme of this book.[9]

It was at this time that the transnational emphasis—stimulated by closer examination of the Latin American experience—emerged as a major theme. This new orientation led to a substantial recasting of the original framework and was formulated in a point paper prepared for a special issue of the *International Migration Review,* edited by Dennis Gallagher, director of the Refugee Policy Group in Washington, D.C.[10]

We further had occasion to discuss our approach in a seminar at the Colegio de Mexico (Mexico City) and to observe refugee settlements in the state of Chiapas. We are grateful to our hosts, who must remain anonymous. Further versions were presented at various scholarly conferences, and a final, memorable week was spent in a mountain retreat, hammering out the last version of the framework, and preparing a detailed outline of this book.[11]

Its completion was delayed by the difficulties of long-distance coauthorship. The regional chapters were written separately but subjected to mutual criticism; the analytical chapters were outlined collectively but written by Zolberg (1 and 9) and Suhrke (10). With additional assistance from the sponsoring foundations, we were able to meet for final workshops in the spring and fall of 1987 and to present our draft manuscript to colleagues at an invitational conference convened at the New School for Social Research in New York City.

All three authors acknowledge their special gratitude to forbearing spouses who put up not only with repeated absences but also, even more patiently, with recurrent visits from one or the other coauthor dropping by for yet another protracted round-the-clock working session. Vera Zolberg bore the brunt of this with unswerving kindness and good humor, often at the expense of her own work. A few good friends also provided moral support at critical junctures, as well as hospitality; among them Christine Birnbaum, University of Paris XIII—Villetanneuse, deserves special mention. Finally, we also thank our respective institutions, the Graduate Faculty of the New School for Social Research, which managed the grants and provided additional research assistance; the School of International Service, American University; and the Colegio de Mexico.

Throughout, our project also benefited from the suggestions of an advisory group whose participants included at various times Senator Dick Clark (former U.S. coordinator for refugees); Richard Day (Subcommittee on Immigration and Refugees, U.S. Senate); Arthur Dewey, deputy assistant secretary, Bureau for Refugee Programs, U.S. Department of State; Patricia Fagen (then Refugee Policy Group); Dennis Gallagher (Refugee Policy Group); Albert Hirschman (Institute for Advanced Study); Philip Johnston (CARE); Charles Keely; David Martin (University of Virginia Law School); Doris Meissner (then executive associate commissioner, U.S. Immigration and Naturalization Service); Michael Posner (Lawyers' Committee for International Rights); Zia Rizvi (then regional representative, UNHCR Regional Office); Saskia Sassen-Koob (City University of New York); Ambassador Walter Stoessel; Dale Swartz (National Immigration Refugee and Citizenship Forum); Julia Taft (consultant); Jerry Tinker (Subcommittee on Immigration and Refugees, U.S. Senate); and Jennifer Whitaker (Council on Foreign Relations). Aguayo and Zolberg also profited from contact with the project on Latin American and Caribbean Immigration and U.S. Foreign Policy conducted by Christopher Mitchell at New York University.

Beyond these collective acknowledgments, Sergio Aguayo wishes to thank Laura O'Dogherty, Mexican Academy of Human Rights; Rodolfo Stavenhagen; Maria Moore; Alfredo Witsschi (UNHCR); Gordon Hutchison, Belela Herrera, Felipe Tomic, and Elizabeth Odio of Project Counseling Service for Latin American Refugees; colleagues at La Jornada, especially Carlos Payan and Carmen Lira; Dr. Roberto Gomez Alfara and Rene Morin of SEDEPAC; Juan Juarez, refugee from Guatemala; and colleagues at El Colegio de Mexico.

Astri Suhrke expresses her gratitude for the patient assistance of the refugees and those aiding them during her fieldwork in South and Southeast Asia since 1979, particularly on numerous trips to Thailand, Pakistan (1984), Sri Lanka (1986, 1987), and Afghanistan (1987, 1988). Until 1985, she drew freely on the active refugee community in Washington, D.C.; after that she benefited from close contact with a smaller but equally concerned community in India. Colleagues who read parts of the manuscript and provided insightful comments are Urmila Phadnis of the School of International Studies, Jawaharlal Nehru University, New Delhi; Jaweed Laiq, lately of Amnesty International, London; and Steven Levine, who regretfully has since left the American University. Two graduate assistants at the American University who were particularly helpful and patient are Andrea Barron and Kum Kum Suneja.

Ary Zolberg thanks Helen Bodian, Human Rights Program, Columbia University, for her helpful suggestions regarding Chapter 1; colleagues at the University of Chicago and the New School for Social Research; and research assistants at the New School, including Cynthia Beaver, Eric Orts, Ansia Petroupoulos, and especially David Vann.

Shortly after this study got under way, Aristide Zolberg was appointed to the University-in-Exile Chair, which was created at the New School in 1984, thanks to a generous gift from the Senate of the City of Berlin (West), to commemorate the founding of the Graduate Faculty of Social and Political Science in 1934 as a haven for German refugee scholars. He is happy to present his contribution to this book as the first product of his occupancy of the Chair.

New York, New York   A.R.Z.
July 1988   A.S.
                                                                               S.A.

CONTENTS

Part One

HISTORICAL AND ANALYTIC PERSPECTIVES

Part One

HISTORICAL AND ANALYTIC PERSPECTIVES

Chapter 1

Who Is a Refugee?

Why Definitions Matter

The definitional problem with which we start is no mere academic exercise but has a bearing on matters of life and death. Although the term *refugee* has deep historical roots, its significance as a legal and administrative category has been vastly enhanced in our own times. The point can be brought home by considering the words that Emma Lazarus used in her poem a century ago:

> *Give me your tired, your poor,*
> *your huddled masses yearning to breathe free*
> *The wretched refuse of your teeming shore. . . .*

Which, among the arrivals thus greeted, were "real" refugees? The need for precise categories did not arise under conditions of unlimited immigration, and so the distinction was not made explicit. However, given the growing numbers, restrictive immigration policies, and limited availability of aid, criteria must be established for distinguishing a set of persons deserving priority with respect to asylum and assistance. *Refugee* has become a category on whose basis international organizations and individual states engage in a process of worldwide triage. Refugee status is a privilege or entitlement, giving those who qualify access to certain scarce resources or services outside their own country, such as admission into another country ahead of a long line of claimants, legal protection abroad, and often some material assistance from private or public agencies.

Confusion arises from the fact that *refugee* has acquired a diffuse meaning in ordinary parlance and a much more precise one in legal and administrative jargon. Jacques Vernant observed as far back as 1953 that "in every-day speech a refugee is someone who has been compelled to abandon his home." Such refugees include victims of an earthquake or a flood, as well as of war or persecution. More generally, the emphasis has been on victimization by events "for which, at least as an individual, he cannot be held responsible."[1] This is still the emphasis today, as in press references to the victims of

3

famine in Africa as "refugees." When conceptualized in this manner, the term covers a large and varied universe of oppressed, suppressed, malcontent, and poor persons, whose movements can be attributed to conditions commonly considered as "push" factors that produce migrations. But a good indication of why this definition is not satisfactory is the distinction in the press of many Western countries between "genuine" and "false" refugees.

On the other side, the prevailing definition in international law displays an air of considerable precision and, in reference to international migrants, is highly selective. According to the Protocol Relating to the Status of Refugees agreed upon by the United Nations in 1967, the term *refugee* applies to "any person" (but only that person) "who is outside the country of his nationality . . . because he has or had well-founded fear of persecution by reason of his race, religion, nationality, membership of a particular social group or political opinion and is unable or, because of such fear, is unwilling to avail himself of the protection of the government of the country of his nationality."[2] This definition, which also applies to people without nationality in the country of their habitual residence, figures centrally in the statute establishing the Office of United Nations High Commissioner for Refugees (UNHCR), and for this reason the set of persons constituted on this basis are generally known as *statutory refugees*. But among those people who genuinely need refuge and assistance, many do not qualify. Is the triage based on this definition warranted? Or should the definition itself be changed to reflect current realities?

We shall return to the protocol and related matters later in this chapter. For now, we point out only that disagreement on these issues is unavoidable, because defining refugees for purposes of policy implementation requires a political choice and an ethical judgment. Research on refugees is also affected by these considerations and so cannot ignore the underlying problems. If refugees are identified simply as the people who have been recognized as such by the appropriate United Nations agency or the authorities of a particular state, research conducted on this basis will consequently help legitimate the ongoing practices and hence exclude a consideration of policy alternatives that might give refugee status to others whose need is even greater. To counteract this, scholars might adopt what some call an *ethnomethodological* stance and accept the self-definition of all those who claim to be refugees. But although this approach might be valid for some purposes, it too would reduce the usefulness of the resulting study for the formation of refugee policy.

Another possibility is to define refugees on a sociological basis, that is, according to criteria grounded in observable social realities, independent of any determination by official bodies or by the refugee's own claims. But this would just move the problem back one step: What criteria should we use to distinguish "genuine but unrecognized" refugees from "false" ones?

This chapter tries to answer the question Who is a refugee? It begins with an analytic review of the Western historical record, identifying the types of social situations that have led to the labeling of particular groups of people as refugees and to the development of commensurate legal categories. The analysis also indicates why only some populations and not others in similar situations were treated as refugees and thereby how the development of codes reflects broader political considerations and discretionary judgments by state authorities. We then consider current legal codes and practices to help clarify today's controversies and to help justify our position in relation to them.

Classic Refugees

Religious Persecution

Although banishment, flight into exile, and the granting of asylum to strangers in need are practices found throughout history, the appearance in early modern Europe of *refugee* as a noun suggests a new awareness of a distinctive social phenomenon. Originating in France in the late seventeenth century, the word *refugee* is recorded as having been used in 1573 in the context of granting asylum and assistance to foreigners escaping persecution.[3] The date suggests that this phenomenon probably referred to the arrival of Calvinists from the adjacent Low Countries, a region where the Reformation had gained considerable support but whose Spanish rulers were engaged in an all-out repression of religious dissent.[4] The English word *refugee* is derived from the French; ironically, it was first used about a hundred years later in reference to the Huguenots, persecuted Calvinists from France who streamed into England immediately before and after the revocation of the Edict of Nantes by Louis XIV on October 18, 1685.[5]

The case of the Huguenots illustrates particularly well the refugee phenomenon.[6] In the early seventeenth century, France was unusual among the European states in having achieved a relatively peaceful coexistence between a Catholic majority and a Protestant minority, which was based on the Edict of Nantes, enacted in 1598 after four decades of civil war. The edict institutionalized a political compromise between Catholic and Calvinist nobles—the latter then amounting to perhaps one-fourth of the aristocracy—whereby Catholicism was reestablished as the state religion but the Protestants achieved a large measure of political autonomy in an archipelago of fortified cities, complete with their own courts of law and military forces. To clinch the compromise, Henry IV—a Calvinist noble who had returned to Catholicism as a condition for assuming the crown—took on the Calvinist Duc de Sully as his chief minister.

However, with each subsequent step in the consolidation of state power, the Protestants' situation came to be viewed as more anomalous. Religious conformity was imposed on the aristocracy in the late 1620s, and Protestant towns such as La Rochelle were shorn of their defensive walls as well as deprived of their political autonomy. Henceforth, the Reformed community survived at the mercy of the king. By the middle of the seventeenth century, French Protestants were reduced to a minority of from 6 to 8 percent, largely bourgeois in character, except for a rural enclave in the south (Languedoc). Having achieved considerable prominence in the economic and professional sphere, the Calvinist bourgeoisie rallied in support of the monarchy during the mid-century confrontation known as the Fronde. Nevertheless, shortly after seizing power in 1661, Louis XIV set out to eliminate Calvinism from France. This undertaking makes sense only in regard to absolutist ideology, as an effort by the king to achieve what he conceived to be a perfectly unified polity.

The revocation of the Edict of Nantes in 1685 was the capstone of a twenty-year-long systematic attempt to undermine every requirement for the survival of the Reformed community, making it impossible for people to be born, work, marry, or die as Calvinists. Except for the ministers, many of whom were sent into exile, the objective was not to expel the Calvinists from France but to force their return to the Catholic fold. On the eve of the revocation, the Calvinist population numbered about 878,000, down to about 4 percent of the French total. In keeping with the tenets of mercantilism, the state prohibited this valuable population from emigrating. Nevertheless, the Calvinists began to leave the country in the early 1680s, and about 40,000 escaped each year between 1685 and 1688. The total outflow is estimated at 200,000 between 1681 and 1720, nearly one-fourth of the Protestants—and by all accounts, the most affluent part of the community. The exiles scattered widely, with most going to Britain and the Netherlands, some to Switzerland and Brandenburg-Prussia, and a few as far afield as Russia, the British colonies of North America, and the Dutch colony in southern Africa. Among the three-fourths who remained behind, some converted; a small number were sent to the galleys; the southern peasants rose up in rebellion; but most led a quiet double life, quietly going about their secular affairs while surreptitiously participating in "desert" congregations until the dawn of tolerance in the mid-eighteenth century. The surviving community was about half its pre-Revocation size.

What made the Huguenots refugees? First, they were people fleeing a life-threatening danger—with "life" referring to spiritual as well as physical existence—but they constituted something more distinctive than an aggregate of individuals in flight, and the danger they faced was distinctive as well. Their plight stemmed from membership in a religious organization targeted for destruction by the governmental authorities of their own country, in peacetime and without any provocation on their part. Although this persecution may have been rooted in the emergence in Europe of a "persecuting society" that actively repressed all forms of deviance, our own analysis focuses more immediately on the dynamics of absolutist state-formation.[7] As persons whose flight can clearly be attributed to the fear of persecution on account of religion, the Huguenots would certainly qualify as statutory refugees under the current definition. Indeed, they provide a historical model of the classic type of refugees, still relevant today.

How relevant it is, however, is one of the questions that this study seeks to answer. On the occasion of the tricentennial of the revocation of the Edict of Nantes, an unofficial publication of the United Nations High Commission for Refugees (UNHCR) emphasized that this historic movement into exile "had many features in common with the situation of refugees today: emergency assistance, protection, refoulement, pirate attacks on 'boat people' at sea, integration problems, resettlement, repatriation."[8] The article concludes with the observation that the Huguenots "also brought great benefits to their countries of asylum." However, it neglects to point out that most of the people with whom the UNHCR is concerned today do not fit this classic type and that the new types of refugees are much more likely to be a burden than an asset to the receiving countries.

What made the Calvinists refugees was not only persecution by Louis XIV but also their recognition by other countries' political authorities as people to whom asylum and assistance were due. The fact that the term *refugee* originated among the receiving countries highlights an ill-understood but fundamental feature of the phenomenon: For a refugee flow to begin, certain conditions must be met in one or more of the states of destination as well as in the state of origin. People cannot leave their country if they have no place to go—a truism that holds for all types of international migration—and the availability of such a place is in turn largely determined by those who control the places of destination, usually governmental authorities.[9] Should a government be bent on persecuting some target group, the asylum policies of other countries may well determine whether the persecution will lead to a refugee flow or to some other outcome, such as acceptance of severe disabilities by the target group, or even mass murder. The experience of many European Jews during the Nazi era is a tragic case in point.[10]

Asylum was available to the Calvinists because whatever made them unacceptable to their state of origin was, on the contrary, supported by some politically powerful groups elsewhere. Most obviously, they were welcome in states that had established some form of Protestantism as their official religion, or in which fellow Calvinists had achieved significant power. A sense of obligation toward fellow Protestants in distress was undoubtedly a leading motive, and although this might be labeled *humanitarianism*, it should be understood that this humanitarianism was decidedly partisan. Within the conflictual international political arena of the sixteenth and seventeenth centuries, the provision of refuge to foreign Calvinists also was an astute move in the game of statecraft. Moreover, in the dawning age of mercantilism, the prospects of gaining a population renowned for its skills and wealth clearly came into play as well, as the UNHCR article cited reminds us.

Extrapolating from these specific historical circumstances to a more general level, we can think of the classic type of refugee as arising from a broader universe than merely the country within which persecution occurs. This universe contains several interacting political entities—let us call them states—controlling territories and the people they contain and varying significantly from one another with respect to some ideological elements (e.g., religion), thus forming a world characterized by certain pluralist features. One such world was that of the ancient Greek city-states, in which the phenomenon of political exile and asylum appears to have been quite common. Another such world arose in Western Europe in the epoch that we are considering, when the region as a whole experienced major upheavals resulting in the formation of competing national states and religions.

The significance of outsiders in determining whether victims of persecution become refugees is highlighted further by the contrast between what happened to the Calvinists from the Low Countries and France, and the approximately 150,000 Jews forced to leave Spain in 1492 for refusing to convert. Some sneaked into neighboring France, from which Jews had been officially expelled at the turn of the fourteenth century; others moved similarly to the Low Countries or quietly joined correligionists living under the pope's protection in his own states. Many more moved to Portugal, whose sovereign saw in them a golden opportunity for economic promotion, but in a few years, they were expelled from that country as well. Most of the Jews of Iberia scattered among the Muslim states of North Africa and the Middle East, which welcomed them for the wealth and skills they brought and where they joined established communities of their own kind.

Like the Huguenots, the Iberian Jews were faced with a life-threatening danger because of their religion. Banishment from one's own country might be thought of as "social execution," paralleling the notion of "social death" that is central to slavery.[11] However, from the perspective of Christian Europe in the late fifteenth century, the Jews were not "innocent victims" of religious persecution but a people guilty of wrongfully resisting legitimate acts of their sovereign, by adhering to a proscribed religion; they therefore deserved their unhappy fate. But because they would qualify as refugees according to the criteria used in international law today, we can think of them as a classic case of *unrecognized* refugees.

But let us note that this judgment is based on a relativistic view of religion—that is, that all are equally deserving of respect—such as that underlying the notion of religious freedom in the American Bill of Rights and other Western constitutions. Because this is a modern conception of religion, not universally shared even today, the statement that "the Jews of Iberia were unrecognized refugees" is accepted as valid only in the context of specific shared understandings. It is precisely the formation of such a community of discourse, within which certain categories of persons are viewed as refugees, that we are seeking to reconstruct. Its development followed a "Kantian" progression, beginning with particularistic judgments of the sort we have just seen, contingent on the circumstances prevailing in a given country at a given time; to which, over time, other categories were added; and gradually becoming more universalistic until, after World War II, the general criteria for identifying refugees were institutionalized in a body of international law administered by a bureaucratic organization staffed by appropriate experts.

Religious refugees proliferated throughout Europe in the sixteenth and seventeenth centuries. In addition to those cited, major streams included Muslim Spaniards, expelled in a series of waves beginning immediately after the fall of Granada in 1492 and culminating in the deportation of 275,000 people across the Mediterranean in the five years after 1609; German Catholics and Lutherans, involving a series of exchanges of religious minorities at the end of the Thirty Years' War, when the innumerable principalities of the Holy Roman Empire attempted to sort themselves out according to the principle that the ruler's religion determined that of his territory as a whole; and Irish Catholics, beginning in the late sixteenth century, and especially in the mid-seventeenth, when many fled to Spain and France in the face of Oliver Cromwell's attempt to deport them to the waste of Western Ireland (Connacht) or, if they resisted, as indentured plantation labor to Barbados. To these might be added the various groups of Protestant dissenters who came under pressure to relocate from England and Scotland to their sovereign's possessions in the dangerous wilderness of the New World. But refugees were generated even in the New World itself, as when French Acadians were expelled from their Nova Scotia home by British authorities after 1755, with many ending up in Louisiana.

These movements halted by the middle of the seventeenth century, partly because after two centuries of enforcement, most of the states concerned had in fact achieved a high degree of religious homogeneity and also because by then Catholic-Protestant differences had lost their significance in regard to international political conflict. As absolutism gave way to enlightened despotism, religious tolerance became accepted on grounds of principle as well as self-interest. Committed to a doctrine of individual rights, the revolutionary regimes that subsequently emerged in America and France emancipated religious minorities from their remaining disabilities. The absence of religious persecution became the hallmark of "civilized" states, and thus anyone who was so persecuted came to be considered a refugee.

Political Opposition

The conflicts of this new age fostered a new type of refugee flow. In the latter part of the eighteenth century, the West—now encompassing the descendants of Europeans who had settled in North and South America—began experiencing another epochal transformation, extending into the political, cultural, and economic spheres, each of which conditioned the others, and involving once again interpenetration of the domestic and international levels.[12] It was both the age of democratic revolutions and the onset of this great transformation that resulted in the emergence of industrial capitalism as the dominant mode of economic organization. A distinctive feature of the conflicts of this period is that they were fought in the nascent language of political ideology, with the objective of preserving or achieving a particular regime and with status groups—the aristocracy, the bourgeoisie—as the most relevant social categories. This ideological dimension entered the international level as well. By the early 1790s, France was seeking to expand in the name of revolution, and most of the other European states were coalescing to contain France in the name of legitimacy. At the same time, internal political divisions became international-ized: English democrats were viewed as French agents, and French conservatives as the servants of Austria or England.

These new waves of refugees in the West were also recorded in linguistic usage. In English, the old term was put to new use in the late eighteenth century: "Since the revolt in the British colonies in America," noted the *Encyclopedia Britannica* in 1797, "we have frequently heard of American refugees."[13] In France, however, the revolutionary experience gave rise to a new term, *émigré*. Unlike *refugee*, it was a term of opprobrium, imposed by those who disapproved of the people departing.

The total number of refugees produced by the French Revolution has been estab-lished at 129,000. On the basis of a population of 25 million, this is a ratio of approxi-mately 5 per 1,000.[14] Of these, 25,000 were members of the clergy, deported for refusing to take an oath of allegiance to the revolutionary constitution. The others consisted of two somewhat overlapping categories: members of the nobility who came under general suspicion during the Terror, regardless of their degree of involvement in the political opposition, and political opponents of successive ruling groups in the various phases of the revolution, or merely those whom they believed to be their enemies. Less well known is that the American Revolution triggered an equivalent movement. Although estimates of the number of loyalists who left for Canada, Nova Scotia, or England run as high as 100,000, R. R. Palmer adopts a more conservative 60,000. On the basis of a population of about 2.5 million (including slaves, some of whom became refugees), this produces a ratio of 24 refugees per 1,000, five times higher than in France.[15]

The refugee flows caused by the revolutionary conflicts of the late eighteenth century differed significantly from the classic type, in that the repression was directed against individuals deemed undesirable or dangerous because of their political opinion—that is, their response to current issues, especially to the objectives to be pursued by the govern-ment and the activities carried out to implement them. This reflected the rise of ideology as a major element of political communities, a process initiated by revolutionary chal-lengers, who justified their attacks on the legitimate authority by appealing to higher principles. But revolutionaries breed counterrevolutionaries; in the face of these chal-lenges, defenders of the status established a doctrine founded on principles of their own. As in the case of religious homogeneity for absolutist states, the achievement of these objectives was evidence of political unanimity. Thus, revolutionary and counterrevolu-tionary regimes were driven beyond the mere neutralizing of opponents to repress sys-tematically any political dissent.

The French Revolution was rapidly internationalized as the new regime launched preemptive moves in preparation for a Europe-wide counterrevolutionary thrust and as involvement in war helped radicalize the regime. With refugees living in what were now enemy countries and participating in operations against France, internal dissent came to be perceived as even more dangerous. As tensions were exacerbated, the domain of repression expanded to encompass *ancien régime* elites as a whole, whose loyalty was questioned because of their position in the social order. The nature of the target thus shifted perceptibly, from a collection of individuals holding certain political opinions to a social group.

Across the Atlantic, the bulk of the outflow consisted of what the American revo-lutionaries called *Tories,* colonial partisans of continued British rule, many of whom fought on the British side in the war, and they even included some slaves, who were rewarded with manumission. As already noted, from the British perspective there was no doubt that these "Loyalists" were refugees. But considered from a contemporary perspective, their status is more ambiguous. The decision to leave undoubtedly reflected widespread apprehension of what the Americans might do once they came to power, but because the people in question left before having lived under the new regime, there was no opportunity for "persecution" to take place. However, the governments of the several states did confiscate the property of those who emigrated, as revolutionary France later did as well, and in many instances, they enacted laws prohibiting their return. Because the impossibility of returning to one's homeland does provide grounds for claiming asylum, it can be argued that many of the Loyalists would qualify as refugees today.

The outcome in this case was tantamount to repatriation, not only to Britain itself, but especially to what are now the Canadian provinces of Quebec, Nova Scotia, and Ontario, where the Loyalists received large grants of land in exchange for guarding the remainders of the British Empire in North America against its southern enemies and for preparing for the next round of conflict. The fact of having desirable places to go to probably stimulated some departures but also contributed to the ambiguity of the movement, by giving it an element of ordinary migration. Overall, much as the case of the French émigrés foreshadows the initial type of refugee flow produced by successful social revolutions, the American experience anticipates the exodus characteristically triggered by wars of national liberation.

Mirroring the cause of the new flows, the response of states was determined essentially by the orientation of their government. It is noteworthy that the issue of refugee policy precipitated a major political crisis in the new American state. In the 1790s, as the world's only successful revolutionary republic, the United States emerged as a potential place of asylum for defeated European democrats. However, the ruling Federalists viewed the arriving British and Irish political refugees as dangerous "Jacobins" and devised legislative barriers both to restrict their entry and to punish their American friends. The campaign to repeal the Alien and Sedition acts in turn contributed to the triumph of the Jeffersonians in 1800 and helped liberalize the American regime.[16]

The comings and goings of political refugees became commonplace in the West in the nineteenth century. The outcomes of the continual confrontations between revolutionaries and counterrevolutionaries, as well as between national independence movements and imperial authorities—the two often being intertwined—led to new flows of refugees or enabled earlier exiles to go home, as did the French émigrés after the Restoration. Michael Marrus has emphasized that politically determined migration during this period "generally concerned *exiles,* individuals who had chosen their political path, rather than large masses of people torn loose from their society and driven to seek refuge."[17] However, the streams of exiles sometimes became quite large and concentrated in time, showing that crises tended to occur in waves, not only because the political conjuncture of most of the Western countries was affected by common transnational processes such as fluctuations in the business cycle, but also because these countries had become a single network of communication, within which events in one country (e.g., the French Revolution of July 1830) could have instant effects elsewhere (e.g., in Belgium, Poland, and even Canada).

The refugees of this period came mostly from the ranks of revolutionary and nationalist movements, which usually were unsuccessful, at least in the short term; havens were therefore limited to the few liberal regimes. Although they did not hesitate to repress indigenous revolutionaries, the governments of the liberal states were generally tolerant of the exiles, who made few demands on them beyond asylum itself, as long as they stayed out of domestic politics and their presence was compatible with foreign policy. After a time, such refugees tended to go home, but occasionally they were asked to move on.

Among the major flows were the Polish rebels of 1830, inspired by the July Revolution, of whom over 5,000 fled after the insurgency was defeated, mostly to France. Another unsuccessful attempt at gaining independence from the Russian tsars triggered another outflow in 1863. Similarly, many of the defeated French Canadian *rouges,* followers of Papineau who had staged an uprising in 1837–38 on behalf of reform, along the lines of Jacksonian democracy, fled to the United States—as did some English Chartists and Irish nationalists. Although no detailed overview is available, by all accounts the Europe-wide mid-century crisis produced tens of thousands of refugees, originating mainly in France, Germany, Italy, and Austro-Hungary and going mostly to Belgium, Switzerland, the United States, and Britain. There were also intermittent trickles from Italy, Spain, and Russia, amounting to substantial numbers over the course of the century. Following the annexation of their region to Germany, about 130,000 residents of Alsace and Lorraine left home in 1871 in order to remain French, but this constituted another type of refugee movement, which we shall examine in the next section.

In the earlier part of the century, Marrus has suggested, "the world of political exiles was that of the relatively well-to-do or, at least, of the once well-to-do" because "national politics and a long-term investment in the business of revolution were not generally possible for ordinary Europeans." Moreover, "it took some measure of affluence to flee abroad in the first place."[18] However, these observations are somewhat misleading with respect to Western Europe, where workers and even peasants participated quite early on in radical social and political movements. For activists from the lower classes, the consequences of defeat were more likely to be incarceration, transportation to penal colonies (such as Australia for the Irish and Algeria for the French), and even massacre, as occurred in Paris in June 1848 and again in the spring of 1871. Later, the increased availability of cheap long-distance transportation made it possible for workers to flee as well.[19] Marrus has pointed out, for example, that in the French civil war of 1871 and its aftermath, 20,000 Parisians died; 35,000 were arrested; and about 45,000 fled, "including men and women from across the social spectrum," mostly to England and Belgium.[20] The failure of the Russian Revolution of 1905 also prompted a massive exodus of politically active workers. As there still were few barriers, most of them flowed with the ongoing immigration tide to England, France, and especially the United States. Nevertheless, the lower classes remained less mobile in the twentieth century, as tragically illustrated by the wholesale massacre of peasants after the defeat of the 1932 uprising in El Salvador.

National Minorities and the Stateless

The latter decades of the nineteenth century marked the beginning of a protracted crisis, lasting until the middle of the twentieth century, which propelled refugee issues to the fore of international concern and gave rise to the institutional apparatus that prevails today. This apparatus is characterized by both a resurgence of the classic types—on a much larger scale and under circumstances that rendered their plight more urgent and more difficult to resolve—and especially by the appearance of a largely new type.

Once again, these flows arose as the by-product of a regionwide upheaval.[21] The global expansion of the international political and economic system entailed a dislocation of the economic and political structures that had provided Europe with a century of peace. Its striving to become an economic and political empire—on the scale of Britain, the United States, and Russia—prompted Germany to embark on an expansionist path. The outbreak of World War I in turn exacerbated all existing tensions, including the social and national conflicts among the belligerents.

World War I had especially dramatic consequences for the Russian, Austro-Hungarian, and Ottoman empires, which formed a huge region spanning Europe and Asia and which had been experiencing for some time the familiar tensions and conflicts that accompany the transition from traditional social and political orders, and the transformation of empires into national states. Internationalization came on top of a number of other features that helped make these upheavals particularly serious. The region as a whole constituted a zone of economic "backwardness" in relation to the world of industrial capitalism, deeply affected by the destructive transformations it wrought, but without the benefits of the rapid increase in per-capita income it brought to the early developers. The region contained very large populations, mostly rural and living close to subsistence, that were beginning to increase more rapidly, and the upheavals came at a time when railroads as well as automobiles increased the possibility of moving large masses of troops and civilians over long distances. At the time the refugee-producing conflicts began, the relevant regions were already producing very large outflows of international migrants. Finally, all three empires had heterogeneous ethnic configurations by the standards of the Western European countries where the nation-state as a political form originated. Attempts to remold these configurations according to this model were therefore bound to run into almost insurmountable obstacles.

The war brought about the collapse and dismantlement of both the Ottoman and Austro-Hungarian empires, as well as the collapse of the Russian tsarist regime followed by revolution and civil war, which in turn produced numerous refugees. In addition, attempts by the successor states to "unmix" their nationalities resulted in the identification of minorities as obstacles to be eliminated.[22]

Reflecting on this experience, Hannah Arendt observed in 1951 that "since the Peace Treaties of 1919 and 1920 the refugees and the stateless have attached themselves like a curse to all the newly established states on earth which were created in the image of the nation-state."[23] Her explanation focuses on the "corruption" of the traditional Western doctrine of human rights which, with the proliferation of national states, gave way to that of nationally guaranteed rights. Implied from the outset in the system of nation-states was that "only nationals could be citizens, only people of the same national origin could enjoy the full protection of legal institutions, that persons of different nationality needed some law of exception until or unless they were completely assimilated and divorced from their origin."[24] But this remained hidden from view until the nation-state formula was adopted to organize political life in states containing ethnically mixed populations, often so inextricably interspersed that it proved impossible to form viable, ethnically homogeneous political entities. The gap between the formula and the social realities generated enormous tensions, out of which emerged two "victim groups," the minorities and the stateless.[25]

The minorities were persons insisting on a nationality different from that of the state in which they lived. This different nationality often happened to be that of a neighboring state. As the doctrine of nationally guaranteed rights came to be equated with the notion of rights guaranteed to nationals only, the minorities were thus turned into political misfits.[26]

The stateless were misfits in an even more extreme sense, in that no matter how national or provincial boundaries might be reorganized, they would always remain residual groups who did not belong to any established nation-state or recognized national minority. The proliferation of stateless persons, of whom the most prominent were the Jews, was the culmination of the nation's conquest of the state. This is why Arendt considered them to be "the most symptomatic group in contemporary politics," people who live necessarily "outside the pale of the law" and hence are vulnerable not only in their states of origin but also in the world at large. Others were deliberately reduced to stateless status when a type of state emerged that "would rather lose its citizens than harbor people with different views."[27] The counterpart to the rise of nationality as the exclusive source of rights was thus that "denationalization became a powerful weapon of totalitarian politics."[28]

As a historical account, Arendt's analysis is problematic in a number of ways.[29] Most important, her insistence on the newness of the victim-group phenomenon in the period following World War I is misleading in that, as we have seen, state-formation in the sixteenth and seventeenth centuries also resulted in the targeting of minorities for persecution. Nevertheless, Arendt brilliantly highlights the essentially political dynamics involved. With the qualifications indicated, the emergence of target minorities as a result of the "nationalization of rights" can be seen as an instance of a more general process, whereby the state's choice of an integration formula determines positive and negative categories of persons and its ensuing relationships with these groups. The formula is the construction of a collective identity encompassing the rulers and the majority of the population; its foundation may be religious, racial, or even ideological, as well as national, but each has distinct implications. In early modern Europe, for example, affiliation with one or another Christian denomination was conceived to be a matter of individual will, leading sovereigns to pressure their religious minorities to conform through conversion or abjuration. This also was the case for Islam and can be seen at work today in fundamentalist Iran, which persecutes Muslim heretics. But if religious categories are founded on ascendancy—traditionally conceptualized as "blood"—they are by definition immutable, and therefore the state cannot achieve its objectives by transforming the deviants into persons of the approved mold. In an earlier era, Orthodox Christians could be made into Muslims, but in the twentieth century, Greeks cannot be made into Turks. Under these circumstances, the adopting of a mononational formula by a multiethnic state entails some form of exclusion, either extreme segregation or expulsion. Moreover, interactions among several states striving to achieve this monistic objective tend to invite mutual hostility and endless attempts at unmixing nationalities.

The leading European powers, which formed a rudimentary international political community, undertook to guarantee from the outside the minorities' elementary rights. First devised as a condition for the minorities' support of Romanian independence in 1856, after World War I this method was included in the League of Nations, through minority treaties imposed on the newly created states.[30] However, these treaties were clearly discriminatory, in that only the new states were bound to such obligations; political resentment against the minorities consequently intensified because their very presence forestalled achievement of full sovereignty. For example, after independence Romania denied citizenship to Jews, despite its treaty obligations.[31] Defined as enemies of the nation, the Jews were prohibited from attending state schools, harassed while carrying out their economic activities, and in many cases forced to relocate. Not only did the Romanian authorities deny the Jews protection, but they even encouraged violence against them. Consequently, out of an estimated 200,000, nearly one-third had emigrated by 1914.

Unlike the Jews, most of the refugees associated with the "unmixing of peoples" remained in their original empires, usually moving from what had become a new state, in which they constituted a minority, to another where their nationality was dominant. Most prominent were the population exchanges following the transformation of the Ottoman Empire into a set of states aspiring to become nations, a protracted process that began with the emergence of Greece as an independent state in 1832 after a decade-long war and that is still far from completed, as indicated by ongoing ethnic struggles in Cyprus and Turkey.[32] Internationalized from the start, when the Greek separatists obtained considerable support from various European powers, the resulting conflicts have remained so all along, as indicated by the Turkish invasion of Cyprus in 1974. Beginning with Greeks fleeing the island of Chios to escape massacre in 1822, the series continued with thousands of Bulgarian revolutionaries and Christian peasants leaving Bosnia and Herzegovina in the 1860s and 1870s, and Muslim settlers from Greece and territories annexed by Serbia and Montenegro in 1878. With the onset of nearly continuous war in the Balkans, target groups proliferated and refugees grew into the hundreds of thousands by the eve of World War I.

The population exchanges between Greece and Turkey in the 1920s illustrate the formation of a new type of refugee, stemming from the organization of a largely involuntary unmixing of peoples under the aegis of international law.[33] Background features include the secular migrations of both Greeks and Turks from their respective homelands within the Ottoman Empire to regions inhabited by the other, and the tensions between Turkey and Greece beginning when the latter achieved independence at the expense of the former and became a client state of Russia and Britain, intent on reducing Ottoman power. Committed to the reunion of all Greek nationals, Greece steadily encroached on Turkish territory, and each of these gains in turn precipitated the flight of a part of the local Muslim population.[34] Turkey and Greece then joined opposite sides in World War I, hoping thereby to promote their respective aims. Being on the victors' side, Greece was awarded the remnants of European Turkey except for Constantinople (Istanbul) itself. Encouraged by the Allies, in 1921 Greece invaded Asian Turkey but was defeated by Mustafa Kemal (later "Atatürk") on the outskirts of Ankara. The Turks then pushed the Greeks back to Smyrna, where in September they laid waste to the Greek sections of the city and massacred the population. About one million refugees fled to Greece during the rout and its immediate aftermath.

The Turkish victory consolidated control in the hands of the Kemalist revolutionaries. Viewing the flight of the Greeks as an unanticipated opportunity to promote the transformation of Turkey into a genuine national state, the government not only refused their repatriation—in violation of international law—but also insisted that remaining citizens of the Greek Orthodox faith leave as well. In return, asserting that it had neither the resources nor the land to resettle these refugees, the Greek government demanded the transfer to Turkey of the much smaller Muslim population of Greece, already reduced from 800,000 to about 400,000 in the wake of earlier episodes of "unmixing." This was acceptable to Turkey, because the lands to be vacated by the Greeks would facilitate their resettlement and because they feared Greek reprisals against the Turkish minority concerned. Moreover, the convention establishing the exchange would retroactively legitimize the Turkish government's violation of international law with respect to its Greek Orthodox population.[35] The regrouping of populations helped end the international conflict and the violence. But in contrast with what was being done in similar situations in other parts of Europe, this regrouping was made compulsory, without any pretense of consulting the population concerned. Although few Greek Orthodox adherents remained in Turkey, a large number of Muslims still were living in Greece.

The most tragic of the target groups were the Armenians, who must figure prominently in any account such as this, not only because many of them became refugees, but also because most did not—a fate that befell also most European Jews two decades later and, more recently, victims of violence similarly trapped in Nigeria, Uganda, Indonesia, Kampuchea, and East Timor.[36] Long prominent in Eurasian long-distance trade, the Armenians were divided between the tsarist and Ottoman empires. In the latter, in the last quarter of the nineteenth century they constituted a Christian minority of 1.5 to 2 million, who controlled a large share of the expanding trade and were prominent at the highest levels of government. Although many remained in their Anatolian homeland, while carrying out their economic activities the Armenians scattered throughout the empire, with substantial clusters in most of the towns and cities. Concurrently, influenced by earlier developments in the Greek community, they became a self-conscious national group. However, in the 1870s Sultan Abdul Hamid sought to stem the empire's decline and disintegration, by reinforcing the central authority vis-à-vis the various national communities. This required, among other things, the "ottomanization" of the administration, an objective in which the Armenians emerged as an obstacle. With the onset of conflict between the sultan and the tsar, the Armenians' loyalty also became an issue. Although the victorious Russians imposed on Turkey a treaty affording protection to the Armenians, this merely compounded Ottoman resentment. Tensions were further exacerbated by the steady arrival in Turkey between 1878 and 1897 of Muslim victims of Christian persecution in Greece, Bulgaria, and Serbia, amounting to perhaps one million.[37]

After nearly twenty years of intermittent repression, which in turn further stimulated Armenian aspirations toward national independence, a large massacre took place in the summer of 1894, triggered by the refusal of an Armenian community to pay tribute to the Kurdish chieftain to whom it was obligated. This was the first of a two-year-long series, culminating in the murder of 6,000 Armenians in Constantinople in August 1896. Estimates of the total number of victims range from 50,000 to 300,000, or between 2 and 15 percent of the Armenian population; many of the survivors fled to Russia or Persia. The use of terror was "rational" in that it forced the Armenians to withdraw from public life and thereby enabled Turkey to escape its treaty obligations, as did Romania with respect to the Jews. More massacres carried out by the reformist Young Turks in 1909 prompted the Europeans once again to intervene on behalf of their protégés, but the new guarantees fell by the wayside with the outbreak of World War I. Acting in the name of national security, in 1915 the authorities disarmed all Armenian soldiers, rounded up and deported most of the leaders, and drove masses of people from the Armenian homelands, adjacent to the Russian empire, to arid wastelands in the south, where they were not expected to survive. Massive deportation was not in itself a new method of persecution. The much earlier cases of the Moriscos, Acadians, and Irish come to mind. What was different, perhaps, was the alliance of modern technology and communication that enabled over a short period of time a vast operation of destruction, whose toll amounted to as high as 800,000, or from one-half to two-thirds of the target population. Hundreds of thousands survivors fled north to Russia or south to Syria, with some turning up in Egypt as well.

A third episode began with the collapse of the Russian empire and the onset of the Russian Revolution, which were viewed by the subject nationalities as an opportunity for achieving independence. Among them were the Georgians, Azerbaijanis, and Armenians, all of whom attempted to create republics of their own, to be united in a trans-Caucasian federation. The possibility of an Armenian state fostered a massive outpouring from Turkey, whose population by the end of 1918 was estimated at 1 million, half of whom were refugees from the south. However, the new state was continuously besieged by its neighbors, and in 1921, Turkey and the Soviet Union settled their differences by dividing up the territory between themselves. The refuge thus turned into a trap. Abandoned by their European protectors, refused admission by Georgia and Azerbaijan, another 200,000 Armenians perished as the returning Turks took their revenge. The objective of the new Turkish state was no longer to subjugate the Armenians, but to rid itself of them. About 90,000 were expelled to Greece, where many were massacred by Turkish armies in the subsequent conflict. Others departed over the next few years for the Soviet Union, which in 1926 reported 94,000 foreign-born Armenians.[38] About 125,000 went to Western Europe, of whom half went to France. The United States recorded slightly more than 100,000 arrivals from Asian Turkey between 1910 and 1921, after which—as the result of immigration restrictions—the level was drastically reduced to an average of about 2,500 a year for the remainder of the 1920s.[39]

The distinctiveness of genocide thus arises from the means employed rather than the objective to be achieved. In the cases of the Armenians and the Jews in Nazi-controlled Europe, as with many other minorities before and after them, the objective was to rid the land of their presence. Turkey initially sought to achieve this by terrorizing the Armenians into flight. In Germany, the Nazis similarly sought at first to rid themselves of the Jews by a combination of expulsion (foreign Jews) and the imposition of conditions that would cause them to leave (German Jews). In both cases, when external conditions made emigration impossible, the persecutor resorted to mass murder. Among these external conditions, particularly with respect to the Jews, was the refusal of other states to accept the target population as refugees. This constituted, in effect, collusion with the persecutor in a conspiracy to deny exit.[40]

The Reinstatement of Barriers Against Exit

One of the hallmarks of the twentieth century is the reinstatement of prohibitions against exit, such as were common in the age of absolutism but now implemented by states with a much greater ability to control movement across their borders. The classic case is the Soviet Union.

Initially, the refugee flows generated by the Russian Revolution far exceeded any generated by violent regime changes in earlier historical experience, not only because the state affected had a much larger population than did any of the others, but also because the upheaval took place within the context of the collapse and transformation of the Russian empire, with consequences similar to those in the Ottoman case. The collapse was protracted, brought about by the catastrophic defeats Russia experienced at the onset of World War I.[41] Already reaching about 2.7 million by the end of 1915, the number of internally displaced persons escalated further to 5 million within the next few months.

The seizure of government by revolutionaries a year later precipitated a protracted civil war involving complex shifting alignments of both social groups and nationalities, which were made more violent by substantial foreign intervention in support of the counterrevolutionary camp. As is almost inevitable under conditions of near-subsistence, the upheaval disrupted basic food production and sanitary conditions to the point that the least unfavorable events might precipitate famine and epidemics, as in fact occurred in 1921. This type of situation is commonly encountered in the contemporary developing world as well. In Russia, the ranks of the uprooted were steadily swollen by masses of army deserters; of civilians escaping White or Red terror or just trying to get out of the way of the fighting; and of fleeing minorities, many of whom poured into provinces that were emerging as successor states. Although estimates of refugees originating in Russia ranged at the time up to 3 million, many of them were displaced Poles and Germans, who were merely returning to their homes, located in what had now become a new country. A more realistic assessment is that the Russian Revolution created about 1 million refugees outside the boundaries of the old empire. Many were defeated counterrevolutionaries who initially made their way to Germany and France, where they evoked considerable political sympathy. The United States, which at that time did not distinguish between refugees and ordinary immigrants with respect to admission, recorded about 92,000 arrivals from Russia between 1917 and 1924, after which the new quota system reduced the flow to about 3,000 a year for the remainder of the decade.

By this time, however, the policies of the receivers hardly mattered, as in the mid-1920s the Soviet Union adopted a no-exit policy, which with minor exceptions it has maintained to this day. Consequently, despite the massive initial flows, over the long term the Russian Revolution generated a much smaller number of refugees than probably would have been the case otherwise, as large numbers probably would have taken flight during the murderous collectivization drives and purges of the 1930s. As it was, these produced only a few individual escapes to Poland, Romania, and the Baltic states; the only mass movement recorded is the exodus of Kazakhs to China in 1933.[42]

As Alan Dowty has pointed out, the roots of the Soviet Union's exit policy can be traced back to prerevolutionary Russia, which never had a tradition of freedom of movement, either inside or outside the country, because this was incompatible with the maintenance of serfdom. Although prerevolutionary Marxists advocated lifting such restrictions, Lenin's views of the state "laid the basis for future controls," in that all citizens were to be considered as "hired employees" of the state and to be required to serve it.[43] Adopted later on by many other states, this stance emerged as the common feature of a disparate array of modern authoritarian regimes, including not only those of the Marxist-Leninist persuasion but also Fascist Italy, Spain, and Portugal, as well as Nazi Germany.

The prohibition of emigration can thus be seen as a normal concomitant of state-directed economic autarchy. This was surely the leading motive in the case of Italy and Portugal (as late as the 1960s), as labor-exporting countries that sought to stem emigration in order to maximize the internal supply of labor and thus reduce its price. The need for such controls is even more urgent in the case of states trying to develop by imposing great sacrifices on the current generation. Beyond this, "the Bolshevik attitude toward emigration was also shaped by civil war and foreign intervention. It was feared that those leaving the country would swell the ranks of the White armies and other enemies abroad. From there it was a short step to equating the wish to emigrate with opposition to the socialist state."[44] This is applicable more generally to tense international conjunctures, including the Cold War and more limited regional conflicts such as that between the United States and Cuba.

But the prohibition of emigration also serves more purely political objectives. Because exit is tantamount to "voting with one's feet," an alternative to protest, authoritarian regimes that claim to rest on democratic consent cannot afford such concrete evidence of alienation.[45] Against this background, emigration may be used occasionally to relieve tensions or to rid the state of some unwanted ethnic or national minority. However, permission to leave is usually disguised as expulsion or coupled with humiliating measures, so as to avoid appearing to grant to undesirables a privilege refused to the majority of nationals.

In ancient times, great walls were built to keep invaders out, but in the twentieth century, they have been built to keep people in. This development is at the root of a major dilemma for liberal states. While denouncing such policies as a violation of human rights, liberal states also deplore the intrusion on the international scene of burdensome refugee flows; hence, they tacitly accept such no-exit policies as a solution to a potential problem. This is highlighted by a paradoxical turn of events, whereby the receiving countries sometimes demand that the refugee-generating countries do a better job of preventing victims of repression from leaving.[46] Adopting a relatively open admissions policy is therefore the necessary complement to advocating freedom of exit.

Refugee Crises and the Emergence of an International Refugee Regime

The First European Crisis

With an estimated total of 9.5 million in 1926, the refugee crisis of the post–World War I years reached a magnitude unprecedented in European experience.[47] Although these numbers are roughly comparable to current counts for the developing world as a whole, when the population size of the relevant countries is taken into account, the European crisis stands out as relatively much greater. Fear of these huge flows contributed to a rush to erect protective barriers, but the specter of a world of closed borders in turn stimulated awareness that there were special international migrants who urgently needed protection and assistance.

The Western nations' generalization of restrictive immigration policies in the latter decades of the nineteenth century amounted to the imposition of a new international regime with respect to population movements in the world as a whole, because the countries that might otherwise have generated various types of outflows had no place to send their people. This remarkably uniform process, encompassing such diverse countries as the United States, Britain, and Germany, was the result of an interaction between two distinct dynamics. One was political and reflected efforts by elites to enhance national identity and solidarity in the face of increasing internal and international tensions, in effect the counterpart of the dynamic that fostered the persecution of minorities.[48] The other dynamic was economic and reflected the efforts by indigenous workers to reduce competition that undermined their living, and by welfare agencies to minimize costs.[49]

Restrictive measures were systematized during World War I in response to security concerns and, after the war, in response to revolution and economic depression. In relation to the overall trend, France emerged as a singular exception; as the most important liberal state with relatively open borders, it admitted nearly 1.5 million foreigners in the 1920s, of whom a large proportion was refugees.[50]

Beginning in 1875, the United States enacted increasingly severe prohibitions against immigration from Asia. A proposal to reduce also the new immigration from Europe, by imposing a literacy requirement, was passed by both houses of Congress as early as 1896, only to be vetoed by the president. The restrictionists then fell back on lesser measures, such as increasing entry fees and imposing additional health and "moral" qualifications. However, at the insistence of congressional representatives from concerned constituencies, victims of religious persecution were generally exempted.[51] The closing of the immigration door thus led to a distinction between refugees and ordinary immigrants that had hitherto been absent from American institutional practice. The literacy requirement finally became law in 1917, when wartime hysteria provided the two-thirds congressional majority needed to override the president's veto. Victims of religious persecution were again exempt. Arrivals from Europe and Western Asia, whose number had fallen to a low of 25,000 by 1919, owing to wartime restrictions on exit and the unavailability of civilian shipping, climbed rapidly afterwards, reaching 677,000 in 1921. In that same year, the United States imposed its first quota on European immigration, with an annual cap of 300,000, or fewer than half the current level. This cap was lowered to 150,000 in 1924, with admissions to be allocated through a quota system based on national origins, designed to minimize the number of Eastern and Southern Europeans admitted. Immigrants from Asia were prohibited altogether. Victims of religious persecution were still exempted from some entry requirements but not from the restrictive quota system, nor did the system provide any means to admit refugees on an emergency basis.

It is against this background that a more specialized regime pertaining to refugees emerged. The League of Nations made it possible to develop international institutions to this effect.[52] In the face of the huge outpouring of refugees from Russia, volunteer-service agencies that were trying to alleviate their immediate problems appealed to the League of Nations to establish a central office operating under its authority. Its ad hoc character is clearly indicated by the designation, "High Commissioner on behalf of the League in connection with the problems of Russian Refugees in Europe" (1921). Under the leadership of Fridtjof Nansen, however, the office also assisted displaced Greeks, Turks, and Bulgarians, by means of exchanges worked out with the League's encouragement.

Nansen and the League viewed these tasks as temporary, with the office to be abolished as soon as the people with whom it dealt were resettled or had returned to their homes. However, while the refugee flows were being absorbed, new ones were being generated, as Europe began to experience severe political instability. Nationalist authoritarian regimes became commonplace from the 1920s on, among both old and new states. The Fascist takeover of Italy in 1922 drove many into exile, as did subsequent waves of repression. But except for prominent political individuals, refugees were difficult to distinguish from the usual Italian emigrants.[53] Similar developments took place in Portugal and Spain at the end of the decade. The Nazi victory of 1933 in turn triggered two distinctive refugee streams, political opponents and Jews, with some overlap between the two. The Nazis started by expelling 10,000 to 20,000 recent immigrants from Eastern Europe, mostly to Poland, whose government also persecuted Jewish citizens.[54] German Jews were subjected to increasingly brutal and comprehensive discrimination, which in effect deprived them of the possibility of making a living. As intended, these measures led to departures, totaling about 150,000 by 1938. Another 126,500 fled Austria following the Anschluss. Nearly half a million Spaniards, both soldiers and civilians, escaped to France following the collapse of the Republicans in early 1939; of these, however, about 150,000 to 200,000 were soon repatriated.[55]

The problems posed by the resurgent refugee crisis were aggravated by the deepening worldwide economic depression, which brought another round of immigration restriction. Because of the problems the Jewish exodus from Germany posed to neighboring countries, the Assembly of the League decided in October 1933 to appoint another High Commissioner, "for Refugees coming out of Germany." This ad hoc measure brought out the political implications of the emerging international regime: The recognition of a group as refugees was tantamount to a formal charge by the international community that one of its members was engaging in persecution. As it was, "in order not to give offence to the German Government," the Assembly formally made the High Commissioner independent of the League, accountable to his own governing body, but Germany subsequently resigned from the League, and the High Commissioner was once again made responsible to the Assembly. In 1938, the Soviet Union in turn objected to any kind of League protection for its exiles.[56]

These rudimentary international institutions were not effective. The first High Commissioner for Refugees from Germany resigned "in the conviction that he was virtually powerless."[57] In 1938, as the crisis became worse, the Assembly decided to set up a single High Commissioner's office responsible for all League work on refugees, but the High Commissioner's limitations were evident from the unwillingness of member states to assume greater responsibilities in dealing with the crisis. Nor were the member states open to persuasion by anyone else, as indicated by the failure of the Evian Conference, convened by President Franklin D. Roosevelt in 1938 on the problem of refugees from Germany and Austria—that is, Jews—to come up with a solution to their plight. Its one contribution was the formation of the Intergovernmental Committee on Refugees, headed from 1939 onward by the High Commissioner himself.

Nevertheless, interwar developments were significant in that they distilled the concept of refugee from the European historical experience to date and made it concrete by creating a set of specialized agencies. These in turn were located in a more comprehensive institution that represented the concept of international community. This process inspired the notion that the international community, that is, the League's member states, collectively were obligated to a category of persons designated as refugees. It is important to note that the idea of refugee thereby gained some independence from the actions of particular states, as the issue raised by the appointment of the High Commissioner for Refugees from Germany indicates. Although the response was still tentative, it was a step toward the formation of more permanent international institutions for dealing with refugees. Another significant step was specifying the rights to which those so identified were entitled—travel documents, education, right to work in the receiving country, and so forth—as codified in a 1933 convention regarding the international status of refugees.[58]

The groups of refugees that came within the domain of successive High Commissioners generally were the classical types, but as already noted, they were considered on an ad hoc basis and "from above." Viewed from the vantage point of the present, the League regime was highly collectivist, responsive almost exclusively to the claims of states and groups (nationalities). It stopped short of devising a mechanism whereby any person might independently lay claim to being a refugee and thus obtain the benefits that the international community now offered to those who achieved that status.

However, under the pressure of subsequent events, a more universalistic regime was started in the late 1930s. Amidst the growing awareness of the high stakes involved, its general purpose was to establish criteria for the refugee groups, which led to an emphasis on political causes. A draft resolution prepared by the Institute of International Law for its 1936 session thus defined a refugee as "any person who, by reason of political events in his State of origin, has either left the territory of that State, whether voluntarily or under expulsion. . . ."[59] In the same vein, the principal contemporaneous study of refugees stated that the refugee "is distinguished from the ordinary alien or migrant in that he has left his former territory because of political events there, not because of economic conditions or because of the economic attractions of another territory."[60] But these criteria evoked considerable resistance by state officials. As one observer reported,

> The customary arguments against accepting a general legal status for political refugees are that it might encourage countries to get rid of their unwanted people and that many might emigrate who would otherwise remain in their countries even under serious disabilities.[61]

Moreover, as was brought out in the preparatory work leading up to the establishment of the International Refugee Organization during World War II, the Institute of International Law's definition, "if adopted, might have meant multiplying the number of refugees *ad infinitum*. Some exact definition seemed essential of what is meant by 'political events'."[62]

The most obvious problem in this respect, still unresolved today, was that with a growing number of states adopting some form of authoritarian rule, much of the globe's population could be thought of as victims of "political events." Moreover, looking back from the perspective of a world in which self-government is the norm, it can be argued that the category of "victims of political events" could also apply to the masses of people then living under colonial rule. Those concerned with the development of refugee-oriented institutions therefore insisted on a definition that would deny refugee status to very large numbers, as this would both jeopardize the possibility of their obtaining special consideration from the international community and undermine established state authority. Accordingly, the author of a study published in 1953 under the sponsorship of the U.N. High Commissioner for Refugees points out that "even . . . if 'political events' can be distinguished from other social phenomena . . . the mere fact that a man has left his country solely because political events there were not to his liking does not suffice to confer on him the status of refugee and any ensuing advantages."[63]

This observation introduced and justified the definition that was actually adopted by the 1951 Convention Relating to the Status of Refugees. According to its author, it follows as a matter of course that "the political events which in the country of origin led to his departure *must be accompanied by persecution or the threat of persecution against himself or at least against a section of the population with which he identifies himself*."[64]

The Second European Crisis

The 1951 convention was the critical event in the institutionalization of the post–World War II regime. It was the capstone of disparate efforts to deal on an ad hoc basis—much as had occurred after World War I—with a European refugee crisis that was even more overwhelming than the earlier one. According to the first comprehensive postwar survey, the total number of Europeans displaced in the six years of war, 1939 to 1945, was around thirty million. At the end of the war, of these, eleven million survivors were outside their country and in need of assistance.[65] At the same time, additional refugees were being generated by postliberation conflicts, such as the civil war in Greece between Communist partisans and the returning royal government, and clashes among countries of Eastern and Southern Europe that had resumed their elusive pursuit of ethnic homogeneity and geopolitically desirable boundaries.

Remarkably, most of these refugees were settled within a few months after the end of hostilities. In some cases there were population exchanges between neighboring countries, similar to earlier ones in the Balkans. But a distinctive element after World War II was the appearance of refugees from the Nazi and Fascist governments, who could hardly be thought of as "innocent victims." In some cases entire ethnic groups came to be viewed as "collaborators," such as the Yugoslavian Croats, who perceived the Nazis' "new order" as an opportunity to liberate themselves from Serbian domination and so supported the puppet government of Ante Pavelic. Many of these collaborators fled with the retreating Germans; unable to return, they were later joined by many other escaping Marshal Tito's retribution, which was hardly limited to proven collaborators. The question of innocence also arose with respect to the largest refugee flow, from Eastern Europe, of over twelve million people of German descent—some old settlers, others recently implanted by the Nazis—who retreated with the German forces or were expelled from Czechoslovakia, Poland, Hungary, Romania, and Yugoslavia. However, their political status did not become an international issue, because nearly all were taken in by the two Germanies then in the making.[66]

Another ambiguous case was the two million Soviet citizens who were outside their country at the end of the war, including prisoners of war, forced laborers, and anti-Soviet activists—mostly non-Russian ethnics from European Russia—who had fought on the German side. Despite vociferous protests, including many from ordinary citizens who had no wish to return under Josef Stalin's rule, the Allies agreed to Soviet demands for their return. Although the bulk of them were sent back very quickly, operations slowed down when it was learned that many were being dealt with harshly merely because of their having lived abroad, as if contact with the outside world were a source of political contamination.[67] In the light of this notorious episode, the assertion shortly afterwards as a principle of the new international regime—that a person's decision to leave "merely because of political events not to his liking" is not sufficient to confer refugee status—acquired a sinister connotation.

International efforts to deal with refugees began once again on an ad hoc basis, but with some advance planning and a more comprehensive scope, encompassing both material and legal needs. The original model was the "relief and refugee" administrations established by the British and Americans in the Middle East early in the war.[68] In 1943, the United States secured widespread international support for the organization of a comprehensive body along similar lines, the United Nations Relief and Rehabilitation Administration (UNRRA), which was to oversee most of the immediate relief and repatriation operations in postwar Europe. But its scope did not extend to the longer-term needs of those who could not be returned, and the agency was soon caught up in nascent Cold War tensions as its American sponsor tried to harness refugee assistance to foreign policy considerations. These controversies, as well as the eruption of new refugee problems outside Europe, discouraged the organization's comprehensiveness.

At the end of 1946, the International Refugee Organization (IRO) was established to deal with "the last million" in Europe, a task it was expected to complete by the end of 1951, after which the agency was scheduled to go out of existence. Within the new agency, the ideological cleavage that shaped the postwar international political system weighed against adoption of a universalistic conception of refugees:

> Western countries sought to include large numbers of dissident and anti-Communist elements; Eastern countries tried to exclude those whom they believed were deadly

political enemies. Both sides agreed that the international community had no obligation to the many millions of Germans who remained unsettled in Europe in 1946.
Beyond this, the IRO reflected a broad compromise between East and West, desig-
nating broad categories of persons to be assisted rather than offering an abstract
definition to be used for all cases.[69]

But in other respects, the IRO was a major institutional innovation, shifting away from the
collective approach that had marked previous international efforts toward a more individual one that was inherently more appropriate to a universalistic orientation. This was
reflected principally in its operational structure, founded on the notion of applicants who
were to be processed by a specialized staff of ''eligibility officers'' in order to ascertain
whether they came within the organization's mandate.[70]

These procedures were carried over into the U.N. High Commissioner's Office for
Refugees (UNHCR), established by the General Assembly in December 1949 as the
successor to the IRO. Although the new organization's mandate was again limited,
initially to a three-year period, many assumed that it would become a permanent
agency.[71] The UNHCR's domain was somewhat more comprehensive than the IRO's,
extending to all displaced Europeans not repatriated or permanently resettled, including
the ambiguous categories noted earlier and excluding only common and war criminals; but
it remained exclusively concerned with Europe.[72] Although there were a number of major
refugee flows originating elsewhere while the UNHCR was being established, they were
either ignored by the international community or dealt with through ad hoc institutional
arrangements.

The first of these waves of refugees came from the Indian subcontinent after the
partition of India in August 1947. As discussed in Chapter 5, the territorial division was
decided on to relieve the rising tensions between the Hindu and Muslim communities.
Because the two populations to some extent overlapped, the partition had created religious
minorities in each of the two new states. With the outbreak of widespread hostilities,
whose toll mounted to over half a million dead, about fourteen million people fled across
what now had become international borders to what they considered their homeland. The
fledgling governments of India and Pakistan were left to deal with a huge resettlement
problem, involving extremely poor populations whose mass dwarfed that of Europe's
refugees, with little assistance from the international community.

The first body of non-European refugees for whom the new international community
did assume responsibility were the homeless and stateless Palestinians, on whose behalf
the General Assembly created the United Nations Relief for Palestine Refugees (UNRPR)
late in 1948. In December 1949 the UNRPR was replaced by the United Nations Relief
and Works Agency for Palestine Refugees in the Near East (UNRWA), still in existence
today. The exodus from the districts that became the state of Israel in the months preceding and following the proclamation of independence in May 1948 numbered between
700,000 and 800,000, amounting to at least three-quarters of the Arab population. Triggered in late 1947 by the breakdown of British authority and rising communal violence,
the movement broadened in April 1948, when Zionist military forces launched preemptive
strikes against potentially hostile Arabs and retaliated against Arab attacks on Jewish
settlements, and again on May 15 when Israel and its neighbors went to war. During this
conflict, many were driven from their homes on grounds of security. After the armistice,
which left Israel with a larger territory than provided for under the partition resolution,
more were expelled or fled to avoid living under Israeli authority.[73] Over the next several

years, most Jews also were expelled or fled from Arab countries in the Middle East and North Africa; of these, about 750,000 resettled in Israel, the rest mainly in France.[74] Because of Israel's law of return or the possession of French citizenship (i.e., those refugees originating in Algeria) all of these people had a place to go to and so did not enter the ranks of international refugees.

Owing to the lack of concern for the plight of refugees on the Indian subcontinent, the exceptional attention accorded to the Palestinians can be attributed less to humanitarian considerations than to the emergence of the Palestine problem as a prominent issue on the United Nations' political agenda. The UNRPR and UNWRA were by-products of the intervention of the United Nations as a third party in the Palestine conflict following the relinquishment by a weakened Britain of its mandatory responsibilities in the wake of World War II. Much like the U.N.'s intervention itself, the UNWRA was largely an instrument of U.S. policy: The agency was designed to resolve the Middle East conflict by turning Palestinians into attractive economic assets in the eyes of Arab receiving states, so as to overcome their resistance to resettlement.[75] However, as discussed further in Chapter 9, the policy failed because of opposition from both the Arab states and the refugees themselves, who over time began to act on their own behalf. Conversely, because of its eminently political character, UNRWA remained peripheral to the postwar refugee organization, as did the United Nations Korean Reconstruction Agency established in 1950, in the wake of the "police action," which closed its doors in 1958.

The principal institutional development was the UNHCR. Despite its initial limitations, over time the agency assumed responsibility for a variety of groups in every region in the world, except for the Palestinians. From a more analytic perspective, its evolution represented significant steps toward the bureaucratization—in the Weberian sense—of international assistance to refugees. The most important of these steps was the formation of a professional staff that had definite objectives.[76] But this in turn made the issue of definition more pressing, as it was necessary to establish operational criteria to enable the staff to carry out their appointed tasks.

Not surprisingly, the issue of scope was "one of the most difficult to resolve."[77] It was agreed early on to remove protection of the "stateless" (left over from the Nansen days) from the High Commissioner's jurisdiction, leaving the office to deal exclusively with refugees. In regard to defining the latter, the choices were between enumerating the categories, as had always been done before, and formulating a broader definition. In keeping with models of bureaucratic development, experienced IRO staff argued in favor of the latter, because the enumerative approach had proved cumbersome to implement. But many of the member states objected to a universal definition on the grounds that it would mortgage the future, as it would mean that new groups of refugees who exhibited the specified characteristics would fall automatically in the embrace of the High Commissioner's office.[78] This debate distinguished between two projects: on the one hand, the statute itself, pertaining to international action and the establishment of an agency for this purpose, and, on the other hand, a convention of member states, directed toward national action and imposing binding obligations on the signatories.

The universalists triumphed on both fronts. According to the resolution adopted by the General Assembly on December 14, 1950, the High Commissioner's mandate extended, first, to persons already considered to be refugees under previous international agreements or under the IRO's constitution; second, to people living outside their country of origin as the result of events occurring before January 1, 1951, and unable or unwilling to avail themselves of its protection "owing to a well-founded fear of being persecuted" or "for reasons other than personal convenience"; and finally and most important, to

> any other person who is outside the country of his nationality, or if he has no nationality, the country of his former habitual residence because he has or had well-founded fear of persecution by reason of his race, religion, nationality or political opinion and is unable or, because of such fear, is unwilling to avail himself of the protection of the government of the country of his nationality, or, if he has no nationality, to return to the country of his former habitual residence.[79]

Essentially the same definition was adopted by the "Convention Relating to the Status of Refugees" enacted in 1951. The most noteworthy change was the joining in the enumeration of "membership of a particular social group" to "political opinion." This was added by the Geneva conference at Sweden's initiative, apparently with no other motive than "to stop a possible gap" in the coverage afforded by the other, more specific categories.[80] However, the obligations undertaken by the signatories were restricted to persons who had become refugees before January 1, 1951, and pertained to Europeans only. The discrepancy between the domains of the UNHCR and of the convention prevailed until 1967, when a protocol was enacted to eliminate time and space limits from the convention.[81]

By capturing the classic types encompassed by the notion of refugee—that is, members of target groups and more active political dissenters—the convention's statute codified essential elements of the Western experience. But it was a major departure from historical precedent, in that the international community assumed for the first time some degree of responsibility for persons who qualified as refugees without any temporal or geographical limitations. The definition on which the statute was grounded became a widely accepted concept in contemporary international law as well as in—by way of the convention and the protocol, the domestic law of the signatories, whose number has grown to include nearly all states in the international community. At the same time, a number of states included in their constitution the right of asylum for political activists.[82]

As noted earlier, the selection of "persecution" as the key operational criterion was in keeping with the desire of the international community to make the status of refugee exceptional, so as to preclude overwhelming numbers. Observe, first, that this omits victims of egregious exploitation. Second, this definition is predicated on distinguishing between the victims of what might be called nefarious political routine, a huge category that includes most of the citizens of repressive states or societies, who form a large part of the world's population, and those who are singled out as targets of extraordinary malevolence by some agent.[83] Although the U.N.'s language does not specify who that agent might be, it was generally assumed from the outset to be the government, "either in that it initiated or encouraged the persecution, or that it could not or did not provide protection to its national from persecutory actions or threats by other elements within this society."[84]

By the same token, this definition suggested that the determinants of persecution were exclusively internal to the appropriate state. Reflecting the fact that international law is founded on the concept of sovereignty—that is, on the notion that the world is divided into a finite set of states with mutually exclusive jurisdiction over segments of territory and clusters of population—this definition contributed to the crystallization of an "internalist" vision of the refugee phenomenon. But such a conceptualization negates the fundamental point of the preceding analysis, namely, that persecution is related to broad historical processes in which complex internal and external forces interact.

The statute, the convention, and the protocol institutionalized elements of a more universalistic regime, but from the beginning they also exhibited features that diverged from universalistic norms. These divergences can be attributed mainly to the emergence of a bipolar world locked in cold war. Aside from the Greek Communists who fled to the Soviet Union after the civil war, from the late 1940s onward, nearly all new European refugees were escaping the harsh economic conditions and political repression accompanying the transformation of the Eastern European governments into Soviet-style regimes. Although these states went to extraordinary lengths to seal their borders, there were waves of departures before the task was completed as well as a massive relocation of people from East to West Germany by way of Berlin—owing to the peculiarities of the four-power occupation arrangements—amounting to some 3.5 million from 1951 until the Berlin Wall was built in 1961 to close this loophole. Movement was otherwise limited to a trickle of escapes, except for the sudden exodus of 200,000 following the crushing of the Hungarian uprising in 1956.[85]

Although the more prominent dissenters among them could make a case for asylum on grounds of persecution for reasons of political opinion, most others could not, as escape from routine oppression was not enough to qualify as a refugee. However, to the extent that the refugees could demonstrate that they were systematically discriminated against because of their class origins (e.g., with respect to educational opportunities and employment), a case for their meeting the convention's criteria could be made. For example, the UNHCR responded to the Hungarian emergency by tentatively according refugee status to anyone coming out, postponing individual determination of "persecution," if needed, to a later time. This was later invoked as a precedent for accepting prima facie evidence of refugee status for large groups in the developing world as well.[86]

The Western states individually also tended to favor people leaving the East. Some Western European authorities judged the convention's language as too narrow for this purpose but were reluctant to stretch it for fear of "devaluating" formal refugee status under the convention. This reluctance gave rise to the so-called B-status, which first developed in Scandinavian legal-administrative practice in the 1960s, under which residence permits were issued on "humanitarian grounds" and other benefits were kept just short of convention standards.[87]

Albeit a major financial supporter of the UNHCR from the outset, the United States shunned the U.N. definition as a guide for its own admissions. Having refused during the interwar period to make special provisions for refugees, the United States shifted to a more generous stance, partly in response to constituency pressures, but mostly as a weapon in the Cold War.[88] First, various measures were devised to stretch existing immigration laws in order to admit European displaced persons. Although the Immigration and Nationality Act of 1952 reenacted existing discriminatory restrictions and still failed to make any provisions for refugees, it gave the attorney general discretionary authority to parole any alien into the United States for reasons of emergency or if "deemed strictly in the public interest." This provision was used repeatedly to admit large numbers from Eastern European countries and, later on, from Cuba and Indochina.

The Refugee Relief Act of 1953 provided for taking in as "refugees" 189,000 persons who could not be accommodated under the small quotas for their respective countries; these categories included Eastern Europeans and German expellees, Dutch ex-colonials from Indonesia, and Greek and Italian victims of natural disasters. The act was identified in a National Security Council memorandum as a device to "encourage defection of all USSR nationals and 'key' personnel from the satellite countries'' in order to "inflict a psychological blow on Communism" and, "though less important, . . . material loss to the Soviet Union'' insofar as the emigration pertained to professionals.[89] The Refugee–Escapee Act of 1957 made additional room for existing applicants from the same groups but also included a more general provision for admitting as refugees in the future those persons fleeing persecution in Communist or Middle Eastern countries.

In 1965 the United States for the first time reserved part of its annual entry quota for refugees, but the definition was revised only in 1980, and subsequent practice indicates that the old policy of attributing refugee status almost exclusively to people from Communist countries still prevails.[90]

Despite these limitations, the legal framework developed by the Western states proved adequate to deal with the population movements of the 1950s and the 1960s with which they were particularly concerned: Europeans from Communist countries and, later, non-European, Chinese, and Cubans. Beyond the humanitarian considerations, it is evident that this suited the political purposes of the Western Alliance at the height of the Cold War. As it was, given the restrictions on exit, the burden to the receivers was not very heavy, except in the case of Germany—which, in retrospect, derived considerable economic benefits from the huge number of workers that this entailed.

Challenges from the Developing World

By about 1960, however, major population movements originating in the developing world created mounting pressures to give them international assistance. The most glaring shortcoming of the international arrangements was the limitation of the convention's domain to pre-1951 Europe, a deficiency that was overcome in 1967. Although the UNHCR itself was not so limited, it faced even more profound problems arising from the very nature of the flows. To this, there was no single solution, because the situations encountered in the various regions differed considerably, as did the local responses to them. Because the flows themselves will be examined in subsequent chapters, these developments will be considered here only as they relate to changing notions of who is a refugee.

Despite the unruliness of its political development, Latin America has produced very few refugees. The protracted violence of the Mexican Revolution in the early decades of the twentieth century undoubtedly helped raise the rate of emigration to the United States above the level induced by economic factors alone, but this historical experience was largely forgotten. As the now-classic 1965 study of the Inter-American Commission on Human Rights notes:

> Throughout the history of Latin America there has . . . been a significant, if not large, number of Latin American nationals who have temporarily moved into exile for political reasons. . . . The political exiles of years past flowed rather easily into the neighbouring Latin countries where culture, tradition and language pose few barriers; furthermore, the political exiles have frequently been of the wealthier elements, and they have not become burdens on the economy of the absorbing state.[91]

However, this generosity by the region's states with respect to their exiles constituted a form of authoritarian collusion because, as Albert Hirschman has pointed out, the provision of easy "exit" helped reduce the intensity of "voice" within each.[92]

Accordingly, there was little responsiveness in the region to the broader concerns of the U.N. convention, and an unwillingness to assume the obligations it entailed. Instead, the traditional orientation was formalized into a common regional policy focusing on asylum seekers rather than refugees, with the criterion for recognition being political activism or, more properly, "political crime" *(delite politico)*.[93] An elaborate system of inter-American law was developed to specify procedures for the individual *asilado,* conditions permitting extradition, inviolability of foreign missions, and the distinction between common crimes and political offenses.

However, the Latin American situation changed dramatically in the 1960s, with the appearance of large international population movements that claimed refugee status and whose social composition was much more diversified. The massive outflows from Cuba and, later, Chile, Nicaragua, El Salvador, and Guatemala severely strained existing legal codes and prompted a call by the Organization of American States (OAS) for more members to accept the somewhat broader obligations of the U.N. convention and to adopt its language in national legislation.[94]

In contrast, postwar developments in Asia replicated the crisis-ridden experience of Europe. Nevertheless, except for the Palestinians, the problem of refugees did not capture the attention of the international community, because most of them found havens in the region. Although few states had formal provisions for asylum—to the extent that those seeking admission were expelled or fleeing "conationals"—they were generally let in. As we shall see in Chapter 6, this was true also for most of those leaving China as a result of its revolution. However, in 1957, the U.N. General Assembly entrusted to the UNHCR the task of assisting large numbers of Chinese in Hong Kong, even though they did not fully satisfy the statutory definition because of complications inherent in the existence of two Chinas.[95] This assistance constituted a precedent that led to a steady expansion of the High Commissioner's domain on an ad hoc basis throughout the developing world. Other groups that were included were Algerians fleeing to Tunisia and Morocco to escape the effects of French counterguerrilla campaigns (1958–61), and Angolans who escaped under similar circumstances to what is now Zaire (1961). This was subsequently applied to other liberation struggles in southern Africa.

Legitimized around 1960 through the umbrella doctrine of "good offices," these practices broadened the institutional concept of refugee. Initiated largely by the UNHCR's specialist staff in response to new problems in the African setting, this development was in keeping with established propositions concerning the role of officials in fostering the growth of government more generally. As Goodwin-Gill reports, conditions of underdevelopment in Africa made individual assessments of refugee status impractical, and the staff also felt that although it might not be possible to establish a "well-founded fear" on an individual case-by-case basis, people should benefit from refugee status when there was no doubt that "political conditions" had compelled the flight of the entire group in question. As noted earlier, a precedent for this had been established for the Hungarian crisis of 1956. On a more political plane, Goodwin-Gill suggested that the approach "was almost certainly influenced by factors such as the desire to avoid the imputation on newly independent states which is carried by every determination that a well-founded fear of persecution exists."[96]

The broadened conceptualization was further formalized in 1969 in the Convention on Refugee Problems in Africa negotiated by the Organization of African Unity (OAU). Article I begins with a restatement of the established U.N. definition centering on persecution and then adds:

2. The term "refugee" shall also apply to every person who, owing to external aggression, occupation, foreign domination or events seriously disturbing public order in either part or the whole of his country or origin or nationality, is compelled to leave his place of habitual residence in order to seek refuge in another place outside his country of origin or nationality.[97]

Reflecting the historical experience of Africa, much as the 1951 convention did for Europe, this formulation came into existence largely as an expression of political solidarity on behalf of the ongoing struggles against white rule in southern Africa, as well as retrospectively in Algeria, which drove large number of persons to seek refuge in other countries. But it also captured the emerging realities of a continent where instability and upheavals of various kinds cast masses of deprived people across international borders in order to stay alive and where man-made calamities interacted with natural catastrophes to threaten the survival of entire communities. The inclusion of foreign intervention and "events seriously disturbing public order" as grounds for according refugee status was tantamount to arguing that victims of such processes are similar to those of persecution and hence equally worthy of special consideration. It can also be understood as a collective claim by African states in regard to the international community. Moreover, as suggested by Goodwin-Gill's observation concerning the UNHCR's expanded role, the broadened definition was also self-serving, as it enabled African states to acknowledge people as refugees without imputing "persecution" to anyone, thus obfuscating the responsibility of the OAU's members in generating the flows.

In the early 1970s the UNHCR's mandate was extended further to include people in refugeelike situations if no other agency were available to provide relief, and it applied in at least one case even to people who stayed in their own country.[98] But the mandate's inadequacies became more problematic in the latter part of the decade, when it appeared that the developing world was producing more and more refugees and that a larger proportion of them would land on the international community's doorstep. Moreover, these flows were no longer confined to their region of origin but impinged on Western receivers at a time when the energy crisis followed by a severe economic downturn prompted a general belt tightening and a feeling that charity must begin at home. It was the conjunction of deteriorating circumstances in the developing world and among Western industrial societies that precipitated the century's third refugee crisis, which forms the subject of this book.

Conclusion: In Fear of Violence

An examination of the historical matrix of contemporary concepts and institutional practices shows that the basic features and relative stability of the current refugee situation can be attributed to a stalemate between contradictory tendencies. On the one hand, there has been a secular evolution from particularistic practices, reflecting the willingness of specific states to grant asylum to individuals and groups of special concern, to a more universalistic definition of refugees and a concomitant institutionalized apparatus for dealing with them, founded on the acknowledgment by a duly constituted international political community of a special obligation toward the categories of persons specified in that definition. At the same time, however, the states that compose this community continue to exercise considerable discretion in implementing the definition and in interpreting their obligations to those acknowledged as refugees.

The contradiction itself reflects divergent global trends: on the one hand, a more widespread adherence to a core of common humanitarian values and, on the other, the increasing economic inequality and persistence of strategic competition among national states. These features of global social organization also account for a comprehensive order pertaining to the general international population movement, which provides the context in which contemporary practices concerning refugees must be understood. Its most relevant features are the maintenance by many states of prohibitions against exit, and the generalization of severe restrictions against immigration, particularly among affluent countries with liberal governments that attract the world's unfortunates. Within a shrinking world subject to violent upheavals affecting large and very poor populations and resulting in the appearance of all kinds of people on everyone's doorstep in search of assistance, it becomes vital to distinguish refugees from international migrants.

Combining the responses to the twentieth-century crises, the current institutional meaning of refugee is a composite of three categories founded on the causes of the refugees' departure. The first two, constituting the U.N. definition, are a formalization of the classic types. They include the refugee as an activist, engaging in some politically significant activity that the state seeks to extinguish; and the refugee as a target, by misfortune of belonging—often by accident of birth—to a social or cultural group that has been singled out for the abuse of state power. The major change in the definition since its inception in the 1950s is the emergence of a third category, the refugee as a mere victim. This covers persons displaced by societal or international violence that is not necessarily directed at them as individuals but makes life in their own country impossible. Although recognized by the League of Nations after World War I, and again by U.N. agencies after World War II, this category was deliberately not included in the 1950 statute, the 1951 convention, or the 1967 protocol. However, it was reintroduced as upheavals in the developing world came to the attention of the international political community in the 1960s, and then was generalized in the "good offices" doctrine. At the same time, the category was formally institutionalized at the interstate level in Africa, where it accounted from the outset for the major part of refugee flows, as our regional analysis will show.

Population movements falling into these three categories are included in our study. Because not all such people have been formally recognized as refugees by international organizations or particular states, we shall sometimes refer to them as "recognized" or "unrecognized" refugees. This does not mean that we are setting ourselves up as a court of hearing to determine the status of individuals or groups; rather, more careful terms minimize the dangers of terminological legitimization as noted in the introduction and are thus a prerequisite of critical thinking about refugees and refugee policy. We shall also propose a definition that arises from the three categories mentioned. But to be relevant to political and ethical discourse about refugees, this definition must be theoretically coherent, meet acceptable normative criteria, and provide a suitable foundation for operational guidelines in making decisions.

Most discussions of what makes refugees distinctive have focused on a combination of two different characteristics of their movement: It is involuntary, as opposed to voluntary, and is occasioned by political, as opposed to economic, causes. In practice, these two are considered equivalent: We thus get a couplet, "voluntary economic = migrants" and "involuntary political = refugees." But this conceptualization is problematic in a number of ways.

With reference to the voluntary/involuntary dimension, Jacques Vernant suggested that to qualify as a refugee rather than a migrant, a person must be "the victim of events for which, at least as an individual, he cannot be held *responsible*."[99] This clearly rules out, say, a common criminal fleeing abroad to escape punishment. Beyond this, the concept of responsibility works reasonably well in the case of target groups, particularly when the group in question is one to which people belong by accident of birth, as with race or nationality. It is also applicable to uninvolved bystanders who are caught up in the cross fire of civil war or similar situations—that is, the category we term *victims*.

This definition is more problematic, however, with respect to the third category, dissenters. Unlike, say, Armenians in Turkey or Jews in Nazi Europe, Huguenots who converted to Catholicism were allowed to live in the same way that all other French did. And so if they rejected this alternative, they must have made a choice, and hence their flight to escape the consequences of their decision cannot be said to be entirely "involuntary." Much the same might be said today, for example, of someone opposing the established regime in Chile, Zaire, or Cuba. Indeed, it is precisely because dissent does entail the exercise of personal choice that those who engage in it are admirable.[100]

Thus it can be seen that the determination of whether movement is voluntary or involuntary must refer ultimately to some doctrine of rights. Indeed, it is understood in international law that the U.N. definition of refugees "encompasses those who are threatened with sanctions for struggling to protect their human rights" as delineated by a variety of instruments, most prominently the Universal Declaration of Human Rights; and despite some remaining ambiguities, this specification is adequate to our purposes.[101]

The voluntary/involuntary dimension also requires a consideration of the costs of staying as against leaving. Although Vernant does not specify what kinds of "events" he has in mind, it is evident that they must be of a grave sort. People who run for their lives are exercising such a limited choice that we usually do not consider their movement voluntary at all. Movement is most clearly involuntary when it is forced—that is, when it occurs as a response to life-threatening violence, exercised by an agent or occurring as a by-product of circumstances. *Violence* includes both clear and immediate physical violence, and coercive circumstances that have similarly threatening effects. *Life* includes both biological existence and social existence, and the basic material and organizational conditions necessary to maintain them. The more immediate and intense the life-threatening violence is, the more clearly a person is a refugee rather than a migrant. This introduces the notion of a degree of need, and it follows that any categories established on this basis are not dichotomous but located along a continuum.

The other dichotomy, economic versus political, is problematic as well. This was already noted by Vernant, who remarks in his 1953 book:

> Today more than at any other period, it is difficult to distinguish between events which are political and those which are not. A man's economic situation is no longer looked on as a "natural" phenomenon, but as a responsibility of the State. The view is steadily gaining ground that the modern State is responsible for the living conditions of its nationals—a perfectly reasonable view given the part played by the State in the organization and direction of the national economy. . . . In a great many States any measure, whatever its nature, is a political event. In recent years, the States initiating strictly controlled economies have enforced drastic changes in the working and living conditions of many sections of their population, arbitrarily directing them to new occupations.[102]

But in fact the difficulty of distinguishing between political and economic migration-inducing events was hardly new, even then.

For example, in the case of the Russian Jews of the 1880s, not only were the economic and political causes of their migration inextricably mixed, but the economic ones also were themselves in part induced by policies designed to undermine the Jews' economic position. Another case in point is that of the Irish during the Great Hunger of the late 1840s.[103] As is well known, the ongoing Irish emigration escalated dramatically after 1846, following a catastrophic food shortage resulting from successive failures of the potato crop, due to a blight compounded by bad winters. Although these conditions were found also in other parts of Western Europe where rural populations relied on the potato as a major staple, the Irish situation was more life threatening because the disaster befell a society that, even in good years, was unable to meet its subsistence needs. Any analysis of why this was so must consider a broad complex of causes, including several centuries of British policy.

From the second half of the sixteenth century onward, successive English regimes decapitated Irish society of its elites and confiscated their lands for the benefit of immigrant colonists and absentee landlords. By the beginning of the nineteenth century, 95 percent of the land was owned by Protestants. In the wake of the Glorious Revolution, Catholics were deprived of their political rights, and British policies toward them paralleled the contemporaneous policies of Louis XIV toward the Huguenots.[104] Because the mercantilist system prevented investment by Protestant landlords in commercial agriculture or other productive undertakings that might compete with England, they derived their income essentially by exacting the maximum rent from subsistence-level tenants. The Irish adapted by producing very large families, enabling some members to engage in migrant labor for cash income and others to grow potatoes on very small plots. Although this was a "rational" solution at the level of the individual family, it worsened conditions for the collective whole, by stimulating a growing demand for land and, hence, steadily increasing rent. The Great Hunger of the 1840s was only the worst of numerous famines. In contrast with England and Scotland, Ireland had no system of public relief: In bad times the only alternative to starvation was emigration. Viewed in this light, the responses of the English landlords and British authorities to the famine itself amounted to an opportunistic deportation policy—as was indeed charged at the time not only by the Irish themselves but also by Americans who objected to the massive influx of immigrants, particularly undesirable because they were both poor and Catholic.

The movement of both the Jews and the Irish was caused by an inextricable mix of political and economic causes; it must be located close to the "involuntary" end of the continuum; and a good case can be made that at specific times they emigrated in order to survive—that the waves between 1846 and 1854 for the Irish, and 1882 to 1885 and 1905 to 1908 for the Jews, can be attributed to "life-threatening violence." But it should be noted that it was necessary for them to do so only because of the unavailability of adequate help *in situ*. If, say, the Irish community in the United States had sent large amounts of food to their unfortunate kinsmen or if the U.S. authorities had contributed such assistance and Britain had accepted it, as well as undertaken relief operations of its own, the life-threatening danger would have been averted, and emigration would have no longer been necessary for survival. With respect to the Jews, economic relief would not have been enough, but one can imagine conditions under which diplomatic pressures might have been successfully applied to the Russian government to cease its actively anti-Jewish practices and to restrain those engaging in pogroms.

In the end, then, the key issue from the perspective of concerned humanitarians is not only whether the movement is involuntary and essentially political but also whether the immediate, intense suffering of the victims can be relieved by helping them in their own country—through policies of their own government or combined with favorable external initiatives—or if relief is possible only by enabling them to move abroad—that is, by providing them with a refuge.[105] This final consideration suggests how theoretical and normative concerns can be integrated into a coherent framework for critical analysis.

The common element that merges the three categories into a coherent set and distinguishes them from others is violence. We shall therefore define refugees as persons whose presence abroad is attributable to a well-founded fear of violence, as might be established by impartial experts with adequate information. In cases of persecution covered by the statutory definition, the violence is initiated by some recognizable internal agent, such as the government, and directed against dissenters or a specified target group. The presence of the victims abroad may be the result of flight to avoid harm or the result of expulsion, itself a form of violence. But flight-inducing violence may also be an incidental consequence of external or internal conflict, or some combination of both, and affect groups that are not even parties to that conflict. Violence may also be inflicted indirectly, through imposed conditions that make normal life impossible.

When defined in this manner, refugees are also distinctive in that they form a category of unfortunates who can be assisted only abroad, unless conditions change in their country of origin. It is because of this that they have a strong claim to a very special form of assistance, including temporary or permanent asylum in the territory of states of which they are not members. Our theoretically grounded definition is thus consistent with ethical considerations, which dictate an approach to the problem of refugees founded on the distinctive and urgent needs of the people concerned.

It is also realistic, in that the operational criteria can be applied to administrative decisions concerning priorities for assistance and admission. For example, they make it possible to distinguish refugees from persons who move as a consequence of natural disaster. Most victims of malnutrition and slow starvation in the developing world should not be considered as refugees because most of them can be assisted *in situ* in their own countries. Given international sovereignty, however, it is often easier to change such conditions for the short term than to change the political economy that is at the root of much of it, or the deliberate political actions that cause flight.[106] People cast abroad by famine are refugees to the extent that the famine is itself a form of violence, as in the case of confiscatory economic measures or extremely unequal property systems maintained by brutal force, the inability to meet subsistence needs because of unsafe conditions, or the refusal of the state to accept international assistance.

One of the main conclusions of this book is that the causes of life-threatening conditions in the developing world stem from an interpenetration of national and transnational, or global, processes. But the world is organized as a set of mutually exclusive states that constitute paramount membership communities, on which individuals normally depend for protection against violence, and for the maintenance of conditions that enable them to survive materially. As people forced to move abroad in order to survive, either because their own state is the cause of their predicament or because it is unable to meet these basic requirements, such people are genuine international outcasts, stateless, in the deep meaning of the term, as suggested a generation ago by Arendt and recently restated by Sacknove.[107] That is the sense in which their predicament stems from distinctively political conditions.

Part Two

REGIONAL STUDIES

Chapter 2

Ethnic Conflict in the New States of Sub-Saharan Africa

A Crisis in the Making

With over 3 million recognized refugees at the beginning of 1987, Africa is today viewed by the UNHCR as the main challenge, absorbing the principal part of its budgetary and organizational resources.[1] Nearly all of them are confined to the region, adding heavy burdens to the world's poorest countries. This problem is compounded by the multiplicity and protraction of refugee-producing conflicts. Although Ethiopia is the source of approximately two-fifths of the current total, the other refugees originated in fourteen different countries, of which nine produced over 70,000 each, some of them as far back as the early 1960s.

The total would be several million higher still if one added international population movements in whose onset violence played a significant role but that for various reasons have not been recognized as refugee flows. For example, there was a major exodus from ex–French Guinea from 1959 onward, stimulated by a mix of deteriorating economic conditions and the exactions of an increasingly brutal political regime, with estimates running as high as 2 million—roughly one-fourth of the population—by the time of Sékou Touré's death in 1984. Most went to Ivory Coast and Senegal, whose leaders maintained an open door but shunned the involvement of outsiders in their relations with Guinea, which discouraged the UNHCR's recognition of Guineans as refugees.[2] The over-100,000 people who escaped from the bloody Macias dictatorship in Equatorial Guinea (ex-Spanish) were initially granted recognition but lost their status after the tyrant was overthrown in 1979.[3] The term *refugees* is sometimes also applied to the mass expulsions of foreign African residents, as occurred in Nigeria in 1983 and again in 1985 after the workers attracted by the oil boom were no longer needed. But despite the element of violence, such expellees differ fundamentally from refugees in that they end up in their own country.[4] Finally, it should be noted that most of the conflicts that produced international flows also occasioned massive internal displacements, with current estimates ranging from a conservative 2.45 million to as many as 8.3 million: The higher count includes about 3.5 million South African blacks and coloreds forcibly relocated by governmental fiat since 1961 to implement the elusive dream of apartheid.[5]

37

Important as these numbers may be, the gravity of the situation does not arise from the size of the flows alone, but from the fact that they have taken place in the context of a multifarious crisis, to which the refugees are related as both cause and effect. As pointed out in a report to the U.N. General Assembly on the role of the UNHCR in Africa:

> What is now generally known as the "African crisis" has brought into focus the interplay of major factors such as natural calamities, armed conflicts within and between nations, regressive economic trends, etc., all of which represent an unrelenting back-drop to the region's refugee problems. These factors, taken individually, are not inherent to Africa alone as cause for large-scale population movements across national boundaries. But what is unique in the African context is that these adverse conditions operate and interact cumulatively to produce a compound crisis of tragic proportions.[6]

This is a suitable epigraph for our analysis, which will start with a brief overview of the origins of the crisis.

Although population displacements induced by violence figured prominently in the earlier history of sub-Saharan Africa, both before and after the intrusion of Europeans, as of 1960 the only major refugee flow on the continent were the 100,000 or so Algerians in Tunisia.[7] As we shall discuss later, the struggles for decolonization of the 1940s and 1950s produced hardly any refugees. From this baseline, the UNHCR figures then climbed rapidly to about 400,000 in 1964, 625,000 in 1966, and 1 million at the end of the decade, by which time African operations absorbed about 70 percent of its budget.[8]

Of these, slightly over half were caused by the violent struggles for liberation in Portuguese Africa. Most of the others originated in a dozen new African-ruled states, with Rwanda, Sudan, and Zaire producing the bulk of the total. At the time, the upheavals appeared to be attributable to exceptional conditions that distinguished these states from the other new states. Zaire's woes were ascribed to a uniquely unfortunate experience of colonialism and decolonization, which led to chaos after independence; Rwanda's to a unique social structure whereby an African ethnic minority ruled the majority, which exploded once the colonial lid was lifted; and Sudan's to its being an impossible political amalgam that straddled the divide between Arab northern Africa and black sub-Saharan Africa.

In the late 1960s, the developing conflict between the imperial regime and the Eritreans striving for political independence moved Ethiopia into the group of major refugee contributors. At the same time, a bloody confrontation erupted in Nigeria. After being subjected to pogroms in the northern region, Ibos from the east fled back to their homeland, which they declared independent as Biafra; the advance of the federal armies into the breakaway state triggered further flight. By the end of the three-year-long conflict, more than three million internal refugees were crowded into a mere 2,500-square-kilometer enclave, their resources exhausted and with almost no access to international relief. Estimates of Biafran dead from hostilities, disease, and starvation exceeded one million, but few escaped abroad because the secessionist region was surrounded early on, precluding any possibility of their leaving, except by air.[9]

Despite this inauspicious start, there appeared to be some grounds for optimism in the early 1970s, as the refugee total remained stable. Of the 1,015,800 refugees from and in Africa recognized by UNHCR at the end of 1972, 57 percent were generated by the continuing struggle in the Portuguese colonies.[10] The only major new case was Burundi, whose social configuration resembled that of contiguous Rwanda. But some of the situations that had produced the largest flows either had been resolved or had exhausted their refugee-generating potential. The civil war in the Sudan was brought to a negotiated conclusion in 1972, and the Portuguese colonies gained their independence in 1975. With nearly all of the refugees from these countries returning to their homes, by the mid-1970s the African total declined to about half a million.

During this period, however, the vast swath of territory running from the Sahel in the west to the Horn in the east was beset by a catastrophic drought. This turned out to be only the first of several over the next decade and a half, possibly reflecting an increasing frequency caused by deteriorating ecological conditions that were produced and aggravated by growing demographic pressure. The resulting famines contributed to the refugee crisis both directly, as desperate people crossed international boundaries in search of relief, and indirectly, as the effects of the famine exacerbated latent or ongoing social conflicts. In Ethiopia, the 1973 famine contributed to the outbreak of a social revolution. Conversely, the violence unleashed by the conflicts compounded the crisis of subsistence.

By 1978, the number of refugees had climbed back to over 800,000 and, in the following year, had escalated to a new high of over 2 million. This was due largely to the further expansion of conflicts in southern Africa and the Horn. But an equally ominous development was the multiplication of substantial flows from a variety of new states throughout the rest of the continent. From the mid-1970s onward, masses of people fled the brutal tyrants who seized power in the Central African Republic, Uganda, and Equatorial Guinea. Concurrently, Chad was engulfed in a multisided internal war, instigated in part by Libyan intervention, and Zaire experienced severe disturbances as well. By 1981, the United States Committee for Refugees, a highly reliable nongovernmental monitoring agency, reported a total of 3,589,340 international refugees from and in sub-Saharan Africa, and the American press referred to 5 million and Massachusetts Senator Edward Brooke advanced an even more dramatic figure of 6.3 million.[11]

Although these numbers have fluctuated in recent years, with some changes in the countries of origin, the basic trends have persisted. The crisis can therefore be divided into three components:

1. Of today's African refugees, approximately one-fourth originated in the southern part of the continent—principally Angola, Mozambique, and Namibia. Although this pool of about 800,000 is the result of disparate flows occasioned by different circumstances in the several countries, southern Africa forms a regional system, dominated by the Republic of South Africa. Its refugee-producing dynamics stem from the common developmental history of the several countries involved, made worse by the activities of South Africa. This will be examined in Chapter 3.

2. Ethiopia, which with 1.2 million refugees is the largest single source, warrants separate consideration (see Chapter 4) because of its distinctive social structure and political experience and the importance of international interactions at the level of the Horn of Africa as a whole in the shaping of the relevant conflicts.

3. The remaining million or so, which includes people who became refugees as far back as the early 1960s, as well as many displaced only recently, originated mainly in Uganda, Rwanda, Burundi, Chad, Zaire, and, beginning in 1985, once again Sudan. The list might be extended to include Equatorial Guinea and French Guinea, the major sources of unrecognized refugees, together with Nigeria and the Central African Republic, which experienced similar conflicts, but without refugees. They form a generic category of "new African states," which will constitute the starting point for our analysis because it provides a baseline for understanding develop-

ments in the black-ruled states of southern Africa also and is relevant to our discussion of Ethiopia.

The Weakest States, the Weakest Economies[12]

As more of the new states of sub-Saharan Africa fell prey to conflicts, analysts tended to move from an approach that emphasized exceptional circumstances, as noted for Zaire, Rwanda, and Sudan, to something akin to "multivariate analysis"—that is, an attempt to identify common factors distinguishing the troubled states from the other new states and account for their instability.[13] But as the crisis spread, this approach gave way to an alternative conceptualization: that most of the region's states share structural characteristics inducive to severe upheavals and that whether or not such upheavals do in fact occur depends on particular circumstances and chains of events.

The emerging paradigm is founded on an apparent paradox: Although the state dominates the social scene, it is itself an extremely weak and fragile organization, with a very limited capacity for managing society and directing change. This is particularly well captured by Thomas Callaghy's characterization of the African state as a "lame Leviathan."[14] This extreme weakness was initially hidden from view, because of the common assumption that an organization's persistence is based on its capacity to perform those tasks required for its maintenance. Therefore, because the African states were in place, it was taken for granted that they met these requirements. But states do not exist in a vacuum; their fate depends substantially on the international environment. Thus the weakest of states may survive if this environment is supportive, as has been the case of the international political community toward the new African states generally.[15] But the other side of the coin is that stronger states may collapse if the international environment invites destructive processes—as we shall see with respect to southern Africa. In some cases, these external effects are difficult to gauge—as we shall see in regard to Chad.

Although the new states contain landlords and peasants, capitalists and workers, the upper stratum usually consists not of a "national bourgeoisie" but rather a "political elite," that is, a group that owes its position to its ability to rule rather than to its control over the means of economic production. Overall, it is political power that provides access to material rewards, rather than the other way around. The hierarchy of privilege is based on the men who, at any given time, literally constitute the state. Their relationships form clientelist networks, which encompass various functional and interest groups—party officials, civil servants, soldiers, traders, and the like—but especially kinsmen and fellow or allied ethnics. Such a combination of elements is characteristic of "patrimonial" systems of rule. Whereas the prevalence of this system throughout history and in many different parts of the world attests to its lasting power, it also shows that patrimonial rule leads to instability because the persistence of any given government depends almost entirely on the performance of the incumbent. Moreover, succession is often troublesome.

This state of affairs has arisen from the legacy of precolonial structures, the impact of colonialism, the consequences of Africa's place in the contemporary world economy, and the response of political elites to the preceding. The resulting structure generates characteristic dynamics that form a common ground, against which specific configurations and their consequences will be examined later in the case studies.

Most new African states consist of culturally diverse social groups, mistakenly labeled as *tribes,* that were combined into distinct territorial entities by European colonial entrepreneurs in response to the dictates of imperial rivalries in the late nineteenth century. Characteristic elements of African social organization were lineage groups, which expanded through "fictive kinship." Lineages often formed village associations, and villages were linked by cults and trade networks, age sets, titles and secret societies.[16] For the most part, these small African societies lived close to a subsistence level.

In contrast with the Eurasian continent, Africa was a land of extensive rather than intensive agriculture; its population was historically small, its land plentiful, but its soil relatively poor. These factors encouraged the persistence of "slash and burn" techniques, which gave the soil the long time required to recover from usage and also encouraged the continual relocation of the social group as a whole.

Reliance on the hoe as the main instrument of agriculture—except in Ethiopia, which had the plow—made it difficult for Africans to accumulate a surplus. Differences between the standard of living of chiefs and the general population, therefore, were not great. Under these circumstances, even a rudimentary state was difficult to form because it required some shift of manpower from primary production to administrative activity. Political dynamics consisted largely of competition among factions. Along with the absence of centralization and the low population density was the possibility of "exit," which gave rise to a process of segmentation, whereby new social clusters were constantly being established by outmigrants on available land. Chiefs tended to rule people rather than land. Where conditions enabled rulers to control the means of destruction (and hence to "sell" protection), the basic pattern was superseded by protostates, as will be noted in the appropriate case studies.[17]

By establishing themselves as the ultimate source of law and order, the colonial authorities superseded the indigenous authorities and thereby undermined their role in African society, even when coopting them as auxiliaries.[18] Consequently, precolonial political structures offered relatively little resistance to the formation of a new system of domination, and the remnants of the "traditional societies" appeared in the new states largely as "ethnic groups."

The experience of colonial rule also gave ethnic identities a new significance.[19] Friends and enemies found themselves in a common political arena; European conquerors fanned animosities among groups in order to facilitate control over them; and some African peoples became allies while others resisted and were treated accordingly.

For purposes of administrative convenience, colonial officials defined *tribes* as mutually exclusive territorial entities, thereby solidifying hitherto fluid boundaries between groups and often creating new groups. This process usually went hand in hand with the institutionalization of a cultural division of labor founded on an application to the African scene of simplistic group psychology. Administrators identified "intelligent" tribes— usually in the area that had had the longest contact with Europe—as potential sources of teachers and clerks and located schools accordingly; they made "docile" tribes into bearers and workers; and they recruited more remote "martial" tribes as military auxiliaries.

These new differentiations were compounded by the spatial unevenness of economic change and the dynamics of political mobilization during the struggle for independence. Far short of anything that might be called development, the objective of the colonial powers was merely to produce exportable commodities. In retrospect, the consequences of the variations in how this was done outweighed the differences in colonial "philosophies" or administrative institutions.[20] One pattern of development was the massive mobilization of African labor for plantations or mines, which was characteristic of colonies with white settlers, mostly in southern Africa. Elsewhere, attempts to transform Africans into a labor force had little success because of the continued availability of subsistence agriculture as an alternative. Colonial entrepreneurs tended to pass over commodities that could be grown only on plantations, such as rubber, whereas African smallholders produced many commodities that elsewhere were grown on plantations, such as coffee, cocoa, or cotton.

Where it was institutionalized, this pattern of production led to the emergence of African petty capitalists, usually concentrated in a region ecologically suitable to the given commodity and hence ethnically distinctive. The incipient class included not only the farmers themselves but also various intermediaries, who used their surplus income to expand their farms and related activities, such as transport, storage, and processing. Expansion usually was accompanied by a shift from family workers to wage workers, often brought in from poorer regions or neighboring countries, resulting once again in inequality along ethnic lines.

The colonial state was dramatically transformed after World War II, under the combined effect of pressure from African political organizations, attempts by European authorities to contain protest by means of repression and accommodation, and efforts to stimulate and orient production in keeping with the dictates of more elaborately planned economies. With what turned out to be little more than a decade to go, France and Britain, and to a lesser extent Belgium, made substantial investments in the expansion of the physical infrastructure and in the development of social, economic, and administrative services, thereby endowing their colonies with some of the accoutrements of the welfare state. Britain and France also trained and recruited Africans to manage higher levels of the state and began to construct an apparatus of representative government.

Overall, the pace of political change was amazingly swift. After a brief period of confrontation and repression in the late 1940s, both the French and the British shifted to a strategy of negotiation, usually with the leaders of the most successful movement. This is why in the absence of white settlers the decolonization of Africa produced few refugees.[21] Aside from the Union (now Republic) of South Africa, which in 1910 acceded to dominion status in the British Empire, as of 1955 the only sovereign states in sub-Saharan Africa were Liberia and Ethiopia. Ten years later, independence prevailed everywhere except for the Spanish and Portuguese colonies; Southern Rhodesia (now Zimbabwe), which that year was declared independent by a government representing the white settler minority; and South-West Africa (now Namibia), held as a U.N. trusteeship by the Republic of South Africa.

The early organizations were usually congeries of associations appealing to diverse groups, loosely united under a "charismatic" leader who was able to translate disparate grievances into a more unified program and who was supported by a cohort of lieutenants. By the mid-1950s many Africans participated in elections and in territorial government, a development that in turn brought about a shift from protest movements to politics founded on the distribution of tangible rewards to supporters. Benefiting from a bandwagon effect and access to both the carrot and stick afforded by governmental power, the leading nationalist organizations easily imposed their hegemony. At the same time, however, the broadened participation and the discovery of the rich rewards of political office fostered a proliferation of political entrepreneurs who cast their appeal in ethnic terms. Distinctions emerged between regimes aspiring to achieve structural change by way of mass mobilization and those operating within the limits of the existing framework of relationships linking Africa to the global political economy; but regardless of orientation,

African political life consisted largely of interaction among clientelist factions, in which ethnic affiliations played a prominent role.

The most extreme manifestation of this pattern of political change during the decolonization phase occurred in the Belgian Congo (Zaire), because the process was telescoped into a brief eighteen months. In the first five years of its existence the new state was beset by multifarious conflicts, several of which sent waves of refugees to neighboring countries. As noted, this case was generally viewed at the time as exceptional; however, it was in some ways a preview of things to come.

The ruling elite's project has been aptly characterized as "self-aggrandizement combined with enough redistribution to maintain its tenuous and vital hold on the state."[22] The takeover of the colonial state's apparatus enabled the organization of clientelist networks through which the state was managed. However, in answer to the demands occasioned by broader mobilization and rising expectations around the time of independence, these resources had to be expanded and these demands met. But because the takeover of the colonial state meant controlling police and military forces, African rulers were able to use coercion to refute these demands and limit costs. They also quickly discovered the full range of authoritarian techniques, from the imposition of legal restrictions on political activity in the name of national security, to the physical elimination of opponents and the replacement of autonomous associations with state-controlled bodies. The authoritarian strategy proved self-defeating, however, as the agents of repression soon learned where the true power lay, and from the mid-1960s onward, within a few years over half of the new states experienced military coups.[23]

Although neoconservative analysts welcomed both the accession of the military as a harbinger of stability and the new development policies more attuned to capitalist imperatives—following the bureaucratic authoritarianism that emerged in Latin America around the same time—their optimism turned out to be short-lived.[24] The error made with respect to political parties was repeated: Contrary to appearances, the military in Africa did not constitute an institution, a social organization with autonomous capacity to exert leverage on society, but, rather, a mere assemblage of men in uniform, whose distinctive feature was that they had access to guns. Ethnic tensions were as prevalent among the military as among the political class they replaced, and in addition, with little or no experience of statecraft, officers were quicker to fall back on brute force. Far from inaugurating an era of stability, coups begat more coups, and the advent of military rule often exacerbated the very conflicts that had provided the pretext for intervention. This was the case in the Sudan and Nigeria, where seizure of power by the military helped bring about civil war.

Paralleling what occurred in the political sphere, both market-oriented and socialist-minded economists initially overestimated Africa's economic prospects, probably because their strategies were implicitly predicated on baseline levels significantly higher than those found throughout most of the continent, and because they shared the commonplace assumptions about the institutional capacity of the new states. A quarter of a century later, Africa's predicament is, unfortunately, readily obvious. In short, all but a handful of African countries are clustered at the lowest end of the world's economic rankings, and even the exceptionally rich barely reach the midpoint of the distribution.[25] Immediately after independence, this situation was alleviated in some cases by continued aid from the former colonial power, support from a variety of previously uninvolved international actors seeking to establish a sphere of influence in the emerging African political arena, and, especially, loans. In a few instances, the state secured income from mineral royalties, but usually it could augment its resources only by shifting from subsistence to export agriculture, while concurrently extracting an increasing share of surplus from the primary producers. This helped assuage those demands to which rulers were most vulnerable, by redistributing income from the rural to the urban sector. But the basic conditions made it difficult to extract as much of a surplus through state action as through capitalist exploitation. Any attempt to do so in a weak state was likely to lead to wholesale "exit" from the commercial economy into the subsistence sector.[26]

The new states' difficulties were made worse in the 1970s by the deterioration of Africa's already extremely marginal position in the international economy, occasioned by a combination of deteriorating terms of trade, the energy crisis, the mounting burden of debt, the corruption of many economic managers and their foreign patrons, and the growing reluctance of investors to face the risks of continued instability when other choices were available. Some countries also faced a crisis of subsistence. This stemmed not merely from unfortunate climatic conditions but also from the degradation of already marginal agricultural environments as the result of overgrazing and overcultivation, as well as from the accelerating shift away from subsistence agriculture to the production of commodities for export. Amplifying these factors was Africa's runaway demography. Food production per capita decreased by nearly 20 percent from 1960 to 1986, with the prospect of continued decline.[27]

There is now widespread agreement that political and economic conditions are unlikely to change much in the forseeable future. Successes are tenuous at best, and failures open the way to catastrophes. Weak patrimonial regimes are subject to two distinct, but often complementary, processes of deterioration. Most obviously, in the face of shrinking resources and an absence of institutional restraints, desperate rulers degenerate into outright tyrants.[28]

The other process might be termed *massive exit* from the state. In Africa today, the possible responses to an extremely exploitative and oppressive state include wholesale escape abroad, secession, and "internal emigration"—withdrawal of major segments of the population into localized and ethnically specific entities that afford the hope of security and economic self-sufficiency. In the most extreme cases, a tenuously amalgamated national society can disintegrate into its component elements. With its existence eternally ensured, the state is reduced to little more than an arena in which groups vie for survival, as if they were microstates in a contentious international system. Under these conditions, collective life is reduced to two fundamental activities, food production and war. Because cheap small weapons are widely available, and warriors are obviously in a position to secure their subsistence without engaging in their production themselves, war-making steadily gains the upper hand. The outcome is a proliferation of warrior bands, verging on a war of all against all.

Weak States and Ethnic Conflict

In the case studies that follow, Chad and Uganda dramatically illustrate, though in somewhat different ways, these processes of deterioration. The two form an unexpected pair, because of their very different pre-European cultures, varied colonial experiences, and contrasting economic configuration, one of them inherently very poor and the other with more promising possibilities. Both countries have generated large refugee flows, so that the relationship between the dynamics of ethnically structured weak states and the formation of refugees can clearly be seen. We should note that this is a sort of clinical approach to the problem and that we are not arguing that Chad and Uganda be regarded as typical or as previews of the future that awaits all, or even most, of the other new states of sub-Saharan Africa. The other case studies illustrate acute versions of two distinct patterns of ethnic conflict, though usually encountered in a more mitigated form: one of them a class struggle among groups that are hierarchically related, in Rwanda and Burundi; the other between a state center and an ethnically distinct periphery, in Sudan. Although these are cases, in the real world each of them shares a boundary with at least one other in the set, as is true also of Sudan and Ethiopia. This means that with the exception of Chad, each is also a country of asylum. From an analytic perspective, this highlights further the linkages between the processes governing the formation of refugees and international politics.

Ethnic Revolution and Counterrevolution in Rwanda and Burundi[29]

Rwanda generated over 100,000 refugees in 1962–63, when the subjected Hutu majority gained control of the government through universal suffrage and tried to destroy the power of the ruling Tutsi minority.[30] Rwanda's explosive social structure was the legacy of its African past, compounded by the policies of German and then Belgian colonial authorities.

The Tutsi (about 15 percent of a 1960 population of about three million) and the Hutu shared many elements of culture, including kinship structure and language. The Tutsi's ruling hierarchy was formed around the end of the seventeenth century when one of the Tutsi lineages mustered sufficient military force to subdue the local population. The state was headed by the Mwami, who controlled the allocation of land through a network of dependent chiefs. Itself the creature of an authoritarian monarchy, the German colonial administration, established in the late 1890s, reinforced the Mwami's position and helped eliminate the remnants of Hutu autonomy. After Belgium took over Rwanda as a mandate under the League of Nations, this policy was further elaborated by state and church officials imbued with traditionalist Catholic ideals. Colonial Rwanda was thus made into a neofeudal state, founded on a rigid dichotomy between "Tutsi lords" and "Hutu serfs," and legitimized by an imaginary distinction between a superior race of immigrant "Hamites" of Egyptian origin and the primitive indigenous Negroes.

Greater control over the people enabled the Tutsi to acquire greater control over the land. This control was used in turn to exact services such as the cultivation of mandatory crops, corvée labor to build the colonial infrastructure, and, in some areas, the recruitment of workers for European plantations. The Tutsi were also given priority over the Hutu in education, which was segregated. Such differences were further compounded as a result of Rwanda's incorporation in the larger world economy, as opportunities to produce coffee for export and to export food crops and firewood enhanced the value of land, whereas the demand for manpower in mining enterprises and plantations in the neighboring Belgian Congo enhanced the value of controlling men. The ranks of the privileged were steadily opened to many Tutsi families, who formerly had been kept down by the ruling dynasty, but were closed to the Hutu, who previously had access to them through clientelist relations with ruling lineages. Colonial policies thus helped sharpen lines that had been more diffuse and, in so doing, eliminated elements of social structure that might have acted as buffers in future conflicts.

The nascent political life in the postwar years contributed to further polarization. With the support of a new generation of missionaries inspired by progressive currents in postwar Catholicism, a Hutu counterelite began to emerge in the 1950s, urging the Belgian trust authorities to institute democratic institutions that would provide a means to overturn the hierarchy. Under pressure from the United Nations, in the late 1950s the Belgians began moving in this direction. At the same time, the Tutsi sought to accelerate the departure of the Belgians before democratization occurred, so as to retain control over the country's future. Ironically, in the final heat, the relationship of the contending groups to the Belgian overlord was sharply reversed. Within the Tutsi community, power moved into the hands of the Union Nationale Ruandaise (UNAR), a militantly anti-Belgian party but with a neotraditionalist ideology. The colonial administration disciplined the Tutsi chiefs who participated in its founding and patronized the launching of a countervailing Parti du Mouvement d'Emancipation Hutu (PARMEHUTU), a wholly Hutu party led by G. Kayibanda. In November 1959, provoked by UNAR assaults, the Hutu rose in local- ities where Tutsi control had been most recently imposed. The insurgency then spread to the rest of the country, causing the Tutsis to flee to safer communities in Rwanda as well as across the border into Urundi (now Burundi), the Belgian Congo (now Zaire), and Uganda, which already had a substantial population of Rwandan migrant workers. The colonial authorities refrained from interfering until the middle of the month, when several companies of constabulary arrived from the Congo.[31] By then there were several hundred dead, thousands of destroyed dwellings, and widespread damage to fields and livestock.

The *jacquerie* of 1959 was a prelude to revolution. Hutu candidates swept the municipal elections of June 1960 and in September 1961 went on to gain control of the national legislature; a republic was proclaimed, with Kayibanda as president. Despite U.N.-imposed arrangements for representation of the Tutsi minority, after independence (July 1962) the PARMEHUTU government eliminated the Tutsi from all command posts and tried to reduce their numbers drastically in every sphere of public life. This action brought about a major exodus to the neighboring countries indicated, with the refugee count increasing from about 1,500 in late 1960 to 130,000 by the end of 1963. About two-thirds of the target group remained in Rwanda, however.

The Tutsi leadership in the diaspora was intent on regaining power. A guerrilla force was formed among the refugees in Burundi, where the Tutsi retained the upper hand. They limited themselves to minor border incursions until December 1963, when a few hundred of the *inyenzi* (cockroaches) staged a larger operation directed at the capital. Quickly defeated, the invasion led to a bloodbath. Possibly as many as 15,000 Tutsi were mur- dered in the next few days, their lands confiscated and redistributed to PARMEHUTU faithful. The remaining Tutsi political leaders were arrested and later executed. The regime also undertook to reduce Tutsi numbers in the schools and government and private employment, to 9 percent, a quota based on their proportion of the total population, as determined by the government.

Fearing more upheavals in neighboring Zaire and retaliation by Tutsi-dominated Burundi and apprehensive of left-leaning Tanzania, the PARMEHUTU regime trans- formed Rwanda into an isolated island, entirely dependent on Uganda for communications and supplies. As a consequence of the persecutions and general economic decline, the refugee total climbed to 185,000 in 1966, about evenly distributed among Zaire (60,000), Uganda (50,000), and Burundi (50,000), with a smaller number in Tanzania (25,000).[32] The Zaire government asked for the removal of Rwandan refugees after they participated in the Mulelist uprisings of the mid-1960s, and over half were subsequently resettled, mostly in Burundi and Uganda.[33]

In Burundi, relations between the Tutsi and Hutu were much less hierarchical. The Tutsi—also about 15 percent of three million—were themselves divided into a pair of castelike groups, the lower Hima and the higher Banyaruguru. Most of the chiefly positions were held by princes of the blood, or *ganwa,* whose power rested on client networks that included Hutu lineages. The transethnic character of these networks prevented political mobilization in the 1950s from crystallizing into a Hutu–Tutsi cleavage. Unité et Progrès National (UPRONA), an alliance led by the Mwami's eldest son, himself married to a Hutu, won a decisive victory in the 1961 legislative elections, and a Hutu was appointed prime minister. The alliance fell apart, however, after its leader was assassinated by a Greek gunman in the pay of his opponents. As independence neared (1962), power reverted into the hands of the Mwami who, alarmed by the revolution in Rwanda, preemptively consolidated the dominant Tutsis. Rwandan Tutsi refugees deemed undesirable by Zaire were encouraged to resettle in Burundi and emerged as stalwart supporters of anti-Hutu policies. Although the Hutu captured twenty-three out of thirty-one seats in the national elections of May 1965, the Mwami replaced the outgoing Hutu prime minister with a Tutsi *ganwa.*

In the following October, Hutu army and gendarmerie officers staged a mutiny but failed to win power. In retribution, Tutsi youth bands killed every Hutu leader they could find. The government machinery nearly collapsed, and the panic-stricken Mwami fled to Europe. The ensuing vacuum provided an opportunity for the army to take power, under the leadership of Captain Michel Micombero, a Tutsi from the lower Hima group, who proclaimed Burundi a republic.[34] As the trend toward Tutsi supremacy continued, Hutu in and out of the military plotted coups of their own. Disclosure of their plans in September 1969 provided a pretext for the arrest and subsequent execution of another thirty Hutu leaders and scores of soldiers. The surviving notables fled to Tanzania. Faced with growing discontent among the Hutu and disadvantaged Banyaruguru Tutsi, in April 1972 Micombero dismissed the entire government and assumed personal command of the state.

Exhorted to action by their exiled leaders, the Hutu then rose up in the capital and the southern provinces. Operating in small bands of 10 to 30 men, the assailants numbered about 10,000 all together. In addition to local activists, they included Hutu refugees operating from bases inside Tanzania. Joining the largely Hutu movement were also members of excluded Tutsi factions, as well as Mulelist refugees from Zaire, including Rwandan Tutsi who had turned against Micombero when he denied them the use of Burundi as a staging base. The rebels rapidly overran provincial capitals in the south and held out for two weeks, slaughtering every Tutsi in sight as well as any Hutu who refused to join the movement. The toll was estimated at over 2,000. Micombero's army then swept through the country in a cold-blooded reprisal. The counterviolence continued for several months, taking on the character of a "selective genocide" directed at the literate strata of Hutu society, especially including secondary school students. Estimated deaths range from 80,000 to 200,000, the victims being overwhelmingly Hutu—from 3 to 7 percent of the target group—but also including some Banyaruguru and Rwandan refugees.[35] However, not only did these murderous actions evoke little international concern, but a number of foreign states even provided support for carrying them out.[36]

An estimated 150,000 Hutu fled abroad. As of 1976, there were approximately 110,500 in Tanzania, 24,000 in Zaire, and about 15,000 in Rwanda.[37] Tanzania-based Hutus staged additional raids into southern Burundi in 1973, but after retaliatory bombardments by Burundi, the Tanzanian authorities moved them further inland. Settled amidst a closely related population, these Hutus were rapidly integrated into the receiving society; integration proceeded apace in Rwanda as well.

Despite the massive killings and refugee waves in both countries, as of the early 1970s most members of the target groups were alive and in their respective country of origin: well over half of the original Tutsi group in Rwanda and as much as nine-tenths of the Hutu in Burundi. In Rwanda, the Tutsi minority served as a stake in factional fights within the ruling stratum. In response to the persecution of the Hutu in Burundi, in 1972 bands of party toughs brutally enforced the quota throughout the school system and among private firms, and in the last months of the year about another ten thousand refugees fled to Rwanda. Kayibanda was overthrown in July 1973. Proclaiming his commitment to the reduction of ethnic tensions, his successor, General Habyarimana, included a Tutsi minister in his government and appointed others to senior posts in the civil service and the army. However, the logic of ethnic power prevailed, and more Tutsi left the country in 1978, complaining that even the established quota system was unfairly administered.

A decade later, conditions for the Tutsi minority appeared unlikely to improve in the forseeable future and might even worsen. General economic conditions continued to deteriorate as the result of extreme demographic pressure, combined with unfavorable conditions for coffee, the main export commodity. Already the densest in Africa (147 per sq. km), Rwanda's population has been increasing at an annual rate of 3.0 to 3.5 percent and in the early 1980s passed the five-million mark. In the absence of any increase in productivity, the country began to experience a crisis of subsistence, which the government proposed to resolve by settling uninhabited regions. At the same time, coffee exports were to be increased by raising productivity without expanding the area cultivated. However, the fact that the area had not been settled previously raised doubts about its suitability, and coffee yields have indeed fallen steadily since independence. From the late 1970s onward, landlocked Rwanda's economic problems were compounded by generalized violence in Uganda. Given the further shrinking of an already miserable pie, pressures to reduce the share allocated to the outgroup mounted, and in 1980 an attempt was made to overthrow the government on the grounds it failed to enforce the quota system.

In 1982 many of the Tutsi refugees who had fled to Uganda were forced to return, and Rwanda also became a country of first asylum for Ugandan Tutsi and the related Hima (see the section on Uganda). An estimated 188,900 Rwandans were living abroad as refugees in 1985. Despite the events of 1982, most of them were still in Uganda (118,000). The other receivers were Burundi (58,000), Zaire (11,000), and Kenya (1,900).[38] In Burundi—which claimed it was hosting over 256,000—the Rwandans, as members of the dominant ethnic minority, readily gained access to the public and private sectors; however, like the Burundians themselves, they were subject to the factionalist conflicts of clientelist politics and faced grave economic difficulties. As of 1985 the UNHCR calculated that about three-fourths were in need of assistance—all of the 51,000 in rural areas and about 10,000 out of 30,000 in Bujumbura—and because of limited possibilities of employment the UNHCR endorsed a proposal by the government to transfer the latter to new rural settlements.[39] The Rwandans in Zaire have become economically self-sufficient and are now being integrated into the receiving society. This is a mixed blessing, however, as oppressive conditions have driven many Zaireans to seek a better life abroad.

After the events of 1972 the political scene in Burundi remained dominated by intra-Tutsi factionalism and latent ethnic tensions. Although a few Hutu were appointed to ministerial positions, most were systematically barred from acquiring a secondary or higher education and were excluded from both the army and the civil service. Micombero was overthrown in 1976 by a faction of Tutsi officers led by his cousin, Colonel Jean-Baptiste Bagaza, who called for ethnic reconciliation and appointed several Hutu to minor ministries. The army, however, refused to admit Hutu. The new government officially abolished the traditional sharecropping system and called on Hutu refugees to return, promising to resettle them on their old land or to give them new homesteads, but did little to implement the policy. Ten years after the abolition, a seasoned observer reported that the traditional patron–client relations still prevailed.[40]

Ethnic tensions mounted in Rwanda in the late 1970s. The Roman Catholic church emerged as the major critic of the government's policy toward the Hutu, but this stance only prompted Bagaza to launch a sustained attack on the church itself.[41] In the spring of 1979, Tutsi university students, under the leadership of Rwandan refugees, lashed out at their Hutu colleagues. Fearing a resurgence of pogroms against educated elites, Hutu students and teachers throughout the country went into hiding or fled to Rwanda. Bagaza then expelled more missionaries, charging that they had collaborated in the circulation abroad of tracts alleging massive arrests and executions. Despite repeated promises of a return to civilian rule, open political competition was unlikely, as it would undoubtedly produce a Hutu majority. Legislative elections were held in 1982 under a system providing for the selection of representatives by local electoral colleges composed of traditional dignitaries and UPRONA cadres, so as to ensure Tutsi preponderance, and indeed, only three Hutu were elected. As one observer reported at the time, "People live in terror. The only force is the army. By design, it is always on maneuvres in the bush, where the Hutu rural majority lives; they are thereby subjected to a series of measures of permanent intimidation."[42]

Here also, the deterioration of general conditions precludes any significant improvement in the target group's situation in the foreseeable future. As of 1980, Burundi was one of the five poorest countries in the world, with a yearly per-capita income as low as $40 in the rural areas and a literacy rate of only 10 percent. The economic conditions fluctuated from poor to worse, depending the size of the coffee crop and the world market. More fundamentally, as in Rwanda, the combination of rapid demographic growth, export agriculture, and low productivity generated a crisis of subsistence. These conditions, together with continued pressure on Bagaza to assuage revanchist factions, led to the expulsion in 1978 of 40,000 to 50,000 Zaireans, mostly Bembe refugees from the 1964 Mulelist rebellion and jobless migrant workers. The vacated lands were allocated to the regime's Tutsi clients, prompting Zaire's retaliatory eviction of Burundian Hutu refugees from the farms on which they were settled by the UNHCR in 1974, on the grounds that these were needed for the returnees. In September 1987, while out of the country, Bagaza was overthrown by Major Pierre Buyoya. Although Buyoya ended the war against the Catholic church, he insisted that Burundi did not have an ethnic problem.[43]

Despite recurrent reports of voluntary repatriation, the 1986 estimate of refugees from Burundi was still 189,000.[44] About 160,000 were in Tanzania, living in three self-sufficient agricultural settlements on land donated by the government, to which the UNHCR turned over supervisory authority. Although it was reported many of the refugees wanted to return home, Tanzanian officials viewed them as permanent settlers and offered them an opportunity to acquire Tanzanian citizenship.[45] Of the remainder, 19,000 were in Rwanda, where de facto integration was also taking place, and 10,000 in Zaire.[46]

The Two Wars of the Two Sudans[47]

The two major waves of refugees originating in Sudan since it gained independence in 1956 stem from the policies that were adopted by successive regimes toward the southern region and that are rooted in the historic stance of northern state-builders: Like their predecessors, the postindependence rulers were determined to incorporate the south but failed to secure the consent of the governed and lacked the capacity to achieve their objective by force alone.

The largest country on the African continent, Sudan stretches for nearly a thousand miles, from Egypt and Libya to Zaire, Uganda, and Kenya. In culture and politics, Sudan spans the Middle East and black Africa. Historically, what is now the north used to be the hinterland of Egypt. In the early nineteenth century it was subdued by Mohammed Ali and incorporated into his Turko-Egyptian state. This provided a staging base for penetration into the southern region, which was effectively annexed in the decades after 1839, when Egyptian navigators found their way across the "Sudd," a huge swampy stretch blocking access to a tropical region inhabited by non-Muslim Negroes, valuable as a source of ivory and slaves for use in Egypt or export via Red Sea traders to Arabia. Considered from a sub-Saharan perspective, however, the south is a black African country, whose diverse peoples have strong cultural and social links with their neighbors all around. In the nineteenth century, communities throughout the region were ravaged by the expanding slave trade, but owing to their organizational capacity for warfare, the Azande and Dinka maintained their integrity as constituted societies.

Shortly after the British occupied Egypt in 1882, the region immediately to the south of Khartoum spawned a fundamentalist movement under the leadership of Mohammed Ahmed, leader of the Ansar sect, who revealed himself as *al Mahdi al Mutazar* ("the awaited guide in the right path") and proclaimed a *jihad* (crusade) against the corrupt Egyptian state. Committed to avoiding overseas adventures, British prime minister William Gladstone's Liberal government relinquished the field to the Mahdi and his successors, who by 1891 controlled most of contemporary Sudan.[48] In the latter half of the 1890s, however, mounting rivalries among European imperialists prompted Britain to undertake a reconquest. In retrospect, the Mahdist state came to be viewed by many Muslims as the first genuinely Sudanese regime. But although some Dinka leaders aligned themselves with the new state to further their own aims, from the vantage point of the south more generally, the new state was merely another incarnation of Arab imperialism. Despite its destruction as a state, the Mahdist achievement survived through the leader's descendants and the Ansar sect, with attendant networks of dependent clients. Also supporting the Egyptian regime against the Mahdists was the Khatmiyah sect led by the Mirghani family, which has also endured.

Far from integrating the country, British policies, guided essentially by the objective of maintaining hegemony in the Middle East, crystallized Sudanese dualism. The Anglo-Egyptian agreement of 1899 restored Egyptian sovereignty but provided for a "condominium" whereby Britain assumed complete responsibility for the government. The north was governed Egypt-style by collaborative elites mainly from the Mirghani camp, and the south was deemed fundamentally different, requiring a distinctive administrative organization. Concerned with limiting the expansion of Islam as well as protecting the southerners from further slave raids, administrators and missionaries encouraged the emergence of a distinct southern culture founded on Christianity and the use of English (rather than Arabic) as a common language. This policy was formalized in the 1920s into a "closed door" policy, whereby northerners as well as foreigners other than the British were not allowed into the south.[49] Conceived largely as a deterrent, this policy was not concerned with promoting development, and so the south remained an area of mostly subsistence husbandry and agriculture.

The first stirrings of nationalism arose in the north in the late 1930s. Emerging political parties clustered around established sectarian nuclei; the Khatmiyah sided with those who opposed British rule in Egypt and favored union with that country, later forming an alliance with like-minded radical secular nationalists known as the National Unionist party. The anti-Egyptian Ansars coalesced with moderate secular nationalists into the Umma party, seeking Sudanese independence in cooperation with Britain. The south remained backward and isolated. Although a few development projects were started, its physical and social infrastructures remained rudimentary. Containing about one-fourth of the population (in 1960), the south had only three secondary schools, compared with sixty-five in the north, and of 1,216 students at Khartoum University, only 60 were southerners.

The institutional profile of the emerging state was shaped by the establishment of a unitary national assembly (1948), within which the south figured only as a cluster of constituencies. Both leading parties courted southern support, but the small southern elite launched its own Southern party, which advocated federation. With the Nasser revolution under way, the British stepped up the transfer of power to anti-Egyptian Sudanese nationalists. The replacement of British officials with northern bureaucrats committed to centralization stimulated further demands for southern autonomy. Umma politicians, who needed the support of southern representatives to achieve independence, agreed to consider moving afterwards to a federal constitution.

Despite political accommodation, independence exacerbated interregional tensions. The spark came from the army. Amidst rumors of an impending mutiny by southern troops against their northern officers, the government dispatched reinforcements to Equatoria Province. Fearing that they would be slaughtered by the northerners, the southern enlisted ranks killed their officers. The mutineers fled and emerged later as the nucleus of a guerrilla force. These events unleashed a wave of attacks against northern merchants and officials throughout the region. Punitive actions followed, prompting more widespread resistance to northern rule.

Claiming the parliamentary politicians' inability to cope with the country's problems, General Ibrahim Abboud staged a coup in November 1958. Far from resolving tensions, however, "military rule eliminated an important institutional nexus wherein bargaining and interaction, however frustrating, did continue."[50] Determined to bring about a final solution to the southern problem, the military government launched an "arabization" policy, which entailed closing all English-language educational institutions (1964) and eliminating all English speakers—that is, the entire southern elite—from the regional administration. Plans were also made to colonize the south with over a million Arabs. With the political parties completely suppressed, relations between the regions continued to deteriorate, and by 1963 the south was engulfed in violence. Over the next several years, the northern army and government-sponsored militias perpetrated a number of massacres against civilian populations. Although these atrocities lent credence to charges of deliberate genocide, they may merely have reflected the Khartoum government's inability to control the remote provinces.

Although the conflict fostered the development of a new southern consciousness, spokesmen remained divided between those committed to a federal solution and the outright separatists. Large groups such as the Dinka, Shilluk, and Nuer were initially not involved in the resistance, and some of their representatives continued to participate in Khartoum politics. Various exile groups arose, of which the most prominent was the Sudan African National Union, operating at various times from Zaire and Uganda. The most important component of the armed resistance was the guerrilla force known as Anya-nya, formed around a core of mutineers of the Equatoria Corps and augmented by army deserters and uprooted schoolboys. Estimates of their numbers (1972) range from ten thousand to twenty thousand. Operating largely as independent bands, the Anya-nya at first lacked an external military patron and so relied mainly on captured weapons and supplies from the Sudanese army. Subsequently, however, some arms became available from Ethiopia, in return for Sudan's support of the Eritrean insurgents, as well as from Israel, which viewed the conflict as an opportunity to weaken Arab control over the Red Sea.

From 1960 on, southern politicians and intellectuals began fleeing to adjoining Uganda and Zaire; massive population movements followed after 1963, as southerners sought havens in regions inaccessible to the ravaging government forces, within Sudan or in neighboring countries. By the end of the conflict (1972), estimates of the internally displaced ranged from 500,000 to as high as 800,000. In 1970, the UNHCR enumerated 170,500 Sudanese refugees abroad: 71,500 in Uganda and 59,000 in Zaire, with another 20,000 each in the Central African Republic and Ethiopia. They included an unusually high proportion of schoolage children, determined to pursue their education.

With the conflict aggravating other problems, the Sudanese government was gripped by severe instability. Overthrown in 1964, the Abboud regime gave way to a succession of ineffectual civilian combinations, until in 1969 a group of younger officers assumed power under the leadership of Ja'far Nimeiri. Striking a tactical alliance with the Sudanese Communist party (SCP), the new government committed itself to structural change within and neutralism without, coupled with a more militantly pro-Arab stance. Again, all political parties were declared illegal. Nimeiri weathered an attempted coup by the Ansar in 1970 and levied severe retribution, prompting about 3,000 to flee to Ethiopia. The following year he prevented another coup, possibly involving the SCP. He then formed his own Sudanese Socialist Union (SSU). At the same time, Nimeiri shifted away from pan-Arabism and sought a rapprochement with the West, stressing Sudan's distinctive "African" identity.

The new orientation would be well served by a settlement of the civil war. In keeping with this, in 1972 Khartoum began negotiations with Joseph Lagu, who had emerged as leader of the main body of the Anya-nya. This resulted in the Addis Ababa Agreement, which provided for the unification of the southern provinces into a single large region, with administrative and political autonomy and the authority to create its own cultural policy. The key institutions were the Regional People's Assembly and a higher executive council, whose president would also serve as a national vice-president. Refugees were granted complete amnesty and aid in resettlement, and the Anya-nya were to be integrated into the armed forces serving in the south. Arabic was to be recognized as the country's official language, but English would be the "working language" of the South.

As of May 1972, the UNHCR estimated Sudan's refugees at 200,000; 145,000 had returned by the end of 1973, and the process was completed over the next two years, leaving only a few thousand in Ethiopia, including some 3,000 Anya-nya who rejected the agreement (mostly Anuak and Nuer) and about 1,000 northerners of the Ansar sect.[51]

Albeit a genuine attempt at accommodation, the agreement did little to overcome the structural flaws that make Sudan nearly impossible to govern as a single state.[52] Although the south received considerable international development aid, this was hardly enough to overcome its relative undevelopment. The largest undertaking was the construction of the Jonglei canal, which in fact benefited mostly the north, as it entailed diverting some of the Nile waters from the Sudd, where much of it evaporated and hence was lost to the north and Egypt. The arrival of Egyptian workers to begin work in late 1974 prompted demonstrations by southerners who feared a renewed invasion.[53] The following year, a group of Anya-nya guerrillas who resisted incorporation into northern army units shot their commander and fled to Ethiopia, where they formed the nucleus of Anya-nya II.

From the perspective of Nimeiri, as of any Sudanese state-builder, the existence of an autonomous southern region could be viewed only as a temporarily necessary evil, to be eliminated at the earliest opportunity. The consolidation of central control was rendered more urgent in the late 1970s by the discovery of huge oil reserves in the northern part of the south. Achievement of this objective was facilitated by the continuing disunity of the south itself. Regional centralization, which redounded to the advantage of the Dinka, prompted resentment from lesser groups, whose representatives—such as Joseph Lagu— therefore advocated redividing the region into its component provinces, a process that would in effect enhance the power of Khartoum. In October 1981 Nimeiri dissolved the southern assembly and dismissed the regional government, installing a caretaker administration favoring redivision; anti-redivision activists were later arrested. Khartoum also decided to locate the principal oil refinery in the north rather than close to the oil fields.

Concurrently, dissension was growing within the north as well, where with the renewed suppression of the traditional political parties the only remaining autonomous political force was the Muslim Brotherhood. By early 1982, "there was growing (and perhaps irreversible) disenchantment with the government in power."[54] Nimeiri dissolved party institutions and further tightened his personal control. These developments stimulated further resentment in the south, manifested by proliferating mutinies among the army rank and file and the defection of a number of prominent officers, including Colonel John Garang. In June of that year Anya-nya II emerged as a significant force in Upper Nile. The number of incidents rose steadily over the next several months, with indications of collusion between southern officials and the insurgents. This triggered once again an escalating spiral of repression and resistance, but without a leader, Anya-nya II could stage little more than banditry.

His position ensured by a military agreement with Egypt—which provided him with a pretorian guard—and increased military aid from the United States, in 1983 Nimeiri tried to bring the south to heel. In June the region was formally redivided; Arabic was imposed as the sole official language, and in September Nimeiri decreed the immediate introduction nationwide of Islamic law (*Sharia*). Nimeiri probably made this move to enhance his popularity with the Arabic masses in the north so as to undercut support for the Muslim Brotherhood, but even though the *sharia* was not widely enforced in the south, the measure pushed the regional conflict beyond the brink.

Thanks to considerable aid from the revolutionary regime in Ethiopia, which was once again retaliating against Sudan for the safe haven it provided to Eritrean insurgents, John Garang's Sudan Popular Liberation Army (SPLA) rapidly overtook Anya-nya II as the leading guerrilla force and eliminated most of its rivals. Rejecting secessionism, Garang aspired to a national revolution, and so the SPLA organized the broader Sudan Popular Liberation Movement (SPLM). Its domain was initially restricted to the Dinka populations of the upper provinces of the south (Bahr-el-Ghazal, Upper Nile, and Jonglei); moreover, geopolitical constraints confined its operations largely to the eastern districts along the Ethiopian border. But the war escalated further in the early months of 1984, when an SPLA force of two thousand to three thousand attempted to sever lines of communication linking the south with the north and to bring petroleum extraction as well as work on the Jonglei canal to a halt by raiding work camps and abducting foreigners. At this time the SPLM claimed that it had gained control over the quasi totality of the insurrection but acknowledged a lack of support in Equatoria.[55]

The violence led to a renewed exodus of refugees to Ethiopia. Border crossings increased in the latter part of 1983, from an average of about one hundred a day to five hundred a day in January 1984, seven hundred in February, and eight hundred in subsequent months. The population of the UNHCR camp at Itang, thirty-five miles from the border, rose from about ten thousand in 1983 to forty thousand by May 1984, when the Ethiopian government allowed reporters to visit the site and interview inmates, whose accounts indicated that the Sudanese forces—referred to by the refugees simply as "Arabs"—were engaged in a systematic terror campaign against Dinka, Awak, and Shilluk villagers, to discourage them from supporting the guerrillas. Most of the refugees were young and male, because they were the principal targets, and in any case only the fittest could undertake and survive the long trek to the camp. Although the journalists reported no signs that Itang was a training camp for the rebels, as charged by Sudanese authorities, it can hardly be doubted that this population constituted a pool for the recruitment of fighters. The Ethiopians, who steadfastly denied supporting the rebels, said that they were bound to accept the refugees and, in any case, were unable to control the flow. But even though this open door policy was in accord with Addis Ababa's political objectives, there were reports of increasing tensions as the refugees competed with the local population for the region's meager resources.[56] Overall, the refugee total increased by an estimated seventy thousand between 1983 and 1985.[57]

Throughout 1984, the Sudanese ruler wavered between lashing out at his opponents and making conciliatory moves so as to establish a new power base.[58] In late 1984 Nimeiri's credibility as an Arab and a Muslim was undermined by revelations that he had collaborated in an operation to evacuate several thousand Ethiopian Jews to Israel (see the section on Ethiopia). Meanwhile, the economy was deteriorating rapidly. The northern region fell prey to a major drought; one-fourth of the army was engaged in the conflict, at a cost of between $300,000 and $500,000 a day; and with annual debt service exceeding the total export revenues, the state tottered on the verge of bankruptcy.[59] Nimeiri's decline prompted renewed activity by his opponents in the north. The traditionally antagonistic parties coalesced under Sadek El Mahdi, an Ansar leader and former prime minister, then in detention. They reportedly tried to establish contacts with Garang as well. Meanwhile the further deterioration of the situation in the south fatally undermined the army's confidence in the regime.

Albeit beholden to Nimeiri for his cooperation in implementing their anti-Libyan policy, Egypt and the United States also began viewing him as a liability.[60] In February 1985 the United States froze further economic aid, except for food relief for refugees; Great Britain, Saudi Arabia, and Egypt followed suit, blaming Nimeiri for the collapse of the Jonglei canal project; and Egypt's President Hosni Mubarak rescinded his military alliance. At the end of March, when Nimeiri left for a visit to the United States, riots broke out in the capital, followed by a general strike. Contacted by Sadek el Mahdi, army leaders agreed not to interfere but instead to join the movement should it prove "irresistible." On April 6 the military took over, promising a return to democracy within six months.[61]

The transitional military council, which included two Christian southerners, stated that ending the civil war was a key priority and offered to talk with Garang. However, the subsequent provisional government sought to undermine Garang's position by undertaking a rapprochement with both Ethiopia and Libya. The latter move prompted a drastic reduction of U.S. aid.[62] Garang insisted on civilian rule as a prerequisite for talks and further emphasized his movement's role as a revolutionary vanguard for all of Sudan. The decline and fall of Nimeiri boosted support for the SNLM, whose forces in mid-1985 were estimated at ten thousand to fifteen thousand. In the latter part of the year these forces moved steadily north and west, as well as into southernmost Equatoria, interdicting the supply of food relief through Kenya.

In keeping with its commitment, the provisional government held countrywide elections in April 1986. But because of the violence, polling was postponed in thirty-seven of sixty-seven southern constituencies, which undermined the legitimacy of the new assembly and government in the eyes of the south. In the north, the elections reflected traditional alignments.[63] Sadek el Mahdi became prime minister of a coalition government with support from the Ansar and Khatmyia camps; it also included a few southerners, leaving the Muslim Brotherhood's Islamic Front as the opposition. Although Sadek had earlier denounced the imposition of the *sharia,* he could not abandon it altogether without playing into the hands of the Brotherhood. This required months of maneuvering, during which there was no possibility of negotiating with Garang. Moreover, given the catastrophic economic situation and steadily falling morale among the government's armed forces, it made sense for Garang to hold out for the regime to collapse completely. Prospects for peace receded as the new government became mired in the Sudd of traditional Sudanese politics. In 1987 Sadek sought to consolidate his crumbling position by having himself elected as the new religious leader (imam) of the Ansars. For this purpose, reenacting Nimeiri's itinerary, he began moving away from the Khatmiyah toward the Muslim Brotherhood, which remains the best organized force in the country. This might lead the government once again to emphasize Sudan's Islamic character, an eventuality that would perhaps consummate its split into two states.[64]

Meanwhile, the war expanded, with both sides resorting to a scorched-earth policy and using food as a weapon. Traditional ethnic tensions escalated into bloody wars as the government resumed the practice begun by Nimeiri during the first civil war, of equipping Maralheen raiders as an anti-Dinka militia, who rode into villages on camels, horses, and donkeys, armed with rifles, submachine guns, and mortars.[65] With no government controls, desperate food shortages fostered banditism throughout the region, with old antagonisms flaring up into bloody clashes that engulfed refugee camps as well (see the section on Uganda).[66] Half the population of the eastern part of Bahr-el-Ghazal—nearly 600,000—was uprooted by the fighting, their cattle decimated and their granaries burned to the ground.

By mid-1986, Wau, the capital of Bahr-el-Ghazal, and Juba were under a virtual state of siege, their populations swollen by a huge influx of refugees from the surrounding countryside. In Juba, the non-Muslim majority supported the rebels and successfully prevented the installation of a new Executive High Committee appointed by Khartoum to govern the south once again as a single region. But the city's Muslim minority reportedly still acted as a colonial elite, and the construction of a huge Islamic center, financed by Kuwait, continued on schedule.[67] Conditions deteriorated further in August, when after the insurgents downed an airplane carrying passengers and cargo from Uganda to southern Sudan, the U.N. evacuated most of its personnel and halted all food shipments into the area. In the latter part of the year, an abundant crop brought immediate relief to the north, but in the south, the determination of each side to starve out the other kept everyone hungry.[68]

People fled where they could, mostly to the north, where reportedly as many as a quarter of a million refugees were encamped around Khartoum, adding to the problems of famine and encouraging further antisouthern sentiment. At the end of 1986 the Sudanese refugee population in Ethiopia numbered 131,599, and by mid-1987 it had reached 179,285—131,156 in Itang, 27,279 in Dimma, 20,000 in Assosa, and 490 in Addis Ababa.[69]

The Fragmentation of Chad[70]

As in Sudan, the protracted conflict that has wracked Chad for the past two decades is rooted in the inclusion in an inordinately large and extremely poor state, of Muslim and non-Muslim populations historically bound as raiders and prey. Here also the depredations occasioned by the slave trade reached unprecedented heights in the latter part of the nineteenth century, when the country was in the throes of yet another conquest. However, in this case, under the impact of colonization the relationship of domination was partially reversed. It was the non-Muslim southerners who inherited the apparatus of the colonial state, dealing themselves the lion's share, and hence the northerners, in the face of deprivation and humiliation, rose up in insurgency. Exacerbated by tyrannical rule, extreme poverty, recurrent natural disasters, and external interventions, the confrontation unleashed a process of fragmentation that engulfed the country in violence.

From a European perspective the region remained of no interest until the French tried to secure a land link between their possessions in West Africa, North Africa, and the Congo.[71] Chad thus emerged as a residual amalgam spanning three climates, with correspondingly different sociocultural regions. Despite its reputation for "Cartesian" administrative uniformity and "Jacobin" assimilationist universalism, France governed Chad as it did its other colonies, making the most of limited means by adapting to local realities; thus colonization did little to unify the country.

The desert zone, known administratively as B.E.T. (Borkou-Ennedi-Tibesti), encompasses half of Chad but contains a mere 10 percent of its people. These nomadic Arabs and blacks are called Toubous but are known to outsiders as Goranes, desert raiders who entrusted the routine tasks of agriculture and husbandry to slaves captured in the Sahel or farther south. Having prohibited raiding, the French governed the B.E.T. as a protectorate entrusted to the military, which established a patron–client relationship with the local notables to whom they distributed goods and services to make up for their loss of income. The nomads continued to circulate quite freely throughout the desert and retained stronger ties to the north—now Libya—than to the more southern parts of Chad.

Of special relevance to the current situation is the ambiguous status of a band of territory totaling 110,000 sq. km (about one-tenth of Chad), known as the "Aozou strip," which includes the Tibesti mountains and adjoining oases.[72] At the time France established itself in southern Chad, the area nominally belonged to Ottoman Turkey but was effectively under the rule of a Mahdist-type movement launched from southern Libya by the Sanussyia religious order, whose leaders established themselves as overlords of the principalities established in the Sahel farther south. France rolled back the Sanussyia from the latter region and, taking advantage of the struggle between Turkey and Italy (1911–

15), later occupied the Tibesti as well. In 1935, as part of an attempt to settle Franco-Italian imperial rivalries and prevent the formation of a German-Italian alliance, French Foreign Minister Pierre Laval conceded the worthless Aozou strip to Mussolini. However, the treaty was never implemented, and later France insisted that it had become null and void.[73] The United Nations, which gained jurisdiction over Libya in 1947, decided that its southern border should eventually be settled by negotiation. After the country became independent, King Idriss, whose rule was founded on descent from the founder of the Sanussiya, voiced claim to the contested region but did not actively pursue the matter. Dormant when Chad in turn achieved independence in 1960, this issue was revived by the onset of an uprising in the Tibesti region in the mid-1960s and moved to the fore after Muammar Qaddafi seized power in 1969.[74]

The Sahel covers about 30 percent of Chad and contains 40 percent of its population, mostly sedentary Muslims of the Tidjanya sect, who speak related Chadic languages but use Arabic as a common language. Beginning in the thirteenth century the area gave birth to a succession of Muslim states that thrived on the export of salt, ivory, and slaves. In the nineteenth century most of them became sultanates of the Sanussi rulers. The French wanted to destroy the link with northern Africa but found that the indigenous variety of Islam provided a reliable foundation for the colonial order and so made no effort to impose Christianity or Western education on the region. As in the British system of indirect rule developed in adjacent Nigeria, which the French officially eschewed, administrative districts reflected the boundaries of sultanates such as Kanem, Baguirmi, and Waddai, and official chiefs were drawn mainly from the ranks of ruling elites. During the colonial period, exactions increased as the chiefs harnessed traditional structures to the collection of new taxes and the production of new export commodities, mainly peanuts.

The south, dubbed by the French as "useful Chad," encompasses only one-tenth of the country's territory but contains one-half of its 4.5 million (c. 1975).[75] It is a tropical zone inhabited by non-Muslim agriculturalists, organized into small-scale societies. The majority of them are linguistically related and generically referred to as *Sara*.[76] As black animists, more "primitive" than Muslims, the Sara were initially regarded by the French as a pool of docile manpower and were recruited with the collaboration of local chiefs for portage and corvée labor in the construction of public works in more promising colonies, as well as for service in the colonial army.[77] In the 1920s the French introduced cotton into Chad, and it became "the pivot around which all the activities of the region were organized and synchronized under the direction of the State."[78] Production was entrusted to a monopolistic parastatal organization, with mandatory family quotas enforced by local chiefs, a system that has largely persisted to the present. But Chad remained so unpromising that the French did not even bother to build a railroad for shipping exports or even a single paved road. The low price and the obligation to plant cotton to the detriment of food crops encouraged insurgencies against the chiefs and emerged as major political grievances in the immediate postwar period.[79] Concurrent with this "voice," there was also "exit": The brutal exactions and the lack of economic opportunity caused considerable emigration to Nigeria, Ubangi-Shari (now Central African Republic), and Sudan, where over 75,000 Chadians were counted in 1955.[80]

Within these limits, in the decade and a half preceding independence, Chad's economic activity did expand somewhat, and the French institutionalized a minimal apparatus of government and social services. Muslims from the Sahel emerged as the commercial middle strata of the southern towns, but the southern underdogs gained access to Western education, which the Muslims generally rejected in favor of secondary and higher education in Sudan or even Cairo. With the onset of africanization, the ranks of the expanding bureaucracy thus came to be run almost exclusively by Sara southerners.

The institutionalization from 1946 onward of popular elections, initially on the basis of limited suffrage, set the stage for the mobilization of the Sara, both to protest colonial conditions and to compete with the Muslims. Their organizational instrument was the Parti Progressiste Tchadien (PPT), a radically anticolonial party led by Gabriel Lisette, a civil servant of West Indian origin.[81] Muslim notables generally supported the Union Démocratique Tchadienne (UDT), patronized by the French authorities. However, somewhat like the Belgians in Rwanda, in the light of developments in North Africa and the Middle East, the French later shifted to promoting the "Christian" south as a counterweight to the "Arab" north. The PPT henceforth collaborated with the administration, whereas a new generation of Muslims attuned to developments in the Arab world launched the Mouvement Socialiste Africain (MSA) and later the more radical Union Nationale Tchadienne (UNT), under the leadership of Ibrahima Abatcha.

In 1957, when Chad was granted internal self-government, the PPT achieved an overwhelming majority in the Territorial Assembly. As its West Indian leader was active mainly in Paris, organizational power fell into the hands of his Sara lieutenant, François Tombalbaye, who became head of government. Tombalbaye proceeded to broaden his base by naming to his cabinet Muslim conservatives threatened by the MSA and the UNT. This move enabled him to eliminate Lisette and gain the upper hand over his PPT rivals. Having done so, in 1962 Tombalbaye dismissed his Muslim ministers and declared the Tidajanya brotherhood illegal. In the following year, a wave of arrests caused major demonstrations in the Muslim quarters of the capital, which in turn were savagely repressed. The Chadian state was thus quickly reduced to a Sara autocracy that monopolized the country's meager public resources. Despite its extreme weakness, the state attempted to collect much higher taxes from the northern regions than the French had and also to follow a more aggressively assimilationist cultural policy, which further antagonized the Muslim half of the country.

These measures led to antigovernment actions throughout the Sahel and an acceleration of the exodus. By 1964 the estimates of Chadians abroad climbed to 250,000 to 500,000, principally in Sudan but also in the Central African Republic, Cameroon, and Nigeria. None, however, were yet recognized as refugees.[82] In 1966, under the leadership of Ibrahima Abatcha, UNT exiles in Sudan organized the Front de Libération Nationale (FROLINAT) with the tacit approval of their hosts. Consisting of a few small guerrilla bands, FROLINAT operated mainly in adjacent Waddai, but it failed to gain support among the local population, perhaps because its leaders were strangers to the region, and so its activities ground to a halt after Abatcha was killed in an ambush in 1968.

The B.E.T. remained under French military administration until 1965. After taking over, the Sara regime not only stopped providing the traditional grants-in-aid but also attempted to turn the nomads into sedentaries, forcing them to do work that was, from their perspective, reserved for slaves. At the end of 1966, a leading notable from the Tibesti and his following crossed into Libya, where he established contacts with FRO-LINAT. Operating with the connivance of Libyan authorities, guerrilla bands under the leadership of his son, Goukouni Oueddei (also Woddei) roamed with impunity across the Tibesti, calling themselves the "Second Army" of FROLINAT. Equipped mostly with World War II weapons from Erwin Rommel's Afrika Korps, they left the Chadian army with only a tenuous hold over the administrative centers. France initially stayed on the sidelines but, after a mutiny of the Aozou garrison in April 1968, offered logistical assistance in retaking the town.

The pinning down of government forces in the far north in turn provided an opportunity to revive FROLINAT activities in the Sahel, where the "First Army" forced the government to evacuate its administrative personnel and prevented the collection of cotton and the delivery of cattle. At the beginning of 1969, the government retained control over only the capital, Fort-Lamy, and the southwest, whereas the B.E.T. and the central and eastern Sahel were in the hands of local warlords.

Despite the common label and the emergence of Dr. Abba Sidick as their spokesman abroad, the many FROLINAT components showed no indication of coalescing into a national organization. As the insurgency spread, fragmentation became apparent in each region. Terrorized by governmental forces and guerrillas and faced with steadily deteriorating economic conditions, people from the eastern districts of the Sahel continued to pour into Sudan, forming a mixed collection of economic migrants and unrecognized refugees, probably numbering over half a million.

In the late 1960s the Chadian conflict was further internationalized. With the insurgents converging on Fort-Lamy, the French agreed to dispatch a well-equipped intervention force on the condition that Tombalbaye reform his administration, for which purpose the French provided a cadre of seasoned colonial administrators, who in effect reassumed control of military and administrative operations throughout the Sahel.[83] At about the same time, Colonel Muammar Qaddafi took power in Libya and renewed the old Sanussi claim, but with greater ideological fervor and subsequently vastly increased means afforded by the oil boom. Moreover, the value of the Tibesti was enhanced by rumors of uranium deposits there.[84] By 1971 the French had successfully contained the insurrections, but after they officially pulled out in June of that year, leaving only a token force, Tombalbaye returned to his usual practices and quickly lost the areas they had regained, abandoning the B.E.T. as well as most of the Sahel, except for the Kanem region.[85] At the same time, the Sahel began experiencing a catastrophic drought.

To best his rivals in the FROLINAT, Goukouni entrusted command of the Second Army to Hissen Habré, a defecting government official. Also a Toubou but from a different clan, Habré was one of the first Chadians to receive training as a high-level field administrator. He rose as a protégé of Gaullist "old Africa hands," with whom he remained in contact throughout the period. Under his leadership the B.E.T. became in effect an autonomous state from which, in the guise of a revolutionary movement, Toubou raiders, now equipped with modern weapons from Colonel Qaddafi, exacted tribute from cattlemen and transients, as they always had done.

In a dramatic turnabout, in late 1972 Tombalbaye himself secretly recognized Libyan sovereignty over the Aozou strip, possibly in the hope of securing Qaddafi's support as ruler of Chad or perhaps, more simply, in exchange for payment. The move became public when Libya proceeded to occupy Aozou and other administrative outposts. Tombalbaye then undertook a complete turnabout in foreign policy as well and, with the assistance of a pretorian guard supplied by Haiti's "Papa Doc" Duvalier, launched a brutal "cultural revolution" directed against the educated strata from his own ethnic group. Among other things, these individuals were forced to give up their Europeanized names as well as to undergo Sara initiation rituals, and the capital was renamed Ndjamena.

Around this time the French decided to abandon the ineffective tyrant to his own fate and began searching for a substitute. Persuaded that Chad could be held together only by a coalition of regional strongmen, in the north the French supported Habré, who had broken with Goukouni over the Libyan annexation and enhanced both his visibility and his bargaining power by capturing some West German and French hostages.[86] On the southern side, perceiving a tacit green light from France, a group of Sara officers led by Colonel Kamougué, head of the gendarmerie, staged a coup in April 1975. Tombalbaye was killed, and General Malloum installed in his stead, but little else changed. France displayed its contempt by dealing directly with Habré, to whom they delivered a ransom in cash and nonmilitary supplies. Under his leadership the Second Army moved steadily southward and by early 1978 came within reach of the capital. Over the next few months the French provided two thousand men to defend Ndjamena but also helped Habré form his own Forces Armées du Nord (FAN). Malloum then agreed to share power with Habré as prime minister.[87] Bringing his men with him to the capital, Malloum formed a mostly Muslim government, retaining only three southerners from among the incumbents.

This French-imposed duumvirate had the catastrophic effect of propelling the regional conflict into Ndjamena itself. After months of rising communal tensions, in February 1979 there was a violent confrontation between Malloum's and Habré's forces, which rapidly engulfed the Sara and Muslim civilian populations as well.[88] Kamougué withdrew to the south, where he established an autonomous state of his own with help from Libya via Brazzaville. Deprived of protection against the rampaging Toubou guerrillas, thousands of southerners fled the capital, to their home villages or across the Chari River to Nigeria and Cameroun. The exodus swept up nearly all civil servants, hastening the collapse of the administration. Hundreds of Muslim residents were in turn massacred throughout the south.

Nigeria, which had entered the fray as well by providing aid to a "Third Army" that sprang up in the east-central districts, imposed itself as a mediator. In November 1979 the Chadians agreed to form a "Transitional Government of National Union" (GUNT), a loose confederation of eleven political-military factions spanning both the governmental side and the insurgents, with Goukouni as president, Kamougué as vice-president, and Habré as minister of defense. But the conflict soon resumed, and Goukouni turned to Qaddafi for assistance against Habré. Libyan armored troops rolled down the length of Chad and at the end of 1980 helped defeat Habré in a renewed battle for Ndjamena that again sent thousands into flight. The following January, Goukouni and Qaddafi proclaimed the "fusion" of their two countries. France did not interfere, merely issuing a stern warning to Libya. Kamougué holed up once again in the south, while Habré withdrew near the Sudanese border, where he began rebuilding his forces with aid from the incoming Reagan administration and its anti-Libyan allies, Egypt and Sudan.

After a decade and a half of conflict, most of Chad was in the hands of local bands of "Suwaar"—revolutionaries—whose major concern was to survive from day to day and to defend themselves against the revolutionaries next door. Competing for support from a shrinking population with diminishing resources, they raised their demands to unprecedented levels and stopped at nothing to achieve compliance. Under the circumstances, a career as a Suwari was the most rational choice, and the number of fighters steadily increased. But this increase in turn reduced the profitability of the fighters' activities, thus beginning an escalating spiral of violence.[89] Those who could, fled. With 396,000 refugees in early 1981 Chad became the second largest source of refugees in Africa, after Ethiopia, but in proportion to population it probably ranked first. About half originated in Ndjamena, reduced to a pile of rubble and without public utilities or services. An estimated 266,000 landed in northern Cameroon, and another 110,000 moved a little farther into Nigeria. About 5,000 southerners fled to the Central African Republic, and thousands more from the east-central districts joined the established expatriate communities in Sudan.[90] Many of the refugees, particularly from Ndjamena, returned home after the fighting stopped, between July 1981 and March 1982, but many of the returnees as well as others were uprooted again when the conflict resumed.

After his victory, Goukouni attempted to consolidate his power and lessen his dependency on Libya, which accordingly sought to replace him with the GUNT foreign minister, who was an Arab rather than a Toubou.[91] There was also pressure from the OAU, the United States, and the new French Socialist government to end the Libyan occupation, with the promise of substitute assistance.[92] At Goukouni's request in November 1981, the Libyans did withdraw to the far north; the OAU provided a peacekeeping force with soldiers from Nigeria, Zaire, and Senegal; and the French delivered logistical aid for use against Habré. But Habré steadily expanded the area under his control and, with the OAU forces standing on the sidelines, retook Ndjamena in June 1982. Tens of thousands again fled to Cameroun.[93] Exiled in Algiers, Goukouni was taken back into the Libyan fold and in mid-1983 returned to the offensive with the assistance of Libyan regulars and Qaddafi's "Islamic Legion," a largely mercenary or impressed force made up of Africans from a variety of countries.[94] In July the legion took Faya-Largeau, Habré's hometown and the gateway to central Chad, two hundred miles south of the Aozou strip. Libya subsequently undertook a de facto annexation of the entire region, issuing its own identity cards and eliminating all traces of Franco-Chadian administrative and cultural institutions.

This prompted an escalation of the American and French commitments. In August 1983 the United States began air surveillance with AWAC operating from Sudan; the Mitterand administration had given the cold shoulder to Habré because of his Gaullist connections but reluctantly joined in to stem U.S. influence. Eventually the French dispatched a three-thousand-man force to establish a "red line" along the fifteenth parallel, approximately the northern limit of the Sahel. In January 1984, after a French plane was shot by a ground-to-air missile, the line was moved one hundred miles northward to the sixteenth parallel. Although taking a firm stand, by choosing this emplacement and preventing Habré from launching any offensive across the line, Paris tacitly condoned Libya's irredentist action.[95]

The shield that France provided enabled the Ndjamena government to restore minimal state operations, establish a budget for the first time in several years, pay its civil servants, and even collect a substantial cotton crop. Accordingly, most of Chad's remaining refugees returned to their homes, spontaneously or with some assistance from UNHCR, which in May 1983 closed its liaison office in Darfur. In early 1984 the count of recognized refugees stood at a low of 16,000.[96] This included about 4,000 in a transit camp established in Benin after Chadians were expelled from Nigeria along with other foreign Africans. The camp reportedly fell under the control of a pro-Libyan faction that used it as a recruiting base for anti-Habré forces.[97]

Even as repatriation got under way, international relief officials estimated that thirty thousand to fifty thousand people left the Libyan-occupied sector for the south because of food shortages and exactions.[98] Moreover, conflict within Habré's domain soon stimulated a new exodus. Although Habré appointed a number of southerners to his government, he did little to allay fears of "Gorane" rule in the southern districts, where Kamogué's forces, left to fend for themselves, were disaggregating into local bands of "Codos" (commandos). Sweeping through the region in the fall of 1984, Habré's men summarily executed hundreds of civilians suspected of sympathy with the rebels, triggering massive flight into the adjoining Central African Republic.[99] At this time the south also was decimated by an unprecedented famine occasioned by drought, insecurity, and the renewed enthusiasm for cotton, which prompted a reduction in the area devoted to food crops.[100]

By the end of 1985 the number of refugees abroad had climbed back to 176,300. The exodus to the Central African Republic reached approximately 50,000; initially piled up along the border, the refugees were later moved farther inland to avoid attacks by Habré's men.[101] Also subject to harassment were about 8,000 to 9,000 fled who joined the residue of earlier waves in Cameroun. About 121,000 new arrivals were enumerated in Sudan's Darfur Province, itself devastated by drought and almost beyond the reach of relief organizations. Reports from the reopened UNHCR camp indicated an unusually large proportion of women and children.[102]

Quite unexpectedly, in the fall of 1984 it looked as if Chad might be peacefully reunited. On September 17, following a year of secret diplomacy, France and Libya announced that they had agreed to a "total and simultaneous" withdrawal, scheduled to begin a week later; but although the French pulled out as agreed, the Libyans did not. Despite a further flurry of diplomatic activity, France again appeared to accept the Libyan *fait accompli*.[103] Chad remained on the shelf throughout the following year, but as the Socialists approached the difficult parliamentary elections scheduled for March 1986, the de facto partition emerged as a serious political liability.

The occupation generated tensions between the Libyans and their clients, and in September 1985 some elements of GUNT clashed with Libyan forces in Faya-Largeau and Fada. The Mitterand administration tried a new diplomatic initiative, but in February 1986—a month before the French parliamentary elections—Goukouni attacked several Chadian outposts south of the red line.[104] French forces based in a neighboring country immediately retaliated by destroying a Libyan airstrip north of the sixteenth parallel, used to supply the aggressors. Libya then bombed Ndjamena, and a few days later France returned once more to Chad, with a fighter-bomber squadron accompanied by a protective ground force ("Operation Hawk"). Concurrently, Ndjamena secured a commitment of increased military aid from the United States.

These developments dramatically enhanced Habré's bargaining power at home and abroad. Famine relief became better organized, and Ndjamena restored its authority over parts of the south, where several of the insurgent factions had coalesced under Colonel Kotigua, who in February 1986 struck a power-sharing agreement with Habré, reportedly as a result of French intermediation. Meanwhile the GUNT continued to fall apart, and toward the end of the year Libya launched an offensive against the ever-troublesome Goukouni, holed up in the Tibesti. Habré saw this as an opportunity to push back the Libyans to the Aozou strip. As a result of the Gaullists' return to power in Paris, he was given a green light, initially to attack on his own but subsequently with increased French operational participation, as well as substantial logistical support from the United States.[105] Beginning with the capture of Fada on January 2, 1987, Habré's forces swept northward with astonishing tactical skill until eight months later, notwithstanding French disapproval, they crossed into the strip and seized Aozou itself. Although the future of the strip was hardly settled, it seemed clear that Chad would not be partitioned along the sixteenth parallel.[106]

Within the reunited country, Habré further broadened his coalition to include Kamougué and other GUNT leaders. With relative stability prevailing for the time being, and a waning of the famine, the refugees once again began returning to their homes. By the end of 1986 the total abroad was down to 122,600. The bulk of them were still in Sudan's inaccessible Darfur Province; but further spontaneous repatriation was reported in the early months of 1987, leaving only about 45,000 under UNHCR jurisdiction, one-third of the original mass.[107]

Tyrannical Rule and Its Legacy in Uganda[108]

Uganda began its descent into hell in 1971, when the authoritarian regime headed by Milton Obote was overthrown by the armed forces under the leadership of Idi Amin. Although this sequence of events was not unusual, in this instance the army leader emerged as a murderous tyrant whose depredations were so destructive of social organization that after his overthrow the country was torn asunder. Uganda's tragedy is even sadder because around the time of independence, it was viewed as one of the more promising African countries, with an adequate administrative apparatus, thanks to relatively progressive British colonialism, competitive party politics, and reasonable economic prospects. Yet in retrospect it is evident that it shared the generic structural conditions delineated earlier. Within this general framework, the onset of severe conflict can be attributed specifically to the incongruous power that one of the ethnic groups achieved, largely as the result of British policies and the institutionalization during the colonial period of a racially segmented economic division of labor, involving the insertion of Asians between the white rulers and the black ruled.

Within the framework of African historical development, Uganda straddles the meeting ground between the Nilotic herdsmen to the north and the Bantu cultivators to the south. As in neighboring Rwanda and Burundi, the region spawned a number of centralized kingdoms, among which by the nineteenth century Buganda had become the dominant force. Although Islam was already well established as the result of penetration from Sudan and the Kenyan coast, Buganda welcomed British Protestant and French Catholic missionaries as diplomatic allies. In the 1890s, Christian chiefs staged an oligarchic revolution against the Kabaka (king). The alliance between the Protestant faction and the British East Africa Company led to the establishment of a British protectorate, which in turn provided a base for British expansion over the rest of what became modern Uganda. The protectorate agreement also enhanced the privileged position of the chiefs and notables, by granting them about half of the land in private holding.

In the initial phase of colonial rule, local administration throughout all but the remote northernmost regions was organized on the Buganda model and staffed by Protestant Ganda chiefs. The Ganda also provided religious personnel to staff the Christian missions. Within the developing colonial state, not only did Buganda enjoy an extraordinarily autonomous status, but also the Ganda "built up an enormous lead in entry into privileged social strata, through education and economic change."[109] A telling indicator is that around the time of independence, with 16 percent of the population, the Ganda held about 40 percent of the higher civil service positions.[110] Accordingly, Uganda's recent history "has been dominated by the twin desire of its peripheral kingdoms and districts both to emulate Buganda and to set a limit to that kingdom's pretensions."[111]

The postwar political awakening initially took the unusual form of a popular monarchical movement, as Ganda peasants looked to the Kabaka for relief from exploitation by their chiefs. At the same time, the Kabaka emerged as the champion of Uganda-wide resistance to Britain's plan for an East African federation that would have placed both

Uganda and Tanzania under the thumb of Kenya's white settlers. After a brief clash, in the mid-1950s the British committed themselves to Uganda's future as an African-ruled country with democratic institutions but within which Buganda would lose its privileged status.

In response, the Buganda political establishment launched its own political party, the Kabaka Yekka (KY), and ordered a boycott of the first nationwide elections, scheduled for March 1961. The other contenders were the Democratic party (DP), with support from Roman Catholics mainly in Buganda but also other districts, and the Uganda People's Congress (UPC), a coalition of Protestant district notables outside Buganda led by Milton Obote, an educated Langi from the less developed north. Although the UPC ran slightly ahead of the DP outside Buganda, all of the Buganda seats went by default to the DP, which thereby gained control of the Legislative Council. Although the DP leader became prime minister, it was evident that the transplanted "Westminster system" could not produce a representative government founded on a substantial majority.

To resolve the impasse, a British commission recommended hybrid constitutional arrangements whereby Buganda would enjoy maximum autonomy. The other three major southern kingdoms would have quasi-federal status, and the remainder of the country would be governed within a unitary framework. The Buganda establishment then agreed to new elections, as the result of which Milton Obote led Uganda to independence in October 1962 at the head of a transethnic but "Protestant" UPC–KY coalition, leaving the DP Catholics in opposition.[112] As part of the deal, a year later Uganda was proclaimed a republic and the Kabaka elected as president.

Despite the constitutional arrangements, the arithmetic of universal suffrage undermined Buganda's position. The partners fell out as Obote exploited Catholic and Muslim dissatisfaction in Buganda to weaken the KY, and the Kabaka conspired to unseat Obote. Obote consolidated his support in the army, whose rank and file were largely recruited from the Nilotic north, among what the British considered "martial races." In April 1966 Obote successfully deployed this force in a violent showdown with the Buganda authorities and rewarded the leader of the operation, Chief of Staff Idi Amin, with promotion to the top post in the army.[113] Amin's ethnic identity remains somewhat mysterious. A Muslim from the north, he labels himself Kakwa, a small group in West Nile Province. However, a more relevant identity is his membership in a group known as "Nubi" or "Nubian," a sort of military caste formed by the descendants of soldiers recruited in the Anglo-Egyptian Sudan by Emin Pasha in the late nineteenth century and later brought south by the British to form the nucleus of a Ugandan army.[114] Recruited into the army as an adolescent, Amin had little formal education. Beginning as a cook, he also became an accomplished boxer and rose quickly through the ranks, becoming one of the first Africans commissioned by the British to officer rank.

Obote proceeded to transform Uganda into a unitary one-party state committed to a socialist approach to development and neutralism in foreign affairs. He concentrated power into his own hands. Paralleling developments elsewhere, Obote's increasing reliance on coercion had the consequence of stimulating the ambitions of the military and enhancing their power.[115] From 1967 on, Obote and Amin each attempted to pack the army with fellow ethnics and to preempt the other's moves. Then Amin seized power on January 25, 1971, and proclaimed himself head of state shortly afterward. In the light of later developments, it is noteworthy that the removal of the socialist Obote was generally welcomed by the West. His successor "was widely judged . . . to be a conservative soldier who counted for his main support on Britain and Israel," which trained the airborne battalion that constituted his praetorian guard.[116] Obote and a few thousand supporters, including elements of the army, fled to fellow-socialist Tanzania.

At first received enthusiastically as a liberator from oppression, especially by the oppressed Roman Catholic supporters of the DP as well as the hitherto largely excluded Muslims, Amin cultivated popular support in the country at large as a representative of the "common man," by lashing out against educated elites. His credit was bolstered further when he defeated Obote's attempt to invade from Tanzania in September 1972. However, the new ruler rapidly went on to establish what amounts to a classic tyranny founded on raw force: "Where Obote had imprisoned opponents, Amin had them physically eliminated; instead of harassing ethnic groups he distrusted, Amin simply massacred them."[117] He secured his base by reducing the power of the civilian police while ruthlessly purging the armed forces of Obote's Langi and neighboring Acholi for the benefit of various groups from his own West Nile district, as well as Nubians and Anya Nya refugee-warriors from southern Sudan.[118] The armed forces became a law unto themselves: "Unless Amin felt that he was personally threatened, he gave his army and police immunity and the most barbaric acts went unpunished."[119]

THE ASIAN EXODUS   Uganda's first refugee flow was triggered on August 4, 1972, when Amin ordered all Asians, regardless of citizenship status, to leave the country within ninety days. The target group numbered about 71,000, of whom approximately 26,000 were Ugandan citizens and another 12,000 had applied for citizenship.[120] Albeit unusually brutal, Amin's enactment was in keeping with developments in the other countries of former British East Africa and with policies initiated by his predecessor.

The Asians settled throughout East Africa as economic intermediaries between the British rulers and their African subjects also functioned as a political buffer, facilitating the maintenance of imperial hegemony by absorbing much of the resentment generated in the course of peripheralization. Severe anti-Asian riots erupted in Kampala in 1958, and incidents recurred afterwards.[121]

At the time of Uganda's independence, at the urging of Britain, Asians were given a choice between retaining their status as British subjects (or "protected persons") or becoming citizens of their African country of residence. Well over half chose to remain British. This stance was understandable, given the Ugandans' long-standing resentment of Asians and the commitment of the new government to the africanization of the public and private sectors, but it was viewed as evidence of the Asians' contemptuous isolation from African life. African governments showed little enthusiasm for granting citizenship to those who did apply.[122] By the late 1960s, Asians had become aware that their days in East Africa as a whole were numbered. But the bulk of them had no place to go, as most of them had never lived in South Asia, where opportunities were in any case very limited, and Britain imposed increasingly severe barriers to their entry, including even holders of British passports.[123] Underscoring the undesirability of Asians, British immigration policy legitimized African hostility toward them and had the effect of provocation.

In 1969, Kenya announced that the eighty thousand noncitizen Asians must leave; however, the government avoided a direct confrontation with Britain by agreeing to spread their departure over a number of years.[124] The Obote government had contemplated a similar action but had been persuaded by Britain to postpone it until those who had neglected to apply for citizenship within the allotted period, or who had been turned down on technicalities, had had a second chance. The government insisted, however, "that Uganda could not envisage a long phasing out of their departure."[125] Negotiations with Britain were still under way when Obote was overthrown. Although the Asian community initially welcomed the coup, the new government stepped up the pressure, and by January 1972 many carriers of British passports had begun to leave.[126]

Amin's brutal order later that year can thus be understood as an especially wanton betrayal of Asians who had made a commitment to Uganda. But from the perspective of the man in the street, it was a "macho" enactment that confirmed Amin's stature as a leader who deserved obeisance. Although Amin at first indicated that he might relent with respect to Ugandan citizens, in the end he did not. Moreover, 12,000 to 16,000 had their citizenship papers confiscated and were thereby rendered stateless. Three weeks before the deadline, the expulsion order was extended to Asians from other African countries as well. The exodus began in mid-September in an atmosphere of terror: 41,840 persons were airlifted out over the next six weeks, with assistance from a variety of countries and the UNHCR. Britain suspended its restrictive policy and admitted 23,840; its total intake of British passport holders from East Africa was 39,371 for 1972 as a whole. India admitted its own passport holders plus 6,000 British; its overall intake reached the British level. Canada accepted 6,000 refugees; Pakistan and the United States 1,000 each; and about 4,000 were sent by the UNHCR to refugee centers.[127] Over the next several years, many Asians from Uganda and other East African countries relocated to the United States as ordinary immigrants. When the exodus was over, only about 1,000 Asians remained in Uganda.

The expulsion of the Asians provided a huge booty for distribution to Amin's loyal followers, particularly in the army, but it also contributed to a further deterioration of the already battered economy. As shortages grew, the character of Amin's rule emerged in sharper relief: "the conduct of regime agents was scarcely distinguishable from that of ordinary criminals, revealing the essential banditry of tyranny."[128] Property was reduced to power, and power came from the barrel of a gun. Army commanders in the major regions set themselves up as "local warlords, combining military, political, administrative, commercial, and agricultural operations into composite *fiefs*."[129] The advent of an unusually high world price for coffee in 1976–78 provided another source of loot for Amin's men, who controlled most of available transport, but the boom soon collapsed, owing in part to a U.S. embargo. With the weakening of the institutions required for operating a modern economy, Uganda's agricultural and industrial production declined drastically while black marketing and smuggling became the rule, giving the edge once again to those with guns. Other Ugandans survived by withdrawing into subsistence production.[130]

Government in the ordinary sense disappeared in Uganda. Amin's whims were enforced by a variety of killer squads, among which the most notorious was the Public Safety Unit, operating with technical assistance from the Soviet Union. The scale of violence escalated as successive attempts to kill Amin were met with more massive retribution, directed in particular against Acholi and Langi northerners. By 1977, estimates of the death count ranged from 50,000 to 300,000. Uganda also began generating a growing stream of refugees, as both surviving members of the targeted ethnic groups and individuals singled out for arrest and murder fled to adjacent countries, Sudan, Zaire, and especially Tanzania, where Obote was allowed to recruit his Uganda National Liberation Army.

Faced with growing dissension in the army itself, in September 1978 Amin recruited another ten thousand Nubi and invaded Tanzania's Kagera salient, on the western shores of Lake Victoria. The invasion was a failure, and in November Amin pulled back. But in early 1979, the Tanzanian army counterattacked with the help of Ugandan exiles. Despite last-minute assistance from about fifteen hundred airlifted troops from Libya, Amin's armed rabble offered little resistance, and after plundering or destroying everything they could, they fled to Zaire and Sudan. Fearful of retribution, much of the population of West Nile followed in their wake.

In April the Tanzanians entered Kampala. This was the first time since the emergence of an independent Africa that one state had used its armed forces to depose the ruler of another. Under a plan agreed upon before the liberation, there was to be a two-year transitional period of rule by a comprehensive coalition, with nonparty elections to be held in 1981 before the withdrawal of the Tanzanian umbrella. But once force has replaced political authority and economic exchange, it is extremely difficult to reverse the process.[131] As the contest for power got under way, the old parties reappeared but now sprouted military wings as well, and the new political formations acquired them also. Despite attempts to limit the size of military forces and to allot each region a quota proportional to its population, the various commanders worked furiously to enlarge their organizations. The one thousand or so soldiers who had been fighting in the spring of 1979 grew to over thirty thousand by fall. Obote controlled about three-fourths of the Uganda National Liberation Army (UNLA); the remainder were mostly members of FRONASA, which began as a splinter of the UPC based mostly in the kingdoms of southwestern Uganda but with some support in Buganda as well. Trained in liberated Mozambique, its cadre espoused FRELIMO's revolutionary program and achieved an unusual level of organizational cohesion under the leadership of Yoweri Museveni, who emerged as the most important new actor in Uganda.

Benefiting from the backing of Tanzania's President Julius Nyerere and hence assured of the benevolent neutrality of Tanzania's occupation troops, Obote quickly gained the upper hand and set out once again to establish a one-party system by coopting and intimidating opposition politicians.[132] However, conditions differed fundamentally from those in the postindependence years, in that the government no longer had a monopoly of force. Several bands of armed resistance arose, among which Museveni's National Resistance Army (NRA) emerged as dominant. Violence spread further as the ethnic groups earlier persecuted for their identification with Obote avenged themselves on those associated with Amin and as factions within the Obote camp vied for power. The country was wracked by five conflicts, of which four generated large waves of refugees and one a wholesale massacre.

THE BANYRWANDA   The designation of Banyrwanda encompasses the Tutsi and Hutu of Rwandan origin, including not only the refugees of the 1960s but also almost a million long-time settlers, mostly in Buganda, where they constituted about 40 percent of the total population.[133] Albeit strangers from the perspective of local communities, at independence time the Banyrwanda acquired Ugandan citizenship, along with all other permanent African residents. It should be noted that this was a collective naturalization under legal fiat and conditions of rudimentary civil registry. As clients of the Ganda, the Banyrwanda generally sided with Buganda, and as Roman Catholics, in the 1960s they supported the opposition DP.

As noted earlier, the presence of this established community facilitated the settlement and integration of Rwandan refugees. But from Obote's perspective, the arrival of a mass of Rwandans was a political threat. He therefore confined the refugees to camps and in 1969 attempted to exclude even the established Banyrwanda from the political process, on the grounds they were not true Ugandans. The target group therefore welcomed Idi Amin, who in turn allowed many refugees to leave their camps and settle on available land. The Banyrwanda went on to play an important role in the tyrant's secret police, and he in turn encouraged their revanchist dreams.[134] Having become identified with Amin, after Obote's return the Banyrwanda were disenfranchised and therefore began supporting their kinsman Museveni.[135]

In early 1982, the Obote government indicated that it wanted all Banyrwanda refugees returned to the camps. Although the UNHCR averted the move, further threats were issued throughout the year, and beginning on October 1, local chiefs and members of the ruling party's youth wing swept through the district, forcing Rwandans out of their homes and giving them a choice of returning to the camps or leaving the country. The vacated homesteads were then looted and burned.[136] About 25 to 30 percent of the people thus affected were refugees, the rest, older settlers. By the end of October, almost 30,000 were confined in camps in Uganda; an estimated 40,000 to 50,000 crossed into Rwanda with 25,000 head of cattle, while 4,000 waited near the border; and thousands more went into Tanzania. Expulsions and flight continued intermittently over the next three years. As of May 1985, 120,000 Banyrwanda were receiving UNHCR assistance in Uganda, including 12,000 who claimed to be Ugandan citizens but had failed to gain recognition as such. There were four camps with a total population of 69,900. The largest, designed for 17,000 people and 22,000 cattle, had swollen to 29,000 and 40,000, and in addition to overcrowding, an exceedingly limited international presence allowed UPC toughs to rule unchecked.[137] During the same period, another 35,000 Banyrwanda living in Buganda were displaced by the violence that erupted within the Luwero Triangle.

Rwanda intermittently closed its borders on the grounds that the refugees were Ugandans, but a total of about 44,000 had been admitted by 1985. At first many of them settled on land belonging to a national game park, from which other Rwandans were excluded, but this fanned local resentment, leaving their future highly uncertain. As of 1985, Rwanda had recognized more than 1,000 refugees as nationals and begun to resettle them; 14,000 had settled on their own, moved to Tanzania, or returned to Uganda; and another 30,000 had remained in camps. Many of them returned to Uganda after the July 1985 coup.[138]

WEST NILE   To avenge the massacre of Acholi and Langi, Obote's followers were determined to sack Amin's home region. Linked to the rest of Uganda by a single bridge, during the transitional period West Nile was occupied by Tanzanian troops and the UNLA was kept out. Many who had fled to Zaire or Sudan in the expectation of massacres returned. Meanwhile, some of Amin's soldiers, now refugees, regrouped in Zaire and Sudan as the Uganda National Rescue Front (UNRF). After Obote seized power again, the Tanzanians were replaced by Langi and Acholi UNLA troops. The UNRF then took the opportunity to invade and, with the aid of the local population, seized control of the district capital. In turn, the UNLA, composed largely of "volunteers," poured across the bridge, destroying the town and killing between 5,000 and 30,000 civilians. West Nile changed hands several times over the next two years, with masses of population moving to and fro with the fortunes of war, between various parts of the region and across international borders. By mid-1983, there were about 60,000 refugees from West Nile in Zaire, where they were subject to harassment by the army, and over 200,000 in Sudan— with one estimate going as high as 350,000.[139] Assistance was provided mostly by Norwegian Church Aid, which had begun working in the area during the protracted

Sudanese conflict. Settlement was facilitated by the fact that the local Sudanese of the same ethnic groups had found refuge in Uganda during their own civil war.

The Ugandan government vacillated among denying the refugees' existence, denouncing them as guerrillas, and encouraging their repatriation—at least for purposes of obtaining international aid on their behalf. A reliable observer of southern Sudan reported no evidence for charges that the guerrillas used the refugee camps as a base.[140] But to the extent that the camps provided support for dependents, leaving adult males free to fight, there is no denying that the camps facilitated the conduct of guerrilla operations.

The UNHCR initially encouraged repatriation, because its Ugandan returnee program was viewed as the key to "durable solutions" on the continent as a whole.[141] By June 1984, 12,000 refugees had returned from Zaire and 900 from Sudan under UNHCR auspices, with perhaps as many as 50,000 returning spontaneously. But at that time UNHCR officials privately admitted that the situation for returnees was still unsafe and suspended the program after a returning Muslim notable was beaten to death by UNLA soldiers. There were raids in both directions across the border and disputes over land and water. The Sudanese government therefore decided that some of the self-settled refugees were a security risk and had to be moved inland. Undertaken after the crops were planted and in the worst part of the rainy season, the move occasioned severe hardship. Repatriation resumed intermittently, with 4,574 returned by mid-1985.

KARAMOJA During the war with Tanzania, thousands of automatic weapons fell into the hands of the pastoralist population of the arid and undeveloped Karamoja region of northeastern Uganda. This precipitated a bloody struggle for power among the leaders of the cattle-raiding bands. Although Obote initially formed an alliance with the emerging strongmen, it fell apart in late 1983 when the Karamojong began directing their raids westward into his adjacent home region. The following spring, the UNLA launched a campaign against the pastoralists, causing a massive flight of people to more remote parts of the area and driving about 20,000 across the border into Sudan and Kenya.[142]

THE LUWERO TRIANGLE The largest of these conflicts took place in an area of central Uganda known as the "Luwero Triangle," formed by the principal roads stretching northward from Kampala. Containing about 750,000 people, largely Ganda, in early 1981 the region gave birth to the two major guerrilla groups that challenged Obote. Sporadic attacks on government installations started after the departure of the last Tanzanian troops in June, and in the spring of 1982, the UNLA launched operations against the growing threat. With aid from a variety of countries, by June 1983 government forces amounted to twenty-eight battalions with possibly 40,000 men. One guerrilla group was quickly eliminated; the other, Museveni's NRA, beat a strategic retreat to the north and west. Much as in West Nile, the UNLA then lashed out against the population and systematically drove civilians from their homes to create a "free-fire zone" inside which anyone could be shot as a "bandit." The army thereby also gained access to the stored coffee crop as booty. Although some retreated with the NRA, most of the inhabitants were trapped. Young men were killed as suspected guerrillas; women, children, and the elderly were rounded up and transferred to detention camps. As of mid-1983, there were thirty-six known camps with between 100,000 and 140,000 inmates; food shortages were widespread; and a number of massacres took place.

At first reluctant to authorize access by international agencies, the Ugandan authorities later appealed for massive assistance. In the face of international criticism, the camps were disbanded, but this move left their former inmates exposed to even worse brutality outside, particularly after new offensives were launched in 1984. By the end of that year, the death toll mounted to perhaps as much as one-fourth of the total population, with a much higher incidence among males in the sixteen-to-forty age group. The conflict produced no international refugees because, as in Biafra, the target population was surrounded by territory loyal to the government.

ACHOLI VERSUS LANGI, AND THE FALL OF OBOTE   From early 1984 onward, the Obote regime began to fall apart. Brutality increased throughout the country as unpaid soldiers robbed to live, and production ground to a standstill, with the estimated per-capita income sinking to about one-third of its 1970 level. Having seized a major UNLA weapons depot, Museveni opened up a second front in his home region. Within the UNLA itself, Acholi and Langi commanders vied for power. The accidental death of the army chief of staff in December 1983 brought these tensions to a head. Obote tried to resolve the conflict by sending the army on campaigns that provided opportunities for looting; he also appointed a fellow Langi as chief of staff and stepped up recruitment from this group. Nonetheless, following a mutiny of Acholi soldiers in the northern region, in July 1985, the army's second in command took power in Kampala. The commanders then formed a Council chaired by yet another Acholi, seventy-one-year-old Lieutenant General Tito Okello, and appointed a government of national reconciliation that was headed by Paulo Muwanga, a Ganda UPC stalwart long associated with Obote but that included as minister of internal affairs Paul Ssemogerere, leader of the Democratic party and a major critic of Obote's human rights abuses. But the Council rapidly degenerated into an unruly assembly of warlords while Museveni advanced toward Kampala, picking up support as the disaffected governmental army dissolved.

Assessing the situation in August 1985, *The Economist* wondered, "Is Uganda Still Worth Calling a Country?" and *Le Monde* spoke of "an East African Chad."[143] Under pressure from Kenya and Tanzania, the Council began negotiations with Museveni. These dragged on through the fall while the NRA secured control of the entire southwestern coffee-producing region, where it established a provisional civilian administration. The rest of Uganda remained in the grip of violence. To bolster its position, the Council struck a deal with the Amin camp, leading to the airlift of 7,000 men from West Nile to reinforce the government forces. The "Former Uganda National Army" ravaged Obote's home district, clashing with Acholi forces throughout the region. Finally, at the end of February 1986, the NRA entered Kampala. The rampaging UNLA fled northward to the Acholi districts, which the NRA occupied in March, starting a fresh outflow of perhaps 25,000 refugees into Sudan's Equatoria Province, mostly the remnants of Tito Okello's Acholi army and their kin.

By mid-1986, peace had been restored to much of Uganda, an achievement that most observers attributed to Museveni's leadership. As one editor put it, "When Museveni and his men came, there was no looting. That was one of the earliest signs that Museveni was different from those who came before him."[144] But despite these hopeful signs, the reconstruction of political and economic institutions was hampered by the memory of murder, catastrophic material conditions, perennial intrusions by Nubi guerrilla bands operating from Sudan, and later a violent millenarian movement arising among the Acholi.[145] Moreover, the NRA soon proved as difficult to restrain as its predecessors had been.

Despite the precarious peace, after Museveni was installed in Kampala, the refugees returned at an increasing pace, particularly from Sudan. This was attributable as much to "push" factors in Sudan as to a "pull" by Uganda. In addition to the usual problems, the resurgence of secessionist activity near the refugee settlements on the East Bank of the White Nile jeopardized the continued supply of the settlements by Norwegian Church Aid and the UNHCR and threatened the security of the camps. In addition, the Ugandan civil war spilled over into Sudan, where the latest arrivals attacked established refugee camps, precipitating flight of the inmates back into Uganda. Overall, by mid-1987, about 160,000 refugees had returned from Sudan, Zaire, and Kenya.[146]

Chapter 3

In the Long Shadow
of South Africa

Southern Africa as a Regional Complex

As noted in the overview of the African crisis, southern Africa started producing major refugee flows in the mid-1960s and has been a leading source ever since. Initially they were occasioned by struggles for national liberation, starting with Angola and Mozambique, then extending to Rhodesia/Zimbabwe, and finally encompassing South-West Africa/Namibia. At the root of the violence was the political economy of settler rule, which prevented negotiated decolonization such as that in other parts of the continent. Another distinctive feature was that all the countries in question were part of an emerging regional system, dominated by South Africa. As a result, violent decolonization became a serially interactive process, in which each outcome altered the configuration of the remaining cases.

Although the refugee populations propelled by the struggles in Mozambique and Zimbabwe quickly returned to their respective homelands after independence, most of the Angolans did not. Moreover, later both Angola and Mozambique generated new waves, even larger than the first. Hence these two countries will be considered anew in the latter part of the chapter, with an analysis of decolonization serving as the background for this second round.

These postindependence flows arose from a distinctive set of circumstances. Because the peoples of the region share many elements of culture with others on the continent, some of the observations concerning state-formation set forth in the preceding chapter are applicable here as well, particularly the prominent role of ethnicity. However, it has been suggested that because it entailed a more extensive mobilization of rural populations, the experience of armed struggle would result in stronger states than elsewhere in Africa.[1] If so, the "weak state" syndrome that is at the root of many of the refugee flows considered so far would lose its explanatory power. But because mobilization tends to occur along lines of ethnic distinctiveness, more extensive mobilization might be expected to result in even sharper cleavages, leaving the new states with a potentially explosive legacy. In addition, liberation movements shaped by the inequities of settler colonialism and forged in battle tend to develop a strong commitment to structural transformation, but developments noted elsewhere suggest that under African circumstances, efforts to carry this out are likely to produce widespread "exit" responses.

These theoretically interesting questions remain largely moot because the development of postsettler African states has been overwhelmingly determined by South Africa's aggressive response to mounting challenges and by the consequent involvement of the superpowers and their allies in the regional conflict. Consequently, in addition to political economy, the analysis in this chapter will also consider international events.

The principal feature of settler colonies was a massive appropriation of land and its subsequent transformation into private property owned exclusively by whites.[2] Mines and large commercial farms or ranches relied on minimal capitalization; their profitability was founded on labor-intensive methods, which required an abundant supply of manpower. This was obtained by denying to Africans the possibility of autonomous subsistence and preventing them from engaging in commercial agriculture.[3] At first, the colonial authorities also imposed some form of labor obligation, and when this became no longer practicable, it was replaced by a money tax that could be paid only by securing wages. The mechanics of procurement led to the characteristic formation of a network of labor migration linking a center with a periphery, that is, a settler-dominated locality with populous regions within the same country or even abroad. The workers' families stayed behind, engaging in subsistence production under deliberately maintained backward conditions. After World War II, the several countries in the region evolved into a more integrated economic system. The Republic of South Africa functioned as a capitalist center, with an increasing share of its gross national product (GNP) stemming from industrial production and returns on capital investments among its neighbors. At the same time, labor recruitment was expanded and integrated.[4]

This distinctive mode of production shaped political developments in the region throughout the twentieth century. The system fostered the institutionalization of extreme status differences between whites and blacks, rationalized by an ideology of racial superiority and backed by an apparatus of state coercion more brutal than that in the "black" colonies considered earlier.[5] Consequently, the processes of social transformation leading to the emergence of Africa's middle strata, operating simultaneously as auxiliaries of the colonial state and its critics, were much weaker. In the absence of white settlers, the metropolitan powers adapted to postwar circumstances by negotiating the transfer of governmental authority into the hands of African nationalists. The white settlers, however, were much more dependent on continued local control and hence resisted any challenge to their privileged status. Initially they uniformly secured the backing of their respective metropolitan governments.

Under these extreme conditions, African protest was expressed mainly through "weapons of the weak," that is, nonconfrontational forms such as withdrawal into subsistence production or emigration, interspersed with rare peasant insurrections, strikes, or boycotts, which were ruthlessly repressed.[6] Because of their greater coercive capacity, settler governments were able to deter organized political protest until well after extensive nationalist movements emerged in the rest of the continent. However, as the pace of decolonization quickened, the balance of organizational costs and benefits shifted toward the African side. The region's earliest political stirrings produced a few of activist exiles, but as the struggles got under way, nearly all the refugees remained in the region, in liberated zones inside their own country or across the border of some newly independent neighbor. The growing availability of havens helped turn the trickle into a flood, and the formation of large refugee pools further facilitated the recruitment of liberation fighters.

The course of the struggles was determined in large part by the degree of external support available, respectively, to the settler minorities and the black liberation movements. In 1967, for the first time, South Africa sent troops to fight on foreign soil against black guerrillas.

Although South Africa has been generating a refugee exodus of its own, discussed briefly in the concluding section of Chapter 4, it will be considered here mostly in its role as the dominant actor in the regional international system.[7] Contrary to what is widely believed, the structural nexus of the apartheid regime was formed over a century ago with the discovery of diamonds and gold in the interior, at the height of British imperialism, when the Afrikaners themselves were as much victims as oppressors and long before they rose to power in 1948.[8] The nature of South Africa's wealth, which was found to include a variety of essential minerals, enhanced the strategic significance of the region as a whole. South Africa's importance was further increased after World War II because of the centrality of its gold to the Bretton Woods structure. Hence the superpowers were drawn to the area as early as 1960, when the colonial status quo in the mineral-rich part of the continent began to crumble with the independence of Zaire and the onset of insurgency in Angola.

As Zaki Laïdi has observed, there was from the beginning a fundamental asymmetry: Whereas from the perspective of the Soviet camp, both ideological disposition and foreign policy interests dictated support of the liberation movements, the Western countries found themselves perched on the horns of a dilemma, from which they have not yet been able to climb down.[9] The evolution of their policies and the consequences of these changes will be discussed at the appropriate point. Until the mid-1960s, with the benefit of benign neglect from the West, South Africa was essentially secure, insulated from newly independent Africa by white-ruled outer bulwarks.[10] Its external activities were generally confined to the economic sphere, except for the de facto annexation of South-West Africa. But as the winds of change began to blow, Pretoria departed from its isolation to assist beleaguered white regimes countering challenges from African liberation movements as well as from the international community. Pretoria's commitment to Rhodesia in 1967 helped contain the uprising for almost another decade. During the same period, South Africa also provided economic support to the Portuguese colonies, which sought foreign investments to develop exports so as to cover the escalating costs of warfare. The major undertaking was the Cunene hydroelectric and irrigation scheme in southern Angola, which would also provide power for the soaring mineral sector of Namibia.

Though still essentially defensive, South Africa's policy was coupled with an innovative "outward strategy" designed to win friends among black-ruled states in order to secure an aura of legitimacy. This was pursued by wielding economic power and playing on the more conservative black leaders' fears of radical challenges. Within its immediate perimeter, South Africa easily asserted its hegemony over the poor, landlocked British High Commission Territories after they achieved independence—Botswana and Lesotho in 1966 and Swaziland two years later; Malawi fell in line as well, for similar reasons.[11]

In light of these experiences, as early as 1966 some informed South Africans began to question the wisdom of an all-out commitment to maintaining white rule throughout the region, but Pretoria maintained its stance until the abrupt ending of Portuguese rule following the revolutionary coup of 1974.[12] Although in the intervening period, South Africa faced the onset of insurgency in Namibia as well as mounting pressures from the international community to relinquish its control over the territory, these challenges remained very limited.

The advent of black rule in Angola and Mozambique forced South Africa to recast its external strategy because Angola is adjacent to Ovamboland—the focus of insurgency in Namibia—and Mozambique shares a short border with South Africa itself and a very long one with Rhodesia (Zimbabwe). At the time, Rhodesia was the most important consideration, because it had the effect of turning white Rhodesia from an asset into a major liability. Quickly adapting to the new circumstances, the South Africans devised a "total strategy" that pursued apparently contradictory objectives: putting pressure on the Rhodesians to come to terms with black majority rule but concurrently intervening to destabilize the new regimes in Angola and Mozambique. These actions and the counter-moves they elicited from other international actors opened a new chapter in the regional system's history and also fundamentally altered the internal situation of each of the countries concerned.

The Struggle Against Settler Regimes

Angola

Although Angola was among the very first African regions to be incorporated into the expanding European imperium as a major source of slaves, it took on the character of a white settler colony only after World War II.[13] After the slave trade was abolished in the middle third of the nineteenth century, Portugal encouraged white settlement and imposed coercive devices to secure an adequate supply of labor. But because of the peripheral character of its own economy, Portuguese capital was not forthcoming and so development of the export sector remained very limited.[14] The corporatist "New State" constituted by Antonio Salazar after 1926 took a mercantilist interest in the colonies. The Portuguese expanded their forced labor drafts and made cotton cultivation mandatory, and they also formed a small stratum of educated African auxiliaries drawn mostly from the *mestiço* (mixed-descent) population and the Mbundu ethnic group living around Luanda. These *assimilados* were granted a relatively privileged status, but as late as 1950 they constituted less than 1 percent of the indigenous population, and only about one-half of 1 percent of African children were enrolled in primary schools.

In the face of continued economic stagnation in Portugal itself after World War II, the state encouraged the immigration of white settlers and provided attractive conditions for them. Angola's white population grew apace, reaching over 300,000 on the eve of independence.[15] International conditions in the early postwar years provided a window of opportunity for expanding coffee production. Some *mestiços* and blacks engaged in coffee farming, but the bulk of it was produced on large Portuguese-owned plantations, for which vast amounts of land were appropriated from African peasants, who were in effect forced to work for the whites who occupied their land. In addition to some established diamond deposits, petroleum was discovered in 1955 and quickly became the country's second largest export.

Additional education was provided to form African auxiliaries, but very few were able to continue beyond the primary level. By the end of the colonial period, the *assimilados* had grown to constitute about 3 percent of the population. About one-third of the appropriate age cohort was enrolled in primary schools, and overall literacy was estimated at 15 percent. Determined to stem the tide of liberalization that was sweeping colonial Africa, the Portuguese provided no opportunity for educated Africans to participate in decision making. Even the ranks of the expanding bureaucracy were staffed mostly by white immigrants. The slowness of colonial development and the persistence of authoritarian rule made for a belated political awakening, but its timing in relation to developments elsewhere made for a rapid transition from limited protest to armed struggle.

The building blocks of Angolan political movements reflected differences arising from diverse positions in the colonial political economy, geopolitical location, ethnic identity, and religious denomination. As of 1960, the African population numbered about five million. Because of uneven ecological conditions, approximately 60 percent were concentrated in two regions, forming a mere 12 percent of territory. The first, in the north, contained the Mbundu and the Kongo. The Mbundu, located east of Luanda, constituted about one-fourth of the total population, but because of their proximity to the colonial center and length of contact with the Portuguese, they were significantly overrepresented among the educated strata and the population of the capital city. The Kongo (about 14 percent) inhabited the provinces adjoining Zaire and the "Cabinda enclave" across the Congo River; they retained strong links with the other remnants of the Kongo kingdom in Zaire and the Popular Republic of the Congo (ex-French). The second concentration, amounting to about two-fifths of the total population, occupied the rich west-central plateau and consisted largely of Ovimbundu, who despite their large numbers were a peripheral group because of their situation in the colonial political economy.[16]

As in Uganda, religious differences acquired political significance. In the Portuguese system, the Catholic church occupied a quasi-official position as the handmaiden of the state. Protestantism was viewed with suspicion by the Portuguese authorities not only because the missionaries were foreign but also because the denominations constituted a sphere of relative autonomy and provided Africans with organizational resources. Around the end of the colonial period, about 40 percent of the African population was nominally Roman Catholic, with heavier concentrations in the western coastal regions and especially among the Mbundu. Another 10 percent were members of various Protestant denominations. Each of these was very localized and hence came to be identified with a particular ethnic group—the Baptist with the Kongo, the Methodists with the Mbundu, and the Congregationalists with the Ovimbundu. Protestants generally played a major role in the struggle for decolonization, but denominational differences among them further reinforced ethnoregional cleavages.

The impact of the postwar economic changes also affected each group differently. By the early 1970s there were some 530,000 wage laborers out of a total population of about 6 million, of whom about half were employed on plantations. Other estimates suggest that in 1971 roughly one-third of peasant heads of families could be classified as semiproletarians.[17] The Ovimbundu were in effect transformed into a migrant agricultural proletariat, supplying most of the approximately 180,000 pickers transported annually to the coffee estates of the northwest.[18] The Kongo provided some workers as well but were more likely to engage in coffee farming of their own. Relatively better opportunities for Africans in the European-dominated towns as well as the desire to avoid forced labor fostered a rural exodus. The population of Luanda nearly doubled within a single decade, providing a critical mass available for political mobilization.

The acceleration of political change in neighboring African countries (especially Zaire) and other parts of the Portuguese colonial empire (Guinea-Bissau) stimulated simultaneously the development of nationalist organizations, as well as Portugal's determination to counteract this process. The first of the movements, which originated among the mostly Mbundu population of Luanda and its hinterland, evolved into the Popular

Movement for the Liberation of Angola (MPLA). Its leadership was drawn from the *mestiço* and *assimilado* strata of government employees, largely Methodist, frustrated by persisting racial discrimination and declining opportunities as a consequence of white recruitment in the civil service. These grievances appealed also to the urban stratum immediately below. As the most culturally Portuguese of the movements, the MPLA had contacts with the metropolitan opposition, including the tiny, clandestine Portuguese Communist party. Operating initially from exile in remote Conakry, where contacts were established with Amilcar Cabral's organization in adjacent Portuguese Guinea, the movement sought "to scare away the Portuguese in a show of urban unrest, similar to that which had brought independence to the Belgian Congo."[19] Subsequently the MPLA moved to Kinshasa and then to Brazzaville. In 1962 its presidency was assumed by Augustinho Neto, a Portuguese-educated physician. As a multiracial and outspokenly revolutionary movement, it attracted widespread political sympathy among leftist circles throughout the west as well as the east and obtained aid from a variety of sources, including Cuba from 1966 and the Soviet Union from 1968.[20] For the most part, the organization concentrated on building up support in its Luanda home base and on external relations. But it also conducted occasional guerrilla operations in the Cabinda enclave and, following Zambia's independence in 1964, opened up an eastern front among the Lunda and Chokwe as well.

The Union of the Populations of Northern Angola (UPNA, later UPA) was launched in 1957 among the Kongo in the northwestern districts adjoining Zaire under the leadership of successful Baptist traders and coffee farmers, in the course of a confrontation with the Portuguese over succession to the Kongo throne. Headed by Holden Roberto, the movement spread rapidly among a population already primed by the political ferment among their fellow-ethnics in Zaire. Anti-Portuguese feelings were exacerbated in the late 1950s by a sharp decline in the price of coffee, which reduced the income of both African workers and producers.[21] In 1961, a massive uprising erupted in the UPA-saturated region, during which hundreds of European settlers were killed. Relying heavily on air power, Portuguese forces terrorized the population into submission at an estimated cost of 40,000 African lives, triggering a massive exodus of the survivors across the border. By 1966, the refugees were estimated at 400,000, amounting to about two-thirds of the local Kongo and 8 percent of Angola's population. More fled to Luanda and other towns, which recorded considerable Kongo immigration in the 1960s.[22]

As of the mid-1960s, the struggle was stalemated. Despite the deployment of considerable manpower and sophisticated equipment contributed by fellow NATO (North Atlantic Treaty Organization) members, Portugal was unable to extinguish the rebellion, but the insurgents could neither maintain territorial control nor achieve unity. Much of the population that stayed behind was resettled in compounds under government control. In 1964, the Portuguese authorities granted asylum to a body of armed refugees from Zaire, the "Katanga gendarmerie," and enlisted them as a mercenary force against the insurgents.[23]

Over the next decade, as the domain of the struggle continued to expand, Angola became an arena for confrontation between the major world camps, whose competition by way of client movements compounded existing cleavages among them. These experiences contributed in turn to the crystallization of a postindependence configuration ripe for further violence. Recruiting from the growing refugee pool, which included many deserters from the Portuguese army, the UPA trained a guerrilla army in Morocco and Tunisia with assistance from the Algerian National Liberation Front (FLN). In 1962, the

UPA struck an alliance with smaller northern groups to form the National Front for the Liberation of Angola (FNLA) and established a government-in-exile in Zaire, whose president was also a Kongo. The FNLA has been termed a "bourgeois" movement, in that its principal objective was the redistribution of settler lands to established African farmers. Its leadership also aspired to reconstitute the Kongo state, in collusion with Kongo peoples in Zaire and the People's Republic of the Congo. In 1962, Roberto began receiving covert funding from the CIA. Three years later, as part of the same operation, Sese Seko Mobutu was installed as leader of Zaire. Afterwards the Zairean army "took on organizing, training, and equipping the FNLA armed forces. In fact Roberto and Mobutu's politics became so closely tied as to be indistinguishable."[24] The FNLA subsequently also received aid from the People's Republic of China which viewed it, as did the United States, as a counterweight to the Soviet-backed MPLA. The Roberto government was initially recognized by the OAU but in 1969 lost this recognition to the MPLA.

In organization, the FNLA was a one-man show focusing on the achievement of military might. By 1974 it emerged as the main fighting force, with about 2,000 guerrillas inside Angola and another 10,000 to 12,000 making forays from Zaire. It made little or no progress in establishing a political base, however, even among the Kongo, because the Catholics were excluded and others resisted what they suspected was an effort to reinstate the Kongo monarchy. In the early 1960s, the organization attempted to broaden its support by co-opting leaders from other ethnic groups not yet mobilized by the MPLA. Jonas Savimbi, an Ovimbundu, was appointed minister of foreign affairs of the government-in-exile but subsequently left to form the National Union for the Total Independence of Angola (UNITA).

The new movement was a loose coalition of the more peripheral ethnic groups, among whom the Ovimbundu were outstanding by virtue of sheer numbers. They resented the *mestiços* and *assimilados* associated with the MPLA, a resentment expressed in an ideology of "black power" using Maoist terms, which earned them some support from China. UNITA was at first based in Zambia but was later expelled because its attacks against the Benguela Railroad interfered with the flow of Zambian exports. It then operated from within Angola itself, with relative impunity because from the Portuguese perspective it was a thorn in the side of the MPLA. Indeed, UNITA may have collaborated with the Portugese.[25] Thus largely by default, by the time of independence UNITA had come to control much of the rich, food-producing central and southern provinces and claimed the support of about 40 percent of the population. The rise of the UNITA dramatically altered the political situation in southern Africa as a whole because it provided friendly territory from which the South-West Africa People's Organization (SWAPO) could initiate a struggle to liberate Namibia.

The situation in Angola was dramatically altered by the revolutionary coup of July 1974 in the Portuguese metropole, which originated among officers radicalized by their experience of colonial war. Despite an attempt by white settlers to take matters in their own hands, the new Portuguese government opted for rapid decolonization. In January 1975, the OAU encouraged an agreement among the contending Angolan movements to cooperate in the forthcoming negotiations. Portugal also recognized all three and agreed to independence as of November 11, 1975, with a transitional government to be established immediately. This triggered the exodus of nearly the entire European population—leaving only about 30,000 out of 350,000 a year later—as well as of many *mestiços* and *assimilados* holding Portuguese citizenship. Consequently, Angola was suddenly bereft of nearly its entire administrative apparatus and economic cadre.

The agreement notwithstanding, political tensions rapidly escalated as the three movements and their respective international sponsors jockeyed to achieve maximum power under the new conditions. Benefiting from the support of the leftist officers who seized power in Portugal, the MPLA expanded its military potential through stepped-up deliveries of arms and equipment from the Soviet Union and other Eastern European countries, operated with the help of an increasing number of Cuban advisers. The MPLA's leaders also unleashed the Katanga gendarmerie against the FNLA. The FNLA in turn sought to preempt control over the future Angolan army and attempted to move into Luanda, where it immediately clashed with the MPLA. To block the latter, the United States also provided some funds to UNITA.

Because of the size of his ethnic constituency, Savimbi saw the possibility of achieving power through national elections. He therefore proposed a government of national unity and engaged in a complex maneuver to obtain international support, distancing himself from SWAPO to conciliate South Africa, while simultaneously effecting a rapprochement with the Front Line states to court the OAU. After failing to achieve his objective, Savimbi formed an alliance with the FNLA and in August 1975 declared war on the MPLA.

On October 23, a South African force invaded Angola in support of the FNLA–UNITA camp; this in turn prompted the Soviet Union to accelerate the flow of military supplies, and Cuba to dispatch several thousand more troops.[26] Although U.S. Secretary of State Henry Kissinger advocated vigorous American intervention as well, the Ford administration's choice of action was constrained by the United States' still-recent Vietnam experience, and so the United States limited itself to covert action in support of UNITA, but even this was later prohibited under the "Clark amendment" enacted by Congress. After hopes for a government of national unity with FNLA–UNITA participation faded, and in the absence of direct U.S. intervention on behalf of its clients, South Africa began withdrawing its forces.

Even though it started out with only about one-fifth of the territory, the MPLA controlled the capital and its immediate hinterland, the oil-producing Cabinda enclave, the port of Lobito, and the eastern rail head and port at Benguela and so managed to establish itself as the dominant force. Cuban troops, reaching about 14,000 by February 1976, made a crucial contribution to the outcome by repelling the FNLA from Luanda while South African forces were approaching from the south. Thus from independence onward, Angola was in effect divided between an MPLA regime based in Luande and a UNITA one in the south. On February 10, the OAU recognized the Luanda regime as Angola's official government. By the end of 1976, the international political community had followed suit, with the exception of the United States and the People's Republic of China.

Broadly speaking, this configuration prevailed over the next decade. With the FNLA on the losing side of a civil war, the Kongo in Zaire hesitated to go home, and the organization may have deliberately obstructed the return of those who wished to do so.[27] Hence most of Angola's half-million refugees remained abroad.

Mozambique[28]

Portugal's other colony in southern Africa was assembled into a single administrative entity from outposts widely scattered along a coastal line that, if stretched out along the east coast of North America, would span the distance from the Canadian border to Florida. Its physical configuration, consisting of relatively fertile river valleys running east to west and separated by arid wastes, provides severe obstacles to any north–south movement. This was reflected in the emergence of three very different patterns of colonial exploitation. In the late nineteenth century, the south was closely linked to the South African economic system by international agreements, under which the Portuguese supplied labor to the South African mines in exchange for the diversion of a major share of the Transvaal's imports and exports to the port of Lorenço Marques (now Maputo).[29] The workers, drawn mostly from among the Tsonga (or Thonga), increased from an initial 40,000 a year to 80,000 by 1908. These numbers remained at approximately this level over the next half-century and then began increasing again, reaching about 120,000 at the time of independence. This amounted to an exodus of 25 to 30 percent of the adult male population of the area concerned. As in Angola, there was a considerable increase in white immigration after World War II, with a concomitant increase in land alienation. Most of the white immigrants settled in the south, where as of 1970 their modest farms accounted for 75 percent of marketed production.[30]

The central region was similarly linked to Southern Rhodesia, with Beira serving as its major port and Mozambique functioning as a labor pool supplying about 25,000 workers. Large European plantations were established after World War II, contributing 57 percent of the region's commercial production. The third region consists of the isolated and undeveloped northern provinces of Cabo Delgado and Niassa, adjoining Tanzania. As in Chad, the mostly Maconde population was impressed into the production of cotton, bought up by the state at a price well below the world market. By 1945 more than one million peasants were supplying enough to meet the needs of the metropole, and cotton had become the colony's major export. A similar system was developed with respect to rice. After the war, the Portuguese encouraged African smallholders, and on the eve of independence they accounted for 65 percent of commercialized production in the north.

The extreme harshness of Portuguese colonialism led to uncontrolled outflows of refugees: As many as 100,000 Africans escaped to neighboring British possessions after the panethnic revolt of 1917, and later there was also a steady stream of illegal emigration to escape exactions and secure work on better terms, encouraged by African and European producers in Nyasaland (now Malawi) and Tanganyika (Tanzania).[31] These massive departures, together with the enforced perennial migration of a large part of the male population and the reorientation of agriculture toward exports, caused a decline of food production, so that famines became more common.

As elsewhere, postwar developments resulted in increased pressures on African labor and resentment among the educated minority that had begun to emerge in the more developed south. Despite Portugal's efforts to insulate its colony, while abroad, Mozambican workers were exposed to local nationalist movements. Early efforts at mass mobilization were met with overwhelming repression. In 1961, Portuguese troops killed about six hundred unarmed peasants staging a peaceful protest in Mueda, a northern administrative center, causing a massive flight into Tanzania. The government went on to prohibit all African organizations of over thirty members, prompting most of their cadres to relocate abroad. In June 1962, the three major groups met in Dar es Salaam to launch the Front for the Liberation of Mozambique (FRELIMO), under the leadership of Eduardo Mondlane, a southerner educated in South Africa, Portugal, and the United States, where he received a Ph.D. in 1960. Despite factionalism and fragmentation, FRELIMO established itself as the leading Mozambican organization and subsequently achieved OAU recognition. One of its distinctive features was doctrinal commitment to interracial cooperation, a position it maintained after independence as well.

Faced with spreading unrest, the Portuguese concentrated on maintaining control over the more valuable and easily defensible south, where they benefited also from South Africa's assistance. Relinquishing the thinly populated regions along the Tanzanian border to the rebels, the Portuguese subjected the rest of the north to a scorched-earth policy, precipitating a massive exodus, and in the central provinces they forcibly relocated over half a million people into fortified villages, as in Angola. The UNHCR refugee count in Tanzania was 10,000 in 1966, then nearly doubled to 19,000 the following year, climbed to 29,400 by 1969, and reached about 50,000 in 1972. Numbers in Zambia were in the 2,000 to 5,000 range.[32]

Despite its largely southern leadership, because of the situation in neighboring countries, FRELIMO remained confined in the north throughout the 1960s, carrying on a guerrilla war from Tanzanian bases under the command of Algerian-trained Samora Machel and Joaquim Chissano, with mostly Maconde fighters recruited *in situ* and from the refugee pool. Support at first came mainly from Tanzania, but FRELIMO also received nonmilitary assistance from the West, including the United States. As the struggle expanded, the Socialist camp increasingly provided training and arms as well. FRELIMO's organizational development can be attributed to its precarious control over a liberated zone in Cabo Delgado, where it reorganized production and restructured society along socialist lines. The outflow of refugees slowed down somewhat after FRELIMO began organizing the liberated areas.

As the struggle wore on, FRELIMO experienced increasing divisions between its field commanders and the political leadership, blacks and *mestiços,* opportunists and the more principled, established smallholders in the north and collectivists, northern "regionalists" and southern "nationalists." The assassination of Mondlane in 1969 by the Portuguese secret police—possibly with the collaboration of some of his FRELIMO rivals—brought matters to a head. In the ensuing struggle, power shifted into the hands of the more radical wing led by the guerrilla commanders Samora Machel and Marcelino dos Santos. In 1973–74, the movement was transformed into a Leninist vanguard party and expelled deviationists, some of whom turned to collaboration with the Portuguese.

Despite a vast increase of Portuguese forces and an expansion of the "protected village" program, under which the authorities claimed to have resettled 1.25 million by 1972, owing to a shift of policy by Zambia and Malawi, FRELIMO finally managed to open a second front in west-central Tete Province, where it threatened the dam under construction on the Zambezi River at Cahora Bassa. By 1974, in collaboration with Zimbabwean insurgents, the guerrillas were able to attack rail and road links linking Rhodesia with Beira on the Indian Ocean, threatening the city itself. Over the next two years, FRELIMO continued to advance southward against a largely demoralized conscript army.

Following the Portuguese coup, unlike in Angola, FRELIMO rapidly established itself as the exclusive holder of power and, with the help of residual Portuguese forces, slammed a lid on the spontaneous political life stimulated by the prospects of independence. In keeping with FRELIMO's ideological commitment, the new government included a number of white and Asian members; nevertheless, most of the settler population also fled.[33] Their African auxiliaries and opponents of FRELIMO had a harder time getting out. By the end of 1974, several thousand had been sent to "reeducation camps," and another three thousand were seized in October 1975. Again in contrast with Angola, with the assistance of international organizations, most of the refugees were quickly brought home; repatriation was completed by early 1977.[34]

Zimbabwe

Former Southern Rhodesia drew its new name, Zimbabwe, from the ancient capital of the Shona confederacy. Although the settlement itself was abandoned in the mid-fifteenth century, the Shona—making up about three-fourths of the country's current population—maintained supremacy throughout much of the region until well into the nineteenth century, when they were defeated by Ndebele conquerors and driven northward by the process of competitive state-formation that engulfed southern Africa, known as the *mfecane*.[35] Drawn to the area around 1890 by hopes of rich gold deposits, the pioneering white settlers recruited by Cecil Rhodes's British South Africa Company clashed head-on with the centralized state recently established by the Ndebele.[36] Defeated in 1893 and again in 1896, the Ndebele were confined to native reserves, and most of the land they had occupied was appropriated by the company for reallocation to European settlers. The Shona also rebelled in 1896–97 and experienced the same fate.

A disappointment to the company, Southern Rhodesia emerged instead as a land of white settlers engaged in commercial agriculture and small-scale gold mining, whose profitability was founded on control over a plentiful source of cheap indigenous labor. In the 1920s the white minority achieved extensive self-government, but short of the quasi-independent dominion status of South Africa or Canada.[37] They institutionalized a legal apparatus of economic exploitation along racial lines, whereby Africans were confined to less than half the total land, restricted to subsistence agriculture, and hence driven to seek wage employment in the European-controlled export sector. This sector used mechanisms to prevent the Africans from bargaining effectively with employers and competing with white workers.

The system was further elaborated during and after World War II, when conditions in Britain and the world market more generally stimulated the expansion of modern commercial farming, led by tobacco, and encouraged import substitution, fostering the emergence of a substantial industrial sector with capital investments from Britain and South Africa. The mineral sector also expanded and underwent concentration, with asbestos, chrome, and coal following gold in importance. Substantial white immigration, mostly from Britain, led to the expansion of the settler community into a critical mass, reaching a quarter of a million in the 1960s, about 5 percent of the total population. These developments required a vast expansion of the African labor force. Beginning in 1950, long-time black occupants who had hitherto been allowed to remain on "white" land were forced to relocate in the already overcrowded reserves. At about the same time, regulations governing African land were modified to facilitate a transition from communal holdings to family-owned farms. But because there obviously was not enough land to go around, the act was designed in effect to create a "surplus" population and encourage its migration to urban areas as wage labor. By the 1960s, somewhat over half of African rural households depended to some extent on cash earned by migrants, but the average African wage was only about one-tenth that of the whites.[38]

To rationalize imperial management, colonial officials advocated unification with mineral-rich Northern Rhodesia and populous Nyasaland, but the settlers initially rejected this because of British commitment to African primacy in the other two colonies. The Central African Federation was finally brought into being by the Conservatives in 1953. Although the British government insisted that it was to be an instrument of "partnership" between blacks and whites, in Africa both understood that the federation was designed to protect the institutional apparatus of white power against the winds of change.

Further proletarianization as well as enlargement of the white-collar sector led to the emergence of more powerful labor organizations, which spawned most of the independence generation of political leadership. Drawn from a variety of ethnic groups, these leaders included Joshua Nkomo, secretary general of the railway union, a Ndebele; Ndabaningi Sithole, active in the teachers' union, a Shona on his father's side but brought up by his mother's family as a Ndebele speaker; and Robert Mugabe, also a teacher and a Shona. In 1957, most of the organized groups coalesced into the African National Congress, inspired by the South African model, under Nkomo's leadership. These political stirrings prompted the enactment of restrictive legislation. Banned two years later, the Congress reemerged in 1960 as the National Democratic party (NDP), advocating majority rule, higher wages, and better education and housing. Held responsible for the mounting urban violence, the new party also was banned, and at the end of 1961 managed another reincarnation as the Zimbabwe African People's Union (ZAPU), again headed by Nkomo. ZAPU drew support not only from Nkomo's home base in Matabeleland and its industrial center, Bulawayo, but also from the multiethnic population of the capital, Salisbury. Ethnic diversity was also maintained at the leadership level to ensure national representativeness.

As both Northern Rhodesia and Nyassaland began progressing toward African majority rule, white Southern Rhodesians increasingly envisaged going it alone. The constitutional conference of 1961, held at Britain's urging in an attempt to save the federation, produced a charter whereby Britain would relinquish its reserve powers in exchange for a commitment to only limited black representation (fifteen assembly seats out of sixty-five).[39] A boycott of the ensuing referendum by the NDP (later ZAPU) brought Southern Rhodesia to the attention of the international community. The U.N. General Assembly, with many new African members, called on Britain to suspend the constitution and initiate discussions leading to independence with majority rule. Nyasaland and Northern Rhodesia pulled out of the federation in 1963 and became independent the following year as Malawi and Zambia. In response, the center of gravity of Southern Rhodesia's white electorate shifted to an even more extremist direction.[40] Emboldened by the elimination of white moderates at the polls and knowing that the new Labour government in Britain would insist on majority rule, on November 11, 1965, Rhodesian Prime Minister Ian Smith proclaimed a unilateral declaration of independence (UDI).

Denouncing this action as illegal, Britain obtained the condemnation of Rhodesia by the U.N. Security Council, with mandatory economic sanctions. But the outlaw regime benefited from numerous loopholes.[41] Moreover, because of the economic development of the postwar period, Rhodesia was able to achieve a fairly high degree of self-sufficiency. With state intervention to provide incentives for evading firms as well as extensive planning, not only did the regime survive, but despite hardships in certain sectors, the country also experienced a decade of sustained economic growth. Liberated from British constraints, the government invoked emergency powers to reduce further the civil and political freedoms of Africans and proceeded to construct a regime akin to South African apartheid.[42]

The development of African resistance was first hampered by the deployment of an effective apparatus of repression, leadership rivalries, and geopolitical constraints, which also limited the possibility of flight. After the 1962 banning, ZAPU was reconstituted in Dar es Salaam, but lingering dissatisfaction with Nkomo's leadership erupted into a full-blown split. After trying unsuccessfully to take over, in August 1963 Sithole and Mugabe formed the rival Zimbabwe African National Union (ZANU). Operating within the very narrow bounds of legality, the two parties remained similar with respect to ideology and organization. But in keeping with the process noted in preceding cases, while mobilizing at the grass-roots level, ZAPU became identified more closely with the Ndebele and the Kalanga (one of the Shona clans), while ZANU emerged as a more distinctly Shona body. The Shona provided ZANU with the larger population base, but clan rivalries were a continuing source of violent clashes at both the leadership and the mass levels.[43]

In response to the UDI, both parties established headquarters in Zambia, from which they planned to launch an armed struggle with financial support from the recently formed OAU Liberation Committee, in the hope of attracting British intervention. But operations remained limited because infiltration required crossing the confining Zambezi Valley or Lake Kariba, where Rhodesian security forces, with South African assistance, were able to concentrate their efforts. Most of the top leaders were eventually detained, and in late 1968 the guerrilla actions ground to a halt. In preparation for the next phase, the nationalists secured external sponsors who provided training and supplies, China for ZANLA, the military arm of ZANU, and the Soviet Union for ZIPRA, the counterpart of ZAPU. Even though they operated separately and often at odds, for purposes of negotiation in 1974 the two movements formed a joint legal front organization within Rhodesia, called the African National Council (ANC), operating under the chairmanship of Bishop Abel Muzorewa.

FRELIMO's success in the adjacent provinces of Mozambique enabled ZANLA from 1971 on to stage operations in the lightly defended areas of northeastern Rhodesia. Following Maoist doctrine, they initially concentrated on gaining the moral and material support of the local population by developing ties with local spirit mediums and respected elders and, at the end of 1972, began mounting attacks against white farmers.[44] The Portuguese coup of 1974 enabled the further expansion of the front along the whole 764-mile border. Upon his release in 1974, the ZANU's Nkomo continued to pursue power, mainly through political negotiation, but after the failure of the Geneva negotiations in 1977, the rival ZIPRA forces rapidly expanded. Trained along more conventional lines by the Soviet camp and operating from camps in Zambia and Angola, the ZIPRA forces limited themselves to quick incursions.

In the mid-1970s Rhodesian security forces were able to carry out a full-scale counterinsurgency war, about half of which was financed by South Africa, with operational support from the South African air force and specialized units.[45] As in Angola and Mozambique, the authorities set up "protected villages"; in 1978, the Rhodesian Catholic Commission for Justice and Peace estimated that over half a million Africans had been forcibly removed from their homes and placed in over two hundred settlements. Africans of military age were also subject to a draft.

These developments, occurring after a new haven had become available, caused a massive exodus of people. In 1975, the UNHCR recorded about 1,000 arrivals a month in Mozambique, mostly Shona from the eastern districts, for a total of 14,500. Estimates then grew geometrically to 27,000 the following year, 42,500 in 1977, 80,000 in 1978, and 150,000 in the last year of the war. Those within the zone of ZAPU activity escaped mostly to Zambia and Botswana, where the refugee count at the end of the war reached 45,000 and 23,000, respectively. All together, in 1980 there were 216,700 refugees abroad, as well as an estimated half-million internally displaced, amounting to well over 10 percent of the African population.[46]

The presence of so many black Rhodesians abroad in turn facilitated the recruitment of guerrillas. The fact that ZAPU and ZANU were considered by the OAU and the United

Nations as legitimate representatives of the African majority, and entrusted by the UNHCR with the operation of refugee camps, made the distinction between refugees and liberation fighters even more difficult.[47] Indeed, it became so difficult that in 1978 the UNHCR stopped assisting ZAPU-affiliated camps altogether, though it did grant them emergency aid. There were recurrent reports that ZANLA and ZIPRA recruiters resorted to coercion, both within Rhodesia and abroad. In effect, as the conflict escalated into full-scale civil war, the two organizations launched a military draft of their own.[48] By the late 1970s, the nationalist armies were active throughout most of the Tribal Trust Areas. Although they never achieved the quasi-governmental power exercised by FRELIMO, within its zone ZANLA organized effective grass-roots political structures.[49]

At the same time, Rhodesia not only pursued guerrillas across the border and sought to destroy their camps but from 1976 on also attacked refugee villages and launched strikes against Mozambican facilities.[50] In retaliation, President Samora Machel closed the border, seized Rhodesian rolling stock, and cut off Rhodesia's access to the Indian Ocean, leaving the country with no surface links to the outside world except the longer routes through South Africa. At the same time, Machel put pressure on ZANU to accept a negotiated solution. Rhodesian intelligence in turn helped organize the Mozambican National Resistance.

Throughout the first decade of UDI, the Smith government bought time by maintaining a negotiating stance but rejected every opportunity for a compromise solution. However, in the light of the changing geopolitical situation brought about by the collapse of Portuguese rule, in 1974 South Africa began urging the Rhodesian government to engage in a negotiated settlement along the lines of a "separate and equal" solution.[51] Britain countered with a plan for African majority rule within two years, which it was hoped would forestall a more radical outcome. This plan was endorsed by Secretary of State Kissinger, who was prompted by the confrontation in Angola to undertake a more active role in the Rhodesian affair. South Africa, on whose help Rhodesia increasingly depended, was enlisted in support of the settlement and accordingly began holding back its military support. At the same time, the Front Line states also urged the nationalists to sit down at the conference table. Once again united into a Patriotic Front, Nkomo and Mugabe rejected the proposal, holding out for direct negotiations with Britain. In the face of this, over the next two years Smith negotiated a settlement with African "moderates"—most prominently Sithole and Muzorewa—which provided for African participation in the government but fell decidedly short of majority rule.

The "internal settlement," with an interim government headed by Bishop Muzorewa, failed because it remained unable to achieve a cease-fire and could not secure international legitimacy.[52] In the face of the war's rising costs, Smith bypassed his own creatures and arranged a secret meeting with Nkomo, who reputedly was more moderate than Mugabe was. The move opened the path to the Lancaster House Conference, which in the fall of 1979 designed an acceptable constitution. Its principal feature was a one-hundred-member assembly, with eighty members elected on a common African roll and twenty seats reserved on a separate white roll for a transitional period ending in 1987. A cease-fire came into effect on December 21.

A major feature of the settlement was that elections had to be held before formal independence, so as to ensure participation by supporters of the Patriotic Front, whose two components decided to campaign as separate parties. At the request of the British government and with the agreement of all concerned parties, the UNHCR undertook to coordinate the speedy repatriation of refugees. During the first phase, with the assistance of the United Kingdom, local authorities, the governments of the asylum countries, the Patriotic Front, and an array of international volunteer-service agencies, 18,203 refugees were repatriated from Botswana, 10,935 from Mozambique, and 4,292 from Zambia.[53]

Thanks to the mobilization it had achieved in the rural areas during the war, ZANU won 63 percent of the votes cast, sweeping all but the two Matabeleland provinces, which went to Nkomo, and obtained fifty-seven out of the eighty black seats.[54] In keeping with British tradition, Mugabe was selected as prime minister designate; he then proceeded to form a coalition government with Nkomo but clearly maintained the upper hand. The second phase of repatriation began at the end of April. At Mugabe's request, the UNHCR coordinated a program for the rehabilitation of up to 660,000 returning refugees and internally displaced persons over a twelve-month period to April 1981. By the end of the year, practically all Zimbabwean refugees had returned to their home country.

Namibia

The protracted conflict in Namibia is the result of South Africa's stalwart determination since the end of World War II to head upstream against the historical current: "In a world in which neo-colonialism and dependent development had already become the dominant strategies of the center vis-à-vis the periphery, Namibia became the last colony, the last application of *mise en valeur* territorial development as a significant contribution to the economy of the metropole."[55] Conceived in flagrant violation of international law, this project could be implemented only by resorting to oppressive economic and political measures, whose burden fell most heavily on the Ovambo people.

In the era of the European partition of Africa, Imperial Germany established a protectorate over all of South-West Africa except for a small enclave at Walvis ("Whale") Bay, annexed by Britain in 1868. The pastoral Nama, Damara, and Herero living in the region of the most intensive European penetration were brutally pushed off the better land to the benefit of German and South African settlers, whose numbers reached about twenty thousand on the eve of World War I. Diamond deposits were exploited as well, with migrant labor impressed by cooperative chiefs. By 1903, Africans were confined to 31 million out of the country's 82 million hectares, while Europeans controlled 42 million—of which 29 million were granted to international concession companies. Subjected to increasingly unbearable pressure, in 1903 the Herero rose in rebellion, followed later by the Nama and Damara. After reinforcements arrived from Europe, the German high commander ordered the extermination of every Herero, armed or unarmed, found within the colony's boundaries. Over the next four years, the eighty thousand Herero were reduced to fifteen thousand starving refugees; half of the Nama and Damara were killed as well. Deprived of their land and cattle, the survivors were impressed as herdsmen for the white usurpers. The central region deemed fit for white settlement constituted a "police zone" within which colonial authorities ruled supreme and Africans were treated as subhumans, except the Rehoboth *Basters* (i.e., bastards), a racially mixed group of Cape coloured immigrants and Nama, who were granted relative autonomy. The rest of the country was administered indirectly through African chiefs. Its most important component was Ovamboland, adjoining Angola, which contained about half of the country's African population.

South Africa's involvement began during World War I, when the governing Anglo-Boer coalition accepted responsibility for British defense efforts in the region and successfully invaded the German colony.[56] Although denied the outright annexation to which it aspired, South Africa was granted a mandate over South-West Africa and allowed to treat it as its own territory.[57] To encourage white settlement, the government offered easy credit and in 1926 created the South-West African Native Labour Association (SWANLA), a recruiting agency operated jointly by the state and the employers, which administered mandatory labor migration to supply mines and ranches, backed by an apparatus of vagrancy laws and criminal sanctions for breach of contract. Most Africans were confined to inadequate native locations whose areas were further reduced whenever white settlers deemed they could use more land. Among these constrained groups, the formerly relatively self-sufficient Ovambo, increasingly squeezed off their land, were in effect transformed into the country's major disposable labor reserve, a sine qua non for its profitable exploitation.

Although the white settler population rose to 31,000 by the end of the 1930s, Namibia's economy stagnated throughout the interwar period.[58] The situation changed dramatically in the post–World War II decades, as international mining interests based in South Africa began accumulating capital at an unprecedented rate, stimulating industrial expansion as well. With the advent of the United Nations, mandates were charged to trusteeships, which entailed an obligation to prepare dependent territories for independence. Rejecting this, in 1946 South Africa moved toward the annexation of South-West Africa. In 1950 the World Court issued an advisory opinion stating that the U.N. General Assembly had the right to supervise South African rule, but in the absence of sanctions, de facto annexation was allowed to continue.

With political control ensured in the face of international inaction, Namibia presented a unique opportunity for ruthless economic extraction to augment South Africa's international purchasing power.[59] Designed without any concern for providing economic opportunities for the country's African population, this strategy resulted in a widening disparity between the per-capita incomes of blacks and whites.[60] The educational system was designed similarly to perpetuate inequality.[61] Little or nothing was done to stimulate productivity in the subsistence sector which, with about half of the labor force and approximately three-fourths of the population around 1975, generated only 2 percent of the territorial product. This enhanced dependence on employment in the export sector, under conditions of extreme exploitation backed by the might of the South African state. Before 1972, all workers seeking employment outside their homeland continued to be recruited through SWANLA. The pay scale was uniform; workers were not allowed to bring dependents; information on their conduct was centralized; and contracts were designed to ensure rotation.[62] Although the contract system applied to only about half of African and colored wage earners, it set the basic terms of employment throughout the economy.

The most important protest movements of the postwar period originated among the Ovambo, who constituted the major part of the migrant labor force. Many of their leaders came from an unusually autonomous religious organization, the Evangelical-Lutheran Ovambo-Kavango Church (ELOK).[63] Although their protests generally centered on work-related issues, the scope of grievances steadily expanded as workers discovered that the objectionable conditions were occasioned by a system. In the mid-1950s, under the leadership of Herman Toivo ja Toivo, Namibian migrant workers in Capetown launched an organization aimed at abolishing the contract labor system altogether. Initially limited to only one of the Ovambo groups, in 1957 this body evolved into the Ovamboland People's Congress (OPC). After Toivo's arrest, the OPC was reorganized by Sam Nujoma and Jacob Kuanga and changed its name to the Ovamboland People's Organization (OPO), with branches in both Namibia and South Africa. Other organizations were emerging as well, including especially the South-West Africa National Union (SWANU), established in 1959 by Herero students.

A major turning point occurred in 1959, when the black residents of Windhoek protested eviction from their old location, close to the expanding city center, to a distant suburb without facilities. Foreshadowing the tragic events in Sharpeville a year later, the police and army opened fire on unarmed civilians, killing eleven and wounding over fifty. In the wake of these events, OPO changed its name to the South-West African People's Organization (SWAPO) and escalated its demands to ending South African administration. While continuing to draw most of its support from Ovamboland, SWAPO broadened its base somewhat to form a popular front encompassing migrant workers and urban Africans more generally.[64]

Namibia's situation was transformed in the 1960s when newly independent African states began participating in international organizations and made the liberation of white-ruled territories their highest priority.[65] This led to a dialectical process: South Africa responded by seeking to integrate Namibia more closely into its own apartheid system, stimulating further development of its internal liberation movement and greater international support for it. The course of the conflict was further spread by the dramatic changes in the regional circumstances already discussed.

In October 1966 the U.N. General Assembly voted overwhelmingly to revoke the South African mandate and to transfer authority over Namibia to the United Nations itself, but the decisive element was intervention by the Security Council which, in Resolution 266 of March 20, 1969, enjoined South Africa to withdraw immediately its administration.[66] South Africa not only refused to abide by any of these or later injunctions but defiantly proceeded to integrate Namibia into its own system by way of the "Oldendaal Plan," complete with *Bantustans* (later "homelands").[67] At first, South Africa was fairly successful in securing the support of traditional authorities for the policy, except among the Herero.[68] The South-West African Affairs Act of 1969 returned to South Africa legislative and administrative authority over virtually all subjects previously under territorial control. The act also reallocated to Pretoria many sources of territorial revenue, in particular the corporate income tax on foreign firms, ostensibly to compensate the South African government for performing its newly assumed functions.

The movement toward full-scale apartheid, occurring at a time when external support had become available, in turn prompted SWAPO to create an armed wing, the People's Liberation Army of Namibia (PLAN). But given Portugal's control of the area adjacent to Ovamboland, the possibilities for action were initially very limited.[69] SWAPO continued to operate legally in Namibia through a separate "internal" wing, as ZANU and ZAPU were doing in Rhodesia. Despite occasional tensions from within and considerable harassment from without, the organization managed to maintain this arrangement for the next two decades.

Further international condemnations in 1971 precipitated a chain reaction that resulted in much broader participation in the Namibian liberation movement. Already unhappy with the Oldendaal Plan, the ELOK hierarchy openly condemned the contract labor system as a form of slavery; Anglicans and Catholics joined in as well; and in mid-December, the majority of Ovambo workers in Walvis Bay and the Windhoek areas walked out, invoking higher authority: "The word of God says Christ died to free all people, but we Ovambo are not free of the contract."[70] Most of the strikers chose to go home rather than fulfill their contract, a decision facilitated by a good harvest. Streaming back into Ovamboland, the workers vented their wrath against collaborative local officials and resolved to try to raise as big a crop as possible to make the region economically autonomous, thereby issuing an even greater challenge to the system.

The work stoppage, which involved about thirteen thousand workers, continued until well into the spring of 1972 and emerged as the most successful labor action in South African history to date. The authorities declared a state of emergency in Ovamboland, which gave the South African police a free hand in rounding up hundreds of strikers and sympathizers for confinement in special camps, where most were tortured and many executed. Unable to recruit sufficient replacement workers from other groups in Namibia and outside, the authorities offered the Ovambo a revised version of the contract system, whereby SWANLA would be replaced by the homeland authorities, "a change that substituted corruptible local individuals for the impersonal cruelty of a large organization."[71]

The situation remained tense throughout 1972 and 1973, when SWAPO staged a successful boycott of elections for Ovambo, as the self-governing homeland was to be called.[72] In 1973, the insurgency became more serious as PLAN guerrillas operating from Zambia destroyed a major SADF arms depot at Katima Mulilo, in the eastern corner of the Caprivi strip. Fielding its largest force since World War II, the SADF swung into action and forced the PLAN troops to withdraw. Concurrently, there were renewed moves toward African political unity. On the occasion of U.N. Secretary General Kurt Waldheim's visit in 1972, Herero chief Kapuuo called a National Convention of Freedom Parties, with representatives of the internal wing of SWAPO, SWANU, the Rehoboth Coloreds' Volkspartei, and his own National Unity Democratic Organization; but SWAPO pulled out in 1975, after the convention adopted a resolution asserting that it was the sole representative of the Namibian people.

The collapse of Portuguese rule precipitated from February 1974 onward an outflow of refugees through Ovamboland into Angola, and from there to Zaire and Zambia; they included students, migrant workers escaping from arrest for participation in strikes, and political leaders.[73] The numbers increased to about two thousand as it became clear that those arriving in Angola would not be repatriated. In a strongly worded memorandum to South African authorities, church leaders blamed them for causing the exodus by failing to provide adequate educational opportunities and for putting the area under emergency rule, with the population at the mercy of the SADF and its brutal auxiliaries. SWAPO's external wing expanded the area of its guerrilla activities along the Angolan border, in collaboration with UNITA. In August 1975, the Ovamboland authorities announced that nobody would be allowed to enter Angola without a permit, and the South African premier announced that SADF forces would remain in the area to help enforce this policy.

In the following October South Africa invaded Angola in support of the FNLA–UNITA side, prompting the latter to cooperate with the SADF to destroy the bases it had shared with SWAPO. The SADF cleared an area 50 miles on both sides of the borders of all its populations to prevent further guerrilla incursions, with the uprooted to be compensated from homeland treasury funds. However, the MPLA successfully defended itself with Cuban assistance, and South Africa pulled back when anticipated help from the United States failed to materialize. Assured of support from the Angolan government as well as its Russian and Cuban allies, SWAPO was therefore able to resume its forays into Namibia. In December 1975 there were reports of attacks on white farmers as far as 150 miles south of the border, indicating that the war would continue.

Structural Transformations Under Siege

"Total Strategy" and "Linkage"[74]

In the fall of 1974, when South Africa began putting pressure on Rhodesia to come to terms with African majority rule, Prime Minister B. J. Vorster suggested a solution for Namibia as well. The U.N. Security Council responded by giving South Africa until May 31, 1975, to terminate its unlawful occupation. This is when Secretary of State Kissinger tried to involve South Africa in a settlement of the Angolan conflict, thus establishing a de facto linkage between the two situations and legitimizing South Africa's claim to special consideration as the guarantor of Western interests in the region. In 1976–77, with Cyrus Vance replacing Kissinger and Andrew Young as the new U.S. ambassador to the United Nations, the United States joined four other Western powers with major interests in Namibian mineral operations (France, the United Kingdom, Canada, and West Germany) in forming a "Contact Group" to confer with South Africa. The objective was to achieve majority rule through U.N.-supervised elections that would include SWAPO candidates, and to secure Pretoria's consent by ensuring that an independent Namibia would not act as a staging base for operations against South Africa, in other words, a southern African version of "finlandization."

But the negotiations dragged on. Pretoria was merely playing for time, awaiting developments in Zimbabwe and meanwhile planning a "total national strategy" with respect to southern Africa as a whole. As delineated after P. W. Botha became South Africa's prime minister in 1978, the strategy's long-term objective was to create a "constellation of states" founded on common economic and security interests. This entailed the negotiation of a series of mutual nonaggression pacts designed not only to prevent black-ruled states from supporting liberation movements but also to encourage them to play a police role on behalf of Pretoria with respect to the African National Congress.[75] Zimbabwe figured as a crucial element in the plan, and it was expected that as a client of white power, Bishop Muzorewa would adhere in due course to the "constellation."[76] However, the project was negated by the ZANU's stunning victory. Moreover, at about the same time, the Front Line states convened the Southern African Development Coordination Conference (SADCC) for the express purpose of reducing dependency on South Africa, and the prospects of this initiative were in turn bolstered by the outcome in Zimbabwe.[77]

Given the political orientation of Angola, Mozambique, and Zimbabwe, it was becoming increasingly evident that South Africa must either forgo its major goal or else bring about a change of its neighbors' regimes. The international constraints limiting its choice of actions, not very severe to start with, were considerably eased from late 1979 on, by the disarray of the Carter administration induced by the Iranian hostage crisis and the prospect of a Reagan presidency sympathetic to South Africa's position. Indeed, the new Reagan administration committed itself to "constructive engagement," a "realistic" approach harking back to the Kissinger strategy of 1976, which included major concessions to the Republic of South Africa in order to secure regional stability.[78] Within this framework, whose adoption was designed also to assuage pressures from the right, the Reagan administration sought to persuade South Africa to accept the Contact Group's Namibia proposal in exchange for the total withdrawal of Cuban troops from Angola. Albeit skeptical of the United States' capacity to deliver, Pretoria had little to lose by going along with "linkage." The new collaboration was sealed by the Reagan administration's veto in August 1981 of a U.N. Security Council resolution condemning "Operation Protea,'' the SADF's largest raid into Angola since 1975. Accordingly, South Africa shifted to a more aggressive destabilization policy, through systematic military intervention and economic intimidation, directed most ruthlessly against Angola and Mozambique but extending to all its other neighbors as well. As Thomas Callaghy observed in 1983, ''South Africa has become the rogue elephant of Southern Africa, and its behavior has been abetted by Western acquiescence.''[79] The resulting conflicts have taken a huge toll in human lives and triggered even more massive refugee flows than in the previous period.

Angola

After independence, the Luanda regime evolved along the characteristic lines of a besieged government operating in an increasingly hostile environment. It was heavily dependent on aid from Cuba and the Soviet Union, whose involvement was justified by recurrent South African intervention, but Cuban troops also functioned as a praetorian guard that made the MPLA invulnerable despite its inability to overcome structural weaknesses.[80] In March 1977, Zaire's steadfast support of the FNLA in turn prompted the Angolan regime to allow the refugee Katanga gendarmerie to stage an attack on their home province, renamed Shaba. The invasion, repelled by Zaire with the aid of Moroccan troops, dispatched with the tacit encouragement of the United States and direct assistance from France, brought about a state of undeclared war between the two countries and precipitated a flow of refugees from Zaire into Angola. The deteriorating situation prompted a further expansion of the Cuban contingent and the further evolution of the MPLA into a cadre party, still under largely *mestiço* leadership.

Owing to the consolidation of its apparatus, the MPLA successfully weathered the succession crisis opened up by the death of Neto from cancer in September 1979. The new president, Eduardo dos Santos, was also from Luanda and of Mbundu origin. Despite the decline of popular support, with the aid of its international allies, the ruling group was able to forge its army (FAPLA) into an effective, battle-hardened force. FAPLA also played an increasingly prominent role in the party.[81]

Mirroring this process, UNITA became increasingly dependent on South Africa for its own survival. Because it needed the Benguela Railroad to export its copper, in 1976 the Zambian government came to terms with the MPLA and prohibited further UNITA operations from its territory. South Africa returned to the fray in May 1978 by staging a raid, 230 km inside Angola, on a Namibian refugee camp, which it claimed was a guerrilla base. A secret battalion of the South African army began operating in southern Angola at this time as well and provided training camps for UNITA fighters inside Namibia. With support from a number of ''friends,'' persuaded by U.S. officials to help Savimbi during the years the Clark amendment was in effect, by the late 1970s UNITA controlled about one-third of the country, including the Ovimbundu central highlands that constituted Angola's ''breadbasket'' and the arid southeast.[82] Although the Benguela Railroad was formally reopened in April 1979, the guerrillas kept it largely inoperative.

Angola inherited the makings of an unusually successful economy, less vulnerable to pressure from South Africa than any other in the region. During the colonial period, the country was almost self-sufficient with respect to food; it received an ample income from exports of oil, diamonds, and coffee; and it had an adequate infrastructure, with direct access to the Atlantic. However, the economy was badly shaken by the departure of the Portuguese and steadily deteriorated under the impact of the protracted internal war as well as the government's misguided policies. As the southern "breadbasket" turned into the center of fighting, Angola had to import about half of its food. The government and UNITA allowed peasants to sow and cultivate but then seized the crop, and so more and more villagers fled to the towns. By the mid-1980s, only 2 to 3 percent of the country's arable land was under cultivation; money was almost useless, and food was so scarce that it took the place of cash. Shortages were particularly acute in the cities as producers withdrew from the central economy, retaining their production for subsistence and local exchange.[83] The decision to transform the coffee plantations abandoned by the Portuguese into nationalized state farms created a crisis in coffee production, because after independence the mostly Ovimbundu migrant workers used their newly gained freedom to tend their family farms. The situation deteriorated further with the onset of violence and as abandoned plantations reverted to forest.[84]

The MPLA regime was saved by the country's mineral deposits, particularly petroleum. Gulf Oil, the major concessionaire—later acquired by Chevron—suspended operations in 1975 at the request of the U.S. State Department but resumed them in 1976–77. Although there was talk of nationalization, a *modus vivendi* was soon reached, and the company invested heavily in further development.[85] Hence, despite the continued decline of production in all other sectors, export revenues soared, accounting for a positive balance of trade in hard currency, which provided the wherewithal to pay not only for food imports but also for Cuban soldiers and Soviet equipment. Ironically, in 1984 the United States became Angola's single largest trading partner, and the Cubans have played a crucial role in guarding American oil installations against raids by South Africa and American-sponsored guerrillas.[86]

Dos Santos effected an opening to the West, which evoked positive responses and some assistance from France and others in the European Economic Community (EEC), but the Carter administration refused to establish diplomatic relations so long as the Cubans remained. The new leader also engineered a rapprochement with Zaire, which expelled the FNLA, thus bringing an end to guerrilla activity in Cabinda and the other Kongo areas. Angola in exchange expelled the Katanga gendarmerie, who found a haven in Guinea-Bissau. Angolan refugees in Zaire were invited to return, with a promise of amnesty; about half reportedly had done so by 1980. As a consequence of their social background, participation in the profitable Zairean economy for many years, and the availability of higher education in that country, many of the *zairenses* quickly rose to high economic and administrative positions. Under the aegis of the UNHCR, Angola, Zambia, and Zaire subsequently agreed to organize further voluntary repatriation. But after 1980, in the face of deteriorating conditions and reports of sanctions despite the amnesty, few Angolans availed themselves of the opportunity.[87]

As indicated, the coming to power of the Reagan administration prompted South Africa to intervene more openly and on a larger scale. A few months after "Protea," a force of about 5,000 penetrated 120 km inland to create a no-man's land north of the Namibian border, occupying most of Cunene Province and driving another 130,000 Ovambo out of the region to swell the ranks of the internally displaced. At the end of 1983 the SADF launched "Operation Askari" with 10,000 troops, its largest intervention to date, with the objective of capturing Lubango and possibly even Luanda. But the FAPLA put up an effective defense, thanks to the monitoring of South African movements by the Soviet Union. UNITA expanded its domain as well, and by the end of 1982, guerrilla groups were reported active over two-thirds of the country and continued to expand northward the following year. With some 5,000 guerrillas and 20,000 followers, UNITA was transforming itself into a semiregular army with training assistance from South Africa and possibly Israel.[88] Like some of the liberation movements of the colonial era, it was becoming a state within a state, with a Maoist organizational structure and its costs met in part by smuggling diamonds and exporting ivory and timber through Namibia to South Africa.[89]

At the behest of the United States, in 1983 South Africa undertook secret discussions with both Angola and Mozambique. On January 31, 1984, Pretoria and Luanda agreed to a cease-fire, the withdrawal of most of the South African troops, and the establishment of a joint force to impose a freeze on SWAPO operations on Angolan territory. Although this was to be a prelude to departure of the Cubans as well, the negotiators soon reached an impasse.[90]

Talks were held on and off over the next two years, but little progress was achieved. The United States continued to play an ambiguous role, carrying on further mediation efforts while simultaneously becoming more involved with UNITA. In July 1985, the Reagan administration finally secured repeal of the Clark amendment; conservative groups stepped up their pressure for intervention, prompting in turn more determined liberal opposition; but the administration did get its way to the extent of securing a free hand in providing substantial covert aid to UNITA.[91] Because "linkage" remained the major issue, we shall discuss developments at the international level in connection with Namibia.

The protracted international stalemate, with all concerned parties willing and able to bolster their stand by means of increased military activity, occasioned a further expansion of internal violence without appreciably shifting the balance of power among the Angolan antagonists. In the mid-1980s the government's armed forces escalated to 110,000; FAPLA now had much less difficulty recruiting because military service was the best way for Angolans to meet their basic economic needs. In addition, with over 30,000 Cuban troops, 1,200 Soviet advisers, and deliveries of an estimated $2 billion worth of Soviet supplies, Luanda was able to affirm its control of the major towns throughout the south and to stage an annual summer offensive. But its actions remained short of decisive because South Africa stood by to intervene whenever UNITA's strategic bases were threatened. Savimbi's forces steadily broadened the domain of their action and could stage raids nearly anywhere in the countryside. American support enabled them to fight off aerial attacks and to open up a second front in the provinces adjacent to Zaire, which resumed its role as the major conduit for military supplies, but they could not hope to overturn the regime so long as it remained under the protection of the Soviet Union and Cuba.[92]

The spreading conflict occasioned massive population displacements, both directly as people fled the affected areas or were forcibly relocated in government-controlled settlements, and indirectly through its contribution to economic hardship. In 1979 there were 178,000 recognized Angolan refugees abroad, 141,000 of them in UNHCR-supervised camps in Zaire. Five years later the total had risen to 301,000—approximately 5 percent of the Angolan population—including 215,000 in Zaire and 86,000 in Zambia. The number then reached 357,000 in 1985 and 376,000 in 1986, 290,000 in Zaire and 86,000 in Zambia. There were also half a million internally displaced, largely Ovimbundu from the central plateau, driven out by war and drought.[93]

About half of the refugees in Zaire were Kongo who had been there for a long time and now included a substantial progeny; many were in the process of becoming ordinary settlers. Another seventy thousand were recent arrivals who had settled in a remote region

of Shaba Province throughout 1984 and 1985, escaping UNITA attacks on poorly defended government towns and fleeing to avoid being drafted by either side. About 10
percent were second-time refugees, Zaireans who had fled to Angola during the 1977
"Shaba war."[94] The Zaire government initially allowed them to settle on undeveloped
land but, because of food shortages and Angolan incursions, moved them farther inland
with UNHCR assistance and regrouped them in camps. The rest were also newcomers
who arrived in Bas-Zaire after the opening of UNITA's second front in northern Angola.

The Lusaka authorities were increasingly reluctant to admit Angolans; although they
claimed high unemployment, food shortages caused by the drought, and a rising crime
problem attributable to illegal aliens, their stand appeared to be dictated mostly by foreign
policy considerations.[95] In mid-1982, Zambia began implementing the voluntary repatriation program agreed upon two years earlier, but the refugees refused to budge. The
following March, the authorities announced their intention of repatriating all of the inmates of Maheba camp, prompting a warning that this would endanger the nine thousand
people involved because of their known pro-UNITA orientation. Some expulsions did
take place later in the year, and several more planeloads were forcibly repatriated in 1984.
Nevertheless, Angolans continued to enter the country in flight from the adjacent fire
zone; about twelve thousand more arrived in North West Province in late 1985, most of
them settling among the local population.[96]

Mozambique

Coming to power after nearly a decade of organizational experience in the liberated areas
of northern Mozambique, FRELIMO was much more committed to structural change than
was the MPLA and could rely on a corps of eight thousand seasoned cadres to pursue its
objectives, but it had little or no organization in the south, including the capital. The
leadership's prime objective was to transform the movement into a ruling party. They
consolidated their apparatus and ruthlessly repressed strikes and other spontaneous attempts to change prevailing economic relationships. Internal purges proliferated as well.
The transition was confirmed at FRELIMO's first postindependence congress in 1977,
which officially adopted Marxism-Leninism and concentrated power in the hands of
Samora Machel, whose conception of his role was symbolized by adoption of the title
Field Marshal.[97] The erstwhile guerrilla army, which had shown signs of unruliness, was
separated from the party and brought under its discipline.[98] By the late 1970s, as many
as ten thousand people were believed to be in reeducation camps, but a few dissidents
inside and outside the ranks of FRELIMO escaped to Rhodesia, Malawi, and even South
Africa.

The distortions of the colonial economy, compounded by the Portuguese exodus, that
occurred despite FRELIMO's interracial character, raised severe obstacles to postindependence development. The new regime's rigid adherence to a highly statist form of
socialism had, however, catastrophic consequences, particularly in the vital agricultural
sector.[99] As in Angola, the Machel government nationalized the property abandoned by
the Portuguese, turning the large plantations into state farms and the settler farms into
cooperatives. The state then expended all its resources on these undertakings, while
completely neglecting the much larger peasant household sector. This inaction led to a
withdrawal of workers and farmers from commercial agriculture into subsistence, causing
a sharp drop in both the production of export crops and government revenues. Although
food production initially increased somewhat, it later declined as a result of violence. At

the 1983 congress, the leadership acknowledged its errors and announced a drastic reorientation toward household producers. The damage had been done, however, and whatever positive results the change might have brought about were negated by drought, floods, South African economic pressures, and the growing insurgency.

In regard to external relations, the government adopted a complex position athwart the regional fault line: While acknowledging economic dependency on South Africa and the necessity of maintaining continuity in its external economic policy, Mozambique did not hesitate to support liberation movements, including not only those fighting to overthrow white rule in Rhodesia but, even more defiantly, South Africa's own African National Congress (ANC).[100] The course of events since independence is largely attributable to the consequences of these choices.

As indicated in the Zimbabwe section, by the end of 1979 Mozambique had provided a base for ZANLA operations and hosted at least 150,000 refugees, who constituted a heavy burden on its already strained economy. Rhodesian troops repeatedly crossed the border in pursuit of the guerrillas, destroying their camps and attacking the refugees' villages as well as Mozambican facilities. Machel retaliated by ordering an embargo on Rhodesian transport and recalling Mozambican workers, but this in turn entailed heavy costs in lost revenues and remittances. The Smith government then enlisted revanchist Portuguese settlers, regionalist opponents of FRELIMO, and disillusioned FRELIMO supporters who had escaped the purges into an organization designed to wreak havoc throughout Mozambique.[101] Under the direction of former Portuguese counterguerrilla personnel and Rhodesian intelligence, in 1977 this blossomed into the Mozambican National Resistance (RENAMO), which staged hit-and-run operations in the border areas. Over time, RENAMO emerged as a catchall for the grievances generated by FRELIMO rule, much like the anticolonial movements that arose throughout Africa in the post–World War II decades. The very same sociogeographical configuration that worked to the benefit of FRELIMO during the liberation struggle now redounded to the advantage of its enemies, who stepped up their appeal to regionalist sentiment in the north and west against rule by the south. By the time Zimbabwe became independent, Maputo was faced with an extensive insurgency.

Pretoria was at first less openly aggressive toward Mozambique than Angola was but nevertheless relentlessly exerted economic pressure to keep Machel in line.[102] In 1978, South Africa's annual quota for workers was reduced from over 120,000 to fewer than half, and wage withholdings turned over to the Mozambique government in gold were henceforth paid at the open rate; consequently, Mozambique could no longer realize a profit on gold sales. The lost revenues amounted to approximately twice its international debt. Although South Africa did begin purchasing hydroelectric power upon the completion of Cahora Bassa in 1977, as it had contracted to do, it reduced its use of Mozambican rail and port facilities, and the tourist trade began to dry up as well. It soon became apparent that although South Africa could destroy the Machel government whenever it wished, it was content to reduce Mozambique to the level of political acquiescence of a Lesotho or Swaziland and to prevent the SADCC project from getting off the ground by discouraging Zimbabwe and Botswana from routing their import–export traffic through Maputo. In this South Africa was quite successful.[103] However, with its own survival at stake, Zimbabwe subsequently decided to protect the railroad and pipeline to Beira with its own troops and became ever more firmly committed to defending Mozambique's integrity.

Although the advent of Mugabe in Zimbabwe provided some relief, RENAMO soon shifted its bases to South Africa. Pretoria also began intervening more directly to halt attacks by the ANC. In January 1981, commandos swooped down on the town of Matola, just below Maputo, and its secret services engineered attacks on foreign sympathizers.[104] Later that spring RENAMO launched a second front along the Malawi border, and by mid-1982 armed bands were making travel difficult in many parts of the country. RENAMO's fighting strength was estimated at about five thousand in 1982, including some white mercenaries, and twelve thousand a year later; rather than a single organization it might perhaps be best thought of as a congeries of warlord bands. The military wing was headed by Afonso Dhlakama ("Jacamo"), a former soldier in the Portuguese army, but the leadership otherwise remained unknown.[105]

By 1983 the insurgents were active in all ten provinces. Aided by South African air reconnaissance and supply drops, their sorties were directed mostly against government installations, but because these included communal villages, they became in effect a terror campaign to turn the population against FRELIMO. The cost of security operations rose steadily, to equal roughly the total value of Mozambique's exports. Maputo was left to fight the insurgency largely on its own, with some military supplies from the East as well as some "nonlethal" aid from the West. But without the revenue and foreign assistance to build up reliable armed forces, as MAPLA was able to do in Angola, the government faced a growing stream of defections. Many fled to Malawi; some joined RENAMO; and others just fended for themselves, with banditry adding to the violence. Mozambique also began experiencing a catastrophic drought and found itself trapped in a tragically vicious circle: The spreading hunger played into the hands of the insurgents, causing more violence which resulted in a further decline of food production and made relief operations nearly impossible.

Practically bankrupt and helpless to fight the war, in late 1983 Mozambique's leadership softened its economic policies and negotiated military cooperation agreements with Portugal, France, and Britain, which began training Mozambican troops in Zimbabwe.[106] At the same time, under strong pressure from the United States, which held out the incentive of substantial food aid, Machel began talking with South Africa. This led to the Nkomati nonaggression accord of March 1984, whereby Mozambique pledged to cease harboring the ANC in exchange for an end to South African intervention.[107] Already in the previous September, the Maputo authorities had announced that South African refugee settlements would be moved away from the border. Following the accord, many were forced to leave the country altogether.[108] Subsequently the two countries also concluded an agreement for the joint exploitation of Cahora Bassa. Despite efforts by some members of his administration to tilt American policy toward RENAMO, in September 1985 President Reagan officially received Machel, and Mozambique became the major recipient of U.S. food aid in Africa.[109]

Nevertheless, the insurgency persisted, in part because in anticipation of the accord the SADF had provided the rebels with large stores of military supplies and because RENAMO had become sufficiently rooted to live off the land.[110] By mid-1985 Maputo and Beira were in effect besieged, and in September 1986 RENAMO launched a 12,000-man offensive from southern Malawi which, if successful, would cut the country in two as well as bring Zimbabwe to its knees; the invasion was reportedly coordinated by the SADF.[111] The Mozambicans also violated the agreement by allowing the African National Congress to return, prompting Pretoria to expel the remaining 52,000 migrants still working legally in South African mines under bilateral agreements.[112]

In late October 1986, President Machel died in a plane crash, together with several other members of the government, on a flight from Lusaka to Maputo that passed unexpectedly over South African territory. The tragedy struck amidst reports that the military hard-liners in South Africa who had opposed Nkomati were readying themselves to engineer Machel's ouster—a possibility enhanced by the success of the Pretoria-instigated coup in Lesotho at the beginning of the year—and gave rise to suspicion of foul play.[113] Although the event was thought to constitute the coup de grâce for the regime, the succession was quickly ensured by long-time Minister of Foreign Affairs Joaquim Chissano, generally considered a "pragmatist" likely to steer a cautious course. The Mozambique government managed to survive and, in the spring of 1987, with the aid of a reported fifteen thousand Zimbabwean troops and the cooperation of Tanzania, defeated the RENAMO offensive against Beira. Zimbabwean businessmen then set about restoring the port to full operation. The government also achieved greater control over the south.[114]

The situation in other parts of the country remained fluid, however, as much of the population shifted allegiance to whichever side exercised the greatest pressure at a given moment. With the government's own forces in disarray, seasoned observers raised the specter of "ugandization." There was also a possibility the major powers might be drawn in. Indeed, critical all along of food aid to a "communist" country, in mid-1987 the right-wing lobby in the United States stepped up its campaign for support of the RENAMO "freedom fighters."[115]

In early 1987 the new leadership took further steps toward an economic rehabilitation program founded on traditional peasant farming, in tune with the most recent dictates of the World Bank, and began negotiations with the International Monetary Fund (IMF) as well.[116] Nevertheless, without peace the possibilities for reconstruction remained extremely limited; the export sector ground to a halt; and Cahora-Bassa functioned at 1 percent capacity. Le Monde dubbed Mozambique the "martyr country," and it appeared as the country with the most negative rate in the World Bank's tally of growth for 1980–85.[117] In August 1987 Mozambique and South Africa agreed to revive their non-aggression pact, but the internal conflict continued.

Driven by an inextricable mix of violence and famine, after a decade of respite Mozambicans once again began to flee abroad. Numbers rose to 44,000 during 1984 and reached between 145,000 and 219,000 the following year, with the major concentrations in Zimbabwe (45,000 to 51,000) and South Africa (100,000 to 160,000). Estimates for 1986 ranged from 255,000 to as high as 430,000. At a conference called by the U.N. secretary general in March 1987 to review the emergency in Mozambique, the UNHCR reported 275,000 refugees, including 175,000 in Malawi. By mid-June the number there had increased to 277,000.[118] Over the same period the internally displaced soared from 400,000 to perhaps as many as 1.8 million. In 1986, close to 4 million persons—one-third of the population—faced famine or life-threatening violence. About 1 million uprooted by the drought were unable to return to their villages because of insecurity; most of the others were forcibly relocated away from their homesteads to areas under government control near the cities and larger towns, where they were dependent for survival on food handouts from a government that completely lacked the capacity to perform this task. In April 1987 the U.N. Food and Agriculture Organization (FAO) reported that the number of people at risk had risen above 4 million, many of them in rural areas cut off by civil war and that massive airlifting would be necessary to prevent a huge death toll.[119]

It is a bitter irony that people who struggled for independence from white settler rule should end up seeking refuge in South Africa where, by all reports, their situation remained precarious.[120] Mostly Shangaans from the south, who set out to join coethnics on the other side of Kruger National Park, the refugees reported that they felt trapped: "On one side FRELIMO demands that they move near the cities on security grounds; on the other [RENAMO] tries to prevent them from leaving, because they constitute a protective screen and a source of food. These peasants have thus become hostages as well as a stake."[121] Already setting out in near-starvation, the travelers faced further grave dangers: Mozambique mined the border to prevent RENAMO penetration, and within the park they were also vulnerable to predators, both wild animals and South African security police. In late 1983, the International Red Cross and the chief ministers of the homelands obtained permission to allow those who made it into the homelands to stay, but they risked immediate deportation whenever they stepped outside these areas in search of work. In 1985, about two thousand a month were intercepted and dumped back into Mozambique, where they once again faced the life-threatening situations that caused them to flee in the first place.[122] The International Red Cross was expelled from South Africa in October 1986, leaving the local voluntary agencies and Gazankulu authorities, highly vulnerable to South African pressure, as the only sources of protection. Without aid many of the refugees joined the illegal labor force, subjected to even more ruthless exploitation than were ordinary contract workers. There were reports of mounting resentment among residents of Gazankulu, where the unemployment rate reached 40 percent.

Refugees in Zimbabwe also arrived near starvation, but then had greater access to international assistance. Of the 70,000 total as of mid-1986, about 25,000 were in UNHCR camps with, according to the agency, excellent prospects for being integrated into the government's regional development strategy.[123] During the same period approximately 16,500 Mozambicans entered the eastern provinces of Zambia. Although they found havens among fellow ethnics, the authorities feared that their presence would create security problems and so insisted on repatriation in principle, as with the Angolans. However, the government indicated that some might be allowed to remain should international assistance be forthcoming and on the condition that they be moved away from the border.[124] Victims of FRELIMO repression have gone mostly to Malawi, where many of them joined RENAMO. Under pressure from Zambia and Zimbabwe, in 1985 President Hastings Banda ordered the refugee-warriors out of the country; they then captured several small towns across the Mozambican border, thereby creating a liberated zone of their own. But as noted earlier, in the fall of 1986 RENAMO launched a major assault from Malawi, and the fighting in turn precipitated a flood of refugees into that country over the next several months.[125]

Playing for Time in Namibia

After the independence of Angola, South Africa attempted to buy time by building up institutions that would lend an aura of legitimacy to its rule, while simultaneously deploying an ever-more extensive apparatus of repression. There was increasing pressure from the international community for a settlement, but this was largely relieved by the coming to power of the Reagan administration in the United States.

The first phase, from 1975 to 1983, involved the establishment of a sort of ethnic confederation, with guaranteed representation of the white minority in both the parliament and the government. It began with the "Turnhalle" conference convened in 1975 by Dirk Mudge, deputy leader of the ruling Nationalist party and a member of its *verligte* (enlightened) faction. SWAPO and the convention refused to attend. While negotiations

between the Contact Group and South Africa were under way, in March 1977 an agreement was announced on a constitution. In preparation for independence, scheduled for
December 31, 1978, Namibia was to have a three-tier system of government founded on
the election of representatives by each of the ethnic communities, but SWAPO exiles were
made ineligible by the requirement of five years' residence for all candidates. The charter
also specified that the Walvis Bay enclave, Namibia's only deep-water harbor, was an
integral part of the Republic of South Africa.[126] The convention firmly opposed the
proposal but maintained an uneasy alliance with the internal wing of SWAPO. In June
Pretoria announced that in light of the ongoing international negotiations, implementation
of the constitution would be suspended; but this did not apply to Walvis Bay, which was
formally annexed. In the following November, various pro-Turnhalle groups, including
Dirk Mudge's white followers, formed the Democratic Turnhalle Alliance (DTA) under
the presidency of Herero Chief Clemens Kapuuo. Somewhat later the Namibian National
Front (NFE) was launched by supporters of the Contact Group plan, who included the
white Federal party under the leadership of Brian O'Linn, backed by the Anglo-American
mining group and its local staff.[127]

Meanwhile, despite a major internal crisis precipitated by the Angolan civil war,
SWAPO was building itself up with supplies and equipment from the Soviet Union and
Eastern Europe, and combat training from the Cubans in Angola. By early 1978, its
strength was estimated at five thousand to ten thousand guerrillas.[128] As the war continued, people on both sides of the border were driven into flight. In 1977 several hundred
Namibian youths fled to Botswana following a boycott of secondary schools in protest
against the end of "Bantu" education, compounded by the decision to impose Afrikaans
as the language of instruction.[129]

In January 1978 the Western nations announced that South Africa and SWAPO had
agreed to a plan for a cease-fire and elections, with the matter of Walvis Bay to be settled
separately. Concerned at this time mostly with developments in Zimbabwe, Pretoria was
merely playing for time and subsequently withdrew its assent. SWAPO, some of whose
leaders favored an exclusively military solution, also broke off negotiations but was
persuaded by the Front Line states to return to the conference table.[130] Tensions between
the DTA and the opponents of Turnhalle exploded into violence. The Ovambo minister of
health was assassinated on February 7, as was Clemens Kapuuo a few weeks later.
Although SWAPO denied responsibility in these matters, there was another wave of
arrests, and more fled abroad. Despite the negotiations, in May the SDAF again struck a
Namibian refugee camp in Angola, about 150 miles north of the border, killing between
five hundred and one thousand persons.

Because of South Africa's continued defiance, on September 29, 1978, the U.N.
Security Council adopted Resolution 435, which established the United Nations Assis-
tance Group for the Transitional Period, charged with assisting the special representative
in carrying out his mandate to bring about independence before the end of 1979, following
U.N.-supervised elections. Stepping up its efforts, the Contact Group proposed posting a
U.N. force in Namibia at the end of February for a seven-month transitional period.
Meanwhile, despite unanimous international condemnation, elections under for the Turnhalle constituent assembly were held in December 1978. SWAPO and SWAPO-Democrats boycotted it. On the eve of the elections, six SWAPO leaders were arrested and
detained under the Terrorism Act following bomb explosions in Windhoek. On election
day itself, South African troops and police guarded the polls and brought in the voters.
The DTA won 82 percent of the votes cast and later indicated its willingness to participate

in U.N.-supervised elections under the right conditions. Emerging as a major issue was the return of refugees to participate in the elections. SWAPO claimed that the refugees numbered thirty thousand to forty thousand, but South Africa reckoned ten thousand to twelve thousand only, with the U.N. leaning toward the South African estimate.[131] In any case, the talks collapsed again in March 1979 when South Africa rejected the notion of allowing SWAPO to establish camps inside Namibia during the transition. Accordingly, SWAPO stepped up its infiltrations.

From Pretoria's perspective, the failure of the "internal settlement" in Zimbabwe created a dilemma in Namibia. U.N.-supervised elections would most likely result in a ZAPU type of outcome, but rejection of the settlement could lead to tougher international sanctions and continued antiguerrilla warfare, swallowing an increasing number of conscripts. Under the circumstances, it made sense to prolong negotiations without reaching a conclusion, the more so as political developments in the United States held the promise of relief from pressure. Concurrently, while admitting a military solution was unlikely, Pretoria invested heavily in maximizing its strategic superiority, so as to bargain from a position of strength. In 1979 South Africa stepped up its attacks against Zambia and Angola so as to contain infiltration into Ovamboland. Repression became more severe in Namibia as well, driving the internal wing of SWAPO into exile. By 1980 a significant part of the SADF was committed to containing the insurgency.[132]

In January 1981, South Africa finally sat down at the conference table in Geneva, but this was apparently another delaying ploy, and after ensuring that the conference would end in failure, Premier Botha postponed further action on Namibia until after the South African general elections, scheduled for April.[133] After his reelection, South Africa launched the major operations discussed in the Angola section. Although "Protea" disrupted SWAPO's command structure, the SADF later admitted having failed to cut off the guerrillas' escape route.

In the intervening period Turnhalle was further implemented, but Pretoria failed to consolidate a cohesive anti-SWAPO coalition.[134] There were in fact indications of growing support for the movement, in activities such as the peaceful Namibia Day rally of September 1981 as well as anticonscription demonstrations by the parents of draftees. This trend was even borne out in surveys conducted by South African polling organizations.[135] With the DTA falling apart, Dirk Mudge and the Council of Ministers finally resigned in early 1983; the National Assembly also was dissolved; and Namibia returned to direct South African rule.[136]

While international negotiations dragged on, the conflict escalated further. Unacceptable to SWAPO, the Angolan government, and the Front Line states, the "American initiative" got nowhere but played into South Africa's hands by validating its claims as the dominant regional power and shifting the onus for delaying a settlement to SWAPO.[137] Early in 1981 the authorities introduced conscription throughout Namibia, except on Owambo. This met with widespread opposition, leading thousands of young workers and students to leave the country, increasing the pool of candidates for SWAPO's U.N.-assisted programs of secondary and higher education as well as for the PLAN cadre.[138] In April 1982, PLAN launched its largest military operation to date, with over one hundred guerrillas armed with SAM-7 missiles and land mines moving south into the Tsumeb area. A year later they were operating two hundred miles south of the border, causing white farmers to flee.

At the beginning of 1984, the UNHCR counted 75,000 Namibian refugees abroad. About 70,000 of them were in Angola, scattered throughout the south as well as in Luanda and Kwanza-Sul Province in the northwest. Another 4,900 were at the Nyangio Center in Zambia. Recognized by the international community as the official representative of the Namibian people, SWAPO was the UNHCR's operational partner for assistance and training programs in agriculture, education, and health. The Zambian camps had a particularly broad range of services. The refugees were also involved in over fifty projects under the Nationhood Program administered by the U.N. Commission for Namibia. Because most of the Namibians were from Ovamboland and had fled because of their active or implicit support of SWAPO, the distinction between refugees and fighters was inherently ambiguous. The guerrillas did not reside in the camps, whose populations consisted largely of their dependents and wounded.[139] This ambiguity was compounded by the fact that the refugee communities were given representation in SWAPO's Central Committee, along with PLAN and the National Union of Namibian Workers. This applied as well to the refugee community's educational institutions, including most prominently the United Nations Institute for Namibia established in Lusaka in 1976.[140]

A new phase was opened by the agreement between Angola and South Africa in early 1984.[141] Most of the Namibian refugee camps in southern Angola were evacuated to the north, and PLAN had to evacuate its bases. The commandos were ordered to regroup in Ovamboland by infiltrating the 800-km border, which South Africa could not fully control, but this made them more vulnerable to counterinsurgency operations, and guerrilla actions rapidly subsided.[142] Seizing the opportunity to negotiate from a more advantageous position, and as a move to avoid U.N. involvement, in March 1984 South Africa proposed a regional peace conference. After searching hesitations, SWAPO agreed to attend.[143]

The conference opened in Lusaka on May 11, 1984, under the chairmanship of Zambian President Kenneth Kaunda. SWAPO clearly emerged as the dominant actor on the African side, with forty representatives indicating their support, as against twenty-four for the "Multiparty Conference" (MPC). Reportedly, South Africa proferred a Botswana type of solution, but the negotiations were torpedoed by SWAPO's Soviet advisers.[144] In the following July direct talks took place for the first time between the major antagonists, but they again failed to reach agreement. South Africa then returned to a more aggressive external stance, resuming intermittent raids into Angola and going as far as dispatching commandos to destroy Gulf Oil's installations in Cabinda. Concurrently, the SADF also staged an attack on Botswana, which shamed even the Reagan administration's apologists into recalling the U.S. ambassador.

In bold defiance of U.S. policy, in mid-1985 Pretoria announced the establishment of an African-led transitional government with authority over Namibia's internal affairs, including the command of twenty thousand troops of the mostly black South-West Africa Territory Force (SWATF). Claiming an emergency, the legislature was to be nominated rather than elected. Although the members selected were mostly black, including a number of former activists, the *New York Times* dubbed the regime installed on June 17, 1985, "the sham of Namibia," commenting that "even in a cynical world, this ploy stands out as extraordinary."[145]

Under the new government repression grew yet more severe. The South African authorities further expanded the SWATF by extending conscription to the entire country, and in March 1985 the five northern homelands as well as those along the Botswana border were declared a security zone. This allowed the armed forces a free rein in terrorizing the local population into submission and gave the authorities greater latitude to restrict freedom of speech and of movement. In March 1986, the Botha government declared that it would begin unilaterally implementing Resolution 435 on August 1, conditional on the withdrawal of Cuban troops, but all parties concerned immediately indicated that this one-sided prerequisite would make the proposal meaningless.

Although SWAPO was hegemonic among the Ovambo population and had widespread support from other Namibians as well, the organization appeared unable to recruit more manpower within the country itself and was also cut off from further access to the refugee pools in Angola. Guerrilla operations nearly ended, except for occasional sabotage. SWAPO's 1987 offensive was quickly defeated. Reversing the usual sequence, the liberation movement focused increasingly on political mobilization, devoting most of its organizational energies to reviving the National Union of Namibian Workers and building up a united front. Thanks in part to the upheavals in South Africa itself, the strategy was quite successful, particularly in the mining sector.[146] UNITA's predominance over much of southern Angola also reduced the flow of refugees to a trickle of escaping activists. But in 1986, the count still hovered about 76,000.[147]

Chapter 4

Separatism, Revolution, and War in Ethiopia and the Horn

Already bearing the sad distinction of ranking as the poorest country in the world, in the past two decades Ethiopia has been wracked by separatist conflicts, a social revolution, and war with neighboring Somalia. The revolution was caused in part by the onset of a major famine, and the violence unleashed by the ensuing social upheavals further undermined the population's ability to meet its subsistence needs. At the end of 1986, there were approximately 1.25 million Ethiopians abroad, mostly in refugee camps in neighboring Sudan and Somalia, but with clusters in the United States (around 45,000), Israel (around 15,000), and a few other Western countries. These dramatic upheavals were caused by an interaction between two distinct processes: competitive state-formation in the Horn of Africa as a whole, involving Ethiopia, Somalia, and Eritrea, and the belated transformation of the ancient Abyssinian empire into a modernizing state.

Competitive State-Formation in the Horn[1]

Because of its historical priority as a state, Ethiopia—known before the twentieth century as Abyssinia—contributed to the formation of the others. Although the country is located geographically on the African continent and Addis Ababa emerged in the 1960s as the headquarters of the Organization for African Unity (OAU), it differs fundamentally from the new states of sub-Saharan Africa in that, as in Asia and Europe, the traditional social order was founded on control by an aristocracy of the land and the peasants who lived on it. The origins of Ethiopia's distinctiveness can be traced to Axum, a maritime trading kingdom that was formed in the first century A.D. from a coastal colony settled around contemporary Massawa (Eritrea) by immigrants from southern Arabia who intermingled with the indigenous African population of what was known to Egyptians as the land of Cush. Axum later adopted Christianity. After maritime trade was ended by the expansion of Islam to the shores of the Red Sea, the kingdom lived off the conquest of pagan lands to the south. Axum itself disappeared, but some of its features were incorporated into an emerging empire, which in the tenth century encompassed two peoples of the Abyssinian highlands, the Tigrayans and, beyond them to the south, the Shoan Amhara.[2] Having gained the upper hand, the Shoans subdued some of the Muslim sultanates entrenched along the eastern and southern fringes of the highlands and also expanded northward toward Eritrea.

The subjects of the sultanates were mostly Somali nomads, who from the thirteenth century onward occupied the vast and largely arid expanse constituting the Horn of Africa proper. In the first half of the sixteenth century, they were mobilized by local Muslim rulers, with backing from the Ottomans, in a *jihad* against the Christian empire. The empire survived, thanks to aid from fellow-Christian Portuguese, who had recently appeared in the region in the course of their movement toward India. Somewhat later, another pastoralist people, the Oromo—formerly known as Galla, an Amharic name they now reject—took advantage of the mutual weakening of the Christian and Muslim states to occupy much of southern and eastern Shoa, as well as lands to the north and west. Some of the newcomers became sedentary, intermarrying with the local population and slowly adopting elements of Amhara culture. Indeed, the later emperors were often of partly Oromo origin, including Haile Selassie.

Notwithstanding its persistence and even expansion, the empire stagnated at an extremely low level of organizational development, owing to material and technological constraints.[3] It is best thought of as a congeries of patrimonial formations, covering a territory of varying extent, among which at any given time some held the upper hand. Local magnates acknowledged the idea of a supreme ruler but lacked a regularized means of determining who that ruler might be at any particular time. Tigre and Shoa remained, for practical purposes, independent kingdoms, themselves subject to recurrent disintegration.[4] Finally, the empire lacked a permanent geographical center; the capital moved with the emperor's household.

In the second half of the nineteenth century, the Horn acquired new strategic value from the perspective of the European imperialist powers; a key event in this respect was the opening of the Suez Canal in 1869.[5] This changed situation enabled ambitious Ethiopian rulers—the Tigrayan warlord Johannes and, after him, the Shoan Menelik—to consolidate their position in relation to internal competitors and to expand their patrimony by external conquest. In the scramble set off by the collapse of Egypt after the Mahdist rebellion in the Sudan (1883), with the collaboration of Menelik, the Italians secured most of Eritrea, in exchange for which they helped him obtain European weapons. These enabled Menelik to conquer the Muslim city-state of Harar that exercised hegemony over the Somali of the Ogaden. The covetous allies, however, subsequently clashed over the lands south of Shoa. With the aid of the French, the Ethiopian emperor defeated the Italians at Adowa in March 1896. The victory boosted the emperor's personal power and ensured that Ethiopia would not only survive as an independent state but would even participate in a division of the spoils.

As emperor (1889), Menelik displayed little interest in Eritrea, which was later consolidated as an Italian colony and thereby launched on a distinctive path of development.[6] But the south was vital to Menelik as a source of coffee and gold for trade with the Europeans, as well as slaves for the Shoans' use and trade with the Arabs.[7] Menelik already had a free hand with respect to the Oromo- and Negro-inhabited lands of the southwest; and the vaguely worded peace treaty of 1897 confined Italy's sphere to an area up to 180 miles from the coast, which left the Ogaden to Ethiopia. The empire thus could expand at a very low cost. The historical Abyssinians now, however, constituted only one-third of the total population, with most of the new subjects being Oromo or Somali

Muslims, and Negro animists. The newly conquered south became a Shoan colony, with allied Oromo notables sharing in the spoils under a system of exploitation that transformed the local population into tenants on their own land, and into chattel in a thriving slave trade.[8]

The effects of partition on the Somalis were more ambiguous. The Somali people have been termed a *pastoral democracy,* consisting of loosely associated clans sharing many cultural elements but without a comprehensive political organization.[9] From one perspective, partition imposed unpredecented divisions: The northern nomads were distributed among three different jurisdictions, French Djibouti, British Somaliland, and Ethiopia (the Haud); and the southerners among two, Italian Somalia and again Ethiopia (the Ogaden). But from another perspective, by bringing together disparate clans into two Somali-dominant entities—British Somaliland in the north and Italian Somalia in the south—partition launched the Somali people on the path of state-formation. These contradictory dynamics shaped the orientation of Somali nationalism in the epoch of decolonization and its aftermath. In particular, they fostered a determination to reunite the fragments, an objective that could be achieved only at the expense of Ethiopia.

Despite halting attempts at modernization from above, notably the founding of a new permanent capital at Addis Ababa and the creation of a handful of ministries staffed by officials selected from outside the traditional ruling families, the Ethiopian empire remained very much a patrimonial one-man show. Menelik's terminal illness (1906) inaugurated a struggle for succession that lasted nearly a quarter of a century. Emerging as the leading contender in the wake of World War I, Ras Tafari Makonnen ascended to the throne by the usual caesarist means and in 1930 was proclaimed emperor under the name of Haile Selassie. Resuming Menelik's efforts to strengthen the imperial center, Haile Selassie considerably reduced the autonomy of regional magnates and of the church and covered the empire with a veneer of modern political institutions; but beneath this, the traditional system largely prevailed.[10]

Between 1935 and 1952, external factors once again intervened to change the Horn's political configuration. These changes were triggered by the imperial ambitions of the Italian Fascist regime, which in 1935 crushed Ethiopia by way of a pincer movement from Eritrea and Somalia. For the first time, most of the Horn was united into a single political entity. Claiming inspiration from the Roman model, the Italians had already imposed on Somalia an elaborate structure of direct administration and built up an extensive network of roads; they also invested heavily in export-oriented agriculture. A similar strategy was applied to Eritrea, which was to become a port of entry and industrial zone for the Horn as a whole, as well as a home for Italy's surplus population. Accordingly, the European population grew from five thousand in 1935 to fifty thousand in 1941. Although they imposed terrible burdens on the Africans, these policies also accelerated processes of social transformation that led to the emergence of nationalist indigenous elites in the postwar period.

In Ethiopia also, starting from a baseline close to zero, in five years the colonial government constructed over three thousand miles of road, much of it paved; public buildings proliferated also. Although the cost was met in part by Ethiopian gold and more vigorous tax collection, which entailed brutal repression, there was a considerable influx of Italian capital as well. Surviving the Italian occupation, these practices provided the restored emperor with vastly enhanced resources to consolidate his state. But the occupation also exacerbated center–periphery tensions after the war. Welcomed in a number of Tigrayan and Oromo districts as liberators from Shoan oppression, the Italians exploited ethnic antagonisms to weaken the Ethiopians' resistance and generally favored the Muslims over the hitherto-dominant Coptic Christians.

After expelling the Italians in 1941, the British emerged as the dominant power in the Horn. They restored Haile Selassie to this throne but established what amounted to a protectorate over Ethiopia and assumed control over Eritrea and Somalia while awaiting their disposition by the international community. Britain's liberal colonial policies as well as its competition with Italy for the population's allegiance stimulated the development of organized political activity. In Somalia, the most prominent group was the Somali Youth League, which advocated an end to Italian colonialism and a reunion of all Somali under a four-power trusteeship. In 1949, however, the United Nations decided on an Italian trusteeship for a ten-year period, at the end of which Somalia was to be independent. Most political organizations in British Somaliland also advocated independence and reunion. While recognizing Ethiopian sovereignty over the Ogaden and the Haud, Britain initially kept them under military occupation. Despite the vocal opposition of Somali groups, in 1954 Britain turned both regions over to Ethiopia, but with the proviso that the nomads would retain their autonomy. But, Ethiopia immediately claimed sovereignty over them, prompting an unsuccessful bid by Britain in 1956 to buy back the area. These issues remained unsettled as of 1960, when Somalia and Somaliland became independent and united into a single state, which lost no time in fomenting separatism among Somalis in neighboring states.

Concatenated Conflict

Eritrean Separatism

Eritrea's emerging political life in the postwar years was shaped primarily by the country's religious cleavage. The British census of 1950—the last to date—indicated about equal numbers of Muslims and Copts.[11] The Christian population consisted mostly of Tigrinya-speaking agriculturalists, concentrated in the densely populated central Eritrean highlands from Asmara southward, adjoining Ethiopia's Tigrayans to whom they are closely related; migrating to the cities, they formed the bulk of Eritrea's industrial labor force. The Muslims were mostly pastoral nomads, living in the northern and western highlands and in the adjacent coastal plain north of Massawa, but some Muslim urban dwellers were also connected with the older trade networks. Paralleling its stance in the Indian subcontinent and Palestine, Britain at first advocated partition, with the Christian half of the population going to Ethiopia and the Muslim half to Sudan. The Christian parties leaned toward a union of Eritrea with Ethiopia, whereas the Muslims demanded independence on the model of Somalia. Moved by bargaining among the great powers rather than concern with Eritrean preferences, in 1950 the United Nations decided on federation with Ethiopia, to go into effect two years later. Eritrea was to maintain its parliamentary institutions and retain a distinct cultural identity, including especially its two official languages, Tigrinya and Arabic. But once international controls were lifted, Haile Selassie drastically reduced Eritrea's autonomy and destroyed its political life, as incompatible with Ethiopian autocracy. The region's further development was hampered as well, because preference was given to industrial projects located in the Shoan Amhara country around Addis Ababa. Finally, in 1962 the emperor secured from a puppet Eritrean assembly a vote for outright annexation.

Eritrean separatism originated as the response of the political class to recolonization and authoritarian rule by Ethiopia after 1952. Initially, its Muslim segments were most affected, but by the late 1950s, Ethiopia's stifling government and discriminatory policies alienated numerous Christian leaders as well. In 1958 a handful of Muslim exiles in Cairo launched an Eritrean Liberation Movement. From 1961 onward, however, this was over-shadowed by the Eritrean Liberation Front (ELF), a group of Muslim nationalists and elements of the mostly Christian labor movement, committed to armed struggle. Bene-fiting from a favorable geopolitical situation, the Eritreans gained access to money, weapons, training, and staging bases for guerrilla operations from Arab states that wel-comed the opportunity to weaken Ethiopia, as it was closely associated with the United States and Israel. From 1964 onward, their supporters included the Syrian Ba'ath. Based in adjoining Sudan, where it began by recruiting Eritreans serving in the Sudanese army, the ELF staged operations against local Ethiopian forces in the western lowlands. Sudan's supportive stance was in retaliation for Ethiopia's support of its own southern rebels. The conflict produced a few refugees. Nearly indistinguishable from the traditional movement of nomads, they consisted largely of Muslim herders, who came with their property and animals and settled into a self-sufficient life near the border.

By 1966, the insurgents had achieved control over most of rural western and northern Eritrea and were challenging imperial forces throughout the region. Though at first very limited, Ethiopia's repressive capacity was augmented by U.S. and Israeli counterinsur-gency training conducted near Asmara, the major American base in the Red Sea theater. In 1967, the imperial government staged a massive offensive, resorting to a scorched-earth policy to terrorize Muslim populations of doubtful political loyalty. This drove an estimated 28,000 refugees into the Sudan, where they constituted a pool for the recruit-ment of additional combatants.[12] In return for an Ethiopian commitment to curtail the transit of Israeli assistance to their own southern separatists, in 1967 the Sudanese agreed to relocate the refugees at least fifty miles from the border. ELF operations were further handicapped by the Arab defeat in the Six-Day War with Israel.

International support grew again after 1969 as a consequence of simultaneous regime changes in Libya, Southern Yemen, and especially Sudan. At this time ELF also began receiving aid from Iraq, which sought to offset the influence of Syria. In order to min-imize conflict among its disparate components, ELF organized the expanding liberated territory into autonomous zones, controlled by distinct ethnoreligious factions. Neverthe-less, around 1970 the urban Christian groups coalesced into the more distinctly socialist Eritrean Peoples Liberation Front (EPLF), leaving the ELF a more Muslim body.[13] This provoked an escalation of the intra-Eritrean conflict, which caused an estimated twelve hundred casualties of its own between 1972 and 1974.

In 1971, following the assassination of the provincial military commander, Eritrea was placed under martial law and subjected to what amounted to a foreign military occupation by twenty thousand troops, about half of the standing army total, poorly supplied and hence left largely to fend for themselves. The air force systematically razed villages, whose inhabitants were driven into "strategic hamlets" organized into antiguer-rilla militia units. At the same time, the emperor stepped up diplomatic efforts to stem aid to the rebels. He secured some cooperation from Sudan, faced with a growing refugee burden, and even from Aden, concerned about the fate of the large Yemeni trading population in Ethiopia. In the short run, Ethiopian policies succeeded in reducing the guerrilla activity, but they also further alienated the Eritrean Muslims.

As the flow increased, the refugees competed with the local population for limited grazing lands; there were now also displaced peasants who could not meet their subsistence needs without land. Sudan therefore turned to the UNHCR, which established its first camp in 1970, 350 km south of Kasala. Khartoum at first shunned the involvement of foreign governments or volunteer-service agencies in refugee affairs, and the western governments showed little interest in the refugee situation in Sudan, partly because of their association with Ethiopia.[14] Consequently, a close partnership evolved between the UNHCR and the Sudanese who, as the exclusive implementors of refugee programs, tried to use international aid to solve their own economic problems. The funds were channeled mostly into capital investments—infrastructure and cash-crop schemes—and the refugees were turned into a reserve of cheap labor for the public sector and private entrepreneurs.

The Ethiopian Revolution[15]

Skillfully exploiting the diplomatic opportunities opened up by the new international configuration, in the postwar period Ethiopia's restored emperor secured vastly expanded resources, which he harnessed to the enhancement of his personal authority within an enlarged and more powerful empire. There can be no doubt that Haile Selassie surpassed the achievements of any of his predecessors and will go down in history as the greatest of all Ethiopian emperors, who also achieved a paramount place among the leaders of the new Africa. But the empire itself was an anachronism, and Haile Selassie's very successes at home and abroad contributed to its destruction.

Ruling with the benefit of British support for the better part of a decade, at their behest the emperor established new administrative, fiscal, and political institutions, including the office of prime minister. When Britain withdrew from the international fray, Haile Selassie secured a firm commitment from the United States by sending Ethiopian soldiers to Korea. Although over the next two decades Ethiopia acquired more of the accoutrements of a modern state, including a popularly elected parliament, these changes were largely superficial. Elections took place without the benefit of freedom of association or of political organization, and Ethiopian ministers remained imperial courtiers rather than government officials. Shoan Amhara dominance was further institutionalized: Other groups were greatly underrepresented, with the exception of the Eritreans, whose recruitment was attributable not only to an abundance of qualified personnel in the more developed region but also to an attempt to minimize separatism by means of co-optation.[16]

The emperor's futile efforts to secure the benefits of modernization without changing the fundamentals are well illustrated by his educational policies: Ethiopia was behind even colonial Africa with respect to educational development as a whole. Around 1960, only about 5 percent of the population was literate, one of the lowest rates in the world. Nor was this about to change, as the country also had one of the lowest proportions of schoolage children in school—about 7 percent compared with, for example, 62 percent in neighboring Kenya. The emperor then launched a crash program designed for the narrow purpose of rapidly increasing the number of university graduates, all of whom were expected to enter government service. To prevent the emergence a radical intelligentsia, higher education was entrusted to conservative Westerners, particularly Americans from church-related colleges. Enrollment in Ethiopian institutions rose to approximately 5,400 students by 1970, with nearly 2,000 more studying abroad. But there was little development at other levels; over the next decade the proportion of youngsters in school rose to about 10 percent, but with rates as low as 3 percent in non-Christian rural areas. Despite all efforts to insulate them, university students both at home and abroad became a major source of political opposition.

The emphasis in the economic sphere, was on industrialization, which was accomplished by according land grants to foreign investors practically free and guaranteeing them monopolistic protection as well as a low-wage labor force that was prevented from organizing unions.[17] From 1963 to 1973, agriculture was allotted only 4.2 percent of combined ordinary and capital expenditures, and most of that went to large commercial farms.[18] Although the government admitted that there could be little agriculture development without land reform, land reform was unthinkable because land formed the basis of the system of political domination. Foreign aid agencies' programs to stimulate small-scale commercial farming led to the expulsion of tenants and the takeover of the scheme by large farmers. Overall, the substantial economic growth of the 1960s brought few benefits to the urban masses, except in Addis Ababa, whose inhabitants were personal dependents of the emperor, and none whatsoever to Ethiopia's peasants. On the contrary, given Ethiopia's demographic expansion and erosion, the neglect of agricultural development steadily narrowed the peasants' margin of survival.

In the early 1970s, drought prevailed across the entire continent, but whereas other African victims received aid from their own governments and the international community, little was offered to the Ethiopians because the emperor insistently denied there was a famine at all. Potential donors, including the United States, refrained from interfering for fear of antagonizing him.[19] But by the end of 1973, famine had claimed between 100,000 and 300,000 people in Tigray and Welo, the hardest-hit provinces; thousands of nomads wandered from their accustomed paths and across international boundaries in a desperate search for the means of survival, thereby aggravating border tensions throughout the Horn. Although the famine evoked considerable concern within the Ethiopian intellectual community, teachers and students who sought to organize relief were explicitly prohibited from doing so and severely punished for disobeying the order. This flagrant violation of patrimonial obligation destroyed the last vestiges of legitimacy that the regime had retained among the new educated generation.

As in any empire, the armed forces constituted a doubled-edged sword: As the ultimate enforcers of the emperor's authority, they were also the most likely source of challenge to his rule. After the British withdrawal, the United States established a major base at Asmara and assumed the major responsibility for developing the army; Ethiopia subsequently became the principal recipient of American military aid in Africa. The emperor also obtained assistance from other sources to build up counterweights, in particular, the Imperial Guard.[20] These precautions proved effective in 1960, when a coup launched by U.S.-educated Girmame Neway with support from the Imperial Guard, headed by his older brother, as well as elements of the police and security services, was defeated by the army and air force, with aid from the U.S. military mission and the embassy.[21]

The long-lived emperor's ability to weather the storm, and the absence of popular support for the coup—probably attributable to the speed of the counterthrust—hid from view the growing fragility of the empire itself. In the absence of structural change, the sheer expansion of the scale of government, and the diversification of agencies vastly complicated the task of managing the imperial system by means of traditional techniques. After 1960, most observers thought the empire would survive only if its ruler instituted fundamental modernization and liberalization policies, but genuine institutionalization and delegation of authority were unthinkable because they would reduce his personal power. Having reduced the traditional elites but distrusting the new, Haile Selassie ruled by maintaining an uneasy balance among competing cliques. After the attempted coup, most plans for political reform were shelved as too dangerous.[22]

Meanwhile, the escalating war in Eritrea, an uprising in the south, and irredentist thrusts by Somalia drained an increasing share of governmental resources and fostered the emperor's growing dependence on the armed forces. This in turn emboldened them to bargain for a bigger piece of the pie, and there were frequent mutinies on behalf of better pay and conditions, to which the emperor generally gave in.[23] With the country in the throes of famine, in early 1974 yet another string of disturbances erupted among the armed forces, beginning among the enlisted ranks and NCOs of a southern army garrison then spreading to an air force base near Addis Ababa, and culminating on February 25 in a generalized uprising of the Second Division in Eritrea. Over the next few months, power among the insurgents gravitated into the hands of self-appointed committees of middle- and junior-rank officers, who formed successive coordination committees at the national level.

The Ethiopian revolution unfolded into a rapid collapse of the *ancien régime* and the much slower formation of a new power center. The lifting of the lid produced an extended "moment of madness," with a flowering of broadly based political organizations and a proliferation of innovative ideological discourse. With the armed forces out of commission, protestors with long-accumulated grievances could act with impunity. Beginning in mid-February 1974, there was an outburst of strikes and demonstrations in Addis Ababa, by prostitutes to priests, but including most prominently urban workers, both labor unions and the unorganized. But the emperor's indecisive reshuffling of government personnel revealed unsuspected weaknesses, and the limited reforms he belatedly proposed were obviously insufficient. In March there was an uprising among Oromo tenants on the big farms south of the capital, probably stimulated by the spontaneous network that formed among teachers and students in small towns throughout the country. More uprisings followed in other parts of the country. By the middle of the year, the provincial administration was nearing collapse.

Appointed as a crisis manager, Prime Minister Endelkachew, a modernist member of the old aristocracy with good connections among the new professionals, solicited the aid of the military coordination committee in containing the popular upheavals, in exchange for a commitment to the establishment of a constitutional monarchy. However, the insurgent officers demanded as a prior condition the arrest of corrupt officials, particularly those responsible for mismanaging the famine. When they failed to obtain satisfaction, the radicals created a second coordination committee, which proceeded to carry out the arrests without official sanction. Known as the Derg (Amharic for "committee"), this body began rounding up its targets in late June 1974. Despite proclaiming their loyalty to the emperor and commitment to a civilian regime, the radicals cut out the imperial institutions one by one, until only the emperor himself was left. Finally, on September 12, the Derg announced that Haile Selassie had been deposed and proclaimed a Provisional Military Administrative Council (PMAC), chaired by general Aman Michael Andom. Himself not a member of the Derg, Aman was flanked by two vice-chairmen, Major Atnafu Abate and Major Mengistu Haile Mariam.

Only two months later, after refusing to order new troops to Eritrea, the PMAC chairman was dismissed and then executed. Most of the emperor's relatives, courtiers, and dependents were imprisoned before they could escape; hence the wave of *ancien régime* refugees was unusually small. Some of those in captivity were later executed; Haile Selassie himself died a year later.

As the patrimonial center built up by Haile Selassie over nearly six decades of rule began to crumble, under pressure of the radical groups that had sprung up throughout Ethiopia, what had started out as a military coup evolved into a social revolution. The crucial turning point was the Derg's radically egalitarian land reform of March 1975, which parceled out large holdings to peasant families and prohibited the use of paid labor in agriculture. This obliterated at one stroke the material base of the *ancien régime* and removed the underpinnings of local and provincial administration. The reform also dramatically redistributed income from the urban to the rural areas, as the peasants retained a much larger share of their production for self-consumption, while the price of food in the cities escalated. In the face of urban discontent, in July the Derg decreed an equally radical "urban land reform" that sharply lowered rents.

In classic fashion, as it constructed a revolutionary government, the Derg clashed simultaneously with defenders of the *ancien régime,* competing revolutionary organizations—including some of its own creatures that got out of hand—and peripheries that sought to increase their autonomy. Immediately upon taking power, the Derg crushed the myriad autonomous associations that had sprung up in the urban areas and prohibited strikes. In conjunction with the land reform, it despatched revolutionary students and teachers to organize peasant associations that would function as both producer cooperatives and units of local government. Many of them escaped the Derg's control, however, and challenged its policies. Similar developments took place in the urban sector. On the first anniversary of the emperor's deposition, parading workers and students shouted antimilitary slogans. Shortly afterwards they launched a general strike, to which the Derg responded with martial law and over fifteen hundred arrests. The military also entrusted to civilians the establishment of a cadre party on the Soviet model. But, the organizers seized the opportunity to create their own, more pro-Soviet, All-Ethiopian Socialist Movement (MEISON).

Around mid-1976, the conflict crystallized around three major actors: Mengistu and his faction in the Derg, together with their rudimentary cadre party known as the Political Bureau, which itself escaped their control; MEISON; and the Ethiopian People's Revolutionary Party (EPRP), a radical offshoot of the student movement that also encompassed remnants of the labor unions. The contest produced nearly two years of extremely violent terror and counterterror, at the end of which Mengistu and his men had gained the upper hand. Beginning as a loosely constituted assembly of about 120 members, broadly representative of all the services and many ethnic groups, by the end of 1976 the Derg had transformed itself into a more tightly structured and smaller executive body, dominated by Amharas, which after further internecine conflict was brought under Mengistu's autocratic control. Over 5,000 secondary and university students, as well as labor militants, were killed in the course of the "red terror," with estimates of the slaughter ranging up to 30,000. A few thousand were able to escape abroad, mostly to the United States under student visas.

The Derg's triumph over the leftist opposition of the 1970s left it in control of the capital and towns, which it consolidated through a dense network of "urban dwellers' associations" (*kebelles*). In the rural areas the situation varied considerably. In the large estates of central and southern Ethiopia, acquired by the expanding empire in the late nineteenth century, the liberation of serflike tenants by means of land reform ensured their fundamental support for the new regime. This inhibited further growth of the Oromo Liberation Front, which had arisen in the 1960s as a tenants' movement. Farther north, in the provinces of historic Abyssinia, where the peasants mostly owned their own land, the situation was different: Gojam joined the revolution, but Tigray and to some extent Gonder spawned insurgencies.[24] Initially, the most promising opposition movement appeared to be the Tigrean Liberation Front, which was formed by the region's aristocratic governor and which became the core of the Ethiopian Democratic Union, a guerrilla movement based in Sudan that was promoted in Washington as prospective "freedom fighters" worthy of support. But precisely because of its Tigrean and aristocratic character, the organization failed to become a rallying point.[25] Within Tigray itself it was eliminated by the more radical Tigrean People's Liberation Forces (TPLF), a more explicitly separatist movement closely allied with the EPLF, from which it received substantial support. The TPLF suffered heavy losses in 1978 but was able to rebuild quickly with an infusion of refugees from the "red terror" and subsequently gained control over much of the province.

The nomads, who were also Muslims, mostly saw the revolution as an opportunity to escape control by the center. Separatist groups in the lowland peripheries included the Somali and Abbo Liberation Front (SALF), the Western Somali Liberation Front (WSLF), the Afar Liberation Front, and the Sidama Liberation Movement, all but the Afar movement supported by Somalia. The most important were the SALF (in Sidamo and Bale) and the WSLF (in the Ogaden), led by returning refugees from earlier uprisings.

By 1977 there were uprisings in nine out of fourteen provinces besides Eritrea, and a strong prospect that these center–periphery conflicts might quite literally tear Ethiopia apart and fatally undermine the viability of the revolutionary center. However, the Derg secured massive assistance from the Soviet Union that enabled it not only to survive the immediate crisis but also to institutionalize the revolution. Although the new government still received military assistance from the United States, in July 1976 the Derg indicated to the Soviet Union its interest in switching patrons. The Soviets already had an alliance with Somalia, but they may have thought it possible to establish close ties with both states simultaneously and undoubtedly decided that if it were not, Ethiopia would be the more valuable client of the two.[26] The crucial organizational changes made by the Derg in the following months were probably prompted in part by ongoing negotiations. By the end of 1976, the PMAC had declared itself Marxist-Leninist and secured a pledge from the Soviet Union of $100 million in military assistance.

Somalia and the Ogaden Conflict

After independence, the question of reunification moved to the forefront of political controversy. But while the bickering politicians charged one another with lacking determination, all of them were bound by a common constraint against irredentist action. In short, political life was shaped by the dynamics of coalition making among the several clan-families and their constituent lineages, in a manner akin to the interactions among ethnic groups in other parts of Africa.[27] The Darod were already the largest of the six clan-families in Somalia, and most of the Somalis in the Ogaden were Darod as well. Hence all other clans shared an interest in avoiding the reality of reunification, and Darod politicians themselves could not pursue reunification too vigorously lest they precipitate the formation of a broad countercoalition.[28]

The external configuration first acted as a constraint as well. Somalia faced a vastly superior Ethiopian military establishment, trained and equipped by the United States, which held out the promise of economic aid in exchange for restraint. Moreover, the newly formed Organization for African Unity—based in Addis Ababa—was committed to maintaining established boundaries and insisted that self-determination apply only to white-ruled territories. Somalia thus encouraged foreign Somali to challenge their respective governments and repeatedly clashed with the latter but refrained from major confrontations and even negotiated regional detente.[29] In 1964 Somalia provided logistical support to the uprising in Ethiopia's Bale Province and after 1970 provided a refugee to the defeated insurgents. It also initiated the formation of the WLSF in the Ogaden itself. At the same time Somalia began to build up its armed forces with assistance from the Soviet Union, which was determined to establish itself in the strategically vital Red Sea region, and its numbers increased rapidly from a mere four thousand at the time of Somalia's independence to eighteen thousand by 1969.[30]

The gap between irredentist rhetoric and restrained action dealt the coup de grâce to Somalia's postindependence political class, already discredited by the lack of economic development and the egregious corruption. In 1969 the army staged a coup with the support of the police. Emerging as head of the Supreme Revolutionary Council was Major General M. Siad Barre, a Darod whose mother was an Ogadeni.[31] Despite rejecting the commitment to regional detente, Siad Barre initially remained very cautious and, even as late as 1975, cracked down on advocates of intervention on the grounds that they invited Ethiopian provocation. But he further stepped up the military buildup with Soviet aid; the manpower level tripled from 18,000 in 1969 to 53,000 in 1977, with special emphasis on armor and the air force. Meanwhile, the stakes in the Ogaden escalated with the discovery in 1973 of natural gas deposits thirty miles on the Ethiopian side of the border.

The 1973–74 drought had catastrophic consequences for the contested region, already tottering on the brink of disaster owing to overgrazing. Although the new Ethiopian government tried to provide some relief to the victims, they did so by concentrating the local population in camps, a highly suspect operation that the army conducted with a heavy hand. Most of the able-bodied men stayed out with their dwindling herds and linked up with the resurgent WSLF, which reoganized itself into separate Somali and Oromo wings. This provoked severe Ethiopian repression, which in turn stimulated more widespread mobilization in support of the guerrilla forces.

By 1976 it was evident that the Derg would, if anything, pursue an even more centralizing policy than its imperial predecessor had. With the bulk of Ethiopian forces tied down in Eritrea and chaotic conditions at the center, Siad Barre could take the risk of a more aggressive policy, the more so as the impending Soviet commitment to the PMAC would soon restore and even reinforce Ethiopia's advantage.[32] In early 1977, Somalia for the first time encouraged the WSLF to engage in direct combat against Ethiopian troops from base camps on its side of the border. By June, the WSLF forces, numbering between three thousand and five thousand, controlled most of the Ogaden and cut the Addis-Djibouti Railroad, Ethiopia's principal import–export route. The Somali armored forces rolled in on July 23 and advanced rapidly toward Jijiga, which fell on September 13, after which the war settled to a standoff on the Marda Pass between Jijiga and Harer.[33] However, a week later the Soviets launched a massive airlift that within a few weeks brought the defensive forces to fifty thousand Ethiopians and eleven thousand Cubans, coordinated under the command of fifteen hundred Soviet advisers. Although the Somalis briefly captured Harer at the end of November, they were unable to hold the city, and their position steadily deteriorated because of logistical weakness. After the failure of a Western-sponsored negotiated settlement, a counteroffensive was launched in late January 1978, with assurances from Ethiopia and the Soviet Union to the United States that they would not attack Somalia itself. Jijiga was retaken on March 5, and the Somalis began withdrawing four days later.

The counterattack precipitated the first wave of refugees into Somalia, as much of the local population fled the effects of the war itself and the anticipated Ethiopian revenge. But, many of the men stayed behind to fight on with the guerrilla forces. Somalia's heavy losses, which amounted to one-third of its prewar army and an even larger share of its materiél, precluded another offensive. Some small units of the Somali army, however, remained in the Ogaden and continued to stage operations with the WSLF.[34] Ethiopia, which lacked the means of establishing a regular military occupation, resorted to a scorched-earth policy designed not only to cut off local support for the guerrillas but also to drive out the pastoralist population so as to make room for the settlement of non-Somali agriculturalists along the relatively fertile river valleys along the border. A similar policy was pursued in Bale Province.[35] Steadily weakening, at the end of 1980 Somalia withdrew the remnants of its army; the Ethiopians drove on to the border; and a second major wave of refugees poured out.[36] The conflict then declined to the level of intermittent border clashes.

The number of refugees in Somalia emerged early on as a contentious issue. In mid-1978, the Somalian government asserted that there were already half a million, whereas the UNHCR estimated only 80,000. Following the second wave, in 1981 the Somalian claim rose to as high as 2 million, but estimates by U.N. experts and international aid agencies ranged between 450,000 and 620,000; the UNHCR settled, for planning purposes, on a compromise figure of 650,000.[37] There were, in addition, about 45,000 refugees from the Ogaden in neighboring Djibouti. Numbers fluctuated over the next several years as the result of both organized and unorganized repatriation as well as new arrivals. About 300,000 returnees were counted in Ethiopia's Haraghe Province as of 1984; 30,000 of them were from Djibouti, repatriated under what many observers insisted were involuntary conditions. In any case, the program was halted at the onset of the 1984 drought.[38]

Somali officials often use statistics as a rhetorical device, and it was to their advantage to inflate the refugee statistics for both propaganda purposes and to maximize international assistance.[39] Moreover, in 1980 many native Somalis were made homeless and destitute by a severe drought and turned to the camps for assistance. International voluntary agencies reported that the camps were open to the population of nearby villages and charged that the police and the army were trucking them in for statistical purposes. In any case, given the extremely low level of administrative organization that prevails in the Horn as a whole and the nomadic character of much of the population affected, it is almost impossible to sort out "native" from "foreign" Somalis or to determine the precise cause of their movement. We believe that as many as one million were displaced from Ethiopia to Somalia by violence and famine at the 1981 high point.[40] According to these figures, the refugees increased Somalia's population by about one-fifth but as much as doubled that of the receiving regions.

From the outset, both official reports and independent observers emphasized the very high proportion of women and children.[41] This is consistent with reports that able-bodied men initially stayed behind to fight on with the WSLF and the OLF. It should be noted, however, that ecological constraints made it extremely difficult to supply the grazing

needs of a much larger number of nomadic herdsmen in Somalia alone. Economic survival thus required the men to wander in and out of Ethiopian territory, where they clashed
with Ethiopian forces, whose objective was precisely to prevent them from making a
living in the area. In February 1983, the quiescent WSLF announced the resumption of
hit-and-run operations, but there were few signs of activity after that announcement. In
keeping with the logic of its irredentist stance, Somalia applied to refugees who were
ethnically Somali a sort of informal "law of return," but by the same token, able-bodied
men were liable to military service. Viewed as impressment, the rounding up of the camp
population brought repeated protests from UNHCR.[42]

Eritrea After the Revolution

The collapse of the imperial regime in 1974 and the onset of revolution brought about a
dramatic change in Eritrea, to the advantage of the secessionists. A de facto cease-fire
went into effect while Eritrean leaders awaited actions by the Derg, which initially
included some Eritreans and others favorable to a compromise settlement. Meanwhile the
organizations consolidated their positions. In January 1975, after the hard-liners had won
out, the ELF and EPLF launched a joint operation against Asmara, successfully fighting
their way into the streets of the city. Ethiopian forces retaliated as they had before, with
air and artillery attacks that killed thousands of villagers and drove tens of thousands more
into Sudan. The following year, the Derg mobilized a huge "peasant crusade" against the
rebels. Although this demonstrated a high level of organizational capacity, the force soon
began falling apart and was routed by the Eritreans and their TPLF allies. An offer of very
limited regional autonomy was then rejected by both Eritrean movements.[43] Taking
advantage of the reassignment of Ethiopia's best forces to the Ogaden, by year's end they
controlled most of the region and the access roads, bottling up Ethiopian garrisons in
Asmara and the ports, where they were supplied by air and sea. For reasons that are not
clear, however, the Eritrean surge then ended.

At the end of 1976 there were an estimated 350,000 displaced persons in Eritrea and
over 100,000 refugees in Sudan, growing to perhaps double that number in the following
year. Many of the refugees were in camps operated by the insurgents, which functioned
as extensions of the liberated zones. The key to the insurgents' success was their ability
to secure logistical support from bases in the Sudan, where, in addition to the camps, they
established hospitals, schools, communication and training centers, and facilities to repair
equipment captured from the Ethiopians and to manufacture ammunition. The EPLF grew
into a well-structured mass organization of 25,000 to 30,000 members, mostly highland-
ers of both religions, of above-average education and organized into peasant and worker
units. Although the EPLF was the more radical of the two movements, its support still
came mostly from the more conservative Arab states.[44] The ELF leadership, on the other
hand, consisted of an uneasy coalition of Muslim traditionalists and younger radicals
linked with the Iraqi Ba'ath. Both organizations experienced considerable internecine
conflict and recurrently clashed with each other as well.

After their victory in the Ogaden, the Ethiopian leadership resumed operations in
Eritrea on an expanded scale, made possible by assistance from its new allies. Although
both the Soviet Union and Cuba welcomed the Eritrean uprising as "progressive" and
continued to urge publicly a political solution, the Soviets showed little hesitation in
switching sides, because the Eritrean ports were a valuable part of the Ethiopian prize.[45]
In March 1978, sixty thousand to eighty thousand Ethiopians were redeployed for a

succession of carefully planned ground, air, and amphibious offensives. The reversal was nearly complete: By the end of the year Ethiopia had retaken all the towns and controlled about three-fourths of Eritrean territory, leaving the insurgents with only the northeastern corner of the region, but with access by road into the Sudan. The offensives dealt the ELF a crippling blow and encouraged the defection of the survivors to the EPLF. These remnants took on a fundamentalist cast, moving close to Iran and purging militant Ba'athists from its ranks.[46]

Much of the population of the reconquered zones withdrew with the guerrillas into Sudan, raising the refugee total to between 280,000 and 400,000. The arrivals coincided with the onset of severe floods and disastrous economic conditions in the receiving region; they included a considerable number of urban dwellers who were unlikely to become self-supporting, and many of them were Christian. In response, the Sudanese government again sought an accommodation with Ethiopia. Concurrently, the refugees were evicted from cities and self-initiated settlements and were concentrated in government-sponsored locations so as to control their political and military activities. But the refugees resisted relocation because the poorly administered government camps were economically unviable and insalubrious. As of 1981, only 20 percent had been resettled under government supervision; nevertheless, these programs absorbed 90 percent of the UNHCR's funds.

In effect, both the EPLF and the ELF continued to operate their camps. Observers, admittedly sympathetic to the Eritrean cause, have drawn a sharp contrast between the deplorable state of Sudanese-run operations and those under the control of the insurgents. One of them, established by the EPLF during its retreat in 1978, was described in the following year as "an oasis of hope for close to 10,000 people."[47] The reports either remain silent on the role of these camps as military bases or explicitly deny any direct links with the operational wing of the sponsoring organizations, but they also indicate that the Sudanese government had no control over what went on in them. Furthermore, it is evident that the political education that the organizers provided was designed to encourage participation in the war and that by sustaining the dependents the camps freed the men for combat. As in Somalia, a very high proportion of the camp households were headed by women.

After 1978 the Eritrean conflict turned into an inconclusive war of attrition, interspersed by equally inconclusive negotiations. Ethiopia repeatedly staged massive offensives to dislodge the Eritreans from their territorial foothold but failed to do so definitively. The Eritreans, in turn, tried in vain to regain the initiative and enlarge their territorial domain. Both sides, however, succeeded in inflicting severe losses on the other. Each successive Ethiopian offensive created more displaced persons. As of early 1984, Sudan estimated there were all together some 460,000 Ethiopian refugees, about 50,000 to 100,000 from Tigre, with the remainder Eritrean.[48]

The host government continued to use the refugees as pawns in its external policy, sometimes tolerating military activities along the border as a way of putting pressure on Ethiopia and sometimes relocating them inland as prelude to a rapprochement.[49] In September 1980, the Derg proclaimed a general amnesty for the Sudan-based guerrillas, with the assurance that they would be allowed to return to their homes after three months of reeducation in a transit camp. Over the next several months, government sources claimed that 10,000 guerillas had accepted the offer and that 70,000 civilians had returned home.[50] After these claims proved unfounded, Western relief agencies became more active. As noted, U.S. aid substantially increased when Sudan emerged as an important element in the containment of Libya and entered into negotiations to establish American bases.

Famine and Its Aftermath

The Soviet-Cuban commitment ensured not only the integrity of Ethiopia but also the survival of the PMAC. Even skeptical observers regard the leadership's organizational achievements over the next decade as extraordinarily impressive, a success probably faciliated by the persistence of imperial traditions, including the authoritarian culture of the Ethiopian church. Attributing the highest priority to the constitution of an effective political cadre, in 1979 the PMAC launched the Commission for the Organization of the Ethiopian Workers' Party (COPWE). Over the next decade thousands of cadres were trained in the Soviet bloc, and many more in political schools in Ethiopia. The PWE was formally inaugurated in 1984, on the tenth anniversary of the revolution, but became fully effective only in 1987, at which time the regime proceeded to establish a full panoply of institutions on the Soviet model. Remaining officials from the imperial regime, or revolutionaries who resisted party discipline, were ousted or defected. Although many of the leaders came from the armed forces, Ethiopia was no longer a military regime but a People's Democratic Republic. Mengistu, however, maneuvered to maintain the army itself as a relatively autonomous body in relation to the PWE, so as to ensure that he would not be eliminated in favor of a more docile Soviet client.

Although the center–periphery tensions persisted, the reorganized state regained the upper hand throughout Ethiopia except in Tigray and Eritrea, to which it was able to hang on only at an extremely high cost that could be borne only because of continued support from the Soviet Union. The state's organizational capacity was harnessed to major structural transformations. Some of these, such as the literacy program, have unquestionably been successful. In agriculture, however, the record is at best mixed and regarded by many as a tragic failure. The main problem is Ethiopia's declining ability to produce a surplus for consumption in the towns—let alone for export—and, in some areas, even to feed the rural population itself. The margin of subsistence has always been extremely thin, with the specter of famine ever present. Despite its good intentions, the land reform may have worsened the situation.[51] The government undoubtedly erred in giving a much larger share of investments to nationalized commercial farms than to the vastly enlarged smallholder sector, which has minimized the incentive to produce agricultural surpluses, by keeping prices very low. The peasants therefore retreated from the market into subsistence production, but under increasing demographic pressures.

These trends, compounded by violence in many parts of the country, has made the country more vulnerable to famine in case of drought, as occurred in 1984. The PMAC was severely criticized for its reaction to the famine: It has been charged that, like its imperial predecessor, the PMAC initially ignored the catastrophe because of its single-minded concentration on the anniversary of the revolution. Although the government relented and eventually appealed for international assistance, it is charged further that it obstructed the work of humanitarian agencies by assigning higher priority to the unloading of military equipment than to food and further denying the agencies' access to the areas of insurgency in Tigray and Eritrea, which were among the worst hit.[52] Under those conditions, many had no alternative but to flee to Sudan.

The most controversial policies were the resettlement and "villagization" programs. Because of the widespread attention they received, it is important to note that the resettlement programs were not invented by the PMAC but by a 1973 World Bank recommendation for the relocation of peasants from Tigrai and other northern areas suffering from population pressure, erosion, and deforestation, to underutilized parts of the south. The fact that these areas later gave birth to secessionist insurrections undoubtedly persuaded the leadership to carry out the recommendation as soon as possible. Preparatory plans provided for voluntary relocation, the participants to receive considerable infrastructural and logistical support from the government. But as late as 1983, officials remained hesitant because the program entailed extremely complex operations, requiring considerable financial and organizational resources. However, with the onset of the famine, the government declared its intention to move 1.5 million people within a year. Then the program came under heavy attack on the grounds that it was politically motivated, involving involuntary impressment and transport under brutal conditions. It was further charged that the regions of destination were overpopulated and unsuitable for the sorts of crops that northerners knew how to grow, as well as ecologically fragile, and that the government failed to provide sufficient food for the settlers until the first harvest. Mounting international criticism led the government to suspend operations in March 1986, but only after some 800,000 peasants had been resettled.

The program is difficult to evaluate because of the lack of qualified observers and reliable data. There is no doubt that the relocation produced extreme hardship—some say as many as 100,000 deaths—and prompted many to flee across the border to Sudan. But it should be noted too that the prospects in the regions of origin were dreadful as well, including starvation for many and an economic dead end for the survivors.

The government's motives for "villagization"—the concentration of peasant households within their own region—were also unclear. Paralleling the creation of *ujaama* villages in Tanzania, the program was designed to boost productivity by offering extension services as well as seeds, fertilizers, and equipment. But it was also a way of increasing state control over the peasants. As first undertaken in Bale and Harague between 1978 and 1984, villagization amounted to an antiguerrilla strategy, similar to that practiced by colonial authorities, to inhibit secessionist insurgency among Somalis and Oromos and to protect Christian settlers against attacks by local Muslims. A more extensive program was undertaken during the 1985–86 interim between the harvesting and planting seasons in provinces south of Addis Ababa, affecting 33 percent of Ethiopia's farming population; 4.6 million peasants, or 12 percent of the total rural population, were relocated in 4,500 villages. That program, too, has drawn considerable criticism, on the grounds that coercion was used and that the government was unwise to institute a disruptive program at a time when the country was suffering from severe food deficits. Moreover, analysts estimate that the long-term effects on agricultural production are likely to be negative. Enforced villagization was cited by many arrivals in northwestern Somalia during this period as the reason for their flight.

The famine drove nearly half a million people to seek relief across the Sudanese border in 1984–85. The population of the camp at Wad Sherife alone soared to 128,000. Movement from Tigray was coordinated by the TPLF, which returned the people to Ethiopia after the crisis was over, having meanwhile used their sojourn in the camps to enlist many into the movement. At the end of 1986, according to the Sudanese government, the number of Ethiopian refugees stood at 677,000; UNHCR assistance for Sudanese refugees as a whole topped $100 million, of which over half was emergency relief operations for famine victims. All but about 100,000 people had been resettled, either self-sufficient in agriculture or employed in the commercial agricultural sector, with a small number in the major cities. However, the catastrophic decline of the Sudanese economy and the resurgence of internal violence encouraged the growing animosity toward the refugees.

The Somalian government also reported another 140,000 arrivals from the Ogaden region from late 1984 through 1986 as the result of famine and villagization; a first wave of 107,000 included both Somali and Oromo, a second some 32,000 Oromos. Several of the receiving centers along the border in northwestern Somalia had to be shut down after an outbreak of cholera in 1986. At the same time, however, Ethiopia and Somalia initiated negotiations to settle their territorial disputes, and Somalia reduced its support for separatist guerrillas. This in turn fostered a sizable repatriation movement, estimated at about 100,000 from 1985 to the end of 1987. After accounting for returnees and new arrivals, international relief agencies estimated the overall number of refugees in Somalia in late 1987 to be 430,000, approximately half the government figure.[53] There were forty-one centers located in four different regions, with populations ranging up to 30,000; the majority of the refugees were women and children.

The UNHCR indicated in 1987 that the remaining refugees had to choose between repatriation and integration. But despite negotiations, it appeared unlikely that the question of the Ogaden would be settled soon, that most of those there now would probably remain in Somalia, whose government has indicated that those who become economically self-sufficient would be granted citizenship. Long-term plans include the transformation of nomadic herdsmen into settled agriculturalists. Suitable land, however, is extremely limited, and conflicts have arisen wherever the refugees appear to be competing with the local population for benefits or scarce resources.[54]

Given the nature of the political process in Somalia, the situation of the refugees varies with their ethnic identity (i.e., Somali or Oromo) and clan affiliation. The situation will remain generally precarious because of economic and political conditions in the receiving country, which have produced refugees from Somalia also. The 1978 defeat precipitated an attempted coup by disgruntled army officers, mostly of the Mayerteyn clan-family, but Siad Barre survived, meting out severe repression and relying increasingly on his own kinsmen, particularly with respect to control of the armed forces. Bolstered by military support from the United States, in 1980 Siad Barre invoked the growing Ethiopian danger and the refugee crisis to reinstate military rule under the SRC. By the following year there were reported to be as many as five thousand political detainees.[55] Mayertein exiles formed an opposition movement based in Addis Ababa, with backing from Libya, and, a separatist movement emerged in the north (former British Somaliland), with support mostly from the Isaq clan that dominates the region. In 1982 the opposition groups united as the National Somali Movement (NSM) and began staging border raids with Ethiopian assistance. The movement gained considerable ground in the north, and as of late 1987 there were thirteen thousand refugees from that region in Ethiopia's Hararghe Province.[56] Somalia faced an impending succession crisis as Siad Barre reached age seventy and was severely injured in an automobile accident. The ensuing conflict was likely to crystallize around clan lines and include the refugees as well.

At the end of 1986, the Djibouti government hosted only 15,287 recognized refugees from Ethiopia, the bulk of them in camps; but there were another 50,000 to 150,000 Ethiopian and Somalian migrants, driven by economic necessity and perhaps violence as well, who were regarded as illegal aliens. The government continued to exert pressure to repatriate the unwanted refugees, and persons outside the camps who applied for asylum were often deported.

Resettlement outside the Horn remains unlikely. Of the estimated 45,000 Ethiopians in the United States, a very small number are from the first wave, that is, officials from the imperial regime who were not executed or arrested, and their families. Most are from the second wave, students involved in or associated with the leftist opposition of 1977–78, who managed to escape as students.[57] Living in limbo, they for the most part obtained extended voluntary departure. Ethiopians have accounted for about 90 percent of African refugees admitted under the 1980 law, but the annual quota was initially only 3,000, later reduced to 2,500. Canada and Australia also receive some Ethiopians under small annual quotas for African refugees, 1,500 and 200, respectively.

Other Western countries have been extremely reluctant to give asylum to Ethiopians, with the exception of Israel, which after the revolution organized the exodus of Ethiopian Jews, earlier known by the Amharic term Falasha but who call themselves Beta Israel.[58] Although the interest of Western Jews in this ancient community originated in the nineteenth century—when they became the object of some philanthropic assistance—the thirty thousand Beta Israelis were recognized as Jews by Israeli rabbinical authorities only in 1975. A poor landless group concentrated in Gonder, they benefited from some degree of imperial protection by virtue of the Solomonic myth. After the revolution, however, they were targeted for persecution by the reactionary EDU for their support of land reform, as well as by the radical EPRP for being Zionists. A few of them began to leave for Sudan, where their presence was hushed up because the government was Islamic. In 1980, Israeli Prime Minister Menachem Begin entrusted to the Mossad (Israeli Secret Service) an operation to relocate the refugees in Israel. About six thousand were spirited out of Sudan between 1979 and 1984, with the cooperation of the Sudanese authorities under pressure from the United States, and perhaps of Ethiopia as well. With numbers escalating as the result of the famine, another seven thousand were taken out in November 1984. The operation ended in January 1985 after it was publicized by the Western press. But, despite public protests, Sudan and Ethiopia quietly cooperated in the removal of several thousand more. Although they were citizens of Israel under the law of return, the Beta Israel were forced to undergo unaccustomed rituals to affirm their religious status, which they protested as humiliating.[59]

African Prospects

The African refugee crisis is best understood as a composite phenomenon that can be divided into three major components, each of which has a distinct configuration composed of deeply rooted structural factors and more circumstantial ones. However, common to sub-Saharan Africa as a whole are structural factors that stem from the continent's ancient history, colonial experience, and situation in relation to the current world economy, making for weak economies and weak states. It is now widely recognized that because of this, Africa faces more severe developmental problems than does any other region of the world, and because this condition pertains to each component, the overall prospects for resolving the refugee crisis in the foreseeable future are not good.[60] Within this gloomy framework, the situation differs somewhat with respect to each component, in relation to which we must distinguish further among (1) the disposition of refugees produced by past conflicts, (2) the likelihood that the conflicts that produced them will themselves be resolved or flare up again, and (3) the probability that other conflicts will erupt among the countries considered as case studies or others that have a similar configuration.

The New States

The problems of weak states with weak economies cannot be remedied by revolution or rapid structural change; weak states do not have the leverage to bring about such change, and the low absolute level of production means that it is difficult to accumulate a critical mass for social investment by even the most devoted of elites. The application of market mechanisms is disastrous as well, because many of the countries concerned are in the grips of an agonizing dilemma, with the choice of concentrating on subsistence, which forecloses prospects of significant investments, or diverting their energies to agriculture for export, thus exacerbating the subsistence crisis, rendered steadily more acute by the onset of rapid demographic expansion.

The few positive exceptions in sub-Saharan Africa appear to be attributed to astute patrimonial management achieved by a mix of carrot and stick, coupled with a willingness to make the best of Africa's bad situation in relation to the international capitalist economy, by eschewing challenges while establishing relationships with patrons willing and able to provide a slightly larger share of benefits. Such a development also provides the wherewithal for political maneuver, making it possible to expand the network of clientele to encompass groups that can exert some leverage. Having weathered the storms of the first quarter-century, a handful of states are on the threshold of moving out of the weakest category.

Others, however, continue to hover on the brink of catastrophe, and sooner or later one or more of these catastrophes will in fact occur, triggering renewed violence and flight.[61] Among those considered in Chapter 2, it is evident that despite the temporary stabilization that led to substantial repatriation, neither Uganda nor Chad are out of the woods. Most of the refugees who originated in Rwanda in the 1960s and Burundi in the 1970s are unlikely to return. Some are well on the way to becoming settlers in neighboring countries (including Rwanda and Burundi themselves), and under appropriate conditions, including sustained international assistance to the receivers, others might follow suit. However, large remnants of the original target populations in the countries of origin could be subjected to renewed attacks. This in fact occurred in Burundi in August 1988.

Sudan's renewed civil war has again produced large flows, and the country as a whole appears on the verge of collapse. A particularly ominous development following Hissen Habré's victory over Libya was Libya's use of Sudan as a base for operations against Chad, a step that further links Africa's enlarged northwestern quadrant with the Middle East arena.[62] Within such a framework, long-established tensions between Ethiopia and Sudan also might flare up into more open international conflict.

Prominent among other new states at serious risk are Zaire and Nigeria, both of which have experienced severe conflicts in the past. Although they are currently dormant, the conditions that brought them about have not fundamentally changed, and new problems have arisen as well. In the case of Nigeria, these prospects are mitigated by the haunting experience of civil war itself, which has acted as a restraint on the key political actors; the subsequent experience of reconciliation; and return to political bargaining, even within the limits of successive military regimes. Zaire, however, which has had nearly a quarter of a century of kleptocratic dictatorship, with no institutional development, emerges as a prime candidate for ugandization. Should this occur, it is likely that the conflicts would rapidly become internationalized and engulf a number of neighbors as well. Ghana, Kenya, and Benin also exhibit regional inequalities that overlap with ethnic differences, a characteristically explosive compound whose dynamics will be examined further in Chapter 9.

Ethiopia and the Horn

The situation of Ethiopian refugees in the Sudan and Somalia, already discussed in this chapter, is unlikely to change in the near future. Even as the sequels of previous catastrophes lingered on, another drought broke out in mid-1987, which once again was particularly severe in Tigray and Eritrea. Although the Ethiopian government acknowledged the problem, both the authorities and the insurgents in effect prevented relief organizations from gaining access to the war zones. This drove additional refugees into Sudan.

In April 1988, Ethiopia and Somalia agreed to a disengagement in the Ogaden, which might in time lead to repatriation of the refugees. However, later that year there were reports that the Somalian government was drafting many of them to fight against the NSM in the north, and the escalating internal conflict drove 300,000 Somalian refugees into Ethiopia. On the Eritrean side, in early 1988 the prevailing stalemate shifted once again to the advantage of the insurgents, who staged a successful offensive against the garrison town of Afabet.[63] Acknowledged for the first time by the Addis Ababa authorities, the EPLF's victory came amidst indications that Ethiopia wished to reduce its dependency on the Soviet Union and that the Soviet leadership was seeking to reduce the high economic and political costs of continued engagement in another endless war in the Third World. Under these conditions, the insurgents' prospects should continue to improve while Ethiopia's bargaining power decreases. Should the Soviet Union significantly reduce its contribution, the Ethiopian government would be left with little choice but to negotiate. But as it is difficult to imagine the Eritreans settling for less than complete independence, and such an outcome remains totally unacceptable to Ethiopia. Because of the risk that an independent Eritrea would pose for Tigre, the conflict is unlikely to be settled in the near future. The most likely outcome is another stalemate or some sort of unofficial cease-fire, with a somewhat enlarged Eritrean liberated zone, that would enable some of the refugees currently in Sudan to return. It should be kept in mind, however, that an autonomous or independent Eritrea would have a configuration akin to Lebanon's, that is, with a sharp division between Christians and Muslims, and as in Lebanon, these conflicts would most probably be internationalized.

Southern Africa

In the absence of significant external interference and given SWAPO's limitations, in the mid-1980s the situation in Namibia remained governed largely by the costs and benefits of various options from the South African perspective. The territory's value is both strategic and economic. It constitutes not only a buffer against Angola and a staging base for destabilization but also insurance against undesirable developments in adjoining Botswana. The economic dimension is more complex. Thanks to the energy crisis and inflation, in the early 1970s both uranium and diamonds experienced a major boom, but this soon collapsed because of depression, the lower value of petroleum, and the rising opposition to nuclear energy among its European customers.[64] At the same time, production costs have soared because of the vulnerability to sabotage of Namibia's main source of energy production at Cunene, and private investments have stopped.[65] Karakul pelt production has also declined because of depression, drought, and war. Nearly one-fourth of the 6,500 white agricultural enterprises have closed down, and the white population fell from 90,000 in 1970 to 76,000 in 1981. These changing circumstances might dispose the leading capitalist interests concerned, which learned to live with independent black governments elsewhere in Africa, to strike a deal with SWAPO with respect to postindependence arrangements.[66] But, from the perspective of South Africa's interests as a state, there is little incentive for compromise. In the late 1970s, the costs of war approximately equaled South Africa's profits from Namibia. The burden was quite easy to bear because Pretoria obtained a $1.1 billion loan from the International Monetary Fund, which roughly equaled the cost of the war in Namibia and Angola in 1981 and 1982. Although the balance later fluctuated, the further institutionalization of representative government along ethnic lines and the wearing down of SWAPO have improved the prospect of turning an independent Namibia into a docile member of the "constellation."[67]

Beginning in late 1984, South Africa's apartheid regime was itself enmeshed in an internal crisis. But rather than leading to retrenchment, the crisis has propelled the hawks to the fore and prompted Pretoria to take even greater risks abroad in order to deter governments that might abet its internal enemies. The hosting of refugees from South Africa and Namibia was made even more costly. As a result of South African pressures, including repeated raids in which a number of refugees were killed, and culminating in the January 1986 coup, Lesotho in effect ceased harboring South Africans affiliated with liberation movements and became a mere transit point. As already noted, South Africa's intervention in Angola and Mozambique was escalated, and in mid-1986 the SADF struck simultaneously against Zimbabwe, Botswana, and Zambia, where one of the targets was the Makeni Refugee Center near Lusaka. A year later, South Africa again struck deep into Zambia, hundreds of air miles from its border.[68]

By mid-1986 it was evident that the Reagan policy of "constructive engagement" in southern Africa was in tatters, and a year later, a panel appointed by the State Department formally released its obituary; nevertheless, the administration remained adamant on "linkage."[69] As indicated in the Angola section of Chapter 3, Washington renewed its support of UNITA to put pressure on Luanda. But, it also resumed negotiations with the Angolan government and tried to secure SADCC support for a settlement by inducing UNITA to allow the reopening of the Benguela Railway. Meanwhile, at the United Nations, with the help of its European allies, the Reagan administration thwarted attempts to impose sanctions on South Africa for its violation of the international community's directives concerning Namibia.[70]

Concurrently, Angola's President dos Santos actively pursued openings in Europe and in August 1987 initiated new proposals for a mutual withdrawal of foreign forces, amidst indications that the Soviet Union and Cuba wished to decrease their commitment in the region. In October, however, South Africa boldly stepped up its involvement and, for the first time in twelve years, acknowledged that it had sent a three-thousand-man expeditionary force to fight alongside UNITA, including notably a battalion of refugee FNLA fighters. The move was interpreted as a signal that on the eve of a new detente, Pretoria would not allow the United States and the Soviet Union to make a deal without its participation. On November 29, the U.N. Security Council unanimously ordered South Africa to withdraw, but far from complying, three months later it further escalated the intervention. In its final months, the Reagan administration succeeded in bringing about a settlement between Cuba, Angola, and South Africa. This was rendered possible by developments in the Soviet Union and in South Africa, which crucially altered their respective stances. The conflict was becoming an expensive drain on the Soviet military budget, at a time when consolidation of the Gorbachev administration allowed disengagement from the developing world on both political and economic grounds.[71] South Africa's intervention was countered by Cuban troops and resulted in a humiliating defeat.[72] At the same time there was mounting domestic opposition to the use of white conscripts in foreign wars. Hence military planners advocated defense of South Africa's own borders as the preferable strategy. Elections are to take place under U.N. supervision, and Namibia is to become independent in 1991, by which time all foreign troops will be withdrawn.

Should international negotiations bring about a pullback from Angola and Namibia, each of them would nevertheless remain in a precarious situation. The de facto division of Angola between zones under MPLA and UNITA control constitutes the prelude for a separatist showdown, whose outcome is highly uncertain because the challengers are armed and would undoubtedly have access to international support.

On balance, although the legacy of struggle perhaps makes for stronger states, it is also more likely that they will experience severe disturbances. Commenting on the violence unleashed by Mugabe against his opponents during the 1985 electoral campaign, David Caute observed: "A depressing feature of violent decolonization is that the liberation forces tend to adopt tactics and attitudes that mirror the oppressor's, as if the rationale of repression had transplanted itself in the victim."[73] However, it is not necessary to invoke mimetic possession as an explanatory mechanism for this tendency. Intensive political mobilization, which in Africa entails as a matter of course the use of ethnic solidarity as a resource, deepens the cleavages commonly encountered throughout the continent. Counterintersurgency strategies or postindependence subversion tends to exploit such divisions as well, further compounding the potential for conflict. Whatever tensions do arise are especially likely to erupt into violence because participants in the struggle for national liberation are armed. And as Kenneth Grundy has put it, "Small weapons are nonbiodegradable. . . . Thousands of weapons are in circulation, and dissidents are quite prepared to threaten the precarious order that has been inaugurated."[74]

Meanwhile, South Africa's own crisis has begun to produce a greater outflow of refugees. In the past, these had been limited to individual political exiles, mostly connected with the banned African National Congress, but they have now been joined by a variety of others, including especially youths seeking to escape sanctions for involvement in demonstrations and the like, or impressment into the apartheid forces. Precise statistics are particularly hard to come by because the receivers are reluctant to reveal numbers, for fear of reprisals.[75] The USCR estimate was 27,900 in 1985 and 34,650 the following year. The leading receiver in 1985 was Lesotho, wich had 11,500 "refugee-like persons," of whom only a small proportion were registered and assisted by the UNHCR. Most of them were expelled following the coup, leaving only 2,500 in 1986. Angola hosted 9,300, of whom 6,500 were in Luanda and Benguela; the implementation agency was the African National Congress itself.[76] Swaziland had another 6,900 South Africans and over 3,000 others, mostly Mozambicans. Tanzania also received about 6,000 South Africans affiliated with national liberation movements, into a well-developed network of institutions, including "freedom" secondary schools.

The situation in southern Africa as a whole has posed a critical challenge to the

UNHCR, whose response has evoked considerable criticism. As reported by Norman Williams on behalf of the Joint Inspection Unit of the United Nations in mid-1986:

> Asylum seekers fleeing apartheid policies and repression . . . find themselves in a unique plight. Those countries surrounded by or bordering on South Africa and Namibia are subjected to military raids, armed subversions, economic destabilization and other beligerant [sic] acts, which force those countries to break international fundamental protection principles relating to refugees and asylum seekers. As such, South African asylum seekers often do not find safe refuge in those countries which are compelled to take cognizance of their geopolitical environment.

The report points out further that with rising numbers since September 1984,

> their vulnerable situation has worsened in first asylum countries. Hundreds of refugees have perished under South African military raids . . . [M]any asylum seekers attempting to leave . . . are either repelled, jailed, or summarily killed by border patrols. The first asylum countries cannot protect the refugees any more than they can protect their own citizens against South African repression.[77]

Concluding that the situation is "nothing short of a crisis," the report goes on to castigate the High Commissioner for having failed to address it "with the seriousness and promptitude it deserves" and points out that no special measures were adopted to alleviate the situation:

> This is regrettable, considering that most South African refugees cannot effectively be protected by countries of first asylum and that they represent perhaps the single large-scale refugee group in the region falling squarely within the mandate of UNHCR, in comparison with persons displaced by drought, who are of concern to other agencies besides UNHCR.[78]

The absence of response by the secretary general to this observation suggests a tacit acknowledgment of failure.[79]

However, a further exchange between the inspector and the secretary general on another point indicates that the problem could not be easily remedied by more effective UNHCR action. In discussing the issue of protection, the JIU report deplores the unwillingness of Western countries to receive significant numbers of refugees from South Africa and Namibia and suggests that there are "immense possibilities" for resettling them in other parts of Africa as well, so as to relieve pressures in the immediate region. But, in his response the secretary general appropriately observed that most of the refugees under consideration do not want to be resettled elsewhere and, in an unusual display of political candor, pointedly remarked that the inspector failed to deal with the role of national liberation movements.[80] In southern Africa as elsewhere, conflictual regional systems inevitably generate warrior-refugees, whose very existence exposes the inadequacy of conventional understandings of the refugee phenomenon.

Chapter 5

Reorganization
of Political Communities
in South Asia

Asia's Refugees: An Overview

Shortly after World War II ended, two huge streams of refugees appeared in the south and the east of the Asian land mass. Neither was immediately related to the ravages of a world war, although the war had hastened the social and political tensions that were at their roots. In the Indian subcontinent, decolonization through partition in 1947 compelled some fourteen million people to move, either seeking immediate safety or hoping to realize a better future in the new Pakistan or the dismembered India. In China, just two years later in 1949, the civil war was drawing to an end, setting off a large population movement from the mainland to the nearby islands. In the first wave, about 1.5 million soldiers, government officials, and civilians associated with the defeated Kuomintang withdrew to the island of Taiwan. Here they demanded recognition not as refugees but as the government of China. Large numbers also sought asylum in Hong Kong, totaling about 1 million over the following decade.

The very large numbers of Indian and Chinese refugees partly reflect the fact that the flows originated in the two most populous countries of the world. After all, the fourteen million who moved with the partition of India represented only 3 percent of the entire population affected. Later refugee movements in Asia have also rapidly mounted into the millions. The current significance of the two early migrations is not that they were particularly large or uniquely brutal but that they appear as classic types: refugees from partition and refugees from revolution. They were the first in a series of similar movements that are associated with the independence and postindependence struggles in Asia and on which they exerted some influence. As such, the mid-century refugees on the Indian subcontinent and the Chinese mainland indicated the two main patterns of later flows in the region, just as the classic refugee flows did in Europe, which were associated with the French Revolution and the breakup of empires in Central Europe.

In the plural states of South Asia, the structure of conflict in the postindependence period was to a large extent shaped by the demands for rights, power, and protection advanced by groups defined along lines of religion, language, or culture.[1] The very large refugee movements in the region—and some that spilled into other regions as well—

resulted from ethnic conflicts of this kind. In their extreme form, the conflicts meant the reorganization of political communities. Partition falls into this category, involving as it did a regrouping of political communities along religious lines. The formation of Pakistan was an expression of an essentially nationalist sentiment, a demand that an "imagined community" be recognized by acquiring distinct territorial and administrative attributes, as one analyst of nationalism puts it.[2] The subsequent breakup of Pakistan into two separate countries—Pakistan and Bangladesh—and the later demand for an autonomous Tamil state in Sri Lanka likewise reflect nationalist sentiments that lay claim to territorial and political recognition.

Each of these conflicts led to large refugee flows. The Bengali war of secession in 1971 generated an outflow of perhaps nine million people who were given temporary refugee assistance in India until most of them returned. The Tamil separatist conflict in Sri Lanka in the 1980s has given rise to a much smaller absolute number of refugees, although in proportion to the Tamil minority population in the island, it is significant. At the height of the conflict in 1985, about 250,000, or 12.5 percent, of the estimated two million Sri Lankan Tamils had left.[3] Of these, about half went to India and the rest to the Western industrialized states. The Tamils were not the first South Asian refugees to claim asylum in large numbers in Europe—they were preceded by the Pakistanis—but they became a highly controversial set of interregional refugees.

Apart from these very large flows, however, it is remarkable how few international refugees have originated in South Asia, despite the high incidence of social and international conflict in the region. Ethnic conflict with territorial overtones in the direction of autonomy or separatism is endemic in various parts of the continent, and so is conflict along ethnic, caste, or class lines that focuses on sharing power or obtaining protection within existing territorial delimitations. Although such conflicts involve physical violence, repression, and discrimination, only limited migrations have followed. These have been mainly within the country or—if international—mostly within the region, for example, by tribal peoples in the northeast of the subcontinent. Apart from the Sri Lankan Tamils, only a few Indians, Bangladeshis, and Pakistanis have moved beyond the region to seek asylum or resettlement in the industrialized Western states. By the mid-1980s, about 10,000 annually sought asylum in Europe, a small figure in relation to the population universe of nearly 950 million from which they came.[4] The reasons for this, as we shall see, can be found in both the structure of social conflict and the international context.

In the more homogeneous states of East Asia, refugee flows have not been related primarily to ethnic divisions—which are subdued—but to the clash of antagonistic class formations in the process of decolonization and modernization. The Chinese revolution was not only the classic case but also a source of continuous international population movements claiming refugee status. After the first waves to Taiwan and Hong Kong, new waves associated with revolutionary excesses followed in the great Leap Forward and the Cultural Revolution. The new order also led to conflict with ethnically distinct people that previously had enjoyed autonomy. In 1959 the Tibetan rebellion was ruthlessly suppressed, causing almost 100,000 Tibetans (a sizable 7 to 8 percent of the population) to flee to neighboring India, where most remained thirty years later.

After the victory of the Chinese Communist party in 1949, other communist parties in the region made slow and painful progress. A devastating war in Korea (1950–53) confirmed the division of the peninsula into two separate states, a communist and an anticommunist half. In Southeast Asia proper—commonly defined as the region between the Chinese mainland and the Indian subcontinent—only in Indochina did revolutionary forces persist, culminating in victory in 1975 in Vietnam, Kampuchea (Cambodia), and Laos. All the countries emerged only slowly from the destruction of protracted warfare, and Kampuchea soon was plunged back into a renewed and possibly even more brutal conflict.

The massive involvement of foreign powers in the Korean conflict and the Indochinese wars served to internationalize the consequent refugee movements. The UNHCR's predecessor, the UNRRA, helped South Korea relocate refugees from communist North Korea and those being repatriated from Japan between 1948 and 1950. With the establishment of the UNKRA (U.N. Korean Reconstruction Agency) during the Korean War, many of the four million people uprooted by the war became the first Asian population to be recognized by the international refugee regime that evolved after World War II. The Koreans did not come under the 1951 U.N. convention (which applied only to European populations), nor would they have qualified as "refugees" under its definition, because of the con-nationality clause (as they moved from one Korea to another). Yet, as Western forces were fighting on the South Korean side under a U.N. flag, U.N. assistance to persons who were displaced by the war or who fled from North Korea was a logical counterpart of the war effort. For this purpose, a special organization was established, just as the UNRWA (U.N. Relief and Works Agency) was set up to aid the Palestinians in 1949.

The Indochinese conflicts generated one of the greatest contemporary flows of internationally recognized refugees, which started to taper off only in the mid-1980s. In the preceding decade, about 1.7 million people left Vietnam, Laos, and Kampuchea, of which 1.3 million were resettled in the United States and other industrialized countries under the protective umbrella of the UNHCR.

Outside Indochina, radical nationalist forces in Southeast Asia failed to capture the leadership of the independence movements. They were subsequently suppressed, physically liquidated en masse (as in Indonesia in 1965), or increasingly marginalized by the economic development strategies adopted by the ruling elites. Social conflict was muted or transformed, in part also by persisting ethnic alignments that cut across incipient class formations. As a result, relatively few international refugees have originated in this part of Southeast Asia. Except for a few political exiles from Indonesia and the Philippines, the only UNHCR-assisted flow of rank-and-file populations has been Muslims from the southern Philippines: about 100,000 in the east Malaysian state of Sabah, of whom about half were aided by the UNHCR in the late 1970s.[5] An estimated 11,000 Papuans from the Indonesian-controlled West Irian who in 1984 had sought refuge in neighboring Papua New Guinea had uncertain status, and international relief agencies were allowed access to them only when there were starvation deaths.[6]

At the westernmost end of the Asian region, where it meets the Middle East, are two cases that each form a pattern unto themselves. Modern Afghanistan and Iran have developed fairly separately from South Asia and are quite unconnected with East Asia, although the current conflict that has ravaged both countries and produced millions of refugees bears some resemblance to the internationalized, revolutionary upheavals of the Far East.

Afghans and Iranians form a large part of the current global refugee population. By 1988, about five million Afghans remained abroad, primarily in neighboring Pakistan and Iran. Estimates of the number of refugees from the 1979 Iranian revolution and the Iran–Iraq war ranged between one and two million. But these figures are highly uncertain, as only a small minority has been granted asylum under the 1951 U.N. convention, and the rest reside abroad under various legal categories or in a legal twilight.[7]

Although the Afghanistan conflict is included in this volume as a case study, Iran is not. It may be noted, however, that although the origins and course of Iran's Islamic revolution differ from the peasant-based communist-led revolutions of Asia, the refugee consequences seem to be broadly similar. Waves of Iranian émigrés consisted initially of highly politicized cadres of the previous regimes or contenders in the succession struggle. Subsequently, much broader population segments tried to leave as the revolutionary regime became radicalized and increasingly repressive, partly in response to external pressures and a devastating war with its neighbor.

The Classic Case: Partition of India

The huge migrations accompanying the 1947 partition of the Indian subcontinent were probably the largest and most concentrated in time that have been recorded in modern history. About fourteen million people moved between 1947 and 1951. This migration may also have been the most violent. About 600,000 were killed and hundreds of thousands injured. To the extent the term *involuntary migration* has an objective meaning, it was here. Millions fled, literally to save their lives from the murderous mobs engaging in orgies of physical violence.

The partition of colonial states was an unusual form of decolonization, even though the size and diversity of British India presented a prima facie case for one or more divisions. In ancient and medieval times, competing political sovereignties had controlled various parts of the subcontinent, without any one of them able to impose a single administrative establishment on the entire area. The British came close, but considerable ethnic and administrative diversity remained and was deliberately cultivated by the colonial rulers in accordance with the maxim of "divide and rule." This was facilitated by several factors. The 1931 census listed 222 language groups, each typically limited to some geographical area.[8] The princely states enjoyed separate administrative status. And religious distinctions cut across most linguistic boundaries, although both the Muslim and the Sikh minorities had some geographic strongholds.

The Muslims who formed Pakistan comprised several cultural-linguistic groups, just as did India's Hindu population. The Muslim—Hindu distinction, which became the basis for partition, was a politicoreligious division that had been associated with ruler–subject relations during centuries of Mogul rule. In the British period the temporal significance of the religious distinction was further accentuated. The two communities generally moved in opposite directions on the socioeconomic scale—Muslims down, Hindus up—and politically they were divided by deliberate colonial strategies, such as the introduction of separate electoral rolls.

It was against this background that segments of the Muslim community formed the Muslim League (1906) and gradually moved to demand a separate state as independence drew near. The Muslim League was increasingly convinced that the Muslims' interests could not be protected in a united India ruled by a Hindu-dominated party, the Indian National Congress. The Congress had all along dominated the nationalist movement and was poised to rule independent India. Its leaders failed to assure the Muslim leaders on crucial succession issues concerning institutional structure and representation during talks in 1937–39 and the final negotiations in 1946–47.[9] The British, for their part, preferred an undivided India as "the road of easy abdication" but were anxious to withdraw once the end of their empire had become inevitable.[10] They thus failed to mediate in a conflict that their own colonial policies had done much to promote, and partition was the result.

The negotiations leading up to independence were extraordinarily acrimonious and contributed to the climate of fear and hate that exploded in violence even before the talks in the Partition Council had ended. The Congress vehemently opposed a partition that would diminish the power of independent India and undermine the party's claim to represent and protect minorities and majority alike. India's extreme diversity, moreover, made it almost impossible to sort out many areas, and the prospect of further fragmentation loomed large. Partition, in short, appeared as yet another divide-and-rule strategem in its consequences, if not its intention.

Although some observers feared that partition would lead to violence and forced migrations, they apparently did not anticipate mass migrations.[11] The future Pakistan would contain the large Muslim population concentrated in the northwest and northeast of the subcontinent, but both India and Pakistan were expected to have large minorities. Because leaders of both future countries took pains to emphasize that they would protect these minorities, large-scale migrations would seem unnecessary.

The liberal official stance on minorities—so different from the newly independent states in Central Europe that emerged after World War I, with unwanted and stateless minorities—reflected important political considerations. Boundary determinations based on commission awards and negotiations in the Partition Council continued right up until the eve of transfer of power in August 1947. A liberal position on minorities could mean the inclusion of additional people and their territory. The Muslim League leaders were particularly anxious to maximize their territory, lest they end up with a "moth-eaten" and "mutilated" Pakistan, as Mohammed Ali Jinnah put it, that even the best of circumstances would be a small power relative to India. The new Pakistan also needed the skills of the Hindu professional class, but a more weighty consideration was the sobering fact that the forty million Muslims likely to remain in India would be hostages of Pakistan's good behavior toward its own Hindu and Sikh minorities.[12] On the Indian side, the Congress had all along opposed partition on the grounds that the Muslim minority would be safe in an undivided, secular India under Congress rule. Jawaharlal Nehru was the strongest advocate of secularism so defined and maintained this position with increasing vehemence as the August transfer date drew near.

Massive migrations of minorities nevertheless took place, and the immediate cause was violence. The initial outbreaks of violence in the two powerful linguistic regions to be divided, Bengal and Punjab, had been associated with efforts to influence the negotiations in 1946 and early 1947; later violence resulted from anger and revenge over the partition agreement. The 1947 clashes started in Punjab, where at first they pitted Sikhs against Muslims. The Sikhs fought the partition of Punjab, as it would divide the Sikh community, its properties, and its shrines. When the partition was announced in principle (June 1947) the Sikhs attacked the Muslims for having brought it on. A virtual "communal war of succession" ensued in which several thousand people were killed, and so the migrations began.[13] Two months later, when independence was declared and the precise terms for the partition of Punjab were made known, Punjab again exploded in violence, this time even more seriously.

In 1947–48, the violence was mainly confined to the Punjab and Delhi, where it caused the immediate flight of several million people. In the eastern wing of the subcontinent, the migrations followed a different timetable but also here were linked to the unfolding violence. When about thirty thousand Indian Muslims were killed in one week in Bihar, the exodus from eastern India to East Pakistan commenced, eventually to reach more than one million. Migrations in the other direction started in earnest after outbreaks of violence in East Pakistan in 1950.

The atrocities created a general climate of fear that undoubtedly accelerated migrations wherever Hindus, Sikhs, and Muslims found themselves in a minority position, but some groups probably would have migrated anyway. Few Hindus welcomed the prospect of living in an Islamic state (although Pakistan was not declared an Islamic republic until 1956), and much of the Muslim bourgeoisie had been in the forefront of the Pakistan movement.[14]

The migration patterns as well as the violence itself were affected by property relations. A larger proportion of the urban than of the rural Muslim community migrated, presumably because their property (if any) was more mobile. When the minority community largely had immovable property (land and shrines), and especially when the property was big (the *zamindar* holdings), the owners tended to move only in the face of imminent, physical violence. In the eastern sector, there was little violence in 1947–48 and relatively little movement into India, as the generally landed Hindu community in East Pakistan, particularly the successors to the powerful *zamindaries,* tried to remain on their properties as long as they safely could. However, communal violence in 1950 propelled almost one million Hindus to cross the border. The same pattern of migrations induced by actual or expected violence was evident in subsequent years, although by now more of the Hindu migrants from East Pakistan were low caste and propertyless, suggesting that the landed classes had left earlier.[15] The massive migrations in the western sector—in which about five million people moved each way in the space of a few months in 1947–48—contained a large proportion of landed classes on both sides; the movements, as noted, took place under conditions of extreme violence.[16]

In part, the violence also resulted from the fact that much property affected by partition was immovable (land and shrines). Under these circumstances, partition faced problems similar to those of decolonization when the colonizers have become landowners: The immovable nature of the property makes disengagement costly, compromise difficult, and violence likely.[17] As land also is a form of property that can readily be appropriated by others, much violence was associated with simple land grabbing. One close observer notes that in the Punjab, "the pogroms on both sides of the border, while couched in religio-political terms, were in large measure aimed at the seizure of property of the minority group. . . . In Pakistan menial and artisan castes were urged to stay. . . . Landlords, on the other hand, were almost invariably threatened with extreme violence."[18]

Once started, the violence took a predictable path in mixed residence areas. Majority pounced on minority in one place, and the minority took revenge in areas where it constituted the majority.[19] But the multiplier effect was possible only because of the conspicuous absence of either a civil authority or a strong, reasonably impartial state apparatus that could impose civil order. The hardest-hit Punjab region had effectively no government, and the army and police were communally inclined. Although a Weberian type of state had not existed in Punjab under the British either, the form that decolonization took produced a complete collapse, and the hasty British withdrawal contributed greatly to the carnage.[20]

The sudden displacement of millions of people caused enormous economic, political, and social dislocations. Camp and urban pavement dwellers grew by the millions ("Only the sun saves Karachi from epidemics," a visiting mission observed),[21] and rehabilitation authorities were rapidly running out of funds. Although an exchange of abandoned or confiscated land was possible in the western sector, there was virtually no land in the eastern sector available to refugees on the Indian side, as those who fled were largely propertyless. New arrivals brought tales of fresh atrocies and sustained the momentum. Yet, both governments still kept the border open until 1952 to give the populations time to sort themselves out. By that time, a mutual passport system was introduced to regulate further population movements. In 1956 more restrictions, in the form of migration certificates, were required by Indian authorities to slow down the continuous inflow from East Pakistan. In the western sector the flow had tapered off earlier.

The legal and operational concept of refugee that emerged from partition was based on the right of people to escape violence targeted along religious lines. In Pakistan, "refugee"—*muhajir*—was included as a category in the 1951 census and defined as a person who had moved to Pakistan as "a result of partition or fear of disturbances connected therewith."[22] *Muhajir* also is the generic term for "refugee" in Urdu and Arabic, as it refers to the movement of the Prophet from Mecca to Medina which constitutes the first refugee movement in Islamic history. A similar concept of refugee is encoded in the only international legal provision regulating population movements between India and Pakistan in these years. Under the 1950 Nehru–Liaquat Pact, the two governments agreed to protect people who moved between the two countries as a result of communal violence (i.e., along religious lines) until the end of the year. Members of religious diaspora—Muslims from India, Hindus and Sikhs from Pakistan—were also the ones who availed themselves of refugee assistance, by registering for relief and rehabilitation.

But other people were also migrating. The traditional outmigration from the densely populated Bengal region to surrounding areas continued after partition. A comparison between these migrants and those defined as refugees shows how the two groups were administratively distinguished and treated at the time. In the eastern sector, both Bengali Hindus and Bengali Muslims continued to move from East Pakistan into India, and they were treated quite differently.[23] The Bengali Hindus had little difficulty crossing the border and generally registered with the relief and rehabilitation authorities. Most of the Bengali Hindus went to the Indian state of West Bengal, but some went to the northeastern Indian states, including Assam. The Bengali Muslims, by contrast, had to dodge border patrols, face summary deportations, bribe their way to obtain identification papers, and lie to the census enumerators about their place of birth (but not religion). Large-scale illegal migration was nevertheless possible and partly encouraged because the migrants represented "vote banks" for the political parties. Most of the Bengali Muslims went to the surrounding northeastern Indian states; in particular, an estimated 600,000 went to Assam between 1951 and 1971.[24]

In practice, then, the Bengali Hindus were treated as refugees, whereas the Bengali Muslims were (illegal) migrants. The definition had the advantage that it could easily be put into operation; it also reflected certain compelling political sentiments in the post-partition era: The traumatic partition and progressively hostile relations with Pakistan made it politically imperative in India to give preferential treatment to Hindu arrivals. Later, foreign policy concerns contributed to a sharp reversal of administrative practice. In 1971, when India and Pakistan were at war, all persons entering India were designated as refugees. After 1971, when East Pakistan had become friendly Bangladesh, no succor was given to the hundreds of thousands of both Hindus and Muslims who kept trying to enter India. The prima facie designation was now "illegal migrant," and many of those caught were summarily deported.[25] The social realities within East Pakistan/Bangladesh had also changed, but hardly so categorically as by themselves to account for the abrupt changes in prima facie designations. Bangladesh was formally at peace, but the internal strife and repression continued. In short, it seemed that undocumented arrivals from a friendly state were "illegal migrants," while those from an enemy country were "refugees."

Ambiguities in the conditions of the migrations of those defined as refugees, as opposed to migrants, also appeared before 1971. The Hindu minority in East Pakistan left in large numbers whenever tension between Hindus and Muslims mounted and when the movement for Bengali rights clashed violently with the Pakistani authorities. In both instances the Hindu minority was vulnerable to violence at the hands of the mob or the state apparatus; they were refugees according to legal concepts in both the subcontinental and European traditions, and also in the sociological sense we have proposed. The Bengali Muslims, on the other hand, were typically migrants, having a long history of migrating into the relatively resource-rich surrounding states, especially Assam. But ambiguities arise because, as with most movements, the groups were not mutually exclusive. The Bengali Hindus also had a long history of migration into surrounding areas. Many undoubtedly took advantage of the ruling definition of refugee to migrate and to make a fresh start. With time an increasing proportion of those who registered as refugees were small traders and artisans belonging to the lower castes and classes.[26] The Bengali Muslims, for their part, were also suppressed during the Bengali rights movements, and some of their leaders in fact obtained exile in India. These differences were not recognized by immigration status accorded on the basis of membership in religious groups.

A more fundamental question concerns the priority given to the need of the refugees, as opposed to the migrants. A person fleeing the fury of mobs, overtly for reasons of religion, is obviously vulnerable in an immediate, life-threatening sense in which economic refugees are not. Yet it can be argued that the conditions of poverty in the subcontinent in the early postcolonial years were so severe as to be perpetually and immediately life threatening. The victims of such structural violence could rarely escape and only minimally adjust. Their moral claim to an escape from violence in this sense seems equivalent to that of people facing physical violence targeted along religious lines, enabling both groups of victims to be aided as refugees. The point—and the resulting dilemma of triage—becomes evident by considering the conditions of one group that was victimized by structural violence of this kind, the *haris* (peasants) of Sind in 1948:

> They live in the most primitive conditions without any conception of social, political or economic rights. They have only one interest in life—food—with which to keep body and soul together. No other problem attracts them because the fundamental problem of living remains unsolved for them. . . . Fear reigns supreme . . . fear of imprisonment, fear of losing his land, wife or life.[27]

The *haris* of Sind who migrated from Pakistan to India in 1947–48 were treated as refugees according to the legal and administrative definitions of refugee at the time, but because they were Hindu, not because they were impoverished. As in the Euroopean tradition, extreme economic poverty was excluded from the operational definition of refugee in the subcontinent. The reasons for this are sharply brought out by the extreme conditions of inequality and population pressures in South Asia. The very poor are also very numerous in a subcontinent where even in the 1980s about half the population of one billion people live below the national poverty lines.[28] To the extent that the national authorities are concerned with alleviating poverty, their first priority is to aid the numerous poor in their own country. Special privilege in the form of relief and resettlement to alleviate mass poverty in neighboring countries is politically impossible in an age of nation-states and the ideological supremacy of "imagined communities." Even the extension of such privileges to refugee members of the religious diaspora is limited by time and resource restraints, as we have seen.

The question still remains why some people, qua victims of extreme poverty, are not included under the over-all ceiling of refugee admissions. The reason has to do with the essence of structural violence, namely, it is structured. Economic violence of this kind is not incidental or random but is a characteristic of certain socioeconomic systems and, to some extent, is necessary for their functioning. In the complex social web of class and caste, the very poor also have a functionally specific role to play. If they escape, production will be disrupted. A combination of fear, lack of resources, and external coercion usually does prevent flight; the extreme form of this phenomenon is bonded labor, as it still occurs in the subcontinent. Because the ruling national elites in the subcontinent represent the propertied classes—drawn variously from the landed elites, the upper echelons of the military and civilian bureaucracies, and the national bourgeoisie—there is no effective political pressure on the authorities to permit the most miserable, but still useful, poor to migrate with the help of the special assistance that refugee status represents.

The concept of refugee in South Asia as it emerged in the spasms of violence during partition thus closely resembles one of the historic European types: the refugee as a victim of physical violence targeted against members of a religious minority. Most became victims simply because they happened to belong to one particular religious community. Usually such individuals were "punished" for a specific act—similar aggression by members of their own community—whether or not they had participated in that action. Within the communally patterned violence, however, there was a more specific targeting according to property relations. Being the most vulnerable, members of the propertied classes were also the most likely to become refugees.

The partition itself has several distinct features that makes it a classic conflict case in refugee annals. As we have seen, the process of transferring political authority and sorting out of properties led to violent clashes among the contending communities. This violence then became self-perpetuating in large measure because of the absence of both civil authority and effective state power. But because the conflict involved the creation of two nation-states out of one, refugees on both sides had a prospective homeland that afforded immediate protection, resettlement assistance, and full citizenship rights for the future. Having a homeland, the refugees from partition were not international refugees in the customary sense. Yet material assistance was desperately needed for refugees who lacked shelter, food, and medicines and who generally were in "a terrible plight."[29] Indian and Pakistani delegates to the United Nations desperately pleaded for aid for their millions of refugees.[30] Some assistance was rendered by the U.N. agencies the World Health Organization (WHO) and the U.N. International Children's Emergency Fund (UNICEF), as well as the International Red Cross and private organizations, but it was a paltry effort. The international refugee regime at the time was explicitly Europe centered and preoccupied with aiding Europeans uprooted, displaced, and persecuted during World

War II. That the partition of India did not connect with the emerging superpower conflict between the United States and the Soviet Union reinforced Western indifference. Throughout the 1950s, the international refugee regime put in place and financed largely by the Western powers assisted only two large refugee populations outside Europe, the Palestinians and the Koreans, for whom separate international refugee organizations were established. It mattered little that the Koreans, like the refugees on the Indian subcontinent, were, technically speaking, not refugees, as they had a "homeland." The needs of these refugee populations were recognized as constituting a legitimate demand on the emerging U.N. system largely for reasons of foreign policy: They were concentrated in strategic conflict areas where the Western powers were deeply involved.

South Asia After Partition

One of the arguments made by the departing British viceroy against partition in 1947 was that a divided subcontinent would fall prey to its own quarrels and invite attack from foreign powers, especially the Soviet Union. With three Indo-Pakistani wars since 1947, the first part of the prediction certainly proved correct, although the second part did not.

Closed in by the Himalayas to the north and surrounded by the Indian Ocean on most other sides, South Asia is a distinct geographic entity. Partly for this reason, the region has many characteristics of a "subsystem." The main feature of this system in its international aspect has been the overwhelming power of India relative to that of the other states in the region. When Pakistan in 1971 was divided into (West) Pakistan and Bangladesh, losing about half its population and a sizable portion of its territory, the regional power structure moved further in favor of India.[31] The other countries in the region came at the very bottom of a conventional scale of power: Sri Lanka, with a population of sixteen million people and an area of only 65,000 sq. km, was about the size of an administrative district in South India. The small Himalayan kingdoms of Nepal and Bhutan, and the Indian Ocean archipelagic state of the Maldives were both geographically and politically dependent and peripheral entities. This power differential between the largest regional power and the rest necessarily shaped the patterns of conflict and cooperation within the region and the external alignments. Pakistan looked to the United States for military and economic support to strengthen its position vis-à-vis India, culminating in a formal defense alliance in 1954 (SEATO, or Southeast Asia Treaty Organization). India for many years kept its distance from the superpowers, pursuing a policy of economic self-sufficiency and political nonalignment. Not until 1971 did it conclude a defense treaty with the Soviety Union. The other regional states adopted nonalignment policies in the shadow of India, and Sri Lanka's subordinate position was formalized in the Indo–Sri Lankan peace accords of July 29, 1987.

The regional balance of power was influenced by the two superpowers, and the United States and the Soviet Union also shaped the settlement of two Indo-Pakistani wars (1965 and 1971). Their interest in the subcontinent subsequently was accentuated by the Soviet war in Afghanistan. China, for its part, became embroiled in one war with India (1962), and Sino-Indian relations have remained tense. But in comparison with the East Asian region, great power rivalries on the subcontinent have been limited and indirect. As a result, the nature of the conflicts and the related refugee flows have reflected less the extraregional than the regional forces and interests.

International Conflict and Refugee Flows

Of the four major international wars on the subcontinent since 1947, three have been between India and Pakistan. The almost ritual hostility between the two countries after independence originated in the competitive state-formation of partition. Pakistan's leaders claimed that India never had accepted the establishment of Pakistan and was bent on its destruction. Indian leaders, for their part, saw Pakistan's very existence as a negation of the concept of a multiethnic, secular Indian state and accused Pakistan of dragging a superpower onto the subcontinent in order to pressure India.

Indo-Pakistan hostilities have generally not led to the formation of international refugee flows. Two of the wars (1947–48 and 1965) were short, conventional affairs. The opposing military forces slugged it out in border regions; the damage was relatively limited; and the status quo ante was soon restored. Although fighting in the border area led to some internal displacement of people, there was ample, secure space on both sides. Without major territorial adjustments or changes in sovereignty, there was no reason that the refugees should cross international borders, and none did. The third war, leading to the establishment of Bangladesh, differed in these crucial respects, and the international refugee flow was accordingly enormous.[32]

Internal Conflict and Refugees

The partition had sorted out some people according to religion, but independent South Asia remained a region of ethnically plural societies in which social change was shaped by the forces of numerous linguistic and religious identities and, in India and Sri Lanka, also by ancient caste lines that only slowly were modified by pressures of modernization. Political organization and conflict largely followed these "primordial" forms of consciousness. Although conflict along these lines was common, only in two instances did large-scale population movements claiming international refugee assistance occur, that is, the separatist struggles in Pakistan and Sri Lanka. India—with its vast millions, myriad of ethnic divisions, enormous poverty, and sharp social inequities—has produced few. There has been some tribal movement in border areas within the region, but little beyond. It is indicative that by the mid-1980s—when the Punjab crisis was deepening and some of the worst Hindu-Muslim clashes in the history of independent India were recorded—there were only about six thousand Indian asylum seekers a year in all of Europe, and these were primarily from one community (the Sikhs).[33]

INDIA   The apparent paradox of a great potential for conflict, but relatively few refugees, is partly explained by the nature of the social structure in India, which looks like a complex grid of ethnic, caste, and class divisions.[34] Simple ethnic or simple class alignments are rare. The propertied classes that had led the nationalist movement—the landed elite, the national bourgeoisie, and the professionals—were themselves multiethnic. If ethnic ties had centrifugal effects, tugging at the federal structure and unitary administration of independent India, class interests tended to pull in the opposite direction. So also did considerations of international power and prestige that provided a bond among the elites. The masses were politically organized mainly on a regional basis, but divisions created by vertical dependencies of caste and class were also important. One result of this complex configuration was to blunt social divisions and to moderate conflict; only a few ethnic tensions developed into sustained insurgencies, and the violent challenge from the revolutionary left had completely faded by the late 1960s.

On the political level, accommodative behavior and a liberal democratic process (except for a four-year interval between 1973 and 1977) strengthened the forces favoring compromise and conciliation. A relatively peaceful reorganization of states along linguistic lines in the 1950s helped meet demands for greater recognition from ethnically defined groups. The dominant ideology in the postcolonial era was progressive and secular, emphasizing equal or preferential treatment for backward castes, tribes, and religious minorities. The general impact was to contain violent social conflict and, hence, the underlying causes of refugee movements. On the other hand, it is clear that the liberal side of the Indian state in part is a "luxury," related to the fact that the institutions of caste and poverty themselves help keep intact a highly inequitable and exploitative social order. In instances when the social or political order was openly threatened, the state has not hesitated to apply armed force ruthlessly, as against the revolutionary Naxalites in the 1960s, intermittently against tribals in the northeast, and in the troubled Punjab region since the mid-1980s.

But even when the state exercises its most coercive functions and excesses ensue, they occur within a legitimizing framework of liberal democratic institutions. This makes it difficult for the victims to obtain refugee status abroad, especially in Western countries which discount the possibility that a democratic and liberal state can "persecute" its citizens. The difficulty of obtaining refugee status has a feedback effect that discourages prospective claimants and limits the outflow.

There is another, somewhat formalistic but still important consideration. Violent social conflict in India has led to some internal population movements. As in 1947–48, fearful minorities seek safety in areas where they constitute the majority. In the 1980s, for instance, Hindu and Sikh migrations meant that the Hindus moved out of the Sikh-dominated Punjab and the Sikhs residing in other Indian states moved in.[35] In 1983, the violence in the Indian state of Assam compelled thousands of Bengalis to flee for safety to the neighboring Bengali-dominated Indian state of West Bengal, where refugee camps were established. Given the diverse ethnic and political configurations of India—constituting, as it does, a subcontinent—assorted ethnic groups in search of security can find local protective majorities. Because all of these local "homelands" are under one national sovereignty, movements that in an area of smaller national sovereignties would be classified as international here become internal.

Considering more closely India's actual and potential refugee flows, the most striking point is that the largest minority—the approximately 35 million Muslims who remained in India after partition—generally stopped migrating to Pakistan in the 1950s.[36] During this period the Indian government under Jawaharlal Nehru's leadership made efforts to establish a secular, progressive state in which the Muslim minority could be integrated on mutually acceptable terms. Communal violence, in which the Muslims as the minority typically suffered most, did occur, although by itself it was not sufficient to compel large numbers to flee across the border for safety, even though Pakistan's liberal immigration and naturalization policy at the time made this a realistic option. When Hindu-Muslim violence increased during the latter half of the 1960s (1,919 persons were killed in 1964 alone), the option to migrate to Pakistan was virtually closed by the restrictions introduced by the Pakistan government in 1965.[37] Thus the failure of the Indian Muslims to migrate to Pakistan is not conclusive evidence of the secular and protective nature of the Indian state regarding minorities. Still, it is clear that central government forces have tended to play a protective, if belated, role in communal riots in which local police and paramilitary forces have abetted or committed systematic violence against the minority.[38]

Whether or not the state can provide the minimally necessary protection is a critical factor that determines minority attitudes toward the state. If violence is seen not as riots, or even local repression, but as a pogrom tacitly approved at the highest level, the need to escape will become paramount. This charge has not been leveled by the Muslims against the Union government, but it has been made by another minority, the Sikhs. In November 1984, the police stood idly by while mobs attacked members of the Sikh community in various Indian states where they constituted a minority. About two thousand were killed in New Delhi alone, and it was widely surmised that local leaders of the ruling Congress party had organized the "riots" to avenge the assassination of Prime Minister Indira Gandhi by extremist Sikhs.[39] Thereafter many Sikh families sought security by migrating to their "homeland," the Indian state of Punjab where they constituted a majority.

In the northeast, relations between the state and tribal minorities have long been problematic, leading to outbursts of violence or prolonged insurgencies. The minorities are here geographically concentrated and traditionally have viewed external authority as an imposition on their semiautonomous status. Faced with the greater administrative penetration of the postcolonial state and threatened by growing in-migration of the lowland people—who for their part sought to escape the explosive population pressures on the land in the Bengal deltaic region—the indigenous people struck back.

In Assam, sporadic violence and internal refugees resulted, the most recent serious clash occurring in 1983. Tension between the indigenous communities and the Bengali migrants, which goes back to the turn of the century, had escalated steadily in the 1970s owing to political competition.[40] The ruling political party had tolerated illegal migration from Bangladesh in order to build up their "vote banks". In the resulting burst of accumulated fury, about 5,000 people were killed, and thousands became internal refugees. Strong nativist pressured forced the central government in 1985 to promise a stricter policy toward migrants, including a commitment to expel the estimated 200,000 to 300,000 illegal migrants who had entered Assam after 1977.[41]

Were this policy to be strictly enforced, it would help solve one conflict, but another would be created. For economic as much as foreign policy reasons, the government of Bangladesh does not accept returnees, claiming that they in fact belong to earlier migration waves that qualify for Indian citizenship. The Bengalis in this case would become classic refugees, a "stateless" expelled minority.

In other parts of the northeast, autonomy–separatist conflicts developed. The tribals had enjoyed a semiautonomous status in the colonial period, and their geographical noncontiguity with the rest of India gave their demand for self-determination a certain logic.[42] The Naga community of half a million people rebelled in 1955; it took twenty years and several accords to end the war. The less numerous Mizo people followed in 1966, and also here it took decades to reach a final accord.[43] Elsewhere the struggle continued. In Manipur, an insurgency has been simmering since the mid-1960s, and in Tripura tribal raiding parties have been killing Bengali settlers with some regularity. Across the border in Bangladesh, the Chakmas were fighting a rearguard action against lowland settlers supported by government forces. About 300,000 Bengali settlers moved into tribal areas between 1977 and 1987.[44] The Chakmas formed an armed movement (the

Shanti Bahini) in 1969, and intensified strife in the mid-1980s led to the inflow of some 50,000 Chakma refugees on the Indian side of the border.

The autonomy–separatist conflicts in the northeast have a distinct refugee profile. Because the tribal populations involved are relatively small, the absolute number of refugees is small as well. Except for the Chakmas, about 15 percent of whom fled across the border in 1986–7, the number of refugees relative to the total population also tends to be small, partly because of the pattern of violence. Much of the northeastern conflict has been intermittent or of moderate intensity. Civilian dislocation has been limited, and the activists have found natural cover in the hills. When hard pressed, the insurgents and related civilians moved across the border; the tribals in India went to Bangladesh (earlier East Pakistan), Burma, and China; and those on the Bangladesh side went to India. Assistance to the insurgents and recognition of the refugees in the host country have been limited so as not to attract attention. A low-profile posture reflects the mutual vulnerabilities of the concerned governments in this corner of the subcontinent. Both India and the erstwhile East Pakistan are wedged into each other in sandwich fashion, with their border areas populated by minority communities with uncertain loyalty to the state.

A few of the leaders went into more or less voluntary exile in London to argue for an international hearing for the movements.[45] But most of the refugees stayed in the region. The question of seeking asylum farther away in Europe or the Americas did not arise, not even when the fifty thousand Chakmas found that they were not particularly welcome in already crowded areas on the Indian side of the border and that the prospect of repatriation was uncertain. The tribal people were held back by their attachment to the land, which was the original reason for the struggle; they also lacked the resources and networks necessary for migration beyond the neighboring region.[46]

Autonomy–separatist movements also developed in the area most favored by India's uneven economic development process. Rapid economic progress associated with the "green revolution" has been at the root of the growing violence in Punjab since the late 1970s. A separatist faction of the prosperous, educated Sikh community also exploited the government's political mismanagement, the increasing politicization of religious sentiments nationwide, and the escalating violence involving Sikhs. Inside the Punjab, there were terrorist-style violence and casualties on all sides. Sikh activists attacked Hindus and Sikh "collaborationists," and police and paramilitary forces sought out actual or suspected Sikh separatists.[47] By 1987 Sikh and Hindu communities outside Punjab also feared random retaliation, and the Sikh community remained deeply embittered after the 1984 massacres of their people.

The consequent population movement has been, first, a clandestine flow of activists to and from Pakistan. The figures are unknown, and the phenomenon is at any rate denied by Pakistan for fear of offending India. Second, an extraregional flow of five thousand to six thousand Sikh asylum seekers was, by the mid-1980s, finding its way to Europe, particularly West Germany, where it created a strong reaction.[48] The annual flow amounted to only a small fraction of 1 percent of India's total Sikh community of 13 million. Evidently, intermittent and random violence was not sufficient to generate a large outflow, especially as Punjab's thriving economy remained largely unaffected by the unrest.[49] Another factor was the discouraging effect of the very low acceptance rate of refugees. In West Germany, not one applicant out of about ten thousand had been accepted as of late 1986.[50] In Great Britain, the acceptance rate was four out of sixty-seven between 1979 and 1985.[51] UNHCR sources suggested that as a group the Sikhs had a weak claim. Sikh activists fearing state retribution were subject not to "persecution" but to "prosecution" under Indian antiterrorist laws or, alternatively, could be excluded as "terrorists." The level of violence was not great enough to justify asylum on the basis of generalized insecurity ("victims of violence"), and the 1984 violence against the Sikhs appeared in retrospect to be an aberration.[52] In short, the credibility of the Sikhs' applications was undermined by the liberal democratic dimension of the Indian state. Moreover, the Sikh community had always been a migrating community with strong diaspora in the industrialized world. Without these resources and networks, they could scarcely move en masse to Europe; this very fact created suspicion that those who now traveled well-trodden migration routes also were ordinary migrants.[53]

Considering the contemporary population movements from India as a whole, one pattern clearly stands out. The only Indian minority group that has applied in large numbers for refugee status beyond the region are the Sikhs, who are also one of the most advanced minorities in the country in a socioeconomic sense and have a long tradition of outmigration. The other main group to become international refugees were the tribal people, and they generally remained within the region. Unlike the Sikhs, the tribal communities have no tradition of migration beyond the region and hence lack the resources and migratory networks that are necessary for an intercontinental search for refugee status. In socioeconomic terms, the disadvantaged position of the tribals and attachment to the native land further discourage movement beyond the region.

PAKISTAN   The new state of Pakistan had several sharp ethnic distinctions that intersected with other social formations to shape the contest for control of the state. An enduring expression of this conflict was democratization versus martial law.

Pakistan emerged after 1947 with a strong state built during the colonial rule but weak political party organizations, and a fairly stark semifeudal economy centered on large landholdings with widespread tenancy. The national bourgeoisie was small and timid, consisting largely of refugees from the partition. Onto this social structure were grafted institutions of liberal democracy. The uneasy fit lasted several years in two widely separated periods (1947–58 and 1971–77); during the rest of the time military rule prevailed. Military rule did not change the basic direction of social change or, initially, evoke much political conflict. The military had made an alliance with important elements of the established elites and tended to arbitrate among a plurality of powerful classes, rather than to dominate them.[54] A sudden national protest in 1969, however, compelled General Ayub Khan to hold elections. In the subsequent years of civilian rule and political liberalization, political consciousness among the masses and the bourgeoisie grew, and civil society was strengthened. The workers and peasants, in particular, were mobilized as the ruling party of Z. A. Bhutto sought to develop a mass base in order to gain an edge in the interelite competition that the ethnic divisions had sharpened.[55] Rapid economic growth associated with a policy of liberalization and an inflow of Western capital stimulated the development of the bourgeoisie and the industrial sector. As a result, when the military returned to power in 1977, it met with greater resistance. Co-optation of civilian elites no longer sufficed, and repression followed.

Critics of the regime under General Zia ul-Haq have compared it with the so-called national security states in Latin America, and the historical origins indeed are somewhat similar. The repression in Pakistan, however, has been less harsh, mainly because the opposition was not very radical, highly organized, or violent. Martial law in Pakistan meant select and gradual repression. In fact, one of General Zia ul-Haq's first actions was to release thousands of political prisoners jailed by the previous civilian government, including many associated with the autonomy struggles of the Baluch and Pathan peoples in the country's far northwest. By 1979, perhaps emboldened by U.S. support after the Soviet intervention in Afghanistan, the repression increased, and in 1981 the state openly flaunted its coercive techniques: mass detentions, public floggings, torture, sentences of amputation, and executions.[56]

Military rule and overt repression led to a sharp increase of Pakistani asylum seekers in Europe. Many were political activists associated with the previous regime, but also a wider spectrum of people criticizing martial law was affected. The numbers were fairly small, however. In West Germany, which had the biggest concentration of Pakistani asylum seekers, about 5,000 applied in 1977. The influx increased gradually until 1980 (6,824 applicants) before falling sharply as the West German government introduced new restrictions.[57]

The Pakistani inflow set off a near-panic reaction in West Germany. With the almost-simultaneous increase in asylum applicants from Turkey, it inaugurated the current period of restrictive European asylum policies, particularly toward Asians and Africans. The inflow of Pakistanis and, later, Turks also precipitated the current debate in Western Europe about the distinction between economic and political refugees.

The Pakistan case in fact was ambiguous. The country had a history of much labor outmigration, estimated at about 2.3 million (or about 40 percent of the total urban labor force) in the late 1970s. The majority went to the Middle East, but considerable early migration to Britain had been followed by substantial "guest-worker" employment in the rest of Europe, especially West Germany, in the early 1970s. Although the "push" factors behind the outmigration remained, the opportunities declined in the mid-1970s when Western European countries terminated their programs. It was at this time that the military seized power in Pakistan. The repression enabled would-be migrants to pose as refugees in the U.N. convention sense, but at the same time, such refugees were undeniably generated by martial law rule and could use established networks to escape along traditional migration routes. The problem for the recipient country in dealing with this mixed flow did not arise from conceptual ambiguity in the origins of flight, unlike other situations in which it could be argued that economic migrations were caused by a deliberate and discriminatory political act amounting to persecution. Rather, the Pakistani movements fitted conventional concepts and prevailing legal definitions of migrants and refugees. The challenge of sorting out individuals according to these categories was primarily administrative, not philosophical.

The other main social conflict in Pakistan was formed by ethnic divisions, which led to a different set of confrontations and refugees. Each of Pakistan's main linguistic groups had a clear territorial concentration: In the west wing of undivided Pakistan were the Sindhi, Baluch, Pathan, and Punjabi, and the Bengali were in East Pakistan on the other side of India. These divisions led to two major separatist movements by, respectively, the Baluch and the Bengali people. One failed and one succeeded.

The struggle for Baluchistan, which so far has failed, resembles similar movements in India's northeast. A community of tribes with a tradition of autonomous rule under the British, most of the 3.6 million Baluchs resisted the penetration of Pakistan's increasingly centralized administration and, with it, land acquisitions by the ruling Punjabi elite in their own province of Baluchistan. Sporadic fighting culminated in a four-year "brutal confrontation."[58] The war (1973–77) was much more intense and destructive than were the campaigns in India's northeast. Around 55,000 Baluchi guerrillas faced 80,000 Pakistani troops with superior firepower. There was extensive aerial strafing, many villages were destroyed, and villagers were rounded up by the army.

At the height of the war, the population displacement was summed up as follows: 30,000 in Pakistani jails, thousands hiding in the mountains, about 250,000 dispersed in the rest of Pakistan, 4,700 in neighboring Afghanistan, and about 5,000 in the Gulf and Saudi Arabia.[59] Some of the tribal guerrilla units moved across the border to Afghanistan, where they were quietly given sanctuary and called "refugees" by the Afghan government to avoid offending Pakistan. But most of the insurgents as well as the civilian population stayed behind. For the few thousand who wanted to leave, the Persian Gulf sheikdoms were attractive because there already was a Baluch community of 350,000 in the area, dating back to late-eighteenth-century migrations. Great Britain also had a small émigré community, big enough for a small Baluch newspaper to circulate, but evidently few fresh arrivals came in between 1973 and 1977. After the war a few leaders appeared in voluntary exile in London to carry on the struggle despite the truce, which did not radically alter the status quo ante.[60]

As in the other autonomy–separatist conflicts discussed so far, this one created remarkably few international refugees. One reason was the strength of the tribal ties to the "homeland," over which the conflict took place. The other important factor is topographical. Although the fighting was intense, it took place in a large and sparsely populated area, adjacent to other parts of the country where the minority could live and work safely.[61] The differences in the Bangladesh case in this respect are marked, suggesting that there is a threshold of space and violence beyond which pressures for massive outmigration will build up, particularly if external forces permit. The determinants of this threshold become clearer when we consider the two South Asian cases in which large refugee flows have materialized: Bangladesh and Sri Lanka.

BANGLADESH   Although the breakup of Pakistan in a sense was a continuation of partition, it also showed the "limit to which separatist problems can be adequately attributed to the decolonisation process or even, more generally, to the legacy of imperial divisions."[62] East Pakistan's secession in 1971 was a classic case of national liberation from a colonial political economy that was sustained in the postcolonial period, with relations of dominance and dependence further reinforced by ethnic divisions. Islam was virtually the only positive bond uniting East and West Pakistan. The East was Bengali, which meant a distinct culture, language, and past that had figured prominently in Indian history, including the nationalist movement. The East also had a slightly larger population than the West did, with 68 million people out of a total of 128 million (1971 figures). Territorial noncontiguity symbolized a deeper division between the two parts. The West had industry and manufacturing, whereas the East had raw materials, mainly jute. The West's capital investments, social welfare expenditures, calorie intake, and per-capita income also were higher than those in the East. The elected or self-appointed national leaders were overwhelmingly from West Pakistan. Some concessions to equity were made. Bengali became an official language alongside Urdu in 1956. The Bengalis, representing 53 percent of the national population, had demanded a greater share of civil and military service positions, and their representation had increased from a miniscule part in 1947 to about one-third in some of the services by the mid-1960s.[63] The army remained overwhelmingly West Pakistani, especially Punjabi, and not without denigrating stereotypical perceptions of the Bengalis.[64]

Political liberalization instituted in 1969–70 brought the situation to a head. National elections placed the conflict squarely in a competitive political arena, from which the Bengalis, being united and slightly more numerous than the disparate western population, came out ahead. Fearing that the Bengalis would use their newly acquired political power to implement regional autonomy and, at any rate, rejecting the prospect of Pakistan's being ruled by the Bengalis, the remaining military and the civilian leaders joined to deny the Awami League its parliamentary right to form a national government. At that point, a relatively peaceful Bengali protest provoked a singularly brutal army suppression on March 25, 1971. The violence marked a critical juncture in the development of the conflict; it was a declaration of full-scale war.

Although Bangladeshis tend to minimize the importance of India's military intervention, it undoubtedly brought to a rapid and decisive conclusion what otherwise would have been a long struggle. Pakistan's armed forces had serious difficulties fighting a war among a hostile population in a territory twelve hundred miles removed from its main base, but they had firepower and an international recognition. If the secessionists had not received direct military aid from India, the war would have dragged on for at least two to three years, according to their own estimates.[65] As it was, the Indian government started to train, arm, and give logistical support to the Bengali guerrillas in April and May, sent in regular Indian forces in November, and in the following month Pakistan surrendered. The case seems to confirm a tendency that has been observed more generally: A secessionist movement can start by its own volition but requires international support to succeed.[66]

By shortening the conflict and helping bring about unconditional independence for Bangladesh, Indian military intervention also decisively influenced the refugee flow. After only a few months in camps, millions of refugees could return home when the war ended. It was a relatively rare case of successful military intervention and not only because the popular insurgency was well advanced. By limiting their own reactions, other foreign powers enabled India to carry out a quick, surgical operation.

It was not a foregone conclusion that the conflict would be confined to the regional powers. Pakistan had a defense alliance with the United States and enjoyed friendly relations with China, which had defeated India in war only a decade earlier. Counterintervention as part of an intruding global competition was not improbable. In fact, India postponed its own intervention in order to secure a Treaty of Peace, Friendship and Co-operation with the Soviet Union, concluded in August 1971. In the end, however, none of the great powers deemed the separatist conflict in the northeastern corner of the subcontinent—bordered on all sides by India—sufficiently important to warrant more than a very limited involvement. The United States sent ships from the Seventh Fleet into the Bay of Bengal in the closing stages of the fighting, but it was too little and too late to deter India, let alone to prevent the breakup of Pakistan.[67] China, for its part, merely stated that the war was an internal Pakistan affair.

Another risk of intervening was that it would set a precedent. In a region of multiethnic states in which various groups, including those in India itself, were clamoring for recognition, only compelling domestic and foreign policy considerations could override the liabilities for India of openly supporting secessionists.

It was, of course, a perfect opportunity to deal a decisive blow to an archenemy.[68] Defeat would weaken Pakistan materially and undermine its ideological *raison d'être*, as Muslims were seceding from Muslims. It would presumably also give India a beholden new state of Bangladesh in a sensitive border region. Since the 1962 war with China,

India had feared Chinese intrusion in the northeast tribal areas separated from the rest of India by Bangladesh.[69] In India, the war would be popular, as hundreds of thousands of refugees pushed across the border with widely publicized horror stories of Pakistani atrocities.[70] As the flow mounted into the millions, the Indian state of West Bengal reeled under the impact, as did Tripura and Assam where a smaller number of refugees ("only" 1.5 million) weighed heavily on the traditional tension between Bengali immigrants and the indigenous communities. Indian intervention on behalf of the secessionists would, if successful, enable the refugees to return home, as the public rationale for intervention indeed carefully stated.

The refugees were an important part of the conflict, both militarily and politically. By keeping the border open, India made it possible not only for refugees to enter, but also for insurgents and volunteers to cross the border freely. India quite openly trained and maintained insurgents within the organizational structure of its own armed forces. The refugees had their own encampments, which provided a large pool of manpower for the insurgents. The diplomatic uses of the refugees to India were equally clear. The millions of refugees that suddenly flowed across the open border served to legitimize Indian intervention and the Bengali claim to independence. The refugees' testimonies to the world mass media detailed Pakistan army atrocities; their flight demonstrated that the Bengali people rejected foreign rule; and their teeming presence on Indian soil called out for a quick solution that would enable them to return.[71]

India's ability to derive political mileage from the refugee situation does not deny its objective reality. Although precise numbers are difficult to establish when millions of distraught people suddenly rush across the border, Indian sources estimate nine million (or 13 percent of East Pakistan's population) arrived between March and December 1971; other estimates are lower.[72] Most of the refugees were Bengali Hindus who were especially open to attacks by the armed forces. Because of their religion, the Hindus were suspected to be the most subversive elements in East Pakistan and the most determined to secure its secession.[73] But suspected insurgents and accidental bystanders among the Muslims were also likely targets in the escalating war. The insurgents had their own targets, principally "collaborators" and among the them the entire Bihari Muslim minority. These were non-Bengali Muslims from the eastern Indian states who had fled the violence of partition and its aftermath. Public massacres of Biharis formed a tragic postscript to the Bangladeshi liberation war.

The large population movements to India reflected the limited internal space available to permit an escape from violence. Bangladesh is a densely populated deltaic region, and India was easy to reach and safe. A huge international relief apparatus was set up under a special coordination organization, the U.N. Focal Point, as the demands exceeded the capacity of the regular UNHCR machinery. International assistance was specifically and urgently requested by India, which declared that it had no means of providing adequate relief by itself. Nevertheless, only about half of the estimated outlay of $400 million was covered by external sources.[74]

As in other successful independence struggles, most of the refugee population quickly returned to its homeland.[75] Some counted and probably uncounted thousands remained in neighboring Indian states where migration and refugee trails already had created sizable Bengali communities. Others became refugees in their "own" land. About 300,000 Bihari Muslims were left in Bangladesh, but as an originally poor, immigrant community that had fared relatively well in united Pakistan, they were now ostracized and harassed and lacked minimal physical and economic security. Many apparently wished to go to Pakistan, but Islamabad claimed that space and resources precluded large-scale repatriation. About 110,000 were admitted in 1974. The rest have rejected halfhearted Bangladeshi offers of citizenship and so live without civil status in semicamps, minimally aided only by the International Committee of the Red Cross (ICRC) and a few voluntary agencies.[76]

SRI LANKA   The struggle for Bengali rights was older than the Eelam movement for autonomy among the Sri Lankan Tamils, and the dynamics of the conflicts were different. In Sri Lanka, the Tamils constituted a small minority that only gradually moved toward an autonomy–separatist stance, and only after several attempts to establish a federative structure had failed. The international context also differed. This time the separatists found no ready external support that could bring the conflict to a speedy conclusion.

Constituting 1.87 million, or 12.6 percent of the population (1981 census), Sri Lanka's indigenous Tamil community was traditionally concentrated in the arid northeastern part of the island. Here, as elsewhere, colonial rule gave rise to new social formations, each vying for the favors of the colonial state. A range of opportunities opened up for the Tamils of the northeast. Upward mobility typically meant outward mobility, and so the Tamils came to dominate the professions and the civil service out of all proportion to their share of the total population.[77] Not surprisingly, the core of the postindependence conflict has been pressure from the Sinhalese majority for downward adjustment of the Tamils' socioeconomic status.

The other Tamil community in Sri Lanka, the so-called Indian or plantation Tamils, was also in a problematic but quite different situation. Having been brought in as colonial labor for the tea plantations, they had little contact with the Sri Lankan Tamils, were not associated with their struggle, but suffered severely in ethnic riots. The distance between the two groups was underlined by their common designations as, respectively, Indian and Sri Lankan Tamils.

For the Sri Lankan Tamils, the postcolonial adjustment process was aggravated by uneven development in many sectors of the economy. Major irrigation schemes in the eastern province led to Sinhalese settlements in traditional Tamil areas that generated fresh tension between the two communities.[78] The state-protected capitalism in the 1970s favored the Sinhalese majority, but their newly acquired privileges were threatened by the economic liberalization policies after 1977.[79] Simultaneously rapid but unevenly distributed economic growth created sizable urban groups of Sinhalese who were available as storm troopers in ethnic riots. Sinhalese nationalism drew its strength from other sources as well. By influencing the anticolonial struggle, Sinhala culture had made a claim to ideological hegemony, which before independence had already been expressed in exclusivist agitation against other minorities on the island (Christian, Muslim, and Malayali).[80] The Sri Lankan Tamils were the last minority to be exposed, but they were a much more formidable one. Indeed, the intensity of the Sinhalese reaction was related to the awareness that in a subcontinental context, it was the eleven million Sinhalese who constituted a small and potentially quite vulnerable minority, facing—across the narrow Palk strait that separates Sri Lanka from India—about fifty million, ethnically self-conscious Tamils in India. India's support for the Tamil militants did little to assuage such fears.

The Sinhalese attacked the Tamil position on two fronts. First, the potentially united Tamil vote was divided and neutralized by disenfranchisement of the Indian Tamils (1948). Second, the status and economic power of the Sri Lankan Tamils were eroded by discriminatory policies regarding language and education. The conflict evolved unevenly, however. After a crisis in communal relations in 1956–58, a relative detente followed in the 1960s as the two communities resumed a political dialogue and no major new discriminatory measures were enacted. But in the 1970s the government introduced a series of "affirmative actions" to help the Sinhalese obtain higher education which, under the prevailing conditions of scarce resources, was at the expense of the Tamils. The reforms in a sense "attacked the basis of security of the Tamil minority"; lacking both political power and a fertile agricultural base, the minority had relied on technical and scientific expertise to advance its career.[81]

The problems in this situation were severe but hardly sufficient for the minority as a whole to favor secession. The Tamils still retained access to privileged higher education roughly in proportion to their share of the population. As "an advanced minority from a backward region," they had a clear interest in not being confined to a small "homeland," except as a last resort to enjoy physical security, as Donald Horowitz has pointed out.[82] They had not been victims of serious mob violence since 1958 (the 1977 violence was mainly directed at the Indian Tamils in the central highlands). They retained an overwhelming numerical preponderance in the northern province (dropping less than 1 percent from 1963 to 91.8 percent of the total population in 1981), although Sinhalese settlers had made inroads in the southernmost part of the eastern province.[83] A section of the younger generation had by the mid-1970s launched an armed separatist struggle, but the moderates still pursued a parliamentary strategy to achieve autonomy, despite increasing disillusionment with the promises held out by the new government that took office in 1977.

Events in 1983 transformed the conflict. The violence in July 1983, whose origins remain obscure,[84] exercised a "step-level function" on the intercommunal conflict similar to the "dark night" of March 25 in Bangladesh: From then on, it was civil war. The "riots" this time were more organized and widespread than before, taking on the character of a five-day state and Sinhalese-sanctioned campaign—in effect, a pogrom—against the Tamil minority. Estimates of the number of persons killed varies from almost 500 (government sources) to 2,000 (independent observers), and 100,000 to 200,000 persons were made homeless.[85] Of the nearly 80,000 who crowded into refugee camps around Colombo, about 70,000 later moved to the relative safety of Tamil-populated areas in the northeast. The internal refugee flows were both a consequence and a cause of interethnic tension, as the refugees brought with them tales of horror that strengthened the appeal of the militant Tamils.

As the conflict intensified, so did the presures for internationalization, mainly from India. In line with its role as a regionally preeminent power, India sought to define the parameters of the conflict and exclude other nations, in particular the United States and its supporters in the region, Pakistan, and China. As it turned out, India's fears were exaggerated. The great powers had little interest in an obscure separatist conflict in a small, nonaligned country that had little strategic relevance to their own rivalries.[86] But even limited internationalization had an escalatory effect. India's support enabled the Tamil militants in a crucial initial stage to rise above the level of making scattered, amateurish attacks to become, by 1986, an organized and much more self-reliant force that exercised de facto control in much of the northern province and seriously challenged the government forces in the east. Indian support included providing a sanctury and training in South India and facilitating access to financial and diplomatic support. But compared with the Bangladesh conflict, it was a secretive and halfhearted effort. Indian officials denied the well-known fact that the militants had established political offices and military training camps in the South Indian state of Tamil Nadu. Indian units at any rate trained only some of the militant groups and did not supply all of the weapons that the militants shipped across to their island bases under the benign watch of Indian authorities.[87]

The caution, which contrasts sharply with India's unconcealed intervention in Bangladesh, matched its diplomacy: India supported claims for limited autonomy but not the more comprehensive demands of the Tamil militants, and certainly not secession. The autonomy–separatist agitation in parts of India had by this time become a serious problem and made it imperative to avoid a radical precedent. Unlike the Bangladesh stiuation, there were no compelling counterarguments. India and Sri Lanka had no outstanding animosities of the kind that made India and Pakistan ritual enemies. A more interventionist Indian role, it was reasoned, could in fact drive Sri Lanka closer to countries that Indian policy sought to keep out of the Indian Ocean region, notably the United States.[88] Even the relatively minor military links that the Colombo government had established with Pakistan and Israel (in the form of arms purchases and technical assistance) caused considerable anxiety in New Delhi.

Domestic considerations, however, favored a pro-Tamil role. The cost of supporting some 125,000 Tamil refugees in South India was barely noticed in an area with a local population of about fifty million, who also were Tamil and sympathized with the struggle of their ethnic "brothers and sisters" in Sri Lanka. No state or central government could afford to ignore this factor which, moreover, was magnified by local political configurations.[89]

The result was a generally inconclusive policy cast in the official mold of mediation that by 1987—four years after the fighting had escalated—had yielded few significant results. India was unwilling to shorten the conflict by decisive intervention in support of the separatists, was equally reluctant to pressure the latter toward a compromise, but was determined to keep out other foreign powers. The conflict had settled into a destructive stalemate. The Sri Lankan government adamantly refused to accept the militants' terms for autonomy but was unable to dislodge them from the "liberated" regions. Popular sentiment on both sides tended to harden with the protracted violence. The Indo–Sri Lankan peace accords of July 1987 and India's subsequent direct intervention by dispatching "peacekeeping forces" to the island brought little respite, only making the patterns of violence more complex.

The refugee profile produced by Sri Lanka's autonomy–separatist conflict is quite distinct. As on the Indian subcontinent earlier, communal violence initially led to internal relocation. After the first serious clashes in 1958, when perhaps 1,000 persons, mainly Tamil, were killed, the government evacuated about 10,000 Tamils to the north. About 2,000 Sinhalese escaped their minority position in the north or parts of the east, by moving south.[90] The violence in 1977 forced about 25,000 Indian Tamils from the central highlands to seek security by resettling in the northeast.[91] After the 1983 "riots," there again was massive internal migration, as about 70,000 Tamils moved north. Only rough estimates of internal refugees in the subsequent years of intensified fighting in the northeast are available, partly because the flows fluctuate according to the military activities. As of mid-1986, a figure of 150,000 was cited.[92]

The outflow spilled across international borders also in the early years. Migration statistics for the 1950s read like a diagnostic chart of social conflict. Between 1950 and 1960, the outmigration of Sri Lankan citizens was slight but steady, except for noticeable increases in 1956 and 1958, the years of crisis in communal relations. Throughout the

1960s, the outmigration climbed steadily to peak dramatically in 1972 after another bout of widespread violence, this time the government's suppression of a radical Sinhalese insurrectionist movement in which maybe eight thousand to ten thousand were killed and fourteen thousand were detained.[93]

Although precise figures for the 1970s are not available, the population outflows after 1983 were of a completely different magnitude. By mid-1986, about 250,000 claimed or were receiving assistance as refugees, of which 125,000 were in India and about 75,000 in Europe, North America, and Australia.[94] The majority of these had left after the 1983 riots. By contrast, the peak year of outmigration in an earlier period was only about 6,000 (in 1972). Also revealing is the movement before and after 1983 to West Germany, a relatively easy country to enter. From 1979 to 1982, a period of intensifying communal strife, the number of Sri Lankans in West Germany, presumably mostly Tamils, increased at the rate of 2,000 per year to reach almost 9,000; after the 1983 riots the increase was in the order of 10,000 annually.[95] All together, the post-1983 outflow amounted to a sizable 12 percent of the minority population.

The refugee flow spilled across Sri Lanka's border partly for reasons of space. In only a few areas of an already small island did the Tamil minority feel reasonably safe and included those parts of the north controlled by the militants and the capital city where the government successively proved its determination to prevent a repeat of the 1983 riots. Elsewhere, the state was seen as failing to protect the Tamils, who feared equally the police, the armed forces, and the Sinhalese paramilitary groups.

About half of the international movement went to neighboring India. Most of the 125,000 who were there by mid-1986 had come by plane immediately after the 1983 riots. About two-thirds of them had independent means or family connections in South India. The "boat people" crossed for the most part to escape heavy fighting in February–March and August–September 1985. These were mainly peasants, fishermen, and small traders who wanted to return (and some subsequently did so) when things calmed down at home. Crossing became more dangerous, however, as the Sri Lankan navy tried to intercept the traffic of militants, and the boat people almost stopped coming. Similar restraints did not apply to persons leaving by plane, which became the only public transportation linking Sri Lanka with the outside world when ferry services to India were suspended after the 1983 riots. Because the Sri Lankan government readily allowed Tamils to leave in this way, class increasingly determined exit.[96] On the entry side there were no barriers, as India maintained a completely open admissions policy for Sri Lankan Tamils. Indian authorities also aided the refugees with various relief and rehabilitation measures.[97]

Being a minority with a high level of education and a sizable middle-class component, the Tamils had the resources to seek asylum also farther afield. Migratory networks established during earlier outmigrations from the 1950s onwards also facilitated the later waves of tens of thousands who sought asylum in Europe and North America. Unlike India, however, the Western industrialized countries did not have an open admissions policy for Sri Lankan Tamils. Tamil asylum applications in the West have proved vexing because first asylum is available in the region and there are conflicting elements in the Tamil refugee experience. Their situation embodies the classic concept of refugees as developed in European practice and law: The Tamils as a group were exposed to violence targeted against the minority and risked being caught in the increasingly generalized battles in the island. But the Tamils are also a migrating minority. In colonial times, upward mobility for the Tamils in the arid North typically meant outward mobility: A few thousand even ended up as civil servants in the British colonial administration of

Malaya. After independence, policies designed to move Tamils down on the socio-economic ladder so as to make more room for the Sinhalese majority provided new incentives for outmigration. Deprivations of this kind combined with the risk of physical violence to convince many Tamils that they had little future in Sri Lanka.[98] Even an autonomous Tamil region in the northeast, were it to be realized, would not be an attractive homeland if the Tamils would be effectively confined to this region alone.

To draw the line between refugee and migration in this situation was problematic. It was not merely that the two groups traveled along similar routes and used the same networks. The migration experience itself had elements of deprivation that resembled the concept of persecution in Anglo-American jurisprudence. More restrictive access for Tamils to education and employment was the result of deliberate policies, and as the conflict wore on, the Tamils could claim that their economic difficulties derived from a punitive political act.[99]

Western countries used the ambiguities in the Tamil situation to restrict asylum. The path to easy asylum—opened by some countries in the aftermath of the 1983 riots—was closed as the Tamils kept coming, even though the absolute number was small.[100] British procedures were tightened in May 1985 after a sudden inflow of 1,500 in that month alone (equivalent to the annual figure of net entries from Sri Lanka in the 1960s) created consternation in the Home Office. West Germany followed suit in 1986 as part of a general restriction. An estimated 36,000 Tamils were in the country at that time. As a rule, Tamils who were denied asylum in European countries were not deported but stayed on in a legal twilight. The United States was more consistent, maintaining all along that the Tamils as a group were migrants and so were not entitled to stay. The exclusionary rule in part derived from foreign policy considerations. Next to Pakistan, Sri Lanka was the region's most supportive government of the United States. Political concerns likewise operated in the contrasting case of India's open asylum and general relief measures for Tamils. A liberal refugee policy was a logical extension of Indian sympathy for the Tamil community and support to the militants. When the Indian government later claimed that its "peace-keeping forces" sent to the island in July 1987 had succeeded in restoring peace and order, the refugees were repatriated, although widespread fighting continued in 1988 and the European countries generally did not compel their Tamil refugees to return. Throughout, the Indian government pointedly excluded the UNHCR and other international organizations from dealing with the refugees. This served to keep a low profile for the refugee presence and was consonant with the other, mediatory dimension of India's Sri Lanka policy.

Returning to the question of why, among the many conflicts arising from ethnic pluralism in South Asia, only in the cases of Sri Lanka and Bangladesh did large international refugee flows result, it is clear that a key factor was the high level of violence within a limited space. But equally important was the "targeted" people's perception of the state as their antagonist. Safety, accordingly, lies on the other side of an international boundary. In both cases, the neighboring state, India, readily provided asylum because of its partisan political involvement in the conflict. In Sri Lanka, however, India's policy reflected the inherent bias of the international system against the regrouping of political communities in the postcolonial era. Lacking sufficient aid to succeed, the separatists remained strong enough to ensure that the conflict instead simmered, with protracted refugee consequences.

In Bangladesh, as in the classic case of partition, the refugee problem was diminished by the existence of a homeland to which the uprooted peoples speedily returned. For the Sri Lankan Tamils, the inconclusive conflict made asylum a long-term prospect, and as "an advanced minority from a backward region," an exclusive homeland in the northeast was at any rate less relevant. Their mounting demand for settlement in the industrialized states also reflected the resources and migratory networks of the Tamil community. As we have seen, another educated and prosperous minority in the region (the Sikhs) similarly sought asylum outside the region, in contrast with the tribal peoples.

Revolution and Intervention in West Asia: Afghanistan

The Saur Revolution in Afghanistan (April 1978) and the subsequent internationalization of the conflict left in its wake destruction, death, and large population movements. At the core of this conflict was the struggle between a revolutionary leadership trying to use a relatively weak central state to effect fundamental socioeconomic and political change in the countryside, and the entrenched local-tribal power centers trying to defend themselves. Given Afghanistan's location—wedged between the southern border of the Soviet Union and Pakistan, an ally of the United States—it was perhaps not surprising that the struggle became heavily internationalized.

Efforts to modernize Afghanistan have always involved a struggle between a weak state at the center and local powerholders in the regions where traditional clan and chieftain leaders held sway.[101] A clan-based preindustrial society, Afghanistan in the twentieth century was also a strongly Islamic country, and Islam was invoked most loudly by those who opposed change.[102] The modernizers and the concomitant growth of central state power came to be associated with secular ideologies such as nationalism, constitutionalism, liberal democracy, and, lastly, Marxism-Leninism. This pattern of conflict was established during the reign of the first, serious modernizer, King Amanullah (1919–29). It was repeated when the Marxist-Leninist People's Democratic Party of Afghanistan (PDPA) seized power half a century after his death.

The PDPA launched a "putschist" revolution which immediately became enmeshed in its own contradictions. The PDPA, established in 1965, came to power through a military coup and started to institute radical social change with a weak party structure, few cadres, and entrenched opposition from the established social forces in the countryside.

The party confronted a society that in important respects seemed unchanged from earlier centuries. About 90 percent of the population of 16 million was illiterate. The GNP per capita was among the lowest in the world, and infant mortality was among the highest.[103] Only about 13 percent of the land was cultivated, owing to difficult natural conditions. The majority of peasants were smallholders. There were some large landowners with sharecroppers, but where sharp inequalities in income and wealth occurred, clan and tribal affiliations helped to mitigate their impact. The entire status quo was sanctioned by Islam as interpreted by village *mullah*.

This order was systematically attacked by the Saur Revolution in 1978–79. Led by the Khalq faction under Nur Mohammed Taraki and later Hafizullah Amin, the regime issued a battery of decrees for greater secularization, improvement in health and education, liberation of women, prohibition of usury, and abolition of many categories of peasant debt. It culminated with a comprehensive land reform (November 1978).

The opposition to the revolution developed in much the same way as it had against King Amanullah. Muslim Brotherhood organizations declared *jihad* against the revolution in the fall of 1978. Village *mullah* denounced land reform as being against the Koran. By early 1979 there were open rebellions in many parts of the country where the supposed beneficiaries of the reforms—the nonprivileged peasants, the landless, and women—rallied around religious and tribal leaders. Antigovernment rebellions took place among the historically dominant Pathans as well as the minority tribes of Tajik, Uzbek, Hazara, and Nuristani, who had relatively more to gain from the policies of cultural pluralism promoted by the new regime.

The problems of the revolution resulted not merely from poor judgment or doctrinaire policies by the PDPA, although that did play a role.[104] Under Amin, the government also became quite violent, much of it turned inwards in bloody party purges. More generally, the party was faced with a number of cruel choices which forced it into a radical direction, starting with the decision to seize power in 1978. The Daoud government's suppression of leftists in early 1978 was the catalyst, leaving them a choice of being "slaughtered, or . . . act[ing] to seize power," even though the revolution thereby might be premature.[105] Once in power, the party leaders recognized that in order to develop the mass rural base that they lacked, they had to attack the existing order by instituting both economic and sociocultural changes. Time was of the essence, as the counterrevolutionary forces were rapidly gaining momentum, with the fighting markedly escalating in the fall of 1979.[106]

The internationalization of the conflict proceeded on two levels. The counterrevolutionaries early on included some Afghan groups based in neighboring Pakistan, which rapidly fell into its traditional role of aiding the rebels against the regime in Kabul.[107] Before the Soviet intervention in December 1979, however, the importance of the Pakistan-based resistance was insignificant in comparison with the opposition inside Afghanistan.[108]

The Soviet intervention with some 120,000 troops transformed the conflict in both its internal and external dimensions. It rapidly became an East–West confrontation in which a foreign-aided front of Afghan rebels (*mujahedin*) fought to repulse the foreign invaders; the Soviets and their PDPA ally, for their part, were pressed to consider saving the pieces by means of an "honorable" Soviet military withdrawal that would leave a friendly, or at least a neutral, regime in power. The attempted revolution that had started it all was forgotten by both sides.

The general reasons for the Soviet intervention seem clear. Afghanistan borders the Muslim-populated Soviet Central Asia. In the eighteenth and nineteenth centuries, the country was an object of continuous rivalry between tsarist Russia and imperial Britain. The Soviet Union was the first country to recognize Afghanistan after King Amanullah in 1919 rejected the limitations on the country's sovereignty imposed by the British in the late nineteenth century. A Soviet-Afghan Treaty of Friendship had already been concluded in 1921, affirming the principle that the two countries' territory would not be used against the interest of the other. The suppression of Muslims in Soviet Central Asia in the 1920s did not destroy the conventional wisdom in Afghanistan that the greater imperialist threat was not the Soviet Union but Britain, with whom the Afghans had fought three wars since 1838. Over the years, the Soviet Union became Afghanistan's principal trading partner and major source of economic and military assistance.

Moscow evidently did not play a role in promoting the coup that launched the Saur Revolution.[109] But once the revolution was about to collapse under the forces of reaction, Moscow intervened. The revolution itself was hardly their main concern, as the first actions of the Soviet-installed leader, Babrak Karmal, were to slow down the pace of social change set by his predecessor. Rather, had the radical Khalq faction continued unchecked, it either would have brought the country to chaos or, by victory for the reactionary forces, placed traditional leaders in charge of the government. Either scenario was unattractive to Moscow at a time when the turbulent events in Iran spelled trouble on another stretch of the Soviet Union's southern border.[110]

The Soviet move to protect its "soft underbelly" had the contrary effect of generating a counterintervention. The Soviet action gave the *mujahedin* legitimacy and a political rationale to organize, with large-scale foreign assistance. The main supporters were Middle Eastern countries, responding to the appeals of the Organization of Islamic Conferences, the United States, and China. The assistance was channeled through Pakistan, which provided crucial support by allowing thousands of rebels to use Pakistan's border area as a sanctuary and staging base. Simultaneously, a huge international relief assistance program was established to aid the almost three million Afghans who by the early 1980s had come to Pakistan to escape the war or join the resistance.

International weapons aid and diplomatic support of the *mujahedin* were clearly insufficient for them to "win" in a conventional sense. The rebels' seven-party alliance based in the Pakistani border town, Peshawar, in vain sought international recognition as a government in exile. Nor did the rebels initially obtain sophisticated weapons. In late 1982 they started to receive mortars, bazookas, and grenade launchers from the United States,[111] and four years later came the sophisticated antiaircraft missiles from the United States and Britain that the rebels long had requested. In 1985–86 the American arms aid program was greatly increased in dollar terms.[112]

Throughout, the assistance remained covert, reflecting a desire by the rebels' foreign patrons not to risk a direct confrontation with the Soviet Union. More useful to great power rivalry was a continuous, stalemated conflict that served to embarass the Soviet Union and drain its resources. Considerations for the host country also suggested a low profile of support. Pakistan feared that the mushrooming rebel presence in its Northwest Frontier Province (NWFP) would invite retaliation, in the first instance by air attacks in the border region and bomb explosions of the kind that occurred with increasing frequency in the mid-1980s. Beyond this loomed the possibility of a war on two flanks, given Pakistan's location between Afghanistan and India, the latter being both an archrival and a friend of the Soviet Union.

The Afghan conflict brought benefits to the Pakistan government that helped compensate for the risks and additional costs of hosting a refugee population of nearly three million people. It meant external recognition and material support for a country that some observers believed was on the verge of disintegration in the early 1980s.[113] The military government's international image—tarnished by the 1979 execution of the former prime minister and a poor human rights record—improved as Pakistan emerged as the frontline state against Soviet expansion in Afghanistan and a generous home for millions of refugees. The U.S. aid program, which previously had been terminated on the grounds that Pakistan appeared to be developing a nuclear weapons capability, was restored. A package of $4.4 billion over five years in military and economic assistance was agreed to in 1981 and renewed in 1987.

The Afghan revolution had created refugees before the Soviet intervention, as about 280,000 had left for Pakistan between April 1978 and November 1979.[114] After the intervention, many more departed before the numbers tapered off in the early 1980s. An estimated 2 million to 2.5 million had reached Pakistan by the end of 1983, 0.5 to 1 million were in Iran, and a few thousand went to Western Europe and the United States.

Three years later the figures for Iran and Pakistan were revised upwards to 1.9 million and 2.9 million, respectively.[115] Inside the country, the war displaced a large number of people from the countryside who sought food and shelter in the towns. The population of Kabul doubled to reach about 2 million.[116]

The international flow consisted of sociologically mixed groups. Initially, members of the *ancien régime* were targeted, and many in fact did not get out. President Daoud and his immediate associates were executed, and others were jailed. By mid-1979 the suppression had increased and had in part turned inwards: Perhaps two thousand members of the rival PDPA party faction (Parcham) were killed by the dominant Khalq faction.[117] After the Soviet intervention, the intensity of the fighting increased sharply; in particular, the use of high-altitude bombing to attack the *mujahedin* compelled entire villages to flee. When the *mujahedin* acquired advanced antiaircraft missiles (Stingers), the government forces came to rely even more on heavy firepower.[118] On the other hand, the fighting was concentrated in only some areas,[119] and signs of normalcy in other areas despite the war were noted in U.S. intelligence reports. By late 1987, the cumulative effect of "massive Soviet use of artillery and high-level saturation bombing" had caused surprisingly little destruction: only "5–10 percent of cultivated area has been damaged since the invasion, concluded the Department of State."[120]

The need to escape the violence of war, in other words, would seem not to be a generalized problem throughout the country but to vary with military offensives in particular regions. The outflow nevertheless was of an unprecedented magnitude in the history of Asian refugee movements, and the fact that almost one-third of the people in a large, sparsely populated country fled to refugee camps in neighboring states requires further explanation. In particular, by moving to Pakistan it was possible to mount a large, popular resistance movement against the regime, whereas the civilian refugee population was supported by a massive international relief assistance program. Traditional ethnic affinities and economic ties also facilitated movement across the border.

The routes from Afghanistan to Pakistan and Iran traditionally have been heavily traveled by exiles, migrants, and traders. Similarities in language and culture had encouraged a substantial labor migration from the western provinces of Afghanistan to Iran during Iran's economic boom in the 1970s, and many elected to stay after the 1978–79 upheavals in Afghanistan. Iran's Islamic revolutionary leaders readily provided asylum to these and later arrivals and generally supported the *mujahedin* struggle against the Soviet-supported, Marxist powerholders in Kabul.[121] In Iran the refugees were located in local residential areas, with the costs largely absorbed by the government. Only in 1983 did Teheran ask for UNHCR assistance to establish a modest international program and in 1986 allowed the UNHCR to have a small resident staff.

On the Pakistan side, the traditional cross-border traffic was even more marked. The Durand line drawn by the British in 1983 separated the ethnically distinct Pathan population into two parts. In Afghanistan, the 8 million Pathans came to form a dominant majority. In Pakistan's adjacent border province (NWPF) the 8.5 million Pathans constituted the local majority, even though they represented only 10 percent of Pakistan's total population. The constellation led to intermittent demands for merging the two into a "Pashtoonistan," and de facto elements of a united entity had always been noticeable. Migrant labor moved from Afghanistan into Pakistan; Afghan nomads crossed in large numbers to bring their sheep to winter pasture; and exiles from both sides found ready asylum. The post-1979 trek from Afghanistan, mainly by Pathans, followed and mingled with these flows.

After Pakistan asked in April 1979 for UNHCR assistance, the latter coordinated much of the international aid to the refugees, but the camps were administered by Pakistan authorities. The UNHCR-channeled aid averaged nearly $75 million annually. The other main relief agency was the United Nations' World Food Program, with an annual budget of $100 million. In addition, over forty international voluntary agencies were working among the refugees. The lead financier in this massive relief apparatus was the United States, which by the end of fiscal year 1986 had contributed over half a billion dollars for Afghan refugees. In 1985 the United States also started a "cross-border" program of $35 million to $40 million annually to support development projects in rebel-held areas inside Afghanistan. Other major donors to the U.N. relief program were U.S. allies (West Germany, Canada, Japan, and Australia), and conservative Islamic states in the Middle East (Saudi Arabia and other Gulf states).[122]

The United States, Saudi Arabia, and China were also the main suppliers of military assistance to the rebels. Support for the Afghan refugees was a logical counterpart to these efforts. Requests for aid to the refugees could draw on deep sources of sympathy in the West: It was humanitarian aid to refugees from a cruel war; it was aid to a people fleeing a foreign intervention; and it was aid to a population fighting the Soviet Union. The essential political underpinnings of the relief effort were highlighted by the very different reception given to another large flow of refugees coming to Pakistan. After 1979, thousands of Iranians crossed into Pakistan, fleeing from the Ayatollah Kohmeini's regime and conscription for the war against Iraq. UNHCR officials in Pakistan have noted many similarities in the degree of life-threatening situations facing the Iranians and the Afghans.[123] Yet there were no camps, no mass relief, and little official recognition for the Iranians. Not until late 1985 was there a slight improvement in the process of registering Iranians for third-country resettlement.[124] The very existence of millions of Afghan refugees, on the other hand, was viewed internationally as a massive indictment of the Soviet-backed PDPA and a legitimation of the resistance, and they were supported accordingly.

Perhaps more clearly than in other refugee situations, the humanitarian and political dimensions of the Afghan refugee situation were mutually reinforcing. The exiled people represented an entire population of women, children, and armed rebels, the latter being allowed free operation on Pakistani soil next to the sprawling camps of their dependents. What we have called a refugee-warrior community, with armed forces and a distinct political leadership and social structure, rapidly emerged.[125] As time passed and the community was strengthened by annual inflows of financial and material aid, the warriors appeared to take de facto control in the border region. The *mujahedin* operated freely on their own terms in the NWFP, where they were among fellow Pathans who had traditionally asserted their independence vis-à-vis the central government of Pakistan, increasingly casting doubt on the central government's ability to assert its power over the refugee-warrior community.

Although precise figures are not available, it is clear that only a small proportion of the Afghan refugees resettled in Western countries. The United States' admissions figures are indicative. As by mid-1988, only about 22,000 had entered as refugees.[126] After the Vietnamese inflow, no Western country was prepared to undertake yet another large-scale refugee resettlement program. Moreover, if the resistance movement were to continue and the prospect of return kept alive, the Afghan refugees would need to remain in the neighboring area of their home country.

Chapter 6

Revolution and Reaction in East Asia

The most striking difference in the national development patterns in East Asia compared with those in South Asia is the importance of class distinctions in relation to ethnic or religious identification. The dynastic states of eastern Asia had a long tradition of ethno-linguistic and religious homogeneity. In China, Korea, and Vietnam,[1] this unity was related to the pervasive Confucian ideology and its parallel unitary bureaucracy; in Japan, the government for centuries patronized Buddhism. In the late nineteenth and early twentieth centuries, social change centered on the decline of feudalism and the emergence of nationalist movements attempting to harness new forces of modernization. Regional divisions at times were formidable obstacles to national unity in this process, notably warlordism in China (1916–27) and progressively decentralized feudalism in Japan before the Meiji Restoration.

Subnational identities did not develop easily because they lacked exclusive ethnic distinctions and were not sharpened by colonial rule. Where subnational distinctions did appear, as in Tibet, Mongolia, and among the Turkic peoples of Singkiang, they defined minorities in the periphery of China that did not set the direction of national development. Instead, the dominant axis of social conflict followed lines of class formation and led to opposing nationalist forces: a revolutionary nationalism seeking radical social change, as opposed to a nationalism prepared to accommodate existing power structures.

External forces shaped this process both indirectly and directly. In some cases, modernizing nationalism was primarily a response to external threats and sought to avoid colonization by imitating foreign technology (Japan). In countries that had been fully colonized by European powers, nationalism in its various forms was a reaction against foreign domination (Vietnam). In China, which was partially colonized by European powers and subsequently invaded by Japan, both tendencies were evident.

By the early to mid-twentieth century it was evident that the contending modernization processes were being resolved quite differently in the various parts of East Asia. Initial gradual change in Japan culminated in a militarist regime and catastrophic defeat in World War II. In Korea and Vietnam, decolonization from, respectively, Japanese and European metropolitan rule brought national bifurcation. Largely owing to foreign intervention, the two countries were divided, each half representing a revolutionary and an accommodative nationalism, respectively. Only in Vietnam did eventual unification follow a protracted, devastating war. Although the communists were victorious in China, almost half a century of civil war and struggle against foreign domination stretched between the collapse of the old Manchu dynasty in 1911 and the communist victory in 1949. And the inauguration of the new order in China meant continuous social struggle and occasional massive upheavals.

The turbulent path of social change and foreign invasions in East Asia during this century meant death, destruction, and the displacement of people on a massive scale. Much of this population movement was internal. A special category was the repatriation of millions of Japanese from the disintegrating Japanese empire in Manchuria, Taiwan, Korea, and Southeast Asia when World War II came to an end. Large international movements of people who claimed recognition as refugees were mainly a result of revolutionary change in China, Korea, and the former French Indochina (Vietnam, Laos, and Kampuchea). Of these upheavals, the radical restructuring of China was the first and arguably the most momentous. The Chinese revolution provided a model of change for Asia's agrarian societies and influenced the global structure of the international strategic system. Less momentous but also of a classic variety were the refugees from China's revolution.

The Classic Case: Revolution in China

The collapse of the Manchu dynasty in 1911 was followed by years of social anarchy and political chaos, on which foreign occupation and civil war intermittently imposed a destructive order. Millions were uprooted, but China's huge size helped contain the population flows within its borders. When the outcome of the civil war became clear, the retreating Nationalist (Kuomintang, or KMT) armies still had space to regroup and bring some of their followers along. Those left behind were, on the whole, absorbed into the new social order, including the refugees from earlier campaigns such as the approximately 650,000 refugees from the countryside whom the Communist armies found huddled in Shanghai when they took the city in early 1949. The Chinese Communist party (CCP) screened out KMT civil and military personnel found guilty of "war crimes" but generally pursued a flexible policy toward populations in previously held KMT areas in order to shore up its own position, especially in the cities. The result of this broad, united front policy was to reduce the flow of refugees as the civil war drew to a close.[2]

The rapid southward retreat of Chiang Kai-shek's armies during "the year of defeat" in 1949 indicated the final refugee path. The KMT hastily withdrew its capital southward from Shanghai to Canton and, finally, Chungking. By this time, Taiwan was already serving as a rear base area for the Nationalists. The allies had agreed at the 1943 Cairo conference to return the island to China after the war; the Nationalists, representing China at Cairo, had duly taken possession of it when the Japanese surrendered. Anticipating that Taiwan might become a future capital of Nationalist China, Chaing Kai-shek had improved civil government on the island—much needed after the brutal repression of the 1947 popular uprising against KMT rule—and moved much of his air force as well as 300,000 troops there in the closing phase of the civil war. When the KMT's position on the mainland collapsed during the final Communist offensive in the southwest in October 1949, most of the remaining KMT armies and followers evacuated to Taiwan.

The approximately 600,000 soldiers and 1 million civilians who withdrew to Taiwan during 1949 were the first "international" refugees from the Chinese revolution. A contemporary account described them as "generals with their defeated or retreating troops, wealthy landlords and businessmen who feared the approaching Communists; and a swarm of government officials, secret police and camp followers."[3] They constituted the civilian and military infrastructure of the defeated regime, including about three-fourths of what had been the entire Nationalist army on the mainland before the big Communist offensive in April 1949.[4]

Although people continued to leave the People's Republic of China in subsequent years, the Nationalist government on Taiwan allowed very few to settle on its newly acquired island. The authorities encouraged individual defections from the mainland and paid million-dollar bonuses to pilots who flew air force planes across, but actively discouraged occasional attempts by more ordinary persons to sail small fishing boats from the mainland to the KMT-held islands of Quemoy and Matsu.[5] A similarly restrictive policy governed resettlement from Hong Kong, which had become the main receiving area for refugees from the mainland. Taiwan accepted only 150,000 for resettlement between 1949 and 1954, even though the British government in Hong Kong was desperately trying to relieve some of its overcrowded refugee colonies of about 700,000 persons. Most of those accepted for resettlement by Taiwan were former members of the KMT army.[6]

Taiwan's refugee policy departed sharply from the government's overall policy toward the mainland regime. Diplomatically, the civil war continued unabated, but, curiously, Taiwan was not prepared to accommodate those seeking to escape its adversary on the mainland. After all, every refugee could have counted as a small propaganda victory over the Communist regime. One reason for the restrictive refugee policy was fear of subversion and espionage, but careful screening of entrants presumably could have resolved that problem. Economic limitations were another initial concern. Back in 1949, U.S. authorities had remarked that the arrival of more than one and a half million mainlanders had "increased the population to a point which the island may not be able to support."[7] As it turned out, Taiwan's economy started to boom in the late 1950s and probably could have sustained a higher intake. Rather, the restrictive policy reflected the limitations of political solidarity (perhaps particularly among the faction-ridden KMT) when it meant sharing resources with refugees. A liberal admissions policy, moreover, would have aggravated the tension between the ruling KMT minority and the six million indigenous Taiwanese and might have encouraged a continuous inflow from China's untapped millions, as Hong Kong's experience indicated.

Apart from the route to Soviet Kazakhstan from the Singkiang border region, virtually the only way for people seeking to leave China illegally after 1949 was through the British crown colony of Hong Kong, which had both a sea and a land border (on the New Territories side) with China, and the tiny Portugese enclave of Macau.[8] The standard work on the subject claims that there was a steady inflow over a ten-year period after the Communist Victory, averaging 90,000 annually, but this seems incorrect: Most of the approximately 700,000 refugees estimated by an authoritative UNHCR study to be in Hong Kong by 1955 had arrived between 1949 and 1951.[9] Thereafter, the inflow dropped sharply but again increased markedly as China experienced internal upheavals associated with the Great Leap Forward and then the Cultural Revolution.

These ebbs and flows suggest the dynamics of refugee movements in a revolutionary situation. Within a few years after the Communists' seizure of power, those most likely to fall into the category of "enemies of the people" had made their choice. In addition to

KMT personnel who did not reach Taiwan during the evacuation, this category included members of the landed gentry who sought to escape dispossession or death as a consequence of the land reform instituted in 1950, as well as those individuals who feared that they would be caught in the wave of repression against "reactionary elements" initiated when China later in the year entered the Korean War. The refugees initially had few difficulties obtaining first asylum in nearby Hong Kong, which long had served as a place of refuge in times of upheavals in China. But as people kept coming and there was no sign of the customary return migration, the gate was shut. Fearing that the small crown colony would be literally flooded with people—refugees in the New Territories of Hong Kong were packed so tightly they seemed to "elbow each other off the precarious cliffs to which they cling"—the British authorities imposed restrictions from 1950 onwards.[10] A small quota of legal migration was retained; everyone else was treated as an illegal migrant and returned if caught.

China did not have a comprehensive no-exit policy. Some legal emigration was allowed, and in 1950 Chinese authorities in fact "sharply criticized" Hong Kong for curbing admissions.[11] A sizable flow of legal travel was permitted between the mainland and Hong Kong which facilitated illegal migration, but it leveled off during the 1950s. It was evident that any kind of population movement became more difficult as the Communist organizational apparatus developed. At the same time, the great masses of the people were starting to experience the benefits of the new order, and the CCP's reliance on a united front strategy served to limit the economic and social dislocations in the early years of the revolution. The emphasis on production over reorganization of ownership entailed a more gradual change and greater accommodation of both the urban bourgeoisie and the landed classes than had been the case in the Russian Revolution. The incentives to leave were reduced accordingly.

Massive outflows materialized later when the revolution went through successive phases of radicalization. The first occasion was the Great Leap Forward, announced in 1958, which involved a rapid collectivization of agriculture. The abrupt imposition of a communal structure seriously disrupted food production, and adverse weather conditions did the rest to create widespread shortages and severe famine in 1960–61.[12] Hong Kong authorities who had been accustomed to a "small but steady flow" of illegal immigrants now watched almost helplessly while thousands of people "forced their way" across the border in April–May 1962.[13] Faced with such pressures and obviously lax exit control on the other side, the Hong Kong authorities adopted a more liberal "touch base policy," whereby persons who managed to get inside the crown colony were allowed to stay. Approximately 150,000 qualified, and a somewhat smaller number were caught by Hong Kong patrols and returned.[14] By next year, however, illegal immigration was back to normal levels, reflecting both an improved food situation in China and tightened border controls on both sides.[15]

A third, distinct outflow was generated in the late 1960s as the revolution again took a radical turn, this time creating profound upheavals and violence that brought the entire country "to the brink of chaos," as Mao Tse-tung himself admitted.[16] The massive antibureaucratic, antiprofessional onslaught of the Red Guards was followed by generalized violence and pitched battles between opposing factions. The first consequence noted in Hong Kong was that traffic at the Lo Wu checkpoint, where the railroad crosses into China, slowed to a trickle. By mid-1966, daily crossings were down to about one hundred persons a day, as opposed to a more normal fifteen hundred. The Red Guards, in effect, were not letting people out. The Cultural Revolution in the first instance meant massive and compulsive internal migrations as part of the implementation of Maoist social policies.[17] A delayed but sustained illegal outflow followed.

By 1967, Hong Kong authorities noted that illegal immigration again was up and again adopted a "touch base policy." When the Cultural Revoltution subsided, both Hong Kong and China reverted to a position whereby all movement between the two was considered a matter of migration, legal or illegal. The new Chinese leadership took a more lenient view of illegal departures, appreciating the financial remittances they produced. But the Hong Kong authorities, reeling under a steady inflow, which reached a peak of eighty thousand legal entrants and an estimated two to three times that number of illegals in 1979, abandoned the "touch base policy," rounded up new illegals, and reduced the inflow.[18]

Considering the enormity and continuity of China's revolution and the size of its total population, an outflow of maybe 3.5 million in the first two decades of the new order is not much.[19] It gives a figure of 6 per 1,000, equivalent to the outflow from the more circumscribed French Revolution. The relatively low figure is even more remarkable because China has a history of large outmigrations caused by centuries of political upheavals and economic misery, which has created a vast international network and a diaspora population (the overseas Chinese).

Many, maybe millions of, potential emigrants did not come out after the Communist revolution because they starved to death or were killed, either in the very first years of the revolution or during the cultural Revolution.[20] During the Cultural Revolution, the magnitude of the "holocaust," as one analyst calls it, is indicated by retrospective official Chinese estimates that 100 million people suffered from "political harassment" between 1966 and 1976.[21] An estimated half a million died.[22] The casualties were on all sides, including thousands of Red Guards killed by the army and workers' militias in the closing phase of the Cultural Revolution. Whole town populations were caught in the cross fire, for example, the estimated 50,000 persons who perished when two towns in Kwangsi Province were totally destroyed in late 1968.[23] Others did not come out because of difficult internal movement and restrictive exit policies, although the Chinese were not consistent in this regard. Liberal exit represented a safety valve and a way to dispose of "reactionary elements," particularly in the early periods of the revolution, at which time the new regime lacked the apparatus to enforce a rigid no-exit policy anyway. Legal travel between Hong Kong and the mainland, moreover, was desirable for economic reasons. In periods of internal radicalization, however, the door was closed. Contacts with foreigners became more suspect, and foreign travel was sharply curtailed.[24] To leave the country illegally represented a renunciation of the revolution and was severely punished. The Red Guard slogan put the matter unambiguously: "You cannot run away from your shadow."

An equally important reason for the limited outflow was the lack of a place to go. Hong Kong and, to a much lesser extent, Taiwan, were the principal areas of refuge. The new arrivals placed an enormous and immediate burden on Hong Kong where the population increased almost 50 percent between 1949 and 1951. As a result, the most accessible first asylum area, Hong Kong, usually had a restrictive admissions policy and regularly turned people back. When entry was made easier, the inflow increased immediately, as when the downward sluice in a water reservoir is opened.[25]

Hong Kong's policy of treating the inflow from China as illegal migration was directly linked to the long-standing refusal by countries in Europe and North America to help by offering to resettle the 700,000 who had arrived shortly after 1949. Even the United States—which had aided the KMT during the civil war in China and was the major supporter of "Free China" on Taiwan—did not find that its role entailed an obligation to resettle many of the refugees fleeing the revolution. Successive American administrations disclaimed any special interest in Chinese refugees, even though the very existence of the Republic of China on Taiwan was largely a result of American support. Indeed, until 1972 the United States refused to recognize the Communist Chinese claim to legitimacy. Only in 1962, when hungry refugees from the Great Leap Forward flooded Hong Kong and the Nationalist Chinese representatives warned in the U.N. that their compatriots would be returned to their "executioners" unless the West relieved Hong Kong, was there some response.[26] The Kennedy administration agreed in 1962 to let Chinese refugees into the United States, and Canada and Australia also accepted some for resettlement. The Western countries' lack of interest is perhaps not surprising in view of a similarly restrictive policy by Taiwan, the government most closely concerned. But the contrast with American policy toward refugees from Asia's second major revolution, in Indochina, is striking, suggesting that the massive refugee resettlement in the latter case is indeed the exceptional response.

The international dimensions of the protracted revolutionary struggle on the Chinese mainland had mixed consequences for the refugees. Despite the hostility that the revolution evoked in the West, those who fled China's new order were met with restrictive asylum and resettlement policies. The evacuation of KMT supporters and their consolidation on Taiwan was possible only because of contending recognition policies that created, in fact, two Chinas. But although the Nationalist refugees could capitalize on the intense international divisions generated by China's revolution, later refugees derived no benefit from the two-Chinas issue and in one respect were directly disadvantaged by it. For several years the Chinese representation issue prevented the UNHCR from assisting hundreds of thousands of refugees in Hong Kong. As long as Taiwan represented China in the United Nations (as the Republic of China, or ROC), the ROC representative argued that aid to refugees from "China" would constitute implicit recognition of the mainland government. Until the legal technicalities were sorted out in the early 1960s, "refugees from China" could not, politically speaking, exist and therefore could not be aided under the U.N. system.

In sum, the various stages of the Chinese revolution generated different kinds of refugees. Early campaigns targeted active political opponents ("activists"), notably the KMT, and victimized individuals because of their membership in a social group (e.g., "large landlords"). Subsequent radicalization of the revolution broadened these categories to include many "bystanders" who were threatened by the Great Leap's reform-induced famine and the Cultural Revolution's uncontrolled violence. In this refugee-generating process, international factors were most visible on the receiving end. Because the refugees did not have a homeland (at least one that would accept large numbers), international unwillingness to provide asylum and resettlement sharply limited the magnitude of the outflow, although at times of internal radicalization, a simple overflow developed. The causes of that radicalization, in turn, were most directly related to domestic developments. Because China's size and resources made it a major international power in its own right in the region, the course of its revolution proceeded in some isolation from the international hostility it evoked.

Revolutionary Southeast Asia

The Western powers, mainly the United States, had made only a halfhearted attempt to forestall the Communist victory in China by supporting the KMT. Although the United

States subsequently accepted the revolution as a *fait accompli,* Washington refused to recognize the Communist government and tried to prevent what it regarded as Communist Chinese expansionism elsewhere in Asia. This involved the United States in a war on the Korean peninsula and in an escalating intervention in Indochina where it transformed the decolonization process into a major international war. The international dimensions came to dominate the Indochina conflicts, determining the longevity and destruction of the fighting and, to a large extent, also the refugee flows that appeared when the wars ended.

Vietnam

The violent history of contemporary Indochina centers on the Vietnamese revolution and the international reaction it evoked. The revolutionary struggle in Vietnam was a precondition and a contributing cause of the subsequent revolution in Kampuchea, as well as the less radical restructuring of Laotian society. Its genesis lies, perhaps, in the processes of nation-state formation that the ancient Vietnamese kingdoms shared with the Thais and the Khmer on the mainland of Southeast Asia. Vietnamese sovereigns ruled over populations that were linguistically and culturally homogeneous and professed the same Buddhist religion. Although the degree of central authority varied over time, a strong administrative apparatus and a coherent ideology made it possible to extract a substantial economic surplus and pursue a policy of national consolidation and expansion. Once the thousand years of Chinese rule ended in 939 A.D., the Vietnamese rulers were able to defeat further foreign aggression and promote an expansionary policy of their own. The imposition in the late nineteenth century of French colonial rule on a polity conscious of this tradition generated an immediate nationalist reaction.

After various neotraditionalist phases, Vietnamese nationalism in the early twentieth century divided along opposing class formations. These represented the principal lines of social divisions, overriding other cleavages such as the administrative and cultural divisions between the North and the South that the French and later the Americans emphasized to legitimate their own involvement.[27] The revolutionary and the reformist forces organized into two main groupings, respectively the Indochinese Communist party (ICP) and the Viet Nam Quoc Daw Dang (VNQDD), with the ICP taking the lead already in the 1930s. The ICP appealed to a disenfranchised peasantry, part of which had been transformed into a ruthlessly exploited labor force in a large tenancy sector and the southern plantation economy. Simultaneously, the colonial erosion of traditional authority patterns, which in themselves had been essentially collectivist, enabled the Communist party to build a wide organizational network in the villages. If these were structural preconditions for a revolutionary situation, events brought on by World War II accelerated them by weakening the state materially and ideologically, thereby undermining the capacity of the ruling force to maintain its power. At a crucial moment in the transfer of power from the defeated Japanese to the victorious allies, the state simply ceased to exist, enabling Ho Chi Minh, on behalf of the Communist-led Vietminh front, to make a unilateral declaration of independence in Hanoi on September 2, 1945.[28]

The French, supported by the United States, were unwilling to recognize the end of an empire by handing over power to the Vietnamese Communists, and the First Indochina War ensued. Lasting for eight years, it was a forerunner of the Second Indochina War to come, as were its refugee consequences.

During the war itself a number of people became internal refugees, but because each side had protected space available and there was a premium on controlling people in a "people's war," the refugees generally did not spill across international boundaries. Some, in the early phase, entered neighboring Thailand.[29] Within Indochina, the dislocation from the fighting was uneven. The most severe battles took place in the northern part of Vietnam where both the Vietminh and the French had secure zones to absorb temporarily displaced people. The most intense single battle (Dien Bien Phu) took place in a sparsely populated mountainous border area with Laos, whereas the entire southern part of Vietnam was a "secondary theatre of war."[30]

After the war, a different migration pattern developed as people sought to escape not the fighting but its political consequences. The July 1954 Geneva Accords accepted as temporary the partition of Vietnam that had emerged during the war. In the North there was a revolutionary nationalist regime, recognized internationally by the socialist countries as the Democratic Republic of Vietnam (DRV), and the South had an accommodative nationalist regime recognized by the Western powers as the Republic of Vietnam (RVN). Allowing for the different social characteristics of the two regimes, the accords stipulated free movement of people between North and South for about one year. As a result, about 1 million persons moved, of whom 900,000 went from the North to the South. Technically, they were not international refugees—both groups shared the same nationality and crossed a demarcation line, not an international boundary—but their motives were the same: a felt need to escape by entering a different body politic.

The population movements had great political and propaganda implications which both sides tried to exploit. In the North, local authorities (but apparently not the central government) sometimes refused to issue permits for people to leave, thereby violating the Geneva agreements.[31] In the South, relatively few persons applied to leave. The most determined efforts to influence the refugee movements were organized by a newly formed, special American unit (Saigon Military Mission, SMM) on behalf of the Southern regime. The objective was to encourage people to leave Communist Vietnam through an elaborate "psywar" campaign conducted in the North. Two revealing incidents are described in detail in the *Pentagon Papers*. In September 1954, SMM agents tried to sabotage the printing presses of a large private publishing firm in Hanoi that had decided to stay and work under Communist rule. The attempt to induce the firm to pack up and leave failed, but a subsequent "black psywar strike" in Hanoi was spectacularly successful. Agents distributed false leaflets "signed" by Vietminh officials with instructions concerning the scheduled transfer of French-controlled zones in the Tonkin area to the Communist authorities. The transfer was said to affect property (to be confiscated), money (to be devalued), and the workers (to be given a three-day holiday to mark the takeover). The next day, refugee registration tripled.[32]

Apart from false fears, people left for two main reasons. The first movement out of the North was essentially an evacuation of people who had been closely associated with the French. At the request of the RVN, and poignantly foreshadowing another evacuation twenty years later, most of the 300,000 were airlifted by the United States to the South. These were soldiers, functionaries, and a large number of Catholics, particularly from the large, semiautonomous dioceses where the bishops under the French regime had "ruled their own domain."[33] Over 600,000 Catholics, or two-thirds of North Vietnam's Catholic population, followed their priests southward.[34] The other main reason that people left in 1954–55 was the land reform instituted in 1954. It was implemented with much violence and many nonjudicial "trials" until the party in October 1956 recognized the excesses and took corrective steps.[35]

The Northern refugees from the 1954 accords belonged to social groups that had been strong supporters of the *ancien régime*—landlords and Catholics. In striking contrast with the Vietnamese refugee flows after 1975, the 1954 flow was not followed by a secondary wave of rank-and-file members of the society, even though the border was open until mid-1955. The Vietminh's patient work in building its grass-roots organization for over two decades had paid off; the masses were inclined to accept the new order. The Vietminh's popular strength also in the South likewise suggests why there was very little refugee movement from the South to the North. According to French and American estimates at the time, by 1954 the Vietminh controlled about two-thirds of the villages and about one-third of the territory in the South. Their supporters had been told to remain in the South after the Geneva Accords, either in preparation for resumption of warfare at a later date (as critics maintain) or because it was genuinely expected that Vietnam would be unified peacefully through a faithful implementation of the Geneva Accords (as supporters argue).

The refugees who left the North became pillars of the Southern regime, whose *raison d'être* was to prevent the consolidation and spread of communism in Vietnam. The Catholics, in particular, lent crucial assistance to the Catholic head of the RVN government, Ngo Dinh Diem, until his assassination in 1963. The economic costs of caring for 900,000 refugees were thus balanced by domestic political gains. The refugees also had a significant public relations impact internationally. Both the Western press and academic reports generally interpreted the southward refugee flow as an indictment of the Communist regime, which presumably was the precise purpose of American efforts to scare people out.[36]

By failing to implement their part of the Geneva Accords, the Western powers and South Vietnam set the stage for the Second Indochina War. This war lasted longer (1960 to 1975), destroyed more life and material goods, extended more widely into all of Indochina, and involved foreign powers more deeply than had the previous war. The conflict became a test case of revolutionary nationalism pitted against an American-led international economic and strategic order. As such, all the great powers made significant investments to ensure a favorable outcome. The Soviet Union and China gave crucial and increasingly sophisticated military aid to the North, as well as large-scale economic assistance. Among the great powers, however, the United States was the only one to send combat troops, reaching nearly half a million men at its peak, and made extensive use of its air force for bombing and chemical warfare. The internationalization of the war was most obviously an Americanization of the war, which in fact was a major reason why its Southern client state eventually collapsed.

The internationalization process had a direct impact on the refugee flows. Most fundamentally, internationalization increased the number of internal refugees by prolonging a war that the Vietminh had almost won in 1945, in 1954, and again in 1962–3—at which point the United States intervened in a massive fashion.[37] Internationalization also meant high-technology warfare that immensely enlarged the fire zone which indiscriminately engulfed civilians. In the South, which now was the primary theater of war, an estimated half of the 20 million population had been uprooted, many of whom ended up in refugee camps in urban areas that were reasonably safe. The population of Saigon had swollen from a modest half a million in 1954 to over 3 million by 1975.[38] While the war lasted, however, internal displacement did not spill over into international refugee movements, and for much the same reasons as those noted for the First Indochina War. Each side had protected space available; the United States, moreover, could hardly condone a large outflow of Vietnamese at a time when American soldiers were fighting on their behalf in Vietnam.

It was only when the war ended in April 1975 that large, international refugee flows appeared. About 1.1 million Vietnamese had left by the end of 1986, which is about 5 percent of the Southern population from which most of the refugees came. Although the absolute figure is large, and certainly seemed so in the receiving countries, proportional to the population it is smaller than many other contemporary international refugee movements in Asia.[39] The outflow was caused principally by the implementation of the new social order in the South, but external factors also played an important role, both in the form of the legacy of the long American intervention and in Vietnam's evolving hostilities with China.

The first and classical *ancien régime* wave was to be expected and was to some extent a continuation of the 1954 movement. Many of the first wave to arrive in the United States were Catholics, originally from the North.[40] This wave mainly took the form of evacuation to the United States in 1975 of about 125,000 Vietnamese closely associated with the South Vietnamese government and the American role in the war. It was followed by a socially similar but much smaller outflow over the next few years (21,100 in 1976–77).

By mid-1978 it was apparent that another, distinct social group could not easily be integrated into the new order in the South, and a second flow consisting of the ethnic Chinese, the Hoa, appeared. Several factors combined to produce a sharp confrontation. The Vietnamese Communist party took a different view of citizenship and citizenship rights than had the previous rulers in the South. This meant that the southern Chinese were losing a relatively privileged foreign resident status.[41] Their prominence in the private economic sector conflicted with the government's new measures to effect a socialist transformation in trade and industry; the Chinese were also placed in a precarious position by the hostilities between Vietnam and its erstwhile ally China. Many of the generally urban Chinese were compelled to relocate to the inhospitable New Economic Zones, created by the Vietnamese government to deal simultaneously with the problem of acute urban overpopulation and severe shortages in agricultural production. But the Vietnamese authorities also tacitly permitted the ethnic Chinese to leave, and so a mass exodus began. Between March 1978 and June 1979, about 163,000 people sought first asylum in Southeast Asia and Hong Kong, and then the flow subsided.

Many more Hoa (about 263,000) went to China. These were mainly fishermen, workers, and peasants from North Vietnam who left because of the growing tension between China and Vietnam, and the growing Vietnamese suspicions that the Hoa were a fifth column. They were not expelled, as sometimes portrayed in the Western press, or initially victimized, as the Chinese media claimed. It was a curious movement with obscure origins, fueled in part by a "psywar" reminiscent of the 1954–55 campaign. This included a rumor campaign of an impending Sino-Vietnamese war and the widespread distribution of mysterious leaflets encouraging the ethnic Chinese to leave, for which no one took responsibility.[42] As governmental relations between Vietnam and China steadily deteriorated, China's demonstrative, publicly expressed concern for the well-being of the Hoa mounted, as did Vietnam's suspicion of their loyalty. In a tacit agreement to solve the problem, the two governments in mid-1978 opened the border for a spontaneous "repatriation" of the ethnic Chinese. Only when the inflow threatened to be continuous, did Chinese authorities close the entry points. In an ironic reversal of roles, China established a "local integration" project to settle the refugees on state farms in southern China. The UNHCR assisted by donating $8.5 million and opening an office in Beijing.[43]

After the July 1979 international conference in Geneva, when Vietnam agreed to try to halt further departures, it became increasingly dangerous and difficult to leave. Moreover, measures against the Hoa developed into a more predictable policy that allowed for some accommodation, and most of the remaining ethnic Chinese in South Vietnam (estimated to be about one million) chose to remain. At this point, a different outflow materialized, consisting of ethnic Vietnamese drawn overwhelmingly from the middle and lower strata to include teachers, clerks, soldiers, peasants, and fishermen. Some associates of the previous regime who had been in "reeducation" camps continued to come out, but the outflow as a whole consisted of a much broader population segment.

In contrast with the ethnic Chinese and the associates of the *ancien régime*—who as social groups were targeted as obstacles to the new order—the persons in the third wave generally were supposed to be the beneficiaries of the revolution. Nevertheless, they left by the thousands. In part, they sought to escape the rigors of socialist reconstruction in a war-devastated economy. The problems were made worse by a series of natural disasters in 1977–78 and a virtual economic embargo by Western countries and the major international lending institutions (the World Bank and the Asian Development Bank), for which Vietnam's membership in the Soviet-led COMECON could not fully compensate.[44] At home, ideological rigidities disrupted agricultural production (at least until the 1979 reforms), and there was renewed mobilization for war, this time in Kampuchea and the border region with China. It may still seem surprising that a population that had endured more or less continuous, brutalizing warfare for the last thirty years would find it so difficult to accept the austerity of relative peace. The many years of war and foreign intervention in themselves provide part of the answer. Millions in South Vietnam had been uprooted by the war to be included in a very different economy and society built up during almost two decades of pervasive American presence. A virtual client population had been created, for whom escape from Communist Vietnam after 1975 was a continuation, not a break, with the past.

Escape was facilitated by a growing network of Vietnamese abroad, as indicated by the increasing number of refugees who were admitted to the United States and other Western countries on the basis of reunification with relatives. This network, and the virtual certainty that the Vietnamese who made it to the first asylum areas in neighboring countries would be guaranteed resettlement in Europe or North America, helped create and sustain a considerable outflow of people who were not directly targeted by the new order but resembled more ordinary migrants. In contrast with the refugees from the Chinese revolution, the Vietnamese had a place to go to, and partly for this reason they kept coming.[45]

The initial reaction of the Western powers was to accept resettlement as the only possible "durable solution" (in the UNHCR terminology). The major first asylum countries—the Southeast Asian states of Thailand, Singapore, Malaysia, Indonesia, and the Philippines—categorically denied the refugees permission to stay permanently. Because the refugees were seeking to escape a new social order, rather than a temporary crisis, no one showed much interest in the UNHCR's tentative efforts to explore mechanisms for their return. The Vietnamese government was unwilling to discusses repatriation except in the context of normalization of relations with the United States, a process that was derailed in late 1978.[46] The U.S. position was that people must not be forcefully returned to Communist Vietnam, and Washington was willing to underwrite a large resettlement program. In 1979–80, the United States was resettling almost twice as many Indochinese refugees as were all other third countries combined (about fourteen thousand a month) and was urging its allies to keep up their intake. Japan, which admitted only a handful of refugees, was persuaded to contribute cash support for the operation of the UNHCR camps in the first asylum areas.[47]

The United States took the lead in assisting the Vietnamese outmigration primarily because of its own prolonged involvement in the war. The suffering of the boat people was highlighted by a media blitz to underscore a sense of obligation to the victims of America's defeat in Vietnam. Additionally, the United States was committed to support the remaining noncommunist countries in Southeast Asia, where the large Vietnamese population inflow appeared overwhelming and threatening. There was also the obvious and not insignificant propaganda implication that the Communist victory in Vietnam—which the United States had tried to forestall at such a heavy cost—must be hollow if the Vietnamese people sought to escape the new order.[48] Although these factors encouraged a liberal refugee policy, conflicting considerations soon appeared. The size of the Indochinese resettlement program was unique in the refugee experience of the developing world. The UNHCR was increasingly concerned that it absorbed an undue share of resources available for needy refugees elsewhere, especially the many millions in Africa, and set an unfortunate precedent.[49] When hundreds of thousands of new refugees poured out of Kampuchea in late 1979, and the United States a few months later was directly besieged by refugees from nearby Cuba, it was clear that a critical turning point in dealing with refugees had been reached also in the United States. Resettlement, whether to the United States or elsewhere, was to be a last resort.

In the U.S. Congress and other circles, fears were expressed that an "on-going refugee/migrant flow" from Indochina was being institutionalized.[50] It was also questioned whether later arrivals of Vietnamese in fact were refugees, as they were neither targeted minorities nor political dissidents but had left for other reasons or to join relatives. But the policy implications of this assessment were limited. Without a broader foreign policy reorientation toward Vietnam, there appeared, in fact, to be little choice but to treat as refugees all Vietnamese who succeeded in reaching UNHCR-supervised camps in Southeast Asia. Without a minimal political dialogue between Vietnam and the receiving countries, persons leaving Vietnam could not be returned even if they by some test were determined to be "migrants" rather than "refugees." The question of deporting Vietnamese as "illegal immigrants" (which was the designation used in many neighboring Southeast Asian countries) consequently was irrelevant. But because the Vietnamese were not welcome to stay in noncommunist Southeast Asia either, resettlement to the West remained the norm.

The flow, however, could be choked at other points. Greater efforts were made to dissuade people from arriving in UNHCR-protected camps, by making the refugee trail more uncertain and difficult. By 1981, the main resettlement countries were reducing their intake quotas, and the first asylum countries progressively instituted "humane deterrence" measures.[51] In a complete reversal of American practice in 1954–55, the U.S. Congress censored activities that might have a "pull" effect on Vietnamese refugees, including broadcasts of the Voice of America.[52] The other main strategy was to restrict exit from Vietnam. Already in mid-1979, when large vessels with ethnic Chinese were leaving Vietnam with the tacit approval of the authorities, the Western nations and the UNHCR had, ironically, pleaded with the government of Vietnam to stop the departures. This was not simply a refugee flow, the recipient countries claimed at the July conference in Geneva, but an unacceptable mass expulsion. Simultaneously, the UNHCR concluded an agreement with Vietnam to facilitate select emigration, which came to be known as the Orderly Departure Program (ODP). Given the strained political atmosphere between Vietnam and the receiving Western countries, the ODP represented the maximum cooperative effort possible. Even this modest scheme had a slow start, but in 1984, ODP departures from Vietnam totaled over 20,000 and for the first time exceeded illegal boat departures.[53] The momentum was maintained the following year with about 25,000 departures but slowed down during 1986–87. Simultaneously, the illegal departure of boats increased as some people tried to "jump the queue" for the ODP.

The ODP was a great improvement on the costly system of illegal departures. Thousands of refugees had drowned in the South China Sea, and many more were attacked or killed by pirates. The ODP also served to deemphasize an anomaly in the entire refugee program. In practice, the mode of departure had become the determining criterion for obtaining refugee status, in that anyone who risked the hazardous journey from Vietnam to Thailand or other first asylum areas was given refugee status without further questions.[54] The ODP opened up another channel in which evaluation of need and the reasons for leaving was possible. Yet by incorporating elements of both migration and refugee programs, the ODP tended to obscure questions of equity and purpose. It gave the recipient countries control over their intake of refugees, while simultaneously making it possible to observe Western standards of human rights, by enabling some people to leave through a safe exit. For the most part, however, those who benefited from the program were not the classical refugees whose life or well-being was directly threatened by the state or its agents. These the Vietnamese government was reluctant to let go, fearing they would mobilize against the state in exile.[55] Political prisoners were generally excluded from the ODP until late 1984, when Vietnamese and U.S. authorities negotiated a special program for them. The United States announced it would take 10,000 former reeducation prisoners, but they were only slowly released. By October 1986, 208 cases had been processed in the ODP, and in the following year 72 more were added.[56] Most of the ODP beneficiaries were family reunion cases that in other circumstances probably would have qualified as immigrants; still, they were treated administratively as refugees in recipient countries that had separate programs for migrants and refugees, as in the United States.[57]

Vietnam, for its part, regarded the ODP as a method of getting rid of undesirable social groups (notably ethnic Chinese and Amerasian children). This was in keeping with the policy in 1978–79 when ethnic Chinese were permitted to leave en masse. Hanoi frankly recognized that refugees were an inevitable by-product of revolutions, as "a sizable stratum of people objectively or subjectively [are] unadjusted to socialism."[58] Still, formal restrictions on exit were imposed, and ethnic Vietnamese faced penalties if caught trying to leave illegally.[59] A restrictive exit policy was partly a matter of prestige; authoritative control included the ability to regulate population movements. At the Geneva meeting in July 1979, moreover, Vietnam had agreed to requests to curb illegal emigration. Vietnamese authorities recognzied that large outflows gave the country a poor international image, discredited the revolution, and could be exploited by its adversaries for political purposes. A case in point was China's public expressions of concern over the outflow of ethnic Chinese from Vietnam. China was trying to create the impression that Vietnam was "terrorising and expelling" the ethnic Chinese, Hanoi claimed, so as to justify its hostile policy, which culminated in the February 1979 invasion of Vietnam.[60]

By the mid-1980s, the initial period of huge outflows had given way to a steady movement. The first shocks of adjustment to the new order had passed, and opportunities for resettlement abroad were becoming restricted. The rate of arrival in first asylum areas in Southeast Asia averaged 21,000 annually. Although it shot up to nearly 40,000 in 1987—creating alarm in Thailand which reverted to the practice of turning away Vietnamese boats—it was still miniscule compared with that of the peak year:[61] In 1979 alone, over 200,000 "boat people" arrived in Southeast Asia and Hong Kong, and another 263,000 had just relocated to China.

Laos

The wars in Vietnam also set the pace and intensity of the revolutionary struggle in neighboring Laos. A minor communist party had been formed during the decolonization process in this semifeudal kingdom of lowland rice cultivators and hill tribes. The party (Neo Lao Hak Sat) had gradually grown in strength during the Second Indochina War and was finally lifted to power by the victory of its Vietnamese counterparts in South Vietnam in April 1975. The Lao revolution was gradual and mild, symbolized by the manner in which the party finally seized power. A coalition government of the princes and generals of the old regime and the "neutralists" had been formed in 1974. It gradually disintegrated in 1975 as the *ancien régime* representatives, watching events in Vietnam, thought it prudent to leave. The king abdicated, and the party proclaimed the "bloodless seizure of power" and the establishment of the Lao Democratic Republic on December 2, 1975.

The new order immediately produced a sizable population outflow, which rapidly acquired the characteristics of a self-sustained migration movement before restrictive policies reduced it to a steady trickle. By the end of 1986, the Laotian camp population in neighboring Thailand was only about 85,000, about half of what it had been in 1979. The annual turnover of the camp population had fallen to a mere 22,000 from the approximately 150,000 persons who annually arrived in camp or departed for third-country resettlement. Before the numbers fell sharply in 1981, however, almost one-tenth of the total population (3.3 million) in this small, landlocked country had left. This was twice the rate of the outflow from Vietnam and stands in curious contrast with the generally mild nature of the Laotion revolution.

Some of the migrations were generic to a revolutionary situation: Supporters of the *ancien régime,* defeated armies, and functionaries left en masse. In addition, particular factors operated in the Laotian situation. Intense bombing during the Second Indochina War had ravaged a country that even under the best of circumstances was one of the poorest in the world. The war also had exacerbated traditional differences between the lowland and hill tribe populations. Both groups contributed to the exodus that developed in the late 1970s. The lowland Lao generally fled poverty and, to a lesser extent, the fairly benign Lao version of socialism; just across the border were established refugee camps that virtually guaranteed onward resettlement in Europe or North America. For the principal hill tribes, the Hmong, a different rationale was relevant. The Hmong had formed the mainstay of the CIA-trained "royalist" forces during the war and continued their resistance after 1975. The new government's policies to integrate these hill tribes were seen as control measures by a traditionally semiautonomous people and only made matters worse. As full-scale war ensued, the refugee camps in Thailand became a sanctuary for the Hmong fighters and their dependents.[62] The long and porous border with neighboring

Thailand, where two-way traffic traditionally had been easy, enabled both lowland people and hill tribes to move across after 1975.

In order to regulate this flow, the UNHCR and Thailand had already in 1977 tentaively agreed to an asylum determination procedure whereby refugees would be separated from migrants and treated accordingly. Mainly because of opposition from American government officials in Thailand, who argued that persons who left communist Laos were, *ipso facto,* refugees, the agreement was not implemented.[63] By early 1981, however, the first asylum and resettlement programs were so strained by the weight of new arrivals that another attempt was made at screening. A "humane deterrence" policy was instituted in January 1981, whereby new lowland Lao arrivals were placed in separate austerity camps outside the resettlement track for an indefinite period of time. It was a rough method of separating migrants from refugees without making a case-by-case determination; in effect, the reasoning was that by making access to the resettlement process more difficult, only genuine refugees would come. The other half of the policy followed in late 1981 when Thailand and Laos concluded a formal repatriation agreement. Throughout, the refugee vocabulary was maintained; all arrivals were referred to as refugees, and those returned to Laos were said to be voluntarily repatriating, so as to avoid the charge of *refoulement.* Critics argued that the vocabulary mystified a process that under normal circumstances would be known as asylum determination and deportation.[64] Yet the policy met the objective of reducing the flow, in a manner that circumvented initial Amerian objections.

The hill tribes were for all practical purposes exempt from the humane deterrence policy, as their primary concern was not to resettle in the West. Although many Hmong initially had followed their leader, "General" Vang Pao, to exile in the United States, severe problems of adjusting to life in industrialized countries discouraged further resettlement. Active resistance to the new regime in Laos, moreover, required the Hmong to stay in the border areas, and so a "refugee-warrior community" developed. The UNHCR-financed refugee camps became comfortable sanctuaries not only for the civilian dependents of the Hmong fighters: The men moved easily in and out of the camps located in a remote area of northern Thailand, with a skeletal Thai supervisory staff.[65] Some Hmong would sign up for resettlement in the belief that this demonstrated their bona fide "refugee" credentials but would not show up when the buses came to fetch them. Later, most simply settled into the camps in a pattern of de facto "local integration." When the Hmong resistance weakened in the mid-1980s, a small inflow continued, averaging about seven thousand a year in 1984–86.

Laos was the only Indochinese country that negotiated a repatriation agreement with the UNHCR. Having always been in the shadow of Vietnam during the war, it was easier for Laos to repair relations with its adversaries after the war ended. Laos and Thailand had resumed a political dialogue soon after 1975, and Lao-U.S. relations remained distant but not overtly antagonistic, in contrast with U.S. relations with Vietnam after 1975. Given a favorable international political context, it was possible also to negotiate about refugees.

The initial objection of American officials in the field points to a general implementational characteristic of American policy, not only toward Laotian refugees/migrants, but also toward Vietnamese and Khmer. Staffing patterns in the American refugee bureaucracy that developed in first asylum countries accentuated the tendency for U.S. refugee policy to become an extension of past American policy. Many officials posted to work in the refugee program from other agencies (State, Defense, AID) had previously been part of the American war effort in Indochina and hence had acquired language and country expertise to deal with Indochinese refugees as well. They generally appeared as a pressure group to move people out of Indochina, that is, to provide the alternative to living under communist rule that had been the objective of the American military intervention.

Kampuchea

Of all the Indochinese revolutions, the one in Kampuchea was the most unexpected. The communist party had been small and almost unknown before 1975 but gained in power when the Vietnam War engulfed also neighboring Kampuchea. The war brought widespread destruction and sharply polarized internal political forces as North Vietnam and the United States sought to bend Kampuchea's declared neutrality to their own advantage. The conflict was intensified by the rightist coup against neutralist Prince Sihanouk in 1970; the progressive paralysis of the new regime enabled the communist Khmer Rouge to enter the capital five years later. When the demoralized, American-supported regime in Saigon collapsed, so did the one in Phnom Penh; the final offensive of the Vietnamese communists in South Vietnam delivered the coup de grâce to both.

The social transformation instituted by the Khmer Rouge was uniquely radical and brutally comprehensive. It involved forced internal migrations, massive purges and liquidation of party cadres, elimination of whole social segments, and Endlösung ("final solution") campaigns against ethnic minorities. As a result of this and the regime's determination to seal the borders, relatively few people escaped from the Khmer Rouge's rule of Kampuchea (1975–79).

The Khmer Rouge had been warned by the Chinese not to build communism too quickly. They should learn from the Chinese Communists' united front strategy, not their Great Leap Forward, Chinese leaders had admonished.[66] The advice was not heeded. The Khmer Rouge claimed that as a small nation (only seven million people), with a history of fighting a losing battle against aggrandizing neighbors, Kampuchea could not afford to be patient. Kampuchea's vulnerability had been underscored by its unwilling involvement in the Second Indochina War, and the Khmer communists who seized power in Phnom Penh after the war were also fiercely nationalistic: It was only through a radical, communistic restructuring of society that Kampuchea could be strong enough to withstand its neighbors as well as more distant imperialists.[67] The foreign policy counterpart was an aggressive-defensive posturing in the region. Tension between Vietnam and Kampuchea was building up as the Khmer Rouge sought assistance from China. External threats, in turn, reinforced domestic paranoia and purges. A vicious cycle was created.

In the nationalist book of the Khmer Rouge, all minorities were suspect. Virtually all the Khmer Muslims were killed (sixty thousand of them in one district alone). The systematic killing of ethnic Vietnamese started in 1977 and intensified the following year after the Vietnamese had made a temporary military incursion into Kampuchea. At that point the Khmer Rouge even launched a radio appeal for the "final solution" to "the Vietnamese problem."[68] Ethnic Chinese were also killed by the thousands. In addition, there were class enemies, the "new people" who could not discard their "bourgeois traits" during their forced transformation to peasant labor; there were traitorous cadres, and people who simply did not work hard enough. Perhaps one million were killed.

Those who succeeded in escaping came mainly from the eastern zone, where the purges and the anti-Vietnamese killings had been most widespread, culminating in open rebellion against the Pol Pot leadership in early 1978. The rebel commanders with their dependent populations moved across the border to Vietnam, where they joined earlier scattered refugees to become the first in a long series of Khmer refugee-warriors. Supported by the UNHCR in refugee camps, the approximately 150,000 Khmer were simultaneously organized, trained, and readied by the Vietnamese for the invasion of Kampuchea which took place in December that same year.[69] As the UNHCR noted, the $3.5 million "local integration" program for Khmer in Vietnam had barely gotten off the ground when most of the Khmer returned home, walking behind Vietnamese tanks that crashed through Khmer Rouge defenses to take Phnom Penh in January 1979.[70]

The Vietnamese invasion created a new stream of refugees, this time going in the opposite direction, toward Thailand. When the Vietnamese arrived, the Khmer society was held together only by force and fear. With invasion and defeat of the regime, everything simply collapsed—people abandoned their communes to look for food and relatives, and others were compelled to follow the retreating Khmer Rouge soldiers. Rice in the fields was not harvested, and an economy that had been restructured to function without money and markets during four years of primitive communism came to a stand-still. There was neither production nor trade, and famine threatened. Although the new rulers were "liberators" in a sense, they were also communists and Kampuchea's historic enemies. As a result, hundreds of thousands of people converged on the border with Thailand toward the end of 1979. With the imminent prospect of thousands of deaths, a massive international relief apparatus came into being and was given extensive media coverage. International sympathy was stirred also because the horrors of the Khmer Rouge regime were becoming known, as was the Thai government's *refoulement* of Khmer refugees earlier in the year, particularly an incident in June 1979 when about 45,000 persons were pushed back to Kampuchea and several were killed.

Some important but little known aspects of this widely publicized picture should be noted. As Michael Vickery's careful analysis shows, the initial population movement toward the border after the Vietnamese invasion was not prompted by war or famine but consisted of three groups: (1) people who had been urbanites before 1975 and were so traumatized by the Khmer Rouge experience that they wanted to go abroad, often to join friends or relatives who had left much earlier, (2) ex-traders who came in order to resume cross-border trade, and (3) individuals who wanted to fight against the Vietnamese.[71] Many persons in this first wave were pushed back by the Thais, but additional people congregated near the border on the Kampuchean side. The catalyst in regard to interna-tional relief and attention was the sudden appearance of over sixty thousand emaciated, nearly dying persons—women, children, and soldiers—who literally fell across the bor-der in October. These were the remnants of the main Khmer Rouge army and its civilian population, who for several months had slowly retreated through malarial-infested jungle regions with little food and medicine.

Their arrival caused an international outcry of sympathy. The international relief apparatus went into high gear, ironically drawing on the sympathy for the past victims of the Khmer Rouge and the widespread international opposition to the Vietnamese invasion of the country. When Thai authorities agreed to keep a stretch of the border with Kam-puchea open for refugees, the thousands who had waited on the Kampuchean side entered to get aid from the international relief apparatus providing free food and medical assis-tance. Many were accepted into UNHCR holding centers from where resettlement to third countries subsequently commenced. By early 1980, about 160,000 were in holding centers, and an estimated 300,000 to 500,000 persons were outside UNHCR protection and the resettlement stream in so-called border concentrations, where they received food and medicine from UNICEF and the International Committee of the Red Cross (ICRC). Numerous voluntary agencies also assisted.

Like the earlier peasant armies of Asia and troops in medieval Europe, the Khmer Rouge soldiers moved with their civilian dependents. They thereby acquired a humanizing facade, particularly when the civilians obviously were suffering from disease and hunger. To aid this community was a humanitarian deed but also a highly political act with agonizing implications. For these reasons, the Khmer relief operation soon became controversial.[72] The most needy refugees on the border were probably the Khmer Rouge and their civilian populations, but to aid them also meant reviving a murderous regime, and one that was determined to continue the war by fighting the new Vietnamese-backed rulers in Phnom Penh. The Vietnamese-backed rulers, for their part, were so strongly opposed to the idea of aid being channeled to their enemy that they threatened to deny UNICEF/ICRC access to starving populations under their own control in Kampuchea if international relief were simultaneously given to the border populations.[73] The international agencies nevertheless insisted that as a matter of principle, they be allowed access to the civilians on both sides in a civil war. The fact that the Khmer Rouge still represented Kampuchea in the U.N. as Democratic Kampuchea made it even more awkward to deny it assistance. In the end, a dual-aid pipeline was laid, one to the border and one to Phnom Penh.

Besides the Khmer Rouge community, the border pipeline fed hundreds of thousands of consumers and traders on the border and made it possible for a varied anti-Vietnamese resistance movement to establish de facto zones of governance. Their armies were simultaneously equipped through a separate channel, the so-called Deng Xiao-ping trail, which the Chinese and the Thais had agreed to open as soon as the Khmer Rouge leaders arrived on the border.[74] With time the resistance formed a broader coalition. The Coalition Government of Democratic Kampuchea was established in 1982; Prince Sihanouk was given a leading position; and the U.N. representation was strengthened. In the field, semipermanent village settlements of about 250,000 people were strung out in the Thai-Kampuchean border region on both sides of the boundary line. From settlements on the Khmer side, well-equipped units consisting mainly of Khmer Rouge soldiers made forays into government-controlled areas.

The fears of the Vietnamese-backed regime in Kampuchea when it fought the border-aid pipeline in 1979 had materialized. It responded by launching annual dry-season offensives against the resistance settlements, each time sending thousands of civilians and their soldiers into Thailand as refugees. On the Thai side they were received by an ad hoc U.N. agency, the U.N. Border Relief Operations (UNBRO), which had taken over the relief and medical assistance in 1982. And so by the mid-1980s, an apparently self-perpetuating cycle of wars and refugees had been formed.

Powerful international coalitions kept the cycle going. Behind the Khmer resistance stood the Chinese, the United States, and the noncommunist countries of Southeast Asia (ASEAN), whereas Vietnam and the Soviet Union supported the Khmer regime in Phnom Penh. It was a replay of the traditional Thai-Vietnamese competition for influence in the Kampuchean buffer state separating the two but was linked to the structure of great-power rivalry in a manner that helped sustain the strife. The Third Indochina War over Kampuchea was in some respects a continuation of the Second Indochina War; the United States and its Southeast Asian supporters tried to stem and roll back Vietnamese communism supported by the Soviet Union, only this time in Kampuchea and with the Chinese leading the tacit coalition against Vietnamese ''hegemonism.''

The relief apparatus on the border in 1979–80 had been crucial to the initial phase of the conflict. Refugee assistance helped lay the foundations for the insurgency against the Vietnamese-supported regime in Kampuchea, and the large refugee population provided legitimacy and manpower for the guerrillas. The United States took the lead in the refugee relief campaign. At the U.N. pledging conferences for relief to Kampuchea, the United States emphasized the need to expand border access and staffed its Kampuchean Emergency Group (KEG) in Thailand with foreign service officers and military intelligence specialists.[75] The political implications of aid was recognized by the main international relief agencies, UNICEF and ICRC, which several times tried to extricate themselves from the border feedings, particularly the distribution points controlled by Khmer Rouge soldiers.[76] They succeeded in late 1982 when UNBRO was established to distribute food and medicine to the border populations in settlements controlled by the Khmer guerrillas. The partisan political nature of the relief operation was now transparent, and the United States paid for almost half of UNBRO's budget.[77]

An alternative strategy was to promote a return of the border population. Although criticized by U.S. officials in Thailand, the UNHCR took the position that most of the Khmer were fleeing from a temporary situation of food shortages and unrest and should be encouraged to return.[78] With the distribution in 1980–81 of hundreds of thousands of resettlement kits, including seeds and tools, the large border concentrations were somewhat reduced.[79] In order to discourage the inflow further, Thai authorities sharply curtailed access to the resettlement pipeline.

Despite the violent recent history of Kampuchea, relatively few persons were formally recognized as refugees and given the option of third-country resettlement. One reason was the so-called compassion fatigue in the recipient countries, which was reflected in the UNHCR's position to encourage return. But it was also self-evident that if the struggle for Kampuchea were to continue, the resistance movement would require a population of Khmer to stay in the proximate area rather than overseas.

Reformist Southeast Asia

Elsewhere in Southeast Asia the Western colonial powers secured a transition to the postcolonial period that for the most part safeguarded their economic, political, and strategic interests. Compared with the case of Indochina, the challenges from revolutionary nationalism were weaker and more easily suppressed, but violent struggles took place in three other Southeast Asian countries. Virtually no international refugees resulted, however.

Communist insurgencies developed in connection with the scheduled transfer of power to the indigenous elites in Malaysia and the Philippines. Although the radical movements in both countries were fragmented by ethnic divisions, they succeeded in holding out for several years against the established elites and their foreign supporters. In Malaysia the British forces fought for over a decade until The Emergency was ended in 1960. The United States contributed decisively but more subtly to the suppression of the Hukbalahap movement in the Philippines in the mid-1950s. The refugee consequences from both insurgencies were limited. As in the early phase of the Vietnam War, both sides had internal space to protect their supportive populations, and the control of people in fact was crucial in order to hold territory. When in the end the insurgencies failed, the question of relocation arose only in connection with the defeated guerrillas and their dependents.

The largely Chinese, Malaysian communists moved across the border to inaccessible jungle regions in southern Thailand, from where they tried to keep up a limited struggle. In the Philippines, the government offered the Huks settlement elsewhere in the country through an amnesty program.[80]

Radical nationalism developed differently in Indonesia, the largest country of the region. After a five-year war of independence against the Dutch, alternating currents of radical and accommodative nationalism prevailed in the first decade of the postcolonial period. It was followed by a growing tension between the two principal sociopolitical forces in the country, the Communist party (PKI) and the army, which came to a head in 1965. At least half a million people were killed in the ensuing clashes. The PKI, and its mass front organizations with a claimed membership of almost 20 million people, were eliminated as a political force. Thousands associated with the PKI were imprisoned, and a decade later maybe 55,000 to 100,000 remained in jail.[81] The army, which had directed or at least tolerated the violence, seized governmental power and retained it.

The question has arisen why so few persons escaped from the cataclysmic events of 1965 to become refugees. As it turned out, the PKI was unprepared for the sudden, widespread assault; the cadres had no flight plans and no arms with which to defend themselves.[82] They also lacked a readily available place of refuge, having neither a safe territorial zone within the country nor easy access to neighboring countries, which were separated from the Indonesian archipelagic state by water. It is also evident that the cadres would not have been welcomed in neighboring Asian states that were ruled by strongly anticommunist governments (Singapore, Malaysia, the Philippines).

By the second half of the 1960s, the first generation of revolutionary nationalists in postcolonial Southeast Asia outside Indochina had been defeated. Grouping themselves as the Association of Southeast Asian Nations (ASEAN), the noncommunist states became linked to the U.S. strategic system in the region and adopted development policies that integrated their economies with the international economic system dominated by the United States and, in Asia, Japan. This meant the formation of neocolonial economic structures and the growth of a national bourgeoisie that, alongside a newly emerging technocratic-bureaucratic sector, played a key role in linking the external and the internal sectors of the economy. Governmental policies emphasized economic growth and very gradual socioeconomic reforms.

The result was extremely rapid economic growth in the ASEAN region in the 1960s and 1970s and some consequent alleviation of poverty.[83] In addition, redistributive policies were undertaken to create stability in sensitive population sectors in Thailand, Malaysia, and Singapore.[84] In these three countries, moreover, institutions of liberal democracy functioned intermittently to permit considerable political activity and to restrain the arbitrary exercise of state power. Social conflict thus was muted, and political struggles typically were nonviolent. Under the circumstances, people claiming refugee status rarely appeared.

In the other two ASEAN countries, Indonesia and the Philippines, the development model of dependent capitalism was implanted in a different soil. Here it exacerbated existing contradictions associated with increasing immiseration of peasant cultivators (Indonesia), and the landlord–tenant relationship and the plantation sector (the Philippines). Dual economies were sharpened, and the extractive foreign presence with it; large scale unemployment or underemployment increased, and almost half the population remained below the poverty line.[85] In response, a second-generation radical nationalism emerged to challenge the indigenous elites and their external support structures.[86]

A restrictive political system was an integral part of this development and served to contain or suppress the contradictions generated in the economic sphere, hence the term *repressive-developmental,* as one noted analyst has called it.[87] The timing and nature of the suppression varied. In Indonesia, the physical elimination of the left in 1965 had been a prerequisite for the army's rise to power, thereby facilitating the subsequent silencing of critics. Some dissenters among the students and in the army were disciplined or imprisoned; roving "vigilante corps" in the early 1980s also had an intimidating effect.[88]

In the Philippines, the introduction of martial law in 1972 sharpened old social conflicts and created new ones. Despite his rapidly eroding domestic power base, the aging President Ferdinand Marcos managed to retain power with the help of American support until he became an embarrassment. He was overthrown in February 1986 in a populist revolt with American blessings. During his martial-law rule, a three-tiered structure of social conflict had consisted of, first, a revived communist insurgency led by the armed wing (New People's Army) of the (new) Communist party of the Philippines, established in 1968. The "band of upstarts" who snatched "the vanguard role from the ageing remnants of an aborted rebellion" (the Huks), was a decade later leading an insurgency that posed a serious threat to both the Marcos regime and the American presence in the Philippine islands.[89] Second, established forces of the old order—the middle classes and the landed oligarchy—increasingly united against the autocratic restrictions and economic favoritism of the martial-law regime. Third, a long-standing difficult relationship with the Muslim minority in the south deteriorated markedly as martial law restricted the scope for political activity. The Moro National Liberation Front launched an autonomy–separatist movement in a struggle that five years later had claimed 50,000 dead and 200,000 internally displaced.[90]

Out of this multiple conflict, only one distinct, sizable refugee stream emerged. In a pattern recalling South Asia's autonomy–separatist conflicts, about 100,000 Moros fled to the neighboring region of Sabah in west Malaysia, where they were settled with UNHCR assistance among fellow Muslims. The ready availability of asylum was related, for other reasons, to a rapidly deteriorating relationship between the governments of Malaysia and the Philippines.[91]

The communist insurgency and the more general repression associated with martial law did not, however, generate many refugees. As in earlier insurgencies in the region, the availability of internal space and the need to control people in a "people's war" served to keep people in place; besides, there was no obvious place to go. Unlike the Muslims, the radical nationalists had no support population in the region, and the cultural-linguistic diversity of Southeast Asia created formidable barriers to movement. As for the activist critics of the regime, the erratic nature of repression enabled many to remain and continue the struggle. But also for the activists the absence of a readily available refuge served to keep the outflow down. Social networks from previous migrations made the United States the most likely place, but Washington's support for Marcos until the very last phase of martial law made it difficult to obtain asylum except for a few well-known dissidents.[92]

There was another large population outflow from the Philippines in this period, but it was universally classified as consisting of migrants. Export of labor became one of the main sources of foreign exchange in the country's worsening economic crisis from the late 1970s onwards, and a main outlet for the increasingly impoverished urban labor and lower-middle classes.[93] Most of them went to the Middle East, but also to other parts of Asia and the United States.[94] Because under martial law, the outflow was directly related to the deteriorating economic conditions, the migrants were truly economic refugees. Their situation was probably not so different from those of many Vietnamese who found their way to refugee assistance and resettlement on that refugee trail.[95] For the Filipinos, however, the question of refugee status did not arise. Western European or North American countries were not flooded with asylum requests, largely because they seemed doomed to fail.

Asian Prospects

When considering the prospects for future refugee flows in and from Asia, it must be recalled that in fact relatively few victims of violent social conflict become international refugees claiming assistance. As we have seen, Asia's insurgencies, ethnic conflict, and even generalized repression have produced relatively few refugees. Structural violence, in the sense of systematic and profound economic oppression, is widespread throughout much of Asia and often associated with physical violence; its victims are likely to remain outside the international refugee stream, as they are powerless to move or certain that their claim would be rejected.

A second important aspect of contemporary refugee flows in Asia is the difference in international support that the various flows have received. Massive international assistance has been extended to the Indochinese and the Afghans, whereas very little has been given to the Biharis, the Chakmas, the Tamils, and the Papuans. One important reason is the differing numbers. Large flows require large-scale assistance, and the combination of revolutionary conflicts with foreign intervention in the Indochinese and Afghan conflicts generated large outflows indeed. But even allowing for variations in the size of the flows, it is evident that the response has been uneven. The entire international refugee regime was mobilized to assist the Indochinese and the Afghans, whereas the Biharis and the Chakmas were virtually overlooked. The key factor in this respect is that the first set of refugees had powerful foreign patrons, which the latter did not.

As we have seen, the availability of asylum or resettlement for refugees is conditioned by foreign policy considerations in the receiving countries. Because the refugees are either participants in the conflict or passive victims of one or the other side, the decision to support them has, at the very least, implicit political intent and consequences. In the last instances, therefore, international support for a given refugee flow reflects the nature of the foreign interests in the conflict that generated the refugees in the first place. Because an elaborate relief or resettlement apparatus also tends to attract people, refugee flows that have powerful external patrons tend to become very large indeed. It follows that any projection of future trends must start from the premise that great-power involvement, on both the conflict and the relief side, will usually generate substantial refugee flows.

ETHNIC CONFLICTS AND REFUGEES   In South Asia, violent social conflict has mainly been expressed along ethnic lines as broadly defined (i.e., including religion, language, and culture). This will likely continue, although there is no evidence of a secular trend toward more ethnic conflict except in the case of lowland peoples versus hill tribes, for whom increasing population pressures on land finds a violent expression.

In ethnic conflicts, a number of intervening variables deflect the search for external protection and flight by activists and victims. The most impact important ones are the intensity of violence; the presence of protected space within, as opposed to the availability of external refuge; and the perceived role of the state as an agent of violence or as a protector. In the plural states of South and Southeast Asia, these factors have operated to limit international refugee flows. In India, Asia's second most populous state, the very size and diversity of the country work against the appearance of international refugees, as various groups can find some security through internal migration. That the South and Southeast Asian states were formally committed to accept ethnic pluralism as part of "the nation" also explains why the classical refugee in European history—the unwanted minority—has not been a characteristic of Asia's plural states.

Minority–majority relations still remain difficult, as evidenced by the Tamils in Sri Lanka, the Muslims in India, and the overseas Chinese throughout Southeast Asia. For the most part, the ethnic Chinese have formed symbiotic ties with the ruling elites; this gives them some protection but does not ensure against discrimination or ethnic riots (e.g., Malaysia in 1969). Except for a small repatriation of Indonesia's Chinese to China in 1954–55, in all of Southeast Asia only Vietnam's Chinese have left en masse and claimed refugee status. This unique event is explained partly by the revolutionary transformation that made the Chinese entrepreneurial class unwelcome, but also by the international context that served to encourage departure and provide a place of refuge for Vietnam's Chinese in China and the West.

Autonomy–separatist pressures are likely to continue among minorities with a territorial concentration, but the two main national regroupings in South Asia (the partition of India and the division of Pakistan) are unlikely to be followed by further fragmentation. As the experience of Sri Lanka's autonomy–separatist movement indicates, separatists may well find enough external support to maintain a protracted struggle, but not enough to succeed. Asia's unsuccessful autonomy–separatist movements have tended to produce few international refugees. However, when fighting in densely populated areas has pushed people across state boundaries, the movements have been of two kinds. The Tamils of Sri Lanka represent the advanced minority with a history of outmigration and resources to seek asylum or resettlement beyond the region. The other is represented by the Chakmas of Bangladesh, a tribal people that move across the border when hard pressed, often to find support from related ethnic groups. Each movement has a distinct difficulty. The Chakmas make demands on poor neighboring countries typically with their own problems in outlying border areas. The Tamils' demand for asylum in the industrialized states is economically less significant but has proved to be politically difficult.

REVOLUTIONARY CONFLICTS AND REFUGEES Migrations from accomplished revolutions have been irreversible and gone beyond the region; in inconclusive struggles, large refugee concentrations have developed as refugee-warrior communities in neighboring countries.

The roots of revolution in contemporary Asia lie in the decolonization process or (in China) its equivalent, which sharpened social contradictions and simultaneously eroded the power of the colonial state. Where revolutionary nationalism failed to assert itself in the independence struggle, it weakened over time. Social forces representing gradual change and an accommodative nationalism were consolidated with an international support structure, and strong states capable of eliminating revolutionary challenges to the existing order developed. In South Asia and much of Southeast Asia, moreover, social conflicts in the economic realm were deflected by ethnic divisions. Asia's only "late" revolutions took place in Laos and Kampuchea; both were exceptional in that they were integrally related to the prolonged struggle in neighboring Vietnam.

Given these conditions, more peasant-based revolutions of the Chinese and Vietnamese type are unlikely to occur in the region. A revolution in India, which could have produced the largest refugee flow of all, is improbable. Refugees from Asia's revolutions, therefore, may soon be a thing of the past. Ten years after the communist seizure of power, outmigration from Laos and South Vietnam had stabilized at a low level. In Kampuchea, as also in Afghanistan, refugee flows depend on a political solution to the continuing military conflict. Insurgencies could be revived, but unlike in Central America, the balance of internal secure space relative to readily available external sanctuaries has in the past sharply limited the international refugee flow from Asian insurgencies.

The Philippines may prove to be the only exception. In revolutionary potential, the Philippines has always been exceptional among the ASEAN countries, and it was the only member state with a rapidly growing insurgency from the 1970s onward. The Catholic church is divided and politicized; tenancy is widespread; and a large rural labor force has emerged in the plantation sector; a significant manufacturing sector also has developed, and with it an industrial labor force to which the radical left is appealing. Social conflict is accentuated by the Philippines' close economic links with the United States and its very visible, large military presence. Signs of cooperation between the Muslim separatists and the communist New People's Army have underlined the challenge to the beleaguered centrist forces that seized power from Marcos. By their own analysis, the revolutionary forces are engaged in a long-term confrontation that likely will involve the United States more directly in its closing phase. If a revolutionary transformation of the Philippines eventually takes place, large-scale outflows of people akin to the Vietnamese or Cuban "model" can easily be envisaged.

Another area likely to be affected by radical social transformations, but for very different reasons, is Hong Kong. The British crown colony is scheduled to become a Special Administrative Region of China in 1997. It is not expected that China will interfere with Hong Kong's prosperous foreign exchange–earning economy, although some prosperous businessmen have taken out insurance by acquiring immigrant status elsewhere. In the event that mainland rule brings economic dislocation or political radicalization with suppression, larger segments of Hong Kong's 5.5 million population might try to leave.[96] Whether they would be received as refugees elsewhere is doubtful. Even in an earlier period of strong international enmity toward the Chinese revolution, Western countries generally refused to accept Chinese fleeing the communist mainland as refugees.

AUTHORITARIAN RULE AND REFUGEES Outside the communist countries of Asia, to the extent that the development patterns will be conflictual, it will probably be in the direction of "repressive-developmental" regimes rather than a revolutionary situation. The likely refugee dynamic has been described as one element of the Philippine and the Pakistan situation. Authoritarian rule in these political systems will likely generate the quintessential political refugee; the activist who is threatened by a suppressive state apparatus, often under conditions of martial law. The magnitude of outflow would depend primarily on the extent of repression in relation to the availability of asylum. Although the activist would fit conventional legal norms of refugee, remarkably few activist opponents of Asian authoritarian regimes on the "right" have in fact become international refugees, not only in the case of Indonesia and the Philippines, but equally in the case of South Korea and Taiwan. The contrast with the Latin American experience is striking and revealing. Although the level of physical repression in the four Asian countries has been erratic and generally less than, say, in Argentina, the neighboring region is also much less congenial to asylum applicants, both on political grounds—which assumes much importance in the case of activist refugees—and from a cultural-linguistic perspective.[97] Unlike Latin America, the countries of East and Southeast Asia have few linguistic and cultural commonalities. To move beyond the region becomes a major undertaking, and except for Indonesia, supportive migratory networks are most readily available in the United States, which also is most likely to reject asylum applicants, as they come from allied or friendly countries. The large, activist communities of Koreans and Chinese in the United States overwhelmingly have immigrant, not refugee, status.[98]

A "repressive-developmental" society also creates large numbers of economic refugees from the dualism and marginalization process inherent in this economic development model. Under prevailing interpretations of refugee, they are unlikely to receive refugee status abroad but, as the Philippine case shows, will appear as migrant labor. Underlying questions of need and equity remain unanswered, especially because a somewhat similar population movement generated by Asia's revolutionary regimes was accepted as refugees in the West.[99] As the Vietnamese and Chinese experiences demonstrate, however, third countries accepted large-scale resettlement only under compelling political circumstances, and increasingly reluctantly. Whether from leftist or rightist authoritarian regimes, future economic refugees from Asia undoubtedly will have more difficulties obtaining assistance as refugees.

Chapter 7

Social Conflict and Refugees in Latin America

Introduction

Social conflict and political exiles are not new in Latin America, but, in the last three decades the intensity of the social conflicts has escalated, and the number of those displaced has reached an estimated four to six million. And there are reasons to believe that these trends will continue.

Latin America is not a region about which one can generalize easily. It contains twenty-five small and large nations comprising, in 1980, 364 million people living under regimes that range from socialism to elected democracy to military dictatorship. The region also is diverse economically and culturally, but its countries' different histories are interrelated through the many regional linkages dominated by the United States.

With the exception of Cuba and a few other countries, most of Latin America gained independence in the first decades of the nineteenth century. Afterwards, the region acquired a reputation for political violence that included coups, assassinations, armed movements, military intervention, and, more rarely, social revolutions. Most of the time, however, the struggle for power was confined to particular circles, and those displaced were few. Accordingly, the Latin American governments created a long-standing tradition of asylum that was "designed to respond to individual cases within the framework of the Inter-American treaties and of the practice developed" by the states of the region.[1] These legal practices included the possibility of territorial or diplomatic asylum and were particularly well suited to protecting deposed leaders and their close collaborators.

In the first half of this century there were only three occurrences of political violence affecting substantial sectors of the population: a social revolution in Mexico (1910–17); the massacre of some eight to ten thousand participants in the Communist-led peasant rebellion in El Salvador (1932); and a conventional war between Bolivia and Paraguay over the Chaco territory (1932–35). However, with the possible exception of the Mexican migration to the United States, the literature makes few references to displaced populations.[2] In this century there also have been major migratory flows that serve as a background to the flows that we shall discuss later.

After 1959, deep social conflicts and mass population flows appeared with growing frequency, and the need to provide adequate responses to them become more and more pressing. In this we shall discuss the most important cases; those of Cuba, Haiti, the Southern Cone, and Central America. A systematic comparison of them is difficult owing to the differences and disparities in the available research and information, but they do have, however, some similarities.

All the social conflicts in these countries have had a struggle over, and resistance to, social change. The results of those struggles have differed widely: In Cuba and Nicaragua a revolutionary vanguard led the forces of social change against dictatorial states and armies that lost their hold, partly as a consequence of international factors; in Haiti a despotic personal dictatorship held power, by sheer force; in the Southern Cone countries, repressive state terrorism was instituted by bureaucratic-authoritarian military regimes; and in El Salvador and Guatemala, peasant rebellions were waged along class lines, resulting in protracted civil wars.

These developments have been explained in different ways: For some, they are the result of Latin culture; for others the product of economic dependency. Here we shall start with one of the basic propositions of modernization theory: Economic changes induce social transformations, which have political consequences. Another theory is the international element, because the existence of a regional system has determined, in different ways, the history of each of the countries that it encompassed.

The conflicts resulting from social change can be explained, first, by domestic factors that have a common historical background. The Great Depression disrupted the export–import character of the economies that had characterized the first decades of this century. Besides highlighting these countries' dependence on conditions in the world economy, another consequence was the reassertion of the role of armies in the political process, as manifested in a spate of coups.

The response to the Depression was a search for import-substituting industrialization that, in principle, would diminish dependence, create jobs for the growing population, and stabilize the economies and the political systems. That policy brought consistent rates of economic growth in the bigger countries (Argentina, Brazil, Mexico) and also redefined the power of the social actors. The army retained power (Mexico is an exception, for reasons pertaining to its revolution), but the private sector and working classes gained new strength, and the state increased its participation in the economy. The political solutions most often found were integrative (co-optative) democracies or populist regimes; both found ways to accommodate the contradictory demands of different classes.

This system worked as long as the economies prospered. By the 1960s, however, this development strategy revealed its structural limitations. For example, only the nature of dependency had changed, and the terms of trade had deteriorated. The economies grew, but without reducing the severe inequalities in income distribution or the gaps in the living standards between the rural and urban populations. The population boom (especially acute in the agrarian economies of Haiti and Central America) only worsened unemployment and marginalism. These factors, plus increased urbanization and education, shaped the new political forces that were confronted with rigid political systems resisting change. These are the domestic foundations of the social conflicts.

During the twentieth century, the regional system has had as its center the United States. Although each country has different characteristics (for example, the countries in the Caribbean are in a different category from those in the Southern Cone), the United States has dominated through coercion and hegemony, the two extremes of a continuum.[3]

Domination through coercion implies the real or potential use of some form of economic, military, political, or other kind of pressure to force a social group or nation to do something against its will or interests. Domination through hegemony means, among other things, that the dominated assume that the relations of domination are natural or that they are in their best interest.

In the 1930s the United States started to show a preference for exercising its domination through hegemony, although the use of coercion is an ever-present possibility. In this system, the United States favors a degree of economic development (what Fernando Henrique Cardoso calls associated-dependent development).[4] Another feature of this system is the increasing involvement and weight of societies in international relations, an area usually controlled by governments. This historically novel element has had far-reaching implications for the operation of the system. With these basic elements in mind we can now briefly summarize each case.

The Cuban Revolution began in 1959. That year a revolutionary vanguard filled the power vacuum left by the breakdown of the state and the collapse of the army. To most observers, it was going to be the usual political revolution—a mere change of government. But it was soon transformed into a socialist revolution that completely reorganized Cuban society, strengthened the power of the state, and changed Cuba's international alliances. Although domestic factors (nationalism, the redistribution of economic and political power, and the quality of leadership) were determinant, a fundamental reason for this evolution was the confrontation between Washington and Havana.

The Cuban Revolution had far-reaching effects in the hemisphere. At one level, it accelerated the emergence of short-lived guerrilla movements in different parts of Latin America, which posed a very serious, real or imagined threat to the established ruling elites and to the regional system. The reaction of the local governments coincided, then, with Washington's policies, guided by the obsession of destroying the Cuban regime and determined to stop the appearance of more Cubas.

Facing Cuba is Haiti, the poorest country in Latin America. In 1957 François Duvalier was elected president and established a family dictatorship that systematically excluded from the political arena the church, the business community, the intellectuals, the trade unions, and the army. He created a repressive exploitative machine that, as we shall see, in some aspects stands completely apart from the rest of Latin America. In 1971 Jean-Claude Duvalier inherited the country from his father. Although the authoritarian Duvalier regime survived for more than three decades, the state was always inherently weak.

During most of these years Washington reluctantly allowed its Cuban obsession to overcome its antidictatorial inclinations and so supported Haiti's deeply anticommunist regime. But after the 1980s, the situation changed, mainly because of the attention that the Haitian "boat people" brought to American society. The U.S. Congress and government now pressured for democracy, a move that coincided with some internal changes that facilitated the gradual return of those domestic forces previously excluded. In 1986 Jean-Claude Duvalier fled the island, but in the absence of organized social forces Duvalierism itself appears to have survived.

Between 1973 and 1976 the army openly took power in three of the most developed Latin American countries: Chile, Uruguay, and Argentina. These coups were the consequence of economic crises, the mistakes of civilian governments, and the strength gained by the army in their fight against leftist guerrillas (in Chile they intervened to topple a leftist government). The assumption of power by the military was not a new phenomenon in the hemisphere, but this time its presence was markedly different because it made an effort to restructure the society completely, using an unexpected degree of political violence.

The military established what are called bureaucratic-authoritarian states, which are characterized by increased executive power, entrusted to highly bureaucratized officials; the exclusion of working-class and popular sectors; the almost complete elimination of political life; and the establishment of strong alliances with foreign capital, mainly originating in the United States.[5]

The rationale used by these regimes was the "national security doctrine," first formulated in Brazil and gained force domestically and through Washington's redefinition of the concept of security. The armies justified their actions on the grounds that it was necessary to clean societies of their illnesses, and this included a total war against ideas. The results were devastating for the countries at all levels and produced major waves of refugees, of a new sort. With the exception of Chile, the armies returned to their barracks in the 1980s, and weak democratic regimes have been struggling to move the countries out of the crisis.

In the long ignored and highly stratified agrarian societies of Nicaragua, El Salvador, and Guatemala, social conflict appeared with unusual intensity, the consequence of economic development taking place under a traditional dictatorship without reforms. In Nicaragua, the Sandinista rebels led a multiclass insurrection against the Somoza dictatorship. Since 1979 they have been attempting to create a completely new model of development that, taking elements from its own history, also includes some elements of the Mexican and Cuban revolutions. The state is more centralized, bureaucratized, and autonomous, but it has never adopted the rigid political stances of the Cuban experience. In El Salvador and Guatemala there are protracted and still indeterminate civil wars very much along class lines: Peasants organized and rebelled with support from other social classes and groups, and they have been fighting against the traditional alliance of landed oligarchies and the military.

The actors in these conflicts include traditional Latin American forces like the army and political parties; however, there are also some historically novel actors such as the Christian groups that have played a protagonist role. In Central America the United States is still playing the role of the dominant power but faces many domestic and external limitations in the exercise of its fiat.

These conflicts are quite diverse, but the fact that they are part of a regional system means that they still are interrelated. That is, each one affects the others in a sort of cumulative way that also affects the United States and the system as a whole, including the dynamics of population displacements.

Mass migrations have occurred in all four of the cases mentioned, with estimates ranging between four and six million people. They have affected the countries differently; for the smaller ones, it has meant a demographic cataclysm. One aspect differentiating the migration waves is the socioeconomic profile of those involved. In general those leaving reflect the diverse social stratification patterns of the various countries. For example, professionals have left the Southern Cone, and peasants and the urban poor have fled Central America and Haiti. A common feature of the three flows occurring in the Caribbean Basin is that they have chosen—and have been able to reach—the United States, which has become the main receiving country.

A common approach in the literature on these flows is to look at the conditions in the country of origin. Usually the discussion is about the importance of political versus economic factors as determinants for departure; the conclusions reached then become the basis for extending and denying recognition of refugee status to an individual or a group.

One of our major arguments is that this approach is inadequate to explain the complex realities with which we are dealing. We shall therefore also explore the political and economic factors behind the migratory policies of the country of origin and especially those in the receiving country. Moreover, most analyses include only governments and international organizations (mainly the UNHCR). We shall also consider these important actors but pay more attention to the role of organized groups in the sending and receiving societies. Finally, we shall also look at the tendency to use refugees as political objects and how, under certain conditions, the refugees can become political subjects, thereby influencing the way in which they are treated and the evolution of the social conflicts that lie at the origin of their predicament.

Cuba

The Impact of a Socialist Revolution

The Cuban Revolution was a watershed for both Cuba and the regional system. Internally, its "social structure, economic life and political institutions were attacked with a thoroughness and at a pace that was unprecedented not only in the history of Cuba, but also in the history of the hemisphere."[6] For the region, the consolidation of the first socialist revolution in the immediate vicinity of the United States sent far-reaching shockwaves throughout the system. The Cuban Revolution also created a massive population flow (from 1959 to 1980, over 900,000 Cubans left the island) that has been well studied and allows us to establish some of the variables that will be used in the other cases.

Cuba is a small island of 44,368 square miles and 9.72 million inhabitants (1981) that developed as a export-oriented agricultural society. Its history has always been influenced by its strategic geographical location dominating the entrance to the Gulf of Mexico. It was the most precious jewel of the Spanish crown in the Caribbean, and it remained a colony longer than did the other Latin countries (until 1898 when the United States finally occupied the island after a seven-month war).[7]

The United States' initial domination of the island fit with the traditional imperial pattern of directly administering the possession. Years later the United States established an hegemonic domination system that, unlike that of Haiti (also occupied by the U.S. Marines in the beginning of the century), did not impede Cuba's relative economic and political development. Such development, however, was controlled by U.S. investors and ambassadors. In this century Cuba evolved under the shadow of the United States.

The domestic factors that led to the political revolution of 1959 can be summarized as follows: In the 1950s the country was besieged by income inequalities and unemployment derived from an economic system centered on the production of sugar, more auspicious for the creation of a rural proletariat than a peasant class. Cuba also had a relatively large middle class.

Fulgencio Batista, Cuba's dictator, appeared at the center of the political scene in 1934 and remained there until 1959. Over time, his regime lost its legitimacy, owing to repeated electoral frauds, constitutional violations, corruption, and repression. Combined with the deterioration of the economy, these developments moved some social sectors to seek alternatives to the dictator, but they always acted within the rules of the Cuban political system.

One of the forces active in the 1950s was a small guerrilla group mainly from urban middle class and led by Fidel Castro, with the support of peasants from the regions where it operated. At the time, the most commonly held perception was that even "Castro's rise to power would not doom the system." His July 26th Movement "emphasized social harmony rather than social conflict," and the main points of all Castro's documents were "always political change, legitimacy and purification of the government."[8] The dictator's repressive response to those opposing him not only proved ineffective but also polarized the political atmosphere. Support for the guerrillas increased, and despite a last-minute effort by the CIA to change the course of events, Batista escaped, and his army was defeated on the political rather than the military battlefield. (A similar chain of events took place in Nicaragua two decades later.)

The prestige of the whole political class vanished, and in January 1959, Castro and his troops entered Havana to fill the vacuum. No one predicted the future course of events; it merely looked like another change of government. However, the power lay in the guns of the rebel army. The new regime soon started to expropriate or appropriate the economic and political power of both Cubans and foreigners and to inaugurate redistributive policies favoring the most disadvantaged; the most radical initial measure was the Agrarian Reform Law of May 17, 1959. The young revolution rapidly organized the support of those who were already mobilized against Batista or who benefited by the revolution itself. But it also gained the moral enmity of those affected domestically and internationally. A self-sustaining dynamic of radicalism began.

Soon after, Washington perceived the Cuban regime as a threat to U.S. economic, political, and military interests. The initial measures, it is true, affected U.S. interests, but what was ultimately at stake was Washington's defense of the basic rules of domination of the regional system.[9] The United States was still driven by conservative, Cold War motives that relied on a broad national consensus and ignored differences between nationalist and communist regimes. So, the overriding motives behind Washington's policies became the overthrow of the Castro regime and the containment of real or potential repetitions of "other Cubas."

The confrontation between Washington and Havana rapidly escalated, and by January 1961 diplomatic relations had been broken. For years to come Washington employed every possible means to destroy the revolution and eliminate its principal leader: among others, assassination attempts against Castro, sabotage, economic blockades, the creation of an exile army, and hemispheric isolation.

The Cuban revolutionaries reacted by defining as their main goal the survival of the revolution. In the early years, this strengthened the resolve of the most radical revolutionaries, who had argued that in order to make significant changes on the island, the rules of domination had to be broken.[10] In regard to that objective, both supporters and enemies agreed that "the first, the best, the supreme political resource" for the revolution's survival was Fidel Castro.[11]

We shall not repeat here the history of the Cuban Revolution or of the deterioration of Washington–Havana relations that almost caused a nuclear confrontation between the super powers in late 1962. They have been already explained in a number of different ways.[12] What matters for our purposes is that in order to survive—and that is the non-negotiable demand of any regime—the Cuban government brought political and economic centralization to Cuba and an alliance with the Soviet Union. Some of the consequences were that the already-divided opposition was eliminated or expelled from the country and that in the process of building socialism, the state gradually absorbed or limited the existing means of expression and the development of civil society. Simultaneously the Cuban economy collapsed owing to errors and the external blockade. The massive re-distribution of wealth and political power polarized society, touching the various social groups and classes in different ways. These internal dynamics are one set of factors determining the exodus of hundreds of thousands of Cubans.

Despite the lack of record keeping and the fact that the exiles have gone to many different countries,[13] it is possible to establish that more than 900,000 Cubans—that is, one-tenth of the population—left their country between 1959 and 1980.[14] These people left the island in waves that became one of the best-studied demographic movements in the region as a whole. Because of this we shall illustrate our argument with only three of the most important episodes.

One of the approaches used to distinguish among the refugee waves is the socio-economic profile of those leaving. From that perspective, immediately after the arrival of Castro in 1959, those who left were the dictator's henchmen and the wealthier, better-educated, more urban, and higher occupational strata. The second wave in the latter half of the sixties came from the middle and lower-middle strata. During the Mariel boat lift (1980), a new component was the members of the marginal sectors, including prisoners and the mentally ill. In short, the two decades of Cuban migration have included a virtual cross section of Cuban society.[15]

To link social conflict and refugees, we must determine the reasons for their departure and their status as refugees. Thus we shall look first at the political and economic conditions inside Cuba. Some in the first wave of people feared imprisonment; others had lost their jobs or sources of income; and many were truly refugees.

After the first group the reasons become more complicated, because it is not easy to separate political and economic factors inside Cuba. Those political factors influencing departure that are cited most frequently are Cuba's centralized political system, the limited freedom to express differences, social pressure on the individual, and the limited autonomy of grass-roots organizations created to defend and implement revolutionary goals. Jorge Dominguez, for example, claims that not belonging to one of the revolutionary organizations became a "political act; those who are refused admission or refuse to join brand themselves clearly and publicly as non-supporters of revolutionary rule."[16]

Thus for the second wave and for the antibureaucracy campaigns from 1964 to 1967, it is impossible to deny that many people did lose their jobs, were transferred to other positions, and resented the campaign against individualism, the restrictions on consumption, and the social pressures to do voluntary work; and many simply wanted to be reunited with relatives who had left the country earlier.

One also cannot deny the limited place for plurality in a system in which the state had a powerful presence. The 1975 constitution, for instance, guarantees the "right to freedom of expression, religion and assembly," but "within the framework of the objectives of the Socialist Revolution." So the exercise of fundamental human rights is limited because the state is determined to organize society and integrate as many people as possible into the organizations that guarantee its survival.[17]

In Cuba there is political persecution. Moreover, there is large group of what Amnesty International calls "prisoners of conscience." In this group are some who have been mistreated because they refused to be part of the "reeducation" programs (the *plantados*). Furthermore, individuals are subject to strong social pressure in their day-to-day lives. But an important difference from other countries is that there is no real systematic persecution of those who think differently.

A review of Amnesty International Reports for this period confirms that Cuba has (or has had) a better human rights history than have Haiti, Argentina, Uruguay, El Salvador, Guatemala, and Nicaragua under Somoza. For example, in Cuba "the current regime excludes deliberate and systematic torture"; there are no political murders; and Cuba does not use the criminal practice of physically eliminating its political opposition.[18]

The bad economic situation was another domestic factor influencing the decision to leave. In Cuba there is a general scarcity of material goods, due to errors of the regime or bureaucratization but also to the strict U.S. blockade. The Mariel boat lift (1980) has been explained mainly by the deterioration of the Cuban economy, although one should not underestimate the "contaminating" effect of visits by Cuban-Americans during the Havana–Washington detente of the Carter years: in 1979 alone, some 100,000 Cubans visited the island.[19]

There are thus both political and economic reasons for the migration. But they must not obscure the fact that many sectors of Cuban society found a better life and greater hopes for the future through the revolution than they had ever known before. The contrast with Haiti is striking; there the present is also extremely difficult, but expectations for improvement are nonexistent. Despite the limitations of its political system and its economic deficiencies, the Cuban Revolution has achieved a more equitable distribution of income than in the rest of Latin America.

Thus, except for a clear minority of political exiles, it is difficult to establish whether Cubans are refugees or economic migrants. Cuban scholars do not consider them to be refugees, and even when they accept the existence of economic motives to explain the flow, they add that it was the United States that manipulated "the consumer desires of some sectors of the Cuban population" who "lacked the knowledge of U.S. reality."[20] Even some American scholars express doubts about this categorization of refugees. Jorge Dominguez, for example, has argued that few of these Cuban immigrants "have ever been refugees in a strict technical sense." Gaston Fernandez concurs that their "common denominator is the unwillingness of the emigrants to live in a socialist society."[21] Virginia Dominguez considers that after the first two years, those who left were "consumer refugees: people who left Cuba because they were used to a standard of living they could no longer have in Cuba."[22]

Another puzzle concerning this migration are the reasons for the Cuban regime to let people leave. Unfortunately, these reasons are difficult to document. The most common explanations are that Havana let people go (at some moments) because this was a "safety valve for potential dissidents and discontent"; because it facilitated the redistribution of exiles' property, the "socialization of the Cuban economy," and the creation of a more homogeneous population; and because the "circulation of elites" strengthened the revolution.[23]

From the Cuban perspective, one of the revolution's fundamental goals has been the creation of a new society, with "new men." That would demand the contribution of those with more skills and a strong and voluntary commitment to the process. Fidel Castro integrated both elements in his explanation: With the migration, Washington hoped to bleed our country of qualified personnel and destroy our revolutionary process. These efforts are linked to the economic blockade and to many other kinds of threats and forms of aggression. The Revolution bravely accepted the challenge and authorized the departure of all those who so desired. We were ready to create a new homeland and to make the socialist revolution with free and willing men and women.[24]

However, it is still unclear why the Cuban authorities continue to impose strict obstacles to leaving.

Cubans wanted to leave for political and economic factors, and the regime let them do so sporadically. The Cubans also wanted to go to a specific destination: the United States. Even the 132,878 who went to Spain, a country with linguistic and cultural similarities, wanted to continue on to the United States, though only 81,616 of them managed to achieve this goal.[25] The attraction can be explained by the creation, from the beginning of the century, of a migratory network between Cuba and the United States. This network was gradually strengthened by close political links (Cuban exiles always found a haven in the United States); by the impact of economic differentials; by identification with U.S. culture; and, once a Cuban community was established, by family ties. After the Cuban Revolution this migratory network became even stronger because so many Cubans settled in Miami, creating a "Little Havana" which constituted an additional "pull" factor.

There is another way of explaining the choice of destination. Cuba is an island, and such an enormous outmigration never would have been possible without a willing importer. Unlike other politically motivated flows, the Cuban flow was an "organized one, based on special arrangements between the two countries."[26] Whereas Cuban migratory policy has fluctuated between periods of openness and restrictions, on the U.S. side there have been only two clearly differentiated moments: from 1959 to the early 1970s an exceptionally liberal admission policy, and from the 1970s onwards a gradually restrictive one.

In the first period, Cuban émigrés were warmly received by both the U.S. government and society. In addition to humanitarian considerations, the United States had an established admissions policy that gave preference to "defectors" from Communist countries. U.S. policy for this initial period, it must be recalled, was consistent with the established practice for Eastern European exiles and their perceived role in the global struggle against Communism.[27]

In the Cuban case, U.S. government refugee policy was deeply conditioned by the more general objectives of its Cuban policy.[28] Cuban officials and scholars have always maintained that the "global political connotations of Cuban migration to the United States is, fundamentally, the result of a regime of confrontation that affects all the elements of bilateral relations."[29] This point of view gradually gained ground in American academic circles.[30] The present consensus is that United States' migratory policy toward Cuba "has always been, and continues to be, an essential part of a much broader set of U.S. political motivations that seeks . . . to constrain the Cuban Revolution."[31]

This approach allows us to "relate refugee-creating conditions in Cuba to United States policy toward the Castro regime, and to relate U.S. willingness to accept so many Cubans as refugees to the objectives of that policy." Thus, at least during the first decade of the revolution, the extremely generous admissions policy "of Cubans into the U.S. served clear foreign policy ends."[32] It must be added that throughout the 1960s, thanks to the absence of quantitative limits on Western Hemisphere admissions, the United States admitted the Cubans as immigrants and not as refugees; for that reason the UNHCR played only a marginal role in the history of the Cuban flow.

In short, Washington "not only welcomed the exiles but encouraged them." They became "symbols around which to engage in building legitimacy to justify foreign policy actions"; they constituted fertile ground to recruit for the CIA's clandestine armies; and they offered means for encouraging "resistance to Communism in Cuba" as well as for damaging the island's economy. For these reasons the Cubans received "specialized attention and care—to a degree rarely or perhaps never seen before with other immigrants."[33] It is clear that for many years Washington created a refugee-warrior community using the Cubans as policy objects. Obviously, if the exiles agreed to such a policy, it was because it fitted their own aims. Washington did not have the ability to destroy the Cuban Revolution, but it did encourage outmigration.

The belief that the Cuban Revolution could be reversed was also important. "Cuba must and will be free within two years," wrote an optimistic U.S. State Department official in 1962. Calculations included the "reasonable expectation" that the Cuban exiles would "return to their homeland within a short span of time." Given these expectations, the exiles became a "key figure in all planning," and a typical comment of the Kennedy years was that they were both a "resource and an opportunity."[34]

By the beginning of the 1970s, domestic conditions in the United States and the international situation had changed drastically. For example, detente was reducing East–West tensions; Cold War excesses were disappearing; U.S. power in the hemisphere (and elsewhere) was diminishing; and new centers of influence were emerging. These processes reinforced the gradual search for autonomy by some Latin American countries, and even Havana reduced its promotion of revolutions.

In this context revolutionary Cuba was seen as less menacing. Furthermore, there was a growing acceptance of the notion that the blockade and punishments inflicted on the island had proved ineffective, and a growing number of Latin governments were reestablishing relations with Havana. The antirefugee mood was another element leading to a new rationalization: To accept Cuban migration was a way of cooperating with the Cuban enemy.[35] The combined result was that Washington started rolling up the worn-down red carpet and closing the door to Cubans.

That change in attitude and policy manifested in the early 1970s, when thousands of impatient Cubans had to wait in Madrid for visas to continue on to the United States. With the arrival of the Marielitos in 1980, there was no longer any doubt: Cubans had ceased to be a "resource and an opportunity," and according to a high-level U.S. official, they became "bullets aimed at this country." The U.S. coordinator for Refugee Affairs, Victor Palmieri, explained the frustrating U.S. dilemma rather bluntly: The U.S. could not "let them [the Cubans] in and could not stop them from coming in, contradictory as it may sound."[36]

In April 1980, three thousand Cubans crowded into the Peruvian embassy in Havana. For a few days, some were flown out to Costa Rica, but then Cuba suspended the flights, and on the twentieth of the same month the Cuban government, in a relatively surprising move, opened the Mariel harbor to those wanting to leave, and some 125,000 did so.

At first, the United States suggested that this was a Latin American problem and that it would cooperate with an international solution but would not become directly involved. It was a comfortable, albeit unrealistic, position because the Cubans wanted to go to the United States where they had a solid constituency and because the Latin American governments did not want them. Washington also sought the good offices of the UNHCR to reach an accord with Cuba, which would have permitted an orderly departure and screening program in Cuba, and to operate a third-country resettlement program from reception centers in the United States.

Just five weeks before Mariel, the United States passed the Refugee Act of 1980. Under this law, each person applying for political asylum would have to be considered individually, and not as a group, as had been the case in the previous Cuban migration. This was, however, politically delicate (if not impossible) because, among other things, there were linkages to be made with the Haitian boat people. Prisoner of its own twenty-year-old policy, the United States finally had to accept the Marielitos and the Haitians under the ambiguous "entrants" category and, in the case of the Cubans, without "control over who was being allowed to enter the country or how many would ultimately come here."[37] This became grounds for the argument that the United States had lost control of its borders.

The Marielitos have been the most controversial political migrants entering the United States. At the end of 1987, 3,730 were still detained by the Immigration and Naturalization Service (INS). Another 4,000 were held in federal and state prisons "on a wide variety of criminal charges, including drug smuggling and sales."[38] Under the migratory agreement of late 1987, some of them would have been returned to Cuba; however, thousands of them rioted in the prisons, forcing Washington to handle each case individually.

After Mariel, Washington tightened its admissions policy still further. In 1981, Under Secretary of State Thomas Enders declared that the United States would stop the Cuban and Haitian flows in the Florida straits, interdicting boats on the high seas and turning them back to their country of origin. But perhaps the epitaph for the liberal admission policy was written in January 1982, when U.S. officials deported a Cuban who sought asylum in the United States and the INS "determined that the individual did not have adequate grounds for a well founded fear of persecution under the U.S. Refugee Act of 1980."[39]

In the preceding analysis we have emphasized the role of the two governments, the most important actors. However, there is evidence that U.S. society, nongovernmental organizations (NGOs), and the Cuban-American community helped shape American immigration policy, although their roles have still not been adequately studied. Whether for humanitarian or ideological reasons, NGOs not only backed Washington's initial hospitality but also were partners in the government's decision to give an extraordinary reception to the Cubans. And over time the Cuban-American community's political influence grew.

Thus, when Washington tried to reduce or control Cuban migration, it found itself constrained by the same forces that it had helped create in the 1960s. The strength of these became clear in 1973 when the Cuban-American community and its allies forced the U.S. State Department to admit some twenty thousand Cubans waiting in Madrid for visas.[40] They also played an important role in the Mariel case, as their actions helped precipitate the disorderly exodus.

In conclusion, the Cuban case clearly illustrates the transnational conditions governing the creation and recognition of refugees: A social revolution led to conditions that expelled people, who had a place to go because of humanitarian and political motives in the main receiving country. Cuba also shows that although governments are the major actors, the influence of other actors—including the refugees themselves—should not be underestimated. Some variation of this pattern will appear as we proceed in our analysis of the region.

Some Effects of the Cuban Revolution

The consequences of the Cuban Revolution created a framework within which the other cases were shaped. First, the revolution threatened the system of domination. Initially, the Cubans promoted armed struggle in other Latin countries. For nationalistic or leftist Latin Americans, Cuba was confirmation that armed struggle was a viable route for the establishment of more egalitarian development and greater independence from the United States. In countries like Guatemala, Colombia, and Venezuela, guerrilla movements were organized with Cuban support, and American policymakers saw them as hostile to U.S. interests.

The guerrilla waves of the 1960s failed for many reasons, but especially because they were unable to obtain the allegiance and support of politically meaningful social groups and because local power elites, already anticommunist and inflexible, implemented ruthless counterinsurgency campaigns with U.S. support. The death of Ernesto "Che" Guevara in Bolivia (1968) symbolized the end of this phase.

In the 1960s, Washington's objectives were the overthrow of Castro and the prevention of "other Cubas." It failed in the first goal but achieved some success in the second. The United States designed a two-track policy for Latin America. At one level, it encouraged liberal economic and political reform through the Alliance for Progress and the Peace Corps. At another, it promoted a redefinition of the "security" of Latin American countries. Nonetheless, as Patricia Weiss Fagan has argued, "one side of the balance, the economic development, proved much more difficult to sustain than the other."[41] Later we shall discuss the implications of this policy for the Southern Cone countries. Here we shall explore some of the consequences of the Cuban Revolution that are less well known but basic to our analysis. The most important is the growing involvement in Latin America of some sectors of U.S. society, such as scholars and religious groups, who had a crucial role in formulating U.S. policies toward Latin America and its refugees.

Another aspect of the American response was to devote abundant resources to the study of the region and to the promotion of peaceful changes. But these government expenditures were permeated by the rebellious climate of the period. Many of the young people who studied Latin America or served in the Peace Corps were more politicized than was the population in general. For some people, going into the Peace Corps (in twenty years more than 100,000 went to the Third World, including Latin America) or to college was a way of avoiding the draft and protesting against the Vietnam War. But one of the legacies of these tumultuous years is a generation of much more sensitive and sophisticated Latin American specialists, who today have important positions in U.S. political life, universities, foundations, and even the federal bureaucracy.

This generation was influenced by Latin American realities. Their initial enthusiasm for the reformism of the Alliance for Progress clashed with local intolerance. These young people gradually became more skeptical of or even rejected the official U.S. policy of intervention and support for military coups in Brazil, the Dominican Republic, and Chile. Their opposition to the emerging and innovative ideas of "dependency theory" (a Latin American product of the 1960s) was another element that made them more sensitive.[42]

For the first time in the history of the regional system, a dialogue was established among societies and helped create alternative agendas to those of governments.

A similar change took place in the U.S. churches, although the process was rather different. In 1961 Monsignor Agostino Casaroli, Pope John XXIII's envoy, gave a speech to the U.S. Catholic leadership. In it, he explained the Vatican's concern about the presence of three enemies of Catholicism in Latin America: Protestant sects, Marxist influence (Cuba), and spiritualist practices. Because of these enemies and the lack of Latin American personnel, he asked the U.S. Catholic church to send 10 percent (a tithe) of its 225,000 priests, monks, and nuns to Latin America as missionaries.

Of the thousands going to the region, many quickly lost their original, innocent belief that faith, organization, and resources were sufficient to bring about change. As Gerald M. Costello explains, they soon understood the meaning of "the specter of oppression," the strength of the resistance to change of the local power structures, and the role of the U.S. government itself. Latin American realities also influenced these missionaries' ideas. What dependency theory did for academics, "liberation theology" (also produced in Latin America) did for religious personnel. Among them, "terms like base communities, liberation theology, consciousness-raising became common language."[43] One indicator of the impact of these ideas is reflected in the fact that close to seventy thousand copies of Gustavo Gutierrez's seminal work, *Theology of Liberation,* were sold in the United States between 1973 and 1983.[44]

These trends had an impact on Latin American social conflicts and the creation of refugees, partly because after the 1970s, the consensus behind U.S. foreign policy gradually collapsed. The causes have been amply documented (the Vietnam War, the civil rights movement, Watergate, and so on). But one factor is generally not included: One of the indirect consequences of the Cuban Revolution was that important sectors of U.S. society became much more knowledgeable about Latin America and established their own foreign policy agendas for the area; that is, they became actors who sometimes obstructed the government. In the open political system of the United States, their existence and activities became particularly important to Haiti and Central America.

Haitian Un-Development

Haiti stands apart in Latin America. It is an agrarian and extremely poor society. From 1957 to 1986 Haiti was ruled by a family dictatorship that excluded traditional political actors and used indiscriminate violence against the majority of the population. The state was inherently weak, and thus was aggravated by international factors. Like Cuba, Haiti lies in a strategic location in the Caribbean Basin and has always been influenced by U.S. intervention. In the years we are considering, it is estimated that close to a million people left the island—one of the silent ways of protesting. A substantial percentage of these people chose the United States as their destination point, which makes it possible to view Cuba and Haiti as a contrasting pair.

With 10,755 square miles and 5.7 million people (1985), Haiti is one of the most densely populated countries of Latin America. In 1957 François Duvalier was elected president with the support of the black middle classes from the capital and provincial towns in a movement against the traditional mulatto domination. In 1971 he left the country to his son, Jean-Claude, who became president for life but had to flee the country in 1986. But behind him remained Duvalierism, which is still haunting the country's future.

Duvalierism is characterized, first of all, by the centralization of power in the capital and the attempts to eliminate (quite successfully for some time) from the political scene the most important social groups: the church, business community, intellectuals, trade unions, and the army. As a result, Haiti lacks an organized civil society. A second peculiarity has been its lack of agrarian and social protest. The reasons for this are, first, most Haitians have been able to rent small plots of land from the group of oligarchs that were a part of the regime and, second, the political system inhibited the possibility of organizing and, thus, reduced the possibility of conflict. Indeed, "rural Haiti's economic organizations [were] conducive to political quietude, not to development activism."[45]

In the countryside such a system is the consequence of *marronage*. The term was originally used to describe the phenomenon of escaping from slavery, but it is now used to describe indifference to political events. Such indifference is the result of a simple but efficient structure of political control that, on the one hand, can be described as "franchise" (licensing): the "assignment of government functions to trusted persons and families within the central government, in cities and throughout the rural areas." Beyond the "minimum requirements of resources and security as defined by the central rulers, local authorities are quite free from outside control to pursue their own financial and security interests."[46]

This was complemented by the extended use of corruption. Alex Stepick, among others, has described the Duvalier regime as a *kleptocracy,* a government by thieves from the highest to the lowest levels (it has been estimated that some 50 percent of the state's income ended up in private hands, and Duvalier's personal fortune has been estimated to be $300 million).[47]

A final feature of the regime is the extended use of repression, because in Haiti, opposition became an "all inclusive term, encompassing real, potential, and perhaps even imagined enemies."[48] In fact, the Duvaliers considered security to be so important that 65 percent of the state's budget was devoted to that purpose, and it was enforced mainly by the forty thousand to fifty thousand Voluntaires pour la Securité Nationale (better known as the dreaded Ton-Ton Macoutes). Soon this became a disarticulated society, repressively governed and ransacked by a minority that had been licensed to extract wealth by sheer force.

The economic effects were devastating. Haiti entered a process of un-development: More than 70 percent of the population lives below the poverty level, and 0.8 percent owns 44.8 percent of the wealth. Haiti has the highest infant mortality rate in the Western Hemisphere and the second lowest calorie intake in the world; 80 percent of the people are illiterate, and 50 percent are unemployed.[49] This situation has been made even worse by erosion and natural disasters such as hurricanes and floods.

External factors have been determinant in Haiti's history. As one historian has contended, "The historical accident of Haiti's location on the Windward Passage has given the country a significance for the United States out of proportion to its size and resources."[50] Like Cuba, Washington also occupied the country from 1915 to 1934, dominating Haiti first through coercion and later through hegemony. One sharp difference from Cuba is that the United States really did nothing to transform Haiti's economic and social conditions.[51] Haiti's fate was to become a pool of cheap labor for the sugar plantations, which flourished with American capital in Cuba and the Dominican Republic. Thus, it can be argued that U.S. actions were determinant in creating the migratory networks that later affected U.S. interests.

U.S. policies were also important to the survival of the Duvalier regime. François came to power just two years before the Cuban Revolution. This chronological overlapping and its geographical proximity put Washington in a dilemma as to whether it should follow its antidictatorial or its anti-Communist inclinations. On balance, the United States shifted to a reluctant support of Duvalier, with periodic cycles of colder relations.

It is generally thought that from 1957 to 1986, some one million people left the Haitian rightist authoritarian regime. The estimates are necessarily speculative because the migration was mainly illegal. But if they are accurate, then the Haitian flow would have been higher than the Cuban in relation to population.

We can distinguish three different waves of refugees. The first started during the first years of the regime: Those leaving were the traditional political exiles, the educated or those from the upper class (who were called "Boeing people"). The failing of the economy and the worsening political situation created a second wave in the early 1960s. Belonging to the professional middle classes, these people went to the industrialized countries, international organizations, and Africa's recently decolonized countries. Their departure created rather grotesque situations: Montreal has more Haitian doctors than does the capital of Haiti, and the Organization of American States (OAS) and the United Nations have more Haitian economists on their payrolls than does the government of Haiti.

The third wave started in the 1970s and received more attention. It was mainly composed of rural and urban poor. By 1978 they started to reach U.S. shores as "boat people" lacking the employable skills of the earlier waves and creating a debate that, as we shall see, linked their fate to that of the Cubans.[52]

One of the distinctive features of this migration is its extreme inelasticity. Glenn Perusek convincingly argues that "Haiti is a classic push case—factors in receiving countries do not determine whether there will be migrants from Haiti."[53] That is, Haiti's economic and political conditions expelled its people and made migration a part of popular culture and a symbol of social status.

The economic decline of the country makes logical the decision to leave, and so the question is whether it is possible to separate economic from political conditions. The answer is not simple and goes to the bottom of determining who is a refugee. In Haiti, as in other Latin American countries, politics is a concept that includes more elements than it does in the industrialized countries. Susan Buchanan summarizes the problem in a report prepared for the U.S. Agency for International Development (AID): "The political aspects involved in Haitians' decision to emigrate are not easily separated from the economic." In the Haitian mentality and experience, "daily life is politics."[54] In other words, wealth was systematically extracted by a political regime based on terror and the division of society. Social groups could not easily organize to improve their economic situation because of political conditions.

Indeed, based on Haiti's human rights record, there was actually a better-founded fear of persecution in Haiti than in Cuba. According to Amnesty International, the situation was terrible: a recurrent pattern of political assassinations; a lack of due process; bad prison conditions, giving Haiti one of the highest prisoner mortality rates in the world; and so forth.[55]

Under these circumstances, many Haitians wanted to leave, and the Haitian government let them do so. The U.S. State Department acknowledges that the "Haitian government has permitted emigration—documented or not—to proceed freely.''[56] The government allowed the first two waves to get rid of the real or potential opposition. But as time passed, this tolerance became greed, because the Duvalierists could obtain economic benefits from the flow.[57] For instance, they received money from each Haitian going to cut cane in the Dominican Republic. This liberal exit migration policy by the Haitian government became an irritant for Washington.

The burden of determining the Haitians' status, then, falls more heavily on the receiving countries. The Haitians went mainly to the United States, the Dominican Republic, Canada, the Bahamas, and France, in some cases following migratory networks created early in the century which, curiously, the U.S. government, directly or indirectly, encouraged at the beginning of the century.[58] The industrialized countries had a more liberal refugee policy than did the less developed countries, mainly because of actions by organized social groups rather than governments.

The Dominican Republic is Haiti's neighbor and the most natural destination for its migrants. Between 300,000 and 400,000 Haitians live illegally in the Dominican Republic, despite its deep anti-Haitian sentiment (demonstrated in the 1937 massacre of some 10,000 Haitians). Since the beginning of the century—and partly as a consequence of U.S. investments in sugar plantations—Haitians have provided from 85 to 95 percent of the sugarcane cutters. Their labor conditions led the English Anti-Slavery Society in 1979 to denounce both countries at the United Nations ''for engaging in organized slavery.'' But just as in the Bahamas (another destination and stopover point), few Dominican voices have defended the Haitians.[59]

Before 1978, the numerous islands of the Bahamas were a natural destination and stopover for the Haitians, as the tourist boom of the 1950s created menial jobs that were filled by Haitians. However, ''when the labor market dried up, and Haitians began to compete with Bahamians . . . the Ministry of Interior authorized raids in residential areas.''[60] There are still some twenty thousand to forty thousand Haitians living illegally in Bahamas, and as in Dominican Republic, there is no mention in the literature of a meaningful defense of Haitians by the local society.

Haiti was a French colony, and some cultural ties have remained. Out of an estimated 9,000 to 10,000 Haitians living in France as of December 31, 1981, the French government had recognized 2,585 of them as refugees, an acceptance rate that is quite high (87 percent of applicants in 1982 and 70 percent in 1983). This policy is explained by the higher educational levels of those who come, their relatively small numbers, and the colonial ties between France and Haiti. However, the principal factor has been the existence of a support network for them in French society.[61]

Canada is both a transit route to the United States and a destination country where some forty thousand Haitians have remained, especially in French-speaking Montreal. Initially, the official policy was restrictionist, on the grounds that the Haitians were economic migrants. In response, the NGOs organized activities such as the 1973–75 antideportation campaign. The defense of the Haitians led to greater flexibility, and in 1980, the minister of immigration, Jacques Couture, stated that the ''cause of the Haitians' refugee problem is especially political.''[62]

Outside the Dominican Republic, the United States has become the principal destination for Haitian migrants. Economic differentials, migratory networks, the closing of some destination points (Cuba and the Bahamas, for example) are some of the factors explaining the United States' attraction. Some estimates put the number of Haitians living in New York City, Miami, Chicago, and Boston at between 300,000 and 400,000.

During the 1950s and 1960s, when the U.S. door was open to immigrants from the Western Hemisphere, Haitians received little attention and were never defined as a political problem. The reason may also have been that those arriving were relatively well qualified and that letting them stay was another way for Washington to show its support—or tolerance—of Duvalier.[63] It was believed that not supporting Duvalier might plunge Haiti into chaos, and the phantom of more Cubas was a powerful policy determinant.

The 1970s' change in attitude toward migration that we attributed to the Cubans also applies to the Haitians. The United States restricted nonimmigrant visas to Haitians, and so the undocumented migration of the poorest increased. The most dramatic aspect of that migration was the phenomenon of boat people which reached a record number of 25,000 in 1980. Their presence sparked a strong debate in the United States about the Haitians' refugee status, and the coincidence with Mariel linked their fate with the Cubans. It is important to clarify the main elements of the debate because it is relevant as well to the response given to the Central Americans.

Haitians created a serious conflict in the United States between the executive and judicial powers, in which civil society was both a catalyst and a major actor. In a kind of rehearsal of the Central Americans' arrival, the debate centered mainly on the status of the arriving Haitians. The U.S. government maintained a policy of refusing them asylum on the grounds that they were economic migrants. Among the arguments employed were that the Duvalier regime was "not a government which was so repressive that being a Haitian entitles one to political asylum. It is not a Pol Pot regime. It is not Cuba" and that nothing happened to those who were deported.[64] For some analysts such a restrictive policy was the result of foreign policy considerations, of the "general anti-refugee mood in the country," of the fear of losing control of the borders and becoming a magnet for other Latin Americans, and of the Haitians' poverty and race.[65]

Whatever the reasons, Washington's admission policy for Haitians contrasted with that for Cubans, creating serious doubts as to its fairness. Comparisons are unavoidable. For example, one official argument for not granting asylum to Haitians was that they had passed through, and found safe haven in, the Bahamas, a criterion not invoked with respect to the Cubans coming from Madrid. And for Haitians, the United States distinguished economic from political conditions, something not done with the Cubans or Eastern Europeans.[66]

The lack of congruence in the official policy was clearly perceived by various private groups in the United States, which became especially important because the Haitians did not display the same organizational capacity as the Cubans did. The churches and other human rights groups formed the backbone of the support for the Haitians. The demands presented on their behalf were that the Haitians' human rights were being violated and that the government had been negatively prejudiced against their asylum petitions. The basis for the open disagreement with Washington was the "fundamental fairness" of a "fundamentally moral question." These groups did not object to the status given to the Cubans; they demanded that the Haitians be "granted legal status and treatment equal to the Cubans."[67]

In the end, these sectors of society were successful; Washington recognized that it was to "blame for the slow pace" of the detentions and deportations. President Jimmy Carter finally granted to the Haitians (and the Mariel Cubans) the legal and ambiguous status of "entrants." The Carter Administration's liberal orientation was a key to the decision: If it defended human rights in Cuba and other places, it would be difficult for it to ignore the Haitian situation. Thus, the presence of the Marielitos influenced the fate of the Haitians.

In contrast, the Reagan administration was determined to block the Haitians' entrance and so established a three-pronged policy: the detention of new arrivals; the interdiction and return of Haitians coming by boat; and the cooperation of the Haitian government in stopping the flow. Interdiction and cooperation with the Haitian government (obtained after some coercion) were successful, but they also accelerated the process leading to the fall of Jean-Claude Duvalier.[68] As a matter of fact, Haiti is unique in the impact that migration had on the political system.

The fall of Jean-Claude Duvalier (but not of Duvalierism) was the consequence of an interaction between domestic and international factors. Internally the deterioration of the economy stimulated an explosion of discontent. Simultaneously, there was a gradual return to the political fore of those institutions and groups that were excluded by François Duvalier: the trade unions, army, intellectuals, business community, and especially the church. Inefficiency and corruption widened the cracks in the cohesion of the ruling class, and the division between mulattos and blacks reappeared.

The trends and tensions that had been accumulating in Haitian society finally came to the surface in the 1980s. For example, the army began to withdraw its support from the regime in part because it resented the preeminence of the paramilitary Ton-Ton Macoutes. At the same time, discontent began to take on more organized forms; in this, the Catholic church's role was crucial, as it was the only truly national force that had resisted the long, dark night of Duvalierism.

Haiti is different in many respects from the rest of Latin America, but the Catholic church there went through some of the same transformations as it had in other parts of the continent. It adopted some elements of popular culture, promoted development, and took up the defense of human rights. In effect, the church distanced itself from Duvalier.

The transition from complicity to opposition is well illustrated when one compares the behavior of Archbishop François Ligonde (a relative of Jean-Claude's wife), who used to set his pistol on the altar just before the beginning of Mass, with that of Pope John Paul II, who on his first visit to Haiti in 1983 stated that "things must change here." This legitimized efforts by the most activist priests who, taking advantage of some internal openings and international support, had been involved in development projects and helped mobilize the young people in 1985 (it was the International Year of Youth). They used Radio Soleil, an extremely important tool in an illiterate society, to politicize society with slogans like "only God is forever" in a not-so-subtle criticism of the president for life. When the government murdered three demonstrators in November 1985, the army did not suppress the violent protests that erupted, especially in the provinces. Finally, Jean-Claude Duvalier fled—in a U.S. Air Force plane—in February 1986.

Without exaggerating, it can be stated that of all the cases studied, Haiti is the one in which migration was a determining factor in the transformation of a regime. First, to the extent that migration acted as a safety valve, when Washington imposed controls in 1980 and outmigration slowed, tensions began to build.

Second, and better documented, is that the arrival of so many Haitians to the United States meant that many groups became involved and interested in the Haitians' situation, both in the United States itself and on the island. Some groups helped the Haitians in the United States but also agitated for change in Haiti, by funding local development projects, pressuring Congress, and denouncing human rights violations. The so-called Mica amendment (1982), inserted in a U.S. Congress resolution, is typical, because it linked migratory policy to foreign aid. In fact it was a compromise between the Florida delegation that wanted to control the influx of Haitians and the Black Caucus that wanted to condition aid on the assurance of human rights improvements.[69] The involvement of American NGOs in support of the local groups is yet another aspect of Haiti's recent history needing research.

In the 1980s Washington wanted to reduce migration and, less worried about the internal effects on the island, pressured Haiti for democratization and respect of human rights. In 1983, three rounds of municipal elections were held in Haiti because, in the words of one employee of the Ministry of the Interior, because the "Americans wanted them." All these facts led Alex Stepick to conclude that "ironically, an immigration policy which began with the fear of criticizing the friendly regime of Duvalier, eventually occasioned its demise."[70]

To summarize, in the 1980s the United States continued to intervene in Haiti's affairs. But it was no longer just the government that was intervening; other social forces were involved as well. That intervention contributed to the deterioration of the dictatorship by creating political opportunities and legitimizing the opposition.

The National Security States in the Southern Cone

The import-substituting industrialization implemented after the 1930s was relatively successful in the biggest Latin American countries. Sustained economic growth strengthened confidence in the model, and the political systems concerned were able to channel political dissent through legal democratic institutions. In the 1960s, 11.5 million Chileans, 27 million Argentines, and 3.2 million Uruguayans "had achieved levels of economic growth, social welfare and political democracy unparalleled among developing nations."[71]

Even so, in 1973 the military took power in Chile and Uruguay—long believed to be the citadels of civility in convulsive Latin America—and in 1976 in Argentina. Although there are important differences in the history of each of these countries, there are some similarities as well.

The bonanza years had increased the role of the state, as well as the power of the private sector and the working classes. When the weaknesses of the model of development became apparent—such as inflation, balance-of-payments deficits, economic vulnerability to external disturbances, and troubles with international creditors—the credibility of the civilian political elites started to collapse.

In a simultaneous development, the security forces had expanded their role during the campaigns against leftist urban guerrilla groups. The armed opposition—originating mostly among the middle classes—was a response to internal factors but had also been influenced by the example of the Cuban Revolution. The confrontation reinforced the sense of insecurity already created by economic problems and further weakened the civilian elites. Indeed, civilian groups came to believe that only military takeovers would reinstate law and order. In Chile, the situation was different. A socialist president was elected in 1970 and undertook to make structural changes by peaceful, legal means. But the ensuing economic crisis, political polarization, and external intervention brought the military to power.

In the Cuba of 1959 nobody expected a social revolution; in the Southern Cone countries of the 1970s few envisaged the depth of the transformations that the armed forces would bring. A fundamental difference from previous coups was that the military attempted to restructure society completely. Their justification was the national security doctrine.

A scholar recently summarized the main influences on this doctrine: the "Brazilian *Escola da Guerra* [war college] is credited with having provided the Latin American military with the most comprehensive elaboration of the national security state, the French military with having demonstrated the practical necessities of counter-insurgency methods, and the United States with a major role in training for counter-insurgency action."[72]

After the Cuban Revolution, Washington defined the terms of the "regional threat." According to a 1965 U.S. Defense Department study,

> the real and present threats to U.S. interests—military, economic and diplomatic—in Latin America are the internal disorder and political instability arising out of the social upheaval now underway in the area and the opportunities these conditions present for exploitation by Communist and other elements hostile to the United States. [Thus] . . . it is now U.S. policy to persuade Latin American republics that the U.S. has the primary responsibility for the defense of the hemisphere against external attack and that their military role is the defense of their maritime areas and the *maintenance of internal security* against Communist and other threats of violence and subversion.[73]

In theory, security was to be accompanied by economic and political development through the Alliance for Progress and the Peace Corps. At the end, however, what remained was security. The United States strengthened and helped change the orientation of those armies, believing that it was possible to educate Latin American military officers on the role of the military in a democratic society. The problem with this assumption was that the nature of the subject did not coincide with the expectations.

At the political level, the objective of the national security doctrine was to uproot the ideas of those defined as the enemies of the nation. Because the military held a very broad view of the conflict, security became an extremely broad concept that attempted to control all situations. Accordingly, the military included more and more sectors in its definition of enemy. This, however, was still not enough. Total security became like a "snowball rolling downhill, continually growing in size" to include those who supposedly had been infiltrated by Marxism. Union members and professionals were added to the proscribed parties, and finally the church itself. In their search for total security, such regimes ended by "marginalizing the majority of a society which will never be secure enough for those in power."[74]

These governments have also been described as "bureaucratic-authoritarian." According to Guillermo O'Donnell and others, these regimes, besides excluding most sectors from the political life, recruited people with highly bureaucratized careers. They also tried to revive economic growth by strengthening their ties with international economic forces.

The UNHCR estimates that there were only some 35,000 refugees from Argentina, Chile, and Uruguay but at the same time acknowledges that there were probably more.[75] Most observers agree that the displacement was massive, but there are no accurate estimates. The most reliable research on the Southern Cone's demographic movements suggests over 1 million departures during this period: approximately 200,000 Chileans, 200,000 Uruguayans, and 650,000 Argentines.[76]

The imprecise numbers can be attributed to several factors: the lack of interest by researchers; the unavailability of official information (the Argentine military, for example, would not provide entry and exit statistics for the country from 1976 to 1981, citing "national security" reasons); the multitude of destination countries (at least forty-four of them); and the great disparity in the figures provided by different organizations, often for political reasons (for example, estimates of the number of Latin Americans in Spain range from 20,000 to 200,000).[77]

Besides the UNHCR and the Intergovernmental Committee for Migrations (ICM) (this intergovernmental organization, among other tasks, facilitates the transportation of refugees), many countries adopted unilateral policies to help Latin Americans escape their countries. Italy and Spain offered the possibility of citizenship to Latin Americans whose ancestors were Italian or Spanish; Canada, New Zealand, and Australia gave them immigrant status; Sweden and Great Britain developed special programs for them; and so forth. Finally, a number of observers have suggested that many Latin Americans did not request asylum for fear of reprisals against family members who had remained in behind.[78]

Despite these gaps in information, some waves of refugees can be identified. The first group was made up of some fifteen thousand Latin American leftists who had found refuge in Chile from the political violence in their countries of origin. When the military took power in 1973, these leftists were joined by Chileans who had taken refuge in embassies and those who had managed to get to Peru (which accepted them as refugees in transit) or Argentina. For the most part, this first group had to be relocated to third countries, in a process that increased the involvement of the UNHCR, the ICM, and other international organizations in Latin American affairs. The Uruguayan exodus also began in 1973. The second wave included the Chileans and Uruguayans, who continued leaving for some years after the coups; many had been incarcerated and had been freed on condition of having secured entry into other countries. Finally, after the 1976 coup in Argentina, Argentineans, Chileans, and many other Latin American refugees escaped from that country.[79]

It is commonly assumed that most of those who left were middle-class urban professionals. This is true of those who went to distant countries (Europe, Venezuela, or Mexico). But this assumption has gradually come to be qualified because recent studies have showed that those staying in neighboring Latin American countries usually had less education.[80]

We shall again divide our analysis between conditions in the countries of origin and those in the countries of reception. The United Nations, the Organization of American States, and a number of researchers and organizations have produced a literature that presents a dreadful picture of arbitrary detentions, lack of due process, systematic use of torture, disappearance of suspects, prohibition of political parties and unions, censorship of the press, and other forms of expression.[81] Even cautiously worded United Nations documents contain unusually harsh comments. For example, the United Nations Economic and Social Council concluded that the state apparatus is "looked upon as the symbol of terror that sprawls the streets of Chile like a haunting nightmare."[82] The UNHCR acknowledged that the "numerous acts of violence perpetrated in Argentina have been attempted not only against Argentineans, but also against foreign residents in the country and notably the refugees."[83]

In Uruguay, political freedoms were suspended in 1973. Initially the army allowed a civilian to hold the presidency, and little international attention was paid to the situation until 1975, when military officers openly took power. Referring to conditions in that country, the British Joint Working Group concluded that "one in every thousand citizens have [sic] been political prisoners" and that "abductions and political murders" took place in the "complete absence of voluntary agencies and human rights organizations." For several years, Amnesty International named Uruguay as the country with the highest per-capita number of political prisoners in Latin America, making it one of the "worst human rights transgressors" worldwide.[84]

Also according to Amnesty International, by 1977 "an atmosphere of terror [had] been established" in Argentina. This view was confirmed by the official commission convened after the return of civilians to the government in 1983: "The terror came from both the extreme right and left." However, the terrorism of the armed forces was "infinitely worse than what they were combating." The "military dictatorship produced the greatest and most savage tragedy of our history."[85] What distinguished the Argentine dictatorship was the "sinister and horrifying" practice of causing its suspects disappear. For a lawyers' mission visiting the country, that was the "most starkly brutal human rights violation in Argentina or indeed anywhere in the world that seeks to be civilized."[86] The exact figure will never be known, but Amnesty International estimated that some fifteen thousand have disappeared, and the autonomous commission documented nine thousand cases.

Repression also had economic aspects. In Chile, both for political reasons and as a part of the neoliberal economic project, there were massive firings of public employees, and anyone who had been detained had trouble finding a job. In Uruguay, bureaucrats were forced to swear their loyalty to the new constitution. In Argentina, thousands of professionals were expelled from universities, research centers, and hospitals.

The economic model that was used led to a deterioration in the quality of basic services. For example, the Chilean "public health service, once the most advanced in Latin America, had been dismantled and with declining real wages and high unemployment, as many as two-thirds of the population is no longer able to pay for the very high cost of medical care."[87]

In summary, the combination of repressive governments and serious economic problems forced hundreds of thousands of Latin Americans to leave their countries. The implementation of their decision was facilitated by the existence of migratory networks within the subregion and from there to Europe (the Southern Cone had been a favorite destination for Southern Europeans).

Latin American countries did take in Latin Americans, but the limitations of the tradition of asylum for the new era of mass migration became evident in the many differences in the legal status granted to them. Brazil and Peru, for example, allowed refugees to stay in a kind of tolerated illegality. Mexico, Costa Rica, and Cuba all legalized their status. Venezuela estimated that 50,000 Latin Americans arrived between 1978 and 1983, but the UNHCR recognized only 737 Latin Americans as refugees (one-third of them were Cubans).[88]

One conclusion of this experience—and one that will be confirmed in the Central American cases—is that Latin American governments are not yet legally prepared, or politically willing, to adapt the tradition of asylum to the new circumstances. In Latin America, the era of open asylum is "coming to a close and the rest of the world" would "in the future be involved in the refugee problem in Latin America."[89]

Latin American events also accelerated the involvement of industrialized societies in Latin American affairs. The interest was linked to the old migratory links of some European countries, especially Spain and Italy. Another, more immediate reason was that the Chilean road to socialism had been followed with attention and sympathy by the European left. Chile's coup d'état alerted several European governments to the need to react to the presence of people seeking refuge in their embassies (diplomatic asylum is a Latin tradition), to requests for assistance to move out of transit countries (such as Brazil or Peru), or to documents that would free prisoners.

Although the initial government reactions ranged from acceptance to rejection, in all of the Southern Cone cases we examined, the UNHCR and private groups played a fundamental role. Without taking them into consideration, it would be impossible to understand why Western European countries decided to accept refugees from such far-away countries. We were unable to obtain enough information about the dynamics of recognition in socialist countries, and so we shall discuss only France, Great Britain, and Spain, which received large numbers of refugees.[90]

The Chilean experiment coincided with a period in which the strength of the French left was growing. After the 1968 student movement, the Socialist party became unified in 1971 and, a year later, agreed to a common program with the Communists. In the 1973 municipal elections, the power of the left became evident. Simultaneously, the Catholic social conscience was also growing in France (as part of the worldwide phenomenon already mentioned). Just as in Italy and other countries, France followed closely the events in Chile, which provoked the most important solidarity movement in France since the Spanish Civil War.

These social forces put pressure on the French government to recognize and receive the Latin Americans. The government showed flexibility also because it had to solve the problem created by the presence of Latin Americans seeking refuge in the French embassy in Santiago. A comparison with Nicaragua shows the importance of social groups to a government's recognition policies. During the Nicaraguan civil war (1977–79), the French embassy in Managua turned down—without much domestic resistance—the requests for diplomatic asylum by some Nicaraguans.[91]

The initial response by Britain's Conservative government was that no non-British subject would be given asylum in the British embassy. From the government's perspective, it was a logical policy because the Latin Americans did not speak English and were fleeing rightist governments from countries with no colonial ties with the United Kingdom. In addition, there yet was no consciousness in the country of the refugee problem in Latin America.

But this policy changed quickly owing to the pressure of social groups. First, London began to accept Latin Americans if they had some "ties with England" or if they were personally acceptable. After the Argentine coup (1976), the policy became even more open: Refugees would be given visas if they were "adopted" by "a British organization" that would take responsibility for them (thus creating a tie with England). According to those interviewed for this study and other analysts, this change was the result of a "significant lobby" that was "instrumental in formulating policy and pressing for its implementation." Years later a member of Parliament summarized the experience in this way: British refugee policy was an "elaborate operation, involving a total reversal of government policies. . . . When the decision was made to admit Chilean political refugees to Britain, the focus of concern moved to the needs of the refugees."[92]

Spain received a significant number of Latin Americans (estimates range from 20,000 to 200,000). Although they were not granted refugee status, they were offered excellent conditions: They were given work permits and granted Spanish citizenship after just two years. One determining factor for the hospitality shown by some groups was that in the 1970s Spain was in its transition to democracy and acknowledged a historical debt to Latin America, which had taken in thousands of Spanish Republicans. Also very important were the cultural ties. Many Spaniards were anxious to demonstrate that they were real Europeans and deserved to enter the liberal-democratic world after the many dark, long years under Francisco Franco.[93]

In short, we find once again that to understand the dynamics of refugees recognition, we must try to see them in a broader analysis that includes conditions in the country of origin and the country of reception, as well as the interaction of domestic and international elements. But it is still difficult to determine the impact and fate of the authoritarian-bureaucratic regimes. Our evaluation does not favor the military's efforts: Economically, their policies crippled local business and increased international dependency, "thereby substantially decreasing national sovereignty." Socially, the ideal of a harmonious society was never achieved, and class antagonisms continue. Culturally, censorship and indoctrination devastated universities and research centers. In the religious sphere, "the Catholic Church, which traditionally had been a conservative bulwark of the status quo, has become more progressive and alienated from the governing elite. Finally, in the judicial sphere, national security ideology replaces society. This is a substantial challenge to the legitimacy of the national security state."[94]

On balance, the military only deepened their country's problems but, recognizing that they had not been successful, have now shown more flexibility. Thus, in the 1980s there has been a trend toward liberalization. The Peruvian military accepted an elected government in 1980, and in Brazil, civilians started returning to power in late 1982. A similar process occurred in Uruguay, and in Argentina an additional element was the military humiliation of the Malvinas (or Falklands) war against the United Kingdom. Only in Chile has the military dictatorship maintained its monolithic grip over society. In all of those countries ruled by civilians the military shadow threatens weak democracies and fragile economies.

From a broader perspective, the migrations and social conflicts in Cuba, Haiti, and the Southern Cone represent interrelated experiences that, influencing one another, constitute an accumulation of trends and experiences. Some of them will be apparent and play a role in the evolution of the Central American wars that have overlapped chronologically with the events described so far. The Nicaraguan rebellion erupted one year after the Argentinean coup, and it was when Mariel was creating headaches for Washington that the Salvadorean exodus began in earnest.

Chapter 8

Social Revolutions and Refugees in Central America

The Roots of Social Revolution

Since the 1970s, social conflict has been ravaging the agrarian and highly stratified societies of Nicaragua, El Salvador, and Guatemala. The dispute is over the changes in models of economic development and political relations, and when stability does return to the region, international relations in the whole subregion of the Caribbean Basin will be altered. The decade-long conflicts have militarized and polarized the societies affected and have displaced between two million and three million Central Americans. A unique feature of the Central American situation is the enormous numbers of those internally displaced.

There are differences in the evolution of the conflicts but also some common roots. Central American economies fall within the classic plantation model: In the nineteenth century these countries were linked to the world economy through the production of coffee and bananas and so were usually referred to as "banana republics." This term was based on the stratified colonial social order, because the Central American societies did not experience the destruction that occurred elsewhere in the process of becoming independent from Spain.

Whereas the rest of Latin America started to follow an import-substitution industrialization strategy in the 1930s, the Central American societies remained basically agrarian. For example, in 1970 the urban population of Central America ranged from 20 to 40 percent of the total population, compared with 66 percent in Argentina or 61 percent in Chile. In the 1960s, Central America made an effort to industrialize (not unrelated to the reforms proposed by the Alliance for Progress) through initiatives such as the Central American Common Market. Those moves brought some changes: Economic activity and the state apparatus grew rapidly and became increasingly complex. As in the rest of Latin America, the demographic boom produced young, urban, and relatively more educated societies.

What did not change, however, was the pattern of unequal income distribution. Worse still, it was exacerbated in the 1970s by the deterioration of foreign trade, the rise in oil prices, the international financial crisis, and even natural disasters, such as the earthquakes in Nicaragua (1972) and Guatemala (1976). Recent United Nation studies estimate that 42 percent of Central Americans live in a state of "extreme poverty."[1]

Thus, with some variations, Central American social conflicts have followed class lines: landlords and peasants facing each other under the shadow of increasingly powerful armies, and with shifting alliances of middle classes and the Catholic church. Another common feature of the Central American countries has been their dependence on external influences. They had been among the poorest and weakest countries of the regional system. U.S. interests thus became the main economic partner and always were influential actors in domestic politics (the United Fruit Company being the clearest example).

U.S. interventionism has been especially clear in Nicaragua. As in Haiti, Washington exercised domination by coercion from 1909 to 1933, a period during which the U.S. Marines occupied the country. U.S. occupation was determinative in Nicaragua's history, one of its legacies being the National Guard, which became the main instrument of control by a family dictatorship that lasted for three generations. The first of the Somozas, Anastasio, structured a regime that also had the support of the landed elite and the United States. The repressive and corrupt nature of *Somocismo* gradually alienated most sectors of the population.

Because the third of the Somozas (another Anastasio) maintained his regime by the use of force, there is a consensus among analysts that opposition to his regime could only take the form of an armed struggle. Augusto Cesar Sandino was a Nicaraguan nationalist who resisted U.S. occupation and who was assassinated by the first of the Somozas. He became a martyr and hero for those dissatisfied with the dictatorship, which is why the armed opposition took his name.

The Frente Sandinista de Liberacion Nacional (FSLN) was founded in 1961, partly influenced by the Cuban Revolution. Led by leftist middle-class people, this revolutionary vanguard obtained the support of some peasants and, in the 1970s, the participation of radicalized Christians. It gradually grew, although it was internally divided into three currents that advocated different strategies and programs.

By the late 1970s the Somoza dictatorship had lost its internal legitimacy, and in 1976, President Jimmy Carter chose it as one of Washington's showcases for human rights activism. The Americans demanded a liberalization of the political system, thus legitimizing the growing opposition. In 1977 Somoza ordered the assassination of a moderate opposition figure, Pedro Joaquin Chamorro (owner of the newspaper *La Prensa*). That event sparked a multiclass insurrection that gradually was taken over by the FSLN, which received the support of Venezuela, Mexico, Panama, and various European countries.

By 1979 the Sandinistas had made remarkable military advances and became a real alternative to Somoza. Washington tried to find a middle-of-the-road alternative between Somoza and *Sandinismo*. In June and July, the main actors, including the United States, reached an agreement whereby Somoza would leave and a provisional president would take over for a few days until a government of national reconciliation started the process of democratization. An aspect of that agreement that is usually forgotten was that Somoza's National Guard would not be disbanded; it would somehow coexist with the Sandinistas.

Somoza left for Miami and later went to Paraguay, where he was assassinated by a leftist Argentinean guerrilla commando. After his departure, the provisional president (Guillermo Urcuyo, an obscure figure) changed the script and decided to remain as president. Confusion followed, and without effective leadership the National Guard and the state collapsed, and the Sandinistas filled the power vacuum. It is important to note that as in Cuba, the National Guard was not defeated militarily. Those fighting on the "southern front" escaped to Honduras, where two years later they became the nucleus of the *contras*.

The Sandinistas started a deep social revolution, but it never reached the Cuban degree of radicalism. For example, they retained a mixed economy and allowed some political opposition. Whereas they organized those mobilized against Somoza and created a powerful army from scratch, as well as centralized power, they also launched an agrarian reform and a successful literacy campaign.

The close relations the Sandinistas have established with Cuba and the support they gave to the Salvadorean and Guatemalan rebels were some of the elements leading the Reagan administration to consider them as an example of Washington's determination to block what it perceived as the advance of communism in the Americas. As part of their effort to destroy the Sandinista revolution, the conservatives launched a covert war against Nicaragua that had as its nucleus a counterrevolutionary army. The *contras* benefited from the internal dissent and the refugee camps in Honduras and Costa Rica. Washington also cut off the Sandinistas economically and tried to cut them off diplomatically.

Although the U.S. government has been unable to overthrow Sandinismo, the level of violence has increased, and the economic situation in Nicaragua has become extremely grave, in part also because of the Sandinistas' economic mistakes. One consequence has been 250,000 persons displaced internally and 300,000 in other countries. One result of the Nicaraguan situation has been the displacement by the *contras* of some 30,000 Hondurans and an increase in political violence in that country, which remains extremely dependent on Washington.

El Salvador presents a different situation. The smallest and most densely populated country of Latin America (618 persons per square mile), this country was traditionally ruled by an alliance of coffee-growing oligarchs and the army, who enjoyed the support of the church and the United States. In 1932, a communist-led peasant rebellion—sparked by the drop in coffee prices that followed the Great Depression—was brutally repressed. Between 10,000 and 20,000 people were killed—a considerable number if one remembers that the total population at the time was only 1.4 million.

In the 1960s, the middle classes started to organize into Christian and Social democratic parties, trying to bring about peaceful reform through elections, but they failed. Simultaneously, peasants and urban groups were being organized by the combined efforts of leftist groups and Christians who had decided to support the poor. As the situation deteriorated and repression grew—some thirty thousand people were killed in the late 1970s and early 1980s by the security forces—these groups created armed and political fronts: the Frente Farabundo Marti para la Liberacion Nacional (FMLN) and the Frente Democratico Revolucionario (FDR).

The Reagan administration also assigned a high priority to defeating the insurgency. To achieve this, Washington supported the weak center and tried to control the extreme right by pushing for social reforms, while also channeling resources and support to the Salvadorean armed forces. After 1982–83 the guerrilla groups had been partially controlled at the cost of militarizing and polarizing society. But the guerrillas were able to survive and, according to some military experts, became the most capable and sophisticated guerrilla army in the history of Latin America.

At the time of this writing (1987), El Salvador is experiencing an economic recession and a military and political stalemate. These have led to some 500,000 persons displaced internally and over 1 million departing El Salvador, mainly for Mexico and the United States. Those estimates means that over 20 percent of the 5 million inhabitants have been displaced by the conflict, the highest percentage in all the cases studied.

Guatemala is the biggest and most important country of Central America, with a population of eight million in 1985, 60 percent of whom are Indians, speaking twenty-two variants of the Mayan language. Guatemala has a sad history, but we shall begin with the October Revolution of 1944, when Jose Arevalo tried to establish a progressive constitution somewhat patterned on the Mexican Constitution of 1917.

In 1950 Jacobo Arbenz became president of Guatemala and tried to continue the reforms intended to transform the country into a modern capitalist state by raising the standards of living of the majority. He respected private property but embarked on an agrarian reform that extended to uncultivated land, thereby leading to a confrontation with both the United Fruit Company, the biggest landowner in the country, and the U.S. government.

Arguing that Guatemala had become a Communist beachhead in the Americas, Washington decided that Arbenz had to leave. The State Department handled the diplomatic offensive, and the CIA the covert operation. The overthrow of Arbenz in 1954 became a watershed in Guatemalan history because it eliminated the political center and polarized political life between left and right. The landed oligarchy and foreign investors took control by establishing a corporatist and repressive state that murdered between 30,000 and 100,000 persons between 1966 and 1982. In fact, for years Guatemala was consistently considered one of the worst human rights violators in the hemisphere.

Gradually the army became the most important actor in Guatemalan political life and made inroads into the economic sphere; it can even be demonstrated that in Guatemala it was most successful in establishing a national security state. But despite the difficult circumstances, resistance was maintained in different ways. In 1960 some army officers rebelled against the military government because of their dissatisfaction with the lack of reforms and the support that the government was giving to the U.S. effort against Cuba (the Cuban exiles that invaded Cuba in the Bay of Pigs operation were trained in Guatemala).

That was the initial nucleus of the guerrilla group Fuerzas Armadas Rebeldes (FAR). It followed the "Foco theory," popular here after the Cuban experience. In 1966 this first guerrilla group was crushed after a cease-fire was arranged with the army. But in the 1970s the armed opposition was more successful in establishing a presence. The FAR was reorganized; the Ejercito Guerrillero de los Pobres (EGP) was created in 1972; and the Organizacion del Pueblo en Armas (ORPA) announced its existence in 1979. In 1982 they all united in the Unidad Revolucionaria Nacional Guatemalteca (URNG).

It is important to note that the creation of these guerrilla groups was preceded by the long and difficult process of organizing a political base in the Indian and peasant communities of the north and on the Pacific Coast. Unlike in El Salvador the Guatemalan guerrilla movement's urban base has remained weak. But it found receptive ears among the impoverished peasantry and also received the allegiance of radicalized Christians.

The Guatemalan guerrillas were also influenced by the example of the Sandinista revolution. In 1980 they numbered some five thousand and considered themselves strong enough to launch more ambitious attacks against the army, which counterattacked with a successful counterinsurgency campaign that paid no attention to human rights considerations or international opinion.

In the mid-1980s the Guatemalan economy was in crisis, and the country was an international outcast. Partly for those reasons the army decided to turn over the government to a civilian, the second since 1954. Vinicio Cerezo, a Christian-Democrat, became president in 1986. The army, however, has remained the real power and has maintained strong control over the countryside. The civilians, thus, have been unable to achieve some of the economic or political reforms needed to solve the country's protracted civil war. By 1987 the army acknowledged that the guerrillas had recovered from their defeat and have some 2,500 armed men. In October 1987, after twenty-seven years of intermittent armed struggle, there were peace talks between the guerrillas and the government, but so far they have not led to real peace.

By 1982 the repression had created massive displacements. At the time, it was estimated that 1 million were displaced internally, mostly peasants, and 200,000 had gone abroad. Of the former, 46,000 have been recognized as refugees in Mexico.[2] The low proportion of external migration in relation to the total displaced is attributable to internal controls and the lack of a migratory tradition.

Among the factors that are especially relevant to the Central American conflicts is the appearance of "new social forces." The term refers to a new, more pragmatic type of leftist coalition that does not follow any external model. During the twenty years between the Cuban Revolution and the Sandinista victory, the Latin American left went through a series of profound changes, owing to the failure of the armed struggles of the 1960s in Guatemala and the obsolescence of the Communist parties. This left does not follow any international master plan orchestrated by the Soviet Union or Cuba. Rather, in keeping with what appears to be an emergent world trend, it is characterized by independence, nationalism, and dispersion.

Besides the leftists, these coalitions include more moderate sectors, especially the Christians. All over Latin America, groups of Catholics, and Christians in general, have redefined their political role and allegiances. Because they are truly national institutions, they have legitimized and given impetus to the forces of change.[3]

Unlike at other moments in its two-thousand-year history, the church today neither seeks, nor is it able, to propose its own nation-state project. It is a partner, not a hegemonic force, who is "accompanying" the poor in a "liberation" process. The limits of religious-political participation becomes clear from a brief look at events in Haiti and Nicaragua. In Haiti, the church both catalyzed and coalesced the anti-Duvalier rebellion; yet when the dictator left the country, the church (in part because it also contains conservative forces) could offer no alternative social or economic project. In Nicaragua, Christians formed a central part of the coalition that overthrew Somoza in 1979, but the church has been divided ever since. One segment backs the Sandinista revolution (with some clergy even occupying high-level posts), and the other maintains antagonistic positions.

The heterogenous origins of these new social forces explains why their declarations and practices are strikingly moderate, especially when compared with those of the Latin American urban guerrilla organizations of earlier decades. They have advocated a mixed economy (although assigning the state an important regulatory function), political pluralism (while trying to construct more direct, popular democracies), religious tolerance, nonalignment, and negotiated agreements with the United States. In comparative terms, these forces are closer to the Mexican than to the Cuban Revolution. This revolutionary moderation is one of the reasons for the region's prolonged conflicts: The new forces have gained broad, multiclass, and international support.[4]

Obviously, these new social forces will affect the structure and operations of the regional system of domination in the Caribbean Basin. More than a threat to U.S. security, they provide greater autonomy for the countries involved, but those limits to the exercise of U.S. domination have been considered unacceptable by conservative sectors in the United States.[5]

Another aspect is the importance of external factors in social change in Central America. These small countries have always been susceptible to foreign influence. Although the governments of countries such as Israel, Libya, and Argentina have also influenced events in the region, space limitations force us to concentrate on only the most important external forces.

The role of Cuba is generally invoked to discredit the new social forces. The Cuban presence takes several different forms: Cuba seems to have been influential in unifying the revolutionary forces, and the importance of its support for the Sandinistas is undeniable. However, there is evidence suggesting that the Cubans, instead of urging radical experiments, have pointed out the importance of an understanding with the United States.

Cuba also exerts a more direct influence, stemming from the results of almost three decades of socialist rule on the island. The achievements and limitations of the Cuban Revolution are now clear for all to see. There have been significant advances in health, education, nutrition, and the redistribution of wealth; but there are also economic waste and inefficiency, limits on individual freedoms, and a costly alliance with the Soviet Union.

Central America is a strategic priority for the United States, whose involvement in the region's history has been a constant since the nineteenth century. The style of domination, as in the Cuban and Haitian cases, has fluctuated between coercion and rights. It perhaps could be said that under Carter, the United States pursued its efforts to dominate by means of hegemony to their limits.[6]

The Reagan administration has tried to reverse the United States' relative loss of power and to reestablish U.S. domination, choosing Central America as the place to "draw the line." Its interpretation of events in the region is based on the belief that they are part of the East–West confrontation and that it is necessary to overthrow the Sandinista regime and defeat the Salvadoran guerrillas. The extremes to which the administration was willing to go were demonstrated by the revelations of the Iran–*contra* scandal.[7]

Today, after seven years of conservative U.S. policy toward the region, the Salvadoran insurgency is still a military option and has developed into the most sophisticated and capable guerrilla force in Latin American history. In Guatemala, the armed opposition took a brutal beating but was not eliminated. In Nicaragua, the Sandinista regime is still in power and has managed to control the counterrevolutionary forces that have fought fiercely, but mostly among themselves and from Miami and Washington. Meanwhile, the economic situation in all of the countries continues to deteriorate, and, most Central American societies are extremely militarized. For example, the Salvadoran army grew by 253 percent from 1979 to 1985 (from 15,000 to 53,000), and the Nicaraguan army grew from 5,000 in 1979 to 62,850 in 1985.[8]

The relative failure of the United States' conservative policy is also due to other domestic and international, legal and political obstacles. First, the United States was faced with new international actors in the region. These are governments opposing Reagan's policies, which have found the Contadora peace plan (originally proposed by Mexico, Venezuela, Colombia, and Panama) or the Arias Peace Plan (named after the Costa Rican president, Oscar Arias) to be more realistic proposals, as they would allow for the possibility of coexistence between Nicaragua and its neighbors, guarantee U.S. security concerns, and prevent interventions in other nations' affairs. These plans also would offer greater relative autonomy to some countries in the regional system of domination.

NGOs from industrialized countries have also played a vital role in Central America. They have channeled resources to development projects and aid to refugees and the displaced, and they have also become direct witnesses to the situation, providing information to their societies and governments. In many cases they have lobbied against conservative policies as well. Many of these organizations started their work in Latin America after the national security states were set up in the Southern Cone and/or as part of the concern in the north over problems of economic and political development.

The actions of these groups are both the cause and the effect of the lack of social consensus in the United States regarding the government's foreign policy objectives. In fact, U.S. society is deeply divided over the interpretation of events in Central America, and this has already altered the rules of domination in the system. Perhaps the most effective obstacles to U.S. conservative designs for Central America have come from U.S. society itself.

A variety of different groups and sectors make up the domestic opposition to Reagan's Central America policy, which will be briefly illustrated here using the Christian churches, whose original involvement in Latin America was outlined in the preceding chapter. In addition to historical factors, the church's role in the region has been strengthened by more immediate factors such as the murders of El Salvador's Archbishop Arnulfo Romero and U.S. nuns in El Salvador; geographical proximity, facilitating a constant pilgrimage to the region; and dialogue with institutional counterparts.[9]

These differences were caused in part because the conservatives' ideological positions have been challenged by Christians on the basis of moral and theological interpretations. For example, the Presbyterian General Assembly passed a resolution that states that "in the midst of the region's political and social tensions," there is "a new religious reform." There, opposition groups read the "Bible in a new way, with a fresh view, as radical," as suggested by Luther and Calvin: "This aspect of liberation, seen through the eyes of the poor and oppressed, means nothing less than an experience of conversion."[10]

In the consolidation of this domestic opposition and in the evolution of the Central American wars, the displaced Central Americans have had a relevant role. They are a consequence of social conflicts, but at the same time, they have influenced them in several ways. This exodus has created networks among the region's societies, which in turn have extended the conflicts beyond Central American borders. In other words, the Central American social conflicts and demographic movements are clearly part of the regional system.

The Central American Exodus

In one decade, social conflict in Nicaragua, El Salvador, and Guatemala has displaced between two and three million people, almost entirely from the poorest sectors of the population. Their experience confirms once again the hypothesis that guided our analysis of previous cases: We must take into consideration conditions in the countries of origin and reception; there is a clear involvement of societies and international organizations in debates about the displaced; and there is a tendency to use the displaced as pawns in the conflict, although it is possible for them to become political subjects. These variables are particularly clear in Central America because the displaced come from two countries ruled by rightist forces (El Salvador and Guatemala) and one by a leftist coalition (Nicaragua).

The characteristics of the Central American population displaced by the conflicts have been relatively well studied. Nonetheless, the fact that a large part of the flow is clandestine means that once again we face the persistent problem of inexact figures. Table 1 shows a difference of 1.4 million people between the maximum and minimum estimates for the populations displaced both inside and outside their countries. Lack of space restricts us from discussing the internally displaced (estimated at 1 million) who are in a difficult situation because they receive little external aid and are perceived by the different governments as actors in the conflicts.[11]

During the past ten years, there have been several, more or less distinct waves of refugees. The first wave was made up of Nicaraguans who sought protection in Honduras and Costa Rica during the popular insurrection against Anastasio Somoza (1977–79). Perhaps because the conflict was intense but brief, only 20,000 of the 200,000 Nicaraguans who had abandoned their country earlier did not return home after Somoza's fall.[12] With the triumph of the revolution, Somoza's supporters left and, after them, those dissatisfied with policies of the Sandinista regime, affected by the economic crisis, or escaping the draft. By 1987, between 300,000 and 500,000 Nicaraguans had left the country to settle, for the most part, in Costa Rica, Honduras, the United States, and Guatemala. They include people from the upper and middle classes but also many from the lower classes.

Just as the first wave of Nicaraguan migration was returning home in 1979, the Salvadorans began to form what would become the largest stream of displaced persons in the region. Although the size of the flow has fluctuated according to the intensity of the conflict, its main component is composed of peasants and urban poor. They have gone to every country, from Panama in the south, Canada in the north, and even Australia. Although the largest number of officially recognized Salvadoran refugees is in Honduras, the majority of the Salvadorans who have left their country are now in Mexico and the United States.[13]

In 1981, as several governments and private agencies began to recognize the seriousness of the Salvadoran migration and took measures to deal with it, the exodus of Guatemalans began. With the greatest intensity between 1981 and 1984, Guatemalans fled to Honduras, Nicaragua, and above all, to Mexico and the United States. The population profile was predominantly peasant, with the added complexity that a larger percentage was also Indian.[14]

One variation worth mentioning here is the Honduran case. Along the country's border with Nicaragua, the Nicaraguan *contras* (whose existence in the area is denied by the Honduran government) have expelled an estimated thirty thousand Hondurans from their places of residence.[15] The worsening of the situation inside Honduras itself has also led some opposition leaders to seek asylum abroad.

There are several domestic reasons for this massive flow, usually invoked to grant or deny recognition to refugees. In Nicaragua, El Salvador, and Guatemala, there is political violence and economic disruption. In Nicaragua, the Sandinista revolution is centralizing power and restructuring some aspects of society, but less radically than in Cuba. Nonetheless, immediately after the revolution's victory, the usual wave of partisans of the old

TABLE 1.   Refugees and Displaced Persons in and from Central America: A Statistical Profile

	Salvadorans	Guatemalans	Hondurans	Nicaraguans	Totals
Internally	500,000[a]*	100,000 to 250,000[b]**	35,000[c]	250,000[d]**	885,000 to 1,035,000
In Panama	900[e]	NA	NA	300[e]	1,200
In Costa Rica	6,200[e]	200[e]	NA	22,000[e] to 100,000 (6)	28,400 to 106,400
In Nicaragua	7,600[e]	500[e]	NA	——	8,100
In Honduras	24,000[e]	1,000[e]	——	43,000[e]	68,000
In El Salvador	——	NA	NA	400[e]	400
In Guatemala	10,000[e]	——	NA	2,000[e] to 20,000[f]	12,000 to 30,000
In Mexico	120,000[e] to 250,000[g]	45,000[e] to 150,000[g]	NA	NA	165,000 to 400,000
In United States	500,000 to 850,000[h]	100,000 to 200,000[h]		40,000 to 80,000[h]	640,000 to 1,130,000
In Canada	5,317[i]	1,189[i]	NA	NA	6,506
In Australia	600[j]†	NA	NA	NA	600
In Belize	3,000[e]	6,000[e]			9,000
Total	1,177,617 to 1,657,617	253,889 to 608,889	35,000	357,700 to 493,700	1,821,786 to 2,795,206
Population[k]	4,768,000	7,963,000		3,272,000	16,003,000
Percentage of displaced in relation to population	25 to 29%	3.10 to 7.5%		11 to 15%	11.6 to 18%

Data 1987

*1985.

**1986.

†1984.

[a]Government of El Salvador data and volunteer agencies' estimates in Universidad Centroamericana (UCA), Jose Simeon Canas, *Desplazados y Refugiados. Version Preliminar* (San Salvador: UCA, 1985).

[b]Government of Guatemalan estimates, in International Council for Voluntary Agencies, "Consultation" (Geneva, 1986).

[c]Honduran Voluntary Agencies, quoted in "Consultation." The Honduran case is so special that its population is not included in the aggregate estimates, in order not to distort the figures.

[d]Social Security Institute and CEPAD, quoted in "Consultation."

[e]United Nations High Commissioner for Refugees, "Number of Refugees as of 31 March 1987" (Geneva, 1987). We have not deducted the 4,300 Salvadorans that repatriated voluntarily to their places of origin in October 1987.

[f]Government of Guatemala estimates (CEAR).

[g]Mexican volunteer agencies, quoted in "Consultation."

[h]Patricia Ruggles and Michael Fix, *Impact and Potential Impact of Central American Migrants on HHS and Related Programs of Assistance* (Washington, D.C.: Urban Institute, Department of Health and Human Services, 1985).

[i]Government of Canada Data, Embassy of Canada in Mexico, 1987.

[j]Government of Australia data, quoted in Universidad para la Paz, *Los Refugiados Centroamericanos* (Costa Rica: Universidad para la Paz, 1985).

[k]The figures are for 1985. Economic Commission for Latin America and the Caribbean, *Statistical Yearbook for Latin America and the Caribbean, 1986 Edition* (New York, ECLAC, June 1987), p. 205.

regime left the country. Many of them (with the exception of those implicated in the repression) fitted the category of classic refugees.

After this first wave, people continued to leave for a combination of political and economic reasons. Clearly, the reforms and gradual organization and reorganization of the society affected the interests of some sectors. In addition, some groups are afraid of becoming involved in the war along the borders (especially settlers in those regions and the young men who do not want to enter the military); others are resisting relocation and the effects of the difficult economic situation. These factors are generally evaluated in the context of the Sandinista's rather benign treatment of dissidents. As Thomas Skidmore and Peter Smith, representing a wide spectrum of opinion, have noted, "All in all, the political record was mixed: the Sandinista regime was no doubt repressive in some ways, but it was also more open and less authoritarian than any Nicaraguan government within living memory."[16]

At any rate, the situation does not lend itself to easy conclusions about the legal status of the Nicaraguans who have left their country. Doubts about their refugee status have grown because of evidence that the counterrevolution has openly used some of the recognized refugee camps as logistical bases.[17]

In El Salvador, the class conflict is extremely violent. For years, the alliance of landed oligarchy and military used repression to resist any social change, with the resulting massive violations of human rights. The 1980s have been a period of full-scale civil war, in which the guerrilla forces have continued to represent a military and political alternative, establishing themselves firmly in various parts of the country. The growth and strengthening of the army have led to a stalemate, affecting the entire country and producing tremendous insecurity and the biggest population displacements in absolute figures and in relation to the population.[18]

In all of Latin America, the Guatemalan army has the darkest human rights record, so bad indeed that the Carter administration suspended military aid to Guatemala in 1977. In the last years of the 1970s and the first years of the 1980s, armed insurgency grew quickly through an alliance of middle-class cadres and impoverished peasants, its largest social base among the Indians. To control that movement, between 1981 and 1984, the army launched the region's most violent counterinsurgency campaigns. It managed to gain relative control over the guerrillas but, at the same time, caused major population displacements. By 1987, the violence had diminished but not disappeared. In fact, without any reforms following it, the stage is currently being set for an even deeper conflict.[19]

The social violence in the three countries is compounded by the worsening economic situation. In the opinion of an expert, "the period of the 1980s has been an economic disaster for Central America." The average annual growth has been very weak; there is inflation (and hyperinflation in Nicaragua); with the exception of coffee, the prices of primary commodity exports have plummeted; gross domestic investment has declined, partly owing to capital flights; there has been no foreign investment; there is a noticeable lack of basic infrastructures such as communications and transportation; and the massive infusion of U.S. aid to some countries has been guided mainly by military considerations.[20] In short, Central American countries "suffer from economic policies that need reforming, war damage, oligarchical political structures, oligopolistic economic structures, brain drain and capital flight." The prospects for the future are equally grim.[21]

Another set of elements to be considered in the exodus are the economic differences between Central America and other countries, and the small size of the Central American countries. These differences are interconnected and together have created a tradition of internal and external migration with firmly established networks that facilitate further displacements. In Central America, migration is part of the ordinary culture, thereby making it easier for anyone to decide to leave. But Guatemala is an exception in some ways. In 1982 the local Catholic church estimated the number of those internally displaced at one million, and yet a small proportion of them sought refuge abroad. Perhaps the explanation lies in the fact that for the Guatemalan Indians, the concept of a border to cross is not as clear as it is for the Salvadorans. One final aspect—usually ignored—is that, at least until late 1986, the borders in the region have been relatively open.

The polarization and politicization of Central America extend to explanations of the population displacements. A strong UNHCR presence in Central America would, in principle, help resolve the problem of who is and who is not a refugee; but although this international organization has done a superb job in some countries, it has also created some confusion.

Let us begin with the figures provided by the UNHCR. In December 1986, it estimated that there were 287,000 refugees (this number does not include estimates of the number of refugees in the United States). The UNHCR has recognized and aided some 112,000, or 39 percent, of its own estimated total.[22] The criteria used by the UNHCR to recognize Central Americans as refugees are ambiguous. Its original mandate was to protect what we have called classic refugees, that is, persons escaping from persecution or having a well-founded fear of persecution. But because most of those who have sought asylum are persons fleeing from conditions of internal disorder or armed conflict, the UNHCR's mandate was extended by the U.N. General Assembly by means of several resolutions.[23] Thus, the UNHCR has at its disposal both a narrow and a broad definition of refugees.

It has applied both definitions in Central America but relied more on the broader one. Some 80 percent of all recognized refugees in the region are protected under the broad definition: the Salvadorans in camps in Honduras; the Guatemalans in Mexico; the Salvadorans in Nicaragua and Costa Rica; and the Nicaraguans in Honduras and Costa Rica.[24] It should be noted that the broad (or prima facie) definition is generally used in cases of massive migrations to neighboring countries; however, UNHCR has used it even when the population in question is not in a border country, such as for the Salvadorans in Nicaragua and Costa Rica.

In other situations, the UNHCR has used the classic definition of individual political persecution (Nicaraguans in El Salvador and Guatemala, and Salvadorans and dispersed Guatemalans in Mexico). But here the confusion grows because, under certain circumstances, the UNHCR does not apply either definition, bowing to governmental pressures despite its humanitarian mandate. For example, in Mexico it assists people only in the capital city, even though there are large numbers of Central Americans in the Soconusco region. Even more disconcerting is how the UNHCR has managed to reduce its presence in the United States to a minimum, ignoring the Central Americans there altogether. These ambiguities are the consequence of the fact that although the UNHCR's mandate is humanitarian, the organization is also amenable to political conditions in the countries where it operates and, in some cases, possibly to its economic dependence on the United States for its budget.

Latin American countries have a long tradition of asylum, but those receiving Central Americans have not been able to find an adequate legal solution to the presence of these masses of poor people that arrive spontaneously. Despite these shortcomings, on balance the Latin American governments have tried to respond positively to the Central Americans. There have been humanitarian considerations behind this attitude, but also political considerations, especially when organizations have favored the Central Americans.[25]

The importance of political factors is especially clear because there are refugees from one "leftist" country and two "rightist" ones. Thus, there are two different responses that we shall outline before we review in more detail the conditions in three different countries. Governments, NGOs, and social groups who reject the Sandinistas tend to show a certain sympathy for or tolerance of those who leave Nicaragua. These same forces also generally support the Salvadoran and Guatemalan governments. Accordingly, the refugees from these countries are treated with hostility and defined as economic migrants, as ideologically undesirable, and/or as guerrilla supporters. This dichotomy is especially clear in Honduras, where there are both Nicaraguan and Salvadoran refugees. The former may move about as they please, but the latter are extremely restricted in their movements and are also harassed.[26]

An opposite response comes from those according some legitimacy to the Sandinistas and the insurgent movements in El Salvador and Guatemala. At the national level, the response is the opposite of the one just described. The Nicaraguan government, for example, believes that its citizens in Honduras and Costa Rica have supported the counterrevolution, while simultaneously providing refuge for Salvadorans and Guatemalans. In Mexico and other countries, some NGOs refuse to give assistance to Nicaraguans, in part because of their own political leanings and in part because doing so would limit their work with other nationalities.[27]

Obviously, the situation is not quite so clear-cut because other factors come into play in each of the countries. We shall examine in greater detail Mexico, Honduras, and the United States because they are the most important receivers and because they present alternative, even paradoxical, situations. For example, Mexico and Honduras have the most UNHCR-recognized refugees, but they have not ratified the Geneva Protocol and Convention; the United States has ratified both instruments and has received the highest number of Central Americans but also has the most restrictive asylum policy.

Mexico has from 300,000 to 400,000 Central Americans on its territory and has been used as a corridor for the hundreds of thousands going to the United States. Forty thousand Guatemalan peasants and 5,000 Salvadorans have been recognized as refugees by the UNHCR, but according to Mexican law there is not a single refugee in the country. Accordingly, they have a different migratory status, awarded by a political decision to give them temporary asylum.

In the summer of 1981, some two thousand Guatemalan peasants arrived in the Mexican jungle. The Mexican government deported them because they did not meet the individual requirements for asylum. The decision aroused a wave of support and solidarity from national and international groups seeking recognition for the Guatemalans.[28] One factor usually excluded from the analysis of this event is that the Guatemalans went to a border area (in the state of Chiapas) where independent, grass-roots movements had long flourished. These showed concern for the refugees' fate. Consequently, the peasants' hospitality and solidarity were not entirely spontaneous but, rather, included an important organizational component, making their support less prone to erosion over time.[29]

In political terms, this was crucial. The actions of these groups served as a reference point that helped coalesce the will of other important actors, as diverse as the UNHCR (which had arrived in Mexico only recently to assist Salvadorans and Latin Americans), government officials, national and international public opinion, left-wing parties, international organizations, and foreign governments, among others.

The government was gradually forced to take more a flexible position, even though, simultaneously, its official agency in charge of refugees (COMAR, the Mexican Commission for Refugee Assistance) imposed greater restrictions on the work of private, foreign and national agencies. These factors led to a tolerance of the Guatemalans that has gone as far as to create an economic integration program in the states of Campeche and

Quintana Roo. There was opposition to recognition among conservative sectors of the Mexican bureaucracy and society, but they lacked the firmness of those who defended the Guatemalans. The Guatemalan government also pressured for the refugees' return, but its prestige was so undermined that its efforts were fruitless. Washington showed only marginal interest in the matter.[30] Soon the interaction of a number of domestic and other factors made possible the existence of the bigger community of UNHCR-recognized refugees in the region.

Honduras is a country where the United States has exercised its domination in a direct, outmoded way. When the first Salvadorans sought refuge in Honduras in 1981, the Hondurans reacted with hostility because the Salvadorans were seen as guerrilla supporters and because there is a long history of mutual hostility between the two nations; as recently as 1969, they were at war.

At the same time, Honduran civil society has neither the vigor nor the plurality of its Mexican counterpart, nor did it show the same solidarity toward the refugees. Nonetheless, the Honduran government finally permitted the creation of refugee camps along the border, owing to pressures by a wide range of international forces, including the UNHCR, international public opinion, and groups of internationalists working with the refugees and representing volunteer agencies from the developed world. Indeed, these agencies have played an important role in refugee affairs, and their presence is a source of deep resentment among some Honduran officials.

Nonetheless, the Honduran dependence on and submissiveness to the U.S. government imposed limits on the government policies toward these NGOs and the Salvadoran refugees. They accepted the existence of refugees in settlements that, to some observers, are "virtual concentration camps" and, to the U.S. State Department, are "closed camps under the protection of the armed forces."[31]

The Nicaraguans in Honduras were also recognized by a combination of the UNHCR's presence, the advocacy of conservative NGOs, and the protection of the U.S. government. A crucial difference is that they are given preferential treatment because they fit the general military and political objectives of the United States government. In sum, many elements governing the recognition of refugees in Mexico and Honduras are not exclusively humanitarian.[32]

Only 5 percent of the estimated number of externally displaced Central Americans have been recognized as refugees. The majority is dispersed and living illegally throughout the entire region. One striking aspect of these people is that some 86 to 88 percent of them are concentrated in Mexico or the United States. There are several reasons for this situation: (1) Political stability and economic differentials make the United States and Mexico, even with the economic crisis, a better option than their countries of origin; (2) social support networks exist in both countries; (3) there is a long migratory tradition; (4) the cost of making the trip by land is low; (5) all the borders from Nicaragua to the United States have been relatively open and easy to cross. The effects of the new U.S. immigration law, passed in November 1986, and of restrictive policies in other countries remain to be seen. Because of the importance of Mexico and the United States as receiving countries, we shall now discuss them in more detail.

The number of undocumented Central Americans in Mexico is unknown: Estimates vary from 120,000 to 500,000. The policy of the Mexican government has been to deny the Central Americans recognition, arguing that they are economic migrants. However, it simultaneously maintains a tacit tolerance of them. A number of reasons explain this ambivalent policy. The Central Americans are not recognized because there has not been a coalition of forces such as the one that pressured for recognition of the Guatemalans. This is partly a consequence of the way in which these people arrived: individually or in small groups, dispersed and less organized. Furthermore, the UNHCR has not displayed much enthusiasm for protecting these individuals.

Other factors explain Mexico's toleration. The first is structural: Mexico's border with Guatemala is relatively open. The coastal plains section of that border (known as the Soconusco region) forms a tight geographical knot that connects Central and North America. Most of the Central Americans in Mexico or the United States have passed through this region, which has a formidable infrastructure of human contraband, made possible by the corruption of low-level authorities. The Central Americans crossing there also count on the support of the Tapachula diocese, which for humanitarian reasons, has developed some assistance programs for the migrants.[33]

The region's productive structure is another factor. The Soconusco is a veritable commercial agricultural empire, which depends on the ruthless exploitation of Guatemalan and other Central American labor. The local landlords favor the Central American workers because they constitute a labor reserve that reduces salaries and increases profits. This limits the possibilities of action by the Mexican government and ensures that it will be difficult—if not impossible—to stop totally the flow of Central Americans into Mexico.

Finally, the Mexican government cannot easily change the nature of the open border. Not only would this go against the tradition of asylum, but it also would contradict Mexican diplomacy. Such a move would be opposed by the Guatemalan government, which does not want the Salvadorans and Nicaraguans to stay indefinitely in Guatemala, now used only as a transit country.[34]

Another aspect of Mexican policy pertains to what happens after the Central Americans cross the Soconusco. Many stay in Mexico, but given their uncertain legal and economic situations and the great attraction of the United States, most have gone there.[35] But the journey from Mexico to the United States is a difficult one because the Mexican authorities have tried to control the migrant flow and prevent border crossings; because the Central Americans face systematic extortion by minor officials and groups who deal in human contraband; and because once in the United States they run the risk of deportation.[36]

Despite the obstacles in getting to the United States, the journey is made easier by a particular structural aspect of the demographic regional system: the need of some U.S. economic sectors for cheap labor, which has created a tradition of undocumented Mexican labor migration. The Central Americans have taken advantage of this structure, and the Mexican government has been relieved of the pressure to develop a relevant policy.

A related aspect is Washington's desire to keep the Central Americans in their region, which has led the United States to support the creation of camps and to insist that Mexico detain the refugees.[37] This explains in part why the Mexican government has not been more flexible regarding Central Americans; to do so unilaterally (i.e., outside the framework of a regional accord), would effectively mean justifying the argument that Mexico is a "safe haven" and hence accepting the role of principal depository of Central American refugees and displaced.[38]

The U.S. reaction to the Central Americans is equally complex and has to be explained at different levels. One level is that the Central Americans have made the United States their main destination. The U.S. government has followed a restrictive admissions policy on the grounds that these people are economic migrants. This policy is consistent with the antirefugee mood and the desire to control its borders, both partially a reaction to the influx of Haitians and Marielitos.[39] There is also the fear of a magnet effect—in which U.S. hospitality would attract more Central and Latin Americans—and concern for the economic and political impact of the Central Americans in the United States.

Another reason has to do with foreign policy considerations. Because Washington maintains that the governments of El Salvador and Guatemala are becoming more democratic, it cannot admit that the population displacements are the result of political violence. Washington has also wanted to build support for its foreign policy by arguing that the existence of the Sandinista regime and the triumph of other insurgent movements will provoke a deluge of refugees into the United States (the "feet-people").[40] An interesting variation of this linkage between foreign and migratory policies can be found in the response to the Nicaraguans in the United States. For several years the Justice Department did not recognize them as refugees, whereas the State Department insisted that the Nicaraguan regime was totalitarian. Finally, in June 1987, the attorney general authorized their stay in the country, albeit with a rather ambiguous status.[41]

Another aspect, more extreme, has been the role of Washington in the creation of Nicaraguan refugee-warrior communities in Costa Rica and Honduras. These groups have their own reasons to oppose the Sandinista regime, but Washington has been instrumental in transforming them into an armed opposition. As part of the effort the *contras* have even forced people to become refugees, and Washington has tried to utilize bona fide refugees for military purposes. For example, in Honduras there is a clear division between the *contra* bases and the refugee communities recognized by the UNHCR. However, there have been attempts to transform them into social bases for the opposition, which has been reflected in a struggle over the location of the refugee camps. The UNHCR maintained its camps at a distance from the border—as it does in other parts of the world—but private agencies, such as Friends of the Americas, with U.S. financing have assisted groups along the border. These programs have attracted refugees away from the camps and back to the border. The latter's efforts, however, have encountered resistance from many governments because the *contras* are perceived as extremely dependent on Washington and because supporting them would create a precedent for supporting external armies against established governments.

The Nicaraguans are an instance of the most extreme use of refugees as policy objects. Such attempts have also been evident with the Salvadorans in Honduras. In their case, the situation is the opposite to the one just described. The U.S. government has wanted the Salvadorans to be relocated far from the border and under tight control in closed camps, arguing that they were providing support for the guerrillas. Obviously, the policy was pursued to collaborate with the Salvadoran army's counterinsurgency campaign.[42] The Mexican government also decided to relocate the Guatemalans away from the border, owing to domestic political factors and as a way of reducing tensions with Guatemala.[43]

In both cases a significant number of Salvadoran and Guatemalan refugees successfully resisted the pressures for relocation. The outcome is explained by their previous experiences in organizing, the fact that they stayed united, and the backing they received from outside actors, which gained support from other sectors. In the Mexican case, this actor was civil society; in Honduras, it was private international agencies.[44] These are examples of how the refugees can become "policy subjects." Although this aspect of the refugee experience has received little attention, there is no doubt that it is possible for the refugees to become important actors in the decisions taken on their behalf.

U.S. government policies have been resisted at all levels by many sectors of U.S. society, which have viewed the process from another perspective. The opposition has been remarkably successful in its organization and strength, but also because it operates in a very open political system. At one level this is another demonstration of how U.S. society is divided over the exercise of domination. It should be added that the breakdown of consensus extends to and is fed by the Central Americans who go to the United States and provide a direct line of communication with the conflicts in their home countries. For example, conservative groups support Nicaraguans, and liberals support Salvadorans and Guatemalans. In fact there is a degree of continuity with the coalitions that formed on behalf of the Cubans and Haitians.[45]

We shall develop these points further by examining the response to the Salvadorans, which in the United States is the most important national group from Central America. Christian churches have been the backbone of support for the Central Americans. Their aid has taken a variety of forms: (1) emergency assistance of all kinds, especially in the areas of greatest concentration, such as California, Texas, and Washington, D.C.; (2) legal protection, including the defense of individual cases and efforts to get Extended Voluntary Departure status for entire nationalities; and (3) direct confrontation with U.S. immigration laws, as expressed in the creation of "sanctuaries" for Central Americans—a medieval concept that, ironically, was revived in the hemisphere as a result of the U.S.-supported coup in Chile. The confluence of these forces has made it politically difficult for Washington to undertake massive deportations of the Central Americans.[46]

The debate over what has become known as the Moakley–DeConcini bill illustrates the divergences between government and society. Those in the United States who support the Nicaraguans, as well as those who support the Salvadorans and Guatemalans, have tried to create a sort of two-year amnesty for Salvadorans and Nicaraguans pending an examination of conditions in their countries of origin. The lack of consensus on what to do with the Central Americans has become evident.

The breakdown of consensus extends to Washington's policies in Central America. This is evident in the general dynamics of social conflict and at the more concrete level of refugee policy. For example, American NGOs such as the Catholic Relief Services have been extremely helpful in supporting the Salvadorans resisting the relocation that is considered important to Washington's overall military policies. American NGOs have also been important in overseeing and putting pressures on the UNHCR's actions, as well as in channeling direct support to the displaced. This presence has had the simultaneous effect of reinforcing the domestic opposition to Washington's Central American policy.

U.S. society is not alone in its involvement in Central American refugee affairs. European NGOs also established strong links with Latin America during the upheavals in the Southern Cone and reinforced their role in Central America. They have given financial resources and political support to local organizations, pressured the UNHCR and local governments, and become transmitters of information concerning events in the region, thus helping mobilize concerned sectors in the industrialized countries.[47]

Viewed in broader perspective, the Central American exodus demonstrates both the interrelation of social conflicts and population displacements, and the relative autonomy of the two dynamics. That is, people have been displaced by social conflict, and the solution to their problems depends on the achievement of peace. However, peace in itself will not mean a return to the status quo ante. Central America has experienced a demo-graphic cataclysm with irreversible consequences for the region as a whole.

The concern of the Mexican government over the possible impact of these population flows into its territory has been one of the motives for its vigorous diplomatic activity for peace and its search for a regional solution to the refugee problem. One whole chapter of the Contadora Peace Proposal is devoted to refugees. Even more important in this regard is the Cartagena Declaration. In November 1984, the governments of the region (with the notable exception of the United States) and the UNHCR met in Cartagena, Colombia, to approve a broader definition of refugees, similar to the one used by the Organization of African Unity. Although it is a nonbinding resolution, it demonstrates the efforts made by Latin American governments to adapt the tradition of asylum to the new conditions of massive displacements.[48]

In the search for a regional solution, what the United States does or does not do is essential, given its role as the dominant power in the regional system and the fact that it has more Central Americans than does any other country. Underlying the U.S. position is the lack of consensus in the country for the exercise of domination and the relative loss of power to influence the events in its immediate sphere of influence. Up to now the position of the U.S. government has been to limit the impact of the definition and regional focus laid out in the Cartagena Declaration.

That is why Washington has blocked the advance of the Cartagena Declaration in several fora, particularly in the UNHCR Executive Committee meeting in November 1985 and the OAS General Assemblies in December 1985 and November 1986.[49] Obviously, such a policy is consistent with the traditional U.S. desire to preserve maximum freedom of action for itself in the regional system. From that perspective, the outcome of the debate on the Central American exodus is linked to a restructuring of the regional system in which, we believe, the role of societal actors will be determinant. The final result will also determine the evolution of future social conflicts and the treatment of the population they will uproot.

Prospects for Latin America

The social conflicts in these two chapters cover a wide range of situations: victorious social revolutions with differing degrees of radicalism, in Cuba and Nicaragua; personal despotism with a weak state, in Haiti; state terrorism in bureaucratic-authoritarian re-gimes, in the Southern Cone; and peasant-based revolutionary challenges, in El Salvador and Guatemala. The profiles of those escaping from the violence engendered by those conflicts vary according to the social structure of each of the countries: a sustained trickle of urban middle-class professionals from the Southern Cone, peasants and urban poor from Haiti and Central America, and a cross section in the case of Cuba.

Although they are distinct phenomena, both the social conflicts and the displace-ments are part of a regional system, with the United States as the dominant country. Thus, each case of social conflict and population displacement is dialectically related to the others, and each event has determined some of the characteristics of the others. The process has economic, political, and international dimensions.

One way of weighing the prospects for the region is to consider some of the major conclusions drawn from the preceding analysis. Social conflicts and population displacements are closely interrelated but have a relative autonomy; that is, politically motivated population displacements are also dependent on factors such as traditional migratory patterns, which are essentially economic and a consequence of economic differences between the countries of origin and destination. For example, the Salvadoran displaced peasants left in bigger numbers than did the Guatemalans because they have a long tradition of migrating outside their overpopulated country.

Another consideration is that those leaving must want to seek asylum. This seems to be determined by the intensity of violence in the country of origin, but in the Southern Cone and Central American cases, many people are hesitant to leave, for fear of reprisals against relatives who stay behind. Of course it is not only a problem of will: There must be an available place to go to and a country willing to receive, or at least tolerate, those escaping from violence. That is why the study of refugees must also consider the determinants moving a government or private group to recognize an individual, group, or nationality as refugees.

Such factors also affect the behavior of international organizations. A review of the gradual involvement and increasing importance of the UNHCR in the region indicates that although its policies are, in principle, guided by purely humanitarian considerations, in each case they also are influenced by economic, political and international factors. The relative lack of involvement of the UNHCR in refugee problems in the United States or its silence regarding the U.S. interdiction of Haitians on the high seas are good examples.[50] Nonhumanitarian aspects are also important to the migratory policies of most governments. Clear examples were the 180-degree change in Washington's policy toward Cubans between the early 1960s and 1980 or Honduras's radically different policies for Salvadorans and Nicaraguans.

Among those determinants of migratory policies we also highlighted the increasing role of societal groups in influencing the reception given to a particular group of refugees by a government. Obviously, in those societies with a stronger associational life, there is more involvement in this process. In a regional system, a phenomenon with far-reaching implications is the growing interaction between Latin and U.S. societies, which is imposing limits on Washington's domestic and international policies. This pattern appeared in the three cases (Cubans, Haitians, and Central Americans) in which the displaced selected the United States as the preferred destination.

Another aspect of the refugee experience is the noticeable tendency of groups or governments to use refugees as political "objects," taking advantage of the fact that they usually have little or no control over their lives, at least temporarily. This utilization may be implicit or explicit and manifest itself in different ways. One extreme form is the creation of refugee-warrior communities (as is the case with the Nicaraguan *contras*); another is the manipulation of statistics, which we find in each one of the situations reviewed.

However, it is also possible for the refugees to influence the policies that affect their future and so become political "subjects." Obviously, their very existence has an impact on the policies adopted toward them. But this concept refers more specifically to the development of conscious and organized actions as refugees, that is, the process of becoming protagonists. Although this issue has not been sufficiently discussed in the refugee literature, the cases we reviewed indicate that for a group of refugees to become "subjects" they must be organized; and this, in turn, depends on official recognition, on support from local or international forces, on the refugees' prior experience and ability to stay together in groups, and on their political, economic, or military importance.

In the case of Latin America these trends must be considered in the framework of the regional system. The United States has exercised its domination through the multiple variants of coercion and hegemony. From this perspective, those elements that should be included are the relative loss of U.S. power in the world, the appearance (or reactivation) of other external actors, and the end of the domestic consensus regarding U.S. foreign policy toward Latin America. The situation created by these broader factors is rather fluid, but there are indications of changes in the way that domination is, and will be, exercised in the region. The use of coercion as a means for the United States to impose its will on the entire system appears to be increasingly difficult, and the displaced people have played a role in bringing this about.

The future of Latin America looks quite grim. Most economic indicators show a stagnation difficult to overcome, and structural problems such as unequal income distribution, marginalism, and reduction in the standards of living are continuing. The mounting external debt and the worsening terms of trade further complicate the situation. Simultaneously, the traditional political systems are showing growing signs of weakness. Finally, there is an ongoing struggle to redefine new models of development whose characteristics are not yet clear because various approaches are emerging in the different countries.

In considering future conflicts and population displacements, we must distinguish two subregions, Latin America and the Caribbean Basin. In the first case there are some countries in which social conflict is already under way or is imminent. In Peru, the confrontation between the little-known Sendero Luminoso (Shining Path) guerrilla movement and the army has created some 300,000 internally displaced peasants that up to now have produced very few external refugees. But should they start leaving, they will try to go to Bolivia, Argentina, and Chile, where the situation is not encouraging.

The economic and political effects of Chile's military dictatorship continues to stimulate exit, primarily to Argentina and Uruguay. But the return to civilian government in the latter two countries has not yet produced democracy or economic recovery.[51] In keeping with established patterns, future population displacements will remain mostly within this subregion, with the possible exception of a few among the middle or upper classes.

The Caribbean Basin is experiencing some social conflicts that in the context of a generalized economic recession are likely to produce refugees who almost surely will choose the United States as their preferred destination. Cuba's economic and political problems persist, as does U.S. inflexibility in its policies toward the island. In late 1987 the two countries negotiated an agreement on migration that according to some estimates, if implemented, would mean that by the 1990s at least another quarter-million Cubans will have come to the United States. Another mass migration also is possible. In any case, Cuba will continue to be a subject of debate in the United States. How the public, Congress, and government react to the Cubans will also affect other migratory flows.

The Haitians are a case in point. Haiti got rid of Jean-Claude Duvalier in 1986, but not of its dreadful economic and political backwardness. Duvalierism and economic prostration remain a terrible reality, and the ill-fated elections of November 1987 indicate that violence is a resource that will be used to resolve political differences. This means that Haitians will probably continue leaving their country, although it seems unlikely that they will find a friendly reception in the United States or in any other countries of the Caribbean Basin.

There are also social conflicts and population displacements in other parts of the basin. As a result of the political convulsions in Surinam, by December 1986, some eight thousand Surinamese had fled to French Guinea. In addition, drug traffickers, the army, the landed oligarchy, and the oldest guerrilla movement in the hemisphere are the main actors in a vicious spiral of violence in Colombia that is already expelling thousands of people and that might well emerge as the most serious social conflict of the 1990s. Mexico's economic crisis raises doubts about the future of its political system. Although the situation lacks the elements for a violent social conflict, it probably will increase the numbers of those trying to enter the United States.

At the moment of this writing, Central America remains the most important case of social conflict and population displacement. In 1987 there were some grounds for hoping that peace had a chance in the region. Several factors created this possibility: the limits on U.S. aggressiveness, created by the Iran–*contra* scandal and the divisions in U.S. society; the military ineffectiveness of the *contras;* the independence shown by Guatemala and Costa Rica; and the survival of the peace efforts launched first by the Contadora plan and later by the Arias plan.

With or without peace, sooner or later, we shall have to confront the problems created by the displaced Central Americans. By mid-1987, two general trends had emerged. The first was restrictionist: Governments are starting to close borders that had previously been relatively open. In October 1986, the Mexican government greatly tightened visa requirements for Central Americans. In November of the same year, the U.S. Congress passed a new immigration law seeking, among other things, to regain control of its borders. In February 1987, Canada tightened its asylum policy, in reaction to the thousands of Central Americans who had fled there from the potential effects of the new U.S. immigration law. In the same period, Guatemala also began to review its immigration policies.

But the other trend went in the opposite direction. With the exception of the United States, all the governments of the region affected by the Central American population flows acknowledged that a regional phenomenon demands a regional solution. That is, they acknowledged the need to adapt the tradition of individual asylum to the new realities of mass migrations. Whether for humanitarian or pragmatic reasons, the governments in question have begun to explore global responses. The most obvious, of course, would be peace. But because peace is still only a hope on the horizon, other measures for resolving the refugee situation are also being studied. We already mentioned the Cartagena Declaration, which was adopted in 1984 and began a process that provides some grounds for optimism. After that meeting some efforts have continued to keep alive the possibility of a more binding and effective record. The Mexican government, for example, pushed for a regional meeting; one was held in Geneva in May 1987 under UNHCR auspices, at which a decision was made to hold a regional conference in 1988.[52]

In the search for peace and regional solutions to the immensely complex refugee problem, the United States government and society will play a determinant role. During the eight years of conservative government, the line has been to preserve a unilateral approach and to try to harness the search for peace and for a regional solution to the refugee problem to U.S. foreign policy objectives. Washington has been unable to achieve complete success but has imposed serious obstacles. As we pointed out, the mixed results are in part the consequence of the involvement of U.S. society in Central and Latin American affairs.

In the last instance the United States is confronting a fundamental dilemma: the adjustment of its exercise of power in the regional system to new circumstances. Conservatives in the United States advocate the use of coercion to reduce what they perceive as the threat created by the deep transformations already under way in Latin America. Liberals consider that U.S. interests could best be served by a policy favoring economic development, political pluralism, and international relations based on mutual respect. The configuration that this hemispheric confrontation takes will gradually shape the regional system and influence the changes in the different societies.

For those concerned with the social conflict and with achieving a humanitarian solution for the refugees' tragedy, the challenge is how to find the common ground between what is desirable and what is possible.

Part Three

THEORETICAL AND POLICY IMPLICATIONS

Chapter 9

Patterns of Social Conflict
and Refugee Movements

The Contemporary Crisis Reconsidered

From the moment of its eruption in the 1970s, the twentieth century's third refugee crisis quickly reached an unprecedented global scope, overwhelming the limited regime formed by the international community in response to the waves of refugees from the European upheavals of earlier decades. In the final chapter, we shall suggest guidelines for devising a more adequate regime, but it is evident that such an undertaking must be founded on an accurate diagnosis of the crisis itself. This can be achieved by disaggregating it into its component elements, using the empirical materials presented in the regional studies to determine what types of conflicts are most likely to generate refugees in the developing world, to specify the nature of the flows, and to assess their relative incidence.

Although the refugee crisis took the world by surprise, our regional accounts indicate that it was in the making for some time, beginning in the years immediately following World War II, when the reconstructed international community thought the evils that had spawned so many refugees in Europe in the first half of the century had been finally uprooted, and it might now proceed to resolve their sequels once and for all. The first of the non-European flows, which arose as a by-product of the formation of new states in the Indian subcontinent (1947), reenacted the "unmixing of nationalities" of the interwar Balkans. This process was repeated immediately afterwards in the Middle East, where the sorting out involved the sudden exodus of many Arabs from newly formed Israel (1948), as well as of Jews from Arab countries, a more protracted process reaching eventually as far afield as the Maghreb. As in the past, refugee problems of this sort rapidly solved themselves to the extent that the minorities had access to a homeland of their own. The fortunate ones now included the Jews, whose tragedy helped overcome their previous status as the collective "odd men out" in a world of national states. However, in a great stroke of historical irony, the solution to their predicament in turn contributed to the creation of a new stateless people, the Palestinians.

In their shadowy existence in the institutional framework devised by the international community to contain them, the Palestinians evolved into a refugee nation that, despite not having a formally constituted state, achieved a statelike capacity for pursuing its political objectives at the international level by a variety of means, including violence. Although this book does not deal systematically with the Middle East, we shall briefly consider the case of the Palestinians in this chapter because of its general theoretical relevance to the experience of other refugees.

The early postwar population exchanges signaled the continuing importance of the formation of new states as a refugee-generating process. But these exchanges were soon followed by huge exoduses from China (1949–51), attributable to social revolution, which in the European historical experience had been the other principal type of refugee-producing upheaval. Related to this were the flows occasioned by the Korean war (1950–53)—a conflict rooted in a revolution from above in the North Korean occupation zone and the subsequent internationalization of regional tensions—and by the partition of Vietnam following the victory of the Communist-led national liberation movement over the French (1954). At the end of the decade the Great Leap Forward (1958) and the brutal repression of Tibetan autonomy (1959) renewed flight from China. It was also social revolution that led to the Cuban exodus that began in 1959, the first massive refugee movement originating in Latin America since the distant Mexican Revolution.

As in the past, the populations uprooted by these upheavals mostly obtained asylum among neighbors, whose generosity was motivated in large part by a desire to roll back, or at least contain, the revolution. This in turn prompted the revolutionary regimes to impose more severe barriers on exit, in effect extinguishing the flow. Consequently, even though the Third World generated huge refugee flows before 1960, with the exception of the Palestinians most of the uprooted were quickly resettled in their region of origin. Because the Palestinians remained under the jurisdiction of the ad hoc agency created in 1949, there was no cause for the international community to become unduly concerned with refugee problems, and therefore no crisis.

But this situation changed in the early 1960s when Africa suddenly moved to the fore with the nearly simultaneous flows resulting from the escalation of the violent decolonization struggle in Algeria (1954–63, but especially from 1959 on), the catastrophic dawn of independence in Zaire (1960) as well as Rwanda (1963), the onset of armed struggle in Portuguese Africa (c. 1961), and the increasingly violent confrontation between north and south in Sudan (c. 1963). Some of the older Asian conflicts flared up as well: There was a renewed flight of Chinese from the extremes of the Cultural Revolution (from 1967 on), and a huge outpouring from Bangladesh in the continuing regrouping of political communities in the Indian subcontinent (1971).

The crisis was caused not only by a steady increase of the number of people who might be classified as refugees but also by the burdens they imposed on the international community. Thus the UNHCR decided to assume responsibility for populations displaced by wars of national liberation under the "good offices" doctrine, a move encouraged by the accession of former colonies to U.N. membership. As in the case of Algeria, the difficult institutional problems posed by the refugee-warriors began moving to the fore as well.

The perception of a global and protracted crisis grew in the mid-1970s with the appearance of massive new flows in both Asia and Africa, attributable to complex internationalized conflicts that engulfed entire regions. For the first time, large bodies of refugees also appeared in Latin America's Southern Cone. This was compounded in the early 1980s by the explosion of long-standing ethnic confrontations in Sri Lanka and Lebanon; the resumption of violence following the breakdown of earlier settlements in

Sudan, Chad, and Uganda; and the flaring up of revolutionary conflicts in hitherto quiescent regions, Central America and West Asia (Afghanistan).

The problems facing the international community were exacerbated by several additional factors. More of the new refugees appeared unable either to return to their country of origin or to find a permanent haven. Also, the swelling of the refugee population in the 1970s came at a period of economic retrenchment for all but oil producers. Because of the greater unemployment, the affluent liberal countries imposed more severe restrictions on general immigration and also became more reluctant to take in refugees for permanent asylum. Consequently, many of the new refugees were confined in rag-tag camps in some of the world's poorest countries, themselves badly hit by the global economic downturn. These camps were another distinctive element of the current crisis. With little opportunity to fend for themselves, the refugees became a greater burden for the UNHCR, which itself depended on constant handouts from a limited number of governments and volunteer agencies. At the same time, the refugees were being transformed from objects into subjects, and many resorted to violence in order to overcome their predicament.

Since the 1940s, violent upheavals in the developing world have generated at least forty million refugees.[1] But the number of people needing protection and assistance at any given time is considerably smaller, because although new refugees are constantly being created, some also cease being refugees, somewhat like the passengers of a bus whose total represents the temporary excess of those who got on at previous stops over those who got off. For example, as of 1987 the refugee "bus" contained only 46,000 Vietnamese, because nearly all of the several hundred thousand who came aboard in 1975 and 1979 had been permanently resettled. But it contained over two million Palestinians, a majority of whom were the children and grandchildren of those who originally fled in 1948. Why some refugees get off easily whereas others linger on for so long can be explained mostly by why they got *on* the bus to start with.

One measure of the crisis is that in the late 1970s there was a step-level increase in the total number of refugees in need at a given time, from a previous range of between 5 million and 10 million, to a higher one of between 10 million and 15 million. At the end of 1987, as estimated by the U.S. Council for Refugees (USCR), the figure stood at 15.4 million.[2] Moreover, as indicated in our case studies, refugees abroad constitute but one segment of the total number of persons uprooted by violence. According to the USCR, the same upheavals also produced at least 17 million displaced internally, bringing the current total of those uprooted to around 30 million, with estimates of the major concentrations as follows (as of the end of 1987).

Southern Africa: 10.5 million uprooted (including 3.6 million forcibly relocated within the Republic of South Africa), of whom 1.4 million are abroad.

Afghanistan: 7.8 million uprooted, of whom 5.8 million are abroad.

Palestinians: 2.8 million abroad (of whom 2.2 million are under UNWRA jurisdiction).

Other Middle East: 2.8–3.2 million uprooted (including by Iran–Iraq war), of whom 1.3 million are abroad.

Sub-Saharan Africa: 2.7–2.9 million uprooted, of whom 800,000 are abroad.

Ethiopia: 1.8–2.6 million uprooted, of whom 1.1 million are abroad.

Central America: 1.9 million uprooted, of whom 850,000 are abroad (including 600,000 unrecognized in the United States, mostly from El Salvador).

Former Indochina: residual 440,000 abroad within region.

The number of refugees in the developing world has continued to rise, mostly as a result of the formation of new states out of colonial empires, and confrontations over the social order in both old and new states.[3] These are analytically distinguishable but often combined in reality to generate complex and extremely violent conflicts. Although the processes are akin to those that produced crises earlier in Europe, they are unfolding in very different settings and under extremely different historical circumstances, so that the outcome is likely to be quite different as well.

In contrast with what happened in Europe earlier in this century, relatively few people in the developing world have been uprooted by ordinary wars between sovereign states, but this does not mean that the root causes of the crisis can therefore be characterized as domestic rather than international. Indeed, a distinctive feature of the contemporary epoch is the formation of a world within which national societies persist but are internationalized to a higher degree than ever before. Consequently the conflicts arise as a product of both internal and external forces linked to form distinctive transnational patterns. This is reflected most dramatically in the prominent role of external intervention in the conflicts that produced the major concentrations of refugees found today.

The Globalization of Social Conflict[4]

Although the origins of the political, economic, and cultural structures that shape the contemporary world can be traced to the emergence in the late Middle Ages of the state and of capitalism as leading forms of social organization in Western Europe, and the subsequent rise of Europeans to world hegemony, it was only in the latter part of the twentieth century that these structures literally encompassed the whole world.

The breakup of the traditional empires and of the more recent European colonial realms created many new states, mainly in Asia and Africa. These were incorporated into an existing international system that consisted of mutually exclusive nation-states which were nominally equal at the level of international law. The last remaining self-sufficient economic zones were incorporated into a global network of trade and production. Indeed, today almost every human household draws much of its subsistence from wages or the sale of commodities and is affected by global market forces. This is true of those in the most affluent and the poorest countries, and even of those in socialist countries that have attempted to develop distinct and more autarchic economic systems.

Finally, all parts of the globe were linked into a single network of rapid and cheap transportation and nearly instant communications. The diffusion of literacy combined with cheap mass reproduction and transmission of words, images, and sounds led to a worldwide common culture. One consequence is that information about political events in one part of the world is readily transmitted to other areas, and so can spark conflicts there without any change in the domestic situation.

This global entity is characterized by an enormous gap between a few capital-rich, technologically advanced, and strategically powerful countries and the rest, whose internal conditions are largely shaped by the external policies of the leading countries and the activities of their firms or export agencies, as well as transnational processes that arise as unintended by-products of these. From an economic perspective, it is becoming increasingly evident that the developing world is best seen as a continuum of countries with differing conditions and prospects. Its upper range includes the Asian and Latin American newly industrializing countries, and its lower end includes most of the countries of sub-Saharan Africa, which are becoming a group with almost no likelihood of achieving even modest development, the global equivalent of an underclass.[5]

The gap between rich and poor has been accentuated by demographic developments. After a period of rapid population expansion, attributable largely to a lower death rate, the industrialized societies entered a phase of much slower growth. Europe (excluding the Soviet Union) reached its historical maximum proportion of world population around World War I, and the United States and Japan did so around 1950.[6] Taking into account the redistribution of population by way of overseas migration, for the Western countries as a whole the peak rates of population growth in the nineteenth century generally coincided with the attainment of a rate of economic growth sufficient to absorb additional workers and also to increase per-capita income. But whereas Asia, Latin America, and Africa had record-high demographic growth in the twentieth century, their economies barely kept pace. The world's poorest countries today have a total fertility rate (births per women) approximately three times higher than that of the rich industrial market economies.[7] Hence, as the world population mounts, an ever-larger proportion of it is poor. Indeed, of the eight major concentrations of refugees today, five originated in states that fall within the World Bank's lowest category of low-income countries, with an average gross national product (GNP) per capita (1985) of U.S \$270. Most of the world's refugee camps are located in these countries, and a large proportion of the refugees that are resettled are in these countries.[8]

A major consequence of these economic and demographic features is the potential for massive "south–north" migrations. Except in a few cases, however, this potential has not been realized. Although the affluent countries have periodically used alien labor from the poorer countries as a convenient solution to conjunctural fluctuations and the like, this was predicated on the erection of a solid barrier against their permanent immigration. But during the economic downturn of the early 1970s, the receivers discovered that such labor could not be easily sent back when no longer needed and so adopted even more restrictive immigration policies, with dramatic consequences for the refugees.[9]

The difficulties inherent in the integration of political communities and the achievement of sustained economic growth are compounded in many developing countries by low resource endowment, undeveloped human capital, and extreme ethnic heterogeneity. Moreover, as pointed out by dependency theorists, the difficulties attributable to internal givens are made worse by effects emanating from the capitalist world economy. Some theorists have gone so far as to assert that processes originating at that level constitute the root causes of both economic and political underdevelopment. Although it is difficult to assign precise weights to the different factors, there is little doubt that the poor countries indeed exhibit structural distortions that stem from their incorporation into the global economic system as the primary producers. With no choice but to participate in the global economic system on disadvantageous terms, the poor countries tend to experience effects such as inflation, fluctuations in commodity markets, and unemployment in amplified form, while reaping only a small share of benefits. Not only does this severely constrain their choices of development policies, but by perpetuating and, sometimes even worsening, unfavorable conditions, it makes it likely that the economic and political transformations these countries experience will generate even greater tensions and conflicts than was the case among their European predecessors, in Europe itself or in those parts of the world where Europeans launched new settlements. The emergence of an increasingly integrated world economy also means that powerful states are likely to intervene directly or indirectly to maintain, strengthen, and protect their interests, including those of their investors.

With the waning of empires, the world's political structure evolved into a system of territorial states, whose populations constitute mutually exclusive membership units, leaving individuals little room for changing the unit into which they are cast by the accident of birth. Although there is talk of an "international community," it is misleading, as the states consider themselves as "sovereign" and acknowledge only very limited involuntary constraints on their behavior, arising from the "law of nations." What community there is arises from voluntary compacts, especially long-term multilateral ones pertaining to a broad range of activities within a specified sphere, including those pertaining to international organizations and the regimes that prevail in such areas as international trade or the recognition of refugees.

With respect to strategic violence, without a central mechanism of conflict regulation such as the Concert of Europe inaugurated by the Congress of Vienna (1815), the state system exhibits distinctly anomic features. The globalization of economic and political rivalries in the latter decades of the nineteenth century—accompanied by technological advancements enlarging the precision, scale, and scope of means of destruction—produced a spiral of escalating violence. After nearly half a century of global warfare, the emergence of two superpowers able to destroy each other nearly instantly led to some stability and restraint in their bilateral relations. Today, this MAD ("mutually assured destruction") standoff also governs relations within and between their respective alliances, encompassing all the industrialized countries of Europe and the Pacific Basin.

But the largest segment of the global system—in both the number of states involved and the share of population they contain—is on the periphery of the two superpowers and is subject to severe international instability and conflict. The expansion of the political-strategic system to include the entire globe implies that even the poorest and geopolitically least significant states will have some value in the games of the major players and that internal government changes in the developing countries will tend to be perceived as having implications for the wider system and will therefore be likely to provoke some sort of response by outsiders. Intervention occasionally takes the form of military action, direct or through substitutes, but more commonly is in the form of hegemonic domination and pressure on political elites to maintain or adopt a particular ideological orientation, often using economic and military assistance as the carrot and its withholding as the stick.

Refugees and the Formation of New States

Violent Decolonization

Reflecting on the dismantling of the European empires in the twentieth century, Geoffrey Barraclough observed, "Never before in the whole of human history had so revolutionary a reversal occurred with such rapidity."[10] Although the expansion of Europe got under way in the fifteenth century, it was only in the latter part of the nineteenth century that the imperial powers established control over most of Asia and nearly all of Africa: around the turn of the twentieth century the United States and Japan followed suit in the Pacific, and the United States also established hegemonic domination over the Caribbean and much of Latin America. The power that enabled the new imperial masters to dominate the world was not only their industrial might and military technology but also their organization as national states, capable of mobilizing vast human resources for a common purpose. The new social groups formed by the disruptive effects of imperialism widely adopted the nation-state model to win support in the struggle against imperial rule. Their aspirations were legitimized by proclamation of the principle of self-determination as the ideological foundation of the new international community in the wake of World War I, and they steadily gained support among democratically minded groups in the metropolitan centers. The process of decolonization was accelerated in the 1940s when, despite the reservations of their Western European allies, the United States and the Soviet Union imposed self-government on the European colonies as part of the postwar settlement. With the founding of the United Nations, decolonization—at least of nonwhite peoples ruled by whites—was institutionalized as a global objective, in that those who opposed it were henceforth placed on the defensive.[11]

In retrospect, it is remarkable how few of the over one hundred transfers of authority that have taken place since the founding of the United Nations resulted from a violent struggle. In most cases, the confrontation between the colonial rulers and the movements seeking to broaden their political participation produced what might be termed *constitutional colonialism,* which provided a framework for gradual devolution—or alternatively, integration into the metropolitan system—and democratization.[12] Now that the process is almost completed, it can be seen that the variation in outcome was largely independent of the government's characteristics or the imperial power's "political culture," its general or local strategic capacity, or the colonial nationalists' organizational strength.[13]

The crucial variable was the willingness of the colonial power to engage in a negotiated transfer of authority. Overall, as discussed in Chapter 3, colonizers were much more inclined to espouse a rigid stance, backed by considerable force, in territories dominated by a plantation economy, in which the production of agricultural commodities was supervised by members of the imperial society on alienated land. This pattern usually required the presence of a body of more or less permanent settlers, and it was also applicable to mining economies that needed a large supply of indigenous labor. These conditions tended to produce more radical nationalist movements, whose objectives included not only political independence, but also fundamental changes in the mode and relations of production. Hence the process of decolonization assumed some of the aspects of a social revolution.

Within the post–World War II global context, these basic structural elements combined to produce a characteristic dynamic: The presence of a large body of settlers inhibited the political flexibility of the metropolitan power, and the revolutionary orientation of the nationalists established links between the local situation and the broader Cold War confrontation. This in turn brought more or less direct intervention from external actors from both camps in support of the antagonists. The challengers could not engage in a protracted struggle unless they could mobilize a significant part of the country's largely rural populations. But even though such mobilization ensured a stronger postcolonial state than otherwise, it also deepened existing class and ethnic cleavages.

These dynamics are best illustrated by the cases of Algeria and southern Africa. Some of the key elements were present also in Indonesia and Indochina, leading to protracted colonial wars; and in Malaysia, Kenya, Madagascar, and Ivory Coast, plantation colonies in which, after a time, the imperial center adopted an alternative strategy. In Malaysia, for example, Britain stood its ground until it was able to defeat a Communist guerrilla movement created by conditions in the rubber plantations and tin mines, and only then did it agree to a transfer of power to the indigenous Malay aristocracy if its own economic role would not be unduly disturbed.[14]

Once under way, wars of national liberation produce large flows of refugees. However, in the case of the first two major post-1945 colonial conflicts, in Indonesia and Indochina, these were almost exclusively internal and hence attracted little international attention. In contrast, Algeria, the three colonies of Portuguese Africa, Zimbabwe, and Namibia all generated sizable external movements. Indeed, it was the Algerian confrontation that prompted the first expansion of the UNCHR's mandate under the "good offices" doctrine.

The phenomenon of refugee-warriors associated with this pattern arose from the unevenness of the decolonization process. In the Algerian conflict, for example, adjoining independent Tunisia provided a haven for Algerian victims of French violence, but the refugee population of over 100,000 included able-bodied men available for recruitment by the Algerian Front de Libération Nationale's military wing, and the camps also provided supporting services for its operations, including care for the wounded. These conditions were used by the French to justify the bombing of Tunisian villages, much as they are today by South Africa in regard to Namibia. Because decolonization is a legitimate objective in the eyes of the international community, however, the refugee-warriors are accorded the benefit of the doubt, and so incursions in pursuit of guerrillas are politically counterproductive, as they tend to evoke almost universal condemnation. Nevertheless, situations of this sort jeopardize the security of refugee populations and create dilemmas for the UNHCR as well as associated governmental and nongovernmental relief agencies.

In every case but Namibia, the Europeans either were defeated in the field or, because of escalating costs and domestic as well as international pressure, decided to withdraw. Following the nationalists' assumption of power, the refugees quickly returned to their homes. But the change of regime triggered in turn a massive flight or expulsion of European colonists, as well as their indigenous auxiliaries and allies, who often included people of mixed racial origins. The major exception so far is Zimbabwe, which retained approximately half its settler population after independence, but this is almost certainly not the end of the story. Because such populations were usually citizens of the metropolitan country, their movement was considered a mere repatriation, and they did not come to the attention of international organizations. In most cases, they obtained some form of aid and compensation from their own government.

However, the non-Europeans often retained a marginal status in the metropolitan country and encountered severe problems of resettlement, akin to those of refugees. Sizable populations of this type are still found in the Netherlands, France, and Portugal. The French case involves approximately 20,000 low-level military and civilian auxiliaries of French colonial authorities—generally known as Harkis—and their families, amounting to 75,000 to 85,000 persons, who chose to relocate in France in 1962–63. Although they were granted French citizenship, this entailed complicated administrative procedures, which had to be carried out without assistance and in the face of indifference and ill will. Moreover, lacking appropriate qualifications, the Harkis have generally fared worse on the labor market than have ordinary Algerian guest-workers and immigrants.[15]

These are nonrecurring flows. Today, all the possible cases have already surfaced and reached a definitive outcome, except in southern Africa, about which little need to be added. Sooner or later, Namibia will become independent under black rule, and most whites—many of whom are South African—will leave. As the conflict in the Republic of

South Africa itself develops, it is likely to generate larger flows of black refugees to neighboring countries.

Ethnic Conflict in the New States

For many of the refugee-generating conflicts that have beset the new states of Asia and Africa since independence, there is a tendency to explain them as "ethnic diversity" or "ethnicity." But only some of the numerous differences in language, religion, and social organization have caused conflicts, and only some of these conflicts have produced significant flows of refugees. Indeed, somewhat paradoxically, countries marked by an extremely high degree of heterogeneity—that is, whose population is distributed among numerous groups—may be less likely to experience the types of conflict that lead to major refugee flows.

The ethnic heterogeneity of most of the new Asian states stems largely from the fact that the traditional empires which preceded them did not strive to develop a uniform culture among their peasant subjects. This was the case in Ethiopia also. Elsewhere in Africa, the territories forming the European colonies were mainly amalgams of small societies or parts of societies, so that in relation to the total population, the degree of heterogeneity tends to be extremely high. Although the colonies' metropolitan centers were organized as capitalist economies and national states, the Europeans governed their possessions with fairly traditional techniques. According to the old Roman adage *divide and conquer,* they used the tensions among the subordinate groups to enhance their own power but also confined the conflicts so as to minimize policing costs and keep the economy functioning. Existing group differences were sharpened by the uneven impact of social and economic change, as regions suitable for producing exports, as well as ports and intervening routes, became differentiated from the less developed hinterlands, and the various groups gained differential access to education and employment, particularly in the public sector. In most territories there emerged "advanced" and "backward" regions, which overlapped more or less with the newly differentiated "advanced" and "backward" ethnic groups.[16]

Another source of heterogeneity was migration. Throughout the tropical plantation belt and in the mineral-rich regions, imperial policies of labor procurement forced the relocation of populations. There initially were slaves, later indentured "coolies," and then mandatory migrant workers under contract; the latter are still encountered in South Africa and Namibia. To them were added ordinary "free" migrations from less to more promising regions within and between countries. They were often accompanied by members of the ruling society voluntarily migrating as supervisors or colonists, and by groups functioning as economic intermediaries between the colonial rulers and the primary producers, usually drawn from ongoing "trade diasporas."[17] Such migrations contributed to the formation of "plural societies" racially distinct groups bound together by a hierarchical division of labor.[18]

Ethnicity is not merely a projection or revival of traditional attachments, sometimes termed *primordial,* but a contemporary construct, responding to the opportunity or perceived necessity of establishing social relations beyond the village or locality. In Donald Horowitz's formulation, as a general consequence of social change, "the network of transactions grew in scale out of all proportion to the reach of preexisting sentiments of community." Under these circumstances, "to respond to the new opportunity structure imposed by the European required assurances of predictability, trust, reciprocity, fair dealing, and help in the event of need in strange surroundings." This was achieved by adapting preexisting social institutions, "particularly informal ones that neither threatened the colonial regime with a new panoply of rights nor taxed its strictly limited administrative machinery," mainly kinship and ethnicity.[19]

Sidestepping Horowitz's unnecessarily functionalist approach, it can be suggested that ethnicity commonly came to be used as an organizational resource, particularly in regard to broadening political participation in the course of decolonization, involving both elections and a greater degree of colonial self-government. As indicated in the African case studies, this often meant the construction of new group identities, sometimes inspired by categorizations established by European administrators. Similarly, in India, Hindus and Muslims acquired new significance as collectivities in countrywide political competition. Independence often precipitated a crisis: "As some groups moved to succeed to the power of the former colonialists, others were heard to claim that self-determination was still incomplete, for they had not achieved their own independence."[20] Moreover, the worldwide spread of norms of equality "made ethnic subordination illegitimate and spurred ethnic groups everywhere to compare their standing in society against that of groups in close proximity."[21] The salience of ethnicity in the new states is also reflected in the segmented economic and political organizational structure of society. Under these conditions, virtually all political events have ethnic consequences. Elections foster mobilization along ethnic lines; military coups are often made to secure the power of some ethnic groups at the expense of others; systems of economic relations tend to crystallize around opportunities afforded and disabilities imposed by government policy on particular groups; and even despotism assumes an ethnic form. Overall, four patterns of ethnic conflict may be distinguished, each of them associated with a distinctive refugee-generating dynamic.

EXPLOSION OF ETHNIC HIERARCHIES   "Ranked" or "hierarchical" ethnic systems are social configurations in which social class usually coincides with ethnic membership. Such systems occur in a variety of forms, of which two are of special interest to us: ruling minorities that exercise political-military power over a subjected majority, and trading minorities that constitute an exploitative "bourgeoisie" in relation to a peasant–producer majority (which itself may be either ethnically homogeneous or diverse).

Pure cases juxtaposing ethnically distinct rulers and ruled as an entire society are rare. They stem historically from slave-importing societies (as in the Caribbean region, including the American South) and from conquest (white settler societies in southern Africa and the Americas; Tutsi over Hutu in Rwanda and Burundi; Arabs over blacks in Zanzibar). The groups are usually interspersed, as spatial proximity is required to enforce domination and to exploit the subjected population.[22] Focusing on comprehensive relationships between the dominant and the subordinate groups, conflict takes on an explosive character, akin to a social revolution. The confrontations are extremely violent: Successful revolutions entail the elimination of the dominant group by means of anticipated flight, wholesale massacre, massive expulsion, or some combination of these as determined by local circumstances. Unsuccessful revolutions bring brutal retribution (e.g., Burundi).

As indicated earlier, most of the situations characterized by domination of a European settler minority led to violent decolonization, leaving, at the present, only Namibia and the Republic of South Africa. Other societywide hierarchies generally exploded early on, soon after the introduction of the principle of majority rule, as in Rwanda and

Burundi. In Burundi, the unsuccessful Hutu revolution prompted a tightening of Tutsi rule, with the government shifting from traditional patron–client relations to outright ethnocracy. A similar violent upheaval occurred on the island colony of Zanzibar, involving an Arab ruling stratum and a black majority. Most of the Arabs were massacred or fled abroad, and the victorious revolutionary leadership subsequently joined Tanganyika, to form Tanzania.

More localized versions of such systems, as in northern Nigeria (Fulani over Hausa), are prone to conflict as well, but the confrontations tend to be more contained, and their outcome depends on the larger political context. Local revolutions almost always fail. Activists may be driven into exile, but these circumscribed conflicts seldom result in a mass exodus. The situation may also be mitigated by a formally liberal regime, which provides some opportunities for remedial action.

Trading minorities were ubiquitous among ancient societies and can still be found throughout Asia and Africa. Relying on kinship and ethnic solidarity, they developed distinctive far-flung networks engaged in intercultural trade. Outside their own homeland, these diasporas do not possess political-military power of their own but usually operate under the protection of a ruling elite in exchange for a share of the profits, in the form of tribute, taxation, or bribery. The rulers themselves may be ethnically distinct—as in the plural societies of colonial Asia and Africa, headed by Europeans, with the trading minorities composed of Levantines in West Africa, South Asians in East Africa, Chinese in Southeast Asia, and the like. Or they may belong to the same group as the majority—as, for example, in Poland where the Jews were the intermediaries between the Polish aristocrats and the peasants, and in most of the new states after the Europeans were expelled or withdrew.

From the perspective of the new ruling elites, whose views in this respect are similar to those of the peasant milieu, trading minorities are ruthless exploiters, who either usurp positions that could be filled by genuine nationals or fail to perform any valid economic function at all. Once deprived of their traditional protection, trading minorities are highly vulnerable to governmental persecution or to pogroms, that is, communal attacks tacitly condoned by the authorities. However, because of their economic resources they may be able to negotiate deals with incumbent authorities, and in some cases, their home state may intervene on their behalf. As seen in the case of the Ugandan Asians, the situation is sometimes complicated by the option of obtaining full citizenship in the country of residence, but the lashing out is independent of the target's juridical status. Massive departures can be brought on by outright expulsions, lack of protection in the face of pogroms, or their equivalent, notably regulations that deprive the minority of the possibility of making a living. Alternatively, if they have access to some homeland or other country that will receive them as immigrants, the minority may leave in anticipation of such measures.

Generally speaking, trading minorities remaining throughout the developing world may be considered in jeopardy. But not all such situations will explode, and some will unfold over a protracted period. For example, after the 1954 partition, the Chinese trading minority in North Vietnam worked out a *modus vivendi* with the Communists, and their southern counterpart came to be linked with the American-supported regime. Considering the South Vietnamese uncooperative after the country was reunited in 1975, the Communist authorities sent many of the southern Chinese to New Economic Zones to become peasants, and undertook structural reforms that eliminated trading intermediaries altogether. These developments also undermined the position of the Chinese minority in the north, a process compounded by the nascent conflict between Soviet-supported Vietnam and China. Consequently, the massive flight of Sino-Vietnamese from the south in 1979–80 was matched by the exodus of 260,000 from the north to China. When South Asians were expelled by Uganda, severe tensions had already surfaced in Kenya and Tanzania. Although governments in the latter two countries have so far refrained from brutal actions, over the past two decades the South Asian communities have steadily shrunk as the result of voluntary departures.

TARGET MINORITIES   In the European experience, as discussed in Chapter 1, efforts by rulers to achieve national unity involved the construction of a cultural formula, usually founded on religion or ascendancy, that grouped minorities with a majority of the population into a collective identity. It was in regard to this process that certain cultural outgroups arose as obstacles to be eliminated. Efforts by the state to transform the deviants into subjects or citizens in the approved mold gave rise to the classic type of refugee, targeted for persecution for reasons of religion or nationality. By the same token, the emergence in a multiethnic or religiously diverse region of a number of states striving more or less simultaneously to achieve the objective implied in a monistic formula tended to result in endless attempts to unmix nationalities.

Although the ethnic and cultural heterogeneity of the new states of Asia and Africa generally exceeds even that of the European "successor" states of the interwar period, aside from the trading groups already mentioned, the formation of classic "target minority" refugees as the result of persecution by the state is quite rare. The only clear cases in recent years are the hypernationalist Khmer Rouge regime, which lashed out at all non-Khmer minorities in Kampuchea, and the fundamentalist Iranian government, which persecutes Muslim heretics.

One major reason for the scarcity of such refugees is that in contrast with many of their European predecessors, most of the new states accepted from the outset the reality of a multinational or multiethnic political community. This can be attributed to the different role of ethnicity in the struggles leading to political independence, and to the prevailing ethnic configurations, which seldom occur in clear majority–minority form but, rather, contain several minorities. Thus, somewhat paradoxically, extreme ethnic diversity normally imposes constraints on political elites, providing incentives to build multiethnic governing coalitions.

Such coalitions are inherently fragile, however, and are subject to constant reshuffling. Over the long run, the various components will cooperate only if they reap tangible benefits from ruling together, as was generally the case during the expansive "development" epoch up to the early 1970s. Under conditions of greater scarcity brought about by the worldwide economic crisis, whose effects were multiplied for the heavy debtor nations, the incentives for cooperation were considerably weakened, precipitating a scramble for power that in a few cases resulted in "ethnocracy." Albeit a form of minority ethnic rule, this has little to do with the process of state-formation but, rather, with the distribution of rewards and hence will be considered in the framework of social order conflicts.

COMMUNAL CONFLICT   Groups that are not hierarchically related may be regionally concentrated or spatially interspersed, and the overall configuration within a state often is a combination of both. Each configuration is associated with a distinct pattern of conflict.

In the first instance, each of the groups is located on its own turf; their competition takes place by way of the center. When this escalates into conflict, the characteristic pattern is separatism, discussed in the next section. In contrast with this, interspersed populations surround one another. This is conducive to periodic confrontations among the groups themselves, which may or may not involve the state. The term *communal conflict* stems from South Asia, where it refers specifically to confrontations between Hindu and Muslim religious communities. But the term can also be used to refer to the ubiquitous and recurrent ethnic conflicts among interspersed communities in Asia and Africa.

A further distinction can be made within the dispersed pattern, between national-level configurations and localized ones. The former are usually the legacy of traditional empires, in which part of the population converted to the religion of the conquering rulers, as occurred with respect to Islam throughout northern Africa, the Middle East, and South Asia. Local versions are mostly the result of recent rural-urban migrations (both internal and external).

Clashes involving parts or all of local communities generate considerable violence, and the resulting conflicts sometimes exact a very high toll in human lives; but they are inherently circumscribed and generate few refugees. To the extent that the state appears to be carrying out its obligation to provide equal protection to all citizens, outsiders consider the violence as a strictly internal matter, and even if they flee abroad, victims are unlikely to achieve recognition as refugees and to secure asylum. In turn, the unavailability of asylum acts as a deterrent to flight. But some communal riots are genuine pogroms, in which the authorities in effect encourage others to do their dirty work by withholding protection from the target and refraining from imposing sanctions on the aggressor. In other cases, the state may simply be too weak to maintain internal peace. But even in such cases, because of the ambiguities involved, members of the target group are unlikely to obtain international protection. In 1968–69 the Malaysian government failed to protect the Chinese from attacks and subsequently gave in to pressures by revising the consociational formula to the disadvantage of the minority. Although this action prompted many Chinese to leave, they had to do so as emigrants rather than as recognized refugees.

Where it prevails nationwide, the interspersed pattern is a source of persistent political tensions that pose problems of political management and that cannot be resolved by means of federal arrangements. One solution has been identified by political scientists as forming a distinctive type of ''consociational'' democracy, in which accommodation among the communities is usually solemnized by a constitutional pact among their respective elites.[23] In the Netherlands, for example, the existence of interspersed religious communities (Protestant and Catholic) gave rise to *verzuiling*—''pillarization''—a system in which the state enables each community to maintain separate institutions (especially education), and the parliament is based on elections at large with proportional representation. In the developing world, a major case in point was the entente established among the Lebanese religious communities under the aegis of France in 1943, with institutional arrangements remarkably similar to those of the Dutch. Another was the constitution devised in Malaysia on the eve of independence to resolve tensions of the plural society identified by J. S. Furnivall.

Consociational solutions are unstable, however, because the arrangements tend to be quite specific and cannot be easily modified in response to changing circumstances. Moreover, the conditions that brought them into being may cease to exist. For example, the collapse of the Lebanese system revealed, in retrospect, that it depended on the continued insulation of the communities from the international conflict raging in the Middle East.

Escalating communal conflicts can lead to an internal "unmixing," which has the effect of transforming the configuration into one consisting of regionally concentrated groups and thus enables the emergence of a separatist movement. The aggrieved group (A) is likely to seek refuge in its putative homeland. Because interspersed populations are involved, the region contains members of the other group (B). The first movement is therefore likely to escalate communal conflicts in the region of destination as well, and hence a reactive regrouping of the B's into their own homeland. This is largely what occurred in Nigeria after the anti-Ibo pogroms in the north in 1966, and in Beirut after the collapse of the Lebanese consociational arrangements.

Contrary to what might be expected in regard to the new states' ethnic heterogeneity, however, massive regrouping leading to separation has rarely occurred. In fact, the only full-fledged cases on record remain the early postwar ones noted at the beginning of the chapter. In retrospect, this suggests that the outcome is the result of special circumstances that have not been replicated elsewhere. In both instances, the configuration involved a polarization between two nationally interspersed communities, embroiled in a long-standing conflict that escalated into large-scale violence as independence neared.

In the case of India, tensions between the Hindu and Muslim communities were aggravated by the introduction of separate electoral rolls. It does not really matter whether this was an ad hoc response by British colonial authorities to problems of political management, or the deliberate instrument of a divide-and-rule strategy; once separate political identities were created, it became almost impossible to maintain intercommunal organizations, and their absence in turn led to the emergence of Muslim aspirations toward a separate state. Whether or not partition would have occurred in an undivided independent India, we do not know, as the British did in fact divide the country before they left.

As noted in Chapter 5, India's was an unusual form of decolonization, which was reenacted in only one other instance, again by the British, in Palestine the following year.[24] Without partition, once a colonial territory became an independent state, international institutions generally weighed in favor of maintaining the status quo, as elucidated further in relation to separatism.

Despite the sorting out, in India many Muslims remained interspersed among the Hindu population and were recurrently attacked by local groups. Committed to secularism and coexistence between the two communities, the state usually stepped in as a protector. But in 1984, the Sikhs began to feel highly vulnerable and so began returning to their homeland in the Punjab while the Hindus began moving out of it. The ensuing conflict has taken on a more territorial character and may evolve further toward secession. Some Sikhs have begun applying for political asylum abroad.

In regard to partition as practiced in the early decades of the twentieth century, the case of Palestine was special from the outset, in that one of the two communities consisted overwhelmingly of recent immigrants. It became unique also in that the other failed to obtain a homeland and thus became a stateless refugee nation. As noted in Chapter 1, the Arab exodus from the parts of Palestine that came under the control of Jewish forces in 1948–49 numbered 700,000 to 800,000 people, at least 75 percent of the relevant population. Another 630,000 remained in their original locations, 130,000 in what had now become Israel and 500,000 in districts controlled by Jordan (the West Bank and East

Jerusalem) or Egypt (Gaza). Of the uprooted, a few thousand of the more affluent scattered among neighboring Arab countries (Lebanon, Jordan, Egypt), but the bulk ended up in refugee camps in Gaza or the West Bank.

Over the next four decades, the Palestinian population retained a remarkably high rate of natural reproduction and experienced further migrations. There were also more departures from the original homeland, some for a second time.[25] As of 1987, the remainder of the 1.4 million Arabs who lived in mandate Palestine at the time of partition together with their progeny had grown into 5.2 million, distributed as follows: 600,000 (11.5 percent) within the pre-1967 borders of Israel; 1.35 million (26 percent) in the occupied West Bank and Gaza; 2 million in continguous Arab countries, including 1 million to 1.4 million (25 to 27 percent) in Jordan as well as 600,000 (11.5 percent) in Lebanon and Syria; 750,000 (14.5 percent) in the Gulf states; and perhaps 500,000 (10 percent) abroad in several non-Arab countries, including the United States. Approximately 2.145 million (41 percent) retained their refugee status under UNRWA jurisdiction, with the largest concentrations still in Jordan and Gaza.

The case of the Palestinians remains historically unique, but their achievement of a degree of political coordination and of a capacity for organized violence prefigured attempts by other refugees to take history into their own hands. The development of the political outlook and organization of the several Palestinian communities was shaped by a changing combination of local circumstances and international conditions.[26] Although the partition resolution called for the establishment of both Jewish and Arab states, inter-Arab rivalries prevented the establishment of a Palestinian government. The strongest objections came from Transjordan, whose king had territorial ambitions in the part of Palestine apportioned to the Jews, and he subsequently annexed the West Bank areas occupied by his own and Iraqi troops at the end of the war. In September 1948, however, the Arab League agreed to the formation of an All Palestine Government, initially based in Gaza but later transferred to Cairo, where it subsisted as a powerless and ineffective client of Egypt. Over the next two decades, Arabs living in Israel as citizens tried to get along without making waves. This was the case also with the indigenous population of Gaza and the West Bank, as well as the upper strata among the uprooted, some of whom obtained citizenship in Lebanon and Jordan.

Meanwhile the refugee collectivity was the object of contending maneuvers. Despite Arab opposition, the United States carried on a barely disguised resettlement strategy through UNRWA. In the face of continued failure, however, this was done in an increasingly desultory manner. The Palestinians generally viewed UNRWA with suspicion as an agency of the United Nations, the body whose decision to partition was at the origin of their predicament. But the UNRWA ration card became a central element in the assertion of a distinct identity, and the educational assistance provided by the agency fostered the emergence of a stratum of university-educated youths, who played a key role in transforming the Palestinians into a conscious national community.[27] In the 1950s the younger men who had participated in the 1948 war formed the Al-Fatah organization, and by the early 1960s there were several guerrilla groups carrying out raids into Israel with some regularity. However, their activities remained largely under the control of the Arab states. The Palestine Liberation Organization (PLO) was established in 1964, originally as an instrument of Egyptian policy, designed to keep unruly elements under control.

The Arab defeat in the 1967 Six-Day War with Israel strengthened the hand of those who argued that the Palestinians should act more autonomously and adopt a more aggressive stance. With a larger territory to defend, containing an Arab population attuned to external developments and resentful of occupation, Israel became more vulnerable to guerrilla attacks. Accordingly, its retaliatory measures hardened the resolve of the Palestinian fighters, whose successes increased their confidence in the effectiveness of violence. Despite factionalism, the several armed groups grew remarkably quickly. Recruiting mostly from the UNRWA camps, and with military and financial support from Eastern European and Arab states, around 1970 the number of loosely federated "resistance" forces ranged between 50,000 and 75,000, of whom perhaps 20,000 were full-time guerrillas.

The largest resistance group was the Jordan-based Al-Fatah, under the leadership of Yasir Arafat. Following a major confrontation with King Hussein of Jordan in 1970–71, the PLO relocated in Lebanon and Syria and strove to reduce its dependency on Arab hosts by establishing a Central Committee and a unified military command. The clandestine force called Black September also began carrying out terrorist attacks against Jordan and Israel, both in the Middle East and abroad. In the 1970s, West Bank opinion gradually turned away from Jordan toward Palestinian autonomy, and a slower evolution in the same direction began taking place among Israeli Arabs as well. Distinguished intellectuals in the diaspora also launched a parliament-like body that enhanced the symbolic importance of a Palestinian nation in search of a state. The disparate Palestinian communities thus coalesced into a linked collectivity, which succeeded in imposing itself as an actor to be reckoned with at the level of the international system.

SEPARATISM   New states commonly experience conflicts over the distribution of power between the *center*—which in multiethnic societies is almost necessarily dominated by a distinctive group or combination—and the *periphery,* which believes that the existing distribution is hindering its existence as a group, both materially and symbolically. Characteristic controversies are over unitary versus federal institutions, and the particulars of federalism; the regional allocation of public and private investments; the balance between national and ethnoregional cultures in the educational system; and, if relevant, the language of public life, including not only the governmental sector but the labor market more generally. Center–periphery conflicts in the new states are aggravated by the ethnic distinctiveness of the regions; attempts to alter the status quo involve separation in a general sense, ranging from greater internal autonomy to outright independence, or reunion with another state.

Separatism is especially likely to arise in situations involving a small number of large groups (in relation to population size) that are regionally concentrated, because the collective actors are so weighty that their interactions are a constant and prominent theme of national politics, and the state itself is almost always a party to the conflict.[28]

In liberal regimes, and if the configuration allows the dissatisfied minority to achieve some power through coalition, the conflict tends to be reformist, leading toward a multiplication of the units and greater power for the components and resulting in settlements that offer a higher degree of internal autonomy and a more equitable distribution of benefits among regions, as in Nigeria and India. But these situations are almost never resolved completely, and as time passes and circumstances change, established settlements are challenged. If the conditions for reformist action are not present, because of the state's authoritarian character or in liberal governments whose configuration renders territorial minorities permanently impotent, as in Sudan (in the early postindependence years) and Sri Lanka, the group may opt to exit from the political community altogether, to constitute a self-governing entity or to join another state.

Regions that became ''backward'' as a consequence of the uneven impact of social change during the colonial period are most likely to spawn secessionist movements. Among these, backward groups that reap few benefits from the center are likely to be in the lead and thus act early on. A classic example is the southern Sudanese (1955–72, 1983–). The East Bengalis fit this pattern as well, but because their distance from the Pakistani center made complete domination more difficult and because they constituted a majority of the population, they initially entertained the hope that numbers could be translated into political clout. It was only when they were rebuffed by the West Pakistanis after winning a majority in 1970 that they resorted to secession. Advanced groups in backward regions, such as the Tamils in Sri Lanka and the Ibos in eastern Nigeria, initially tend to seek out opportunities in other regions of the country and so have little interest in secession. However, they are particularly likely to be targets of violence from the groups with whom they compete and, if their aspirations are blocked, may well turn to separatism as a last resort.

Because they normally control the center, advanced groups in advanced regions are unlikely to start secessionist movements, but they may turn to this solution if excluded by others, as in the case of the Baganda in Uganda after Obote came to power. A major exception is Eritrea, an advanced region where secessionism started early. Horowitz attributes this to the fact that the initiative came from Muslims, that is, the more backward group in the advanced region. But a more persuasive reason is Eritrea's formative experience as a separate colony and later trusteeship, with the prospect of achieving independence in the forseeable future but whose progress along this path was abruptly arrested when turned over by the United Nations to Ethiopia.

A common factor of secession in Biafra, Bangladesh, and southern Sudan was the coming to power of a military regime inaccessible to the political influence of the secessionist region. The formation of a wholly ethnically based party system may have the same effect of producing inaccessibility, especially if the majority group that controls the center is itself divided by intraethnic party competition, which encourages intransigeance toward potential secessionists (e.g., Sri Lanka, Sudan, Burma, Chad).[29] Outbreaks of violence catalyze separatism, as do the loss of group members through assimilation and the migration of ethnic strangers into the potentially separatist region.

Whatever the impulse, whether they formed early or late, and whatever strength they mustered, so far only one of the numerous secessionist movements that has arisen in the new states—Bangladesh—has resulted in an actual separation of the ethnic group's homeland from the established political community. In some cases, this is the result of the movement's success in achieving some of its objectives: For example, after seventeen years of struggle, the southern Sudanese gained a measure of autonomy in 1972 (but lost it again a decade later, leading to a revival of separatism). And although the northern Chadians did not establish a new state, they did succeed in capturing the center itself, as did the northern Nigerians from 1966 on. But when the conflict has escalated to the level of armed struggle, the absence of secession can be attributed mainly to the state's ability to defend its integrity and defeat the challengers.

In this respect, international factors are clearly decisive. Whereas the emergence of separatist movements is determined largely by internal factors, their success is contingent on obtaining a level of external support that is in fact seldom available. Because of the legitimacy of established states in the international political system, the governmental side possesses inherent advantages, such as external support in the form of diplomatic recognition, and financial and legal facilities for the acquisition of weapons. By the same token, whereas the diversity and competitive logic of the current international system enable most secessionist movements to find external patrons of some sort, the conservative nature of the system tends to limit that support to a level short of what is required for success.

Because changes of boundaries usually have more limited implications for the distribution of power and values in the international system than do changes of regime, the internationalization of such conflicts is much more circumstantial, depending on the location of the state or states involved in relation to the prevailing international alignments. The great powers seldom become involved, but if they do, it is likely to be in support of the government. For example, the conflict leading to the establishment of Bangladesh attracted only superficial great-power attention, although it meant the breakup of an existing country that was at the time allied to the United States. The Nigerian civil war evoked considerable world attention but little active international involvement. Biafra received limited humanitarian assistance but almost no military aid from abroad, whereas both Great Britain and the Soviet Union provided some support to the central government. In the case of Katanga's secession from the ex–Belgian Congo immediately following independence in 1960, the secessionists secured external support in the form of a largely white mercenary force, but the international community intervened determinatively on the side of the government.[30] When irredentist Somalia invaded the Ogaden, the Soviet Union intervened massively on the side of Ethiopia. And despite Somali entreaties, the United States refused to provide to its aggressive client the military assistance required to keep its prize.

The most likely source of support for secessionists are "irredentist" neighbors. A manifestation of competitive state-formation, irredentism arises when a state seeks to reunite part of its "nation" currently under the jurisdiction of another state, by capturing the territory. Yet despite the enormous potential of irredentism in Asia and Africa, because so many groups straddle international borders, its incidence has been much lower than among the "successor" states of interwar Europe. The only clear cases to emerge so far are Somalia in relation to the Ogaden, and Libya in relation to northern Chad.[31] In this respect, as with cultural minorities, the new states' multiethnic character acts as a constraint: Irredentist initiatives are likely to be taken only by fairly homogeneous states, Horowitz suggests, because otherwise the interventionist policy would become a divisive issue. He also observes that a common feature of the few cases of irredentism that have arisen in the developing world is rule by an autocrat with personal links to the coveted group or territory.

Aside from irredentism, neighbors may actively support foreign secessionists on strategic grounds, as India did in the case of Bangladesh in order to weaken Pakistan. In effect, this is what the Republic of South Africa is doing by aiding and abetting UNITA which, though not originally a separatist movement, has an ethnoregional base and, with deteriorating prospects, might well opt for secession from Angola.

Without such direct interests, neighbors have more limited motives for supporting the separatists than do the separatists themselves for fighting, and their support is likely to fall well short of what is required for victory. This is partly because of the residual commitment of the new states to the boundaries they inherited, particularly in Africa. A case in point is the adamant stance of the Organization of African Unity on the issue of Eritrea. Beyond this, separatists are constrained by possible countermeasures: Chad was able to stop Sudan from aiding Muslim separatists and, more recently, to inflict damage on Libya, with aid from France and the United States. Similarly, Sudanese aid to Eritrean secessionists was moderated by Ethiopia's assistance to the southern Sudanese.

Whereas the Bangladesh case suggests that successful separatism might be associated with a distinctive pattern of short-lived refugee movement, temporarily involving flight from violence and subsequently an unmixing with settlement in the new homeland, the more common unsuccessful separatist challenges tend to produce more problematic refugees. There are usually at first a few activist exiles, who have little difficulty finding havens. But if and when the struggle moves into the military phase, actions by the antagonists foster much larger waves: The separatists encourage able men to leave in order to join the struggle, whereas states facing separatist guerrillas typically attack the source group as a whole, any member of which is considered an actual or potential supporter of insurgency. Matters may therefore evolve into a "target minority" situation. Because the separatist group is usually located near a state's international borders, many in the target group usually succeed in getting out. Indeed, entire populations may flee the fire zone and systematized repression, as in Eritrea and the Ogaden. The major exception was Biafra, which produced few refugees because the Ibo homeland was hemmed in by ethnoregional groups loyal to the Nigerian central government, some of them loyal because they feared "minorization" within an Ibo-dominated Biafra should the secessionists succeed.

Despite their failure to achieve their objectives, such movements can persist for a long time because the state that is challenged seldom has the resources required for effective repression and containment. On the other hand, the separatists—by definition——benefit from some degree of popular support and have the advantage of operating on their own terrain. As noted, they usually also manage to secure at least some aid from a patron. International assistance to the antagonistic camps has the effect of enhancing their respective capacity and hence to widen the fire zone as well as to prolong the conflict. This was dramatically manifested in the case of the Eritreans, whose struggle against Ethiopia, compounded by occasional internecine strife between Christians and Muslims, has been going on for a quarter of a century, outlasting major regime changes in both Ethiopia and Sudan and a reversal of the great powers' position in the region.

These protracted or recurring confrontations tend to produce large masses of refugees, who typically find asylum in neighboring countries, except for some segments of "advanced minorities" that often find their way farther afield. The UNHCR's expanded interpretation of its mandated role has helped reduce the recognition problems of refugees fleeing from the violence generated by separatist conflicts, as has the Organization of African Unity's broad definition. However, to the extent that neighboring states are opportunistically involved in the conflict and face severe economic and political problems of their own, the refugees find protection and support uncertain.

Refugees and Conflicts over the Social Order

Rooted in inequality and oppression, conflicts over the social order are a struggle between dominant and subordinate classes, whose most extreme manifestations are full-scale social revolutions, that is, "rapid, basic transformations of a society's state and class structures . . . accompanied and in part carried through by class-based revolts from below."[32] Like full-fledged secessions, revolutions are rare historical events, but the underlying conditions that produce these cataclysms also produce the more frequently encountered limited upheavals. All the successful revolutions that have taken place in Asia, Africa, and Latin America since the end of World War II, as well as most of the attempted ones, have resulted in major international population movements. Conversely, of the eight/refugee concentrations found today, five can be traced in whole or in part to revolutionary conflicts. Successful revolutions lead to counterrevolutionary attempts, and the emergence of revolutionary movements—or merely the fear of revolution—also generate repressive preemptive measures. These related conflicts also produce refugees.

But the historical and theoretical significance of violent confrontations should not be allowed to obscure the fact that protest against the state—the exercise of "voice"—is only one possible response to oppression, and usually the riskiest. The alternative is "exit"—in common parlance, to get out from under or to vote with one's feet.[33] This has in fact emerged as a major factor, particularly in the case of weak states that cannot confine their populations, giving rise to substantial outflows whose status is particularly problematic.

CONDITIONS FOR REVOLUTION IN AGRARIAN SOCIETIES[34]   As pithily stated by Barrington Moore in 1966, "the process of modernization begins with peasant revolutions that fail. It culminates during the twentieth century with peasant revolutions that succeed."[35] But Moore then went on to express skepticism as to whether the conditions that made for a successful peasant revolution in China were to be found anywhere else and reflected that, pending a detailed study of Latin America and Africa, the Indian case "leads one to ask whether the great wave of peasant revolutions, so far one of the most distinctive features of the twentieth century, may not have already spent its force."[36] Two decades later, despite a proliferation of studies stimulated in large part by the Vietnam War, the answer is by no means clear: There have been fewer revolutionary upheavals than expected in some parts of the world, but more in others. Nonetheless, the new literature provides suggestions that can be used to answer Moore's question.

First, social revolution is now widely recognized as a phenomenon specific to certain types of societies. According to Moore, "an agrarian bureaucracy, or a society that depends on a central authority for extracting the surplus"—such as traditional China and tsarist Russia—is most vulnerable to peasant rebellion, whereas a "highly segmented society that depends on diffuse sanctions for its coherence and for extracting the surplus"—such as the Ottoman Empire, or India today—is nearly immune, "because opposition is likely to take the form of creating another segment."[37] Feudal systems, like those in medieval Europe and Japan, fall somewhere in between. Once modernization begins, however, the involvement of the upper class in commercial agriculture tends to reduce the likelihood and intensity of peasant revolutions. This is also the case with "revolutions from above," as occurred in Japan and Germany. In that sense, "revolution" should be seen as a phenomenon of the transition to capitalism, rather than of industrial capitalism itself, as conceived of in classic Marxist theory.

Placing greater emphasis on cultural features of different societies, S. N. Eisenstadt reached similar conclusions concerning the importance of a developed "center" and an orientation that fosters a "coalescent" pattern of change. This is the reason that revolutions occurred in the West, but not in the great patrimonial empires and city-state societies.[38] With respect to the contemporary situation, Eisenstadt points out the classic type of revolution-prone society has all but disappeared. But he suggests that revolutions may also occur among "neopatrimonial" personalistic patronage states, which are vulnerable to economic downturns or military pressures. Although the goal of the opposition may be only to bring down the government, the regime as a whole may also collapse, opening the way for a popular movement that leads to far-reaching changes. Examples include Mexico (in 1911), Batista's Cuba, and Somoza's Nicaragua.

Theda Skocpol has argued persuasively that revolts turn into revolutions only when the state breaks down. In the classic cases, this did not occur as a consequence of pressures generated by the revolutionary movements themselves, but because the regime had external problems that exceeded its capacity to cope. Defeat in foreign wars was particularly costly, both in strict financial terms and because it meant a loss of legitimacy. Deprived of the protective carapace provided by the state, the dominant classes became vulnerable to direct revolts from below, which under these altered circumstances effected changes in class relations "that otherwise would not have occurred."[39] This circumstance can obviously be broadened to include a variety of stressful undertakings, including expensive preparations for war and Pyrrhic victories, or tensions and fiscal problems resulting from prolonged internal wars, as in imperial Ethiopia with respect to Eritrea.

Skocpol observes further that more recent social revolutions "have invariably occurred in countries caught behind more economically developed competitor nations," because the center exerts greater pressure on the peasantry and is itself subject to severe stress, equivalent to the pressures induced by engagement in war.[40] Jack Goldstone believes that economic pressures arising from worldwide long waves in population growth and prices in fact explain the triggering mechanism of European revolutions better than does Skocpol's "lost wars" idea and suggests that "if this hypothesis is correct . . . much of the Third World, particularly Africa, may well experience an extended period of revolution, similar to that of Europe in 1789–1848, in the next few decades."[41]

Given a vulnerable agrarian state, under what conditions do peasants in fact rebel? As James Scott has pointed out, "if anger born of exploitation were sufficient to spark a rebellion, most of the Third World (and not only the Third World) would be in flames." Whether exploited peasants actually rebel "depends on a host of intervening factors—such as alliances with other classes, the repressive capacity of dominant elites, and the social organization of the peasantry itself. . . ."[42] Moore himself rejected hypotheses that emphasize deteriorating conditions, absentee landlords, and landless labor, because they focus too much attention on the peasantry instead of on the actions of the upper classes. Although suggesting that strong solidarity among the peasants and weak ties with landlords facilitate rebellion, Moore insists that whether the revolutionary potential among the peasantry "becomes politically effective depends on the possibility of a fusion between peasant grievances and those of other strata. By themselves the peasants have never been able to accomplish a revolution."[43] What allies such peasant discontent can find "depends upon the stage of economic development that a country has reached and more specific historical circumstances; these factors also determine the point at which the allies turn on the peasant movement to draw its teeth or suppress it."[44]

With respect to the character of grievances, Moore suggested that "what infuriates peasants (and not just peasants) is a new and sudden imposition or demand that strikes many people at once and that is a break with accepted rules and customs."[45] Scott has elaborated this into a theory of "moral economy," arguing that peasant rebellions arise from indignation and rage provoked by violation of the "subsistence ethic."[46] Normally peasants acknowledge an obligation toward the upper classes or the state as providers of vital services that protect them against famine and the like. Such violations include the failure to perform these, or what peasants consider undue exactions. It stands to reason that stepped-up capitalist transformation fosters more egregious violations and that this is further exacerbated by unfavorable conjunctures.

Attempts to identify particular patterns of social organization that make peasants more rebellion prone have not been very successful. Eric Wolf found that "middle peasants"—smallholders or tenants who live in communal villages outside the direct control of landlords—possess greater tactical power, as do more generally those who live in geographically marginal areas relatively inaccessible to the authorities.[47] Similarly, Scott has suggested that the propensity of some peasants to participate in revolutions is due to their relative autonomy in relation to a hegemonic center.[48] The instruments through which hegemony is exercised are especially weak among precapitalist small-holders, sharecroppers, or tenants, who have village- and kin-based social networks and a more traditional world view, the more so if they are geographically remote from the center.[49] Other things being equal, isolated peasantries are therefore the most explosive. But much like Moore, Wolf concluded that "ultimately, the decisive factor in making a peasant rebellion possible lies in the relation of the peasantry to the field of power which surrounds it. A rebellion cannot start from a situation of complete impotence."[50] Poor peasants may rise in rebellion if some external agents challenge the power that constrains them, and rich peasants may lend support if the challengers prove capable of destroying incumbent power holders, as was the case in Mexico, Russia, and China. Scott also ends up by stating that "any general statement relating peasant social structures to the potential for rebellion would be questionable."[51]

Diverging from the reigning skepticism, Jeffrey Paige has attempted to demonstrate that social organization is determinative and reached conclusions almost diametrically opposed to the preceding: Smallholders are individualistic and basically conservative, and the situation with the greatest revolutionary potential is that in which landowning elites use wage labor to work their land, as in sharecropping and migratory labor systems. Rural proletarians have an incentive for class solidarity, because they can improve their condition only through collective actions such as strikes. Therefore, they are more responsive to socialist or nationalist agitation, as demonstrated in Angola, Peru, and Vietnam.[52] But Paige in turn has been severely criticized on a variety of theoretical and empirical grounds. Most relevant to our discussion is Skocpol's demonstration that Paige's own discussion of actual cases indicates that differences in political behavior "depend not so much on the income sources of the cultivators as upon the larger societal and political contexts within which these agrarian lower classes are located."[53] Nevertheless, Paige's hypothesis concerning the adamant stance of upper classes whose income and position depend on their direct control of land and labor is undoubtedly valid.

One clear conclusion from all this is that "the political role of the peasantry . . . depends on the actions of other groups. Peasant rebellion might provide the 'dynamite,' but other groups must provide the organizational basis before rebellions become sufficiently large in scale to usher in major political and economic changes."[54] In particular, a good theoretical case can be made for the sine qua non of a Leninist vanguard organization whose task is to channel the potential power of peasant rebellions toward strategic objectives. As Scott has observed:

> It normally does violence to the historical factors to attempt to distinguish between peasant revolution and peasant insurrection or between peasant communism and peasant protest or violence. What classically makes for a peasant revolution or peasant

communism is not the motives or values of the peasantry . . . but rather the nature and ideology of the radical intelligentsia or party that manages to attach itself to a massive form of popular discontent.[55]

Although Samuel Popkin has challenged the basic premise of the moral economists concerning the "subsistence ethic," he reaches a similar conclusion with respect to the vital contribution of external organizers, who help overcome the "free rider" problem that usually impedes collective undertakings, by providing collective goods as a by-product of individual action.[56] As an example, Joel Migdal has shown that Communist parties gained adherents among peasantries not because of the inherent attractiveness of their ideology but because they were the most effective groups in organizing peasants for land reform and protecting traditional village communities from state or landlord depredations.[57]

Beyond this, Charles Tilly has emphasized the spatial dimension of such organization: "A revolution is likely only when opponents can mobilize the massive resources necessary to take command of a geographical area and effectively wrest power from the old regime."[58] Similarly, Skocpol has pointed out that organizers seeking to mobilize peasants require a marginal area beyond the state's repressive reach, such as Cuba's Sierra Maestra.[59] The point might be reformulated somewhat to indicate that the most suitable areas are those simultaneously inaccessible by the authorities but accessible from abroad for the movement of personnel and the delivery of supplies, particularly weapons. This is well illustrated by the geopolitical aspects of recent revolutionary upheavals in Central America.

The significance of external organizers and geopolitical considerations points to the importance of the international context more generally. Social conflict in the developing world almost always attracts significant foreign involvement because of the linkages within the global state system between regime orientation and international strategic alignments. As Kenneth Grundy has put it, "a major revolutionary armed struggle for predominance in a strategically important part of the world is like a mortally wounded animal; it attracts the buzzards of international politics."[60] Established ruling classes have external allies and supporters among the states arrayed in defense of the status quo. Conversely, revolutionaries tend to have links with those who challenge the existing international order. It is particularly important to note that in contrast with separatist conflicts, which are usually of only local interest, revolutionary conflicts attract the attention of superpowers with a substantial capacity to pursue their objectives in the farthest corners of the globe. Understandably, each side seeks to strengthen its hand by securing support from external allies, and given the dynamics of contemporary world politics, opportunists with some resources are not difficult to find.

To state the obvious, U.S. governments have tended to oppose revolutions, whereas Soviet governments have tended to be favorably disposed toward them. Intervention to defend an incumbent government against a revolutionary challenge, to promote a revolutionary movement, or to support a newly established revolutionary regime is more likely if the country involved has some strategic significance. But it should be noted that "strategic" is a very subjective and flexible concept. Moreover, the expansion of industrialization and of the domain of strategic interactions makes for a wide availability of weapons, which in turn facilitates the geographical spread and the escalation of conflicts into protracted violent confrontations.

DYNAMICS OF REFUGEE FLOWS Refugees are generated in the first instance by the generalized violence and dislocation that typically accompany the onset of the revolutionary upheaval process itself, regardless of its outcome. Violent conflicts are likely to be more destructive today than in the past because both governments and their opponents have access to firepower in all its forms. Furthermore, as our case studies have shown, the impact of violence on poor and densely populated countries is particularly catastrophic because it often reduces agricultural production below the subsistence level. Given the availability of roads, bicycles, and trucks, even very poor peasants are today much more able to move away from violence than their forebears could. How many of them become refugees is largely a function of location in relation to international borders, existing migratory networks, and the disposition of relevant neighbors.

The prospect of a successful revolution often triggers the exodus of the old ruling class and their associates, threatened with or afraid of retribution. They fall within the distinctive type that E. F. Kunz has termed "anticipatory refugee movement."[61] Many members of the elite who were not politically active come under general suspicion as well because, having been conditioned by the sharp social cleavage that made the society revolution prone in the first place, revolutionaries tend to make judgments in terms of collectivities rather than individuals. In any case, the losers usually find unbearable their life without their previous privileges. The elite wave is likely to be numerically small, often consisting of people who manage to bring out independent means of support—or have taken the precaution of amassing some savings abroad against an eventuality such as they now face—and always have at least nominal foreign patrons. They easily qualify for refugee status under the U.N. protocol and experience little difficulty in finding countries of asylum. Movements of this type are usually irreversible.

This initial outflow is often followed by a second outflow, larger than the first and extending downward to encompass a variety of groups and strata suffering the exigencies of revolutionary reconstruction. Although the policies pursued by revolutionary regimes are in principle designed to effect redistribution, the government is often led to impose great sacrifices on the population in order to extract the resources needed for social investments. Such hardships are aggravated by the fact that such policies are generally carried out in a hostile international economic environment. Under these circumstances a very large number of people may seek to leave, provided that they have minimal assurances of finding reasonable resettlement elsewhere. The cases of Vietnam and Cuba exemplify this mechanism, although in both cases postrevolutionary problems were intensified by other factors as well. States that oppose the revolution are likely to provide the necessary havens, and refugee flows will materialize accordingly. However, the political benefits that arise from a demonstration that the revolution lacks support may be offset by the costs of receiving a large mass of refugees, as in the case of Honduras with respect to Nicaraguans, and of the United States regarding Cubans from the mid-1970s onward.

In anticipation of or in response to this, most revolutionary states tend to impose severe obstacles on exit. As indicated in Chapter 1, an extreme version of this pattern emerged in the Soviet Union. A combination of political-strategic and economic considerations also determined the adoption of no exit as a policy baseline by subsequent revolutionary regimes, but it was implemented with greater or lesser severity and consistency in response to changing circumstances, including the policies of receivers. Exit may be encouraged to get rid of opponents or to embarrass antagonistic states. The United States' perception of Cuban refugees shifted over time from that of defectors who were useful in the propaganda war to "bullets aimed at Miami." And after Mariel, President Ronald Reagan tried to win support for his Nicaraguan policy by evoking the specter of an invasion of the United States by Central American "feet people."

In the light of recent experiences, the "encouragement to defect" stance of the Cold War years may be a thing of the past. Concomitantly, postrevolutionary states may adopt a more permissive exit policy if it appears that putative receivers will refrain from using such flows as a propaganda weapon.

A variation of this scenario occurs when the problems of revolutionary reconstruction are compounded by the military operations of counterrevolutionary forces. The resulting insecurity and added impositions by the revolutionary regime, especially military mobilization, cause even more people to leave. These flows are encouraged by the counterrevolutionaries and their patrons because they also provide a source of military manpower. The Nicaraguan case provides a partial illustration. Although the formation of a second wave may have been hampered by the reluctance of the United States to admit Nicaraguans as refugees—following domestic opposition to the massive admission of Cubans and Indochinese in 1980—there were signs in the mid-1980s that the refugees were emerging as a consequence of the Sandinista draft.

Direct military intervention by external actors, or substantial military contributions from them, works in the same direction. But it is much more intense because it gives the antagonists additional firepower and thus results in enlarging the fire zone, without helping form the social base and legitimacy that are necessary to conclude the conflict. Recent examples that have resulted in large refugee flows include Soviet intervention and Western counterintervention in Afghanistan: Soviet and Cuban intervention in Ethiopia (initially because of the Ethiopia–Somalia war but later because of internal conflicts in Ethiopia); and U.S. assistance to the government of El Salvador.

The Waning of Revolutions and the Persistence of Rebellions

The general answer to Barrington Moore's question thus appears to be that as with separatism, the situations most likely to explode into full-fledged revolutions have already done so, producing the major waves of refugees we have encountered. But the developing countries are likely to experience more limited types of social order conflicts that will produce some refugees. This can be stated more precisely by dividing revolutions into subtypes corresponding to more particular configurations.

POSTCOLONIAL STATES   Many of the recent upheavals categorized as revolutionary pertain to European-ruled colonies in Asia and Africa, already considered under the heading of "violent decolonization." The cleavage between European rulers and the indigenous population differed qualitatively from that which ordinarily separates lords and peasants. Overall, white rule was less hegemonic and more coercive. The colonial situation made it much more likely that counterelites would arise at the center, and their shared racial identity with the masses facilitated their organizational tasks. Moreover, the colonial rebels had widespread support in the international community. In any case, these situations cannot be replicated because of the passage of "world time"; decolonization is now almost complete.

Because it consisted of foreigners who could return to their homeland, the old ruling class was expelled with relatively little difficulty, and thus the first wave of refugees tended to be quite limited and relatively unproblematic. Where the postliberation government undertook radical structural transformations, the consequences were the same as in revolutionary regimes proper. Whether or not a second wave of refugees materialized was contingent on the government's disposition, its ability to control departures, and the availability of a place to go.

But the postliberation course of events has been overdetermined by international politics. Acceptance of the new regime by the former colonial power and by neighbors, as in the cases of Algeria and Zimbabwe, reduced the likelihood of violence and concomitant outflows. But external pressure on or intervention to intimidate the regime into altering its political orientation, or even to replace it, had the opposite effect, as seen in the tragic examples of Vietnam and, more recently, Angola and Mozambique.

The more common form of colonialism effected significant changes that combined elements of a technocratic "revolution from above," capitalist commercialization, and the formation of a more accessible political center. Populist and progressive at their inception, after they came to power most nationalist movements became more authoritarian and conservative but nevertheless undertook some of the structural transformations associated with social revolution. This path is well exemplified by India. Developments of the past two decades have confirmed Moore's judgment that revolution is unlikely but have not sustained his belief that India would experience steady decline and evolve toward a Prussian or Japanese (1920s) outcome. Rather, the government appears to have solved basic problems of subsistence—albeit without significant improvement in the condition of the most deprived—and continues to hover about the middle of the liberal-authoritarian continuum, with occasional lurches toward one pole or the other. What violence there is stems mostly from center–periphery and communal tensions, as indicated in the preceding section.

Revolutions are even less likely in postcolonial states that are recent amalgams of disparate, small societies, composed mostly of smallholders, as in most of black Africa. In effect, these countries do not constitute societies organized around a center. They have no institutionalized social order but, rather, a ruling stratum with a very limited capacity for bureaucratic exaction from what are still largely self-contained residual communities. Social conflict focuses on political management rather than on economic production. Intraelite competition leads to structural instability at the center, manifested by frequent coups and countercoups. And popular protest tends to be localized or to take the form of withdrawal from the state.

AGRARIAN STATES OF EAST ASIA Organized into well-integrated large-scale societies, which combined sharply differentiated cultivator and noncultivator classes with a centralized bureaucratic state, East Asia had the most appropriate conditions for revolution outside the European orbit. Although Meiji Japan avoided this fate by means of a revolution from above, China's Manchu dynasty failed in its attempt to follow suit, as did the Nationalists in the 1930s, who were hampered by the Japanese invasion and the militarization required to meet it. Highlighting the important role of international factors, a critical element in China was the consolidation of a revolutionary state in the Soviet Union, whose agents "left no stone unturned to accelerate China's revolutionary avalanche."[62] Contrary to the ideological pronouncements of its leadership, the People's Republic of China itself displayed little interest in promoting revolution among its neighbors but generally sought to achieve its international objectives by conventional diplomatic and military means. The revolutionary regimes that came to power in the region either stemmed from colonial confrontations and their sequels, as in Vietnam and the other countries of former Indochina, or from a revolution from above induced by Soviet occupation, as in the case of North Korea.

In all the cases discussed in Chapter 6, large internal refugee flows were generated during the revolutionary civil war, and international flows during the postrevolutionary consolidation. These have now been absorbed, except for the Indochinese residue. There remains the possibility of a flow from Hong Kong when the British lease expires. This outcome, however, is being "discounted" in advance by a steady flow of emigrants, tantamount to an informal version of the "orderly departure" arrangements discussed in the next chapter.

Where neither revolution nor violent decolonization took place, the conditions that led to revolutions in the region during the first three-quarters of the twentieth century have by now been largely corrected. Taiwan and South Korea experienced revolutions from above of the more conventional kind, which effected significant changes with respect to landownership and enabled a remarkably successful transition to industrial capitalism. It is noteworthy that in both cases, at the most critical time of the transition, the state's capacity was enhanced by the United States, which also provided international protection. The resulting socioeconomic configuration allows for a range of variation along the liberal-authoritarian continuum. At present both countries have bureaucratic-authoritarian governments that are conducive to limited flows of refugees. Other countries in continental Southeast Asia—Thailand, Malaysia, and Singapore—benefited from extremely rapid economic growth in the 1960s and 1970s, which made possible redistributive policies that had a stabilizing effect. These countries' evolving social structure fostered the emergence of tenuous liberal political institutions, which under stress might also shift in a repressive direction.

Indonesia and the Philippines are especially likely to experience large-scale and protracted upheavals in the foreseeable future.[63] However, in neither case is there a cohesive counterelite that might harness massive popular discontent to a revolutionary undertaking. And the combination of a weak center with an unusual archipelago configuration is conducive to a centrifugal dynamic, with endemic localized confrontations that are likely to encourage internal displacements but few international refugees.

ARCHAIC AGRARIAN STATES Most revolution-prone "agrarian-bureaucratic" states had their revolution long ago or underwent some profound changes that took them out of the category. Leaving aside the oil-rich kingdoms and principalities of the Middle East, around 1960 there were only a handful of ancient agrarian states that, for one reason or another, were not subjected to full-scale colonial transformation and survived more or less intact. They include Ethiopia, Afghanistan, Nepal, Thailand, and Morocco. Thailand was already mentioned as having undergone significant change in recent decades, and Morocco has done so as well. Later, both Ethiopia and Afghanistan did experience revolutions.

However, our studies indicate that in both cases, the center was so weak as to call into question these countries' categorization as "agrarian bureaucratic." Rather, Ethiopia and Afghanistan approximate Eisenstadt's hybrid agglomerate of patrimonial and feudal structures with a weak center, which is unlikely to experience revolution but, instead, tends to fall apart and smolder without explosion. Indeed, that is the course Ethiopia began to follow after the imperial regime—which initiated a very limited revolution from above—collapsed as the result of extraordinary stress induced by a combination of internal and external challenges. There were peasant uprisings, but no revolutionary counterelite to take advantage of the situation until the military Derg emerged. Initially the Derg's control over the center was tenuous at best, and over the periphery it surely declined further from the already-low imperial level. Three years into the process, around 1977–78, the most likely outcome was the loss of the Ogaden to Somalia, soon to be followed by the loss of Eritrea, and probably Tigre as well. There can be little doubt that the weak regime, which was also under attack from both left and right, could not have maintained itself in the face of such dramatic failures. Soviet intervention was determinative. Not only did it reverse the course of both wars, but it also guaranteed the stability of the revolutionary leadership during what turned out to be a decade-long process of constructing an adequate administrative and political cadre. The revolution generated a characteristic first wave of refugees, most of whom quickly obtained asylum in Western countries, including especially the United States. Subsequent tensions were manifested mostly in the form of center–periphery conflicts, resulting in a number of separate outflows from peripheral regions.

Afghanistan is more clearly a case of revolution from above, which resembles its Turkish and Egyptian predecessors. The weak *ancien régime* did not collapse but was overthrown by a coup. The army, in tandem with the Communist party, then undertook a radical transformation of the social order. But here also, because the center was so weak, their efforts provoked a generalized peasant uprising in defense of the status quo, under the leadership of local notables. The new government faltered, and there is every reason to believe it too would have collapsed in the face of armed resistance except for, once again, timely Soviet intervention.

Ironically, the theoretical literature on peasant revolutions provides a particularly good explanation for the success of the "counterrevolutionary" uprising in defense of the traditional social order: The movement spread easily to Afghanistan's largely autonomous local communities, and organizational links were quickly established between the peasants and counterelites with a strategic plan, the material wherewithal to implement it, and a geopolitical base from which to operate. In this case, however, the base was in a foreign country. Outrage among peasants was undoubtedly the fuel, but it was massive assistance from the United States and the collaboration of Pakistan that determined the transformation of rebellious peasants into the world's most effective refugee-warrior community. Because the Soviet intervention has been almost universally condemned, the resistance has been legitimized, and the UNHCR tolerates the ambiguous character of the camps.

But with respect to this configuration as well, "world time" has intervened to minimize the incidence of future upheavals: There are in effect no Ethiopias or Afghanistans left for revolutions, except perhaps in the Middle East.

LAND-BASED DICTATORSHIPS   Land-based dictatorships combine two features: (1) a political regime approximating Eisenstadt's "neopatrimonial" state, that is, rule by an autocrat and a body of henchmen; and (2) Paige's socioeconomic order, featuring an upper class essentially dependent on direct control over land and unable to give up more of the product without reducing its own share. The combination is found in very poor countries with little or no industrial development, concentrated ownership of land, and a dramatic population increase that intensifies pressures on the land, producing considerable urban migration, much of it channeled into an informal sector. Although the first element can be found throughout much of sub-Saharan Africa, cultivators there tend to be smallholders. In a study covering Latin America and Asia (excluding the Middle East), Roy L. Prosterman has suggested using the proportion of landless as an index for predicting rural instability, with 30 percent as the threshold of "substantial danger" and 40 percent as the "critical" level. As of the mid-1970s, the critical group included the Philippines, Indonesia, East and South India, northeastern Brazil, Nepal, and Nicaragua. The substantial group included Bangladesh, Pakistan, Honduras, and Guatemala.[64] Taking into consideration political variables, the pattern is especially pertinent to the Philippines under Marcos (particularly central Luzon), Pakistan, and the Latin American countries that have not had the benefit of significant land reform. These include the troubled trio in Central America—Nicaragua under the Somozas, El Salvador, and Guatemala, and possibly Colombia and Paraguay.[65]

Cuba and Nicaragua are the obvious revolutionary prototypes. In keeping with the theory, in both cases the revolution's success was based not so much on the spontaneous peasant rebellions but more on the emergence of a counterelite capable of providing the required organizational leadership for unleashing such power and harnessing it to the implementation of a revolutionary strategy. The state and its army broke down, less from external stress than under the impact of the revolutionary upheaval itself. A critical element was the opening at the appropriate time of a "window of opportunity": the withdrawal of the protection that the United States has traditionally offered to cooperative dictators in the region.

Because these conditions rarely occur in the appropriate combination, low-legitimacy, neopatrimonial regimes more commonly persist amidst considerable instability, experiencing occasional intraelite coups and recurrent popular rebellions. They are able to carry on protracted internal wars, often with aid from the United States or some other patron in the Western camp, but are unable to extinguish the rebellion. Note that this mirrors the situation of weak revolutionary regimes that survive only with support from the Soviet Union or another socialist power and that the situation is similarly conducive to endemic violence. Whether large flows of refugees are generated depends largely on geopolitical circumstances, that is, the nature of the terrain where the confrontation between government and rebels occurs. A location near international borders allows for relatively easy escape in the event of violence and for regrouping.

An important feature of the pattern, inherent in the underlying socioeconomic conditions, is that the exodus is codetermined by acute economic need as well as manifest violence, thus allowing potential receivers to question whether the victims are "genuine" refugees. This is compounded by the fact that the repressive regime is usually an associate or client of the state in which the victims seek asylum. A leading illustration of this problem is the predicament of Salvadorans seeking asylum in the United States.

Bureaucratic-Authoritarian Rule

Despite the usage popularized by Washington-area political scientists, *authoritarianism* should not be thought of as a distinct regime type but, rather, as an element of political process shared by many different systems of rule and associated with a variety of socioeconomic formations.[66] Among them are the military-headed "bureaucratic-authoritarian" regimes found among countries in the middle range of the world income distribution, in all parts of Asia as well as Latin America, and particularly in those countries that have achieved a modicum of industrialization (newly industrialized countries, or "NICs"). Under ordinary circumstances, these do not generate massive refugee flows but, instead, an intermittent trickle of activist exiles, who are mostly polticians and intellectuals persecuted for speaking and acting on behalf of democracy and who usually find asylum among neighbors or some of the affluent liberal states.

Even a limited violation of liberal norms has, however, a dangerously corrupting effect, in that it weakens civil society and tempts ruling elites to rely more on coercion to achieve their objectives. The military bureaucratic-authoritarian regimes that came to power in the Southern Cone of Latin America and Brazil in the 1970s, possibly in consequence of heightened pressures emanating from the hemispheric international political economy, availed themselves of existing institutions to construct especially brutal national security states. This was sometimes prompted by the emergence of an opposition intent on provoking a revolutionary upheaval by unleashing urban or rural violence. But even in its absence, military elites readily used potential revolutionary challenges as a pretext for using terror against targets that extended well beyond activists to encompass the social groups and strata from which they might be expected to emerge. In a manner reminiscent of European fascism and the Stalinist phase in the Soviet Union, the resulting "culture of fear" brought with it unprecedented levels of personal insecurity which functioned as an effective mechanism of control.[67]

Although probably most intensive in Uruguay, such repression was particularly extensive in Chile, where in reaction to the achievement of significant structural transformations by the Allende regime, the national security state undertook what amounted to a counterrevolution. As pointed out in the case studies, with the biggest countries of Latin America simultaneously veering in an authoritarian direction and because the target groups were larger than in the past, Latin America's customary neighborly asylum was inadequate. The United States, which considered the perpetrators to be "friendly governments" and provided the training and assistance that enhanced the military's capacity to mete out violence, was unavailable either as a country of first asylum or for resettlement. Hence the largest proportion of the refugees was deflected toward Europe and other parts of Latin America. More recently there has been a trend toward democratization, both in Latin America and Asia, but this is unlikely to go very far and would remain subject to reversal.

Weak States: Exit and Implosion

Quite distinct from the preceding are the one-party civilian or military governments particularly common in sub-Saharan Africa. Generally, the rulers of these extremely weak states, which are also among the world's poorest countries, lack the institutional resources required for national security regimes. Under the increasing stress occasioned by the exhaustion of political spoils or a deteriorating international conjuncture, relatively broadly based authoritarian rule tends to degenerate into a more brutal "gangster government" or "kleptocracy," as in Haiti under the Duvaliers. In Africa, for reasons already indicated, the likely version is ethnic tyranny, as in Uganda (Amin and Obote), Chad (Tombalbaye), the Central African Republic (Bokassa), and Equatorial Guinea (Macias). Faced with great danger and without organizational resources, oppressed urban and rural masses have little choice but to try to get out from under the government altogether, that is, to resort to "exit" rather than "voice." Albeit in appearance apolitical, exit constitutes one of the most effective weapons that poor people can wield against an exploitative state.[68]

If the international configuration allows, exit may result in a massive exodus. In the case of ex-French Guinea (under Sékou Touré), departures amounted to an estimated one-fourth of the total population over a quarter of a century. Probably the most extreme case on record is Equatorial Guinea (ex-Spanish Rio Muni and the island of Fernando Po), during the decade-long dicatorship of Francisco Macia Nguema, instituted in 1969 during the waning years of Spanish colonial rule.[69] The country had an estimated population of 325,000 in 1968 but only 250,000 in 1982. Nguema reportedly killed 50,000 people and enslaved 40,000 others for work on state-owned coca plantations, seized from departing Spanish settlers. Despite the obstacles to exit, which included interdiction of the coast by a Soviet fishing fleet, over 110,000 people managed to flee to Gabon, Cameroun, and Nigeria—approximately one-third of the total population. Economic and political conditions failed to improve after Nguema's overthrow in 1979, and as of the mid-1980s most of the refugees were still abroad.

Substantial numbers fled Haiti under similar circumstances, to neighboring Caribbean countries or the United States, until harsh measures were taken by the receivers to stem the flow. It is particularly important to note that here also, the very character of the root causes makes it impossible to distinguish between flight from violence and flight from hunger.

An alternative path is internal withdrawal, in which peasants concentrate on production for subsistence while withholding from the state what it claims as its due. Engaging in what Scott aptly characterizes as "Brechtian" or "Schweikian" behavior, peasants normally seek to avoid confrontations. However, the rulers of very poor countries may well find themselves in a situation equivalent to that of Paige's noncultivators dependent on land for their income: That is, because extortion is the noncultivator's primary source of livelihood, they are engaged in a zero-sum game and cannot afford to give in. Notwithstanding their rational preference for dodging, the peasants may thus find themselves in confrontation with the state and have no choice but to use violence in self-defense. In this manner, withdrawal from the state may trigger a violent implosion, a division of both rulers and ruled into primary solidarity groups vying with each other in a desperate search for security. As violence becomes a major means of survival, it tends to feed on itself. This process may foster the proliferation of armed factions, leading to the emergence of a warlord system, as occurred in seventeenth-century Germany, in China at the beginning of the twentieth century, and more recently in Chad and Uganda. Although the violence unleashed by this process is more likely to result in many deaths, it may produce refugees as well, as those lucky enough to be located near internationl borders cross them to save their lives.

Chapter 10

Toward a Better International Refugee Regime

In the early 1980s, the expression *root causes* became widely used for the underlying social and international forces that generated refugees. Along with it, a notion developed that a better refugee regime meant fewer refugees. To reduce the incidence of human suffering and, more concretely, the demand for blankets, food, and medicine—not to mention asylum and permanent resettlement places—the international community was called upon to "avert" refugee flows, as the 1980 U.N. resolution put it, by modifying the underlying causes.

Having discussed in some detail the nature of refugee-producing conflicts, we must now consider what such preventive measures might entail and whether they are possible and, indeed, desirable.

The Root Causes of Refugees

The Debate

The "root cause" debate was initiated in the U.N. system by a heated discussion in the General Assembly's Special Political Committee in 1980. It was followed by a study of mass exoduses, prepared in 1981 under the auspices of the former High Commissioner for Refugees, Sadruddin Aga Khan.[1] Five years later, a Group of Experts established by resolution of the General Assembly issued a report entitled "International Co-operation to Avert New Flows of Refugees."[2] Outside the U.N., an Independent Commission on International Humanitarian Issues was formed in 1983 to start the process of building an international consensus, along the lines of the previous Brandt, Palme, and Brundtland commissions dealing with contemporary issues of major importance. Cochaired by Sadruddin Aga Khan and the Crown Prince of Jordan, Hassan Bin Talal, the commission issued a report on refugees in 1986.[3]

The two reports prepared under the auspices of the former High Commissioner emphasize economic underdevelopment as a fundamental cause of contemporary refugee flows. Recognizing that the majority of these flows originate in the developing world, it is argued that economic imbalances and overall poverty in the "South" is conducive to political instability and recession that often compel people to flee. In the wake of wars, moreover, problems of reconstruction aggravated by economic stringencies have the same effect. War and political strife in itself are also considered underlying causes of refugee flows. The third major factor is the improvement in communication and transportation, which encourages potential refugees from the developing world to seek asylum in the hope that they will get a sympathetic hearing in the liberal, industrialized countries (referred to here as the "North").

It follows that only if we deal with the problems of poverty and inequity can we hope to strike at the roots of the international refugee problem. The objective of a preventive strategy would be to "widen the choice for the potential refugee, including that of not leaving" his or her country in the first place.[4] As the former High Commissioner noted in an interview,

> . . . unless you really address the problem of development, you are never going to be able to circumscribe movements of people, whether they are refugees for economic, political, or ecological reasons—and basically the root causes combine . . . If we sent proper technical assistance, if there was transfer of appropriate technology, if one focussed on the rural areas rather than the cities, if the quality of life and life support systems were improved, you would begin to address the problem as it should be addressed.[5]

The reasoning is familiar from the public policy debate about refugees that began in the 1980s.[6] In recognition of the vast task identified, however, the two reports' final recommendations are quite modest. They address proximate, rather than root, causes and procedural aspects of international conflict resolution. An international campaign to strengthen respect for human rights is recommended, as is the need to improve the early warning and mediatory capacity of the U.N. secretary general. But because refugees still will be appearing in large numbers, both reports conclude by emphasizing better management of asylum policies, relief assistance and search for "durable solutions" in the form of permanent settlement in a host country, or repatriation.

The report of the Group of Experts appointed by the U.N. General Assembly is more specific and accusatory. Drawing on the General Assembly's resolutions authorizing its establishment, the group cites economic underdevelopment "inherited from colonialism" and aggravated by the world economic situation as a major root cause. As a result, the economies of the South suffer balance-of-payments problems, deteriorating terms of trade, indebtedness, and inflation. Environmentally related problems of desertification and deforestation aggravate the situation. The result is generalized conditions of insecurity that threaten the basic conditions of survival, compelling large numbers of persons to flee. The group considers these people, as well as the victims of natural disasters, to be refugees. Second, the group identifies colonialism, and "oppressive, segregationist and racially supremacist regimes"—in particular the apartheid regime in South Africa—as the other major cause of refugee flows.[7] The group's recommendations, by contrast, are quite bland, merely exhorting the international community to abide by the U.N. Charter and its practices.

More pointed recommendations emerged during the consciously partisan debate in the 1980 U.N. General Assembly's Special Political Committee on efforts to avert new flows of refugees. The debate—which, being the first of its kind, became known as "the root cause debate''—was sparked by Western initiatives in the U.N. to censor Cuba and Vietnam for encouraging mass outflows. The discourse was shaped both by the traditional East–West ideological division and the newer North–South cleavage. Taking the lead in the debate, the West German representative argued that man-made mass outflows were caused by deportation and willful discrimination against groups of people on the basis of race, religion, ethnic origin, or political views. By emphasizing factors internal to the country, and the role of the government in the exercise of persecution, the interpretation followed closely the causal implications of the convention's definition of refugee. Only the charge of de facto expulsions was added. To avoid such flows in the future, the Western-led coalition in the U.N. called for an expanded code of conduct and a series of guidelines for states to follow. The code would be given the status of a Declaration of Friendly Relations, to which states would be encouraged to adhere. The entire U.N. apparatus, from the specialized agencies to the Security Council, should be brought to bear on the deviant states to ensure implementation.[8]

The initial response from the radical South was to take the proposal at its face value. Would not diplomatic censorship of this kind also apply to persecution against majorities, in the form of apartheid in South Africa and Pretoria's control over Namibia? In concrete terms, this meant support for complete U.N. sanctions against South Africa. Were Western countries also ready to identify the establishment of Israel as a cause of Palestinian refugees, and take concrete, ''preventive'' measures, starting by establishing a U.N. inquiry into Israeli human rights practices in the West Bank?[9] More generally, it was argued that the development of an equitable international economic order and an economically autonomous South would contribute to peace, stability, and consequently fewer refugees. The North could show its good faith by supporting existing agendas for a new international economic order (NIEO) and a new global information order.

Poverty and Refugees

The emphasis on economic underdevelopment as a cause of refugees, and the need for a new international economic order in order to get at the roots of the current refugee problem, calls for a correction. Our findings indicate that contrary to U.N. debate, economic underdevelopment is by itself not a major cause of refugee flows.

The simple notion that poverty produces refugees is inconsistent with the fact that situations of extreme economic deprivation usually have not generated population outflows claiming international refugee status (e.g., the poor in India or Burkina Faso). Even poverty in the form of structural violence—that is, extreme, systematic, and sustained economic deprivation—by itself and in the first instance typically produces powerlessness.[10] When migratory movement occurs, it is most likely to take the form of internal migration that requires few resources, or if it is international, the poorest will be the last to leave (as in the case of Haiti). International population movements attributed to severe food shortages caused by foolish policies and unfavorable weather, as is happening in parts of Africa, present problems different from those of refugees requiring protection and possibly resettlement and so are aided accordingly with international famine relief.

Under prevailing international definitions of refugees, victims of structural violence are not likely to be given refugee status; population flows making claim to such assistance therefore rarely materialize. Recognition policies in this respect have the characteristics of a self-fulfilling prophecy. In extreme cases, it is true, internal conditions are so appalling as to create a simple overflow of needy people seeking basic security elsewhere, as in the cases of people fleeing weak states with tyrannical regimes in Africa. In these situations, the distinction between flight from violence and flight from hunger is in practice erased, as noted in the previous chapter. In an earlier period when the international refugee regime was poorly developed in Africa, such flows were treated as migrants (e.g., the mass exodus from Sékou Touré's Guinea). Later there was a greater tendency to treat them as refugees (e.g., from Equatorial Guinea).

Considering the circumstances under which victims of poverty, or its more precise form, structural violence, appear in the international refugee queue, it appears that these are conditioned both by the expansion of an international refuge regime able to render assistance and the objective conditions in the country of origin. First, when structural violence coincides with politically directed, physical violence—wars, state repression, abuse against minorities, and the like—the needy can draw on asylum and relief programs made available primarily in the context of the political nature of the strife (e.g., Chad, El Salvador). Second, and sometimes concurrently, the small margin of survival in many parts of the South ensures that war will create a compounded disaster of man-made and nature-made destruction that compels very large numbers of people to seek basic necessities elsewhere (e.g., the Mozambique region and the Horn of Africa). Third, victims of structural violence can successfully claim refugee status en masse when there is an opportunity for "pairing" cases, that is, when they can claim on the basis of equitable treatment with another at least superficially similar group (e.g., Haitians with the Cubans in the United States in 1980).

In complex conflict situations, a root cause strategy attempting to improve economic conditions in the home country is relevant but has obvious limitations. In cases of famine and internationalized war, a root cause strategy must be formulated at the international political level to establish the prerequisites for peace and development. When massive internal poverty is related to the structure of political power and production, reforms without fundamental change in the political economy will have marginal results.

In special situations, economic hardship directly contributes to refugee flows, as four well-known contemporary cases demonstrate. Societies in a postrevolutionary or postliberation phase are particularly vulnerable. Problems of reconstruction and consolidation can easily be made worse by external punitive measures, generating internal pressures for the population at large to leave the country in the face of widespread economic deprivation or a radicalization of the revolution (as seen in Cuba, Vietnam, Nicaragua, and, with disastrous results, Mozambique). Because the flows originate in highly politicized situations, the people are likely to claim and often obtain refugee status. In such cases, the policy implications for outside states are clear: Termination of support for the *contras*, and the creation of a more benign international environment, including rendering aid rather than instituting a blockade, would reduce internal pressures and the consequent population flows.

The role of economic underdevelopment as a cause of refugees must also be addressed from the broader perspective adopted by the Independent Commission on International Humanitarian Issues. To what extent have the characteristic imbalances of economic underdevelopment contributed to violent political conflicts of the kind that historically has caused large refugee flows? As indicated in the previous chapter, the relationship between structured economic inequalities and violent social change is extraordinarily complex, whether it concerns the development of a revolutionary situation, patterns of ethnic conflict, or the foundations of authoritarian rule. A restructuring of international economic relations along NIEO lines is not a precise instrument to reduce such conflict and related refugee flows. In fact, most reforms demanded under NIEOs could just as well sharpen as reduce internal conflict, by contributing to uneven development processes. The same applies to economic aid policies, which tend to have an uncertain or unexpected impact on the structure of social conflict unless carefully targeted.

This is not to deny that international redistributive agendas such as NIEO and a liberal aid policy are desirable per se. They should be supported for many reasons, but not because they are likely to reduce international refugee flows, especially in the short run. Thus, for the South to argue that more development aid, or a reshaped international economic order, is necessary to deal with the root causes of refugee flows, is to stretch the logic of social conflict. Equally tenuous are expectations in the prosperous North that more generous aid policies can buy insulation from the refugee fallout of conflicts in the South. Such policies can, however, help reduce the burden in developing countries that receive large and sudden influxes of refugees from neighboring states. Here the costs of providing asylum are inflated by conditions of general underdevelopment and, without compensatory economic schemes, will certainly generate new conflicts.

Root Causes and Social Change

The U.N. debate underlined the essentially political nature of the refugee phenomenon. The receiving countries tended to take an "internalist" perspective, blaming the countries of origin; the latter claimed that external forces ultimately were responsible. Both perspectives were colored by the dominant ideological cleavages of the time, in the last instance because root causes in fact are the constituent elements of social change and historical development. Deep disagreements in this area are to be expected. A revolution, for instance, is a root cause with a well-defined range of enemies and supporters. It would be naive to expect that a broad, international front could be formed to attack the root causes of refugees generally, or even in a single conflict complex such as in South Africa. Attempts to create a consensus in the U.N. accordingly produced a rhetorical General Assembly resolution that concluded the root cause debate.[11] The Expert Group, for its part, sought to escape the divisive issues of cause by dealing with the consequences of conflict, that is, by considering improved assistance for refugees.

A more realistic approach must start by recognizing the essential political and normative nature of the root causes. For a start, the call for a root cause approach in itself has a conservative-preventive implication. As the history of refugee movements demonstrates, refugees are a by-product of social change, and only one item on a much broader canvas of suffering and progress. Orientation toward the fate of refugees must be tempered by an awareness of this larger picture. A revolution, for instance, should not be judged merely by the tragic but historically necessary fact that it produces refugees.

The point is not always appreciated by humanitarian organizations devoted to aiding refugees, which frequently complain that nations pursue their conflicting interests with little regard for the possibility that refugees may result. Though well motivated, this concern ignores the historical connection between social change and refugees. To avert flows would be the equivalent of trying to oppose social change. In the aggregate, this of course is impossible, and in particular cases it may well be undesirable. To stifle change may freeze a repressive social order or contribute to systemic social inequalities. In the longer run, both conditions are likely to produce their own refugees, in the form of individuals fleeing oppressive conditions or revolutionary upheavals. In some circumstances, also, violent change may be a necessary path toward a more just social order. As Barrington Moore's classic study of social change points out, even liberal democracy originated in violent change.[12] An emphasis on conflict prevention, like an uncritical stress on "law and order," has legitimized repressive and socially reactionary regimes. In the face of empires, wars of national liberation may be necessary and desirable, as may revolutionary movements in semifeudal societies, and violent resistance to repressive, authoritarian regimes. In these situations, an outflow of refugees is arguably the most humane form of adjustment.

From this perspective, the emphasis on "averting flows" in the U.N. debate is unfortunate. It suggests opposition by the wealthy and powerful North to radical, and especially violent, social change in the South and, at any rate, unwillingness to accept the consequences in terms of providing support for asylees and refugees. The simplest way of "averting flows," it will be recalled, is for both the sending and the receiving countries to slam the door shut.

Clearly, some approaches to reducing conflict can readily be identified. Whether they should be adopted in particular situations must be determined by a broader calculus of what constitutes a just and desirable development. Whatever is ultimately decided, however, action must be informed by an awareness of likely human suffering associated with various strategies. It is in this instrumental sense that we present some policy implications derived from the structural analysis of conflict and related population movements in this book.

Dealing with Root Causes

Institutional Reforms

As long as refugees in our world are defined with respect to violence in the political sphere, the most proximate causes of such population movements will, in fact, be political. A whole range of conflict-reducing principles are relevant here.

In multiethnic, plural societies, policies of moderation associated with liberal-democratic political traditions can encourage flexibility and mutual adaptation among conflicting ethnic groups. Relevant strategies focusing on the political framework in which ethnic conflict occurs can take basically two forms: (1) a recognition of existing ethnic cleavages through process or institutional reforms (e.g., decentralization, or coalition-formation among community elites) or (2) a weakening of existing cleavages by providing incentives for the formation of new groups across ethnic lines or the fragmentation of existing groups. Ethnic conflict can also be modified by various distributive policies designed to change the balance of socioeconomic opportunities and rewards.[13] Ethnic group leadership itself, whether of the majority or the minority, must show moderation. An ethnic community that attempts to capture or utilize the state apparatus primarily for its own benefit will encourage fear and rebellion among excluded communities. This has been the origin of most contemporary secessionist conflicts. But minorities, for their part, cannot realistically expect to secede. As Crawford Young points out, both the international system and the national elites that control the existing state machinery are so "resolutely hostile to such an alternative" that the most the separatists can expect to obtain is represented by the Sudan situation: an uneasy stalemate with promise of cultural autonomy, "at an enormous cost in human suffering and a decade of development foregone.''[14] The alternative of limited autonomy may be acceptable in some majority–minority cases. For instance, the 1987 autonomy provision in the Nicaraguan constitution was included after a less protracted struggle and apparently has had the desired effect of encouraging the Miskito on the Atlantic Coast to return and cooperate with the government.

In societies divided by sharp socioeconomic inequalities, policies of redistribution and social justice in a social-democratic tradition are obvious strategies to reduce fundamental conflict in the longer run. More immediately and concurrently, political reforms are essential to accommodate new social forces that emerge in the economic development process. The difficulties of introducing a reformist "track" in a political economy characterized by sharp contradictions should not be minimized. But, for example, as the experience of reformist Southeast Asia indicates, the complexity of social forces engendered even in heavily dependent economies provides opportunities for moderating forces and alignments to emerge. In certain circumstances, greater democratization may develop in relatively peaceful ways from authoritarian political systems, as the reverses of "national security regimes" in Latin America show.[15]

Of most direct concern from a refugee perspective is the degree to which certain fundamental human rights are respected. This includes, above all, freedom from the most immediate forms of life-threatening violence: mass killings, torture, "disappearances" at the hand of the state apparatus or "encounters" with so-called security forces, exposure to mob attacks, and the danger of being caught in the cross fire. Victims of such violence have historically sought protection beyond the state; few would dispute that they are so entitled. Because the elemental justification for the modern state, at least since Hobbes, is its ability to provide reasonable security for its citizens, the strongest pressures must be exerted on governments not to lash out at their own people. Otherwise, as the history of refugee flows shows, the international community—in practice, other states—will be called upon to provide such protection for people turning up at their borders.

The Role of External Parties

For external parties, the challenge is actively to support policies of moderation in all these spheres and, beyond that, to build structures of peace in regional conflict areas. External parties have a legitimate and necessary role to play insofar as the very structure of social conflict in the contemporary world is international. As the case studies in this book underline, refugees escape from regimes that typically have external supporters or, more subtly, have emerged under conditions shaped by external strategic and economic interests. The opposing social forces also have foreign alignments, which often become the foremost patrons of the refugees. In conflicts that have led to huge outpourings of refugees, foreign involvement has been blatant, as in Afghanistan and Central America.

The international dimension of the causes of refugee movements has not been recognized in prevailing legal concepts and definitions. As we showed in Chapter 1, factors internal to the country of origin predominate in conventional interpretations of persecution. An internalist emphasis also has influenced public perceptions of the origins of refugee movements. This not only is incorrect but also obscures the point that external parties by action—or inaction—can significantly influence the processes that generate refugees. Refugees do not appear simply because they are persecuted by government X or victimized by brutalizing rulers in weak states; such governments and states exist within a necessary structure of international support. It follows that outside parties and humanitarian groups concerned with refugees must make foreign policy a matter of abiding concern.

This could entail support for policies of moderation in other states with respect to ethnic conflicts, distributive social justice, democratization, and human rights, as we discussed. An active stance in this regard should not be opposed simply because it constitutes a degree of interference in the internal affairs of another state. A great deal of interference is inherent in the normal interactions of a highly interdependent world. The challenge is to turn it in positive directions. For instance, a forceful human rights policy linked to economic and diplomatic actions would be appropriate, as would collective sanctions against an unbending regime such as the one in South Africa, which not only maintains brutalizing policies within its own country but also must take a major responsibility for refugee-producing conflicts in southern Africa as a whole.

More direct intervention with military means can be justified in order to terminate an extremely oppressive regime or to help burst a historical boil, so to speak, by shortening the agony of change. The rationale is compatible with a liberal political philosophy and the instrumental logic of the "just war doctrine," but the dangers and dilemmas of intervention are also reflected in contradictory principles in contemporary international law.[16] On balance, international law clearly upholds the principle of nonintervention as a fundamental pillar of international order. Any consideration of international intervention for humanitarian purposes must be at the U.N. level, in order to avoid a destructive, competitive cycle of interference. In practice, however, collective U.N. interventions in a divided world have been rare. Unilateral interventions with a noble purpose have had mixed results, as they also served to strike a blow at traditional rivals (Vietnam in Kampuchea, India in East Pakistan, Tanzania in Uganda) and have generated further strife.

Most kinds of interventions are highly problematic. Unilateral intervention tends to become competitive no-win situations for the intervening powers, whereas opportunistic interventions that are not designed to "win," but to fan regional strife for other reasons, place a heavy burden on the local parties. Interventions involving the extensive use of military force (by proxy or directly) typically produce protracted and devastating conflicts with difficult refugee situations. The refugee consequences of interventionist policies were graphically depicted in a map designed by the UNHCR to show the world's largest refugee problems in the mid-1980s. Five explosive areas were marked: Indochina, Afghanistan, the Horn of Africa, southern Africa, and Central America.[17] In all these cases social conflict had been internationalized by the intervention of either regional states or the superpowers and in the process had expanded into devastating regional conflict systems from which poured forth a perpetual stream of refugees.

Regional Peace Systems

Given a concern for refugees, the main principle of foreign policy must be military nonintervention. But beyond this negative injunction, it is essential to work actively to establish regional structures of detente and peace. All the five explosive areas listed by the UNHCR as major refugee-producing centers also have well-developed peace agendas formulated through the U.N. or regional fora to terminate hostilities. The same applies to Palestinian refugees (who are not under the UNHCR jurisdiction), whose tortuous history has demonstrated that an international political initiative is an inescapable requirement if one is to solve the refugee problem. The principles of nonintervention and self-determination form the centerpiece of these various peace proposals. In situations where the refugees are active participants in the conflict, a durable solution for such refugee-warrior communities is critical for the peace efforts.

For the states and organizations concerned to alleviate the sufferings of refugees on humanitarian grounds, these peace efforts constitute an essential policy agenda. To illustrate, we shall discuss three of them.

An advanced peace agenda has been developed for Central America. The Contadora initiative, launched in January 1983 and eventually including eight major regional countries (Mexico, Colombia, Panama, Venezuela, and, in a secondary support role, Brazil, Argentina, Peru, and Uruguay), sought to defuse the conflicts in El Salvador and Nicaragua and to prevent an escalation in Guatemala. The scheme was based on the dual principles of nonintervention and deescalation of the conflict, by banning foreign advisers and foreign bases, limiting the acquisition of defense materials, and prohibiting irregular forces operating across national borders. Some general principles of domestic politics were also laid down for the governments in the region to observe (respect for institutions of liberal democracy), but the emphasis was clearly on the international aspects.

Perceiving the initiative as a threat to its position in the region, the United States blocked it. The proposal would have undercut the Reagan administration's main policy instruments in the Central American conflicts: assistance to the Nicaraguan *contras* operating from neighboring Honduras and Costa Rica, demonstration of force against Nicaragua from the two neighboring countries, and the supply of weapons and military advisers to the Salvadoran government. The regional states then responded by formulating a new initiative to end hostilities and enhance their autonomy via-à-vis North American hegemony. The Arias plan (named after the Costa Rican president Oscar Arias, for which he was awarded the 1987 Nobel Peace Prize) was signed by the presidents of the five Central American republics in August 1987 and called for a cease-fire in all of them within ninety days. Though less comprehensive than the Contadora scheme, the Arias plan was likewise based on the principle of nonintervention. It prohibited external support to rebel forces and specifically banned aid to groups seeking to overthrow regimes in neighboring states. The plan supported forces of political moderation within states, notably by stipulating an end to emergency regulations. There were no limitations on foreign military assistance to existing governments, however, thus permitting continued U.S. aid to its allies in the region and Soviet and Cuban assistance to the Nicaraguan government.

The main effect of the Arias plan, if fully implemented, would be to neutralize the operations of Nicaraguan *contras* who depend on external sanctuaries (in Honduras and Costa Rica) and U.S. supplies. As a result, the initial response from Washington toward this plan also was negative, making it more difficult for the local signatories to the accords to comply.

With respect to Afghanistan, negotiations under U.N. auspices started in 1982, and the outlines of a peace formula took shape quite soon. The main "instruments" of peace were to be withdrawal of Soviet forces from the country, the simultaneous cessation of foreign military assistance to the rebel forces based in neighboring countries, and the return of the three million to five million refugees located in Pakistan and Peru.

For almost ten years, however, the main protagonists were unwilling to make the required concessions to the principle of mutual nonintervention. On the Soviet side, it was a question of securing a friendly regime on its southern border, a question that became increasingly urgent over time as the United States and other adversaries were building up a virtual client Afghan army of Islamic fundamentalists and tribal leaders in neighboring Pakistan. The United States, for its part, found it useful to have the Soviet Union bogged down in an unwinnable war in Afghanistan, which perhaps eventually would compel the rival superpower to withdraw in defeat.

By 1986–87 the internal reforms in the Soviet Union and a rebel offensive, made possible by the supply of sophisticated weapons, brought about a change in Soviet policy toward Afghanistan. Moscow was willing to withdraw on the terms of the Geneva formula even if it meant that a friendly regime could not be secured in Kabul. General Secretary Mikhail Gorbachev's announcement on February 8, 1988, was the decisive declaration to this effect. Although Pakistan, anxious to be rid of the refugees and the rebel forces, wanted to install the rebel leaders in a coalition government in Kabul before the Soviets' withdrawal, the American response appeared conciliatory, recognizing that the Geneva formula represented the only path to great-power disengagement from the conflict.

Two months later, the governments of Afghanistan and Pakistan signed a peace agreement incorporating the original Geneva formula. The two parties pledged not to interfere in each others' internal affairs and to facilitate the return of refugees. The Soviet Union undertook to withdraw its military forces within nine months, starting on May 15, 1988, and, along with the United States, became a guarantor of the peace accords as a whole.

It soon became evident, however, that the two superpowers would not cut all military ties with their clients. The United States insisted it had a right to continue supplying weapons to the rebels as long as the Soviet Union provided similar support to the regime in Kabul. For although the accords enabled the Soviet Union to withdraw its troops gracefully, the question of who should rule in Kabul remained unsettled and, in fact, had never been on the agenda in Geneva. The war among the Afghans thus continued.

As the Soviet withdrawal progressed, it opened the door for a protracted, internal conflict in Afghanistan or, alternatively, a fragmentation of the country into zones ruled by various warlords. Either situation could be made immeasurably worse by continued foreign intervention in the form of competitive arms supplies. By providing their respective clients with military hardware, the superpowers will primarily ensure that the civil war continues at a high level of destructiveness.

The primary objective of outside parties must therefore be, first, to ensure an implementation in spirit as well as letter of the mutual nonintervention stipulated by the Geneva peace formula and, second, to pursue a diplomacy of moderation in the post-Geneva period. This could entail some measure of support for moderate political factions on both the Kabul and the rebel side and a willingness to sideline irreconcilable elements among former clients. Some factions of the People's Democratic Party of Afghanistan (PDPA) regime in Kabul might have to be relocated for permanent exile in the Soviet Union. On the rebel side, segments of the Muslim Brotherhood (especially the Hezb-i-Islami) that have vehemently opposed any conciliation with the PDPA might remain in permanent exile in Pakistan or elsewhere. Although Islamabad has firmly rejected this possibility, irreversible refugee flows, as we have seen, in fact constitute a typical historical outcome in situations of revolutionary social change.

In southern Africa, the compounded conflict can be divided into five, distinct refugee-producing situations: (1) internal war in Angola that has been exacerbated by progressive internationalization from the competitive U.S. and Soviet interference during the national liberation phase, and onwards; (2) South Africa's struggle with SWAPO, the main indigenous force fighting to liberate Namibia from the South African mandate, which has been declared illegal by successive U.N. and World Court orders since the inception of the U.N. in 1945; (3) the internal conflict in South Africa proper; (4) punitive raids by South African forces against regime opponents in exile linked with the African National Congress; and (5) an internal conflict in Mozambique, internationalized and aggravated by South African support for local *contras*.

Although the conflict in South Africa proper has produced relatively few refugees, those in neighboring Namibia, Angola, and Mozambique have generated large and continuous waves. The internationalization of the conflicts in Angola and Namibia is chiefly a result of the "total national strategy" pursued by the minority regime in South Africa, designed to create a wider security belt outside its border in order to maintain itself. Pretoria's continuous hold on Namibia is part of this strategy but also rests on the rationale of economic imperialism.

The prerequisite to a reduced conflict in southern Africa is that South Africa be contained within its borders, excluding Namibia. In this respect, the United Nations has taken an unequivocal stand: The near-universal condemnation of South Africa's occupation of Namibia has been given institutional form in the establishment of various U.N. commissions to assist Namibia to nationhood. Support for this position is an elemental root cause strategy with respect to refugees in southern Africa.

To attack the basis of the problem by forcefully instituting radical social change within South Africa proper is more ambitious and politically difficult. A case can be made for making efforts to deal with South Africa's international role separately. The relevant model is the 1984 Nkomati nonaggression pact between Mozambique and South Africa. As the model demonstrates, however, the approach has clear moral-political trade-offs. Black African states can buy peace from South Africa by not aiding African National Congress (ANC) rebels, thereby helping Pretoria establish its "security belt." This amounts to implicit recognition of and support for the apartheid regime.

The alternative is to press for more intervention to compel political change within South Africa proper. The U.N. record on mandatory sanctions in this respect is admittedly poor. The arms embargo endorsed by the U.N. in 1977 has not been fully observed: Growing efforts to institute mandatory economic sanctions ten years later remained blocked by the United States and Great Britain in the U.N. Security Council. Nevertheless, the policy of sanctions should be supported. South Africa is an outstanding contemporary case in which intensified conflict seems necessary to bring about the desired social change, even though large flows of refugees may well materialize in the process. It illustrates the point made earlier, that a concern to avert refugee flows by itself must not be a primary consideration.

As the three conflict scenarios from Africa, Asia, and Latin America demonstrate, both preventive root cause strategies and approaches to durable solutions for refugees must initially be formulated at the international political level. This is particularly clear with respect to the durable solution that the UNHCR considers to be the best, that is, repatriation. The point was well illustrated by the inconclusive efforts to deal with Indochinese and Cuban asylum seekers: Without foreign policy adjustments that permit a modicum of political understanding between the receiving and the sending countries, repatriation is impossible.

Dealing with the Flows

Even the most determined attack on the root causes of refugee flows will not—and should not attempt to—avert international refugee flows. The problem of dealing with the flows satisfactorily thus will remain. In this regard, the structural-historical analysis outlined in previous chapters suggest some general policy implications. They do not pertain to immediate, operational questions of providing material assistance or determining asylum claims; rather, they concern broader policy directions relevant to public and private agencies dealing with refugees. We shall first revisit the question of definition and address the issue of politicization of refugee status. These questions will then be considered in light of the global North–South dimension of the contemporary refugee situation, which— to take a phrase from Louise Holborn's study of refugees in an earlier period—has given rise to "special problems of our time."

The Definitional Question Revisited: Who Is a Refugee?

Our analysis of contemporary refugee movements delineated three sociological types of refugees: (1) the activist, (2) the target, and (3) the victim. As discussed in Chapter 1, the classic activists are dissenters and rebels whose actions contribute to the conflict that eventually forces them to flee. The targeted refugees are individuals who, through membership in a particular group, are singled out for violent action. And the victims are randomly caught in the cross fire or are exposed to generalized social violence. What all three have in common is fear of immediate violence—violence resulting from conflict between state and civil society, between opposing armies, or conflict among ethnic groups or class formations that the state is unable or unwilling to control. Whether the individuals are activists or passive bystanders simply caught in the conflict is immaterial from the point of view of their immediate security. Their need clearly could be the same regardless of the cause, and has demonstrably been so in many of the cases analyzed. It follows that in a historical and normative sense, the three types of refugees are equally deserving. The activist, the target, and the victim have an equally valid claim to protection from the international community.

The international refugee regime has to some extent recognized the moral equivalence of the three types. The U.N. Convention's definition accommodates the first two but has no provision for the victim. On the other hand, victims were in practice recognized as refugees in the European experience, both in earlier centuries and after World War II. The victims were also acknowledged in the institutional response to Third World refugees through the expanded mandate of the UNHCR in the 1960s and the general practices of first asylum countries in Asia, Africa, and Latin America. Legal codes in Africa and Latin America were also adjusted to allow for mere "victims" (in the 1969 OAU convention and the 1984 Cartagena Declaration).[18] The UNHCR introduced the notion of "victims of violence" in the mid-1980s to plead for asylum seekers in other regions.[19]

From this perspective, the restrictive tendencies evident in North American and West European asylum practices in the 1980s, toward a narrow interpretation of the convention's criterion of persecution as the basis for refugee status, are highly questionable and have been deplored by UNHCR officials.[20] To deny "mere victims" the opportunity to escape from violence is not only morally untenable but runs counter to broader historical trends. It is also open to charges of discrimination on racial and political grounds, as the restrictive tendencies have been most clearly evident with respect to spontaneous asylum seekers of non-European origin who come from noncommunist states.[21]

A partial corrective is evident in the development of various forms of refugee status short of convention status, notably the B-status common in Scandinavia and the Netherlands which extends most of the convention's privileges "on humanitarian grounds"; the beneficiaries often are the equivalent of what we have called victims.[22] In the early 1980s, B-status was given to many Tamils and Iranians in Europe. In countries without B-status, temporary stay was granted to applicants who did not meet the convention's criteria but were deemed to be at risk if returned to their country of origin. In the United States, the Extended Voluntary Departure granted in cases of generalized violence in the home country is another form of indirectly recognizing victims of violence. A grudging acceptance of validity claims other than the convention's type is also implied by failure to deport applicants whose request for formal refugee status has been turned down, as in West Germany's general policy toward Iranians and Afghans.[23]

An optimal policy would start from the explicit premise of moral equivalence among all three refugee types; the administration of protection and services should also be formal and explicit rather than leaving the beneficiary to an uncertain or semilegal status. Equally important, however, is the need to limit the number of prospective beneficiaries. It will be recalled that with the development toward a universal definition of refugees in the 1930s, it was stressed that some "exact definitions" were necessary to prevent the number of refugees from multiplying *ad infinitum*.[24] Half a century later the point has, if anything, become more self-evident. Because it represents a privileged form of migration, refugee status can be given to only a limited number of people. The question then arises whether the concept of violence lends itself to discriminating interpretations that permit setting priorities.

We submit that it can and that the central ranking principle must be the immediacy and degree of life-threatening violence. Those most exposed must be given preferential access to protection, which becomes the most basic of rights.[25] Farther along in the queue, relief could be given as far as resources and political will permit. More specifically, this would mean that priority be given to individuals or groups who find themselves in extremely threatening situations: civilians in battle areas, likely targets of death squads and pogroms, political prisoners under threat of torture, members of rebel or dissident groups on "wanted" lists, and the like. Proscription on cultural expressions such as lack of freedom of religion would come much farther down on the list, except when it is associated with life-threatening forms of violence.

Situations in which the economic prerequisites for sustaining life have suddenly been removed equally constitute life-threatening violence, and such victims need protection. This definition would include the poverty-stricken masses of the developing world, the victims of structural violence who are systematically pressed toward starvation levels, and the victims of drought and famine, with or without the compounded effect of warfare. It may be objected that such a definitional basis of refugee is totally unrealistic; in particular, the resource-rich countries of the North would not want to relieve famine or massive poverty in the South by means of a large-scale relocation of people.

The objection seems unfounded. Most victims of famine and starvation who today cross international borders remain in neighboring countries, where their claims to life-sustaining support generally are recognized by the international relief or refugee regime. Groups accused of being economic refugees who have claimed asylum in the industrialized countries are not the ones who are most economically destitute and would hardly be admitted as victims of violence even if economically based violence were included in the definition (e.g., Tamils and Zairians in Europe, Salvadorans in the United States). These groups may be victims of general poverty or downward mobility, but they are hardly in an immediately life-threatening situation for economic reasons. In fact, they have means to travel, some by airplane. (This is not to deny, of course, that they may be in immediate physical danger at home and on that ground qualify for refugee protection abroad.) As we have seen, the most needy victims of economic violence usually do not become intercontinental refugees, although they may move within the region. To include them in a formal definition of refugee requires, above all, innovative thinking about how to channel aid to the local areas in which they are most likely to remain.

The rule must be that victims of economic, that is, structural, violence must be helped first in their own country. Observance of the *in situ* clause, discussed in Chapter 1, is necessary to prevent neighboring and often poor developing countries from becoming overloaded by an influx of desperately poor people seeking relief and not to encourage an international restructuring of populations that in an age of nation-states is politically unacceptable. Most often, immediate relief, if not structural reform, can be offered, as most governments have at least a nominal commitment to improve the life of their subjects. Economic relief, of course, does not deal with the root causes of the problem, any more than does providing asylum to refugees. The assistance in both cases addresses symptoms but must proceed alongside efforts to modify the origins of violence. By the same logic, when an entire people is mercilessly exploited by a ruler or an unjust social order—that is, systemic structural violence—the only possible recourse is sanctions in support of fundamental social change, as we discussed.

The violence-based definition would lead us to a universe of refugees somewhat different from those recognized by prevailing standards. Although the purpose of this book is not to establish a detailed eligibility determination, the most obvious discrepancies in the early 1980s were in Central America and the Caribbean. Under our count, most Salvadorans and many Haitians would be accepted as escaping from life-threatening violence, whereas many Cubans would not. In other regions, we would put many Iranians and Tamils (increasingly also Sinhalese) high on the list, whereas Laotians, ethnic Vietnamese, and also some ethnic Chinese from Vietnam generally would go farther down.

The right to protection based on the need to escape violence is not absolute. Special problems arise in the category of the activist refugees, in that it must be determined whether their actions were morally worthy—"a political crime"—or merely a criminal act for private gain. International law has long recognized that asylum or refugee status applies only to political crimes, and the U.N. 1951 Convention's Article 1(F) contains some general exclusionary parameters in defining eligibility for refugee status.[26] In an earlier period, the question arose mainly in connection with war crimes and Nazi collaborators. Currently it relates especially to terrorism: state terrorism, international terrorism, and terror against the state. Efforts by states and international organizations to codify practice in this area has focused on international and antistate terrorism, for example, hijacking, hostage taking, and attacks on diplomats. Increasingly these have been declared common rather than political crimes in international instruments of codification. As Guy Goodwin-Gill notes, this tendency "is a potential source of difficulties," as it may lead to deportations of individuals likely to be "persecuted."[27] By excluding terrorism by the state, the codification also sets up double standards.

The concept of political crime must be understood in relation to some vision of a just order, just as the concept of refugee must be understood in relation to some doctrine of rights.[28] In practice, the normative dimension will vary across societies, as reflected in different municipal laws on extradition and the popular notion that one community's "freedom fighter" is another's "terrorist." The broader dilemmas that this poses for refugee and asylum policy cannot be dealt with here. But at a minimum it must be recognized that to admit, say, an ex-agent of the state's repressive apparatus or an activist who has attacked civilian targets in his struggle against the state at one level is morally equivalent; ultimately the choice will depend on normative-political considerations in the recipient society.

Politicization and Demystification

A degree of mystification is inherent in all social processes. In refugee policy, in which the trend toward a universal definition has emphasized the humanitarian element in formal statements of policy, but the implementation of policy is unavoidably influenced by political considerations, the potential for mystification is especially evident.[29] Although mixed motives determine the policy process, humanitarian goals tend to be exaggerated, as they have a legitimizing function. In fact, the major international organization dealing with refugees, the UNHCR, has a vested interest in not clarifying the political motives and consequences of refugee policy because the organization is totally dependent on discretionary funding from the member states. As the latter often have particular refugee groups that they wish to assist, or overlook, the UNHCR strives painfully to be neutral. The UNHCR discourse is cast in entirely humanitarian terms.[30] In this situation it is all the more important for other groups, inside or outside the refugee community, to be conscious of the complex forces at work when recognizing and aiding groups identified as refugees. In other words, a demystification process is required. This is important not only to foster a more rational refugee policy but also to ensure that well-meaning individuals and groups do not become unwitting instruments for ends of which they would not approve.

Even though refugees have political uses in the countries of origin, we are concerned here with the policy implications in the receiving countries.[31] In tracing the historical origin of the concept of refugee in the Western experience, we noted the relevance of political considerations to the receiving country. The first "modern" debate about international refugees—occasioned by the establishment of the UNHCR's precursor, the International Refugee Organization (IRO)—also was intensely political, reflecting the major power configurations and ideological divisions at the time. During the IRO's operation (1947–50), almost 2.7 million people were given protection and material assistance. Most of them had Eastern European or Baltic nationalities, and most were resettled in the Americas and Australia. As the resettlement occurred in the atmosphere of a deepening cold war, the West considered it a humanitarian question of helping people who wished to escape Soviet communism but coincidentally thereby to demonstrate the superiority of Western political liberalism. Recognizing this, the Soviet Union fought the IRO step by step, insisting that these were people dislocated by war who should be returned to their homeland.

The deliberations leading to the establishment of the UNHCR in 1951 unfolded in a similar spirit. The Soviet leaders strongly opposed the creation of an international refugee regime that they were certain would be used against the Soviet Union, and the East–West conflict cast a long shadow over refugee policy in the receiving and sending countries for years to come.

As detailed in the case studies, refugee policy became an important instrument in U.S. policy toward Cuba (by arming exiles for revanchist expeditions and later encouraging outmigration) and toward Vietnam, in which U.S. policy went to the extreme of actively trying to generate refugees in order to create confusion for the adversary after the 1954 Geneva Accords. But although the United States arguably has used refugee policy more consistently as a foreign policy instrument than some other countries have, the phenomenon is indeed widespread.[32] Most countries, for instance, have their "Haitian-Cuban syndrome"; that is, they accord differential treatment to asylum applicants making similar claims for assistance. For example, in Pakistan in the early 1980s, the Iranians were given stepmotherly treatment, whereas a massive relief apparatus was mounted for the Afghans. Next door in India, the Afghan refugees were barely tolerated, whereas the Tamil refugees were given full support. In Honduras, the Salvadoran refugees received almost no protection, whereas the Nicaraguan rebels and their dependents operated freely with much support.

The various instances reflect the more general, instrumental value of refugee populations in relation to the foreign policies of the recipient countries. In "cold wars," they serve a propaganda function. The classic recognition of this function was noted in an American National Security Council document in 1953 which pointed out that the "escape of people from countries in the Soviet orbit inflicts a psychological blow on communism."[33] In "hot wars," the refugees can be of more direct use, especially when the refugee population forms a refugee-warrior community, by establishing an armed wing from its members. Widespread international support for the Namibian refugees, for instance, helped isolate and weaken the apartheid regime in South Africa. Much of the support for the Afghan refugees was the humanitarian counterpart of military aid to Afghan rebels seeking to oust the Soviet-installed regime in Afghanistan.

Refugee policy is rarely determined exclusively by foreign policy considerations of this kind. The connection is most obvious when the recipient countries have been deeply involved in the original conflict from which the refugees are escaping. The displaced people form the link between foreign policy and refugee policy, either as they seek support from erstwhile external patrons (e.g., the Vietnamese from the United States) or are denied assistance for lack of political patronage (e.g., Salvadorans in the United States). More commonly, humanitarian and political considerations intervene to modify policy in very complex patterns, as indicated by the Western and Arab attitudes toward the Palestinians after World War II. For instance, substantial Western financial support for the refugee agency designed to assist the Palestinians was viewed by large segments of the refugee population as detrimental to their interests, as the UNRWA promoted resettlement rather than recovery of the Palestinian homeland.[34]

The many faces of refugee policy should not obscure the key point that whether or not intended, foreign policy is always an element. The connection derives from the international context. In a world of competitive nation-states, the movement of people across an international border, in response to a conflict within, must to some degree affect the relations among nations. A second reason is the nature of the refugee phenomenon itself. The three sociological types of refugees—activist, target, and victim—are arranged on a scale from the politically active to the passive. But support for any one has political implications. To give asylum to the activist (dissenter, "freedom fighter," or rebel) is obviously an act of political solidarity. To aid an ethnic or social group that has been targeted because of its ascriptive characteristics is an expression of sympathy with the victimized and simultaneously a condemnation of the government for failing to prevent—

or for engaging in—persecution. Even the provision of safe haven to bystanders caught in the cross fire has a political dimension, because the refugees will tend to flee in the direction where they expect to find protection and sympathy. For instance, allowing for distance and other obstacles of movement, refugees in civil wars can flee to the government side or the rebel side. Hence, even apolitical masses of refugees to some extent vote with their feet.[35]

It has been suggested that the recognition process can be depoliticized through terminological adjustments. For instance, instead of the term *refugee,* with its implied condemnation of the government in the country of origin, one might substitute the term *internationally assisted person.*[36] By itself, however, this term is likely to compound the confusion and mystification. More meaningful is the introduction of greater nuances in the refugee vocabulary to ensure more congruence between legal categories and the sociological phenomena. To give asylum on "humanitarian grounds" (B-status) or to "victims of violence" (the new UNHCR category in the 1980s). denotes that the beneficiaries are more distant from political conflicts in their homeland than are the activist refugee.

Also, language serves to mystify rather than clarify the social processes it depicts. In refugee matters, this tendency has been especially pronounced, partly because the standard refugee lexicon is highly normative and thus self-evidently legitimizing (e.g., "refugee" connotes someone victimized who is deserving of help, and "persecution" obviously is a malevolent act to be condemned). Used categorically, such designations are important instruments of power, because they signify critical differences in rights for the beneficiary. Whether resulting from a legal-political determination process or used in general parlance and the press with reference to a particular population, the term *refugee* implies that the beneficiary has a rightful claim to certain privileges stipulated by international law. Groups considered to be migrants have other rights at the discretion of the national authorities, whereas those labeled "illegal migrants" have no rights at all. The instrumental use of language to legitimize differential treatment for client populations has been particularly noticeable in the Indochinese case, but the phenomenon is universal.[37]

Greater awareness of linguistic mystification is the basis for an informed public debate and a rational refugee policy. The starting point is to observe that the sociological existence of a refugee (whether an activist, a target, or a victim) is independent of the legal recognition that may be extended, or withheld, for a variety of political reasons in addition to the claimant's sufferings. It follows that there are legal refugees and illegal refugees—just as there are equivalent categories of migrants—and that some groups that are recognized or referred to as refugees may not deserve the term and the treatment. Failure to make this elementary distinction still pervades much of the literature, with the resultant faulty analysis of policy.[38]

Nevertheless, the increasing debate over refugee policy in Europe and North America in recent years has brought a greater awareness of the political aspects of humanitarian policies. It was brought out most clearly in the Central American context, in which the refugee situation was so politically charged that voluntary agencies were pressed to take sides by working for refugees from either "the left" (Nicaraguans) or "the right" (Salvadorans and Guatemalans), but not simultaneously both. The politicization of official U.S. refugee policy, moreover, was so blatant and unfairly discriminatory that it gave rise to a large civil disobedience movement in the United States, in the form of the sanctuary movement (see Chapter 7).

But what lies beyond demystification? One option is to aid only refugees of one's choice for consciously partisan political reasons (say, Afghans or Palestinians but not both). Another approach is the neutral posture that the UNHCR seeks to maintain, by aiding refugees fleeing from all kinds of political systems and representing a range of political persuasions. The UNHCR's approach is in conformity with the historical trend toward a universal definition of refugee, against which an explicitly partisan refugee policy is, historically speaking, a regression—in U.S. terms a return to the pre-1980 legislation, when a refugee was primarily defined as someone who was escaping from a communist country. There is also a third option. Refugee populations from large and internationalized social conflicts will usually have powerful international patrons. Other outflows—the Chakmas and the Haitians of this world—will be relatively neglected. It follows that the groups that fail to find patrons, or that fall between the cracks of international rivalries, are above all the ones that become a collective responsibility and need an improved international refugee regime. To assist this neglected population, reforms might be patterned after existing UNHCR programs for especially vulnerable groups but writ large; internationally apportioned quotas of financial assistance, asylum, and resettlement all would be relevant. As marshaling international support for the already most neglected populations may prove difficult, however, the most important move would be to enlarge the independent financial basis of the UNHCR, by expanding nonearmarked funding that the UNHCR can allocate at its own discretion. Although such contributions by the mid-1980s was on an upward trend (commitment for all UNHCR programs in 1985 was 24 percent above that of the previous year), the organization still faced the "worst financial crisis of its 35-year history," according to the secretariat.[39]

Special Problems of Our Time

Refugee-Warrior Communities

"What is most worrisome about the current refugee burden is not only the sheer number of refugees, . . . but also the long periods of time that they have spent in asylum," wrote the deputy of the UNHCR, W. R. Smyser, in an article in *Foreign Affairs* in 1985. His mid-decade assessment was that the long-lasting refugee presence in many countries had "fundamentally altered the nature of the global refugee problem" by imposing extraordinary aid demands on the UNHCR and receiving countries. He estimated there were about seven million refugees under the UNHCR's purview (excluding the Palestinians), mostly in camps. The strongest and most enterprising, usually the men, succeeded in escaping from the cycle of dependency, but the most vulnerable and dependent ones remained.[40]

This picture captures an important part of what has become a special problem of the contemporary refugee situation—prolonged exile for millions, whose prospect of return is blocked by seemingly insoluble conflict such as that in Afghanistan, Central America, Kampuchea, the Horn of Africa, and southern Africa. These are the new Palestinians.

In one major respect, however, the description is faulty. The new Palestinians—like the original Palestinians—are not merely a passive group of dependent refugees but represent highly conscious refugee communities with a political leadership structure and armed sections engaged in warfare for a political objective, be it to recapture the homeland, change the regime, or secure a separate state. In recognition of their nature as being both dependent objects and actor-subjects in their own right, we have called them *refugee-warrior communities*. Their existence raises problems not merely of obtaining sufficient relief money, as the UNHCR notes, but also of posing profound ethical and policy dilemmas that the UNHCR, because of its dependent position, cannot confront.

These dilemmas are acknowledged in international law which recognizes a conflict between refugee status, on the one hand, and political activism, certainly of the belligerent kind, on the other. Although the activists are a classic type of refugee, once in exile their political activities must be kept within bounds. Although the U.N. Convention is cautious on this point (Article 2 requires only that the refugee conform to the laws and regulations of the host country), other segments of international law are not. The OAU refugee convention is both specific and sweeping: A separate article (Article III) prohibits "subversive activities" by verbal means or by arms, and in the preface the African states declare that they are "anxious" to distinguish between refugees seeking a peaceful and normal life and those—nonrefugees by implication—who flee "for the sole purpose of fomenting subversion outside." Similar principles have been reiterated in various U.N. General Assembly resolutions, by the Council of Europe, and in the 1967 Declaration on Territorial Asylum.[41]

In international law, refugee-warriors clearly are a contradiction in terms and proscribed. In fact, several major contemporary refugee populations are associated with an armed struggle. Most commonly, there are separate physical facilities for the armed wing and for the refugees. This is the case in southern Africa, the SWANLA (South-West Africa's National Liberation Army) being the armed wing of SWAPO, maintaining bases in Angola where also a large number of Namibian refugees are concentrated. The same obtains in Pakistan, where the Afghan *mujahedin* are training and operating from their own bases, and the old men, women, and children are concentrated in other camps supported by the UNHCR. In Central America, the Nicaraguan *contras* are in some cases living with their families in camps, elsewhere not; a more extreme case is the Khmer rebel bases on the Thai-Kampuchean border where the guerrillas are physically integrated with and control "their" villages, called *border concentrations* in the local refugee lexicon. Entire settlements move back and forth across the border, depending on the level of hostilities with the Vietnamese-supported forces in Kampuchea.

Allowing for varying degrees of separation between the civilians and the armed wing, these communities nevertheless have some common features. To exist, they require sanctuary in a neighboring country permitting military operations from its territory. Without a friendly base, the community in exile can only be refugees, as in the case of the Salvadorans in Honduras. But with a sanctuary for the warriors and relief assistance for the refugees, refugee-warrior communities can develop. The genesis of the classical type, the Palestinians, was the displacement of an entire society, a pattern also found in various subsequent movements, notably the Khmer, the Afghans, the Eritreans, and the Namibians. Although sometimes accompanied by their animal flocks as well, they usually lack the means for even subsistence production in exile. Because such people are heavily dependent on aid to stay alive, they lay claim to and usually receive substantial humanitarian relief. A different genesis is suggested by the Nicaraguan *contras*, whose transformation into a refugee-warrior community resembles the other classic type, the defeated Kuomintang armies in China. The soldiers of the *ancien régime* form the core of the community: With international support rendered on explicitly political grounds, they are able to bring out and support also their dependents and other civilians opposed to the new order.

Because the warriors are engaged in military operations across the border that associate the host country in an act of war, communities of this type cannot persist for long unless they secure substantial external partisan support. In fact, they frequently receive material and diplomatic assistance from external patrons in recognition of their use as foreign policy instruments in related international rivalries.

That condition has obtained through the ages. What is different about the contemporary world that makes refugee-warrior communities a special problem of our time, is, first, the existence of a highly developed international refugee regime that can sustain large-scale civilian populations in exile for years, and, second, the dominant ideology of democratic nationalism which makes a civilian refugee population a necessary adjunct for the warriors. Even when the refugees—the old people, women, and children—are physically separated in camps from the warriors, the two are linked, in that the refugees constitute a legitimizing population for the warriors. The presence of a large population in exile is taken as a physical testimony of support for the warriors, at least in the sense that they represent a rejection of the other side in the conflict (whether represented by a rival regime, an ethnic group adversary, or an occupation regime).

The civilian population also provides a recruitment pool that enables the rebel army to reproduce itself. As the community becomes established, it tends to grow by providing opportunities and even incentives to others to become politically active. Individuals in exile may find that the most socially meaningful and economically rewarding activity is to join the militants. For many children growing up in camp and knowing nothing but a dependent, degrading, and fundamentally insecure existence, joining the battle is the only relevant future.[42] When the camps also are close to or part of the front—as are the Palestinian or Afghan refugee camps—war becomes the dominant reality for the entire exiled population; the armed militants appear as protectors of the community, thus forging more closely the links between the refugees and the warriors.

The warriors' attempt to control the return of refugees is another expression of the great importance that they attach to the legitimizing function of the civilian populations. In both the Afghanistan and the Kampuchean conflicts there have been battles for control over the refugees between the rebel forces and their adversaries. The Nicaraguan *contras* are known to have prevented refugees from returning.[43]

Because the refugee-warrior situation erases the distinction between humanitarian and political activity established in international refugee law, the existence of such communities poses difficult policy dilemmas for external assistance. The UNHCR maintains that the problem can be reduced by physically separating the sociologically distinct parts of the community: the warriors to one side and the refugees to the other. At the same time, the camps are located away from the border, as in the case of the Nicaraguans under UNHCR auspices in Honduras. When a separation or relocation is difficult (the Nicaraguans were promptly moved back toward the border with the assistance of U.S. government financing, as discussed in Chapter 7), the UNHCR may pull out. This was the response of the international relief organizations, ICRC and UNICEF, when they discovered that rice rations distributed to women and children on the Thai-Kampuchean border were quickly appropriated by the men, with or without arms.

The "pure" refugee-warrior community tends to become the ward of its foreign patrons, sometimes with the establishment of ad hoc bodies that solicit broader support, with the patrons' full awareness of the refugees' political activity. Thus, some of the Nicaraguan refugees were aided by the Friends of America; the United Nations Border Relief Organization (UNBRO) was set up to supply the Khmer on the Thai-Kampuchean border; and a separate agency, UNRWA, was established for the Palestinians, the first modern refugee-warriors.

This strategy is also relevant to refugee-warrior communities that are superficially separated into their component parts, but that retain their original sociopolitical links. A decision to support the refugees must be informed by an awareness of the warriors' aims. On this basis, a choice can be made to support one group of refugees but not the others (e.g., SWAPO-Namibians or Nicaraguan *contras*), whether bilaterally or through earmarked funding to the UNHCR. Another option is to recognize a humanitarian obligation to support the civilian population, regardless of the armed wing's political objectives. In that case, policy should at the very least desist from also supplying arms to the warriors and should actively support the peace agendas. The concept of a sustainable refugee policy is relevant here;[44] refugee policy must be measured against the yardstick that it does not directly contribute to the creation of future refugees by keeping alive the cycle of conflict.

A related issue concerns the provision of humanitarian assistance to the civilian populations in rebel-controlled territory within a country. Although this approach reduces the external "pull" and hence the number of international refugees,[45] it is also evident that across-the-border programs constitute a flagrant intervention in a country's internal affairs and so must be evaluated for both its political and its humanitarian implications.

Refugee-warrior communities, in sum, represent a transformation of refugees from being mere objects to being simultaneously actors and subjects in their own right. Although for the refugees this is in most respects a desirable development, for outside parties it complicates both aid policy and political-diplomatic approaches to the conflict's settlement.

Refugees and North–South Relations

The notion of an international refugee crisis that appeared in the early 1980s reflected a dual development. The coincidental crises in Afghanistan, Indochina, and the Horn of Africa, as well as the escalating war in Central America, generated massive refugee flows into neighboring countries. The developing countries demanded, first, that the rich countries of the North help carry this burden, either by taking in people or footing the bill, or a combination of both. Second, the industrialized countries themselves attracted large numbers of spontaneous asylum seekers from the developing world. Not only the United States, with its geographic proximity to Central America, but also Europe and Canada were confronted with flows of Third World nationals arriving uninvited and without papers, sometimes by the planeloads or by clandestine boat landings on their shores.[46]

The rapidly increasing demands for asylum from developing-country nationals created a profound reaction in the North, mainly in an exclusionary direction. It was argued that most of the asylum claims were spurious, representing a thinly disguised movement of "economic migrants" rather than "political refugees." The point was made plausible by travel patterns (as we have seen, migrants and refugees often used similar routes) and by historical timing: The increase in asylum applications lodged in Europe came after restrictive labor migration policies were introduced in the mid-1970s. To apply for refugee status was initially a relatively easy process, and in several countries the applicants received work permits and social service benefits while the application was pending. The system was obviously open to abuse and encouraged a political backlash against the very fundamentals of a liberal refugee policy in the North.

As indicated by the structural analysis of social conflict in the previous chapter, it is doubtful if the large numbers of refugees in the early 1980s were part of a steady, upward trend. On the other hand, patterns of violent social change remain, and even the most determined attack on root causes will not reduce refugee flows to a trickle. The challenge to liberal opinion in the industrialized states at this juncture is to formulate a critical, discriminatory, and yet just policy. By mid-decade, the responses were still working themselves out. Whatever final shape they eventually assume in the various national settings, the general parameters of a liberal refugee policy in the context of contemporary North–South relations seem clear enough.

The extremes must be ruled out. A completely open door would encourage a large-scale resettlement from the South to the North, something not even the most radical proposals for North–South reform envisage; to shut the door completely to asylum is equally untenable, and no country in fact takes this position. The moral obligation of the North to share the global asylum burden rests on its enormous resource capabilities relative to those of the South and on the transnational dynamics of social conflict in the contemporary world, which at least to some degree makes the North coresponsible for the upheavals in the South. A liberal asylum policy, moreover, is derived from the commonly accepted belief that if nations institutionalize an indifference to conflict and suffering elsewhere, the social fiber of their own societies will suffer. Finally, it seems self-evident that if liberal societies uphold as a moral imperative the right to escape violence, they must provide more than token asylum to victims of violence. In this sense, the right to asylum acquires the nature of a basic human right, as Amnesty International maintains.[47] The problems of devising a just selection process under conditions of triage constitute a separate issue; we submit that the degree of violence can be made the basis of selection whereby the most vulnerable are given preference.

The underlying obligation to provide asylum means that the rich countries cannot buy themselves out of a first asylum role simply by providing generous financial assistance to those developing countries that carry most of the first asylum burden, a practice known as the Japanese position, in reference to Japan's policy toward the Indochinese refugees.[48] Still, as long as the rich countries admit relatively few asylum seekers, the moral logic of a liberal refugee policy will demand that compensatory financial assistance be given to those that provide safe haven under conditions of extreme resource restraints.

It is within this general normative framework that the specifics of refugee policy in the industrialized states must be considered. The issue here at the forefront of the policy debate in Europe and North America in the 1980s concerned asylum determination.

The Asylum Challenge

For the North, the asylum question proved extremely vexing. It came on top of existing demands for resettlement places for Indochinese quota refugees and new demands from the UNHCR and ad hoc bodies such as the International Conference on Assistance to Refugees in Africa (ICARA) for aid to African refugees.[49] But the asylum seekers also appeared threatening because their arrival was uncontrolled, in contrast with the quota refugees who were resettled in an organized way through the UNHCR. Asylum applications in Europe increased by 140 percent between 1983 and 1985, and in several countries the upward trend continued unabated.[50] In West Germany, which was a major recipient country, the upswing was even more dramatic (Table 2). Because West Germany, for

TABLE 2. Asylum Applications in the Federal Republic of Germany

1976: 11,123	1983: 19,700
1977: 16,416	1984: 35,300
1980: 107,825	1985: 73,300
1982: 37,423	1986: 94,500

Source: Compiled from UNHCR data, Geneva; Hans-Ingo von Pollen, "Die Entwicklung der Asylbewerberzahlen im Jahre 1983," Zeitschrift für Ausländergerecht und Ausländerpolitik, 2 (1984); Horst E. Theis, "Aktuelle Fragen des deutschen Asylverfahrens," Soziale Arbeit, April 1978, pp 145–53.

reasons of international relations, refused to recognize the division of Berlin as an international boundary, there was free access to West Germany via Berlin. This became a major gateway for asylum applicants from developing countries as well as East Germany and, along with a constitutionally grounded liberal asylum policy, made West Germany the main European destination for Third World applicants.

In the early 1980s a sizable number of Eastern Europeans (from Romania, Poland, and Hungary) were among the applicants, but the increase of non-European applicants was higher and had by mid-decade reversed the ratio completely. In 1985 there were fewer applicants from all of Eastern Europe than from Iran and Sri Lanka alone. The new influx threatened to transform the social composition of Western Europe's refugee population, which by mid-decade was overwhelmingly of European origin. About two-thirds of the then registered 700,000 refugees were from Eastern Europe; the second largest group was the Indochinese, who had come under controlled conditions as quota refugees; and the third group was the Latin Americans, most of whom had arrived under UNHCR auspices as quota refugees following the 1973 coup in Chile. By contrast, the new arrivals from the Middle East, Southwest Asia, and Africa were spontaneous (i.e., direct) asylum seekers. A few were given U.N. Convention refugee status; some were allowed to stay "on humanitarian grounds" (B-status); but the majority lived in a legal twilight, or as perpetual asylum seekers.[51] Increasingly, efforts were made to prevent them from lodging applications in the first place.

The exclusionist response in Europe took basically two administrative forms. One was typified by the British approach which emphasized preventing prospective asylees access to the border where they could submit an application. A characteristically "insular" approach, the policy took shape in 1985 and involved stringent visa requirements, additional difficulties of submitting asylum applications at the point of entry for those succeeding in breaking the initial barriers, and sanctions against carriers that transported individuals to Britain without proper papers.[52] The other approach was exemplified by West Germany's "open door" policy. For reasons of East–West relations, access to the border was kept open, but the legal-administrative process of asylum determination within was tightened after 1984. Previous liberal work and support schemes for the applicant while the case was pending were reduced; limitations on physical movement and poor living conditions were introduced; and the application process itself was speeded up.[53]

Another variation on the open door approach unfolded in the United States. The border with Mexico—the main gateway to the United States from the developing countries of the Americas—was, in practice, relatively open, and in contrast with Europe, residence and employment was fairly easy even without formal permits. As against this de facto openness was an increasingly selective interpretation of the new Refugee Act of 1980. Although the act universalized the criteria for refugees in the U.S. legislation, its implementation reflected partisan political considerations. During the Reagan administration, virtually no Salvadorans were given formal asylum status, and Haitians were regularly deported. Nevertheless, the Salvadorans kept coming, creating a curious dualism in refugee statistics. The official figures of arrivals from Latin America dwindled rapidly from an already diminutive 2,017 (FY 1981) to 602, 668, and 160 in the next three years. At the same time, it was estimated that 600,000 to 700,000 Salvadorans were illegally in the United States, having left their country after the intensified civil war but, according to U.S. official opinion, were not to be recognized as refugees, as they had left "for economic reasons."[54]

Each of the three approaches to asylum had its weaknesses. In the United States, the extreme politicization of asylum determination in contravention of existing legislation led to a formalistic policy divorced from law and social reality. The result was a gathering of civil protest that gave sanctuary to hundreds of thousands of illegal refugees. The U.S. sanctuary movement was the largest and most dramatic of this kind, but smaller movements also developed in various European countries to negate particular asylum decisions perceived as blatantly unjust.

A more fundamental threat to the liberal concept of asylum arose from the insular approach typified by British practice. By making it difficult for the applicant to reach a point where an application could be submitted, the policy jeopardized the very principle of asylum. In practice, it meant that the case for asylum often was not heard; carried to its logical extreme it would prevent all escape from violence.

Optimally, therefore, a liberal asylum policy must rest on a combination of an open door policy and a discriminating hearing process. Only by allowing a wide entry point is it possible to give a reasonable hearing to individuals claiming that they are refugees. On the other hand, the hearing process must be sufficiently sensitive to discriminate reasonably quickly among individuals with different validity claims. In practice, this suggests some version of the West German practice. Elements of the model have been adopted in some European countries, and the principle of "open door—discriminating process" furnished the guidelines for the development in 1987 of new refugee legislation in at least one Western European country.[55]

The incidence of spontaneous asylum seekers in industrialized states could be reduced by expanding the UNHCR's quota system, that is, controlled resettlement through the UNHCR of exiled populations deemed unlikely to be repatriated. For the asylee, a quota system means less uncertainty regarding the future; for the country of final settlement, it means greater control in the admissions process; and for the first asylum country, it means that asylum can be extended with some assurance that the refugee burden will eventually be shared. In all aspects, therefore, the quota system is a method of managing international refugee flows in a humane and equitable manner.

In the past, the main developing-country refugees to come under a quota were the Indochinese and the Chileans after the 1973 coup. Both groups had powerful supporters abroad which made it possible to organize large-scale resettlement. Without such support, the UNHCR can only establish smaller quota refugee programs, as it has done for some political prisoners and for a few Iranians in the 1980s and has tentatively explored for the Tamils.[56] In the absence of political will in the North, large schemes cannot be implemented, including a distribution of asylees and refugees worldwide according to some criterion of wealth and responsibility by the receiving countries.[57]

Well-meaning concern to develop an equitable sharing formula must not ignore the basic fact that not all developing country refugees will want to be resettled in the industrialized North. Although the figures of Third World asylum seekers in Europe and North

America seem large to the receiving societies, they represent only a tiny fraction of the global refugee population. In reality, only a small minority of refugees seeks asylum and/or resettlement outside its region of origin. The large Central American inflow to North America appears exceptional in this respect. As the African and Asian records show, there are many reasons why refugees wish to remain in the region, including sociocultural familiarity, political activism, and the hope of quick repatriation. Large-scale resettlement outside the region cannot be a preferred solution, as the UNHCR stressed after its experience with the Indochinese program.[58]

Nor should it be forgotten that developing countries generally have been willing to accept the major part of the global asylum burden. Only in two cases have there been significant protests. After the latter half of the 1970s, Mexico and the Central American states wanted the United States to accept a greater share of the refugees fleeing civil strife in El Salvador, Guatemala, and Nicaragua, the rationale being that the United States was rich, close, and in large part responsible for the conflicts generating the refugees.[59] Except for the geographic factor, a similar reasoning was invoked by the noncommunist Southeast Asian countries to refuse long-term asylum to Indochinese refugees. Their resolve was demonstrated with much effectiveness, by towing refugee boats out to sea.

Given the inescapable reality that the majority of the developing countries' refugees will remain in the South, the richer states must, at a minimum, accept a greater financial obligation to assist the countries of first asylum in the South. The division of labor has a historical precedent: After World War II, a war-devastated Western Europe demanded that the resource-rich North America absorb most of the financial outlays for refugee relief, as Western Europe provided the asylum.[60] Four decades later, Europe, North America, Japan, and a handful of others constitute the resource-rich North and must pay accordingly, not only on ethical grounds, but also to reduce social conflict in recipient countries that could compound the refugee problem. The concept of a sustainable refugee policy introduced in the discussion of refugee-warrior communities is relevant also in this respect: Refugee policy must be held up against the negative yardstick that at least it should not contribute to greater refugee flows in the future.

NOTES

Preface

1. William Petersen, "Migration. I Social Aspects," in *International Encyclopedia of the Social Sciences* (New York: Macmillan, 1968), vol. 10, pp. 286–92; Brinley Thomas, "Migration. II. Economic Aspects," ibid., pp. 292–300; Louise W. Holborn, "Refugees. I World Problems," ibid., vol. 13, pp. 361–73; Judith T. Shuval, "Refugees. II Adjustment and Assimilation," ibid., pp. 373–77. Note that the authors of the article on migration are men, on refugees women. Although the editors of the encyclopedia evidently thought of "migration" and "refugees" as wholly different subjects, Petersen pointedly rejects the "arbitrary and misleading definition" of migration adopted by the United Nations in 1953, which deliberately excluded refugees, and points out that refugees constitute a large portion of total international population movements (p. 290). Brinley Thomas makes a similar observation, but then goes on to focus exclusively on nonrefugee movements. Consequently nowhere in the encyclopedia is there a discussion of the causes of refugees.

2. E. F. Kunz, "The Refugee in Flight: Kinetic Models and Forms of Displacement," *International Migration Review* 7, 2 (Summer 1973), pp. 125–46.

3. Barry N. Stein and Sylvano M. Tomasi (eds.), "Refugees Today," *International Migration Review* 15, 53/54 (Spring–Summer 1981); and Gilburt D. Loescher and John A. Scanlan, "The Global Refugee Problem: U.S. and World Response," *The Annals* 467 (May 1983). The latter contains A. R. Zolberg, "The Formation of New States as a Refugee-generating Process," pp. 24–38.

4. Charles B. Keely, *Global Refugee Policy: The Case for a Development-Oriented Strategy* (New York: Population Council, 1981), p. 25.

5. Leon Gordenker, *Refugees in International Politics* (New York: Columbia University Press, 1987).

6. Aristide R. Zolberg, "Contemporary Transnational Migrations in Historical Perspective: Patterns and Dilemmas," and Astri Suhrke, "Global Refugee Movements and Strategies of Response," in Mary M. Kritz (ed.), *U.S. Immigration and Refugee Policy: Global and Domestic Issues* (Lexington, Mass.: Heath, 1983).

7. Sergio Aguayo, *El Exodo Centroamericano: Consecuencias de un Conflicto* (Mexico, D.F.: Consejo Nacional de Fomento Educativo, 1985).

8. "Social Conflict and Refugees in the Third World: The Cases of Ethiopia and Afghanistan," unpublished manuscript, 1984.

283

9. See *Refugees: Dynamics of Displacement: A Report for the Independent Commission on International Humanitarian Issues* (London: Zed Books, 1986).

10. "International Factors in the Formation of Refugee Movements," in Dennis Gallagher (ed.), "Refugees: Issues and Directions," *International Migration Review* 20, 2 (Summer 1986), pp. 151–69. Gallagher also enabled us to present our ideas to the Washington refugee community at the Carnegie Endowment in Washington in February 1985.

11. Presentations were given at the Eighth Annual Legal Conference on Immigration and Refugee policy organized by the Center for Migration Studies (CMS) in Washington, D.C., March 1985; at a conference on "Sociology of Exile" convened by Peter Rose at Smith College the following May; and at the July 1985 meetings of the International Political Science Association in Paris. The CMS paper was published as Aristide R. Zolberg and Astri Suhrke, "Genesis of Refugee Movements in the Third World: Implications for U.S. Policy," in Lydio F. Tomasi (ed.), *In Defense of the Alien,* vol. 8 (New York: Center for Migration Studies, 1986), pp. 150–59.

Chapter 1

1. Jacques Vernant, *The Refugee in the Post-War World* (London: Allen & Unwin, 1953), p. 5.

2. Guy S. Goodwin-Gill, *The Refugee in International Law* (Oxford, England: Clarendon Press, 1983), pp. 5–6.

3. *Le Petit Robert* (Paris: Société du Nouveau Littré, 1978), p. 1641.

4. Unless otherwise indicated, the material in this section is drawn from Aristide R. Zolberg, "State-Formation and Its Victims: Refugee Movements in Early Modern Europe," presented as a Verhaegen Lecture at Erasmus University, Rotterdam, 1982. The successive waves originating in the Low Countries over the century extending from the 1540s to the 1630s probably amounted to the largest flow of European refugees on record in relation to the country of origin's population size. Overall, it entailed the relocation of about one-fifth of the population of the southern provinces that remained under Spanish rule (approximately contemporary Belgium) to the northern ones, which in 1609 gained their independence as the United Provinces (approximately contemporary Netherlands).

5. *Oxford English Dictionary* (Oxford, England: Oxford University Press, 1971), p. 2468.

6. Major sources used include Janine Garrisson, *L'Edit de Nantes et Sa Révocation: Histoire d'une Intolérance* (Paris: Seuil, 1985); *Les Huguenots* (Paris: Archives Nationales, 1985); Emmanuel LeRoy Ladurie, "Avant-Propos" to Bernard Cottret, *Terre d'Exil. L'Angleterre et Ses réfugiés, 16e–17e siècles* (Paris: Aubier, 1985), pp. 1–52.

7. It has been suggested that in between 950 and 1250, Western Europe "witnessed a fundamental and irreversible experience in the attitude to deviants," leading to the formation of a "persecuting society" that is "the forerunner and origin of the atrocities of the religious wars and executions of the Reformation period, and the Holocaust of the twentieth century." (M. T. Clanchy, in *Times Literary Supplement,* January 11–17, 1987, p. 990, reviewing R. I. Moore, *The Formation of a Persecuting Society* (Oxford, England: Blackwell, 1986). On absolutism, see especially Perry Anderson, *Lineages of the Absolutist State* (London: New Left Books, 1974).

8. *Refugees,* September 1985, p. 17.

9. Aristide R. Zolberg, "International Migrations in Political Perspective," in Mary M. Kritz, Charles B. Keely, and Silvano M. Tomasi (eds.), *Global Trends in Migration: Theory and Research on International Population Movements* (New York: Center for Migration Studies, 1981), pp. 5–7.

10. There is little doubt that the Nazis' original objective with respect to Jews in Germany and later in the Europe they controlled was expulsion. The unwillingness of most other countries, including the leading liberal democracies, to take in Jewish refugees is well documented also. What is less clear is the precise role that the unavailability of an alternative place for the Jews played in shifting Nazi policy to the "final solution." On these matters, see Hannah Arendt, *The Origins of*

Totalitarianism (New York: Harcourt Brace Jovanovich, 1973), esp. pp. 269–90; David S. Wyman, *Paper Walls: America and the Refugee Crisis* (Amherst, Mass.: University of Massachusetts Press, 1968); and David S. Wyman, *The Abandonment of the Jews. America and the Holocaust, 1941–1945* (New York: Pantheon Books, 1984).

11. Orlando Patterson, *Slavery and Social Death: A Comparative Study* (Cambridge, Mass.: Harvard University Press, 1982).

12. Eric J. Hobsbawm, *The Age of Revolution, 1789–1848* (New York: Mentor, 1962).

13. *Oxford English Dictionary,* 1971, p. 24681.

14. Robert R. Palmer, *The Age of Democratic Revolution* (Princeton, N.J.: Princeton University Press, 1959), p. 188.

15. Ibid., p. 188. Unfortunately, Palmer does not provide the data on which he bases this estimate. It is noteworthy that he uses his finding to argue that "there was a real revolution in America, and that it was a painful conflict, in which many were injured."

16. A. R. Zolberg, "The Roots of American Refugee Policy," *Social Research* 55, 4 (Winter 1989), pp. 649–78.

17. Michael R. Marrus, *The Unwanted: European Refugees in the Twentieth Century* (New York: Oxford University Press, 1985), p. 15. Unless otherwise indicated, information on nineteenth-century European refugee flows is drawn from this work.

18. Ibid., p. 20.

19. On the transportation of the Irish to Australia, see Robert Hughes, *The Fatal Shore* (New York: Vintage, 1988), pp. 181–202.

20. Marrus, *The Unwanted,* p. 24.

21. This analysis is broadly drawn from Karl Polanyi, *The Great Transformation* (Boston: Beacon Press, 1957); and Geoffrey Barraclough, *Introduction to Contemporary History* (Baltimore: Penguin, 1967).

22. The expression "unmixing of peoples" has been attributed to Lord Curzon, with reference to the Balkan Wars (Marrus, *The Unwanted,* p. 41).

23. Hannah Arendt, *The Origins of Totalitarianism,* new ed. (New York: Harcourt Brace Jovanovich, 1973), p. 290. For a fuller discussion of her contribution, see Zolberg, "The Formation of New States."

24. Arendt, *Origins,* p. 275.

25. Ibid., p. 268.

26. Their predicament was compounded when the great powers imposed on the newly created states a variety of minorities treaties as a condition for their recognition, with additional guarantees by an outside body, the League of Nations. As a result, the minorities were blamed for preventing the new states from achieving the full national sovereignty to which they aspired.

27. Arendt, *Origins,* p. 278.

28. Ibid., p. 269.

29. In particular, most of the formally stateless Europeans originated in Russia and included many antirevolutionary émigrés of Russian nationality ("White Russians"). They came under the protection of the high commissioner for Russian refugees and were accorded "Nansen" passports under the League of Nations. Arendt's suggestion that anti-Semitism was more virulent in the "successor states" than elsewhere is surely questionable. For example, during the interwar period, Jews achieved full citizenship in both Poland and Hungary and, despite the prevalence of anti-Semitism, participated prominently in their economic, cultural, and political life. Their situation in Russia improved after the revolution as well. And finally, it is hardly necessary to point out that Germany, where the doctrine of national rights was developed most systematically, was hardly a "successor" state.

30. Marrus, *The Unwanted,* p. 34.

31. Ibid., pp. 33–35.

32. Ibid., pp. 40–50.

33. Ibid., pp. 96–106.

34. Greek acquired Thessaly in 1881, Crete in 1908, and Macedonia—whose population was about evenly divided between Greek Orthodox and Muslims, which were the administrative categories used throughout this episode—plus several important islands as the result of the Balkan wars in 1913.

35. Signed on January 30, 1923, the convention was to become official upon the conclusion of a peace treaty, which in fact took place about a year and a half later, providing for the return of Western Thrace to Turkey.

36. Sources for the Armenian case include Marrus, *The Unwanted,* pp. 75–81; Robert Melson, "A Theoretical Inquiry into the Armenian Massacres of 1894–1896," *Comparative Studies in Society and History,* 24, 3 (July 1982), pp. 481–509; Leo Kuper, *Genocide* (New Haven, Conn.: Yale University Press, 1981), pp. 101–19; Philip D. Curtin, *Cross-Cultural Trade in World History* (Cambridge, England: Cambridge University Press, 1984), pp. 179–206.

37. Kuper, *Genocide,* p. 118.

38. Eugene M. Kulisher, *Europe on the Move, War and Population Changes, 1917–1947* (New York: Columbia University Press, 1948), p. 51 and n. 50.

39. U.S. Bureau of the Census, *Historical Statistics of the United States, Colonial Times to 1957* (Washington, D.C.: U.S. Government Printing Office, 1960), Series C 88–114, pp. 56–59.

40. Arendt points out that the Nazis relied heavily on such collusion for the pursuit of their policies (*Origins,* p. 269 and footnote on same page. See also Wyman, *Paper Walls;* and Henry L. Feingold, *The Politics of Rescue: The Roosevelt Administration and the Holocaust, 1938–1945* (New Brunswick, N.J.: Rutgers University Press, 1970).

41. Marrus, *The Unwanted,* pp. 53–61; Kulisher, *Europe on the Move,* pp. 54–56. As the armies fell back before German advances, huge masses of panicked civilians followed in their wake. Moreover, like their Ottoman counterparts, the tsarist authorities forcibly relocated two large population groups that might welcome the Germans as liberators—the Jews of the Pale and the Volga Germans, descendants of eighteenth-century colonists. Dumped into regions already suffering from war-induced deprivation, these unwelcome strangers were usually set upon by the local population.

42. Kulisher, *Europe on the Move,* p. 97.

43. Alan Dowty, *Closed Borders: The Contemporary Assault on Freedom of Movement* (New Haven, Conn.: Yale University Press, 1987), pp. 63–67.

44. Ibid., p. 68.

45. In addition to Dowty, see the discussion by Albert O. Hirschman, "Exit, Voice, and the State," in his *Essays in Trespassing: Economics to Politics and Beyond* (Cambridge, England: Cambridge University Press, 1981), pp. 246–65.

46. Recent cases in point are Indochina and Cuba, as discussed in the regional chapters. Other instances include a plea from the government of the Crown Colony of Hong Kong to China and some strong signals from the West to Polish general Wojciech Jaruzelski in 1983. The terms *confusion* and *dilemma* were used by William Shawcross in reference to the Western positions at the 1979 conference on Indochinese refugees, in *The Quality of Mercy, Cambodia, and Holocaust and Modern Conscience* (New York: Simon & Schuster, 1985), pp. 93–94.

47. Marrus, *The Unwanted,* p. 51; Kulisher, *Europe on the Move,* pp. 248–49.

48. These are not mutually exclusive: The United States, for example, simultaneously prohibited immigration from Asia and in World War II persecuted Japanese citizens.

49. *Welfare agencies* is a short-hand term referring to both the private and public sectors and to both local and national governments. For a more extensive theoretical discussion, see Zolberg, "International Migrations," pp. 3–27; and A. R. Zolberg, "Dilemmas at the Gate," paper presented at the American Political Science Association meeting, Denver, 1982. Some of the empirical details are presented in A. R. Zolberg, "International Migration Policies in a Changing World System," in William H. McNeill and Ruth S. Adams (eds.), *Human Migration: Patterns and Policies* (Bloomington: Indiana University Press, 1978), pp. 265–79. The United States and Germany led the way in the 1880s, one by means of measures explicitly directed against the importation

of contract labor from China—but in effect, prohibiting Chinese immigration altogether—and the other by barring the way to incoming Poles, including both agricultural workers and the Jewish exodus, as well as deporting many who had arrived earlier. In England, where nearly all controls on the entry of aliens had been swept away by the great wave of liberal reform, the arrival of poor Jews from the East in the 1880s, mostly in transit to the United States but of whom enough stayed behind to establish a substantial community in London, stimulated efforts to erect new barriers, culminating in the enactment of the restrictive Aliens Act in 1906. This was reinforced in 1910 and made much more severe at the onset of World War I. The "white dominions" (Canada, Australia, New Zealand, and South Africa) followed suit.

50. The explanation for French exceptionalism lies in the widely shared concern of elites with their declining population—particularly in the face of demographic growth in Germany—and subsequently exacerbated by the immense losses of men in World War I. In this perspective, immigration was seen as an asset rather than a liability. Most of the refugees were "White Russians."

51. E. P. Hutchinson, *Legislative History of American Immigration Policy 1798–1965* (Philadelphia: University of Pennsylvania Press, 1981), p. 108. Similar exonerations were included in subsequent legislation as well; however, the quota acts of the 1920s specifically did not accord priority of entry to refugees.

52. The concept of *international regime,* which has gained wide currency in the scholarly literature of international relations, refers to principles, norms, rules, and decision-making procedures around which actor expectations converge within a broad sphere of activity, such as international trade. For a recent discussion, see Stephen D. Krasner, "Regimes and the Limits of Realism: Regimes as Autonomous Variables," Krasner (ed.) *International Régimes* (Ithaca, N.Y.: Cornell University Press, 1983), pp. 1–22.

53. This amounted to 1.5 million within the first five years, after which Mussolini imposed restrictions on exit in the name of national pride and economic autarchy (Marrus, *The Unwanted,* p. 125).

54. Ibid., p. 130; Bismarck ordered a similar expulsion in 1885. On Poland between the wars, see Pawel Korzec, *Juifs en Pologne: La Question Juive Pendant l'Entre-Deux-Guerres* (Paris: Presses de la Fondation Nationale des Sciences Politiques, 1980).

55. Marrus, *The Unwanted,* p. 193.

56. Vernant, *The Refugee,* p. 25.

57. Ibid.

58. Louise W. Holborn, *Refugees: A Problem of Our Time: The Work of the United Nations High Commissioner for Refugees, 1951–1972* (Metuchen, N.J.: Scarecrow Press, 1975), p. 15.

59. Vernant, *The Refugee,* p. 6, n. 3.

60. Sir John Hope Simpson, *The Refugee Problem—Report of a Survey* (London: Oxford University Press, 1939), p. 4.

61. Louise W. Holborn, "The Legal Status of Political Refugees, 1920–1938," *American Journal of International Law,* 32 (1939), pp. 680–703.

62. Vernant, *The Refugee,* pp. 6–7, n. 31.

63. Ibid., p. 6.

64. Ibid., p. 7.

65. Kulisher, *Europe on the Move,* p. 305. Other surveys include two by Joseph B. Schechtman, *European Population Transfers, 1939–1945* (New York: Oxford University Press, 1946); and *Postwar Population Transfers in Europe, 1945–1955* (Philadelphia: University of Pennsylvania Press, 1962). There is also a summary in Marrus, *The Unwanted,* pp. 296–345.

66. Schechtman, *Postwar Population Transfers,* p. vii; Marrus, *The Unwanted,* p. 193.

67. This episode is the subject of Nikolai Tolstoi, *The Silent Betrayal* (New York: Scribner, 1978). Interest was revised by the publication in 1986 of the same author's *The Minister and the Massacre,* in which he asserts that the late Harold Macmillan bore a major responsibility for the return—a charge questioned by other historians (*New York Times,* June 10, 1986, and *The Economist,* August 23, 1986).

68. Marrus, *The Unwanted*, pp. 317–24.

69. Ibid., p. 341.

70. Vernant, *The Refugee*, p. 35.

71. Holborn, *Refugees*, p. 68.

72. Vernant, *The Refugee*, p. 40.

73. Nearly everything pertaining to numbers and causes of the Palestinian exodus is controversial. The estimates used here are from Janet L. Abu-Lughod, "The Demographic Transformation of Palestine," in Ibrahim Abu-Lughod (ed.), *The Transformation of Palestine* (Evanston, Ill.: Northwestern University Press, 1971), pp. 139–64; and Janet L. Abu-Lughod, "Palestinians: Exiles at Home and Abroad," *Current Sociology* (forthcoming, 1988). See also Laurie A. Brand, "Palestinians out of Palestine: An Examination of the Origins of the Palestinian Refugee Problem and the Status of Palestinians in Diaspora," paper presented at the Fourth International Conference on Refugees in the Islamic World, Bellagio, October 1987. On the conflict itself, see Simha Flapan, *The Birth of Israel: Myths and Realities* (New York: Pantheon, 1987), esp. pp. 83–118.

74. H. H. Ben-Sasson (ed.), *A History of the Jewish People* (Cambridge, Mass.: Harvard University Press, 1976), pp. 1066–77; H. H. Smith (ed.), *Israel: A Country Study* (Washington, D.C.: U.S. Government Printing Office, 1979), pp. 304–5.

75. See Edward H. Buehrig, *The UN and the Palestinian Refugees: A Study in Non-territorial Administration* (Bloomington: Indiana University Press, 1971); and David P. Forsythe, "The Palestine Question: Dealing with a Long-Term Refugee Situation," *Annals of the American Academy of Political and Social Science*, 467 (May 1983), pp. 89–101.

76. The signal importance of staff in this sense is also emphasized by David Kennedy in "International Refugee Protection," *Human Rights Quarterly*, 8 (1986), pp. 1–9.

77. Holborn, *Refugees*, pp. 73–77.

78. Ibid., pp. 76–77.

79. Goodwin-Gill, *The Refugee*, p. 6.

80. Atle Grahl-Madsen, *The Status of Refugees in International Law* (Leyden: Sijthoff, 1966), vol. 1, pp. 217–20.

81. Goodwin-Gill, *The Refugee*, pp. 270–76.

82. Two French constitutions (1946 and 1958) provide asylum to persons persecuted "by reason of actions in favor of liberty"; the German Federal Republic's basic law does so as well. The 1949 Hungarian Constitution states that foreign citizens "persecuted for their democratic attitude or their activities in the interest of the liberation of the peoples" will be given asylum, and Soviet law contains similar provisions. A number of developing countries do so as well.

83. A word of clarification is required here, as Marrus, *The Unwanted*, p. 358, has attributed this distinction to "Political scientist Aristide Zolberg." What Zolberg actually does in the 1983 article cited by Marrus ("The Formation," p. 26) is first to observe that such a distinction is inherent in the U.N. definition and then to characterize it as "valid and feasible." However, with respect to the latter point, research leading to the present book has led Zolberg to qualify his judgment.

84. Holborn, *Refugees*, p. 95.

85. Marrus, *The Unwanted*, pp. 360ff.

86. Leon Gordenker, *Refugees in International Politics* (New York: Columbia University Press, 1987), p. 39.

87. Goran Melander, *Flyktning i Norden* (Stockholm: Norstedt and Söners Forlag, 1979). For a more extensive discussion of these matters, see Astri Suhrke, "Global Refugee Movements and Strategies of Response," in Mary M. Kritz (ed.), *U.S. Immigration and Refugee Policy: Global and Domestic Issues* (Lexington, Mass.: Heath, 1983), pp. 157–62.

88. The development of postwar U.S. refugee policy is definitively treated in Gil Loescher and John A. Scanlan, *Calculated Kindness: Refugees and America's Half-Open Door, 1945–Present* (New York: Free Press, 1986).

89. National Security Council, "Psychological Value of Escapees from the Soviet Orbit," Security Memorandum, March 26, 1953.

90. Recent studies of the subject include Dennis Gallagher, Susan Forbes, and Patricia Weiss Fagen, *Of Special Humanitarian Concern: U.S. Refugee Admissions Since Passage of the Refugee Act* (Washington, D.C.: Refugee Policy Group, September 1985); and Norman Zucker and Naomi Zucker, *The Guarded Gate: The Reality of American Refugee Policy* (San Diego: Harcourt Brace Jovanovich, 1987), pp. 209–64.

91. Organization of American States, *Report on the Political Refugees in America;* Prepared by the Secretariat of the Inter-American Commission on Human Rights, OAS/Ser. L/V/II.11, doc. 7, rev. 2, September 1, 1965.

92. Albert Hirschman, *Exit, Voice, and Loyalty* (Cambridge, Mass.: Harvard University Press, 1972).

93. Hector Gros Espiel, "El Derecho Internacional Americano Sobre Asilo Territorial y Extradicion en Sus Relaciones con la Convenion de 1951 y el Protocol de 1967 Sobre Estatuto de los Refugiados," rev. 1, working document prepared for the May 1981 conference at UNAM, Mexico City.

94. Organization of American States, "Instrumentos Regionales en Materia de Asilo. Asilo Territorial y Extradicion. La Cuestion de los Refugiados ante las Posibilidades de una Nueva Codification Interamericana" (Preliminary study prepared by the Office of Development and Codification of International Law for the May 1981 conference at UNAM, Mexico). More ambitious suggestions advanced by semiofficial and private organizations call for the incorporation of the OAU's definition into the inter-American legal system.

95. Goodwin-Gill, *The Refugee,* p. 7.

96. Ibid., p. 8.

97. Ibid., p. 281.

98. Gordenker, *Refugees,* p. 40. The extension was occasioned by the formation of Bangladesh in 1971 and applied to people who crossed from East Pakistan into India; the within-country case referred to is Cyprus (1974).

99. Vernant, *The Refugee,* p. 3 (emphasis added).

100. In the same vein, it was asserted at a recent conference that "exiles must always be distinguished from refugees" because "they don't have the collective innocence of victims" (As reported in the *Times Literary Supplement,* May 15, 1987, p. 516).

101. A. Grahl-Madsen, "Identifying the World's Refugees," in *Annals of the American Academy of Political and Social Science,* 498 (May 1983), p. 13. A major source of ambiguity is that in the sphere of political dissent, it is often difficult to draw the line between a struggle to protect one's human rights and the commission of a crime. For example, many countries require military service of their citizens, and international law recognizes such requirements as legitimate, and so leaving one's country to escape punishment for refusing to serve is generally not admitted as grounds for according asylum. Yet there is also an ancient tradition of distinguishing between "just" and "unjust" wars, and since World War II it has become well established that under appropriate circumstances, citizens are morally obligated to refuse service to their state.

102. Vernant, *The Refugee,* p. 5.

103. The most recent comprehensive study of Irish emigration is by Kerby A. Miller, *Emigrants and Exiles: Ireland the Irish Exodus to North America* (New York: Oxford University Press, 1985).

104. Ladurie, "Avant-Propos," p. 48.

105. The crucial distinction between people who can be helped *in situ* and those who can be assisted only abroad is borrowed from Michael Walzer, "The Distribution of Membership," in Peter G. Brown and Henry Shue (eds.), *Boundaries: National Autonomy and Its Limits* (Totowa, N.J.: Rowan and Littlefield, 1981).

106. Although this is not our immediate concern, it should be noted that on the basis of the criteria established, asylum should be accorded to populations whose physical environment has

deteriorated to the point of being permanently unable to sustain life—as in cases of extreme desertification.

107. Andrew E. Sacknove, "Who Is a Refugee?" *Ethics* 95 (January 1985), pp. 274–85.

Chapter 2

1. *New York Times*, February 16, 1986, p. E3 (hereafter cited as *NYT*). Basic data are from U.S. Committee for Refugees, *World Refugee Survey: 1986 in Review* (Washington, D.C.: American Council for Nationalities Service, 1987) (hereafter cited as *WRS*, with appropriate year).

2. This stance was due to the persistence of a special regional framework founded on the common membership of these countries in ex-French West Africa. On the Guinean exodus, see Robert O. Matthews, "Refugees and Stability in Africa," *International Organization* 26, 1 (1972), p. 63. The estimate cited is from *Le Monde*, July 7 and September 17, 1982 (hereafter cited as *Monde*).

3. *NYT*, December 9, 1982; C. M. Eya Nchama, "La Décolonisation de la Guinée Equatoriale et le Problème des Réfugiés," *Genève-Afrique*, 20, 1 (1982), pp. 114–21.

4. The outflows from Nigeria involved about 2 million in 1983 and 700,000 in 1985 (some of them returnees from the first expulsion). The largest number were Ghanaian, with others from Benin, Chad, and Niger (*NYT*, May 13, 1985; *The Economist*, May 4, 1985). One of the earliest documented expulsions occurred in the Ivory Coast in 1958; see Aristide R. Zolberg, *One-Party Government in the Ivory Coast* (Princeton, N.J.: Princeton University Press, 1964), pp. 245–49; and Herschelle Sullivan Challenor, "Strangers as Colonial Intermediaries: The Dahomeyans in Francophone Africa," in William A. Shack and Elliot P. Skinner (eds.), *Strangers in African Societies* (Berkeley and Los Angeles: University of California Press, 1979), pp. 67–83.

5. This brutal displacement is continuing. See, for example, "Apartheid's Refugees Lose Ground to Bulldozers," *NYT*, May 29, 1986.

6. United Nations General Assembly, 41st sess., "Role of the Office of the United Nations High Commissioner for Refugees in Africa," JIU/REP/86/2, March 1986, p. 1.

7. For example, in the early nineteenth century, the southern part of the continent was engulfed in a process of competitive state-formation known as the *mfecane*, which drove escaping populations northward into what is today Zimbabwe. The Arab and European slave trades triggered innumerable flows of refugees, largely lost to history. The imposition of European rule in the late nineteenth and early twentieth centuries did so as well, as Africans periodically tried to escape the harsh exactions, which included forced labor, the diversion of agricultural activity from subsistence to cash crops, military service, and unaccustomed taxation. The subsequent reorganization of Africa into mutually exclusive territorial entities governed by competing European powers entailed the imposition of restrictions on international movement. From the time of imperial consolidation around the end of World War I until the end of the colonial period, Africans were for the most part confined to their territory of origin, except when their rulers promoted international labor migrations or allowed small numbers to seek education abroad.

8. Matthews, "Refugees," pp. 63–64. A more comprehensive estimate for 1966 enumerated a much higher total of 920,838 refugees for sub-Saharan Africa alone; see Hugh C. Brooks and Yassin El-Yahouty (eds.), *Refugees South of the Sahara: An African Dilemma* (Westport, Conn.: Negro Universities Press, 1970), pp. 293–95; 2,500 North African refugees in sub-Saharan Africa have been deducted from the figures cited therein. Aderanti Adepoju provided an earlier analytic overview similar to the present one; see his "The Dimension of the Refugee Problem in Africa," *African Affairs*, 81, 322 (1982), pp. 21–35.

9. Harold Nelson (ed.), *Nigeria: A Country Study* (Washington, D.C.: U.S. Government Printing Office, 1981), p. 60.

10. UNHCR figures as cited in W. T. S. Gould, "Refugees in Tropical Africa," *International Migration Review*, 8, 3 (1974), pp. 413–30.

11. In a letter to *NYT*, December 13, 1981.

12. The principal sources for this section include Thomas M. Callaghy, "The State as Lame Leviathan: The Patrimonial Administrative State in Africa," in Zaki Ergas (ed.), *The African State in Transition* (New York: Macmillan, 1986); Robert H. Jackson and Carl G. Rosberg, *Personal Rule in Black Africa: Prince, Autocrat, Prophet, Tyrant* (Berkeley and Los Angeles: University of California Press, 1982); John Lonsdale, "State and Social Process in Africa: A Historiographical Survey," *African Studies Review*, 24, 2–3 (June–September 1981), pp. 139–225; Crawford Young, "Patterns of Social Conflict: State, Class, and Ethnicity," *Deadalus*, 111, 2 (Spring 1982), pp. 71–98; Aristide R. Zolberg, *Creating Political Order* (Chicago: University of Chicago Press, 1985), A. R. Zolberg, "The Structure of Political Conflict in the New States of Tropical Africa," *American Political Science Review*, 62, 1 (1968), pp. 70–87.

13. See, for example, Ruth Berins Collier, *Regimes in Tropical Africa: Changing Forms of Supremacy, 1945–1975* (Berkeley and Los Angeles: University of California Press, 1982).

14. See note 12.

15. This point was made as early as 1966 with respect to Zaire: "If in order to maintain the political community as it was defined as of June 30, 1960, the Congo had been forced to rely exclusively on the operation of endogenous processes, this community would not have survived for very long after that date. . . . Much as a firm might go bankrupt in a completely free market, so the Congo might have disappeared as an entity in a neutral international environment. But the contemporary international political system is never neutral in this respect. The situation of a country like the Congo is more like that of a firm in a modern capitalist economy which can appeal to some government board to secure temporary or permanent protection against the free play of market forces. The final decision of the board can be viewed as one in which the firm itself participates . . . but in the main it is the result of an interplay of factors over which the firm itself has relatively little control. In this case, the board acted favorably." A. R. Zolberg, "A View from the Congo," *World Politics*, 19, 1 (October 1966), p. 143. Along similar lines, Robert H. Jackson and Carl G. Rosberg have drawn attention to the positive contribution of the international environment to the persistence of the new African states more generally, by ensuring their juridical existence. See their "Why Africa's Weak States Persist: The Empirical and the Juridical in Statehood," *World Politics*, 35, 1 (October 1982).

16. This section is based largely on Jack Goody, *Technology, Tradition, and the State in Africa* (Cambridge, England: Cambridge University Press, 1971); and Bill Freund, *The Making of Contemporary Africa: The Development of African Society Since 1800* (Bloomington: Indiana University Press, 1984). The plow, where it existed, increased the area that a person could cultivate and made possible the accumulation of a surplus. Hence it fostered fixed holdings, rendered land more valuable, and stimulated the growth of differences in wealth and life-styles. Without the plow, and because land was not scarce, land rights were less highly individualized, and so there was little incentive for accumulating land itself.

17. Goody points out (*Technology*, pp. 39–56) that in the savanna regions of Western Africa, for example, the possibility of horse life and the availability of iron weapons, initially through trans-Saharan trade, led to the emergence of a cavalry. Only the wealthy could maintain horses, but because among them all had equal access, the characteristic form of domination was an aristocracy founded on a differentiated stratum of noble warriors, as among the Fulani scattered along the southern shore of the Sahara from contemporary Mauretania to Cameroun. In the coastal regions, access to guns through involvement in the seaborne European trade, particularly in slaves, enabled political entrepreneurs to erect more centralized autocracies, as in Ashanti and Dahomey.

18. On the whole, African chiefs had greater difficulty maintaining their position under colonial conditions than had traditional rulers in other parts of the developing world whose status was anchored in property relations. Moreover, the domain of their authority usually encompassed only a small segment of the newly defined territory's population. But in some cases they were able to take advantage of their privileged situation to become landlords (e.g., Rwanda, Buganda).

19. The following points have been made by a number of observers. See especially Young, "Patterns of Social Conflict"; Jean-Loup Amselle and Elikia M'Bokolo (eds.), *Au Coeur de*

l'Ethnie: Ethnies, Tribalisme et État en Afrique (Paris: La Découverte, 1985); Aristide R. Zolberg, "Tribalism Through Corrective Lenses," *Foreign Affairs*, 51, 4 (July 1973). A more general analysis will be made in Chapter 9.

20. For more discussion of these variations, see Lionel Cliffe, "Rural Political Economy of Africa," in Peter C. W. Gutkind and Immanuel Wallerstein (eds.), *Political Economy of Contemporary Africa*, 2nd ed. (Beverly Hills, Calif.: Sage, 1985), p. 123. It should be noted that the Kenya Highlands, parts of the Belgian Congo, and prewar Ivory Coast also experienced the "southern Africa" pattern. The argument is not that the patterns that actually came into being were intended as such from the first. As with the workers in the process of industrialization, Africans sometimes played a part in determining the outcome (e.g., Ivory Coast, Kenya).

21. Kenya deviated slightly from the general model with respect to timing. The repressive phase lasted until the mid-1950s, and it was only in 1960 that the British acknowledged Jomo Kenyatta as an *interlocuteur valable*.

22. Frederick Cooper, "Africa and the World Economy," *African Studies Bulletin*, 24, 2–3 (June–September, 1981), p. 84.

23. For a discussion of the processes leading to military takeover, see, for example, A. R. Zolberg, "The Military Decade in Africa," *World Politics*, 25, 2 (January 1973), pp. 309–31.

24. Prominent advocates of the military as a stabilizer include Ernest W. Lefever, *Spear and Scepter: Army, Police, and Politics in Tropical Africa* (Washington, D.C.: Brookings Institution, 1970); and Samuel P. Huntington, *Political Order in Changing Societies* (New Haven, Conn.: Yale University Press, 1968). Bureaucratic authoritarianism is discussed in Chapters 7, 8, and 9.

25. Leaving aside the Republic of South Africa, the highest-ranking African country is currently the People's Republic of the Congo, which appears as no. 64 on the World Bank's list of 119 reporting countries. See International Bank for Reconstruction and Development, *World Development Report 1987* (New York: Oxford University Press, 1987), p. 202.

26. Goran Hyden, *Beyond Ujaama* (Berkeley and Los Angeles: University of California Press, 1980; and Goran Hyden, *No Shortcuts to Progress* (Berkeley and Los Angeles: University of California Press, 1983).

27. FAO estimate cited in *Monde*, September 7–8, 1986, p. 13.

28. Jackson and Rosberg, *Personal Rule*, pp. 80–81.

29. The principal sources for this section are René Lemarchand and David Martin, *Selective Genocide in Burundi* (London: Minority Rights Group, 1974); Jean-Pierre Chrétien, "Hutu et Tutsi au Rwanda et au Brundi," in Amselle and M'Bokolo (eds.), *Au Coeur*, pp. 143–66; Claudine Vidal, "Situations Ethniques au Rwanda," in Amselle and M'Bokolo (eds.), *Au Coeur*, pp. 167–84; M. Catherine Newbury, "Colonialism, Ethnicity, and Rural Political Protest: Rwanda and Zanzibar in Comparative Perspective," *Comparative Politics*, 15, 3 (April 1983), pp. 253–80; René Lemarchand, *Rwanda and Burundi* (New York: Praeger, 1970). For the most recent period, these are supplemented by annual volumes of *Africa Contemporary Record* (New York: Africana Publishing, misc. years) (hereafter cited as *ACR*).

30. Bantu languages generally use different prefixes to denote the land (e.g., *Bu*rundi, *Bu*ganda), its people (the *Wa*tusi, *Ba*hutu, *Ba*ganda; sing. *Mu*tusi, and the like; and their language (e.g., *Ki*swahili). It is now acceptable in general writing to use the root alone (Tusi, Hutu, Ganda, Swahili) for most purposes.

31. On the significance of the locus of origin, see Newbury, "Colonialism," p. 270. In the ensuing sweep, the Belgians arrested many more Tutsi than Hutu. Whether the Belgians' behavior was due to a sheer lack of means or was a Machiavellian move remains moot; see Lemarchand, *Rwanda and Burundi*, p. 167.

32. USCR estimates in Brooks and El-Yahouty (eds.), *Refugees*, pp. 293–95.

33. Edward Bustin, "The Congo," in Brooks and El-Yahouty (eds.), *Refugees*, p. 187. The uprising referred to occurred in the Kwilu area of Zaire in 1964–65 under the leadership of Pierre Mulele, strongly influenced by Maoist doctrine. Its ethnic base was among the Mbun and Pende;

see Irving Kaplan (ed.), *Zaire: A Country Study* (Washington, D.C.: U.S. Government Printing Office, 1979), pp. 147–48.

34. The proclamation of a republic led to an improvement of relations with Rwanda. In 1967, they agreed—together with Zaire—that armed refugees should lay down their weapons within a month and would be allowed to return home without punishment, albeit not forced to do so. However, in 1968 Zaire broke off relations with Rwanda following Kayibanda's refusal to hand over white mercenaries who had fled from Bukavu the previous November (ACR 1968–69, p. 193).

35. Lemarchand's estimate in *Rwanda and Burundi* is 80,000 to 100,000; Warren Weinstein cites 100,000 to 150,000, in a review article in *Journal of Modern African Studies*, 14, 1 (1976), p. 161; 80,000 to 200,000 is from Leo Kuper, *Genocide: Its Political Use in the Twentieth Century* (New Haven, Conn.: Yale University Press, 1981), p. 164 (from Victor D. DuBois). It should be noted that a debate arose concerning the role of the United States in the tragedy. Roger Morris (as cited in Weinstein, "Review") has contended that the United States, which at the time provided 80 percent of the market for Burundi's coffee, could have restrained Micombero's government by threatening a boycott, but this is very unlikely. Weinstein agrees with the judgment of most journalists that the U.S. ambassador could have done much more by alerting international opinion. The ambassador himself denies this. See Thomas Patrick Melady, *Burundi: The Tragic Years* (New York: Orbis Books, 1974). Lemarchand points out that the U.S. embassy provided whatever little international publicity the situation received at the time. All of them, however, are critical of the OAU, which justified its passivity on the grounds this was a purely internal matter.

36. Details of international support can be found in Lemarchand and Martin, *Selective Genocide*, pp. 19, 29. Viewing the uprising as a continuation of the Mulelist rebellion, Zaire sent its army to help Micombero ensure control of the capital. France, seeking to expand its influence within francophonic Africa, provided helicopters and pilots. Tanzania, in an apparent misunderstanding, supplied small arms and ammunition; and some assistance was forthcoming from China and North Korea as well.

37. *ACR*, 1974–75, p. B255; 1977–78, p. B175.

38. *WRS*, 1986.

39. *WRS*, 1985, p. 42.

40. As reported by René Lemarchand in *Africa South of the Sahara* (London: Europa Publications, 1985), pp. 247–48.

41. As reported in *ACR*, 1979–80, Burundi may have in fact allowed Libyan aircraft to land while reinforcing the faltering Amin regime (p. B156). During the war between Idi Amin and Tanzania, reports that three thousand Hutu refugees were fighting on the Tanzanian side gave rise to rumors that as many as thirty thousand were armed and trained for an invasion of Burundi. Conversely, Hutu refugees in Rwanda accused the Burundian army of providing aid to Amin's forces and of enlisting Tutsi refugees in Uganda for attacks on their camps.

42. *Monde*, October 6, 1982, as quoted in *ACR*, 1982–83, p. B107. The reports of returns are from *WRS*, 1985, p. 42. See also report in *NYT*, June 4, 1987, and letter from former Ambassador T. P. Melady, June 17, 1987.

43. Reports in *Monde*, September 6–7, 8, 11, 30; *NYT*, September 4, 20; *Le Monde Diplomatique*, October 1987, p. 12.

44. *WRS*, 1986.

45. *NYT*, March 29, 1984, p. 8.

46. *ACR*, 1981–82, p. B242. In 1981, Rwanda revised its nationality law to allow Hutu refugees from Burundi to become permanent residents, but it was reported later that refugees or even their Rwanda-born children were not allowed to become citizens. In June 1985, troops fired on a group of refugees, but this appears to have been an isolated incident.

47. Historical background is from Harold D. Nelson (ed.), *Sudan: A Country Study*, 3rd ed. (Washington, D.C.: U.S. Government Printing Office, 1982). The interpretation of the first Sudanese civil war is drawn mostly from Crawford Young, *The Politics of Cultural Pluralism* (Ma-

dison: University of Wisconsin Press, 1976), pp. 489–501, which is itself founded on the major secondary literature available as of 1975.

48. The famous Charles Gordon, who as military governor of Khartoum in the 1870s effectively interdicted upstream transport of human beings, was dispatched to Khartoum with orders to organize the evacuation of Egyptians and foreigners. Upon arriving, however, he determined that withdrawal was impossible without reinforcements, and despite the absence of support from London, he remained in Khartoum on the grounds that Sudan was vital to the security of Egypt. This prompted the sending of a relief column which, as is well known, arrived too late.

49. Consideration was even given to separating the region from Sudan altogether, linking it perhaps with Uganda or making it into a separate colonial entity within an East African federation to be ruled from Nairobi.

50. Young, *Cultural Pluralism*, p. 496.

51. Counts vary; the *WRS*, 1985, refers to eleven thousand Sudanese refugees who have been in Ethiopia for over ten years (p. 49).

52. The basic source for the period to mid-1984 is the report by Charles Meynell in Minority Rights Group, Report no. 66, *Uganda and the Sudan* (December 1984), pp. 22–27. The author of this section (A. Zolberg) also benefited from participating in the Conference on the Horn of Africa held at the Wilson Center, Washington, D.C., June 17–20, 1987. In keeping with conference rules, however, draft papers are not cited directly.

53. "Sudan: Return to Arms," in *Africa* (London), April 1984, p. 9.

54. "Introduction" (dated October 1982), in Nelson (ed.), *Sudan*, p. ii.

55. Interview with Joseph Oduho, Paris representative of SPLM, in *Le Monde*, April 27, 1984.

56. Information based on dispatches by Judith Miller in *NYT*, May 6, and Agence France-Presse, as reported in *Monde*, May 9, 1984.

57. *WRS*, 1985, p. 49.

58. See the series by Eric Rouleau in *Monde*, December 23–26, 1984. Following a series of strikes by members of the leading professions in April 1984, Nimeiri imposed a state of emergency and subsequently replaced his cabinet by a "Council of the Republic" as a prelude to the proclamation of an Islamic constitution. Waves of arrests followed, with offenders brought before special tribunals, and there were amputations and floggings under *sharia* law. In the face of this, Nimeiri's lone remaining ally, the Muslim Brotherhood, distantiated themselves from him as well. In a desperate attempt to gain other friends, Nimeiri then abandoned the Islamic constitution project, rescinded the state of emergency, and released some of his opponents, most prominently Sadek el Mahdi. In the early months of 1985 it was rumored that the implementation of *sharia* law would be suspended, but in late January a seventy-six year old moderate opposition leader was publicly hanged on grounds of heresy.

59. Judith Miller, in *NYT*, April 15, 1985.

60. Their stance was ambiguous; following a reported Libyan air raid on Omdurman in March 1984, Egypt sent troops to guard Sudanese airports, and Washington dispatched two AWACS and stepped up the delivery of military matériel via Egypt. But Meynell (*Uganda and the Sudan*) states that by this time, "several members of Mubarak's government . . . regarded Nimeiri as a liability" and reports that the following June, President Reagan's roving ambassador General Vernon Walters told Washington "that it was no longer possible to reason with Nimeiri" (p. 26).

61. The basis account is from the series by Eric Rouleau, "Le Printemps Soudanais," in Monde, June 18, 19, 20, 1984. To what extent, if any, the United States played a hand in these events or was consulted in advance by military leaders, is not clear.

62. Diplomatic ties with Ethiopia were restored in June 1985, and a military pact was struck with Libya in July, causing considerable concern in Washington. Given the geopolitical situation, Ethiopia controls almost entirely the delivery of arms and supplies to the insurgents and offers them their only safe haven. *The Economist* pointed out that Ethiopia exercised much more control over Garang than the Sudanese did over the Eritrean and Tigrean insurrections, which benefited from a

wide network of international support from Arab and Western countries (May 18, 1985). On the U.S. response to the rapprochement with Libya, see *The Economist*, July 19, 1986, p. 23.

63. Emerging as the leader with 97 out of 301 seats was the nationalist Umma party, based in the western provinces of Darfur and Khodorfan and drawing strength from the Ansar religious movements that have followed Sadek's family since the days of the Mahdi. Next was the Democratic Unionist party, a front for the rival Khatmyia, under the leadership of the pro-Egyptian Mirghani family, with 64 seats, leaving the Muslim Brotherhood's Islamic Front a distant third with 28 seats.

64. Jean Gueyras in *Monde*, June 10, 1987.

65. Sheila Rule in *NYT*, June 6, 8, 1986. In the early months of 1987 there were further reports of wholesale massacres of Dinka villagers as far north as Darfur Province, at the hands of government-equipped Rizagat tribal militias (*Monde*, April 17 and May 14, 1987).

66. Notably the Acholis, who straddle the border between Sudan and Uganda, wreaked vengeance on Ugandan refugee camps from which UNHCR had evacuated its personnel (see the section on Uganda).

67. "Le paradis perdu de Juba," in *Monde*, June 15–16, 1986.

68. The famine continued, not only because of the inherent difficulties of transport under conditions of civil war; there also was a tug-of-war over the delivery of food to besieged Wau, swollen with a huge refugee population, where order had broken down as people fought for the little food that was available. Food became a weapon in another sense, in that the government organized the Mundari into a 40,000-man-strong armed militia in return for food supplies (*The Economist*, April 18, 1987). There were also reports that whatever little food got to the south was seized by hungry soldiers, and the SPLA charged that the government moved in troops and supplies under cover of food relief; this was confirmed by Oxfam (*Monde*, February 11, 1988).

69. UNHCR Refugee Update, June 18, 1987. The UNHCR reported that prompt emergency responses and effective cooperation between the government and the various international agencies as well as NGOs enabled the refugees to achieve and maintain good standards in health, nutrition, and shelter.

70. The principal sources for this case study are Christian Bouquet, *Tchad: Genèse d'un Conflit* (Paris: L'Harmattan, 1982), covering the period to 1979; Robert Buijtenhuijs, *Le Frolinat et les Révoltes Populaires du Tchad, 1965–1976* (The Hague: Mouton, 1978), which stops in about 1976; and René Lemarchand, "The Politics of Sara Ethnicity: A Note on the Origins of the Civil War in Chad," *Cahiers d'Etudes Africaines* (1980), pp. 449–71. Mr. Buijtenhuijs kindly supplied additional comments in an interview with A. Zolberg in Paris, January 1984. Information on more recent developments is taken from appropriate volumes of *Africa Contemporary Reports* and press reports in the *New York Times, Le Monde,* and *The Economist*.

71. Following a confrontation at Fashoda (Sudan) in 1899, Britain and France settled matters by agreeing that the Nile basin would go to one and the Lake Chad basin to the other. After various administrative experiments, in the late 1930s, present-day Chad was demarcated as an administrative entity within French Equatorial Africa.

72. The account is based on Bernard Lanne, *Tchad: La Querelle des Frontières* (Paris: Karthala, 1982).

73. Although the French parliament enacted a law authorizing the president of the republic "to ratify and, if the occasion arises, to implement" the treaty, Franco-Italian relations deteriorated after the invasion of Ethiopia and the negotiation of the Rome–Berlin "axis." In 1938 Italy renounced the agreement as falling short of its imperial ambitions.

74. In 1955 Libya and France signed a "good neighbor" treaty, providing for recognition of boundaries as specified in prior agreements, which made no reference to the 1935 instrument.

75. The demographic data in this section are estimates from the "human geography" elaborated by Bouquet (*Tchad*, pp. 163–75), who points out that after independence the authorities prohibited all independent research on the distribution of ethnic groups but publicized partial reports of official studies that implied that the southerners constituted a majority.

76. As is often the case in Africa, Sara is a recently constructed term, which probably originated as a reference to peoples from the region who fell into the hands of slave traders. It then gained currency during the colonial period to designate the whole of the local populations and finally came to be used by the populations themselves "as a symbol of their common cultural and social awareness, and as the hall-mark of their political solidarities in the face of continuing threat from the Muslim North." (Lemarchand, "The Politics of Sara Ethnicity," p. 452.

77. The heaviest demands were made during the construction of the railroad linking Brazzaville to Pointe-Noire in the interwar period, when as much as half of the labor force perished. A substantial number were also recruited by the Free French for service in North America and Europe, creating a body of dissatisfied veterans who became involved in collective action in the postwar period.

78. According to a former French official, P. Hugot, as quoted in Lemarchand, "The Politics of Sara Ethnicity," p. 456.

79. In 1946, for example, the Sara community of Fort-Lamy petitioned for the removal of the incumbent French governor, "the man . . . who dared order an inordinate increase in cotton plantings year after year, to the detriment of subsistence crops. . . ." (Quoted in ibid., p. 456).

80. Buijtenhuijs, *Le Frolinat*, p. 61.

81. On postwar politics generally, see Virginia Thompson and Richard Adloff, *The Emerging States of French Equatorial Africa* (Stanford, Calif.: Stanford University Press, 1960). Because of the intricacies of the representative system, African politics reflected to some extent metropolitan political alignments. The PPT was affiliated with the French Africa–wide Rassemblement Démocratique Africain (RDA), which at the time had close ties with the French Communist party, but in the early 1950s, RDA representatives in Paris were co-opted by French centrists, notably François Mitterand.

82. Nelson, *Chad*, p. 21.

83. The decision to intervene was reportedly taken by President Charles de Gaulle nearly alone, in what must have been one of his last official acts before resigning in the face of defeat in a referendum (Buijtenhuijs, *Le Frolinat*, p. 209).

84. This remains a nebulous issue. The Tibesti's promise was founded on its proximity to uranium deposits in Niger; however, unless the deposits were to prove especially rich, it is doubtful that they would lend themselves to economic exploitation at current and anticipated world prices. There has also been talk of rich phosphate deposits.

85. However, six hundred "advisers" remained behind, with a protective umbrella of over one thousand paratroopers and airmen. In 1963 a new French base was established at Sahr as well.

86. They included a French woman anthropologist, F. Claustre. Habré sought to exchange the hostages for weapons and supplies so as to make himself the overall leader of FROLINAT. He obtained payment of a ransom by Bonn and, despite ordering the execution of a French negotiator, may have also reached a covert understanding with certain French policymakers, who saw him as the best hope for Chad.

87. Interpretation based on Bouquet, *Tchad*, pp. 152ff. Around this time Paris may have also struck a secret deal with Qaddafi, involving recognition of Libyan hegemony over northern Chad in exchange for the promise of oil concessions to Elf-Aquitaine, which would guarantee to France an accessible source of energy outside the Middle East (cited in *ACR*, 1980–81, p. B22, on the basis of a report in *Jeune Afrique*, December 24, 1980).

88. While giving priority to the protection of their own citizens and major installations, the French forces reportedly threw their weight toward Habré and Goukouni, who had now also broken with Libya, against Malloum and other FROLINAT factions.

89. P. Doornbos, "La Révolution Dérapée: La Violence dans l'Est du Tchad (1978–1981), *Politique Africaine*, 2, 7 (September 1982), pp. 5–13; and discussions with Buijtenhuijs.

90. Figures from USCR.

91. *ACR*, 1981–82, pp. B18–27.

92. Like its predecessors, the Mitterand administration was eager for an accommodation with Libya but ruled out an outright takeover of Chad, as this would jeopardize France's standing as the patron of French-speaking black Africa. However, the Socialists preferred Goukouni to Habré, whom they considered a client of the right as well as more recently of the CIA. They eliminated the old hands who had run African policy as the Elysée Palace's private preserve since the days of General de Gaulle, but they lacked knowledgeable replacements.

93. Herb Boyd, "Chad: A Civil War Without End?" *Journal of African Studies,* 10 (1983–84), p. 121; see also Mansour O. El-Kikhia, "Chad: The Same Old Story," *Journal of African Studies,* 10 (1983–84), pp. 127–35.

94. Legion members captured by Habré in September 1984 told French journalists that they were Sudanese going to Libya in search of work (*Monde,* October 9, 1984).

95. France's decisive move may have been taken to prevent greater involvement by the Reagan administration in its traditional sphere of influence. However, the two Western powers soon worked in tandem, enlisting the participation of Zaire and Morocco as well (André Fontaine in *Monde,* July 1 and 12, 1983); *NYT,* August 19, 1983).

96. Although repatriation was essentially voluntary, thousands were swept from Nigeria in the wave of foreign expulsions and ended up in transit camps in Benin.

97. Laurent Zecchini in *Monde,* May 11–12, 1986.

98. *NYT,* February 26, 1984.

99. Reports in *NYT,* November 9 and 10, 1984, citing Amnesty International. See also Paul-Marie de la Gorce, "Risques Accrus d'Interventions Étrangères au Tchad," *Le Monde Diplomatique,* February 1987, pp. 12–13.

100. Jean-Claude Pomonti in *Monde,* September 22, 23, 24, 1984; see also reports on October 3 and November 9. Lake Chad, which never reached more than half its previous size after the great drought of 1973, shrank by half again in 1984. The deteriorating situation also occasioned a huge exodus from the most severely affected rural areas to Ndjamena, whose population doubled within a year to 400,000. But relief was nearly impossible because the ferry across the Chari River, which links Chad to transportation networks in Cameroon and Nigeria, was rendered inoperative by the low water level. Delivery costs were extremely high because of the great distances and because trucks must devote much of their capacity to carrying their own fuel, and the difficulties of transport were compounded by the reigning insecurity.

101. Report by Maria Hutchinson, *Refugees,* 13 (January 1985), pp. 8–9.

102. See the report from a Voice of America correspondent reprinted in *Refugee,* no. 14 (February 1985), p. 39; and from *The Times* (London) in *Refugee,* no. 23 (November 1985), p. 34.

103. Eric Rouleau in *Monde,* September 19, 1984. The key actor was Mitterand's confidant Roland Dumas, who told Qaddafi as early as August 1983 that France would not attack Libyan troops so long as they stayed north of the "red line." This assurance was tantamount to French recognition of a Libyan annexation of the territory to the north. The agreement evoked protests from Habré, who reportedly was informed only a few hours before the general public was and who insisted that it was insignificant because men of the "Islamic legion" were being passed off as indigenous insurgents. French field commanders expressed skepticism as well. After a brief delay, Libya announced that it was leaving, and on November 10 the French announced the pullout had been completed. However, a few days later Washington released intelligence reports indicating that most of Libya's 5,500 men were still in place, insisting this was confirmed by French sources. Mitterand rushed to meet Qaddafi in Crete and subsequently claimed that the problems had been ironed out. But two weeks after the meeting, intelligence reports again indicated that the Libyans had not budged (from reports in *NYT* and *Monde*). Although later developments lent credence to the possibility that France's tolerance was a clever ploy—in the expectation Libyan control over the north would unravel on its own account—at the time the affair looked like a major blunder, indicating France's willingness to sacrifice Chad's national integrity to its Arab and Mediterranean policy. Analysts suggested that the African networks of the Elysée Palace and the Quai d'Orsay had

been kept out of the decision-making process altogether (*Monde*, December 8–9, 1984). The policy exposed the Mitterand administration to severe criticism, not only from its enemies, but also from its friends, and seriously weakened its credibility in black Africa.

104. Most Western press reports suggested that he did so with Qaddafi's encouragement, but de la Gorce (*Monde Diplomatique*, February 1987) maintains that the initiative was Goukouni's and that its catastrophic failure earned him Libya's distrust.

105. Under "cohabitation," President Mitterand and Prime Minister Jacques Chirac competed for credit as patrons of black Africa. A cartoon by Plantu showed Mitterand and Chirac in the guise of Tintin's twin policemen, the first telling Habré, "You can count on us" and the other retorting, as usual, "I would say even more, you can count on us" (*Monde*, November 16–17, 1986). With French intelligence reporting that Habré was firmly in the saddle and enjoyed considerable support in his home region within the Libyan zone as well, Mitterand affirmed in mid-November that the conflict was losing its civil-war character and turning into a mere confrontation between Chad and Libya. In September it was reported that France had turned down an offer of U.S. logistical support for an attack on the Libyans, but the aid was sent anyway and the French air force subsequently ensured its local distribution. The increase in French troop cover to 2,200 relieved Habré of the need to maintain a constabulary force at the center and enabled him to send his best troops to the north. On December 18, French planes parachuted food, fuel, and ammunition into the western Tibesti in support of a FANT column sent to relieve Goukouni's besieged guerrillas. Taking advantage of this confrontation, Habré launched a major attack against Fada, in the east, from a forward base established with French assistance immediately south of the sixteenth parallel. Fada fell on January 2, 1987, opening the way to Faya-Largeau. Habré's forces then went on to take the air base covering Faya-Largeau, well north of the sixteenth parallel, reportedly with the aid of French special forces, and took Faya-largeau itself on March 27.

106. On August 29, 1987, Libya retook the town of Aozou, using the same tactics as the Chadians had, prompting *The Economist* to baptize the conflict "the yo-yo war" (September 5, 1987, p. 39). A cease-fire was reached on September 11, and peace negotiations were launched under OAU sponsorship. France continues to call for international arbitration with respect to the future of the strip.

107. *WRS*, 1986. The number of refugees in the Central African Republic decreased to 15,000 and in Cameroon to 5,000. There remained also 4,900 in Nigeria and 4,000 in Benin. See also the report by Ekber Menememcioglu in *Refugees*, no. 40 (April 1987), pp. 33–34.

108. Basic sources include Young, *The Politics of Cultural Pluralism*, pp. 149–56 and 216–73; Aidan Southall, "Social Disorganisation in Uganda: Before, During, and After Amin," *Journal of Modern African Studies*, 18, 4 (1980), pp. 627–56; John Lonsdale, "Uganda: Recent History," in *Africa South of the Sahara* (London: Europa Publications, 1983); Peter Woodward, "Ambiguous Amin," *African Affairs*, 77 (1978), pp. 153–63; Minority Rights Group, *Uganda and Sudan* (London: December 1984); USCR, *Human Rights in Uganda: The Reasons for Refugees* (Washington, D.C.: U.S. Government Printing Office, August 1985); Amnesty International, *Ouganda: Exécutions Extra Judiciaires, Torture et Emprisonnement Politique* (Paris: Amnesty International, 1982); and Jackson and Rosberg, *Personal Rule in Black Africa*, pp. 252–65.

109. Young, *Cultural Pluralism*, p. 221. Coffee is grown in a belt stretching inland across the northwestern shore of Lake Victoria, located mostly in Buganda, which had the effect of further compounding the advantages of the group as a whole and, within it, of the chiefly class. Colonial economic development followed mostly the African smallholder pattern, with coffee and cotton as the main cash crops. In the mid-1960s, coffee and cotton accounted together for 43 to 45 percent of monetary gross domestic product (GDP) and for one-half and one-fourth of exports.

110. Ibid., Table 7.1, p. 239.

111. Lonsdale, "Uganda," p. 863.

112. In April 1962, once again, the UPC slightly outpolled the DP outside Buganda; within the kingdom, however, the DP was thoroughly trounced by the KY. In Crawford Young's terms, politics was "reduced to a three-person game conducted in a communally defined arena," whose

logic forced leaders into coalition building. Because Buganda and the UPC had not yet directly confronted each other, the solution "was an alliance between these two uneasy partners." (Young, *Cultural Pluralism,* p. 254).

113.   He dismissed the Kabaka as president, seized full executive powers, arrested several cabinet members, and abolished all federal arrangements. In response, the Buganda authorities demanded that the central government leave the capital city, Kampala, which is on Buganda territory. Obote then ordered the army to storm the Kabaka's palace. There were heavy casualties on both sides. The Kabaka himself escaped to England, where he later died of alcoholic poisoning. Obote had the army commander arrested to make room for Amin.

114.   The mystery of Amin's origins and its implications are discussed by Woodward, "Ambiguous Amin." Amin's Nubi identity may account for the unauthorized assistance that he gave to the southern Sudanese resistance movement, the Anya Nya, before the coup, at a time when Obote sought improved relations with the new left-wing military regime in Sudan. It even is possible that it was this very issue that precipitated their final confrontation and triggered Amin's preemptive coup. As it was, five hundred Anya Nya refugee-warriors are reported to have played a crucial part in the coup, and fifteen hundred more were recruited into the Ugandan army immediately after Amin took power.

115.   This assessment of Obote's record of office differs from that of Crawford Young (published before Obote's return to power), who states that "Obote labored with an energy and ingenuity that deserved a better reward to find an integrative political formula for Uganda which rested on more secure bases than personal authoritarian rule. He was anxious to find a formula for electoral legitimacy; yet the constraints were severe. . . ." (*Cultural Pluralism,* p. 266).

116.   *ACR,* 1972–73, p. B 269.

117.   L. A. Kayiira and E. Kannyo, as quoted by Jackson and Rosberg, *Personal Rule,* p. 255.

118.   Donald Horowitz, *Ethnic Groups in Conflict* (Berkeley, Calif.: University of California Press, 1985), pp. 487–92, 497–99; "Uganda's descent into ethnocracy" is summarized in Table 9, p. 491.

119.   Lonsdale, "Uganda," p. 864.

120.   Most Asians in East Africa were British subjects or British protected persons, by virtue of being born in, or of a father born in, a British possession or Commonwealth country; a very small number were citizens of India or Pakistan. At the time of independence, British Asians were given the option of obtaining a British passport or becoming citizens of their country of residence. Some were granted this status automatically, whereas others had to apply within a specified period. Given the long-standing communal tensions, the advantage of retaining a British passport were evident. Relatively few household heads applied for local citizenship, and among those who did, many took out insurance by having their wife retain a British passport. As of 1969, only 44 percent had become citizens of Kenya, and about 35 percent of Uganda. Onkwar W. Marwah and James H. Mittleman, "Alien Pariahs: Uganda's Asians and Bangladesh's Binaris," paper presented at the International Congress of Africanists, Addis Ababa, 1973, p. 8.

121.   The main sources used on the Asian issue are ibid.; Donald Rothchild, "Kenya's Minorities and the African Crisis over Citizenship," *Race,* 9, 4 (1968), pp. 421–37; Michael Twaddle (ed.), *Expulsion of a Minority: Essays on Ugandan Asians* (London: Athlone, 1975); Yash Tandon, "The Asians in East Africa in 1972," in *ACR,* 1972–73, pp. A3–A19. Although appearing as a single community from the European or African perspective, in reality the Asians formed a number of heterogeneous clusters, originating in various parts of the Indian subcontinent and differing in both religion and language. Each of the various subcommunities played a distinctive role, ranging from running modest shops in towns and outlying villages, to providing technical and supervisory personnel for railroads and other public services, and financing and operating large agricultural and industrial companies.

122.   Although Tanzania rendered Asians redundant by nationalizing most industries, plantations, and commercial circuits, Kenya and Uganda steadily narrowed their sphere of activity by making citizenship a requirement for licensing and employment in the public sector. Further, they

granted preference to black citizens over others in the name of africanization. Many applications for citizenship were turned down on technicalities, and processing was lengthy.

123. The Commonwealth Immigration Act of 1968 imposed a voucher requirement on heads of households and, in the face of growing pressures on Asians to emigrate, established an annual quota of only 1,500 vouchers for East Africa as a whole—that is, about 7,500 persons. The prospect of the new law precipitated a rush of several thousand Asians from Kenya to beat the deadline. Many who arrived afterwards were denied entry, shuttled around the world, and eventually allowed into Britain under harsh and humiliating conditions designed to deter others (*ACR*, 1970–71, pp. B119–20).

124. It was reported the two countries secretly agreed to an orderly transfer over a seven-year period. In 1971 Britain raised the annual quota of vouchers to 3,500, with another 1,500 to clear the backlog. Although India insisted that holders of British passports were Britain's responsibility, it eventually admitted Kenyan Asians, regardless of their status.

125. *ACR*, 1970–71, pp. B194–95. If all those entitled exercised the option, about 35,000 more Asians would become Ugandan; this would leave about 10,000 with Indian passports, mostly older people who would return to India, and about 25,000 with British passports, mostly younger and better educated, to whom Uganda expected that Britain would accord entry.

126. *ACR*, 1971–72, p. B233. The new regime shortly launched an anti-Asian press campaign and subsequently took a special census that was popularly believed to be conducted on behalf of Britain so as to organize departures but in fact provided an occasion for harassment. At this time, 23,242 produced proof of Ugandan citizenship. There were a number of confrontations between Amin and representatives of the Asian community over the next few months.

127. Twaddle (ed.), *Expulsion*, p. 208; Tandon, "The Asians," p. A 14.

128. Jackson and Rosberg, *Personal Rule*, p. 258.

129. Southall, "Social Disorganisation," p. 642.

130. The total volume of exports fell from 350,000 metric tons in the late 1960s to less than 120,000 in 1980. The monetary agricultural sector, which had grown at an average annual rate of 4.6 percent in 1963–70, declined by an average of 1.6 percent a year in 1970–78. In contrast, subsistence agriculture grew at an estimated average 4 percent in 1963–70 and declined to only 3.4 percent in 1970–78. Jane Carroll, "Uganda: Economy," in *Africa South of the Sahara*, p. 867.

131. The same applies to the economic sphere; writing in mid-1980, Aidan Southall deplored the speed with which the new elite exploited its power, "jockeying with one another to amass fortunes while they can," and suggested that "a whole generation of youth . . . has been led astray into bad habits from which they cannot escape. . . . Many young men of good middle-class background now behave like congenital thieves even to their own families." Asking, "Where can the vicious circle be broken?" he answered, in Hobbesian fashion, "At first sight a new and dependable security force seems the most fundamental prerequisite." There were, he suggests, "suitable Third-World, non-aligned, and Commonwealth countries willing and able" to supply this, but the transitional government did not resort to this solution, probably because President Nyerere, seeking to offset increased Kenyan influence in the region, "prevented a serious demand from being made" ("Social Disorganisation," p. 648).

132. In May 1980, his commanders in the UNLA staged a coup against the transitional government and opened the way for his return to power. Elections were moved up to December 10, 1980, and held on a partisan basis. The balloting was reasonably free, but when early returns showed the DP to be in the lead, the UNLA made it clear nothing but a UPC victory was acceptable. Obote ended up claiming seventy-two seats to the DP's fifty-one, with one going to the UPM, and filled forty-two of fifty cabinet posts with Protestants.

133. They included the descendants of late nineteenth-century Tutsi invaders and their Hutu clients but most were relatively recent arrivals, the residue of a labor migration encouraged by the British in the 1920s to work in Uganda's coffee groves and cotton fields. Also involved in the conflict were the Bahima, a pastoralist group indigenous to Uganda, closely related to the Tutsi—

that is, Burundi's Hima—whose clients are the Bairu. As Catholics, they too sided with the Democratic party, while the mostly Protestant Bairu supported Obote.

134. Although he subsequently relented, these actions heightened concern in Rwanda of another invasion by Tutsi refugees and prompted the construction of a connecting link to the Tanzanian road network (*ACR*, 1971–72, p. B181).

135. This section is based on USCR, *Human Rights in Uganda: The Reasons for Refugees;* and *ACR*, 1982–83. The Bairu, who saw the return of Obote in 1980 as an opportunity to settle scores with their Bahima masters and "foreigner" exploiters—that is, Rwandan Tutsi refugees— gave overwhelming majorities to Obote's candidates and became a mainstay of the new regime.

136. *ACR*, 1982–83, p. B249. On the occasion of Uganda's May Day rally, the Rwandan and Ugandan leaders issued a joint communiqué affirming mutual respect for territorial integrity and their intention of cooperating "to restrain bandits and refugees from using each other's territory as a base for either military or political activities against neighboring countries." In September, immediately after the release by Amnesty International of a report on human rights violations in Uganda, the government accused Rwandan refugees of organizing for the purpose of fomenting political trouble, as well as cattle rustling and smuggling.

137. *NYT*, December 18, 1983; *WRS*, 1985, p. 50.

138. *ACR*, 1982–83, p. B246; *WRS*, 1985, pp. 46–47.

139. The high figure is from Barbara Harrell-Bond, as cited in Minority Rights Group, *Uganda and Sudan*, p. 9.

140. Ibid., p. 10.

141. Ibid.

142. *Monde*, June 20–21, 1984.

143. *The Economist*, August 3, 1985, pp. 27–28; *Monde*, August 24, 1985; Victoria Brittain, "Comment l'Armée de Résistance Nationale Vint à Bout d'un Régime Discrédité," *Le Monde Diplomatique*, March 1986, pp. 21–22.

144. As reported in *NYT*, August 14, 1986.

145. The new government initially took a number of measures to relieve the plight of the urban masses, with the consequences that as of August 1986 the country was on the verge of bankruptcy. Prices paid to coffee producers were set so low that most of the crop was smuggled to Kenya. Later on there were indications of some willingness to abide by recommendations from international organizations in order to secure loans (*NYT*, August 14, 1986; *Monde*, August 26, 1986; *The Economist*, September 20, October 11, 1986, January 31, May 23, 1987.

146. *Refugees*, May 1986, pp. 9ff; February 1987, p. 16, and May 1987, p. 7.

Chapter 3

1. Patrick Chabal, "People's War, State Formation and Revolution in Africa: A Comparative Analysis of Mozambique, Guinea-Bissau, and Angola," *Journal of Commonwealth and Comparative Politics*, 21, 3 (November 1983), pp. 110–27. This will be discussed further in Chapter 9.

2. Lionel Cliffe, "Rural Political Economy of Africa," in Peter C. W. Gutkind and Immanuel Wallerstein (eds.), *Political Economy of Contemporary Africa*, 2nd ed. (Beverly Hills, Calif.: Sage, 1985), pp. 121–23. Within what is today the Republic of South Africa, European-owned land grew from 19.8 percent of the total area in 1860 to 45.2 percent a century later—when whites constituted about one-fifth of the population—with the proportion reaching as much as 94 percent in the Orange Free State. As of 1960, the level was 37.0 percent in Southern Rhodesia, whose whites amounted to only one-twentieth of the total, and 47.9 percent in South-West Africa, where the proportion of whites was one-eighth. The areas reserved for African occupation ranged from a high of 44.7 percent in Southern Rhodesia, which was then still ruled by Britain, to 25.4 percent in South-West Africa, and only 6.4 percent in the republic. Computed from tabular data in

A. J. Christopher, "Official Land Disposal Policies and European Settlement in Southern Africa 1860–1960," *Journal of Historical Geography*, 9 (1983), pp. 371, 373. See also Roger Riddell, "Zimbabwe's Land Problem: The Central Issue," in M. Morris-Jones (ed.), *From Rhodesia to Zimbabwe* (London: Frank Cass, 1980), pp. 1–13. Similar conditions prevailed in Portuguese Africa as well, particularly in Angola, which on the eve of independence (1974) had the largest concentration of white settlers after South Africa itself. See Irving Kaplan (ed.), *Angola: A Country Study* (Washington, D.C.: U.S. Government Printing Office, 1979),pp. 209–11.

3. Bill Freund, *The Making of Contemporary Africa: The Development of African Society Since 1800* (Bloomington: Indiana University Press, 1984), pp. 118–35. For a theoretical analysis of the system, see Michael Burawoy, "The Functions and Reproduction of Migrant Labor: Comparative Material from Southern Africa and the United States," *American Journal of Sociology*, 81 (March 1976), pp. 1050–87.

4. As of the late 1960s, Botswana, Lesotho, Malawi, and Mozambique were highly dependent labor reserves. All of Swaziland's mines and industrial enterprises were in the hands of South African capital.

5. Such a process is hardly unique to the southern African region but is encountered wherever economic development is founded on a racial division of labor. See, in particular, George M. Frederickson, *White Supremacy: A Comparative Study in American and South African History* (New York: Oxford University Press, 1981). For a detailed and lucid treatment of the use of law as an instrument of inequality, see Claire Palley, "Law and the Unequal Society: Discriminatory Legislation in Rhodesia Under the Rhodesian Front from 1963 to 1969," pts. 1 and 2, *Race*, 12 (1970), pp. 15–47, 140–67.

6. See James C. Scott, *Weapons of the Weak: Everyday Forms of Peasant Resistance* (New Haven, Conn.: Yale University Press, 1985).

7. Larry Bowman identified this in 1968 as a "subordinate state system," which is an entity that "can be best analyzed and understood in terms of its own interrelations." "The Subordinate State System of Southern Africa," *International Studies Quarterly*, 12, 3 (1968), p. 231. However, he overestimated the relative autonomy of the subsystem. On linkages with the world at large, see Timothy M. Shaw, "South Africa, Southern Africa, and the World System," in Thomas Callaghy (ed.), *South Africa in Southern Africa: The Intensifying Vortex of Violence* (New York: Praeger, 1983), esp. p. 53.

8. See the review by Leonard Thompson in the *New York Review of Books*, June 11, 1987, p. 20, of William Minter, *King's Solomon's Mines Revisited: Western Interests and the Burdened History of South Africa* (New York: Basic Books, 1987).

9. See Zaki Laïdi, *Les Contraintes d'une Rivalité: Les Superpuissances et l'Afrique (1960– 1985)* (Paris: La Découverte, 1986), translation forthcoming, University of Chicago Press).

10. This section is based on Larry W. Bowman, "South Africa's Outward Strategy: A Foreign Policy Dilemma for the United States" (Athens: Ohio University Center for International Studies, 1971).

11. Beyond this, the Afrikaner leaders established various levels of "dialogue" with a few African states, particularly the Ivory Coast and the Malagasy Republic, and somewhat paradoxically, with Biafra during the Nigerian civil war. Although in 1971 the Organization for African Unity voted twenty-eight to six to reject "dialogue," the fact that the debate occurred at all and that unity failed to prevail was a relative success from South Africa's point of view.

12. Referring to Rhodesia, an editorial in *Die Burger* suggested that the UDI was "something which could have had its uses, but which in the time ahead can become more and more of a hindrance. . . ." The following year, the foreign editor of the *Rand Daily Mail* suggested: "In many ways, a ring of black states economically beholden to South Africa can provide a far better protective cushion against the North than the odd arc of white colonies which, being colonies, tend to invite attention and trouble. . . ." Cited by Bowman, "South Africa's Outward Strategy," 1968, p. 252.

13. The principal source for historical background and basic givens is by Harold Kaplan

(ed.), *Angola: A Country Study* (Washington, D.C.: U.S. Government Printing Office, 1983), chaps. 1 and 2, pp. 3–115. From the late sixteenth century onward, the northernmost part of the country, then under the control of a Kongo state, became a major source of slaves for Portuguese traders. Approximately a century later, the Portuguese established a colony farther south at what is now Luanda, from which they went into Mbundu territory by way of the Cuanza River. In the seventeenth century another slave port was established yet farther south at Benguela, among the Ovimbundu.

14. Some coffee and rubber plantations were established along the coast, and in the 1920s, construction of the Benguela Railroad, to link the minefields of the Belgian Congo's Katanga Province to Lobito, opened up the interior and enabled diamond mining in Angola.

15. Of the economically active, approximately 6 percent were local capitalists, managers, or high-ranking officials; 53 percent were employees (mostly governmental); and 41 percent were farmers or petty traders. See W. G. Clarence-Smith, "Class Structure and Class Struggles in Angola in the 1970s," *Journal of Southern African Studies,* 7, 1 (1980), p. 113.

16. This was the case also with the Lunda-Chokwe (about 8 or 9 percent) adjoining Zaire's Shaba Province, as well as smaller groups abutting on the Zambian and Namibian border.

17. Clarence-Smith, "Class Structure," p. 112.

18. *Africa Contemporary Record* (New York: Africana Publishing, 1978–79), p. B 682 (hereafter cited as *ACR,* with appropriate years).

19. Clarence-Smith, "Class Structure," p. 116. In 1961, they attempted to free political prisoners from a Luanda jail and provided the leadership for an uprising of cotton workers in Malange district, east of Luanda.

20. Cuba was first drawn to the region by the Zaire rebellions of 1964–65, which may have prompted an expedition by Che Guevara. In 1966 Havana provided a pretorian guard for the new radical government established in Brazzaville, where the MPLA later established its headquarters. To what extent this involvement entailed consultation with the Soviet Union is unclear. Maurice Halperin has suggested that Cuba's world role "was its own reward," even if it was in tune with Soviet interests. See his "The Cuban Role in Southern Africa," in John Seiler (ed.), *Southern Africa Since the Portuguese Coup* (Boulder, Colo.: Westview Press, 1980), pp. 25–47.

21. These conditions are precisely those identified by Jeffrey Paige as conducive to agrarian revolutions in the contemporary Third World. See his *Agrarian Revolution: Social Movements and Export Agriculture in the Underdeveloped World* (New York: Free Press, 1975). It should be noted also that in effect, African producers competed with Portuguese for manpower, as was the case in the Ivory Coast, where the conflict fostered the rise of Félix Houphouet-Boigny in 1944. See Aristide R. Zolberg, *One-Party Government in the Ivory Coast* (Princeton, N.J.: Princeton University Press, 1964).

22. According to the count prepared by the USCR for Hugh C. Brooks and Yassin El-Yahouty (eds.), *Refugees South of the Sahara: An African Dilemma* (Westport, Conn.: Negro Universities Pres, 1970), p. 295. This should be taken as an order of magnitude. The same source gives a figure of 300,000 for 1967, without accounting for the difference, but the USCR estimate went back up to 412,500 in 1968 and rose to 567,000 in 1970 for Angolan refugees as a whole. The UNHCR recorded a total of 413,810 in 1970–71, almost entirely in Zaire. Substantial numbers were also known to be in the People's Republic of the Congo but remained inaccessible to U.N. enumerators. Census estimates for the decades 1960–70 indicate losses as high as 60 percent in Kongo-inhabited districts bordering on Zaire. Kaplan (ed.), *Angola,* p. 64.

23. These were armed followers of Moise Tshombe who in 1960–63 headed a secessionist regime in Katanga Province (later Shaba) backed by South Africa, Portugal, and international mining interests. Kaplan (ed.), *Angola,* p. 138.

24. Ibid., p. 124.

25. The assertion concerning collaboration up to 1972 or 1973 is cited by Clarence-Smith, "Class Structure," p. 120, from Franz-Wilhelm Heimer, *Der Entkolonisierungskonflikt in Angola* (Munich: Weltforum-Verlag, 1979), p. 111.

26. Charles K. Ebinger, "External Intervention in Internal War: The Politics and Diplomacy

of the Angolan Civil War,'' *Orbis*, 20, 3 (Fall 1976), pp. 669–99. The exact sequence of inter-vention remains controversial. As early as October 1974, there was a South African plan to foster the emergence of a ''greater Ovamboland'' encompassing regions on both sides of the border, as a buffer between a friendly Angola and a white-controlled South-West Africa shorn of SWAPO. See John Seiler, ''South Africa in Namibia: Persistence, Misperception, and Ultimate Failure,'' in Callaghy (ed.), *South Africa*, p. 167. The International Institute of Strategic Studies suggested that the Soviets had been the first to provide major arms supplies to the MPLA but that Cuban combat troops were brought in only after South Africa invaded. According to Gabriel Garcia Marquez (in an account published in 1977 by the *Washington Post*), Cuba's decision to intervene was taken in May 1975 at the request of Neto, who lacked troops and arms. The first ships arrived in early October, one month before the Portuguese withdrawal, but the major commitment was made in November (Halperin, ''The Cuban Role,'' pp. 25–47). See also the review by Michael Massing of Ryszard Kapuscinski's *Another Day in the Life*, in the *Times Literary Supplement*, May 8, 1987; and letters to the editor published May 22 and July 10.

27. The suggestion is from Gaim Kibreab, *African Refugees* (Trenton, N.J.: Africa World Press, 1955; originally published by the Scandinavian Institute of African Studies, Uppsala), pp. 29, 55.

28. This brief overview is based on the following works: Harold D. Nelson (ed.), *Mozam-bique: A Country Study* (Washington, D.C.: U.S. Government Printing Office, 1985); Allen F. Isaacman, *Mozambique: From Colonialism to Revolution, 1900–1982* (Boulder, Colo.: Westview Press, 1983); Barry Munslow, *Mozambique: The Revolution and Its Origins* (London: Longmans, 1983); Tony Hodges, ''Mozambique: The Politics of Liberation'' in Gwendolen M. Carter and Patrick O'Meara (eds.), *Southern Africa: The Continuing Crisis*, 2nd ed. (Bloomington: Indiana University Press, 1982), pp. 57–92.

29. This was doubly profitable: Having procured this labor by coercion, the Portuguese were paid for it in gold. Because the transaction was reckoned at the official price for the metal, which was much below the actual price, they were able to resell it and pocket the difference.

30. Data from a 1979 study by D. Wield as reported by Barry Munslow, ''State Intervention in Agriculture: The Mozambican Experience,'' *Journal of Modern African Studies*, 22, 2 (1984), p. 208. In 1970, 4,200 Portuguese estates accounted for half of the cultivated land, and 1.3 million families working less than two ha (five acres) shared one-fourth of the total.

31. Munslow, as cited in Kibreab, *African Refugees*, pp. 18, 76.

32. UNHCR reported variously 47,500 and 58,000 as of December 31, 1972. See W. T. S. Gould, ''Refugees in Tropical Africa,'' *International Migration Review*, 8, 3 (1974), p. 415; and Neville Rubin, ''Africa and Refugees,'' *African Affairs*, 73, 292 (1974), p. 299). USCR, in Brooks and El-Yahouty (eds.), *Refugees South of the Sahara*, reported another 20,000 in Malawi in 1967. This was either an error, or they all had gone home by 1969, or the host government deemed it more prudent to remain silent. None were recorded in 1972.

33. The white population decreased from 280,000 in early 1974 to 80,000 or fewer by the time of independence, and only 10,000 three years later. Although most returned to Portugal, a sizable number relocated in Rhodesia and South Africa, where they remained available for mobi-lization on behalf of white rule.

34. *World Refugee Survey: 1976 in Review* (Washington, D.C.: American Council for Na-tionalities Service, 1977) (hereafter cited as *WRS*, with appropriate years).

35. Freund, *The Making*, p. 34.

36. The historical background is drawn from Harold D. Nelson (ed.), *Zimbabwe: A Country Study* (Washington, D.C.: U.S. Government Printing Office, 1983); Patrick O'Meara, ''Zimbabwe: The Politics of Independence,'' in Carter and O'Meara (eds.), *Southern Africa;* John Day, ''The Insignificance of Tribe in the African Politics of Zimbabwe–Rhodesia,'' in W. H. Morris-Jones (ed.), *From Rhodesia to Zimbabwe* (London: Frank Cass, 1980), pp.   .

37. British reserve powers prevented local whites from ruling out black political participation on the basis of racial principles and contributed to the establishment of a higher degree of political

freedom than in South Africa. But the crown did not insist on the primacy of African interests in the colony's development. In effect, Africans were disenfranchised by arduous means and literacy tests, much as in the American South.

38. As of the late 1970s, about 38 percent of African wage earners were in agriculture, 14 percent each in domestic service and manufacturing, 6 percent in mining, and 6 percent in other services. The labor force was supplemented with foreign Africans, growing to about 200,000 in the 1970s, two-thirds of them in agriculture—where they constituted approximately one-third of the farm labor force. There was also a labor migration from Southern Rhodesia to the gold mines of South Africa, reaching over 30,000 in 1976.

39. Reformist currents in the white camp remained very weak. Prime Minister Garfield Todd, who in 1958 supported extension of the franchise to all male Africans with ten years of education, was subsequently voted out of office by his own party. The conference marked a watershed, in that for the first time the British and Southern Rhodesian governments agreed to African participation in deliberations. Nkomo's initial agreement, in violation of the NDP's commitment to majority rule, precipitated a crisis in the party, which was resolved when he rejected the compromise. The NDP then ordered black voters to boycott the referendum and called an unofficial poll of its own, in which nearly half a million voiced their opposition, but the constitution went on to be approved by the white electorate, about two to one.

40. Prime Minister Edgar Whitehead lost the 1962 elections after promising to name one African cabinet minister if reelected and carrying out a land reform, whereby about half the land was open to settlement by all Rhodesians. The new government was formed by the populist Rhodesian Front party, dedicated to obtaining complete independence, regardless of British wishes and without any concessions to the black majority. But the following year, Prime Minister Winston Field was replaced by the more adamant Ian Smith. After securing a mandate for independence by means of a referendum, in 1965 Smith led the party to an even greater victory.

41. South Africa and Portugal tacitly ignored sanctions from the very beginning and provided full access to the outside world. Individual firms engaged in international trade stood to gain from evasion, and in 1971, the U.S. Congress enacted the Byrd amendment to the Defense Procurement Act, which mandated a repudiation of sanctions.

42. A major instrument to this effect was the 1969 Land Tenure Act. Supplemented by vagrancy laws, it confined Africans to the Tribal Trust Areas unless employed in urban areas and established in the latter a "township" system whereby black males were forced to carry passbooks. Also in 1969, white voters approved a new constitution that explicitly provided for racial separation.

43. The issue of ethnic cleavage in Zimbabwe politics is a subject of considerable controversy. The basic "ethnic cleavage" interpretation of the ZANU–ZAPU split is presented by Terence Ranger in "Rhodesia's Politics of Tribalism," *New Society*, no. 49 (1979), pp. 496–97. As the title of his own article indicates, Day has attempted to rebut this; however, he comes close to throwing the baby out with the bathwater and ends up acknowledging the possibility, advanced by Ranger, that there are now in the politics of Zimbabwe "newly invented 'tribes' " (p. 106). Our account generally follows Patrick O'Meara in Carter and O'Meara (eds.), *Southern Africa*, pp. 29 and 41, and is consistent with the analysis of the role of ethnicity in African collective action made in the preceding chapter.

44. See especially the account by Terence Ranger, "The Death of Chaminuka: Spirit Mediums, Nationalism and the Guerrilla War in Zimbabwe," *African Affairs*, 81 (July 1982), pp. 349–69.

45. From 1976 on, whites aged eighteen to twenty-five were subject to military service for eighteen months but in fact served almost continuously. There were also a variety of white and black "auxiliaries." O'Meara suggests "a total potential strength well over 100,000," including (as of 1978) 4,000 regular African troops plus about 6,000 African policemen or special anti-guerrilla scouts. In Carter and O'Meara (eds.), *Southern Africa*, p. 45. Martyn Gregory referred in 1980 to a regular Rhodesian army of 15,000 men plus 20,000 white-led territorials and 20,000 to 30,000

auxiliaries. See his "The Zimbabwe Election: The Political and Military Implications," *Journal of Southern African Studies*, 7, 1 (October 1980), p. 29.

46. *WRS* and UNHCR reports for the appropriate years.

47. At the end of 1977, for example, a group of journalists taken by Nkomo to a UNHCR-administered children's camp outside Lusaka, with funding from a variety of international NGOs, reported that the children were receiving political indoctrination along with primary schooling in basic subjects. *The Times* (London), December 15, 1977.

48. For example, *The Times* (London), January 21, 1977. ZANLA's strength grew from under one hundred men in the early 1970s to seven hundred by 1976 and about three thousand the following year. Its forces eventually soared to an estimated thirty thousand, with over ten thousand operating in Rhodesia by late 1979. ZIPRA's strength rose concurrently from under one thousand men in the mid-1970s to some twenty thousand by the time of independence (Nelson, *Zimbabwe*, p. 252, based on Rhodesian estimates).

49. Lionel Cliffe and Barry Munslow, as cited in Martyn Gregory, "Zimbabwe 1980: Politicisation Through Armed Struggle and Electoral Mobilisation," *Journal of Commonwealth and African Politics*, 19 (1981), p. 69.

50. For example, UNHCR report for 1978, p. 28. In Mozambique after 1974, the camps were administered by the host governments, and there were recurrent Rhodesian raids from 1977 to the end of the war, leading to a division of the camps into smaller settlements (1977 UNHCR report, para. 121; 1978 report, para. 98; 1980 report, p. 21). See also Nelson, *Mozambique*, pp. xxix, 67.

51. This can be thought of as an application to the racial sphere of what political scientists have called a *consociational* arrangement. The literature on this topic centers on the figure of Arend Lijphart; see especially his *Democracy in Plural Societies* (New Haven, Conn.: Yale University Press, 1977). Lijphart has specifically advocated consociationalism as a solution in southern Africa.

52. It was rejected by U.N. Ambassador Andrew Young on behalf of the new Carter administration. By mid-1979, 90 percent of the country was under martial law; war expenses accounted for nearly 40 percent of government funds; and most ominously, mounting casualties triggered white emigration.

53. United Nations General Assembly, 35th sess., *Report of the UNHCR* (1980), pp. 29–30.

54. See Gregory, "The Zimbabwe Election," pp. 17–37; and Gregory, "Zimbabwe 1980," pp. 63–94.

55. Reginald H. Green and Kimmo Kiljunen, "The colonial Economy: Structures of Growth and Exploitation," in Reginald H. Green, Kimmo Kiljunen, and Maria-Liisa Kiljunen (eds.), *Namibia: The Last Colony* (Burnt Mill, England: Longman, 1981). The edited work was a basic source for this case study, together with Elizabeth S. Landis and Michael I. Davis, "Namibia: Impending Independence?" in Carter and O'Meara (eds.), *Southern Africa*, pp. 141–42.

56. Like other subject nationalities within the British empire—including the Irish and the French Canadians—most of the Boers (now known as Afrikaners) opposed going to war on behalf of the British Empire. When the invasion was ordered, former Boer generals, who had accepted offers of German support for the reestablishment of the independent Boer republics, led their troops in rebellion, but the scheme failed. See Harold D. Nelson (ed.), *South Africa: A Country Study* (Washington, D.C.: U.S. Government Printing Office, 1981), p. 35.

57. Accordingly, from 1925 on the country was governed by an all-white territorial assembly and represented in the South African parliament exclusively by whites as well; racial segregation was rationalized and legalized; and the Ovambo were brought firmly under European rule.

58. It was not until 1938 that its gross domestic product (GDP) exceeded the 1920 level. Namibia's gem diamond fields were the richest in the world, but the Depression caused a drastic reduction in demand, and in order to maintain prices, Anglo-American brought production to a complete stop. At the same time, ranching collapsed as a consequence of drought.

59. Diamond mining grew in importance as the output of South African deposits declined or became more costly. The production of base metals (copper and lead) was vastly expanded, with the Tsumeb complex becoming the country's largest employer of labor. Uranium was developed as

well. The other major sector was ranching; almost entirely controlled by whites, it produced cattle for export to South Africa and Karakul sheep pelts for the London fur market. But areas suitable for subsistence agriculture steadily deteriorated because ranching was usually more profitable. Its GDP grew sixfold between 1945 and 1955 and almost tenfold over the next two decades. At the end of this period, Namibia's economic relationship with South Africa was a typically colonial one: At least one-third of its GDP went to foreign capital and labor, and its GNP was at 30 percent less than its GDP, indicating that a high proportion of local wealth was being exported (From the *Financial Mail*, South Africa's leading economic weekly, as quoted in *ACR*, 1973–74, p. B395).

60. As of 1962, the last year for which separate figures for Namibia and South Africa have been published, the ratio was 21 to 1, larger than in South Africa itself. As of 1975, Namibia's gross territorial product was around $1.25 million. Assuming a population of approximately one million, this made for a per-capita income of about $1,250, above the world average and very much above the range in independent African states. But the total income of Africans and Coloreds amounted to only about 15 percent of the territorial product, or $125 to $150 per capita (estimates cited in *ACR*, 1976–77, p. B783).

61. Green et al. (eds.), *Namibia*, pp. 108–9. Education was completely segregated, and the Bantu sector was oriented to "practical" needs. The per-pupil expenditure was one-tenth that of the white sector. In 1977, 72 percent of African children aged five to fourteen were reported as attending school. Although this was a high proportion by African standards, three-fourths dropped out by the end of the first four years, and only 2 percent continued beyond eight. Schooling began in "native" languages, giving way to Afrikaans exclusively from the fourth year onward. English was actively suppressed so as to enhance the difficulty of studying abroad. As it was, in 1974, less than 1 percent of Africans and Coloreds completed secondary school, as against 11 percent of whites, and there were only a few dozen Namibian university students, almost entirely in South Africa.

62. Marcelle Kooy, "The Contract Labour System and the Ovambo Crisis of 1971 in South West Africa," *African Studies Review*, 16 (1973), pp. 83–105; see also Rauha Volpio, "Contract Work Through Ovambo Eyes," in Green et al. (eds.), *Namibia*, pp. 112ff.

63. During the German period, the "police zone" was the exclusive preserve of the German Evangelical Church (Lutheran), in effect an arm of the state, but the authorities relinquished the Ovambo region to the Finnish Missionary Society which, though also Lutheran, had no colonial interest of its own. In later decades, the Finns developed a strong commitment to education, the formation of an indigenous clergy, and the emancipation of women. In 1954, ELOK became independent of the Finnish mission. Its membership numbered about 250,000 in 1980, close to half the relevant population (Justin Ellis, "The Church in Mobilization for National Liberation," in Green et al. (eds.), *Namibia*, pp. 132–35).

64. Kimo Kiljunen, "National Resistance and the Liberation Struggle," in Green et al. (eds.), *Namibia*, p. 150. Another attempt was made to unite SWAPO and SWANU in 1963, but this foundered when SWANU refused to organize the joint military units recommended by the Organization for African Unity, and the two organizations also remained divided by their distinctive ethnic bases. SWANU subsequently underwent a leadership crisis and lost the support of both the Herero Chiefs' Council and dissident chiefs. It became in effect an organization of students in exile, almost exclusively Herero, which has uneasily sought to devise a "third way" between South Africa–backed parties and SWAPO.

65. As early as 1960, Ethiopia and Liberia initiated an action against South Africa before the World Court, but the proceedings dragged on for six years, at the end of which the Court ruled in favor of South Africa on narrowly technical grounds. By this time, however, African membership in the United Nations had grown considerably, and new initiatives were launched.

66. Gérard Cros, *La Namibie* (Paris: Presses Universitaires de France, 1983), pp. 49–53. The 1966 vote was 114 to 2 (South Africa and Portugal) with 3 abstentions (France, the United Kingdom, and Malawi). The following year, the U.N. General Assembly turned over its authority to the South-West African people, created a United Nations Council for South-West Africa, ap-

pointed a high commissioner charged with bringing the country to independence in June 1968, and asked the Security Council to take appropriate measures to enable the United Nations to discharge its newly assumed responsibilities. On June 12, 1968, the General Assembly proclaimed that South-West Africa would henceforth be called Namibia. The following year, Resolution 276 established that the continued South African presence was illegal and invited the World Court to rule on the juridical consequences of this for member states. On June 21, 1971, the Court declared (13 to 2) that because of the illegal character of its continued presence, South Africa was indeed under obligation to withdraw immediately, and, further (11 to 4), that member states were under obligation to recognize this illegality. On October 20 of the same year, the Security Council endorsed the Court's opinion. The vote on Resolution 301 was 13 for and 2 abstentions (France and the United Kingdom).

67. Landis and Davis, "Nambia," in Carter and O'Meara (eds.), *Southern Africa,* p. 147. Published in 1964, the plan reduced the autonomy of the local white population and imposed on Africans a system of separate territorial entities such as was being established within the republic itself in accordance with the logic of apartheid. As in the original model, this meant not only extreme racial segregation but also a sort of apartheid among blacks themselves, by forcing them to relocate to ethnically homogeneous territories. Under the Native Nations Act of 1968, about 60 percent of Namibia was declared white territory, including the best farming land, all urban centers, most of the known significant mineral deposits, the entire seacoast (with alluvial diamonds), and almost all of the infrastructure (roads, railways). The remainder was divided into numerous homelands designed as the exclusive preserve of each of the country's African "nations." Most of these were not economically viable and could become operational only after massive relocation. Relatively little was done to implement the system as a whole, however, and subsequent developments revealed clearly that the main objective was to contain the "Ovambo menace" by imposing on them home rule on the Transkei pattern, founded on a reinforcement of the authority of politically reliable chiefs.

68. *ACR,* 1971–72, pp. B534–35. Of the 60,000 Herero, 24,000 lived outside their designated homeland. Protest was voiced under the leadership of their traditional chief, identified with resistance since German times. The chief died in 1970 at age one hundred; his successor, Klemens Kapuuo, also opposed apartheid.

69. Military training started in Egypt as early as 1962. Penetration was possible from Zambia through the Caprivi strip, but the accessible area contained no significant targets. The insurgency first came to notice in 1966, when the organization's headquarters in Dar es Salaam announced that PLAN had attacked an administrative center in Ovamboland and a South African military camp in northwest Namibia. Mass arrests followed, and in 1967 South Africa enacted its Terrorism Act, retroactive to 1962, under which numerous SWAPO supporters, against whom no existing statutory or common-law crimes could be proved, were brought to trial. By 1968 South Africa claimed to have mopped up all the guerrillas, but low-level activity continued intermittently.

70. From the diary of a striker cited as evidence by the prosecution in support of a charge that religious leaders encouraged the strike, as quoted in *ACR,* 1972–73, p. B418. There are obvious parallels with the emergence of protest movements in other parts of colonial Africa or in the American South.

71. Landis and Davis, "Namibia," p. 153. Although workers could no longer be assigned to particular employers against their will, the worst features of the old system remained. Moreover, having lost direct centralized control over recruitment, employers organized, with government encouragement, to prevent wage negotiations. Accordingly, although the homeland tribal authorities endorsed the new system, the workers themselves did not, and many of those who returned to work later went on strike again, declaring they had been misled. Out of necessity, however, most Africans eventually complied. Ironically, later developments revealed that the continued confinement of workers in homogeneous compounds and the rotation system in fact facilitated their political mobilization (Kiljunen, in Green et al. (eds.), *Namibia,* p. 50).

72. With 43,000 eligible to vote (out of a population of approximately 350,000), the turnout

was only 1,300. In the migrant workers' township outside Windhoek, participation was only 100 out of 10,000. A wave of arrests followed. In keeping with efforts to legitimize Owambo, suspects were handed over for trial in tribal courts, which ordered 300 to 400 of them to be flogged in public. A group of bishops challenged the legality of these practices, but they were upheld by the South African court of appeals. The trials continued into 1974, when another attempt was made to elect an Owambo assembly. This time, as the result of greater intimidation, participation reached about 60 percent.

73. The U.N. Council for Namibia, under the leadership of Sean McBride, began to attract more support. Its Decree no. 1, issued on September 27, 1974—but approved by the General Assembly only five years later—sought to keep mining companies from exhausting Namibia's natural resources before its independence. With a Labour government in power, the United Kingdom now joined the Security Council majority in denouncing South Africa.

74. This section relies heavily on Thomas Callaghy (ed.), *South Africa in Southern Africa: The Intensifying Vortex of Violence* (New York: Praeger, 1983).

75. Robert M. Price characterized the policy succinctly with the phrase "New Strategy: Old Goals." See his "Pretoria's Southern African Strategy," *African Affairs*, 83 (1984), pp. 11–32; also R. Davies and D. O'Meara, "La 'Stratégie Totale' en Afrique Australe: La Politique Régionale de l'Afrique du Sud Depuis 1978," in *Politique Africaine*, 19 (September 1985), pp. 7–28.

76. Malawi and Swaziland would follow, and Lesotho and Botswana would have little choice but to join as well. The architects of the strategy believed that the group might be subsequently extended to include Zaire, Zambia, Mozambique, and even Tanzania, leaving out only Angola. Angola, because of its oil and diamonds, which could be exported without going through another country, had the most viable economy in the region.

77. Christopher R. Hill, "Regional Co-operation in Southern Africa," *African Affairs*, 82 (1983), pp. 215–39.

78. Its architect was Chester A. Crocker, who served as an African specialist on the National Security Council under Kissinger and as foreign policy adviser to presidential candidate George Bush. After publishing a critique of the Carter administration's southern African policy in *Foreign Affairs*, he was appointed assistant secretary of state for Africa. On the policy generally and on Crocker's role, see the profile in the *New York Times*, June 9, 1987 (hereafter cited as *NYT*); Michael Clough, "Beyond Constructive Engagement," *Foreign Policy*, 61 (Winter 1985–86), pp. 3–24.

79. Callaghy, *South Africa*, p. 267.

80. Shortly after it came to power, the Neto government faced an attempted "leftist" coup by a faction backed by student and labor organizations, with widespread support in the Luanda region prompted by growing food shortages and resentment of the privileges of the new, mostly *mestiços*, bureaucratic class. But the coup was defeated by loyal troops with the aid of Cubans. In October 1976, President Neto signed a twenty-year friendship and cooperation treaty with Moscow and entered into various agreements with Cuba as well.

81. FAPLA was initially mostly filled with volunteers, but after 1978 recruitment dropped below replacement levels, owing to low and irregular pay, the dangers of counterinsurgency warfare, and the shrinking population base of governmental support. The regime then resorted to conscription, with reportedly counterproductive effects. As of late 1977, the International Institute for Strategic Studies estimated the Angolan armed forces strength at about 31,500 (*ACR*, 1977–78, p. B503; Kaplan (ed.), *Angola*, pp. 167, 171–72). However, the Cubans remained an essential reserve force and provided a vital political insurance for the regime as well as administrative and technical specialists to replace the Portuguese. In the early 1980s, the Cuban presence amounted to 19,000 troops and 6,500 civilians engaged in health, education, and construction. At the same time, over 2,000 Angolan pupils were being educated in Cuba (*ACR*, 1982–83, pp. B597, B650–52). The army provided one-third of the delegates to the party congress of December 1977—the first one in the organization's history—and over half the members of the newly chosen Central Committee. The persistence of this trend was confirmed at the second congress, held eight years later in

December 1985. Relations between party and administration were streamlined through a supergovernment consisting of the Central Committee and officials from selected specialized departments. An organizational transmission belt was organized from the top down to mobilize the masses. But its membership steadily declined, reaching a mere 16,500 in 1980. A campaign to increase it to 30,000 made little headway in the face of deteriorating conditions, and there was much talk of corruption and growing internal factionalism, culminating in another political purge in late 1982.

82. Savimbi visited the United States in November 1979, under the sponsorship of Freedom House. On that occasion he met with Kissinger, who had urged intervention on his behalf at the time of independence. Reports that emerged during the Iran–*contra* hearings indicated that Colonel Oliver North had operated in Angola around 1975 and suggested that some of the $30 million obtained from Iran arms sales that did not reach the Nicaraguan *contras* may have gone to UNITA instead (*NYT,* December 1, 1986).

83. Food imports absorbed about one-third of export earnings. Another 600,000 tons were brought in as aid, possibly involving Africa's most expensive emergency food program, whereby international organization planes fly 400 tons of food weekly into the fertile central highlands; landing strips had to be swept of mines every morning, food convoys were shot up, and at least one aid worker was killed.

84. Production declined to less than 10 percent of the independence level. The government attributes its inability to reconstitute a labor force to willful action by the UNITA insurgents and their South African allies. See Augusto Caetano, vice-minister in charge of coffee, in *Le Monde Diplomatique,* October 1986, p. 29. However, a better explanation is that change of ownership from the Portuguese to the state made little difference with respect to conditions for plantation workers. It might be noted that the experience of other African countries indicates that it is possible to develop a thriving coffee sector on the basis of smallholders. Most of the coffee is now exported to the German Democratic Republic; however, about five thousand tons a year reportedly go to South Africa, through Zaire and East Africa, in exchange for South African manufactured goods (*Africa Research Bulletin,* February 15–March 14, 1984, p. 7183).

85. As of 1986, about 70 percent of Angola's petroleum was produced by American companies, dominated by Chevron, which had invested $1.3 billion out of a projected total of $2 billion, the largest American investment in a country with which the United States had no diplomatic relations. The diamond mines, operated during the colonial period as a mixed enterprise (DIAMANG) with the participation of the South African company DeBeers, initially brought in substantial income to the government, but production later declined drastically because of the mines' location in the zones of conflict and the government's inability to control contraband. Liquidated after heavy losses, DIAMANG was replaced by ENDIAMA, fully controlled by the state, but production remains extremely low (*NYT,* December 28, 1985, p. 14, January 31, 1986, p. D1, and December 1, 1986, p. D14; *International Herald Tribune,* November 28, 1986; *The Economist,* August 30, 1986; *Le Monde Diplomatique,* two-part report on Angola, October and December 1986).

86. In January 1985, a South African commando force was ambushed at Malongo, in northern Angola. Although it claimed to be merely an intelligence-gathering operation, one of the men later confirmed that the target was Gulf Oil (*NYT,* May 29, 1985). In 1984, the United States bought 53 percent of its oil exports and provided major loans. Although it was totally self-contained, in keeping with government guidelines the Chevron operation has been increasing its recruitment of Angolan personnel. Despite the campaign of U.S. conservatives and the enjoinments of the U.S. government, Chevron insisted it would stay because other Western multinationals are waiting in the wings to take over. Should U.S. regulations hamper further financing of its operations, Chevron would turn to Europe. In the fall of 1986, Congress passed an amendment to a Defense Department authorization bill prohibiting the department from purchasing petroleum products from American oil companies doing business in Angola, as well as a resolution asking the president to use his authority under the Export Administration Act to curtail American business transactions that conflict with

American security interests in Angola. Accordingly, the Export–Import Bank stopped making new loans (*NYT*, December 1, 1986, p. D14).

87. Estimates of returnees ranged from 200,000 to 350,000 (*ACR*, 1980–81, pp. B644, B653).

88. *Le Monde Diplomatique*, March 1984, p. 13. The report was based on the discovery of Israeli weapons instructors in Zaire, whose army does not use Israeli weapons.

89. *Africa Research Bulletin*, February 15–March 14, 1984, p. 7183; *The Economist*, various reports, 1983–85.

90. The Angolan government resisted pressures to form a coalition government within which UNITA might emerge as the dominant partner. After consulting with Cuba, on March 19 President dos Santos set forth the terms for the removal of 25,000 Cuban troops: first South African withdrawal, then a Namibian settlement, and finally a commitment to end aggression. It has been suggested that the Soviet Union was content to let the situation continue so as to maintain Angola's dependence and orthodoxy, on the Afghanistan model (*Le Monde Diplomatique*, March 1984, p. 14). The United States created an impasse by demanding instead that the Cubans withdraw first (Flora Lewis in *NYT*, March 22, 1984). From the perspective of the State Department negotiators, UNITA was dispensable; however, they underestimated Savimbi's resilience as well as South Africa's commitment to him. To prevent being sacrificed, Savimbi launched a number of spectacular actions, undoubtedly with South African assistance. In February 1984 UNITA captured seventy-seven foreigners at the DIAMANG mining complex; in April they blew up a Cuban-occupied building in Huambo; and in August they claimed credit for blowing up Soviet ships in Luanda harbor, an action undoubtedly carried out by South African frogmen. Negotiations ultimately failed owing to resistance by both sides. Invoking continued SWAPO operations, in August South Africa suspended its withdrawal.

91. The Angolan issue moved to the fore at the end of 1985, when conservative organizations announced that they were planning to make aid for Angola their primary foreign policy objective in 1986, paralleling earlier action against the Panama Canal treaty. "Citizens for America" sponsored a meeting of four anti-Soviet insurgent movements in UNITA-held Jamba to found the "Democratic International"; the financial angel of this undertaking was New Yorker Lewis Lehrman. In January 1986, Savimbi was the guest of honor at a three-day Washington meeting of the Conservative Political Action Conference, attended by President Reagan and former Ambassador Jeanne Kirkpatrick. Savimbi was given a level of VIP treatment rare for a nongovernment person. This campaign gave rise to an Op-Ed war in the *New York Times*. Opponents of intervention included the Congressional Black Caucus and Richard Moose, assistant secretary of state for African affairs in the Carter administration, who insisted the United States must recognize South Africa as the primary source of the region's instability, of which the Communists were the main beneficiaries (see *NYT*, October 25, November 12, November 20, December 9, 12, 16, and 27, 1985; January 20 and 30, 1986). There were also reports of considerable disagreement within the administration. Defense and the CIA preferred overt "nonlethal" aid, but the State Department objected on the grounds that overt aid would undercut the United States' credibility as a mediator between Angola and South Africa with respect to Namibia. Yet diplomatic success required that Savimbi be able to maintain pressure on the Angolan government. Hence administration strategists decided to try to help the rebels unofficially and to seek congressional approval for $15 million in covert aid. Secretary of State George Schultz and Undersecretary Crocker were reportedly committed to this approach as well. On February 7, 1986, the House Select Committee on Intelligence asked the president to reconsider helping UNITA, arguing that covert aid represented a major decision in American foreign policy, which should be made openly with congressional approval. But on February 18 it was announced that UNITA would receive $15 million from CIA funds for antitank and antiaircraft missiles, an action that did not require formal congressional approval. Congress was in a position to block this by subsequent action, as it had done for Nicaragua, but a bill to that effect was defeated in the House the following September, making a victory for the administration. The administration also suggested that it might be in the national interest for Chevron to terminate its operations, and

a group of Republican congressmen filed suit to bar the Export–Import Bank from disbursing the loans it had made to Gulf Oil, on the grounds that Angola was a Communist country.

92. At the end of July 1985, FAPLA launched a major attack, starting from the eastern town of Luena along the Benguela Railway, and aimed at Cazombo near the Zambian border, which UNITA admitted losing on September 18. A second thrust was initiated from Menongue in the south-central region against the UNITA supply depot at Mavinga, farther to the southeast. UNITA claimed to have repelled the attack after a close call and asserted that for the first time the Angolan units were led by Portuguese-speaking Russian officers. The government insisted that Savimbi had to call in South African commandos to help him stave off defeat in the south; Western diplomats were reported inclined to accept the Angolan government's view. The South Africans said that they were mainly attacking SWAPO, but this is not very believable in the light of a decline of SWAPO activity during the previous year (*The Economist*, June 14 and August 30, 1986). It has again been suggested that the Soviet Union restrained FAPLA because a decisive Angolan victory would reduce the country's dependency (Le *Monde*, September 3, 1985) (hereafter cited as *Monde*). There was also increased sabotage in the Cabinda enclave, prompting the assignment of additional Cubans troops during 1986 to protect the Chevron installations. Angola reportedly received 2,000 more Cubans in preparation for the 1987 summer offensive, bringing its total strength to 37,000 Cubans, as well as another $1 billion in Soviet aid (*Monde*, May 14, 1987, reporting from the *Washington Post*). In mid-1987 UNITA claimed a strength of 65,000 and control over a "liberated zone" with a population of over 1 million. Though aided by South Africa, the organization was largely self-sufficient, financing itself by selling valuable timber and diamonds. However, the towns were controlled by FAPLA (Jacques de Barrin in *Monde*, May 27, 1987).

93. *WRS*, 1979, 1984, 1985, 1986; UCSR, *Uprooted Angolans: From Crisis to Catastrophe* (Washington, D.C.: U.S. Government Printing Office, August 1987).

94. Responsibility for implementing the project was borne by the World University Service, Canada. A reported 16,000 of 30,000 had been replaced by September 1985; another 2,500 returned to Angola (*WRS*, 1985, p. 51; UNHCR Fact Sheet, Zaire, September 1986, no. 10). See also reports in *Refugees*, no. 11 (November 1984), pp. 8–9, and no. 16 (April 1985), pp. 17–18. On the situation of the refugees in Zaire, see the report by James Brooke in *NYT*, February 10, 1987. The official refugee count in Zaire decreased by half in 1985 following a reassessment of Angolans in Shaba after their resettlement in other area, owing to the reluctance of some to move away from the border and the inclusion of many Zairian returnees in the original count. But the influx continued, and the count was up again to 240,500 at the end of the year, of whom 41,000 were assisted (Office of the UNHCR, *UNHCR Activities Financed by Voluntary Funds: Report for 1985–86 and Proposed Programmes and Budget for 1987. Part II. Africa* (New York: UNGA, A/AC.96/677, Part II, July 31, 1986), p. 86.

95. As noted earlier, Zambia's stance in relation to the Angolan conflict reflects its dependence on the Benguela Railroad. UNITA and Angolan refugees became undesirable when Zambia effected a rapprochement with the MPLA. On similar grounds, Zambia also rejects refugees from Zaire, Zimbabwe, Malawi, and Mozambique while granting asylum to those from South Africa and Namibia.

96. *WRS*, 1985, p. 41; UNHCR, *Activities*, 1986, p. 92.

97. Although Machel was generally regarded as a "charismatic leader," on his death in 1986 *The Economist* (October 25, 1986) commented that his Marxism was half-baked, and his leadership undisputed only for lack of a believable rival. A similarly harsh judgment is hinted at in Horace Campbell, "War, Reconstruction and Dependence in Mozambique," *Third World Quarterly*, 6, 4 (October 1984), p. 852.

98. Elise Forbes Pachter, "Contra-Coup: Civilian Control of the Military in Guinea, Tanzania, and Mozambique," *Journal of Modern African Studies*, 20, 4 (1982), pp. 600–3.

99. It is hardly surprising to read this in *The Economist*, but the indictment from the left is extremely severe as well. Campbell, for example, asserts bluntly: "In effect, the inability to ground their ideas in the concrete reality of the social conditions of production led to economic formulations

and policy directives which compounded the already tenuous hold that Frelimo had over the economy." ("War," p. 854). Much in the same vein, Barry Munslow concludes: "The neglect of the peasant-family sector was arguably the most damaging aspect of agricultural policy," attributing this to an overzealous desire to socialize the countryside ("State Intervention," p. 215). These analyses are confirmed by Claude Meillassoux and Christine Verschuu, who point out the absence of support for community villages as production units and the authoritarian regrouping of peasants in new "protected villages"—attributing the growing distance between the leaders and the population to "rigid Marxist dogmas." They also indicate an accentuation of class formation, as small southern landowners whose development was blocked by Portuguese settlers now tended to control much of the state and party apparatus ("Les Paysans Ignorés du Mozambique," *Le Monde Diplomatique,* October 1985, pp. 14–15).

100. The first aspect is illustrated by President Machel's declaration at a press conference in May 1979 that the long common border between the two countries was a reality that could neither be ignored nor altered. Accordingly, Mozambique would not participate in sanctions. New agreements for coal exports were signed in that year as well (*ACR,* 1979–80, p. B735).

101. Campbell, "War," pp. 839–67.

102. For a full discussion of the evolution of economic relations between the two countries, see Michel Cahen's analysis of the economic aspects of the Nkomati accord, in *Estudos de Economia* (February 1986) (original French version provided by the author).

103. Contrary to SADCC hopes, the flow of international transit traffic through Mozambique declined by 80 percent from 1973 to 1983, and port traffic dropped by about 70 percent, with most Zimbabwean firms switching to Durban. From a World Bank survey quoted in *International Herald Tribune* (Paris), April 5–6, 1986.

104. Notably the assassination in 1982 by letter bomb of the prominent political scientist Ruth First, who was also the wife of ANC leader Joe Slovo.

105. Colin Legum, "The Southern African Crisis," *ACR,* 15 (1982–83), pp. A18–19; *The Economist,* March 30, 1985.

106. The Thatcher government's assistance was intended to protect the large British investment in both countries, including especially the British-owned pipeline linking Beira with Zimbabwe.

107. The agreement also suggested that in Pretoria the diplomats prevailed over the generals (Alan Cowell in *NYT,* October 24, 1986; *The Economist,* October 25, 1986).

108. The extent of the ANC presence at the time has not been ascertained. In early 1984 estimates of the South African refugee community ranged between 150 and 500 (*Refugees,* no. 2, February 1984, p. 7, and April 1984, p. 17).

109. RENAMO advocates included CIA Director William Casey, White House staffer Patrick Buchanan, and Philip Ringdahl, who directed African affairs on the National Security Council staff (*NYT,* May 20, 1987).

110. Moreover, on Machel's visit, a "senior U.S. official" stated that members of South Africa's 700,000-man-strong immigrant Portuguese community—many of them ex-settlers—were aiding the rebels in violation of the agreement, and Pretoria itself acknowledged that its forces were maintaining contact with RENAMO leaders (*NYT,* November 9, 18, and 25, 1984). Although South Africa attempted to follow up by encouraging a coalition between Machel and the RENAMO, this came to nought.

111. *Le Monde Diplomatique,* December 1986, p. 17.

112. *The Economist,* October 18, 1986, p. 43; the order was carried out the following spring (*NYT,* March 6, 1987).

113. Commandos reportedly infiltrated into Maputo shortly before Machel's death and again in May 1987, when they raided ANC targets (*NYT,* May 30, 1987).

114. This section is based on reports in *NYT* (December 6, 1986; January 22 and 30, 1987); *The Economist,* October 25, 1986, and March 7, 1987; *Monde,* November 5, 1986. Tanzania became the major entry point for military assistance. In addition, *Monde* (April 17, 1987) reported

that a contingent of about one thousand Tanzanian soldiers established itself at the beginning of 1987 in Quelimane, capital of Zambezia Province. However, because of financial costs, Tanzania's contribution had to remain limited.

115. State Department officials reported in March 1987 that they had squelched conservative efforts (*NYT*, March 16, 1987). However, the claim proved premature, as the campaign was revived a few months later under the leadership of Senator Jesse Helms and with the support of Senate minority leader Bob Dole, focusing on opposition to the nomination of career diplomat Melissa Wells as the new ambassador to Maputo (*NYT*, May 19, 20, 25, and 30, 1987). Wells was utlimately confirmed.

116. See the interview in *Monde*, March 4, 1987.

117. According to this, Mozambique's output shrank by nearly 10 percent a year from 1980 to 1985 (*The Economist*, July 18, 1987). See the lengthy report in *Monde*, July 16, and *NYT*, August 30, 1987.

118. *WRS*, 1984, 1985, 1986; *Refugees*, May 1987, pp. 7, 42–43; July 1987, p. 7; U.S. Committee for Refugees, *Refugees from Mozambique: Shattered Land, Fragile Asylum* (November 1986).

119. See also the report of the situation as of March 1987 by John Hammock, executive director of Oxfam America, in *Oxfam America News*, Spring 1987, pp. 1 and 4. However, *The Economist* reported in its March 7 issue that with the attack on Beira broken, maize might flow in from Zimbabwe's large surplus.

120. The numbers game is very complex. The UNHCR figure of 20,000 (*Refugees*, January 1987) is by all accounts unduly low. The estimates of concerned NGOs ranged up to 175,000 (*WSR*, 1986). South Africa claimed it had received 60,000 refugees and 160,000 illegal immigrants—a distinction that others rejected. The "illegals" are Mozambicans without work contracts, who include many people driven out by the violence. NGOs reported 45,000 in the Gazankulu Homeland, based on estimates by the local authorities, but a Red Cross official spoke of only 15,000. The remainder were in other homelands, 25,000 in Kankwane and about 5,000 each in Lebowa and KwaZulu.

121. Michel Bole-Richard in *Monde*, December 18, 1985.

122. *WRS*, 1985, p. 46; *Refugees*, 40 (April 1987), pp. 27–29.

123. For an account of the situation along the border in 1984, see the report from a Reuters correspondent, reprinted in *Refugees*, no. 5 (May 1984), p. 37. The UNHCR's official assessment is from UNHCR, *Activities*, 1986, p. 98.

124. *Refugees*, no. 31 (July 1986), pp. 11–12.

125. For the offensive, see *The Economist*, October 18, 1986. Mozambique claimed 200,000; officials of international relief agencies reported 40,000 to 60,000 (*International Herald Tribune*, Paris ed., November 20, 1986; *NYT*, December 5, 1986). A report in *Refugees* suggested that it is extremely difficult to distinguish refugees from the local population and that people move back and forth in accordance with the fortunes of war. There were also an estimated 300 recognized refugees and asylum seekers in the urban areas (no. 29, May 1986, p. 15).

126. Connected to Capetown by a railway and 1,200 km of modern highway, Walvis Bay has modern shipping facilities for mineral exports and fisheries. It also possesses considerable strategic significance in relation to the South Atlantic.

127. *ACR*, 1977–78, p. B836. Polarization on the African side was intensified as SWAPO withdrew from the convention, taking with them the Rehoboth Volkspartei and NAPDO, as well as the Nama chiefs, while Clemens Kapuuo and the Ovambo leader, Pastor Cornelius Ndjoba, began enrolling members of their ethnic groups into organizations of their own, the National Union Democratic Organization and the Ovambo National Independence party.

128. *ACR*, 1979–80, p. B846. Initially, despite UNITA's cooperation with South Africa in the border region, the SWAPO leadership in Lusaka adhered to its established pro-UNITA stance, in tune with Zambia's own position and arising as noted earlier from dependence on the Benguela

Railway. This provoked a rebellion by the guerrilla rank and file and PLAN officers, which was repressed by Zambian authorities. In April 1976, a dozen SWAPO leaders were arrested on charges of plotting against President Sam Nujoma and subsequently transferred to Tanzania, while perhaps as many as one thousand guerrillas were rounded up by the Zambian army and interned (Landis and Davis, "Namibia," in Carter and O'Meara (eds.), *Southern Africa,* p. 165). Some exiles also returned to join the DTA.

129. *ACR,* 1976–77, p. B777; Green and Kiljunen, "The Colonial Economy," pp. 107, 164, 167. About twenty thousand Angolans crossed into Ovamboland in June 1976 as the result of a joint Cuban-MPLA campaign against UNITA. But many Namibians in turn fled from that region into Angola when the SADF emptied the border villages to create a security zone. Community facilities and hospitals were closed down, and anyone found in the no man's land was to be shot on sight.

130. As part of the ongoing negotiations, in May 1978 Tanzanian President Nyerere released Andreas Shipanga and the other dissenting SWAPO leaders interned since 1976; Shipanga then formed the SWAPO-Democrats (SWAPO-D), who allied themselves to the NNF, claiming they would obtain 40 percent of the votes should U.N.-supervised elections be held.

131. *ACR,* 1979–80, p. B829.

132. Although conscription in South Africa is limited to whites, there were about 2,000 blacks in the permanent force units, as well as thousands more Coloreds and Asians. In June 1980 a large operation was carried out by a strike force of white and black light infantry against the SWAPO nerve center in Angola, between Lubango and Cassinga, demolishing their strongholds and seizing about 100 tons of Soviet supplies. The SADF claimed that this dismantled SWAPO's military infrastructure in southern Angola, leaving PLAN leaderless and disoriented, and reported that an increasing number of guerrillas were giving themselves up under an amnesty plan. Over 170 guerrillas were killed each month during 1980, and the cumulative total of South African military dead since the beginning of hostilities in 1966 passed the 400 mark.

133. The conference also provided some international recognition for the DTA government. See Seiler, "South Africa," in Callaghy (ed.), *South Africa,* pp. 175–76. None of the significant "middle parties" (Swapo-D, SWANU, NNF, or the new NIP) took part.

134. By 1981 the three-tier system of government was fully in place, with municipal councils at the bottom, a middle level of eleven ethnic legislatures, and a council of ministers composed of one representative of each of the ethnic communities represented in the National Assembly, including whites. The latter gave a majority to the Nationalist party, indicating mounting opposition to the dismantling of the apparatus of racial segregation, which was part of the Turnhalle project. In September 1981 all departments of government were formally repatriated from Pretoria to Windhoek, but the South African administrator general still controlled the police and local armed forces, with reinforced powers. The NNF and SWAPO-D planned to merge as the Namibian People's Organization/Namibian National Union but failed. The National Independence party and the Rehoboth block withdrew from the NNF, and the outcome of the April 1980 party congress indicated that SWAPO had no serious rival (*ACR,* 1980–81, p. B753).

135. *ACR,* 1981–82, p. B670. The military command announced on July 15, 1981, that conscripts who identified themselves as SWAPO supporters would be treated as conscientious objectors.

136. The Ovambo-based NDP withdrew from the DTA in February 1982, followed a month later by its Damara component. The slow progress of desegregation created tensions among both white and black components of the DTA and NNF, and there were growing tensions between the DTA government and the administrator general over resistance to the creation of an integrated municipality in Windhoek.

137. Seiler, "South Africa," pp. 176–78. The Contact Group itself was divided on these proposals, with Thatcher-ruled Britain in support, whereas France (with a new Socialist government), Canada, and West Germany expressed reservations.

138. *ACR*, 1981–82, pp. B721, B727. Official sources claimed that one-fifth of all soldiers in Namibia by mid-1981 were conscripts, but the proportion in the war zone was much higher. Around this time, it was estimated that PLAN had six thousand to eight thousand guerrillas in Angola and six hundred active in Namibia proper. The disparity persisted, leading some observers to suggest that a major part of SWAPO's men were in fact operating as quasi mercenaries for the MPLA (*The Times*, London, July 15, 1981; *The Economist*, March 30, 1985).

139. Interview with H. P. Asheeke, deputy permanent representative, SWAPO Permanent Observer Mission to the U.N., New York, May 21, 1987.

140. SWAPO Information Bulletin (Lusaka), February 1987, pp. 13–19. Functioning as an unusual university in exile, in its first decade UNIN produced nearly one thousand middle-level cadres, some of whom went on to further university education in Africa and abroad and prepared— in cooperation with SWAPO, the office of the United Nations Commissioner for Namibia, and the United Nations Development Program—a comprehensive document on reconstruction and development planning to be implemented after independence. The institute has been labeled as a SWAPO training camp. When its director, Hage Geingob, was accused of directing funds to the organization, he explained that he and other administrative staff had been detached from SWAPO and were properly paying taxes on their U.N. salaries to their government in exile.

141. The overview that follows is from I. Diener, "La Namibie après Lusaka," *Politique Africaine*, 19 (September 1985), pp. 32–35.

142. These were entrusted to a 2,000-to-3,000-strong unit known as *koevoet* (crowbar) who, according to a settler campaigning for human rights, sometimes wear insurgent uniforms to seek out guerrilla sympathizers and pay children to inform against their parents. SWAPO reportedly kills informants in retaliation (*NYT*, March 23, 1984). A total of 179 guerrillas were reported killed from mid-February to early May, including 6 or 7 by the Joint Commission. As of mid-1984, South African sources estimated that SWAPO had 7,000 to 8,000 combatants, of whom about half were fighting UNITA, and about 1,000 operating in northern Namibia. Governmental forces amounted to about 30,000, including police and military, both South African and Namibian. The six years of operations had claimed about 10,000 victims to date, including 850 civilians, 1,000 soldiers (216 in combat since mid-1979, the rest in mines or accidents), and about 8,000 guerrillas. SWAPO, however, claimed a cumulative count of 2,865 South African casualties as of 1983. A report published in *The Nation* (May 11, 1985) estimated 10,000 Namibians killed and the deployment of 100,000 South African troops.

143. Herman Toivo ya Toivo was released after sixteen years of detention and was provided with travel documents to visit Nujoma and others in neighboring countries. He charged that this was designed to sow confusion within SWAPO by enhancing the credibility of the internal parties that were credited with his release. On March 12, Nujoma and the Angolan government accepted inclusion of the internal parties but rejected the linkage with UNITA and hence the proposal itself. On May 4, Nujoma indicated he was ready to meet with South Africa and no longer opposed the participation of the internal parties. In return, the South African administrator general announced the release of fifty-four SWAPO prisoners and authorized the Joint Commission to visit Namibian prisons (*NYT*, March 9, 12, and 23, 1984).

144. Simon Jenkins in *The Economist*, March 30, 1985.

145. Editorial, *The Economist*, June 22, 1985.

146. SWAPO press statement, Luanda, April 15, 1987; *NYT*, June 21, 1987. It should be noted, however, that SWAPO insists that the war in Namibia is continuing. This was emphasized also by the SWAPO spokesman in the interview noted earlier. In January 1986, arsonists destroyed the offices of the Council of Churches, after which the site was rezoned for residential use only. Vandals attacked the building housing a progressive newspaper as well as the offices of the Namibia Literacy Program. Louis Freedberg, "Stirrings in a Forgotten Land," *The Nation*, June 21, 1986, pp. 849–51.

147. Seven thousand were in Zambia, and nearly all of the remainder were in Angola. *UNHCR Fact Sheet*, Southern Africa, September 1986, no. 6.

Chapter 4

1. The principal sources for this section are Christopher Clapham, *Haile Selassie's Government* (New York: Praeger, 1969); John M. Cohen, "Ethiopia: A Survey of the Existence of a Feudal Peasantry," *Journal of Modern African Studies,* 12, 4 (December 1974), pp. 665–72; Richard Greenfield, *Ethiopia: A New Political History* (New York: Praeger, 1965); Robert L. Hess, *Ethiopia: The Modernization of Autocracy* (Ithaca, N.Y.: Cornell University Press, 1970); Donald Levine, *Greater Ethiopia: The Evolution of a Multiethnic Society* (Chicago: University of Chicago Press, 1974); I. M. Lewis, *A Modern History of Somalia* (London: Longman Group, 1980); Herbert S. Lewis, "The Origins of the Galla and Somali," *Journal of African History,* 7 (1966), pp. 27–46; Harold D. Nelson (ed.), *Somalia: A Country Study* (Washington, D.C.: U.S. Government Printing Office, 1982); Harold D. Nelson and Irving Kaplan (eds.), *Ethiopia: A Country Study* (Washington, D.C.: U.S. Government Printing Office, 1981); Margery Perham, *The Government of Ethiopia,* 2nd ed. (London: Faber & Faber, 1969); Bereket Habte Selassie, *Conflict and Intervention in the Horn of Africa* (New York: Monthly Review Press, 1980); Edward Ullendorff, *The Ethiopians,* 3rd ed. (London: Oxford University Press, 1973).

2. Although effective imperial rule seldom, if ever, extended to the entire zone, the idea of empire was substantiated around the turn of the fourteenth century when contenders for the throne, building on an ancient and widespread tradition according to which the Queen of Sheba originated on the African side of the Red Sea, sought to legitimize themselves by demonstrating descent from Solomon. The victorious Shoan Amhara also insisted that as members of the House of David, they were distant cousins of Jesus—much as their Muslim neighbors claimed descent from Mohammed.

3. See Cohen, "Ethiopia"; and Gene Ellis, "Land Tenancy Reform in Ethiopia: A Retrospective Analysis," *Economic Development and Cultural Change,* 24, 3 (April 1980), pp. 685–91. The societies of the Abyssinian plateau possessed the plow but not the wheel; arable land was scarce; agricultural production barely, if at all, met the needs of subsistence; and long-distant communications and transportation were hampered by the mountainous terrain. Notables, including church officials, squeezed some sort of surplus from the peasantry, but before the twentieth century, the process of extraction did not yield the critical mass necessary for the emergence of a centralized state. On the basis of observations in recent times, it can be inferred that the general population held inalienable and hereditary shares in land of their kinship group, known as *rist.* Notables, including clergy, eked out some sort of "surplus" from this by way of *gult,* a grant from higher authorities to their officials that, in exchange for service, authorized them to the labor of *rist* holders under their control. Although the system is usually labeled *feudal* or *semifeudal,* the appropriateness of this concept has been challenged on the grounds that *gult* was, in theory at least, not hereditary.

4. As Perham, "The Government of Ethiopia," has suggested, "The power of the monarchy may be visualized as a magnificent and lofty throne which was always standing ready for the dynast who had the military power and ability to climb up into it" (p. 76).

5. The canal "made the Red Sea one of the world's great highways, and its barren coasts at once assumed strategic and economic importance. In the interior the source of the Nile began to arouse European interest and ambitions. Great stretches of territory waiting for annexation by the first comer lay along both the sea and the river and Ethiopia stood between them" (ibid., p. 52).

6. Richard Sherman, *Eritrea: The Unfinished Revolution* (New York: Praeger, 1980), p. 12.

7. In the mid-1930s there were probably between 300,000 and 500,000 slaves in Ethiopia as a whole (Perham, "The Government of Ethiopia," p. 232).

8. One-third of the land, together with the labor of its inhabitants, was granted to the church to foster its expansion into the pagan areas, and another third was allotted to soldier-settlers. Most of the local population was gradually reduced to tenancy (Greenfield, *Ethiopia,* p. 172). See also John Markakis and Nega Ayele, *Class and Revolution in Ethiopia* (Nottingham, England: Spokesman, 1978), pp. 23–26.

9. The largest effective political units were clans, ranging in size from 10,000 to 100,000 members, associated with particular areas of pasturage, and further grouped into four major clan-

families with somewhat more precise geographical locations. For purposes of political and military action, the Somali combined and recombined through factions established among close kinsmen on the basis of common blood-compensation.

10. As Perham, "The Government of Ethiopia," pointed out, the Ethiopian government "had still three characteristics of medieval finance. There was nothing resembling a budget or any centralized accounting. Secondly, no clear distinction had been developed between the sovereign's private finances and those of the state. . . . Thirdly, a great deal of the revenue was still in kind and in labour and thus for the most part had to be levied and used locally by methods which gave every opportunity for abuse" (p. 190). Much the same could be said for the army.

11. By the late 1970s, estimates ranged between 2.0 million and 3.5 million, still about evenly distributed among the two religious groups but with perhaps a trend toward a Muslim majority (Sherman, *Eritrea,* p. 3).

12. This section is based largely on Richard Greenfield, "An Historical Introduction to Refugee Problems in the Horn," *Horn of Africa,* 2 (October–December 1979), pp. 14–26, as well as other articles in the same issue; and "Tragedy in the Horn," special issue of *Horn of Africa* 4, 1 (1981).

13. The resulting dynamic is reminiscent of Chad: "The leaders of the zones, far from helping each other, were rejoicing at the defeat of one another. Not only were they collecting money from the local population through taxes, fines, and donations, but also were accumulating property for the future by looting cattle and other property from the people they ruled" (Sherman, *Eritrea,* p. 140).

14. Dan Connell, "Eritrea: The Politics of Refugees," *Horn of Africa,* 2 (October–December 1979), pp. 4–7. Moreover, after the assassination of the U.S. ambassador by Black September terrorists in 1973, the United States cut off all aid and imposed on Sudan what was tantamount to an economic blockade.

15. The major sources for the prerevolutionary period are Clapham, *Haile Selassie's Government;* Hess, *Ethiopia;* and Nelson and Kaplan (eds.), *Ethiopia;* as well as Robert S. Love, "Economic Change in Pre-Revolutionary Ethiopia," *African Affairs,* July 1979, pp. 339–56. For the revolution proper, in addition to Markakis and Ayele, *Class and Revolution,* they include Fred Halliday and Maxine Molyneux, *The Ethiopian Revolution* (London: Verso, 1983); Marina Ottoway and David Ottoway, *Ethiopia: Empire in Revolution* (New York: Africana Publishing, 1978); John W. Harbeson, "Socialist Politics in Revolutionary Ethiopia," in Carl G. Rosberg and Thomas M. Callaghy (eds.), *Socialism in Sub-Saharan Africa* (Berkeley, Calif.: Institute for International Studies, 1979), pp. 345–72; Patrick Gilkes, *The Dying Lion: Feudalism and Modernization in Ethiopia* (London: Julian Friedman, 1975); Michael Chege, "The Revolution Betrayed: Ethiopia 1974–79," *Journal of Modern African Studies,* 17, 3 (1979), pp. 359–80; and Ryszard Kapuscinsiki, *The Emperor: Downfall of an Autocrat* (New York: Vintage, 1984). Despite its self-presentation as reportage, Kapuscinsiki's book is a brilliant interpretative essay, using (without acknowledging) basic works by Perham, Clapham, and Greenfield, among others, to construct a poetic vision of an anachronistic autocracy and its disintegration. In the final analysis it is perhaps best viewed as an important work of contemporary political theory. Sources for developments in the 1980s include annual issues of *Africa Contemporary Record,* and papers presented at the Conference on the Problems of the Horn of Africa, Woodrow Wilson Center, Smithsonian Institution, Washington, D.C., June 1987. These include particularly papers by John Cohen, John Harbeson, Patrick Gilkes, and Christopher Clapham—all of which were previews of larger forthcoming works.

16. Clapham, who has examined the matter more carefully than anyone else has, concluded that Haile Selassie's administration "developed in Shoa from the household of a Shoan Emperor and as part of a policy of centralisation on a Shoan base. The highest posts have therefore tended to go to Shoans . . ." (*Haile Selassie's Government,* p. 75). By his reckoning, the proportion of Shoans in the upper reaches of government hovered around two-thirds—approximately six times what the proportionality to population would allow. The dominance of the Amhara more generally was also visible in the new institutions, which provided a channel for recruitment into the modern

sector. A survey conducted in 1959–60 indicated that although the Amhara constituted a mere 20 percent of the total population, they accounted for 55 percent of all students in Ethiopia's secondary schools and colleges (Levine, *Greater Ethiopia*, p. 249).

17. The basic source for this is Love, "Economic Change." Industry was dominated by the textile, food, and beverage industries, the sectoral share of gross domestic product attributable to manufacturing rose from 2.2 percent in 1960 to 4.5 percent in 1972–73. However, one estimate suggests that by 1967, 75 percent of the private capital in manufacturing was in foreign hands, with a similar situation in trade.

18. Markakis and Ayele, *Class and Revolution*, p. 55, n. 22. In the same vein, allocation to the peasant sector in the Third Five Year Development Plan, 1968–73, amounted to only 1 percent of the projected total expenditures. This, moreover, was to be allotted to the development of large commercial farms. Nelson and Kaplan (eds.), *Ethiopia*, p. 147.

19. Personal observation, A. Zolberg, December 1973.

20. Sweden developed the air force, and Norway formed a coast guard, Israel, paratroopers, and India, a new military academy. Nelson and Kaplan (eds.), *Ethiopia*, pp. 243–44.

21. The conspirators' motive was perhaps best expressed by the general's reply to the judges who sentenced him to death: "I have done what you say, but I am not guilty. Ethiopia has been standing still, while our African brothers are moving ahead in the struggle to overcome poverty." As reported by Donald Levine, "Haile Selassie's Ethiopia—Myth or Reality?" *African Affairs*, 8, 5 (May 1961), p. 11.

22. Clapham, *Haile Selassie's Government*, pp. 24–25; Levine, "Haile Selassie's Ethiopia," p. 14.

23. However, Love has suggested that the armed forces' share of the national income, and particularly the army's, in fact deteriorated between 1967 and 1974 ("Economic Change," p. 348).

24. This necessarily cursory assessment of the land reform and its effects fails to do justice to the subtleties of the analyses on which it is based. These include John H. Cohen, "Analysing the Ethiopian Revolution: A Cautionary Tale," *Journal of Modern Africa Studies*, 18 (December 1980), pp. 685–91; Ellis, "Land Tenancy Reform"; and Peter Koehn, "Ethiopia: Famine, Food Production, and Changes in the Legal Order," *African Studies Review* (April 1979), pp. 51–72. An updated assessment was presented by Cohen (on behalf of himself and Mils-Ivar Isaksson) at the Woodrow Wilson Center conference.

25. It formed the core of the Ethiopian Peoples' Democratic Alliance, which reportedly received half a million dollars from the CIA from 1981 to 1986, but proved to be ineffective (See Op-Ed by Jerry Tinker, head of Senator Edward Kennedy's legislative staff, in the *New York Times*, August 16, 1986 (hereafter cited as *NYT*).

26. The basic source for armed forces in the Horn is by Paul B. Henze, "Arming the Horn, 1960–1980," Working Paper no. 43, International Security Studies Program (Washington, D.C.: Woodrow Wilson Center, July 1982).

27. I. M. Lewis, "The Politics of the 1969 Somali Coup," *Journal of Modern African Studies*, 10, 3 (October 1972), pp. 383–408; David Laitin, "The Political Economy of Military Rule in Somalia," *Journal of Modern African Studies*, 14, 3 (1976), pp. 449–68. Despite considerable foreign aid, the country experienced little or no economic development. For all practical purposes, access to office was the sole avenue to economic success, and the political arena became quite literally a marketplace: "The corruption of the civilian regime had reached egregious proportions by 1969, to a degree that was an insult to the morality and the intelligence of most Somalis. The last election in March 1969 was rife with candidates openly and unabashedly buying their parliamentary seats. Afterward the ruling party 'bought out' the opposition members, and this kind of cynicism filtered down to the bureaucracy" (Laitin, "The Political Economy," p. 453).

28. This analysis is based on David Laitin, "The Ogadeen Question and Changes in Somali Identity," in Donald Rothchild and Victor A. Orunsula (eds.), *State Versus Ethnic Claims: African Policy Dilemmas* (Boulder, Colo.: Westview Press, 1983), pp. 331–47.

29. In February–March 1964, armed encounters erupted all along the Ethiopian-Somalian border, but Somalia subsequently accepted an OAU cease-fire which imposed a 10-to-15 km-demilitarized zone on either side of the frontier. After yet another bout of conflict with Ethiopia in 1965–67 and a confrontation with France over Djibouti in 1966, which also ended in failure, Somalia began exploring detente with its neighbors, saving face by applying to join the East African Community within which all Somalis might be reunited. The deterioration of economic conditions due to the closing of the Suez Canal, which severely curtailed banana exports to Europe, also weighed in favor of detente at this time. At the same time, they withdrew support from Somali nationalists in the Ogaden and the Kenyan NFD.

30. Nelson, *Somalia*, p. 39; Robert F. Gorman, *Political Conflict on the Horn of Africa* (New York: Praeger, 1981), pp. 36–39; Henze, "Arming the Horn."

31. The SRC was committed to the elimination of "tribalism" and corruption, as well as to economic development along socialist lines. The new regime's achievements were mixed (Laitin, "The Political Economy," 1976).

32. Gorman, *Political Conflict*, pp. 68–72. The Soviet Union, which was on the verge of making a major commitment to assist the Derg, reportedly sought to avoid conflict, inducing Fidel Castro to arrange a secret meeting between Mengistu and Barre in March 1977. Nonetheless, the Soviet Union's vastly enlarged commitment to Ethiopia probably helped bring about the war (Henze, "Arming the Horn"). U.S. policy may have contributed to the conflict as well. After the unsuccessful Cuban-sponsored negotiations, Siad Barre made overtures to the Arab world, including Saudi Arabia, and thereby to the United States. The United States indicated interest in a rapprochement and held out the promise of military assistance, but it has been suggested that the negotiators failed to make clear that the aid was conditional on moderation with respect to the Ogaden. Alternatively, the Somalis may have reckoned that the United States would back them once war against a Soviet-backed government got under way. As it was, once the conflict erupted, the Soviet Union stepped up its assistance to Ethiopia, whereas the United States backed away from the Somalian side (Gorman, *Political Conflict*, pp. 70–72; *Newsweek*, September 26, 1977).

33. At this time, the Somalian and WSLF combined strength was estimated at fifty thousand troops, of whom fifteen thousand were irregulars, but it was difficult to distinguish within the Somalian army between natives of Somalia and Ethiopian Somalis, as the WSLF had long served as a conduit for recruitment of Ogaden youths into the Somalian army.

34. The demographic structure of the refugee population in Somalia, as discussed below, is consistent with reports that when the massive outflow of refugees began, the bulk of the able-bodied males remained behind, "living with their cattle or fighting among the ranks of the various anti-Ethiopian liberation fronts." *Le Monde*, July 21, 1981 (hereafter cited as *Monde*). In early 1979, the U.S. Department of State estimated there were all together between twenty thousand and thirty thousand active guerrilla fighters in the region. By the end of the year, the WSLF had secured most of the rural areas and towns south of Jijiga. As of mid-1980, a seasoned observer spoke of the superimposition within the Ogaden of two regimes, Ethiopian and Somali—in a manner reminiscent of Vietnam. Dan Connell, quoted in *Horn of Africa*, 4, 1 (1981), p. 44.

35. *Africa Contemporary Record* (New York: Africana Publishing, 1979–80), p. B306 (hereafter cited as ACR, with appropriate years). *Horn of Africa*, 4, 1 (1981), p. 43; *NYT*, October 14, 1981.

36. At the same time, there was a leadership crisis in the WSLF, resulting in the emergence of a new group less closely tied to Mogadishu. Nelson (ed.), *Somalia*, p. 247. There was also a greater willingness by the Somali government and the WSLF to recognize the Oromo Liberation Front as a distinct presence and to readjust their past rhetoric on the Oromo question (Hebte Selassie, *Conflict*, p. 124).

37. A report submitted to the U.N. secretary general in early 1984 in preparation for ICARA-II stated: "There are 700,000 refugees at camps and at least an equal number of spontaneously settled refugees in various urban and rural areas of the country." On this basis, refugees account for approximately one-fifth of the overall population of Somalia and constitute nearly half the popu-

lation of some regions contiguous to Ethiopia (U.N. General Assembly, A/CONF.125/2, March 23, 1984, p. 119). In addition, the ICARA report indicates that there are 1,600 Ethiopian refugees in Kenya and 25,000 in Djibouti; U.S. Committee on Refugee estimates are 1,500 and 31,500, respectively. It should be noted, however, that Somali aggression brought about a rapprochment between Kenya and Ethiopia and that Kenya is therefore likely to minimize the number of Ethiopian refugees on its territory. *Horn of Africa,* 4, 1 (1981), p. 52.

38. The returnees from Djibouti included 13,216 under UNHCR auspices and the others "spontaneous" (from reports in UNHCR, *Refugees,* January 1985–April 1986). For a critical view, see Roberta Aitchison, "Djibouti: A Model for Repatriation?" *Cultural Survival Quarterly,* 7, 2 (Summer 1983), pp. 48–51, cited also in United States Committee for Refugees, *Refugees in the Horn of Africa* (Washington, D.C.: USCR, January 1988), p. 23.

39. For example, in the late 1970s, the country's population was generally estimated at around 4.5 million, of whom approximately half were under age fifteen. But when a long-overdue general election was finally held in December 1979, officials reported that nearly 4 million votes had been cast in favor of President Siad Barre and his ruling party.

40. Because neither Ethiopia nor Somalia ever had a proper population census, there are no reliable figures on how many people there were in the regions of origin or of destination before the war. The ethnic Somali population of the Ogaden proper was estimated to be on the low side of one million in 1976. Allowing for an outflow that included nearly all women and children, we get a potential maximum of three-quarters of a million. To this, however, should be added Oromos from outside the Ogaden (i.e., Bale Province) who constituted a substantial share of the refugee total. *Horn of Africa,* 4, 1 (1981), p. 46.

41. In late 1979, G. Melander found that only 9 percent of the refugees were adult men. A Somali government survey of April 1981 showed 60 percent under age fifteen, 20 to 30 percent women, and the rest elderly men. The extremely high proportion of children was confirmed by the U.S. Public Health Service sample survey conducted in mid-1980, which also noted a low proportion of males in the fifteen-to-twenty-five age group (Nelson (ed.), *Somalia,* p. 128).

42. *The Economist,* January 9, 1988, p. 38. In September 1982, UNHCR officials reported that the Somali refugee commissioner admitted his government had forced Ogaden refugees to join the army after the recent border incidents (*NYT,* September 22, 1982). It is noteworthy that the investigation that led to this admission was initiated as the result of complaints by camp inmates, a fact that suggests that some, at least, in the Somali refugee community were questioning the warrior role.

43. This section is based on Nelson and Kaplan (eds.), *Ethiopia,* pp. 42, 214–15, 265–66; and Sherman, *Eritrea,* pp. 99–111, 155. The EPLF, with about fifteen thousand troops in the field, was strongest in the east, whereas the EFL, claiming an effective force of twenty thousand, concentrated its operations in the southwest, near the Sudan border.

44. Its fighting force included many deserters from the Ethiopian armed forces and women combatants. It was organized into highly mobile units of about twenty, with considerable firepower, sometimes combined into combat teams, several of which may have formed a combat force, and further into a battalion. Leaders at each force level were chosen by election; troops were reported to be well disciplined and efficient, demonstrating impressive individual initiative. Its weapon inventory consisted primarily of Soviet equipment captured from Ethiopian forces, including anti-aircraft missiles, mobile medium- and long-range artillery pieces, and a number of T-54 tanks, used primarily in fixed positions as artillery. Sudan had initially been supported by Libya as well; however, Libya's policy in the Horn was increasingly determined by Qaddafi's hostility to the Sudanese leader. When tensions mounted between the Sudan and Ethiopia, Qaddafi switched his support from the Eritreans to the Derg. In 1976, Ethiopia and Libya backed a coup against Numeiri, which prompted Sudan to increase its support for the guerrillas. Aden (South Yemen) also publicly endorsed the Ethiopian Derg when it turned to the Soviet Union in mid-1977, but the leadership appears to have been divided on this issue, and as of early 1980, Aden again extended its facilities to the Eritreans (Sherman, *Eritrea,* p. 155).

45. Cuba initially held back, but in September 1978, proclaimed the Ethiopian Derg a "genuinely progressive force" that deserved support against the Eritreans, who were now said to be acting on behalf of an "international reactionary conspiracy" of conservative Arab states (ibid., p. 152).

46. Baghdad then shifted its support to the EFL–EPLF. In response, the ELF turned to Syria, which—given the rapprochement between Syria and Ethiopia engineered by the Soviet Union after the cooling down of relations between Moscow and Baghdad—placed its leaders in a good position to initiate contacts with Ethiopia. Denounced by the EPLF as a betrayal, these overtures triggered retaliatory actions. Dissatisfied with the moderate stance of the ELF–PLF chairman, Iraq urged one of his associates to form the Peoples Liberation Forces–Revolutionary Council (PLF–RC).

47. Connell, "Eritrea," 1979; see also *Horn of Africa*, 4, 1 (1981), pp. 26, 68, 84; and Aderanti Adepoju, "The Refugee Situation in the Horn of Africa and Sudan," *Issue*, 12, 1–2 (Spring–Summer 1982), p. 32.

48. An additional 200,000 Ugandans and 5,000 Zairians in the south brought the total refugee population to 665,000. (UN A/CONF.125/2, March 23, 1984, pp. 143–77). These figures—with the addition of a few thousand from Chad—were generally accepted as valid by observers and relief agencies (e.g., British Refugee Council, May 1984). Most of the Tigreans and about 250,000 Eritreans were located in Kassala Province, adjoining the border; about 100,000 Eritreans in Khartoum and surroundings; and another 100,000 Eritreans, who left by the northern route, were concentrated along the coastal highway leading to Port Sudan, including 55,000 in the city itself. *Horn of Africa*, 4, 1 (1981), p. 24; Sherman, *Eritrea*, pp. 99–105.

49. The negotiations culminated in Numeiri's visit to Addis Ababa the following November. As a consequence of the new Sudanese policies, the formerly adamant EPLF indicated its willingness to open negotiations with Ethiopia; the ELF–EPLF followed suit. In early December, however, Ethiopia launched yet another offensive, and it was reported once again that it was dropping booby bombs on the Eritrean countryside to terrorize the civilian population, stimulating additional flows of refugees into Sudan. Concurrently, the EPLF drove a reported 5,000 ELF followers from its newly acquired territorial domain into Sudan as well, where the number of refugees now approached 500,000. The further ascendancy of EPLF made ELF even more eager for a settlement with Ethiopia.

50. *ACR*, 1980–81, p. B171; *Horn of Africa*, 4, 1 (1981), p. 26. The rapprochement between Sudan and Ethiopia was short-lived, as the Derg soon negotiated a threatening treaty with Libya and South Yemen. In response, the Sudanese government renewed its commitment to the Eritreans and launched an effort to unify the various movements. Although all four groups participated in a meeting in Tunis in March 1981, they remained divided.

51. This is based on Cohen's presentation at the Woodrow Wilson conference, 1987. By guaranteeing plots to the peasants in their own locality, it had the effect of concentrating peasants in areas that were already overpopulated. Although many families gained land, much of it was extremely marginal, and because of the prohibition on hiring agricultural labor, better land could not be worked more intensively, and so the overall output declined.

52. A summary is presented in USCR, *Refugees in the Horn*.

53. The official figures are cited in UNHCR, *Refugee Update: Refugees in the Horn of Africa and Sudan*, New York, June 18, 1987; the estimate is in USCFR, *Horn*, p. 23.

54. Statement by Guy Prim, UNCHR deputy representative in Somalia, *Refugees*, November 1987, p. 33.

55. The United States' reluctance to provide military assistance waned in the face of the Iranian crisis and the Soviet invasion of Afghanistan, which boosted the importance of Somalia as a component of the United States' Persian Gulf defense. In August 1980, the United States leased the vacated Soviet base at Berbera (Gorman, *Political Conflict*, pp. 208–12).

56. UNCHR, *Refugees*, December 1987, p. 19. The Reagan administration, which had welcomed Siad Barre to Washington as an esteemed ally in the spring, immediately launched a weapons airlift of its own in support of Somalia. Despite warnings that stepped-up U.S. aid for

Somalia might increase Soviet support for an Ethiopian counterinvasion, which the Soviet Union had so far opposed, the conflict has remained at the level of perennial border clashes and occasional air raids (David Laitin, op-ed, *NYT*, August 16, 1982).

57. Peter Koehn, "The Migration of Post-revolution Exiles to the United States: Determinant Factors and Policy Implications in the Ethiopian Case," paper presented at the twenty-sixth annual meeting of the African Studies Association, December 1983.

58. David Kessler and Tudor Parfitt, "The Falashas: The Jews of Ethiopia," *Minority Rights Group Report*, 67 (July 1985).

59. *NYT*, March 25, 1985; *The Economist*, September 28, 1985.

60. For a sympathetic and realistic assessment of prospects, see Robert J. Berg and Jennifer Seymour Whitaker (eds.), *Strategies for African Development* (Berkeley and Los Angeles: University of California Press, 1986).

61. The countries discussed appear on *The Economist*'s roster of "Countries in Trouble" (December 20, 1986, p. 70):

Hyper-risk: Ethiopia, Sudan

Very high-risk: Uganda, Zambia, Nigeria, Zaire

High-risk: Ghana, South Africa, Zimbabwe, Kenya, Tanzania

62. *Monde*, November 26, 1987; *NYT*, March 23, 1988.

63. *NYT*, March 27, 1988.

64. Diamonds and uranium accounted for about half its gross domestic product as well as tax revenue, and three-quarters of exports (1980). Despite efforts by the international community to preserve the Namibian people's patrimony, the mineral companies sought to extract a maximum before independence. Rössing Uranium, a multinational company mainly owned by South Africa, Britain, and France, was one of the great economic successes of the decade, with a twice-a-week airlift of uranium oxide via Angola and Algeria to Paris, for distribution to nuclear authorities throughout Western Europe as well as, reportedly, the Soviet Union. Diamond mining is controlled by DeBeers, which is itself affiliated with the Anglo-American Corporation, South Africa's biggest gold producer; mining was cut by about half in the early 1980s to maintain world prices.

65. Transmission lines from Racana Falls Dam to the south have been repeatedly blown up and are almost impossible to defend. Accordingly, a high-tension power link to the western Cape has been pushed ahead at a very high cost.

66. The European power companies that constitute the major customers of Namibia's uranium were concerned mainly with ensuring the availability of supplies when demand expands again in the future. Hence they inclined toward striking a deal with SWAPO with respect to postindependence arrangements. As noted earlier, in the diamond sector, Anglo-American adopted a flexible policy with respect to majority rule, believing that it could live with an independent black government, as it has been doing in other parts of southern Africa and Tanzania. But it has been charged that its DeBeers affiliate is in fact stripping Namibian deposits of their best gems, as insurance against the future (according to a commission of inquiry appointed in 1982 by the South African administrator general, as reported in *NYT*, March 8, 1986; and *Libération*, Paris, March 11, 1986.

67. Jim Morrell, "The International Monetary Fund and Namibia," *Africa Today*, 1st and 2nd qtrs., 1983, p. 17. Given the evolution of costs and revenues in the early 1980s, the balance probably became negative, but costs must have gone down again after the Lusaka accords and the success of UNITA. Moreover, it should be kept in mind that defense costs would not necessarily decline very much after Namibian independence, because South Africa would have to protect its flank.

68. *Refugees*, no. 31 (July 1986), pp. 11–12. Because the raid took place a week before the South African elections, it was suggested that it was an attempt to appease the extreme right (*NYT*, April 26, 1987).

69. Michael Clough, "Beyond Constructive Engagement," *Foreign Policy*, 61 (Winter 1985–86), pp. 3–24; *NYT*, February 14, 1987.

70. On April 9, 1987, the United States and Britain vetoed a U.N. Security Council resolution that would have banned trade with South Africa; West Germany voted against, with France, Italy, and Japan abstaining; and SWAPO reportedly rejected proposals for milder resolutions that would have imposed temporary sanctions in the hope of avoiding the veto (*NYT*, April 10, 1987).

71. The increased cost was occasioned by the drop in Angola's oil income. On Soviet disengagement, see the excerpt from *International Affairs* (Moscow) published as an Op-Ed in *NYT*, January 7, 1989.

72. It was reported that direct Cuban involvement in the fighting was undertaken, with the tacit consent of the United States, as a way of bringing pressure to bear on Pretoria (Pamela Falk Op-Ed in *NYT*, August 10, 1988).

73. David Caute, "Mugabe Moves to One-Party Rule," *The Nation*, February 22, 1986, p. 204.

74. Kenneth Grundy, "The Social Costs of Armed Struggle in Southern Africa," *Armed Forces and Society*, 7 (1980–81), p. 453.

75. United Nations, Joint Inspection Unit, "Role of the Office of the United Nations High Commissioner for Refugees in Africa," JIU/REP/86/2; Geneva, March 1986, p. 5 (hereafter cited as JIU Report, 1986).

76. U.N. Office of the UNHCR, *UNHCR Activities Financed by Voluntary Funds: Report for 1986–86 and Proposed Programmes and Budget for 1987, Part II, Africa*, A/AC.96/677, Part II, July 31, 1986, p. 86 (hereafter cited as UNHCR Activities, 1986); *WRS*, 1985, 1986; *Monde*, May 22, 1986.

77. JIU Report, 1986, p. 5.

78. Ibid. Accordingly, the report's final recommendation is that a special fact-finding mission be despatched to the Front Line states to study ways and means of relieving refugee pressures on them (para. 82, p. 24).

79. In the light of the JIU's criticism, it is noteworthy that shortly after its publication, in response to the May 19, 1986, raid on Gabarone (Botswana), the UNHCR's public information organ, *Refugees*, published a major dossier on southern Africa entitled "The Protection of Refugees: Priority Number One." (no. 32, August 1986, pp. 19–31). Reports from the various receivers indicated a growing fear of retribution. Botswana indicated that although it would not reject South African refugees, despite the raid, they must not use their status to mount attacks on their country of origin. Mozambicans in Zambia were moved after refusing repatriation, and Lusaka similarly insisted that it would maintain an open policy but that the arrivals "must be genuine refugees."

80. JIU Report, 1986, p. 13; U.N. General Assembly, "Comments of the Secretary-General," A/41/380/Add.1; September 11, 1986, p. 7.

Chapter 5

1. The term *ethnic* is sometimes used to include all these distinctions, but the more common, subcontinental usage is to have separate designations for religion (namely, communal) and caste, leaving only language and culture as "ethnic" dimensions. The term will be used here in the latter manner. See Urmila Phadnis, *Ethnicity and Nation-building in South Asia* (New Delhi: Sage, forthcoming).

2. Benedict R. O. G. Anderson, *Imagined Communities—Reflections on the Origin and Spread of Nationalism* (London: New Left Books, 1983).

3. Because Tamils reside abroad under a variety of administrative categories, estimates are uncertain. This figure is based on U.S. Department of State, *Country Reports on the World's Refugee Situation: Statistics* (Washington, D.C.: U.S. Government Printing Office, 1985); *Tamil Refugee* (London: Central British Fund for Tamil Refugees Rehabilitation), various issues; and S. Guy de Fontgalland, *Sri Lankans in Exile* (Madras: Cerro Publications, 1986).

4. The number of asylum seekers in Europe from India, Bangladesh and Pakistan totaled 8,609 in 1984 and 12,680 in 1985 (UNHCR, Geneva).

5. Sadruddin Aga Khan, *Study on Human Rights and Massive Exoduses*, United Nations, ECOSOC, E/CN.4/1503, December 31, 1981, p. 24.

6. Ian Bull, Herb Feith, and Ron Hatley, "The West Papuan Challenge to Indonesian Authority in Irian Jaya," *Asian Survey*, 26 (May 1986), pp. 542–48.

7. Shahrough Akhavi, "Emigrants, Immigrants and the Islamic Republic of Iran: Exiles and Refugees Under the Khomeini Regime," paper presented at the International Conference on Refugees in the Islamic World, Bellagio, October 11–15, 1987. See also U.S. Committee for Refugees, *Iranian Refugees: The Many Faces of Persecution* (Washington, D.C.: U.S. Government Printing Office, December 1984).

8. The British documentation of linguistic diversity in the census was seen by Indian writers as a form of imperialist propaganda designed to erode the legitimacy of an all-Indian nationalist movement. See R. Palme Dutt, *India Today* (Calcutta: Manisha, 1983), p. 295.

9. Uma Kaura, *Muslims and Indian Nationalism* (New Delhi: Manohar Book Service, 1977), covers the 1939 negotiations in particular.

10. P. N. S. Mansergh, "Some Reflections on the Transfer of Power," in C. H. Phillips and M. D. Wainwright (eds.), *The Partition of India* (London: Allen & Unwin, 1970), p. 50.

11. Outbursts of violence and related migrations commenced in late 1946 before the negotiations leading to partition had been completed. A few voices warned that partition would lead to "rivers of blood," notably that of Maulana Azad, cited in Chaudhri Muhammad Ali, *The Emergence of Pakistan* (New York: Columbia University Press, 1967), p. 195. The British viceroy later claimed that although violence was anticipated, the "scale and extent" was not. Lord Mountbatten papers, cited in H. V. Hodson, *The Great Divide* (London: Hutchison, 1969), p. 403. Indeed, if the toll had been anticipated, how could the British have gone ahead with the partition? The point remains controversial and is linked to the haste of the British withdrawal. Prof. Bimal Prasad of Jawaharlal Nehru University in New Delhi, a leading authority on partition, maintains that massive migrations were *not* expected (oral communication, October 1985).

12. Chaudhri, *The Emergence of Pakistan*, p. 158.

13. Hodson, *The Great Divide*, pp. 272 et passim.

14. Zafar Imam, "Some Aspects of the Social Structure of the Muslim Community in India," in Zafar Imam (ed.), *Muslims in India* (New Delhi: Orient Longman, 1975), pp. 70–112.

15. Marcus F. Franda, *Population Politics in South Asia*, pt. II, American Universities Field Service (AUFS), 16, 3 (1972), pp. 3–4; see also Muhammad Ghulam Kabir, *Minority Politics in Bangladesh* (New Delhi: Vikas, 1980).

16. Sikh and Hindu refugees from West Punjab (Pakistan) were mainly landowners and peasants. They left behind properties of almost 4 million acres of agricultural land. Some had lost huge holdings (714 families accounted for half a million acres of abandoned land). Among the Muslim refugees, a relatively larger proportion was artisans, as indicated by the smaller amount of land abandoned in the Indian Punjab (2.4 million acres). M. S. Randhave, *Out of the Ashes* (Bombay: n.d.), p. 93. The author served as a senior civil servant in Punjab.

17. See Jeffrey Paige, *Agarian Revolution* (New York: Free Press, 1975). The property structure also helps explain why an organized population exchange was not seriously contemplated. The idea was briefly considered in the Partition council as a means of avoiding violence but was abandoned as impractical because the assymetry of immobile property between the populations to be exchanged was too great. Penderel Moon, *Divide and Quit* (London: Chatto & Windus, 1964), p. 275.

18. Stephen L. Keller, *Uprooting and Social Change* (Delhi: Manohar Book Service, 1978), p. 102.

19. The pattern was set already in August 1946. As the negotiations over partition broke down, Hindus and Muslims fought it out in the streets of Calcutta, with the Muslims apparently taking the worst beating. Farther East, in East Bengal, the Muslims attacked the Hindu minority, which sparked Hindu attacks on the Muslim minority in the nearby Bihar region.

20. The British are often blamed for executing a hasty and sudden partition, owing to the

general (or malevolent) indifference of a retreating colonial power or because the pro-Indian colonial authorities wanted to weaken Pakistan from its very inception. Chaudhri, *The Emergence of Pakistan*, p. 131; Ian Stephens, *Unmade Journey* (London: Stacy International, 1977). One British response is that violence was an inevitable concomitant of partition; if independence had been delayed, "the sword would only have fallen a few months later." R. J. Moore, *Escape from Empire* (Oxford, England: Clarendon Press, 1983), p. 331.

    21. U.S. Congress, House of Representatives, Committee on the Judiciary, *Refugees in India and Pakistan* (Washington, D.C.: U.S. Government Printing Office, May 1954), p. 6.

    22. Shahid Javed Burki, "Migration, Urbanization and Politics in Pakistan," in W. Howard Wriggins and James G. Guyot (eds.), *Population, Politics and the Future of Southern Asia* (New York: Columbia University Press, 1973), p. 166.

    23. About 2.3 million people arrived between 1951 and 1970, according to official Indian sources. Pran Nath Luthra, *Rehabilitation* (New Delhi: Ministry of Information and Broadcasting, 1972), pp. 18–19. Franda, *Population Politics in South Asia*, p. 2, gives a somewhat lower estimate.

    24. Nearly 200,000 people were deported between 1960 and 1970, according to government sources. Cited in *Indian Citizens vs. Foreign Nationals* (Gauhati, Assam: Asom Jagriti, 1980), p. 8, a publication of Assam's long-standing nativist movement against Bengali immigrants. The Assamese were about equally opposed to Muslims and Hindus from Bengal; yet Assam had refugee camps and even land resettlement schemes for Bengali refugees. Such refugees were generally Hindu; the Muslims from Bengal were considered illegal immigrants, and their number was estimated by census officials on the basis of abnormal growth rates in districts with a heavy Muslim population. Myron Weiner, "The Political Demography of Assam's Anti-Immigrant Movement," *Population and Development Review*, June 1983, pp. 279–92; Chib Sukhdev Singh, "Assam Problem: A Geopolitical Analysis," *Asian Profile*, 15 (July 1981), 88:152–61. Sanjib Baruah, "Migration, Ethnic Accommodation and Ethnic Conflict: Political Stability and Turmoil in Assam, India," unpublished manuscript, University of Wisconsin, Madison, 1986, is a careful analysis by an Assamese.

    25. From 1975 to 1985, an estimated 4.4 million "illegal immigrants" had crossed into India from Bangladesh and managed to remain. Around 30,000 were apprehended and returned in 1984 alone. *The Statesman*, November 6, 1985. By comparison, in the entire period between 1946 and 1970, only 3.9 million "refugees" crossed this border into India.

    26. Franda, *Population Politics in South Asia*, pp. 3–4; see also Kabir, *Minority Politics*.

    27. Tenants in Pakistan as described by a member of a government committee to investigate land reform in 1948–49. Cited in Tariq Ali, *Pakistan: Military Rule or People's Power* (London: Jonathan Cape, 1970), p. 98.

    The term *structural violence* is used in the sense developed by Johan Galtung, "Violence, Peace and Peace Research," *Journal of Peace Research*, 6 (1969), pp. 167–91.

    28. By 1980, an estimated 256 million people (48 percent of the rural population) in India, 52 million in Bangladesh (78 percent), and 38 million in Pakistan (58 percent) were living below the country-specific poverty lines in rural areas. The rural populations constitute the vast majority of the national populations. Inderjit Singh, "The Landless Poor in South Asia," paper prepared for a seminar sponsored by the World Bank, Rural Poverty in India, Gulmarg, Kashmir, May 1985, p. 1.

    29. Jacques Vernant, *The Refugee in the Post-War World* (London: Allen & Unwin, 1953), p. 738.

    30. Louise W. Holborn, *Refugees: A Problem of Our Time: The Work of the United Nations High Commissioner for Refugees, 1951–1972* (Metuchen, N.J.: Scarecrow Press, 1975), p. 82.

    31. Before the 1971 division of Pakistan, India was about three times as large as Pakistan and had almost five times its population and about six times its GNP; and regular Indian armed forces outnumbered Pakistan's forces by about 4 to 1. After 1971, the ratios were respectively 4 to 1

(territory), almost 9 to 1 (population), 10 to 1 (GNP), and 3.3 to 1 (armed forces). Based on the 1965 and 1975 figures from U.S. Arms Control and Disarmament Agency, *World Military Expenditures and Arms Transfers, 1965–74, 1966–75* (Washington, D.C.: U.S. Government Printing Office, 1975).

32. The same pattern appears in conflicts in the area involving China. One short Sino-Indian war, fought in sparsely populated mountainous regions, was followed by restoration of the status quo ante (1962) and produced no international refugees. China's annexation of Tibet (1950) and, above all, its forceful affirmation (1959) produced thousands of international refugees, as Tibetans loyal to the Dalai Lama streamed into India.

33. A total of 5,655 applied for asylum in 1985, and preliminary figures for 1986 suggested a slightly higher total for that year. (UNHCR, Geneva).

34. For the perspectives of two leading Indian social scientists on this point, see M. N. Srinivas, *Caste in Modern India* (Bombay: Media Promoters, 1962), esp. chap. 7, pp. 98–111; and Rajni Kothari, *Politics in India* (New Delhi: Orient Longman, 1970), esp. the balance between "dominance and accommodation," chap. 8, pp. 293–337.

35. The state government of Punjab had by early 1986 registered 26,000 Sikh refugee families arriving from other parts of India. At least 1,000 Hindu families had moved out from Punjab between 1983 and 1986. *Facts About the Punjab Situation* (Chandigarh: State Government of Punjab, 1986).

36. I am indebted to Professor Imtiaz Ahmed at the Jawhahrlal Nehru University for the discussion of Muslims in India.

Apparently some migration continued after partition but was considered "negligible" by one standard source. (Zafar Imam, *Muslims in India,* p. 76). A Pakistani government publication of 1957 claims that Muslims from India had arrived continuously since 1947 but provides no details. *Ten Years of Pakistan, 1947–1957* (Karachi: Pakistan Publishers, 1957), p. 239.

37. A Pakistan source claims that there were 550 Hindu-Muslim riots between 1950 and 1964. G. W. Choudhury, *Pakistan's Relations with India 1947–66* (London: Pall Mall Press, 1968), pp. 174–75. That is now seen as an undercount by Indian sources. One careful study by a former high police official found 620 incidents between 1954 and 1963, although the total casualties were low (244 killed). The year 1964 was a watershed. Clashes and fatalities increased sharply to 2,222 incidents and 1,537 killed between 1965 and 1971. P. R. Rajgopal, "Communalism and Communal Violence," unpublished manuscript (New Delhi: Centre for Policy Research, 1986), p. 8.

38. In the Meerut massacres in May 1987, the provincial armed constabulary of Uttar Pradesh was found by Amnesty International to be responsible for at least eighty deaths and many disappearances. (*Indian Post,* November 20, 1987). The Meerut events were an extreme version of a familiar pattern.

39. "Who Are the Guilty?" People's Union for Democratic Rights and People's Union for Civil Liberties, New Delhi, 1984. The report by the human rights group indicted the leadership of the ruling Congress party. A government-appointed commission blamed the police alone. *Times of India,* February 25, 1987.

40. Myron Weiner, *Sons of the Soil* (Delhi: Oxford University Press, 1978), chap. 3; also author's various interviews in Assam in December 1985.

41. The policy was stipulated in the 1985 Assam Accord. The Assamese state government, controlled by a local, nativist party, later claimed that the central government was deliberately dragging its feet. The latter responded that implementation of the accord was a slow process, requiring the identification of illegal residents and the building of a border fence to reduce illegal crossings.

42. Also India is divided; Bangladesh (earlier East Pakistan) lies between the northeastern Indian states and the rest of the Union.

43. The Naga war was the most destructive. In the worst period, from 1956 to 1958, about fourteen hundred Nagas were killed, according to Indian figures. Neville Maxwell, *India, the Nagas and the North-East,* Minority Rights Report no. 17, 1980. The Mizo struggle was more moderate.

The Mizo National Front had only a couple of thousand armed men, of which one thousand surrendered in 1971, the last to give up was a group of five hundred, including women and children who trekked back from Bangladesh in 1986. Casualties were limited. However, the insurgency meant considerable dislocation for the community, as the Indian Army used the standard counter-insurgency strategy of regrouping villagers in "safe" units. See A. C. Ray, *Mizoram, Dynamics of Change* (Calcutta: Pearl Publishers, 1982), pp. 163 et passim.

44. The U.S. Department of State Human Rights Report for 1987, cited in the *Times of India,* February 11, 1988.

45. For example, Z. A. Phizo of the Naga National Council and Laldenga of the Mizo National Front. London is the home for leaders of assorted autonomy–separatist parties in the former British India, including the Khalistan and Baluchistan movements.

46. The Chakma case recalls another well-known case of tribal refugees' actually refusing to move even when they were offered a ready-made assisted passage, namely, many of the Hmong from Laos.

47. According to official figures, 1,181 extremists had been arrested and 64 killed by the state forces during the first ten months of 1986. The following year the numbers went up: 328 extremists were killed in police "encounters," and 3,750 were arrested. The extremists in turn killed 910 persons, including 95 policemen. *Indian Express,* November 7, 1986; *The Hindustan Times,* January 15, 1988.

48. The majority of Indian asylum seekers applied in West Germany, where the trend for the 1980s are as follows: 1980—6,693 applicants; 1981—no data; 1982—2,817; 1983—1,548; 1984—1,083; 1985—no data; 1986—6,554. UNHCR, Geneva; and Hans-Ingo von Pollen, "Die Entwicklung der Asylbewerberzahlen im Jahre 1983," *Zeitschrift für Auslandergerecht und Auslanderpolitik,* 2 (1984), pp. 110–12.

49. Bumper harvests in fact accentuated the storage problems. "Punjab Glut," *Times of India,* August 31, September 1, 1986; also author's interviews with farmers and businessmen in Punjab, February 1987.

50. "Kein Herz für Inder," *Der Spiegel,* September 22, 1986.

51. Data provided by the British Refugee Council (London).

52. Author's interviews, UNHCR Geneva, March 1987.

53. As European restrictions increased in the latter 1980s, so did the costs of being able to submit an application. In a series of articles on asylum applications in 1986, *Der Spiegel* provided information on costs for various false documentation packages (September 30, 1986).

54. Hamza Alavai, "The State in Post-Colonial Societies: Pakistan and Bangladesh," *New Left Review,* 74 (1972), pp. 59–82.

55. Aijaz Ahmad, "Democracy and Dictatorship," in Hassan Gardezi and Jamil Rashid (eds.), *Pakistan: The Roots of Dictatorship* (Delhi: Oxford University Press, 1983), pp. 40–85.

56. Amnesty International, *Pakistan: Human Rights Violations and the Decline of the Rule of Law* (London, 1982).

57. Horst E. Theis, "Aktuelle Fragen des deutschen Asylverfahrens," *Soziale Arbeit,* April 1978, pp. 145–53; and von Pollen, "Die Entwicklung der Asylbewerberzahlen," pp. 110–12.

58. Selig Harrison, *In Afghanistan's Shadow: Baluch Nationalism and Soviet Temptation* (Washington, D.C.: Carnegie Endowment for International Peace, 1981), p. 3. See also Robert Wirsing, *The Baluchs and Pathans* (London: Minority Rights Group, Report no. 48, 1981).

59. Report by the Standing Committee on Refugees, Asia Committee, British Refugee Council, London, 1974.

60. Additional Baluch were probably in the general stream of Pakistan migrant/refugees fleeing Zia's repression. In 1979, the Baluch movement in Pakistan again went underground, and leaders of the Baluch Student Organization were arrested. Harrison, *In Afghanistan's Shadow,* p. 42. Earlier relations had been good.

61. Baluchistan has 42 percent of (West) Pakistan's total land area and less than 4 percent of its population.

62. W. H. Morris-Jones, "Realities and Dreams: Ebb and Flow in the Politics of Separatism," paper presented at the Sri Lanka Foundation Institute, Colombo, August 6, 1985, p. 9.

63. By 1966, Benglis held 34 percent of the prestigious Pakistan Civil Service positions, 20 percent of the nonofficer ranks in the air force and the navy (but many fewer of the officer positions) in 1963, and 5 to 7 percent of the army positions. Rounaq Jahan, *Bangladesh Politics: Problems and Issues* (Dacca: University Press, 1980), pp. 7–8.

64. A (West) Pakistani officer sent to the East in 1971 records one of the Pakistani generals as saying, "We will not allow these black bastards to rule over us." Siddiq Salik, *Witness to Surrender* (Karachi: Oxford University Press, 1978), p. 29. President Ayub Khan's views of the "downtrodden race" of Bengalis are revealed in *Friends Not Masters* (London: Oxford University Press, 1967), pp. 189–91.

65. Lawrence Lifschultz, *Bangladesh: The Unfinished Revolution* (London: Zed, 1979), p. 26; Talukder Maniruzzaman, *The Bangladesh Revolution and Its Aftermath* (Dacca: Bangladesh Books International, 1980), pp. 123.

66. I am indebted to discussions with Donald Horowitz on this point.

67. In India the U.S. naval movement nevertheless created a profound stir, and in Washington it also was seen as a major initiative. See Raymond Garthoff, *Detente and Confrontation: American-Soviet Relations from Nixon to Reagan* (Washington, D.C.: Brookings Institution, 1987).

68. See Mohammed Ayoob and K. Subrahmanyam, *The Liberation War* (New Delhi: Chand, 1972). Subrahmanyam was a major advocate of this view.

69. The China factor is emphasized by a close Bangladeshi observer, Mizanur Rahaman Shelly, *Emergence of a New Nation in a Multipolar World: Bangladesh* (Dacca: Universities Press, 1979), pp. 51 et passim.

70. The Indian Council of World Affairs recorded some of them in its publication *How Pakistan Violated Human Rights in Bangladesh* (New Delhi, 1972).

71. A U.S. Senate Committee report called it a "massive, man-made disaster." U.S. Senate Committee on the Judiciary, Subcommittee to Investigate Problems Connected with Refugees and Escapees, *Crisis in South Asia* (Washington, D.C.: U.S. Government Printing Office, November 1971), p. 55.

72. Zia Rizvi, a senior UNHCR official involved in the U.N.'s "Focal Point" operation to aid the refugees, feels that the Indian estimates are much too high (interview, Geneva, June 1984).

73. Atrocities were detailed in the Indian press. See Franda, *Population Politics in South Asia*, p. 9.

74. Holborn, *Refugees*, p. 768.

75. According to Government of India figures, 9.8 million refugees had been repatriated by March 31, 1972, leaving only 59,178 in camps. Ministry of Labour and Rehabilitation (Calcutta Branch), *Report*, April 4, 1972.

76. Ben Whitaker, *The Biharis in Bengal* (London: Minority Rights Report no. 11, 1982).

77. A decade before independence in 1947, the Tamil-held proportion of pensionable public service posts was twice the Tamil proportion of the population as a whole. Robert K. Kearny, *Communalism and Language in the Politics of Ceylon* (Durham, N.C.: Duke University Press, 1967), p. 70.

78. Committee for Rational Development, *Sri Lanka, The Ethnic Conflict* (Colombo: Navrang, 1984), pp. 58–60.

79. A. Sivanandan, "Sri Lanka: Racism and the Politics of Underdevelopment," *Race and Class*, 26 (1984), pp. 34 et passim.

80. Kumari Jayawardena, *Ethnic and Class Conflicts in Sri Lanka* (Colombo: Centre for Social Analysis, 1985).

81. Radhika Coomaraswamy, "Through the Looking Glass Darkly," in Committee for Rational Development, *Sri Lanka* (Colombo: Sri Lanka, 1983), p. 190. The following figures on university admissions indicate the Tamils' relative deprivation: In 1969, Tamils held 78.8 percent

of the positions in the engineering and medical faculties. After "standardization" of the entrance scores in 1974, they were reduced to 16.3 and 25.9 percent, respectively.

82. Donald Horowitz, "Patterns of Ethnic Separatism," *Comparative Studies in Society and History,* 23 (1981), pp. 165 et passim.

83. Calculated from *Inter-racial Equity and National Unity in Sri Lanka* (Colombo: Marga Institute, 1985), p. 41. The figure includes a small number of Indian Tamils.

84. Eric Meyer, "Seeking the Roots of the Tragedy," in James Manor (ed.), *Sri Lanka in Change and Crisis* (London: Croom Helm, 1984), pp. 137–52.

85. British Refugee Council, "Tamils in Sri Lanka," mimeo. (London, 1984), p. 10. T. D. S. A. Dissanayaka, *The Agony of Sri Lanka* (Colombo: Swastika Press, 1983), p. 93, sets the death toll at 471. (The author was at the time the official spokesman in the Ministry of Foreign Affairs). The intercommunal Civil Rights Movement of Sri Lanka estimates over 2,000. Christian Michelsens Institutt, *Menneskerettighetene i Norges hovedsamarbeidsland, 1985* (Bergen, Norway, 1985), p. 196.

86. Indian claims that the United States planned to establish a base at the eastern port of Trincomalee went unsubstantiated. Minor links were established with the Middle East conflict when the Jayewardene government received military technical assistance from Israel, and some of the militant groups (People's Liberation Organization of Tamil Eeelam and the Eelam People's Revolutionary Liberation Front) developed training and other ties with militant Palestinian groups. The arrival of a few British mercenary military advisers in Sri Lanka caused great anxiety in India, as did the limited Pakistani military assistance to Colombo.

87. Interviews in Madras, January and June 1986. The local and foreign press visited the training camps that the Indian government denied existed. See, for example, *The Statesman* (Calcutta), November 7, 1985; and the *New York Times,* June 9, 1986. Much of the support came from the state authorities in Tamil Nadu, led by the influential chief minister M. G. Ramachandran. In April 1987, for instance, M. G. R. (as he was known) wrote a check for 40 million rupees ($3.3 million) in "humanitarian assistance" to the largest group of militants, the Liberation Tigers of Tamil Eelam.

88. See, for example, *Mainstream* (New Delhi), August 6, 1983.

89. The state government, formed by AIADMK, was pressed by its local opposition, the DMK, to "do more" for the Tamils in Sri Lanka. The Congress-ruled central government, for its part, was reluctant to offend almost the only regionally based party that supported it in national politics.

90. *The Times* (London), June 1–6, 1958; Sivanandan, "Sri Lanka: Racism and the Politics of Underdevelopment," p. 18. The death toll is taken from Dissanayaka, *The Agony of Sri Lanka,* p. 8.

91. *The Times* (London), August 24–28, 1977.

92. This refers to people who received dry rations from the Ministry of Rehabilitation, including about fifty thousand Sinhalese. (Colombo, interview, July 1986). An earlier Tamil estimate claims that an additional thirty thousand Tamils did not receive any assistance from the government. *Tamil Refugee* (London: Central British Fund for Tamil Refugees Rehabilitation, January 1986), p. 6.

93. The statistics are not broken down per ethnic group. Net outmigration in 1956 and 1958 was 1,597 and 2,244, respectively, and the annual average net outflow for the other years between 1950 and 1960 was 440 persons. This does not include "Indian estate labour" and "other Indians"; i.e., mostly Indian Tamils who were repatriated to India under the 1954 Indo-Ceylon agreement and who accounted for the bulk of the net outmigration of about 160,000 in 1950–60. In the next decade (1960 to 1970), the annual average was much higher (1,419), followed unaccountably by an almost equally large net inmigration in 1971 and a sudden, unprecedented net outmigration of 6,341 in 1972. Patrick Peebles, *A Handbook of Historical Statistics* (Boston: G. K. Hall, 1982), p. 71.

94. Based on *Tamil Refugee,* October 1985, p. 6; *Times of India,* August 27, 1986; Department of Immigration and Ethnic Affairs, Canberra, communication of November 28, 1984; U.S.

Committee for Refugees, *Time for Decision: Sri Lankan Tamils in the West* (Washington, D.C.: U.S. Government Printing Office, June 1985), pp. 15–16.

95. *Times of India*, August 28, 1986; Statistisches Bundesamt Wiesbaden, *Bevölkerung und Erwerbsstätigkeit, Ausländer*, 1979, 1983 (Stuttgart u. Mainz: Verlag Kohlhammer).

96. Based on interviews with refugees and relief organizations in Madras and Madurai, January and June 1986.

97. See Fontgalland, *Sri Lankans in Exile*, pt. II.

98. By the mid-1980s, Tamils in both Colombo and the Northeast would cite a long list of friends and families who had left because they felt they "had no future" in Sri Lanka. Interviews, Colombo and Trincomalee, July 1986.

99. Recall that this was the formulation used on behalf of the Haitians in the United States by Judge Lawrence King in *Haitian Refugee Center v. Civiletti* (1980). A similar rationale had been frequently invoked to give refugee status to émigrées from socialist countries.

100. In 1984, there were thirteen thousand Tamil asylum applicants in all the European countries (UNHCR, Geneva; interview, July 1985). The equivalent figure for later years is not available.

101. Louis Dupree has described it as "a process of alternating fusion and fission." *Afghanistan* (Princeton, N.J.: Princeton University Press, 1980), p. xix. The lineages of the weak state is traced by Vartan Gregorian, *The Emergence of Modern Afghanistan* (Stanford, Calif.: Stanford University Press, 1969).

102. Ashraf Ghani, "The Afghan State, Islam and Legitimacy," paper presented at the conference Islam and Public Life, Asia Society, Washington, D.C., March 1984.

103. GNP per capita was estimated in the U.S. $55 to $90 range in a 1982 publication. *Afghanistan, Area Handbook* (Washington, D.C.: U.S. Government Printing Office, 1982), p. xxiii. UNICEF estimated infant mortality (under one year old) to 215 per 1,000 (1965) and mortality for children under five to almost double that rate. *The State of the World's Children*, UNICEF, 1987.

104. See, for example, Nancy Peabody and Richard S. Newall, *The Struggle for Afghanistan* (Ithaca, N.Y.: Cornell University Press, 1981). Other sources emphasize the alienation of the Marxist-Leninist intelligensia from the rest of society, in contrast with the traditional Islamic literati; Micheline Centlivres and Pierre Centlivres in a discussion with Pierre Bordieu, "Et si On Parlait de l'Afghanistan," *Actes de la Recherche en Science Sociales*, 34 (September 1980); also Sayd Majrooh, "The Philosophical and Psychological Dimensions of Afghan intellectuals in Exile," paper presented at the International Conference on Refugees in the Islamic World, Bellagio, October 11–15, 1987.

105. Feroz Ahmed, "The Khalq Failed to Comprehend the Contradictions of the Rural Sector," *MERIP* Reports, July–August 1980, p. 13. West European leftists took a similar view; see Fred Halliday, "War and Revolution in Afghanistan," *New Left Review*, 119 (1980), pp. 20–41.

106. See Beverly Male, *Revolutionary Afghanistan* (New York: St. Martin's Press, 1982).

107. The Muslim Brotherhoods (Hezb-i-Islami and Jamiat-i-Islami) had moved to Pakistan when they were banned by the Afghan government in the early 1970s. Fifty years earlier, British-ruled Pakistan had supported tribal leaders and clansmen who were trying to depose the modernizing King Amanullah, by allowing the rebels to raise an army on the British side of the Durand line (the border between present-day Afghanistan and Pakistan). The rebels succeeded. The analogy with later events was pointedly noted by Pakistani intellectuals. See, for example, Abduallh Malik, "The Afghan Revolution," *Viewpoint*, April 29 and May 6, 1979.

108. To justify its intervention, Moscow claimed that there was large-scale external aid to the rebels. The Pakistan-based rebels did appeal to the Middle Eastern countries, the United States, and China for help but, according to Western news reports, had limited success before the Soviets intervened.

109. U.S. intelligence sources assessed the relationship at the time as follows: The PDPA "took its overall ideological guidance from Moscow," but the Soviets merely "had foreknowl-

edge'' of the coup. Anthony Arnold, *Afghanistan: The Soviet Invasion in Perspective* (Stanford, Calif.: Hoover Institution, 1981), p. 68.

110. There is also some evidence to suggest that Moscow wanted to remove Amin, who was becoming too independent. Selig Harrison, "Dateline Afghanistan: Exit Through Finland," *Foreign Policy,* 41 (Winter 1980–81), pp. 163–87.

111. *New York Times,* May 4, 1983.

112. According to news reports, the covert weapons program averaged $100 million in the early 1980s and increased to 250 million in 1985 and an estimated $600 million in 1987.

113. Stephen P. Cohen, "Pakistan: Coping with Regional Dominance, Multiple Crises and Great-Power Confrontation," in Raju G. C. Thomas (ed.), *The Great-Power Triangle and Asian Security* (Lexington, Mass.: Heath, 1983), p. 61. Cohen refers in particular to the ethnic pulls.

114. Beverly Male, "A Tiger by the Tail: Pakistan and the Afghan Refugees," in *Refugees: Four Political Case Studies,* Canberra Studies in World Affairs no. 3 (Canberra: Australian National University, 1981), pp. 38–39.

115. U.S. Department of State, "Afghanistan: Eight Years of Soviet Occupation," (Washington, D.C.: U.S. Government Printing Office, December 23, 1987), pp. 31–32. The figure for Iran was provided by the government of Iran. Until late 1986, the UNHCR had no on-site representative working with the Afghan refugees in Iran. The figure for Pakistan has fluctuated according to administrative events. In 1983–84 the Pakistan government registered no new arrivals in the NWFP, in order to encourage people to move farther inland. A later count produced a downward revision of earlier figures. In 1986, the Pakistani government had registered 2.7 million refugees.

116. L. O. Coldren, "Afghanistan in 1984," *Asian Survey,* 25 (1985), p. 170.

117. Interview with PDPA, press section, in Kabul, November 1987.

118. Interview with Western diplomatic sources, Kabul, November 1987.

119. U.S. intelligence assessments concluded that a stalemated situation had developed in many parts of the country by late 1983. Kabul and Soviet forces increasingly concentrated on holding the major towns and a few key areas (e.g., to keep open the Salang road connecting Kabul with the Soviet border). Local leaders were left to rule in their respective regions, provided that they did not become obvious staging centers for the *mujahedin.* U.S. Department of State, "Afghanistan: Four Years of Occupation," Special Report No. 112 (Washington, D.C.: U.S. Government Printing Office, December 1983). Regime sources claimed that Soviet forces by 1987 were stationed in only seventeen of the country's twenty-nine provinces. Speech by President Najibullah to the *loya jirgah* in Kabul, November 30, 1987.

120. U.S. Department of State, "Afghanistan: Eight Years of Soviet Occupation," p. 23.

121. There was less guerrilla-staging activity on the Iranian side. On the other hand, some Afghan *mujahedin* apparently were put on the trains for the Iraqi war front, having been told by their Iranian hosts that they were heading for the Afghan border.

122. U.S. Department of State, *World Refugee Report,* 1986, p. 47.

123. Interview, Islamabad, January, 1984.

124. Most Iranians lived in a legal twilight with meager resources in Pakistan. UNHCR officials processed a very few whom they could reasonably expect to resettle in third countries. In late 1985, resettlement prospects improved somewhat when the United States started to process Iranian refugees in Pakistan (previously they had been referred, in a Catch-22 manner, to the U.S. mission in Rome). The U.S. program was principally for the Baha'i, a small religious minority in Iran.

125. See Chapter 10 for a further discussion of the refugee-warrior community and its implications for refugee policy.

126. Figures supplied by the U.S. Department of State, Bureau of Refugee Programs, September 8, 1988 (oral communication). See also Astri Suhrke, "Contrasting Patterns of Asian Refugee Movements: The Vietnamese and Afghan Syndromes," in James T. Fawcett and Benjamin

V. Carino (eds.), *Pacific Bridges: The New Immigration from Asia and the Pacific Islands* (New York: Center for Migration Studies, 1987), pp. 95 et passim.

Chapter 6

1. Although Vietnam commonly is classified with Southeast Asia, for purposes of this discussion it belongs more properly with East Asia.

2. Suzanne Pepper, *Civil War in China* (Berkeley and Los Angeles: University of California Press, 1978), pp. 410 et passim.

3. Fred W. Riggs, *Formosa Under Nationalist Rule* (New York: Macmillan, 1952), p. 48.

4. As estimated by American advisers. L. H. Chassin, *The Communist Conquest of China* (London: Weidenfeld & Nicolson, 1965), p. 228.

5. Author's interview with local officials on Quemoy, November 1982.

6. Louise W. Holborn, *Refugees: A Problem of Our Time: The Work of the United Nations High Commissioner for Refugees, 1951–1972* (Metuchen, N.J.: Scarecrow Press, 1975), p. 679.

7. U.S. Department of State, *U.S. Relations with China* (Washington, D.C.: U.S. Government Printing Office, 1949), p. 309.

8. In the aftermath of the Great Leap Forward, about 100,000 people from China's Singkiang region moved into Soviet Kazakhstan, with Soviet encouragement. (Majority) Han Chinese settlers were moving into Singkiang in large numbers, squeezing out the indigenous people. June Dreyer, *China's Forty Millions* (Cambridge, Mass.: Harvard University Press, 1976).

9. The claim for a continuous outflow is made by Holborn, "Refugees," p. 661. This is not supported by the annual reports of the Hong Kong government, which give detailed attention to refugees/illegal migrants. From 1952 to 1955, only one inflow is mentioned, when in 1952 the Hong Kong authorities decided to test the waters by temporarily abandoning quota restrictions on legal inmigration. The resultant rush (56,000 came in a seven-month period) led to the restoration of previous restrictions. *Annual Report, 1956.*

10. Hong Kong, *Annual Report,* 1953, p. 11.

11. Hong Kong, *Annual Report,* 1950, p. 10.

12. Jean Chesnaux, *China. The People's Republic. 1949–76* (Sussex, England: Harvester Press, 1979), p. 100. It has later been estimated that 20 million to 25 million people died of hunger. Harry Hardin, *China's Second Revolution: Reform After Mao* (Washington, D.C.: Brookings Institution, 1987), p. 12.

13. Hong Kong, *Annual Report,* 1961, p. 209; 1962, p. 212.

14. Holborn, *Refugees,* pp. 661, 694, claims that 300,000 crossed and 200,000 were returned in 1962. Hong Kong authorities maintain that 142,000 entered illegally but gives only an incomplete figure for persons apprehended and returned (an estimated 62,000 in a six-week period).

15. Food production had actually started to pick up the previous year (1962). Ramon Myers, "Agricultural Developments," in Harold Hinton (ed.), *The People's Republic of China* (Boulder, Colo.: Westview Press, 1979), pp. 180–83.

16. Jürgen Domes, *China After the Cultural Revolution* (London: C. Hurst, 1975), p. 11.

17. Thomas Bernstein, *Up to the Mountains and Down to the Villages* (New Haven, Conn.: Yale University Press, 1977).

18. Fox Butterfield, *China: Alive in the Bitter Sea* (London: Hodder & Stoughton, 1982), p. 419. The post-Mao leadership in China used the issue of illegal emigration to bargain for economic aid from Hong Kong, suggesting that China could not prevent "eye-eyes" from entering Hong Kong as long as China's standard of living was low, but capital and know-how from Hong Kong to the new Special Economic Zones in China's border provinces might alleviate the problem. David Bonavia, *Hong Kong 1997* (Hong Kong: South China Morning Post, 1983), pp. 50–51.

19. Based on the first census in 1954 that counted a total population of 580 million. The net outflow was even smaller, as maybe 400,000 to 500,000 so-called overseas Chinese returned to live

in China in the 1950s and 1960s. See Stephen Fitzgerald, *China and the Overseas Chinese* (Cambridge, England: Cambridge University Press, 1972), p. 4.

20. Sinologists are reluctant to cite figures. One standard American source maintains that during the 1950–52 land reform period, "many thousands" who were not in the landlord category were (mistakenly) "liquidated economically or physically" and that "hundreds of thousands" were "sentenced to prison or executed" in the 1950 campaign. Harold Hinton, "China," in George McTurner Kahin (ed.), *Major Governments of Asia* (Ithaca, N.Y.: Cornell University Press, 1963), p. 54. However, another noted analyst says that violence was used "selectively" and only as "a last resort," especially compared with Stalin's Russia. Tang Tsou, "Revolution, Reintegration and Crisis in China: A Framework for Analysis," in Ping-ti Ho and Tang Tsou (eds.) *China in Crisis* (Chicago: University of Chicago Press, 1968), vol. 1, p. 303.

21. Butterfield, *China*, p. 17.

22. Hardin, *China's Second Revolution*, p. 12.

23. Domes, *China After the Cultural Revolution*, p. 14.

24. For instance, visas for travel to Hong Kong were not issued during the 1952 "Five Anti-Campaign," which particularly affected the business community. A. Doak Barnett, *Communist China: The Early Years* (London: Pall Mall Press, 1964), pp. 133–39.

25. The Hong Kong authorities decided to test the pressure by temporarily abandoning quota restrictions in 1952. The result was a net inmigration of 56,000 in a seven-month period, whereupon Hong Kong closed the gate. Hong Kong, *Annual Report*, 1956, p. 6.

26. Holborn, *Refugees*, p. 694.

27. This section draws particularly on Paul Mus, *Sociologie d'une Guerre* (Paris: Editions du Seuil, 1952); John T. McAlister, Jr., *Vietnam: The Origins of Revolution* (New York: Knopf, 1969); and Ngo Vinh Long, *Before the Revolution* (Cambridge, Mass.: MIT Press, 1973).

28. This is virtually a textbook case of the theory of revolution presented in Theda Skocpol, *States and Social Revolutions: A Comparative Analysis of France, Russia, and China* (Cambridge, England: Cambridge University Press, 1979).

29. Almost 50,000 Vietminh supporters came to Thailand from Laos and Kampuchea in 1945–46. With the Thai government of Phibul Songkram later turning pro-American, Vietnamese refugees were no longer welcome. Peter A. Poole, *The Vietnamese in Thailand* (Ithaca, N.Y.: Cornell University Press, 1970), pp. 46–47.

30. *The Pentagon Papers*, Senator Gravel ed. (Boston: Beacon Press, 1971), vol. 1, p. 29.

31. An administrative practice dating back at least to the French period required permit for travel from one province to another in Vietnam. Both the DRV and the RVN required permits for people to leave under the provisions of the Geneva Accords. B. S. N. Murti, *Vietnam Divided* (Bombay: Asia Publishing House, 1964). The author served with the International Control Commission in Vietnam.

32. *The Pentagon Papers*, p. 579. Apparently there were also leaflets warning against an American nuclear strike against the North, prompting many to leave. Murti, *Vietnam Divided*, p. 83.

33. Especially in Phat Diem and Bui Chu. Murti, *Vietnam Divided*, p. 73 et passim.

34. *The Pentagon Papers*, p. 290.

35. Bernard B. Fall, *The Viet-Minh Regime*, 2nd ed. (New York: Institute of Pacific Relations, 1956), pp. 118–35.

36. This was also true for standard historical works on the period, for example, Ellen J. Hammer, *The Struggle for Indochina 1940–55* (Stanford, Calif.: Stanford University Press, 1966), p. 345 et passim.

37. For a careful documentation supporting this thesis, see James P. Harrison, *The Endless War: Fifty Years of Struggle in Vietnam* (New York: McGraw-Hill, 1983).

38. David Wurfel, "Indochina: The Historical and Political Background," in Elliot L. Tepper (ed.), *Southeast Asian Exodus: From Tradition to Resettlement* (Carleton University, Ottawa: Canadian Asian Studies Association, 1980), p. 106.

39. If we take out the 263,000 who went from North Vietnam to China, the ratio will become even lower. The equivalent figure for a few other Asian refugee movements are Tibet, 7 to 8 percent; Bangladesh, 10 percent; Sri Lankan Tamils, 12 percent; and Afghanistan, nearly 30 percent. At the other end are the refugees from China and the Baluchi struggle, with less than 1 percent each.

40. Gail P. Kennedy, *From Vietnam to America: A Chronicle of the Vietnamese Immigrations to the U.S.* (Boulder, Colo.: Westview Press, 1977), p. 47.

41. Most ethnic Chinese in the South preferred to retain their Chinese citizenship which exempted them from military service and did not create many disadvantages. In the Socialist Republic of Vietnam, however, there were no citizenship rights without citizenship, including the right to a ration card which had become a growing necessity after the collapse of the America wartime economy in Saigon. The issue came to a head in February 1976, when in preparation for elections, all persons were asked to declare their nationality. Nayan Chanda, *Brother Enemy* (New York: Harcourt Brace Jovanovich, 1986), p. 30.

42. Nanda, *Brother Enemy,* p. 243; Charles Benoit, "Vietnam's Boat People," in David W. P. Elliott (ed.), *The Third Indochina Conflict* (Boulder, Colo.: Westview Press, 1981), pp. 151–52.

43. UNHCR, Executive Committee, *Report on UNHCR Assistance Activities in 1979–80 and Proposed Voluntary Funds Programmes and Budget for 1981,* A/AC.96-577, August 14, 1980, p. 151.

44. International food aid valued at $2 million, delivered to Vietnam in 1978 through the UNHCR, was a token modification of the economic isolation of Vietnam by countries outside the COMECON, which Vietnam joined in June 1978.

45. On the "rational" aspect of the Vietnamese refugee/migration movement, see Rebecca Allen and Harry H. Hiller, "The Social Organization of Migration: An Analysis of the Uprooting and Flight of Vietnamese Refugees," *International Migration Review,* 23 (1985), pp. 439–451.

46. Vietnamese officials told UNHCR mission members in Ho Chi Minh City that they would consider repatriation on a case-by-case basis, but no one took up the offer (author's interviews in Canberra and Bangkok, January 1984).

47. At the 1979 Geneva conference, convened to consider the Indochinese refugee question, which had assumed crisis proportions with large outflows of ethnic Chinese, the Japanese pledged $60 million, equivalent to almost half the cost of the UNHCR's budget for Indochinese refugees in 1979 (not including special emergency relief for Khmer).

48. The point was made explicitly; Assistant Secretary of State Richard Holbrooke told the House Foreign Affairs Subcommittee on Asian and Pacific Affairs of the U.S. Congress on May 6, 1980, that "the clearest indication of the bankruptcy of the policies that Hanoi is following is the large number of people who continue to seek the opportunity to leave Vietnam and other Indochinese nations where Vietnamese policies are being implemented." Statement, mimeo.

49. On this point, see also U.N. ECOSOC, *Study on Human Rights and Massive Exoduses,* p. 37. In 1979, the UNHCR's Indochina program in first asylum areas (exclusive of special emergency relief for Khmer) absorbed almost half of its entire budget of $281 million. UNHCR, Executive Committee, "Assistance Activities for 1980," A/AC/96/577. The Vietnamese were then the most numerous among the Indochinese refugees, about 300,000 having arrived in first asylum areas as against about 150,000 Laotians and 34,000 "old" Khmer." Four years later, the Vietnamese constituted the single, largest group of all the approximately 114,000 refugees resettled internationally under UNHCR auspices, and the Indochinese together represented 76 percent of the total. UNHCR, Executive Committee, "Report on the Resettlement of Refugees," UNGA, A/AC.96/640, August 9, 1984.

50. U.S. Senate, Subcommittee on Immigration and Refugee Policy, *Refugee and Migration Problems in Southeast Asia: 1984,* August 1984, p. 2, citing an earlier staff report of the subcommittee dated January 1982. The first comprehensive U.S. criticism of the Indochinese refugee program on these grounds was probably a 1981 report of a study mission headed by a retired, senior State Department official, Marshall Green.

51. "Humane deterrence" meant prolonged camp existence or more difficult access to UNHCR camps where resettlement processing was carried out.

52. The Voice of America (VOA) strongly denied that its coverage of resettlement policies and rescue at sea had been part of "any overt or covert attempt to . . . encourage Vietnamese . . . to leave their native lands and to seek refuge in the United States or in other Free World nations." Statement by M. William Haratunian, deputy director, VOA, to the House Committee on Foreign Affairs, October 5, 1981, mimeo.

53. U.S. Senate, *Refuge and Migration Problems,* p. 12.

54. See Astri Suhrke, "Indochinese Refugees: The Law and Politics of First Asylum," *Annals of the American Academy of Political and Social Sciences,* 467 (1983), pp. 102–15.

55. *New York Times,* September 2, 1984.

56. U.S. Department of State, Bureau for Refugee Programs, *Monthly Report,* October 1986 and October 1987.

57. Of 114,148 ODP cases pending with the U.S. embassy in Bangkok in mid-1984, about 86,000 were "family reunification," and 21,000 were individuals with established links to the previous regime or a record of "reeducation," that is, persons at known risk under the new order. Between 1980 and 1984, about 15,000 of the 22,000 ODP arrivals in the United States were admitted as refugees, the rest came as immigrants. U.S. Senate, *Refugee and Migration Problems,* pp. 13–14.

58. *Vietnam Courier* (Hanoi), August 1979, p. 8.

59. Benoit, "Vietnam's Boat People," pp. 157 et passim.

60. China's later indifference to the killings of ethnic Chinese by the Khmer Rouge, then Beijing's ally, lends credence to Hanoi's charges on this point.

61. The monthly averages for 1984 were 2,174 (boat), 2,361 (ODP); 1985, 2,059 (boat), 1,242 (ODP); for 1986, 1,775 (boat), 2,256 (ODP). U.S. Department of State, Bureau of Refugee Programs, *Monthly Report.*

62. The U.S. government alleged that the Laotian government forces, with Soviet advisers, used chemical warfare against the Hmong. The famous "yellow rain" claims were never conclusively proved. See U.S. Department of State, *Chemical Warfare in Southeast Asia and Afghanistan,* Report to the Congress from Secretary of State Alexander M. Haig, Jr., March 22, 1982; and Julian Robinson, Jeanne Guillemin, and Matthew Meselson, "Yellow Rain: The Story Collapses," *Foreign Policy,* 68 (1987), pp. 100–17.

63. Interviews with U.S., Thai, and UNHCR officials in Bangkok, February–March 1980. See also U.S. Congress, Joint Economic Committee, *Indochinese Refugees: The Impact on First Asylum Countries and Implications for American Policy, A Study,* November 25, 1980.

64. U.S. Senate, *Refugee and Migration Problems in Southeast Asia,* p. 10.

65. Author's interviews, Ban Vinai (the largest Hmong camp), March 1980. See U.S. Congress, *Indochinese Refugees,* p. 4. In 1979, China's offer to take 10,000 Indochinese refugees from first-asylum areas included 2,700 hill tribes people who were resettled in border areas between China and Laos. The UNHCR viewed it as a successful project, in which the new arrivals blended easily with the local, similar ethnic population. For the Laotian government it meant more insurgents in its northern border area. See Suhrke, "Indochinese Refugees," p. 107; Chanda, *Brother Enemy,* pp. 379–80; and UNHCR, Ex.Comm. "Assistance Activities for 1980," p. 153.

66. Chanda, *Brother Enemy,* pp. 43, 348.

67. See Ben Kiernan and Chanthou Boua (eds.), *Peasants and Politics in Kampuchea 1942–1981* (London: Zed, 1982), esp. chap. 9.

68. Chanda, *Brother Enemy,* p. 251.

69. Ibid., pp. 217–18.

70. UNHCR, Ex. Comm., "Assistance Activities for 1980," p. 191.

71. Michael Vickery, *Cambodia 1975–1982* (Boston: South End Press, 1984), p. 33.

72. Elaborated in Linda Mason and Roger Brown, *Rice, Rivalry and Politics: Managing Cambodian Relief* (Notre Dame, Ind.: University of Notre Dame Press, 1983).

73. William Shawcross, *The Quality of Mercy* (New York: Simon & Schuster, 1984), p. 158.

74. Chanda, *Brother Enemy*, p. 348.

75. Author's interviews, KEG, Bangkok and Aranyaprathet, February 1980. Colonel Michael Eiland, a Vietnamese expert who later held a high-ranking intelligence position in the Department of Defense, played a key role.

76. Mason and Brown, *Rice, Rivalry and Politics*, pp. 142 et passim.

77. The United States contributed about $10 million to $12 million annually in cash, plus food aid in kind to UNBRO between 1982 and 1985. Voluntary agencies working on the border which previously had been funded by the U.S. government were now paid through UNBRO. U.S. Department of State, *World Refugee Report*, September 1985, p. 27.

78. Interview with senior UNHCR officials in Bangkok, January 1980 and January 1981.

79. The Sadruddin Aga Khan report claims that 370,000 persons had benefited by the returnee program, *Study on Human Rights and Massive Exoduses*, (United Nations, ECOSOC, E/CN 4/1503, December 31, 1981) p. 24. Interviews with UNHCR officials in Bangkok, January 1980, and New York, March 1984, suggest that there was little control over the program. Families were given resettlement kits on the Thai side of the border and registered as "spontaneous returnees" before they moved toward the Kampuchean side.

80. The Hukbalahap in the Philippines were settled in the southern Mindanao area. An estimated two thousand to three thousand soldiers of the Malayan Communist party withdrew to the southern border provinces of neighboring Thailand with the tacit acceptance of Thai and Malaysian authorities. This neat solution to the problem of disposing of near-defeated guerrillas was made possible by an unusual ethnic-political constellation. See Astri Suhrke, "Irredentism Contained: The Thai Muslim Case," *Comparative Politics*, January 1975, pp. 187–204.

81. Ten years later, Amnesty International estimated that 55,000 to 100,000 untried political prisoners remained in jail, many on the notorious Buru prison island. In the meantime, an unknown number had died. The Indonesian government claimed in 1979 that all untried *tapols* had been released. Julie Southwood and Patrick Flanagan, *Indonesia, Law, Propaganda and Terror* (London: Zed, 1983), p. 3. Five years later Amnesty International estimated that 300 "A-Category" prisoners (i.e., who had been tried) remained in jail. Amnesty International, *Report, 1984* (London, 1984), p. 226.

82. Rex Mortimer, *Indonesian Communism Under Sukarno* (Ithaca, N.Y.: Cornell University Press, 1974), pp. 389 et passim.

83. *Asia-Pacific Report* (Honolulu: East-West Center, 1986), pp. 34 et passim.

84. Successive Thai governments with U.S. assistance spent large sums to develop economically the insurgency-prone northeast. The Malaysian government launched a major economic redistribution in favor of the indigenous Malays after the race riots in 1969, and Singapore's educational and social service policies were designed to develop skilled and content workers, without which the city-state's traditional entrepôt economy could not survive.

85. According to 1981 World Bank figures, about 41 percent of rural Filipinos lived below the poverty line. The relative and absolute trends were clearly toward deeper poverty at the end of President Marcos's rule. In Indonesia, 51 percent of the rural population lived below the poverty line. Only a fraction of the rapidly increasing labor force, to which almost two million were added annually, could be absorbed by a stagnating agricultural sector and a slowly growing manufacturing sector.

86. For a Philippine representation, see Vivencio R. Jose (ed.), *Mortgaging the Future* (Quezon City: Foundation for Nationalist Study, 1982).

87. Herbert Feith, "Repressive-Developmental Regimes in Asia," *Prisma*, 19 (1980), pp. 11–27.

88. Donald K. Emmerson, "Indonesia in 1983," *Asian Survey*, 24 (1983), pp. 136–49. Amnesty International estimated that four thousand "suspected criminals" were killed in an "officially sanctioned" anticrime campaign of extrajudicial killings in 1983. Amnesty International, *Report 1984*, p. 225.

89. Francisco Nemenzo, "An Irrepressible Revolution: The Decline and Resurgence of the Philippine Communist Movement," paper delivered at the University of Hawaii, November 23, 1984, p. 2.

By the early 1980s, the NPA had six thousand guerrillas with a support base of "several hundred thousand to several millions," according to U.S. intelligence estimates. Larry Niksch, "Internal Conditions in the Philippines. Deterioration and Its Causes," *Pacific Basin Economic Review*, 2 (1982), p. 69. The author was at the time a senior analyst with the U.S. Congressional Research Service.

90. R. J. May, "The Philippines," in Mohammed Ayoob (ed.), *The Politics of Islamic Reassertion* (London: Croom Helm, 1981), p. 220.

91. The Philippine government had revived an old claim to sovereignty over Sabah. The conflict was internationalized beyond the region as well. Islamic states worldwide expressed support for the Philippine Muslims, including a strongly worded resolution at the 1973 Islamic Conference of Foreign Ministers in Libya. See Astri Suhrke and Lela G. Noble, "Muslims in the Philippines and Thailand," in Astri Suhrke and Lela G. Noble (eds.), *Ethnic Conflict in International Relations* (New York: Praeger, 1977), pp. 186 et passim.

92. For example, the former senators Benigno Aquino and Raul Manglapus. The United States' acceptance of Philippine asylum applicants increased proportionately with Washington's disenchantment with President Marcos. Over 300 cases were approved annually in 1983 and 1984. By comparison, only 380 cases were approved in the entire 1946–75 period. U.S. Department of Justice, Immigration and Naturalization Service, *Statistical Yearbook of the Immigration and Naturalization Service 1983, 1984* (Washington, D.C.: U.S. Government Printing Office, 1984, 1985).

93. Over a longer time period, the wage trends were also negative for the workers. Real wages of skilled and unskilled workers declined from 1950 to 1976, accompanied by a redistribution of income from labor to the propertied classes. Mahar Mangahas and Bruno Barres, *The Distribution of Income and Wealth: A Survey of Philippine Research* (Manila: Philippine Institute for Development Studies, 1979), pp. 69–70.

94. The outflow of contract labor from the Philippines averaged about 60,000 annually in the second half of the 1970s (1975–78) but then rapidly increased to average 300,000 in the early 1980s (1980–83). Lionel Demery, "Asian Labor Migration: An Empirical Assessment," in Fred Harold and Masra M. Shah, (eds.), *Asian Labor Migrations: Pipeline to the Middle East* (Boulder, Colo.: Westview Press, 1986).

95. I am indebted to Belinda Aquino of the University of Hawaii for discussion on this point.

96. In another category are about 11,500 non-Chinese residing in Hong Kong who may become stateless with the transfer. The majority of the crown colony's citizens are ethnic Chinese who will automatically acquire Chinese citizenship in 1997. *New York Times*, August 17, 1986.

97. In theory, South Korean and Taiwanese activists could seek asylum in North Korea and China, but that would mark an extreme course of action. In fact, much of the opposition in both South Korea and Taiwan is not associated with the rival state but is left-democratic and, in Taiwan, is also a movement of indigenous Taiwanese against the (KMT) mainlanders.

98. See the discussion of Koreans and Chinese in "The Politics of Exile," a special issue of *Third World Quarterly*, 9 (1987). As in the Philippine case, South Korean refugees in the United States in the early 1980s were mostly famous political leaders, notably presidential candidate Kim Dae-jong who also had been in exile in Japan.

99. The rationale given by the U.S. government recalls the 1980 ruling by Judge Lawrence King in favor of the Haitians (which the U.S. government contested), namely, that their economic misery was a result of a political decision and hence constituted persecution. According to a State Department spokesman, the economic distress of the Indochinese seeking refugee status "very frequently relates to their status or class membership under the previous non-communist government. [State Department reports] document the degree and types of persecution in Indochina." James N. Purcell, Bureau for Refugee Programs, testimony before the Subcommittee

on Immigration, Refugees and International Law, House Committee on the Judiciary, September 16, 1988.

Chapter 7

1. ACNUR, "Documento de Trabajo (Version Provisional)," Coloquio sobre la Proteccion Internacional de los Refugiados en America Central, Mexico y Panama: Problemas Juridicos y Humanitarios, Cartagena, Colombia, November 19–22, 1984, pp. 2–3.

2. For Mexico, see Lawrence A. Cardoso, "La Repatriacion de Braceros en la Epoca de Obregon, 1920–1932," *Historia Mexicana*, 26, 4 (April–June 1981). For El Salvador, see Thomas A. Anderson, *Matanza: El Salvador's Communist Revolt of 1932* (Lincoln: University of Nebraska Press, 1981); Tommie Sue Montgomery, *Revolution in El Salvador: Origins and Evolution* (Boulder, Colo.: Westview Press, 1982); and Sara Gordon, "Crisis Politica y Organizacion Popular en El Salvador, 1970–1980," Ph.D. diss., UNAM, Mexico, 1986. For the Chaco War, see Philip Raine, *Paraguay* (New Brunswick, N.J.: Scarecrow Press, 1956); and David H. Zook, Jr., *The Conduct of the Chaco War* (New Haven, Conn.: United Printing Services, 1960).

3. For the original formulation of these concepts, see Antonio Gramsci, *Note Sul Machiavelli* (Roma: Editori Riuniti, 1975); and Perry Anderson, "Las Antinomias de Antonio Gramsci," *Cuadernos Politicos,* 13 (July–September 1977). For a more recent formulation, see Guillermo O'Donnell, "Apuntes para una Teoria del Estado," *Revista Mexicana de Sociologia*, 4 (October–December 1978), p. 1159. The concepts of domination, hegemony, and coercion were formulated to explain social relations within a country. In this work we are using them to explain a regional system.

4. This concept complements our theoretical formulation because the relations between the United States and Latin America cannot be explained as a vulgar extraction of wealth. The style of domination favoring consensus means a degree of economic development. This idea goes beyond the original dependency argument. Fernando H. Cardoso, "Associated-Dependent Development: Theoretical and Practical Implications," in Alfred Stepan (ed.), *Authoritarian Brazil: Origins, Policies, and Future* (New Haven, Conn.: Yale University Press, 1973), pp. 149–57.

5. The concept of bureaucratic-authoritarianism, initially developed by Guillermo O'Donnell, is elaborated in the collection of essays edited by David Collier, *The New Authoritarianism in Latin America* (Princeton, N.J.: Princeton University Press, 1979).

6. Richard Fagen, Richard A. Brody, and Thomas J. O'Leary, *Cubans in Exile: Disaffection and the Revolution* (Stanford, Calif.: Stanford University Press, 1968), p. 100.

7. For U.S. historical involvement and interest in Cuba and the Caribbean, see Richard W. Van Alstyne, *The Rising American Empire* (New York: Norton, 1960); and Walter LaFeber, *The New Empire: An Interpretation of American Expansion, 1860–1898* (Ithaca, N.Y.: Cornell University Press, 1971).

8. Jorge I. Domínguez, *Cuba: Order and Revolution* (Cambridge, Mass.: Harvard University Press, 1979), pp. 128–30.

9. A U.S. State Department officer wrote in 1962 that the "real threat of Castro has always been that he would unleash the forces of social revolution in Latin America under leadership inimical to the United States." William J. Vanden Heuvel, "Cuba: Its Refugees and Its Liberation" (Washington, D.C.: U.S. Department of State, September 6, 1982), p. 2. In 1980 President Carter said that the "real Cuban threat is that it considers it offers a model." *Action: Bulletin of the Caribbean/Central American Action*, 5, 1 (July 1980).

10. Some Cuban leaders had very clearly in mind the lessons of the toppling of Guatemala's president Jacobo Arbenz in 1954 by the CIA. Ernesto "Che" Guevara, one of the revolution's most important leaders, lived through that experience which left a deep mark on him.

11. Dominguez, *Cuba,* p. 196. Also, author's interviews with Cuban officials.

12. For some, like Tad Szulc, "from the outset, Castro went about turning Cuba into a

Marxist-Leninist state, with the collaboration of old-line Communists and the new Communist cadres he was creating within his rebel army." "Fidel Castro's Years as a Secret Communist," *New York Times Magazine*, October 19, 1986, pp. 12–14. For others, like K. S. Karol, Fidel Castro "was not a communist," and there "never was a secret government" with a master plan to socialize Cuba. "Fidel al derecho y al reves," *La Jornada Libros*, January 24, 1987.

13. Eric N. Baklanoff, "International Economic Relations," in Carmelo Mesa-Lago (ed.), *Revolutionary Change in Cuba* (Pittsburgh, Pa.: University of Pittsburgh Press, 1971), p. 269.

14. For the number of Cubans who left the island, we consulted different sources. It is well documented that 778,246 Cubans entered the United States from 1960 to 1983. Christopher Mitchell, "Immigration and U.S. Foreign Policy in the Caribbean Basin: An Introduction," unpublished manuscript, October 1986, p. 2. According to the records of the Madrid office of the Inter-Governmental Committee for Migration (ICM), 132,878 Cubans entered Spain from 1960 to July 1984, and 81,616 continued on to the U.S. and Latin America. Author's interview with Maria Teresa Hualde, ICM, Madrid, August 14, 1984. There are Cuban communities of varying sizes in many countries. The UNHCR estimates that there are from 20,000 to 30,000 Cubans in Latin America. Thus, even considering the possibility of double counting those who went from Spain to the United States, the figure amounts to around 900,000.

15. For a discussion of the waves and criteria, see, among others, Robert L. Bach, Jennifer B. Bach, and Timothy Triplett, "The Flotilla Entrants: Latest and Most Controversial," *Cuban Studies*, 11, 2 and 12, 1 (July 1981–September 1982); Fagen et al., *Cubans in Exile*, p. 23; Mario A. Rivera, "The Cuban and Haitian Influxes of 1980 and the American Response: Retrospect and Prospect" (Washington, D.C.: A Report of the Cuban-Haitian Task Force, November 1, 1980); Gaston A. Fernandez, "Comment—the Flotilla Entrants: Are They Different," *Cuban Studies*, 11, 2 and 12, 1 (July 1981–September 1982).

16. Dominguez, *Cuba*, p. 264.

17. Amnistia Internacional, *Informe 1976* (Barcelona: Ediciones 62, 1977).

18. Amnesty International, *Report, 1977* (London: Amnesty International Publications, 1977). This statement is confirmed in the Amnesty reports from 1975 to 1986.

19. Among others, see Nelson Amaro and Carmelo Mesa-Lago, "Inequality and Classes," in Mesa-Lago (ed.), *Revolutionary Change*, pp. 366–67; Barry Sklar, "Cuban Exodus—1980, the Context," Congressional Research Service, Washington, D.C., Library of Congress, August 25, 1980; and Max Azicri, "The Politics of Exile: Trends and Dynamics of Political Change Among Cuban-Americans," *Cuban Studies*, 11, 2 and 12, 1 (July 1981–September 1982).

20. Redi Gomis and Rafael Hernandez, "Retrato del Mariel: El Angulo Socioeconomico," paper presented at Seminario Migraciones Latinoamericanas hacia Estados Unidos, CEA–LASA, Havana, May 15–17, 1986, p. 14.

21. Jorge I. Dominguez, "Cooperating with the Enemy? U.S. Immigration Policies Toward Cuba," paper prepared for New York University's project on Immigration Policy and U.S. Foreign Relations with Latin America, June 1986, p. 7. Fernandez, "Comment," p. 16.

22. As quoted in John Scanlan and Gilburt Loescher, "U.S. Foreign Policy, 1959–1980: Impact on Refugee Flows from Cuba," *The Annals, 467 (May 1983), p. 125.*

23. For a more developed formulation of these arguments, see James W. Malloy, "Generation of Political Support and Allocation of Costs," in Mesa-Lago (ed.), *Revolutionary Change*, p. 35; Scanlan and Loescher, "U.S. Foreign Policy," p. 127; and Dominguez, *Cuba*, pp. 141, 165.

24. As quoted in Juan Valdez Paz, "La Integración de la Comunidad Cubana en los Estados Unidos: El Proceso de Aculturación," paper presented at Seminario Migraciones Latinoamericanas hacia Estados Unidos, CEA–LASA, Havana, May 15–17, 1986, pp. 31–33. Translation mine.

25. About the fate of the Cubans in Spain, see CISPLA, *Latinoamericanos: Refugiados Politicos en España* (Valencia, Spain: Imprenta Provincial, 1982); Cuadernos INAS, *Integración Social: Los Refugiados en España* (Madrid), 3, 11 (July–September 1983); and the articles in the *New York Times*, December 30, 1964; May 26, 1966; February 7, 1971; and November 8, 1973.

26. Silvia Pedraza Bailey, "Cubans and Mexicans in the United States: The Functions of

Political and Economic Migration,'' *Cuban Studies,* 11, 2 and 12, 1 (July 1981–September 1982), p. 83.

27. For example, a 1953 National Security Council document argued that the ''escape of people from countries in the Soviet orbit inflicts a psychological blow on communism—it serves as a disturbing influence within the Soviet orbit and counters Communist propaganda in the free world.'' National Security Council, ''Psychological Value of Escapees from the Soviet Orbit,'' Washington, D.C., March 26, 1953.

28. Gil Loescher and John A. Scanlan, *Calculated Kindness: Refugees and America's Half-Open Door: 1945 to the Present* (New York: Free Press, 1986), chap. 4.

29. Gomis and Hernandez, ''Retrato del Mariel,'' p. 48.

30. According to Lisandro Perez, it was Silvia Pedraza's work that ''established—really for the first time in the literature—the political functions of migration from Cuba, particularly for the U.S.'' ''Comment—Cubans and Mexicans in the United States,'' *Cuban Studies,* 11, 2 and 12, 1 (July 1981–September 1982), p. 100.

31. Robert Bach, ''U.S. Foreign Policy and Cuban Migration,'' paper presented at Seminario Migraciones Latinoamericanas hacia Estados Unidos, CEA–LASA, Havana, May 15–17, 1986, p. 2.

32. Scanlan and Loescher, ''U.S. Foreign Policy,'' p. 127.

33. The quotations for this paragraph come from Scanlan and Loescher, ''U.S. Foreign Policy,'' p. 127; Pedraza, ''Cubans and Mexicans,'' p. 84; and Azicri, ''The Politics of Exile,'' p. 59.

34. Vanden Heuvel, ''Cuba.''

35. A typical commentary was made by Agustin Tamargo, a Miami Spanish-language radio commentator, who said that the late-1987 migratory agreement between the United States and Cuba ''strengthens Castro's hand at a time when his regime faces its worst economic and political crisis in decades.'' *New York Times,* November 22, 1987. Also see Scanlan and Loescher, ''U.S. Foreign Policy,'' p. 125; Rivera, ''The Cuban and Haitian Influxes,'' p. A-16; and Bach, ''U.S. Foreign Policy,'' p. 18.

36. As quoted in Bach, Bach, and Triplett, ''The Flotilla Entrants,'' p. 30.

37. Ronald Copeland, ''The Cuban Boatlift of 1980: Strategies of Federal Crisis Management, *The Annals,* 467 (May 1983), p. 143.

38. *New York Times,* November 22, 1987.

39. Richard Copeland and Patricia Weiss Fagen, *Political Asylum: A Background Paper on Concepts, Procedures and Problems* (Washington, D.C.: Refugee Policy Group, December 1982), p. 43.

40. See the *New York Times,* November 8, 1973, and April 23, 1972.

41. Patricia Weiss Fagen, ''The United States and International Human Rights,'' *Universal Human Rights,* 2, 3 (July–September 1980), p. 29.

42. For a complete development of this process, see Sergio Aguayo, ''El Conflicto Centroamericano en la Sociedad Estadounidense,'' en *México-Estados Unidos, 1983* (México: El Colegio de México, 1983).

43. Gerald M. Costello, *Mission to Latin America: The Successes and Failures of a Twentieth Century Crusade* (Maryknoll, N.Y.: Orbis Books, 1979), pp. ix, 5, 16.

44. Author's interview with John Eagleson (Orbis Books), Maryknoll, N.Y., April 27, 1984. The book was also chosen by the Protestant publication, *Christian Weekly,* as one of the twelve most important theological works among the fifteen thousand published in the United States in the 1970s. *Time,* November 26, 1979.

45. Marian McClure, ''The Catholic Church and Rural Social Change: Priests, Peasant Organization, and Politics in Haiti,'' Ph.D. diss., Harvard University, 1986, pp. 21–32.

46. Ibid., p. 28.

47. See Serge Gilles, ''Haiti à L'Encan: Un Pays au Bord de l'effondrement,'' *Le Monde Diplomatique,* August 1982; and Alex Stepick, ''Unintended Consequences: Rejecting Haitian Boat

People and Destabilizing Duvalier,'' unpublished paper, Florida International University, February 1987, pp. 3–4.

48. This quotation is taken from the supporting text for Judge Lawrence King's decision in favor of the Haitians. United States District Judge, James Lawrence King, Final Order Granting Relief, Florida, July 1, 1980, p. 115.

49. For Haiti's basic data, see, among others, Gilles, "Haiti à L'Encan''; McClure, "The Catholic Church''; and *Newsweek,* February 1, 1982.

50. As quoted in Susan H. Buchanan, "Haitian Emigration: The Perspective from South Florida and Haiti,'' report submitted to the United States Agency for International Development, Washington, D.C., 1982, pp. 11, 104. This work is essential to understanding Haitian migration.

51. This is the argument of Susy Castor, *La Ocupacion Norteamericana de Haiti y Sus Consecuencias (1915–1934)* (Mexico: Siglo XXI, 1971).

52. There is agreement on the description of the waves. See, for example, Roger Rondeau, "Qui a Peur des Réfugiés Haïtiens?'' *CJN,* May 1983; and Alex Stepick, "Unintended Consequences: Rejecting Haitian Boat People and the Demise of Duvalier,'' paper presented at Seminario CEA–LASA, Havana, May 15–17, 1986.

53. Glenn Perusek, "Haitian Emigration in the Early Twentieth Century,'' *International Migration Review,* 18, 65 (Spring 1984), p. 6.

54. Buchanan, "Haitian Emigration,'' p. 104.

55. This summary of conditions in Haiti is based on Amnesty International's annual reports from 1975 to 1986.

56. John A. Bushnell, deputy assistant secretary for Inter-American Affairs, and Stephen E. Palmer, Jr., deputy assistant secretary for Human Rights and Humanitarian Affairs, to the Subcommittee on Immigration of the House Judiciary Committee, "Haitian Migration to the U.S.'' (Washington, D.C.: U.S. Department of State, June 17, 1980).

57. See, for example, *Washington Post,* August 28, 1982.

58. The military occupation of Haiti and Cuba, and U.S. influence in the Caribbean were determining factors in the establishment of the migratory networks. See Perusek, "Haitian Emigration,'' p. 12; Susy Castor, *Migracion y Relaciones Internacionales (el Caso Haitiano-Dominicano)* (Mexico: UNAM, 1983); and Uli Locher, "Migration in Haiti,'' in Charles R. Foster and Albert Valdman (eds.), *Haiti—Today and Tomorrow: An Interdisciplinary Study* (New York: University Press of America, 1985).

59. The literature on the exploitation of Haitians in the Dominican Republic is ample. See Castor, *Migracion;* Frank Marino Hernandez, *La Inmigracion Haitiana* (Santo Domingo: Ediciones Sargazo, 1973); *Washington Post,* August 28, 1982.

60. Buchanan, "Haitian Emigration,'' pp. 41, 85.

61. "Haiti,'' *Objectifs Immigrés* (France) no. 56 (June–July 1984); Thierry Quinsant, "Haitiani in Francia,'' UNHCR, *Rifugiati,* Rome, March 1984; *Le Monde,* February 11, 1984; author's interview with UNHCR representative, Henriette Taviani, Paris, June 15, 1984; author's interviews with Haitian exiles in Paris, June 1985.

62. Francine Berneche and Jean-Claude Martin, "Immigration, Emploi et Logement: La Situation de la Population Haïtienne dans Certaines Zones de la Region Métropolitaine de Montreal,'' *Antropologie et Sociétés* (Canada), 8, 2 (1984), pp. 5–29.

63. There is a small but solid bibliography on Haitian migration to the United States. Two basic works are by Stepick, "Unintended Consequences''; and Buchanan, "Haitian Emigration.'' A good journalistic summary appears in Nicole Bernheim, "La Vigoureuse Immigration Haïtienne aux Etats-Unis,'' *Le Monde,* October 7 and 8, 1983.

64. For a summary of the arguments of the U.S. government, see Bushnell and Palmer, "Haitian Migration to the U.S.''; *Newsweek,* February 1, 1982; and Buchanan, "Haitian Emigration,'' p. 36.

65. See, for example, Scanlan and Loescher, "U.S. Foreign Policy,'' p. 314; John Tenhula,

"Boat People Flee Haiti to U.S.," *1980 World Refugee Survey* (New York: U.S. Committee for Refugees, 1980); Stepick, "Unintended Consequences," p. 11.

66. Dennis Gallagher, Susan Forbes, and Patricia Weiss Fagen mention that "Eastern Europeans cite loss of employment as an essential motive for their decision to leave. The interviewing officers agreed in these cases that the loss of employment was political in nature." Dennis Gallagher, Susan Forbes, and Patricia Weiss Fagen, "Of Special Humanitarian Concern: U.S. Refugee Admissions Since Passage of the Refugee Act" (Washington, D.C.: Refugee Policy Group, September 1985), p. 55.

67. Copeland, "The Cuban Boatlift," p. 146. For an example of the kinds of arguments used by organizations that defended the Haitians, see Church World Service, "Haitian Refugees Need Asylum: A Briefing Paper," April 1980.

68. The argument regarding the impact of migration on the downfall of the dictator is well developed by Stepick, "Unintended Consequences."

69. The reconstruction of the factors leading to Duvalier's fall is based on McClure, "The Catholic Church"; Stepick, "Unintended Consequences"; and interviews with Gerard Pierre-Charles, Mexico, 1986.

70. Stepick, "Unintended Consequences," p. 37.

71. Jeffrey M. Puryear, *Higher Education, Development Assistance, and Repressive Regimes* (New York: Ford Foundation, February 1983), p. 2.

72. Patricia Weiss Fagen, "Repression and State Security," Unpublished manuscript, 1987, p. 36.

73. Office of the U.S. assistant secretary of defense, "Study of U.S. Policy Toward Latin American Military," memorandum for the special assistant to the president for National Security Affairs, Washington, D.C., U.S. secretary of defense, February 25, 1965, pp. 1 and 29.

74. Robert Calvo, as quoted in Margaret E. Crahan, "National Security Ideology and Human Rights," in Margaret E. Crahan (ed.), *Human Rights and Basic Needs in the Americas* (Washington, D.C.: Georgetown University Press, 1982), p. 105.

75. Interviews with UNHCR officers, Geneve, May 1987.

76. Jorge Balan, "International Migration in the Southern Cone" (Washington, D.C.: Georgetown University, CIPRA, October 1985).

77. The disparity in the figures was confirmed in interviews with many of those who played a role. Among others, Philip Rudge, British Refugee Council, (London), June 1984; Maria Pia Durante, UNHCR (Rome), June 1984; Elisa Perez Vera, Madrid, July 1984; and Senator Justino Azcarraga, President Comisión Española de Ayuda a Refugiados, Madrid, July 1984.

78. Joint Working Group for Refugees from Latin America, "Refugees and Political Prisoners in Latin America," London, October 1979, pp. 1–2; and interviews held in England, Spain, Italy, France, Denmark, Sweden, and Norway. See also Erasmo Saenz, "Les Cadres Socio-politiques de l'Adaptation de Réfugiés Latino-Americains en France, 1964 à 1979," thèse pour le doctorat de 3ème cycle. Université de la Sorbonne Nouvelle (Paris III), Paris, 1983.

79. In reconstructing the story of the Latin Americans, long conversations with Guy Prim of the UNHCR were invaluable, as he experienced the entire process. Of equal importance were contributions from Gordon Hutchison (coordinator of the Project Counseling Service for Latin American Refugees, Costa Rica), Felipe Tomic (ICM), and Belela Herrera (UNHCR). See also ACNUR, *Refugiados de Chile* (Ginebra: ACNUR, 1975).

80. On the profile, see, among others, Joint Working Group, "Refugees from Chile," *La Formation de Réfugiés* (Paris: Ministere de L'Education, 1980); Juan Carlos Fortuna and Nelly Niedwork, "Emigración y Retorno en el Uruguay: 1968–1980" (Montevideo, 1986), pp. 5–8; and Armand B. Magallanes, "Quelle Insertion Professionnelle pour les Réfugiés Politiques Latino-américains en France? D'après une Expérience de Terrain à la CIMADE" (Paris: Institut de Travail Social, 1983).

81. Among others, see *Reports on Human Rights Practices for 1979* (New York: Lawyers

Committee for International Human Rights, *1980); Inter-American Commission for Human Rights,*
Informe Sobre la Situacion de los Derechos Humanos en Chile, OEA/Ser.L/V/11.66 doc. 17,
Washington, D.C., September 27, 1985; and Joint Working Group for Refugees from Chile in
Britain, "Refugees from Chile: An Interim Report," London, December 1975.

82. As quoted in Joint Working Group for Refugees from Chile in Britain, "Refugees from
Chile," p. 36.

83. Joint Working Group, "Refugees and Political Prisoners in Latin America," p. 6.

84. Ibid., pp. 7, 8.

85. Amnesty International's annual reports from 1975 to 1986. Joint Working Group, "Refugees from Chile," p. 18; *Nunca Más,* "Introduction," reprinted in *La Jornada,* December 10,
1985; and Saenz, "Les Cadres," pp. 122–23.

86. As quoted in Joint Working Group, "Refugees from Chile," p. 9.

87. Joint Working Group, "Refugees and Political Prisoners in Latin America," p. 27.

88. The studies carried out under the auspices of the UNHCR-ILO were particularly helpful
in writing this section. See UNHCR-ILO, "Labour Migration and Integration of Refugees in Latin
America. Final Report," Geneva, 1985; Lelio Marmora, "Migraciones Laborales e Integración del
Refugiado en Argentina," UNHCR-ILO, Buenos Aires, 1985; Lelio Marmora, "Migraciones
Laborales e Integración del Refugiado en Costa Rica," UNHCR-ILO, Buenos Aires, 1985; and
Lelio Marmora, "Migraciones Laborales e Integración del Refugiado en Venezuela," UNHCR-
ILO, Buenos Aires, 1985.

89. Joint Working Group, "Refugees from Chile," p. 38.

90. For the policies of other European countries, see, among others, Svante Lundberg,
"Refugiados Latinoamericanos en Suecia," (Norrköping: Statens Invandrarverk, 1977); Tuija Nie-
melä, "Primeros Servicios y Condiciones de Vida de los Refugiados Chilenos en Finlandia,"
Helsinki, 1979; Tom Critchley, "They Order It Better in Holland," *New Statesman,* 9 (July 1976),
pp. 43–44; Mark J. Kurlansky, "The Chileans in Belgium," *The Bulletin,* 7 (March 1980); Service
D'Information Tiers-Monde, "Les Refugies en Suisse," Lausanne, June 1982; Austria Documentation, *Austria as a Country of Asylum* (Vienna: Federal Press Service, 1981).

91. The description of the French case is based mainly on Saenz, "Les Cadres," pp. 46,
54–56, 157, 264, 301, 307; and author's interviews in Paris with Latin American exiles.

92. Anne Browne, "Latin American Refugees: British Government Policy and Practice," in
Britain and Latin America: An Annual Review of British–Latin American Relations (London: Latin
American Bureau, 1979), pp. 28–30; *The Economist,* January 5, 1974; and interviews with Gordon
Hutchison and members of the British Refugee Council.

93. For the Spanish case, we drew on press reports from that period and interviews with Guy
Prim of UNHCR (Geneva); Antoni Yuc (Barcelona); and Maria Teresa Hualde, Elisa Perez Vera,
and Justino Azcarrate (Madrid).

94. Crahan, "National Security Ideology," pp. 117–18.

Chapter 8

1. As quoted by Richard E. Feinberg and Bruce M. Bagley, *Development Postponed: The
Political Economy of Central America in the 1980s* (Boulder, Colo.: Westview Press, 1986), p. 3.

2. From the large bibliography on the Central American conflict, we recommend the following works: Feinberg and Bagley, *Development Postponed;* Edelberto Torres-Rivas, *Interpreta-
ción del Desarrollo Socioeconómico Centroamericano* (San José, Costa Rica: EDUCA, 1973); *Una
Política Alternativa para Centroamérica y el Caribe* (Managua: INIES–CRIES, 1983); CECADE–
CIDE, *Centroamérica: Crisis y Politica International* (Mexico: Siglo XXI, 1981); Tommie Sue
Montgomery, *Revolution in El Salvador: Origins and Evolution* (Boulder, Colo.: Westview Press,
1982); and Josef Goldblat and Victor Milan, "Conflict and Conflict Resolution in Central America," *Bulletin of Peace Proposals,* 17, 3–4 (1986).

3. On the origins of Christian involvement in these new social forces, see especially Phillip

Berryman, *The Religious Roots of Rebellion. Christians in Central American Revolutions* (Mary-knoll, N.Y.: Orbis Books, 1984); and Jorge Cáceres Prendes, "Radicalización Política y Pastoral Popular en El Salvador: 1969–1979," *Estudios Sociales Centroamericanos,* San José, Costa Rica, September–December 1982.

4. For the contents of the programs proposed by the new social forces, see, for example, FDR–FMLN, "Programa de Integración y Plataforma de Gobierno Revolucionario," *Guazapa,* February 10, 1984; Unidad Revolucionaria Nacional Guatemalteca, "Proclama Unitaria (January 1982)," in Comité Guatemalteco de Unidad Patriótica, *Documentos de la Unidad Guatemalteca,* n.d.

5. Robert E. Osgood, "The Revitalization of Containment," *Foreign Affairs,* February 1982, p. 466.

6. The principles of the Carter foreign policy are contained in "Discursos de James Carter"; "Capítulo VI de Platafórma Democrata"; "Segundo Informe sobre Relaciones Estados Unidos-América Latina"; and "Recomendaciones para un Nuevo Enfoque de las Relaciones Internacionales del Grupo Ad Hoc," *Cuadernos Semestrales,* CIDE, no. 1 (1977-I).

7. For more on conservative thinking, see "Plataforma Republicana," *Cuadernos Semestrales,* no. 8 (1980); "Informe del Comité de Sante Fe," *Cuadernos Semestrales,"* CIDE, no. 9 (1981). For an analysis of the Caribbean Basin initiative, see Sergio Aguayo y Cesareo Morales, *El Futuro de la Cuenca del Caribe Segun la Administración Reagan* (Bogotá: FESCOL/–Departamento de Ciencia Politica de la Universidad de los Andes, 1982).

8. Cor. Adolfo Arnoldo Majano, *Fuerzas Armadas en Centroamerica* (Mexico: Estudios del Centro Latinoamericano de Estudios Estrategicos, 1987).

9. For example, the Rev. Bryan Hehir, representative of the U.S. Catholic Conference, stated to the U.S. Congress that "the Bishops of the United States see the conflicts in El Salvador from the point of view of the Church in that country." Washington, D.C., February 25, 1981.

10. "Resolution," *Church and Society,* July–August 1983, pp. 84ff.

11. For those readers interested in the situation of the internally displaced, see Americas Watch Committee (AWC) and Lawyers' Committee for International Human Rights, *El Salvador's Other Victims: The War on the Displaced* (New York: AWC, 1984); Americas Watch Committee, *Human Rights in Guatemala. No Neutrals Allowed* (New York: AWC, 1984); *Guatemala: Revista Cultural del Ejercito* (Guatemala: Ministerio de la Defensa Nacional, January–February 1985); "Guatemalan Displaced Persons Needs Survey Covering Huehuetenango, Quiche, Western Peten and Playa Grande: Final Report," USAID, Project no. DR-520-84-04; and L. R. Moore, "El Salvador: Estrategias de Integración Social para Poblaciones Desplazadas y Marginadas: Labores Realizadas, Conclusiones, Recomendaciones: Informe de Misión," El Salvador, Programa de Naciones Unidas para el Desarrollo, Proyecto ELS/83/004, 1984.

12. Office of the U.S. Coordinator for Refugee Affairs, *Proposed Refugee Admissions and Allocations for Fiscal Year 1983. Report to the Congress* (Washington, D.C.: U.S. Department of State, September 1982), p. 24.

13. Although information is lacking on the profile of Central Americans without official recognition, some surveys confirm that most are from low-income sectors. See Sergio Aguayo, *El Exodo Centroamericano* (Mexico: SEP/FORO 2000, 1985); Johanna Gauthier, "Informe Sobre Encuestas con Centroamericanos en la Ciudad de México," Mexico, 1985; Dora Rapold, "La Lucha por la Supervivencia," paper presented at Encuentro de Talleres del Programa Interdisciplinario de Estudios de la Mujer, El Colegio de México, March 10–12, 1987.

14. Sergio Aguayo and Laura O'Dogherty, "Los Refugiados Guatemaltecos en Campeche y Quintana Roo," *Foro Internacional,* 27, 2 (October–December 1986); and S. Aguayo, H. Christensen, L. O'Dogherty, and S. Varesse, *Social and Cultural Conditions and Prospects of Guatemalan Refugees in Mexico* (Geneva: UNRISD/El Colegio de México, 1987).

15. International Council of Voluntary Agencies, "Consultation," Geneva, 1986.

16. Thomas E. Skidmore and Peter H. Smith, *Modern Latin America* (New York: Oxford University Press, 1984), p. 308.

18. Author's interviews with local agencies and UNHCR personnel from 1983 to 1987.

19. In April 1987 after the deadly guerrilla attack against the El Paraiso military garrison, some American officials "predict that the United States will spend at least the next decade propping up the little Central American country," *New York Times*, April 5, 1987.

20. For a discussion of the human rights situation in 1987, see The Honorable George C. Edwards and William J. Butler, Esq., *Guatemala: A New Beginning. Report of a Mission on Behalf of the American Association for the International Commission of Jurists* (New York: American Association for the International Commission of Jurists, 1987).

21. Stuart K. Tucker, "Trade Unshackled: Assessing the Value of the Caribbean Basin Initiative" (rough draft), paper prepared for the International Commission on Central American Recovery and Development, Overseas Development Council, November 1987.

22. Ibid., p. 30.

23. The figures come from UNHCR, "Number of Refugees, December 31, 1986."

24. Especially resolutions 39/140 of December 14, 1984; 35/46 of November 25, 1980; and 32/67 of December 8, 1977.

25. Part of the analysis of UNHCR criteria comes from Laura O'Dogherty, "Los Refugiados no Reconocidos: Un Problema Regional," *La Jornada*, November 25, 1986.

26. Gil Loescher, *Humanitarianism and Politics in Central America*, Working Paper no. 86 (Notre Dame, Ind.: Helen Kellogg Institute for International Studies, University of Notre Dame, 1986).

27. See Americas Watch Committee and Lawyers' Committee, International Human Rights and Washington Office on Latin America, *Honduras: On the Brink* (New York: AWC, 1984); *Washington Post*, November 11, 1982; and *Newsweek*, November 8, 1982.

28. In fact, an NGO's work plans are closely related to its interpretation of the conflict. (Interviews with NGOs throughout the region from 1982 to 1987.)

29. For an excellent review of the legal situation of Central Americans in Mexico, see Joan Friedland and Jesus Rodriguez y Rodriguez, *Seeking Safe Ground: The Legal Situation of Central American Refugees in Mexico* (San Diego: University of San Diego, 1987).

30. Interviews and field work in Chiapas from 1981 to 1987. Also see Sergio Aguayo, *Chiapas y la Seguridad Nacional Mexicana* (Mexico: Centro Latinoamericano de Estudios Estratégicos, 1987).

31. This argument is developed in Sergio Aguayo, "Los centroamericanos olvidados," *Nexos*, November 1986.

32. For the situation of Salvadorans in camps in Honduras, see *Washington Post*, November 11, 1982; and *Human Rights International Reporter*, 8, 1 (September–November 1982). Regarding the way in which the State Department justifies Honduran policy, see *Country Reports, Fiscal Year 1984* (Washington, D.C.: U.S. Department of State, 1985), p. 102.

33. Interviews with Honduran diplomats and private NGOs in 1984 and 1987.

34. Interviews and field work in Tapachula, Chiapas, from 1981 to 1987.

35. Interviews with Mexican officials in Tapachula, Chiapas, January, 1986.

36. The summary of the situat on on the northern border is from Sergio Aguayo, "La Situación de los Migrantes Centroamericanos en la Frontera de Baja California Norte," Tijuana, B.C., 1981; and field work and interviews along the northern border, February, 1987.

37. Interviews in Mexico's northern and southern borders from 1981 to 1987.

38. In 1983 Ambassador H. Eugene Douglas, then head of refugee affairs, stated clearly that the official U.S. policy is "designed to encourage and maintain the tradition of asylum of [Latin American] countries [where] there is a long tradition of political asylum." H. Eugene Douglas, U.S. coordinator for refugee affairs, "Congressional Briefing Paper and Talking Points on Refugees and Potential Refugees in and from Central America" (Washington, D.C.: U.S. Department of State, May 17, 1983).

39. Interviews with Mexican officials close to the situation, 1981 to 1987.

40. For the development of this argument, see Gil Loescher and John A. Scanlan, *Calculated*

Kindness: Refugees and America's Half-Open Door: 1945 to the Present (New York: Free Press, 1986).

40. This argument was used publicly by President Ronald Reagan. See *Washington Post,* June 21, 1983. Afterwards, other conservative politicians and officials, such as Senator Jesse Helms, have also mentioned it. Even in 1987, in his testimony before Congress, Oliver North used it to justify his activities (*La Jornada,* July 14, 1987).

41. Regarding U.S. motives, see Ronald Copeland and Patricia Weiss Fagen, *Political Asylum: A Background Paper on Concepts, Procedures, and Problems* (Washington, D.C.: Refugee Policy Group, December 1982); Marge Thoennes and Joel Verner, "Los Salvadoreños y el Asilo Político en Estados Unidos," *Foro Internacional,* 26, 1 (1985); Lars Schoultz, "Central America," unpublished manuscript, University of North Carolina, 1987; Dennis Gallagher, Susan Forbes, and Patricia Weiss Fagen, "Of Special Humanitarian Concern: U.S. Refugee Admissions Since Passage of the Refugee Act" (Washington, D.C.: Refugee Policy Group, September 1985); and Gary MacEoin and Nivita Riley, *No Promised Land, American Refugee Policies and the Rule of the Law* (New York: Oxfam America, 1982).

42. R. Camarda, D. Loeb, and S. Hansell (eds.), *Forced to Move: Salvadoran Refugees in Honduras* (San Francisco: Solidarity Publications, 1986); and Demetrio Paredes, "La Reubicación de los Refugiados Salvadoreños en Honduras: Un Paso Hacia la Intervención," *Estudios Centroamericanos* (San Salvador, 1984).

43. On Mexico's motives, see Sergio Aguayo, "Refugiados, una Prueba para el Sistema Político Mexicano," *Perfil de la Jornada,* May 23, 1985; Aguayo and O'Dogherty, "Los Refugiados"; and Mario Arriola, "Mexico y el Problema de los Refugiados guatemaltecos," *Carta de Política Exterior Mexicana* CIDE, 3, 2, México, 1983; and CEESTEM, "Mexico en la Encrucijada de Guatemala," in Adolfo Aguilar Zinser (ed.), *Informe de las Relaciones Mexico–Estados Unidos,* 1, 3, México, 1982.

44. Interviews with officials from the UNHCR and private agencies; San José, Costa Rica, September 1986.

45. Patricia Weiss Fagen and Sergio Aguayo, *Central Americans in Mexico and the United States: Unilateral, Bilateral, and Regional Perspectives* (Washington, D.C.: Center for Immigration Policy and Refugee Assistance, 1988).

46. On the responses of U.S. society, see Fagen and Aguayo, *Central Americans;* Aguayo, *El Exodo,* chap. 10; W. K. Duval, D. S. De Haan, D. H. Larsen, M. Lehman, and P. A. Taran (eds.), *Seeking for Safe Haven: A Congregational Guide for Helping Central American Refugees in the United States* (New York: Church World Services, Immigration and Refugee Program and Lutheran Immigration and Refugee Service, 1985); Renny Golden and Michael McConnel, *Sanctuary: The New Underground Railroad* (New York: Orbis Books, 1986); and Gary MacEoin (ed.), *Sanctuary: A Resource Guide for Understanding and Participating in the Central American Refugees Struggle* (New York: Harper & Row, 1985).

47. Interviews with private agencies from industrialized countries, 1983 to 1987. This section is based on the experiences of Sergio Aguayo, who has been a member of the Latin American Consultative Committee of the Project Counseling Service for Latin American Refugees, a coalition of European and Canadian NGOs.

48. For the Final Declaration, the speeches made at the meeting and other related documents, see *La Protección Internacional de los Refugiados en América Central, México y Panamá: Problemas Jurídicos y Humanitarios: Memorias del Coloquio* (Cartagena, Colombia: ACNUR/Centro Regional de Estudios del Tercer Mundo/Universidad Nacional de Colombia, 1984).

49. Interviews with UNHCR and government officials who have participated in this effort, 1984 to 1987.

50. Interviews with UNCHR officials in Washington, New York, and Geneva, 1985, 1986, and 1987.

51. This evaluation is based on an analysis of the Southern Cone developed in Project Counseling Service meetings in Zurich, June 4–5, 1987.

52. "Grupo de Consulta Sobre Opciones de Solución en Favor de los Refugiados Centro-americanos," Documento Final, Geneva, May 25–27, 1987.

Chapter 9

1. The baseline is G. Beijer's rough estimate of 22 million in Asia between 1945 and 1967. "Modern Patterns of International Migratory Movements," in J. A. Jackson (ed.), *Migration* (Cambridge, England: Cambridge University Press, 1969), p. 18.

2. *World Refugee Survey: 1987 in Review* (Washington, D.C.: American Council for Nationalities Service, 1988), pp. 30 ff (hereafter cited as *WRS* with appropriate year). The total includes 13,296,460 "refugees in need of protection and/or assistance" (Table 1, p. 31), and 2,112,000 persons "in refugee-like circumstances" (Table 2, p. 32).

3. In retrospect, it is evident that by focusing exclusively on the formation of new states, A. R. Zolberg's article, "The Formation of New States as a Refugee-Generating Process," *The Annals,* 467 (May 1983), pp. 24–38, created the misleading impression that this process accounted for most of the refugees in the developing world.

4. Although akin to the "world-system" approach developed by Immanuel Wallerstein, our conceptualization eschews the functionalist notion of a system striving to meet its needs and also recognizes the existence of an international system of states that generates distinctive political-strategic processes with a dynamic of their own. See the further discussion in A. Zolberg, "Origins of the Modern World System: A Missing Link," *World Politics,* 33, 2 (January 1981), pp. 253–81; A. Zolberg, " 'World' and 'System': A Misalliance", in W. R. Thompson (ed.), *Contending Approaches to World System Analysis* (Beverly Hills, Calif.: Sage, 1983), pp. 269–90; and A. Zolberg, "Beyond the Nation-State: Comparative Politics in Global Perspective," in J. Berting et al., *Beyond Progress and Development* (London: Bowker, 1987).

5. Besides "industrial market economies" with an average GNP of U.S. $11,810 (1985) and "high-income oil exporters" (U.S. $9,800), the World Bank ranks its members as "low-income countries" (U.S. $270), "lower middle-income" (U.S. $820), or "upper middle-income" (U.S. $1,800). Of the thirty-seven countries in the lowest group, twenty four are in black Africa; the others are the four countries of the Indian subcontinent, four in southeast Asia (former Indochina and Burma), plus China, Bhutan, Nepal, Afghanistan, and Haiti. Conversely, leaving aside South Africa, only six countries of sub-Saharan Africa are classified as "lower middle-income" (Mauritania, Liberia, Ivory Coast, Nigeria, Cameroon, and the People's Republic of the Congo). Moreover, all but the latter fall below the average for the group. The remaining Asian countries and those of Latin America range across all the other categories. See *World Development Report 1987* (New York: Oxford University Press, 1987), pp. 202–3.

6. E. A. Wrigley, *Population and History* (New York: McGraw-Hill, 1969), p. 205; Colin McEvedy and Richard Jones, *Atlas of World Population History* (Harmondsworth, England: Penguin, 1978).

7. *World Development Report 1987,* Table 28, p. 256; when India and China are excluded, the ratio goes up to 3 to 1.

8. The exceptions are the Palestinians, the Central Americans, and those uprooted by the war between Iran and Iraq.

9. See, generally, Mary M. Kritz (ed.), *U.S. Immigration and Refugee Policy: Global and Domestic Issues* (Lexington, Mass.: Heath, 1983), esp. the contributions of Zolberg, Portes, and Bach.

10. *An Introduction to Contemporary History* (Harmondsworth, England: Penguin, 1967), p. 153.

11. A good overview of this subject is presented by Rupert Emerson in *From Empire to Nation* (Cambridge, Mass.: Harvard University Press, 1960). It should be noted, however, that the principle was extended neither to whites ruled by whites (e.g., Northern Ireland), nor to nonwhites ruled by nonwhites (e.g., Eritrea)

12. The British version, institutionalized in India and Ceylon during the interwar period and subsequently applied to much of Africa with a telescoping of time, led to dominion status and subsequently independence within the Commonwealth. The French alternative emphasized democratization and gradual incorporation into the metropolitan system, as with Martinique, Guadeloupe, and the towns of Senegal. The United States was "British" with respect to the Philippines, "French" in relation to Hawaii, and ambiguous on Puerto Rico.

13. Although it is the case that authoritarian Portugal invested heavily for over ten years to retain its African colonies, the liberal Netherlands also waged war for five years in Indonesia. With respect to its Asian empire, Britain agreed to a negotiated transfer of power in India, Ceylon (Sri Lanka), and Burma but fought nationalist guerrillas in Malaysia. And when demands for self-government arose in Africa, the Ceylon model was deemed applicable to the Gold Coast (Ghana), Nigeria, and Sierra Leone, but not to Kenya or the Rhodesias. Similarly, France stood its imperial ground in Indochina and Algeria but was willing to negotiate a transfer in Morocco, Tunisia, and black Africa.

14. Similarly in Kenya, the British initially adopted a "plantation" strategy and intervened in support of the settlers against a nationalist movement with the appropriately radical orientation. However, the guerrillas failed to expand beyond their core ethnic group or to obtain external support, and after defeating the uprising, Britain here also switched to a negotiated approach. Somewhat in the same vein, France's Ivory Coast was organized in part as a plantation colony (with respect to coffee), an experience that fostered the emergence of a radical nationalist movement. However, in the wake of post–World War II reforms, the nationalists—with indigenous petty producers in the lead—secured the abolition of forced labor on which the economy was based. This undermined the European plantation sector and led economic development in the direction of a trading colony, whose political development was dominated by a party oriented to the interests of indigenous petty producers.

15. Gilles Keppel, *Les banlieues de l'Islam* (Paris: Seuil, 1987), pp. 322 et passim (reporting research by Saliha Abdellatif, André Wormser, and Gabriel Martinez). It is estimated that less than one-tenth of all eligible auxiliaries moved to France.

16. These distinctions are elaborated by Donald Horowitz, *Ethnic Groups in Conflict* (Berkeley: University of California Press, 1985), p. 234.

17. On the general mechanisms underlying such formations, see Philip D. Curtin, *Cross-cultural Trade in World History* (Cambridge, England: Cambridge University Press, 1984). For a general analysis of labor migrations, see Aristide R. Zolberg, "Wanted but Not Welcome: Alien Labor in Western Development," in William Alonso (ed.), *Population in an Interacting World* (Cambridge, Mass.: Harvard University Press, 1987), pp. 36–73.

18. The concept was developed by J. S. Furnivall in various writings, including especially *Colonial Policy and Practice* (Cambridge, England: Cambridge University Press, 1948), pp. 303–12. His insights have been further elaborated by M. G. Smith; see in particular Leo Kuper and M. G. Smith, *Pluralism in Africa* (Berkeley and Los Angeles: University of California Press, 1969).

19. Horowitz, *Ethnic Groups,* pp. 76–77.

20. Ibid., p. 4.

21. Ibid., p. 5. Horowitz insists that what is at stake is "worth"—in the Weberian sense, a matter of status rather than class: "In the modern state . . . the sources of ethnic conflict reside, above all, in the struggle for relative group worth," exacerbated by the juxtaposition of "backward" and "advanced" groups noted earlier (p. 143). However, the precedence of "honor" over more material considerations in competition for control of the state is impossible to demonstrate and in practice not very relevant. As a number of our case studies indicate, under conditions of great scarcity, groups that achieve power often seek to reorganize distribution for the benefit of people of their own kind. Indeed, Horowitz himself acknowledges that the stakes are broader than "worth," pointing out that "the permeative character of ethnic affiliations, by infusing so many sectors of social life, imparts a pervasive quality to ethnic conflict and raises sharply the stakes of ethnic politics" (p. 8).

22. Ibid., pp. 25–30.

23. The concept is associated with the name of Arendt Lijphart, who developed it as a formalization of the arrangements found in his native Netherlands with respect to the Orthodox Protestant, Liberal Protestant, and Roman Catholic communities; see especially his "Consociational Democracy," *World Politics,* 21, 2 (1969), pp. 207–25.

24. The case of the two colonial federations, French West Africa and French Equatorial Africa, is more ambiguous. As the result of the joint efforts of France and some African territorial leaders, they became independent as a dozen separate countries. However, because these were not ethnic homelands, the division did not give rise to "unmixings."

25. These included (1) some returnees to Israel between 1949 and 1967, possibly totaling 100,000; (2) an unknown number of departures from Israel during the same period, including the expulsion of tens of thousands of Bedouins; (3) at least 200,000, and possibly as many as 400,000, uprooted from the West Bank and Gaza in the wake of the 1967 war, some of them becoming refugees for a second time (the higher estimate is from Brand, the lower from Forsythe, who adds that 20,000 were permitted by the Israelis to return to their former homes); (4) sizable migratory movements to economically promising Arab countries, particularly in the Gulf, as well as to non-Arab countries outside the region; and (5) smaller displacements occasioned by political conflicts between Palestinian activists and host Arab governments. For references concerning population figures, see Chapter 1.

26. The principal sources for the following are William B. Quandt, "Political and Military Dimensions of Contemporary Palestinian Nationalism," in William B. Quandt, Fuad Jabber, and Ann Mosely Lesch (eds.), *The Politics of Palestinian Nationalism* (Berkeley and Los Angeles: University of California Press, 1973), pp. 45–78; and David P. Forsythe, "The Palestine Question: Dealing with a Long-Term Refugee Situation," *Annals,* 497 (May 1983), pp. 89–101.

27. Laurie A. Brand, "Palestinians Out of Palestine: An Examination of the Origins of the Palestinian Refugee Problem and the Status of Palestinians in Diaspora," (paper presented at the Fourth International Conference on Refugees in the Islamic World, Bellagio, 1987), p. 13.

28. Horowitz, *Ethnic Conflict,* p. 40.

29. Crawford Young, *The Politics of Cultural Pluralism* (Madison: University of Wisconsin Press, 1976), p. 502.

30. Founded on local ethnic confrontations, the secession was actively instigated by powerful international economic actors (the Union Minière conglomerate) as well as more surreptitiously from associated governments (Belgium itself, South Africa). Because of the importance of the province as a source of revenue, this jeopardized the viability of the new state as a whole; and the collapse of the Congo in turn threatened to destabilize the entire central African region, strategically vital because of its mineral wealth.

31. Horowitz has observed (*Ethnic Conflict,* p. 229) that contrary to expectations founded on the European experience, "troublesome irredentas have been few and far between, whereas troublesome secessions have been abundant. The few irredentas that have broken into warfare have been virulently fought, as have many of the wars of secession. Yet almost none of the secessionist or irredentist movements has achieved its goals." He also includes Afghanistan in relation to Pakistan's northwestern province.

32. Theda Skocpol, *States and Social Revolutions: A Comparative Analysis of France, Russia, and China* (Cambridge, England: Cambridge University Press, 1979), p. 4.

33. The conceptualization of "voice" and "exit" as alternatives was developed by Albert O. Hirschman, *Exit, Voice, and Loyalty: Responses to Decline in Firms, Organizations, and States* (Cambridge, Mass.: Harvard University Press, 1970).

34. Useful overviews of recent developments in the literature have been presented by Jack A. Goldstone in "Theories of Revolution: The Third Generation," *World Politics,* April 1980, pp. 425–53; and "The Comparative and Historical Study of Revolutions," *Annual Review of Sociology,* 8 (1982), pp. 187–207; and Theda Skocpol, "What Makes Peasants Revolutionary?" *Comparative Politics* 14 (April 1982), pp. 351–75.

35. Barrington Moore, Jr., *Social Origins of Dictatorship and Democracy: Lord and Peasant in the Making of the Modern World* (Boston: Beacon Press, 1966), p. 453.

36. Ibid., pp. 482–83. Moore explains that revolution is unlikely in India because its agrarian structures are in major respects quite different from those of China. Thus "a turn to the right or fragmentation along regional lines, or some combination of these two, seems much more probable. . . ."

37. Ibid., p. 459.

38. S. N. Eisenstadt, *Revolution and the Transformation of Societies: A Comparative Study of Civilizations* (New York: Free Press, 1978). "Coalescent" change is bundled up, as distinct from "segregative" change, in which change in various cultural and institutional spheres is relatively unconnected; it is usually found in societies that recognize "a high level of tension between the transcendental and the mundane order."

39. Skocpol, *States,* p. 285.

40. Ibid., p. 286.

41. Goldstone argues that this factor provides a better explanation for European revolutions than does Skocpol's "lost wars." (In his "The Comparative and Historical Study of Revolutions," p. 205).

42. James Scott, *The Moral Economy of the Peasant: Rebellion and Subsistence in Southeast Asia* (New Haven, Conn.: Yale University Press, 1976), p. 4.

43. Moore, *Social Origins,* p. 479.

44. Ibid., p. 480.

45. Ibid., p. 474.

46. This arises in the context of a comprehensive "moral economy," grounded in technical and social relations of production designed to deal with perennial food shortages, which shape the peasants' views of what claims on their product are tolerable or intolerable. For Scott, the peasantry does not include migrant laborers, plantation workers, and many landless day laborers whose position in the social structure is akin to that of a proletariat. Although his analysis is based on empirical case material from Southeast Asia, he suggests that the findings are more broadly applicable.

47. Eric Wolf, *Peasant Wars in the Twentieth Century* (New York: Harper & Row, 1969), p. 290. His general thesis is that they were a response to the destructive effects of incorporation into the capitalist world-economy on both the subsistence economy and traditional authority structures, combined with rapid population growth. His analysis is based on a chronological sequence of six case studies, Mexico, Russia, China, Vietnam, Algeria, and Cuba.

48. James Scott, "Hegemony and the Peasantry," *Politics and Society,* 7, 3 (1977), pp. 267–96.

49. Scott insists that contrary to the common assumptions of urban dwellers, peasants are not isolated in villages but interact across standard marketing areas. Religion itself cannot be relegated *ipso facto* to the sphere of hegemonic institutions: All great religions can be read both ways, with the possible exception of Hinduism, and in any case the religion of peasants differs significantly from that of urban elites, even if it is nominally the same. It often includes "rituals of profanation," as in the European Halloween and Carnival. Supplying their own food, peasants meet many of their other needs such as clothing and shelter directly as well, in contrast with factory workers who depend on wages that they must exchange. In Gramscian terms, they are not organically dependent on capitalist organizers. Landlords often do nothing but collect rent, so that if they were to be eliminated, the net effect on the tenants' life would be to allow them to retain what they now pay. Residual social ties of kinship, religion, and local trade—to which ethnicity should be added as well—provide the foundations for collective action.

50. Wolf, *Peasant Wars,* p. 296.

51. Scott, *The Moral Economy,* p. 203.

52. Jeffrey Paige, *Agrarian Revolution* (New York: Free Press, 1975). Paige elaborated a model of rural society involving two classes, cultivators and noncultivators, defined in terms of their

352   NOTES TO CHAPTER 9

relations to the factors of production, land and capital. The independent variable was the source of income, either land itself or capital (for noncultivators) and wages (for cultivators). The model was then tested by means of multivariate analysis, using "export enclaves" rather than countries as the units of analysis, and further with case studies.

53. Skocpol, "What Makes Peasants Revolutionary?" p. 357. See also Arne Disch, "Peasants and Revolts," *Theory and Society,* 7 (January–March 1979), pp. 243–52.

54. Craig Jenkins, "Why Do Peasants Rebel? Structural and Historical Theories of Modern Peasant Rebellions," *American Journal of Sociology,* 88, 3 (1983), p. 512.

55. Scott, "Hegemony," p. 291.

56. Samuel L. Popkin, *The Rational Peasant: The Political Economy of Rural Society in Vietnam* (Berkeley and Los Angeles: University of California Press, 1979). Viewing Vietnamese peasants as "rational problem solvers" within the framework of neoclassical political economy, Popkin has suggested that whether they turned into maximizing capitalists or stalwart revolutionaries depended on how their interests were affected by changing conditions. For a vigorous discussion of Scott and Popkin, see Bruce Cumings, "Interest and Ideology in the Study of Agrarian Politics," *Politics and Society,* 10 (1981), pp. 467–95.

57. Joel Migdal, *Peasants, Politics, and Revolution* (Princeton, N.J.: Princeton University Press, 1974).

58. Charles Tilly, "Revolutions and Collective Violence," in Fred Greenstein and Nelson Polsby (eds.), *Handbook of Political Science* (Reading, Mass.: Addison-Wesley, 1975), vol. 3, p. 503.

59. Skocpol, "What Makes Peasants Revolutionary?" p. 302.

60. Kenneth W. Grundy, "The Social Costs of Armed Struggle in Africa," *Armed Forces and Society* 7 (1980–81), p. 463.

61. E. F. Kunz, "The Refugee in Flight: Kinetic Models and Forms of Displacement," *International Migration Review* 7, 2 (Summer 1973), p. 131.

62. John King Fairbank, *The Great Chinese Revolution: 1800–1985* (New York: Harper & Row, 1987), p. 204.

63. Both were rated as "high risk" in a "countries in trouble" survey made by *The Economist,* December 20, 1986, p. 70.

64. Roy Prosterman, "A Simplified Predictive Index of Rural Instability," *Comparative Politics,* April 1976, pp. 339–53.

65. The Latin America or Caribbean countries whose 1985 per-capita GNP was below the "upper middle-income" level (i.e., < $1,640) and whose industry contributed no more than one-third of GDP are, in order of ascending income: Haiti, Bolivia, Honduras, Nicaragua, Dominican Republic, El Salvador, Paraguay, Costa Rica, Colombia, and Chile. IBRD, *World Development Report 1987,* Tables 1 and 3, pp. 202–7. For a good current overview of Central America, see the series of articles in the *New York Times,* September 6–8, 1987. Costa Rica and Honduras passed land reform laws as early as 1962; Nicaragua in 1979, as part of the Sandinista program; El Salvador in 1980; but Guatemala not yet. The pressure for land is greatest in El Salvador because its population density, more than 670 people per square mile, is much greater than that of the rest of Central America. All the countries of the region had projected rates of annual growth of population for 1985 to 2000 of above 2.5 percent, with the exception of El Salvador (2.0). For Latin America as a whole, although the rural labor force declined between 1950 and 1980, the surplus was channeled into an urban "informal proletariat" (i.e., casual labor and the like, not protected by even minimal labor legislation). At the same time, the proportion of the rural labor force within the informal proletariat went up as well. See Alejandro Portes, "Latin American Class Structures: Their Composition and Change During the Last Decades," *Latin American Research Review,* 20, 3 (1985), pp. 7–39.

66. For a synthesis of the vast literature on the subject, see Juan J. Linz, "Totalitarian and Authoritarian Regimes," *Handbook of Political Science* (New York: Addison-Wesley, 1975), pp. 175–411. On specific regions, see David Collier (ed.), *The New Authoritarianism in Latin America*

(Princeton, N.J.: Princeton University Press, 1979); and Herbert Feith, ''Repressive-Developmentalist Regimes in Asia: Old Strengths, New Vulnerabilities,'' *Prisma*, 19 (1980), pp. 9–55.

67. The concept of a ''culture of fear'' has been elaborated by the Joint Committee on Latin American Studies of the Social Science Research Council. See the report by Joan Dassin, ''The Culture of Fear,'' *Items*, 40, 1 (March 1986), pp. 7–12; and the chapter by Patricia Weiss Fagen, ''Repression and State Security,'' prepared for the committee's forthcoming book.

68. James C. Scott, *Weapons of the Weak: Everyday Forms of Peasant Resistance* (New Haven, Conn.: Yale University Press, 1985); ''Everyday Forms of Peasant Resistance,'' *Journal of Peasant Studies*, 13 (1986), pp. 6–35; ''Resistance Without Protest and Without Organization: Peasant Opposition to the Islamic Zakat and the Christian Tithe,'' *Comparative Studies in Society and History*, 29, 3 (July 1987), pp. 417–52.

69. Sources include C. M. Eya Nchama, ''La décolonisation de la Guinée Equatoriale et le problème des réfugiés,'' *Genève-Afrique*, 1 (1982), pp. 75–128; Suzanne Cronje, *Equatorial Guinea—The Forgotten Dictatorship: Forced Labor and Political Murder in Central Africa* (London: Anti-Slavery Society, 1976); René Pélissier, ''Autopsy of a Miracle,'' *Africa Report*, 25 (May–June 1980), pp. 10–14.

Chapter 10

1. Sadruddin Aga Khan, *Study on Human Rights and Massive Exoduses*, United Nations, ECOSOC, E/CN.4/1503, December 31, 1981.

2. UN.A/41/324, *International Co-operation to Avert New Flows of Refugees*, May 13, 1985.

3. *Refugees: Dynamics of Displacement*. A report for the Independent Commission on International Humanitarian Issues (London: Zed, 1986).

4. Heading in Sadruddin Aga Khan, *Study on Human Rights*, p. 53.

5. *The Hindu* (New Delhi), August 20, 1987.

6. This is not to be confused with a ''development-oriented'' refugee policy, a term used by Charles Keely in a well-known contribution to the refugee policy debate in the United States in the early 1980s. In his *Global Refugee Policy: The Case for a Development Oriented Strategy* (New York: Population Council, 1981). The term refers to resettlement strategies of refugees within the developing world. Keely argues for long-term development aid rather than relief assistance.

7. A/41/324, p. 11.

8. A/SPC/35/SR.43, December 10, 1980, p. 4.

9. Statements by the representatives of Democratic Yemen and Jordan, A/SPC/35/SR.46, December 12, 1980, pp. 8–9.

10. The term *structural violence* is used here in the sense developed by Johan Galtung; see Chapter 5, note 27.

11. The resolution ''strongly condemns all policies and practices of oppressive and racist regimes as well as aggression, alien domination and foreign occupation, which are primarily responsible for the massive flows of refugees. ''A/RES/35/124, January 28, 1981.

12. Barrington Moore, Jr., *Social Origins of Dictatorship and Democracy: Lord and Peasant in the Making of the Modern World* (Boston: Beacon Press, 1966).

13. For a comprehensive discussion of strategies, see Donald Horowitz, *Ethnic Groups in Conflict*, pt. 5, ''Strategies of Conflict Reduction'' (Berkeley: University of California Press, 1985).

14. Crawford Young, *The Politics of Cultural Pluralism* (Madison: University of Wisconsin Press, 1976), p. 523.

15. See Guillermo O'Donnell, Philippe Schmitter, and Laurence Whitehead, *Transitions from Authoritarian Rule: Latin America* (Baltimore: Johns Hopkins University Press, 1986) and accompanying volumes in this series.

16. See Stanley Hoffman, *Duties Beyond Borders* (Syracuse, N.Y.: Syracuse University

Press, 1981); and Hedley Bull (ed.), *Intervention in World Politics* (Oxford, England: Clarendon Press, 1984). A central doctrine of "just war" holds that there must be some proportionality between the value of ends and the costs of means.

17. See the centerpiece in *Refugees,* no. 24, December 1985.

18. The Cartagena Declaration of November 1984 was approved by Latin American governments for use in the Western Hemisphere but has been consistently opposed by the United States.

19. The category was used primarily for asylum seekers in Europe who did not fit a strict convention definition, notably Iranians and Tamils.

20. Interviews, UNHCR, Geneva, March 1987.

21. Asylum policies are discussed more fully in the last section of this chapter. Note that the quota refugees accepted for resettlement through the UNHCR were exempt from these restrictive trends.

22. Göran Melander, *Flyktning i Norden* (Stockholm: Norstedt & Söners Forlag, 1969); Atle Grahl-Madsen, "Identifying the World's Refugees," *Annals of the American Academy of Political and Social Science,* 467 (May 1983), pp. 11–23.

23. Zentrale Dokumentationsstelle der Freien Wohlfahrtspflege für Flüchtlinge, Bonn, discussions, June 1985.

24. See Chapter 1.

25. Compare Henry Shue's argument in *Basic Human Rights* (Princeton, N.J.: Princeton University Press, 1980), that economic rights (to life-sustaining activities) are more basic than are political ones (freedom of speech, assembly). We contend that escape from violence is a prerequisite for both.

26. The article excludes persons from the benefits of asylum/refugee status if they have committed war crimes or crimes against humanity, and if they have committed "a serious nonpolitical crime" or acts contrary to the purposes and principles of the U.N. The U.S. 1980 Refuge Act excludes from the definition persons who have "participated in the persecution of any person." Sec. 201(a). The principle that a "political offense" but not common criminality entitles a person to asylum has been incorporated in two regional conventions bearing on asylum, the 1954 Caracas Convention on Territorial Asylum and the 1957 European Convention on Extradition.

27. Guy S. Goodwin-Gill, *The Refugee in International Law* (Oxford, England: Clarendon Press, 1983), p. 61. The UNHCR, Geneva, in early 1987 prepared an in-house study on terrorism that favored a narrow definition of "political," that is, justifiable, crime.

28. See Chapter 1, p. 33.

29. Refugee legislation in the United States before 1980, as well asylum legislation in Eastern Europe, was not based on the universal definition in the U.N. convention but was openly partisan and political. A formal trace of partisanship is left in the admission clause in the U.S. 1980 act which specifies that some refugee groups may be of "special humanitarian concern to the United States." Sec. 207 (a) (3c).

30. To illustrate: The current High Commissioner, Jean-Pierre Hocke, opened a seminar with prominent international personalities by characterizing the UNHCR's task as follows: "The humanitarian gesture is, by definition, performed after the event, with perseverance and selflessness in an attempt to assist someone whose flesh and whose dignity have been wounded." The seminar was entitled "Assistance to Refugees: Humanitarian Action and Political Considerations," *Refugees* (Geneva), July 1987, p. 8.

31. Domestic political benefits include easier adjustment to social change and the departure of political rivals. Large-scale outflows may serve foreign policy objectives of creating chaos in neighboring countries, as Cuba and Vietnam were accused of doing in 1979–80.

32. Norman Zucker and Naomi Zucker, *The Guarded Gate: The Reality of American Refugee Policy* (San Diego: Harcourt Brace Jovanovich, 1987), esp. pp. 209–64.

33. National Security Council, "Psychological Value of Escapees from the Soviet Orbit," Washington, D.C., March 29, 1953.

34. See Chapter 1, p. 24.

35. Thus, the U.S. government holds that most of the persons displaced by the conflicts in El Salvador and Guatemala have ''sought the protection of their own governments in areas relatively free from externally initiated aggression, random violence and combat'' [office of the U.S. Coordinator for Refugee Affairs, *Proposed Refugee Admissions and Allocations for Fiscal Year 1986* (Washington, D.C.: U.S. Government Printing Office, September 1985)], p. 15. The guerrilla leaders maintain that most of the displaced seek security away from the government forces, as the latter represent the major security threat.

36. Grahl-Madsen, ''Identifying the World's Refugees,'' p. 22.

37. After 1980, the U.N. and Western lexicon for the Khmer on the Thai-Kampuchean border was as follows: The Khmer were divided among ''border concentrations,'' ''holding centers,'' and ''refugee camps.'' Only the latter were considered to have the rights of ''refugees,'' including guarantees against forceful return and the option of resettlement elsewhere. The holding center population was in limbo until the mid-1980s, and the border concentration people had no rights, as they were not given the prima facie designation of refugee. Their partially supervised return to Kampuchea was called *relocation;* the question of involuntary repatriation in the U.N. convention's sense did not arise, as the population had not been designated as refugees in the first place. The distribution of people among the three camp categories was determined largely by the time of their arrival at the border and the ease of access beyond. The Thai authorities, for their part, employed language indicating that the Khmer (indeed all the Indochinese) were ordinary migrants (*pooawpaiyop* in Thai); hence any right was extended at the discretion of the Thai government. Thailand was at the time not a signatory to the 1951 U.N. convention or its protocol.

Conversely, the term *refugee* was consistently used in the United States in both popular and administrative parlance for the Vietnamese, suggesting inherent rights to assistance and prohibition against return.

38. A 1982 publication by two leading scholars in the field illustrates a typically uncritical mixing of sociological and legal definitions. Refugees are described as ''among the world's most disadvantaged people''; they ''do not voluntarily leave their homes to seek economic opportunity in another country''; and ''they flee because of persecution or fear of it.'' G. Loescher and A. D. Loescher, *The World's Refugees: A Test of Humanity* (New York: Harcourt Brace Jovanovich, 1982), p. 1.

39. *Refugees* (Geneva), November 1985, pp. 5, 9. Only a small proportion of the UNHCR's budget is a regular contribution apportioned by the U.N. General Assembly (2.8 percent in 1985). The rest comes from voluntary contributions from the U.N. member states. This makes for a dependent and precarious position, as the previous high commissioner, Poul Hartling, emphasized.

40. W. R. Smyser, ''Refugees: A Never-Ending Story,'' *Foreign Affairs,* Fall 1985, pp. 157–59.

41. Goodwin-Gill, *The Refugee in International Law,* pp. 225–26.

42. On the subject of refugee children, see R. L. Punamaki, ''Childhood in the Shadow of War. A Psychological Study on Attitudes and Emotional Life of Israeli and Palestinian Children,'' *Current Research on Peace and Violence,* 5 (1982), pp. 26–41; ''Children in Situations of Armed Conflict in Africa: An Agenda for Action. Selected Papers from a Conference in Nairobi July 6–10, 1987,'' The African Network for the Prevention and Protection Against Childhood Abuse and Neglect; and the ongoing Joint Project on Children and War, undertaken by the International Catholic Child Bureau (Geneva) and the Columbia University Center for the Study of Human Rights. A preliminary study is now available: Margaret McCallin, *Report of a Pilot Study to Assess Levels of Stress in a Sample of 90 Refugee Children in Central America,* (Geneva: International Catholic Child Bureau, 1988).

43. The regimes in Kabul and Phnom Penh regularly charged that the rebels were preventing the refugees from returning and gave much publicity to the return movements that actually took place. By the beginning of 1988, for instance, President Najibullah cited the return of 110,303 Afghan refugees as evidence that the government's policy of ''national reconciliation'' was working (*New Kabul Times,* February 3, 1988). Rebel leaders in Pakistan claimed that the remaining almost

3 million refugees had escaped the Kabul regime and remained in Pakistan of their own free will. The claim was upheld by the U.N. special rapporteur of the Commission on Human Rights dealing with Afghanistan, Felix Ermacora. His 1987 report maintained that given the conditions on the border, "it is difficult to imagine the possibility of holding refugees back if they really want to leave" (U.N. General Assembly, *Situation of Human Rights in Afghanistan,* Report of the Economic and Social Council, A/42/667, October 23, 1987, p. 11). Nevertheless, the rebel leaders had considerable power. They had the guns and were manning checkpoints at the border crossings as well as on major roads inside Afghanistan. They also issued the identification cards that the refugees needed to be registered as a "refugee" in Pakistan. See Aristide Zolberg and Astri Suhrke, "Social Conflict and Refugees in the Third World: The Cases of Ethiopia and Afghanistan," paper presented at the Center for Migration and Population Studies, Harvard University, March 22, 1984, pp. 24–26. Sources close to rebel leaders have admitted that they naturally did not wish the refugees to return to the government zones (author's interview, New Delhi, January 1986). Returnees have confirmed that they returned at considerable personal risk (author's interview, Kabul, December 1987).

In the case of the Indochinese refugees, foreign personnel working in Lao refugee camps in Thailand found that there was considerable pressure from self-styled Lao leaders against those who opted for repatriation (Indochina Resource Center, Washington, D.C., various personal communications, 1980–81). A 1983 U.S. intelligence report on the Khmer border concentrations and holding centers likewise suggested that the Khmer Rouge cadres were preventing the refugees from returning. The findings were considered highly embarrassing within the U.S. government, which at that time supported the Khmer resistance, and so was promptly classified (interview with author of the report, Washington, D.C., March 1983).

44. The concept is inspired by the notion of "sustainable development," as used by the World Commission on Environment and Development to denote a development policy that "meets the needs of the present without compromising the ability of future generations to meet their own needs." *Our Common Future,* Report by the World Commission on Environment and Development (Oxford, England: Oxford University Press, 1987), p. 43.

45. The argument has been made especially in the context of the Afghan refugee situation in which the United States established an across-the-border program in 1985 (see Chapter 5).

46. Small boats landed clandestinely on Canada's northeastern coast in 1987, unloading Tamils and Sikhs who applied for asylum. The landings caused a near-panic reaction and paved the way for the introduction of restrictive refugee/asylum legislation in the parliament later in the year. Planeloads of Iranians arriving in Norway with false passports caused a similar reaction in this small, far-northern corner of Europe. In one incident in November 1987, forty Iranians arrived in Oslo on a scheduled flight from Turkey, all with false passports and requesting asylum.

47. With specific reference to restrictive asylum practices in the industrialized states, Amnesty International's 1987 report argues that access to submit an application is a basic human right.

48. See Chapter 6, note 47.

49. The International Conference on Assistance to Refugees in Africa (ICARA) was convened by the UNHCR in 1981 and 1984 to solicit financial contributions and consider the special problems of African refugees.

50. Figures for nineteen European countries, 1983–85: UNHCR, Geneva.

51. Statens Flyktningesekretariat (Oslo), *Årsmelding,* 1984, p. 3. The limited acceptance of new asylees is further suggested by the small overall increase in Western Europe's registered refugee population in this period (only 72,000 from 1983 to 1985), even though asylum applications in this period totaled nearly 165,000.

52. British authorities introduced visa requirements for Indians, Pakistanis, and Sri Lankans in May 1985 after a large number of Tamil asylum seekers had arrived in the first half of the year. A stay of immediate deportation required the intervention of a member of Parliament. Britain was also the first, in early 1987, to propose comprehensive carrier sanctions.

53. The restrictions led to outcries in 1984 that asylum applicants were kept behind barbed

wire in virtual concentration camps. The West German government also took steps to close the Berlin loophole to Third World citizens, by asking East German authorities to impose restrictions on their side. The genesis of the West German open policy is discussed in T. Alexander Aleinikoff, "Political Asylum in the Federal Republic of Germany and the Republic of France: Lessons for the U.S.," *Journal of Law Reform,* 17, 2 (1983), pp. 183–231.

54. Office of the U.S. Coordinator for Refugee Affairs, *Proposed Refugee Admissions and Allocations for Fiscal Year 1986,* p. 15.

55. In Norway. Some European countries started early in the 1980s to improve their staffing by having specialized adjudicators with relevant area and language expertise to determine asylum claims. According to American legal experts, the practice could well be emulated by the United States. David Martin, "Comparative Policies on Political Asylum: Of Facts and Law," in Lydio F. Tomasi (ed.), *In Defense of the Alien* (New York: Center for Migration Studies, 1987), pp. 105–12.

56. By 1987, the efforts continued, but with limited success, to develop a quota refugee system for Iranians from the main first asylum countries of Turkey and Pakistan. A quota system was established for political prisoners from Chile, whose release the UNHCR was negotiating in 1987. The UNHCR also has established quotas on an ad hoc basis for various small groups deemed especially vulnerable or difficult to place.

57. Atle Grahl-Madsen, *Territorial Asylum* (Stockholm: Almqvist & Wiksell, 1980).

58. The Indochinese program was costly, absorbed a disproportionate amount of UNHCR and donor-country resources, induced "compassion fatigue" in the industrialized states, created severe problems of adjustment across sociocultural barriers, and after a while, acquired self-perpetuating tendencies. See Chapter 6.

59. Hence the Mexican authorities did little to prevent Salvadoran refugees from crossing into the United States from Mexico.

60. The demand was rebuffed. When the UNHCR was established in 1951, the West European states also demanded that it be endowed with extensive powers to solicit, receive, and allocate financial assistance. The United States successfully opposed this, arguing that the UNHCR's main function was to extend protection. Louise W. Holborn, *Refugees: A Problem of Our Time: The Work of the United Nations High Commissioner for Refugees, 1951–1972* (Metuchen, N.J.: Scarecrow Press, 1975), pp. 68–69.

INDEX

Garang, John, 53, 54, 55
Garcia Marquez, Gabriel, 304*n*26
Geingob, Hage, 316*n*140
Geneva Accords, 162, 163, 267
Genocide
  of Armenians, 15, 16
  of Hutu in Burundi, 47
  minorities in Kampuchea and, 170
  of Namibian people, 86
  in Sudan, 51
Geopolitical circumstances, 249, 255
Georgia (nation), 16
Germany. *See* Federal Republic of Germany;
    Imperial Germany; Nazi Germany
Ghana, 122
Goldstone, Jack, 247
"Good offices" doctrine, 28, 30
Goodwin-Gill, Guy, 28, 29, 271
Goranes, 56
Gorbachev, Mikhail, 267
Gorden, Charles, 294*n*48
Gordenker, Leon, *Refugees in International
    Politics*, vii
Governments, role of, 186–90, 194–95. *See also*
    Asylum policy; Political considerations;
    Refugee policy
Grass-roots movements, 215
Great Britain. *See* United Kingdom
Great Hunger of the 1840s, 32
Greece, 14–15
Green, Marshall, 335*n*50
Grundy, Kenneth, 124, 249
Guatemala
  Cuban support for guerrilla movement in, 191
  political conditions in, 213
  refugee flows from, 28, 211, 213, 215
  roots of revolution in, 183, 207
  rural instability and, 255
Guerrilla activity. *See also* Refugee-warrior
    communities
  in Angola, 77, 78, 91–93, 311*n*90
  in Central America, 206, 207–8, 209
  in Chad, 58–59
  in Eritrea, 107–8
  in Ethiopia, 112
  in Latin America, 182, 185, 191, 198
  in Mozambique, 80–81
  in Namibia, 88, 89, 95–97, 99, 100, 102
  in Pakistan, 142
  Palestinians and, 241–42
  in Somalia, 113, 320*n*34
  in Sudan, 52, 53–54
  in Uganda, 69
  in Zimbabwe, 83–85
Guerrillas
  as quasi mercenaries, 316*n*138
  vs. refugees, 101

Guevara, Ernesto "Che," 191
GUNT. *See* Transitional Government of National
    Union
Gutierrez, Gustavo, *Theology of Liberation*, 192

Habré, Hissen, 59, 60, 61–62, 298*n*105
Habyarimana, 48
Haiti
  authoritarian regime in, 182, 192–94
  compared with Cuba, 187, 190, 192, 193–96
  conditions in, 187
  impact of migration on political system in,
    197–98
  indifference to political events in, 193
  political role of church in, 208
  prospects for, 222
  refugee flows from, 192, 194–96
  U.S. domination and, 193
  U.S. immigration policy and, 190, 194–96, 281
Halperin, Maurice, 303*n*20
Haris of Sind, 133
Harkis, 234
Hassan Bin Talal, 258
Helms, Jesse, 314*n*115
Henry IV, 5
Herero people, 86
Hezbi-Islami, 267. *See also* Muslim Brotherhood
"High Commissioner for Refugees from
    Germany," 20
"High Commissioner on behalf of the League in
    connection with the problems of Russian
    Refugees in Europe," 19
Hirschman, Albert, 27
Hmong people, 168–69
Hoa, 164
Ho Chi Minh, 161
Hocke, Jean-Pierre, 354*n*30
Holborn, Louise, 269
Homelands
  access to, 149–50, 227
  in India, 137, 138
  Namibia and, 88, 89
  Pakistan refugee flows and, 142
  political mobilization and, 308*n*71
Honduras, 215, 216, 255, 273
Hong Kong
  Chinese refugees and, 28, 126, 127, 157, 158,
    159–60
  Prospects for refugee flows from, 178, 253
Horn of Africa. *See* Eritrea; Ethiopia; Somalia
Horowitz, Donald, 146, 235–36, 243, 244
Hostages for weapons exchange, 296*n*86
Huguenots, 5–7
Hukbalahap movement, 173, 337*n*80
"Humane deterrence," 166, 169, 336*n*51

Voluntary/involuntary movement dichotomy, 31
Volunteer agencies. *See* Nongovernmental
   Organizations

Waldheim, Kurt, 89
Wallerstein, Immanuel, 348n4
Walvis Bay, 99
Walzer, Michael, 289n105
War, as root cause, 259
Warrior bands. *See* Guerrilla activity;
   Refugee-warrior communities
Weak states. *See* New African States
"Weak state" syndrome, 72
"Weapons of the weak," 73
Weinstein, Warren, 293n35
Welfare agencies, 286n49
Wells, Melissa, 314n115
Western countries
   Afghan refugees in, 152, 154
   asylum for advanced minorities in, 150, 194
   asylum for Ethiopian refugees and, 120
   Chinese refugees and, 160
   economic embargo of Vietnam and, 165
   intervention in Latin American and, 202
   Latin American refugees and, 200
   political considerations and, 272, 273
   as receiving countries for southern African
      refugees, 125
   refugee status for Indians and, 137
   resettlement of Vietnam refugees in, 165–66
   restrictive immigration policies and, 18,
      269–70, 278–79, 280–81
   Sikh refugees and, 139–40
   South Asian refugees and, 127
   southern Africa as dilemma for, 74
   Sri Lankan refugees in, 148
Western Somali Liberation Front (WSLF), 112,
   113–15, 320n34
West Germany. *See* Federal Republic of Germany
Whitehead, Edgar, 305n40
WHO. *See* World Health Organization
Williams, Norman, 124
Wolf, Eric, 248
Women, proportion of, in refugee camps, 114–15,
   116, 119

World Bank, 97, 118
World Court, and South Africa, 307n65, 308n66
World economy
   globalization of social conflicts and, 230–32
   international response to refugee crisis and,
      229
   new African states and, 44
   root causes and, 259
   tribal distinctions in Rwanda and, 45
   underdevelopment and, 231–32
World Health Organization (WHO), 134
World War I, and Eastern European empires, 12
"Worth," 349n21

Young, Andrew, 90
Young, Crawford, 263

Zaire
   Angolan refugees in, 92, 93–94, 312n94
   conflict in, 38, 39, 43
   international political system and, 291n15
   as receiving country, 46, 47, 48, 49, 52, 66,
      68, 89
   refugee flows from, 91
   as at risk, 121–22
Zambia
   Angolan conflict and, 312n95, 314n128
   as receiving country, 81, 83, 84, 86, 89, 93,
      94, 98, 101
   South Africa and, 123
Zanzibar, 236, 237
Zia ul-Haq (general), 140–41
Zimbabwe
   European-owned land in, 301n2
   independence and, 42
   internal settlement in, 85, 100
   Mozambique and, 80, 95, 98
   prospects in, 124
   as receiving country, 97
   refugee flows from, 84
   South Africa and, 74, 75, 90, 123
   struggle against settler regime in, 82–86, 234